MICHELIN
CHARMING PLACES TO STAY

1 000 Charming hotels and guesthouses in France

SUMMARY

REGIONAL MAPS

- ALSACE
- AQUITAINE
- AUVERGNE
- BURGUNDY
- BRITTANY
- CENTRE AND UPPER LOIRE VALLEY
- CHAMPAGNE-ARDENNE
- CORSICA
- FRANCHE-COMTÉ
- ÎLE-DE-FRANCE AND PARIS
- LANGUEDOC-ROUSSILLON
- LIMOUSIN
- LORRAINE
- MIDI-PYRÉNÉES
- NORD-PAS-DE-CALAIS
- NORMANDY
- PAYS-DE-LA-LOIRE
- PICARDY
- POITOU-CHARENTES
- PROVENCE-ALPS - FRENCH RIVIERA
- RHÔNE-ALPES

Symbols used in the guide

 Number of the establishment
in the guide and on the regional map:
blue for hotels
red for maisons d'hôte

 Hotel

 Maison d'hôte

 Hotel or maison d'hôte offering rooms
at a maximum price of €45 per night
for a double room

 The little extra that makes the hotel
or maison d'hôte different

The guide

Michelin's 1000 Charming Hotels and Guesthouses features a selection of establishments at reasonable prices throughout France, chosen by our inspectors for their authenticity, character, warmth and setting. The most expensive rooms cost no more than €110, most of the prices are below €80 and a third of the establishments offer rooms for less than €50.

A few words, indicated by our symbol, highlight the little extra that we particularly liked: "Exploring the underwater depths of Scandola nature reserve", for example.

How the Guide works

The guide is divided into 19 French regions. Within these regions, the establishments are listed in ascending order of the number of the *département*: Aquitaine, for example, is split into the *départements* of Dordogne 24), Gironde (33), Landes (40), Lot-et-Garonne (47) and Pyrénées-Altantiques (64). Within the *département*, towns or villages where we list an establishment are given in alphabetical order and the establishments are numbered in this order. Hotels are marked in blue 🏠 and maisons d'hôte in red 🏠.

Maps

The maps of France at the beginning of the guide shows the 19 regions and their *départements*.

At the beginning of each chapter is a regional map with the hotels marked as blue dots and the maisons d'hôte as red dots; each dot has a number which corresponds to the number at the top of the establishment's description. The maps and directions in this guide use the metric system for reasons of practicality; as a reminder 1km = c.0.6miles.

Maisons d'hôte

Maisons and chambres d'hôte are, loosely speaking, bed & breakfast establishments with between three and six rooms. Often converted mills, country houses, farmsteads or hunting lodges, and typically in quiet countryside or the residential area of a town, they are also the private homes of the people who will welcome you and endeavour to make your stay as pleasant as possible. We definitely recommend booking ahead, particularly during the summer or the long spring weekends. You should also call if you think you may arrive late in the evening.

Hotels

Many of our hotels are in converted castles, mansions, convents, abbeys and the like. As with the chambres d'hôte, all have been selected for their character, tranquillity and hospitality. There is no point, however, in attempting to compare a simple seaside holiday home with rooms at under €40 with accommodation in a luxurious medieval château: each has its own distinctive charm. Most hotels have a restaurant and offer half-board rates (i.e. for dinner and accommodation). If they do, we point this out: the establishment will confirm the details. Remember to confirm your reservation if you're running late – guests are usually expected to arrive by 6pm.

The information provided by the maisons d'hôte and hotels and reproduced in good faith should be considered as an indication only. Despite our best efforts, it is always possible that some of the information is not complete or accurate. Michelin Travel Publications cannot be held responsible for such changes.

Tables d'hôte

If a hotel or restaurant has dining facilities, we say so. Some maisons d'hôte offer a "table d'hôte". This home-cooked set menu at a fixed price may be served to you at your own table, or you may join the rest of the guests at a communal table.

Prices

All prices are inclusive of tax and service, the prices indicated in this guide were supplied to us by the proprietors of the hotels in 2004 for the year 2005 and may thus be liable to change during the year. Prices refer to the high season. Such prices are not contractual and Michelin Travel Publications may under no circumstances be held responsible for any possible changes.

Rooms: The prices given are the highest and lowest rates for a double room in high season. Always confirm the price when booking. Out of season, many establishments offer special deals; again, its best to ask when making the reservation.

Breakfast: Breakfast is sometimes included in the price of the room. Whenever this is not the case, we have indicated the price of breakfast per person.

Deposit and Instalments

Visitors should be aware of the conventional difference between a deposit ('arrhes' in French) and an instalment ('acompte'). In the first case, the customer may cancel his booking and so forfeit his deposit; if the hotelier is unable to provide his guest with the room, he repays double the amount his customer paid. An instalment, on the other hand, is considered a binding commitment to pay the whole tariff.

Credit Cards

If an establishment does not accept credit cards, we indicate this in its entry. Note that in giving your credit card number to secure your reservation, you are entitling the hotelier or owner of the maison d'hôte either to charge an instalment equal to the minimum tariff for your stay, to be reckoned against your final bill, or to take payment for what you have ordered and reserved, in such cases where the reservation is not cancelled within the time determined by the hotelier or the owner of the maison d'hôte.

Access and Facilities

For each establishment we give details of
• how to get there from the nearest town.

• facilities including television, swimming-pool, tennis court, sauna, children's games and an indication of whether dogs are allowed.
• handicapped access where special adaptations or arrangements have been made.

Places with that little bit extra

Three themed indexes can be found at the back of the book:

Low price: this index lists all the establishments which offer double rooms at under €45 a night.

Wining and dining breaks: all the gastronomic establishments whose cooking we found particularly good.

Activity breaks: this includes all the establishments which have a swimming pool and also offer at least one other sport (hiking, riding, tennis, golf, canoeing etc.).

Index

In addition to the themed indexes, all of the establishments are listed in alphabetical order.

Exploring France?

Don't forget to stock up with the latest Michelin REGIONAL and LOCAL maps and titles from The Green Guide Collection. Michelin also offers an online route-planning service at www.ViaMichelin.com.

Your viewpoint

We have aimed to make this guide practical and readable and trust that it will accompany you on family outings and romantic weekends: it's written for you and you can help to make the next edition even better. Please point out any errors and ommissions you spot and fill in the questionnaire at the back of the guide: all your comments and suggestions for new addresses are very welcome.

ALSACE

Alsace is perhaps the most romantic of France's regions, a place of fairy-tale castles guarding the foothills of the mountains, gentle vine-clad slopes and picturesque dolls' house villages perched on rocky outcrops or nestling in lush green valleys. From Colmar's Little Venice with its flower-decked balconies and famous storks to Strasbourg's Christmas market whose multicoloured lights illuminate the magnificent cathedral or the half-timbered houses of Little France reflected in the meanders of the River Ill, an inner warmth radiates from Alsace that even the cold winter winds cannot chill. So make a beeline for the boisterous atmosphere of a brasserie and sample a real Alsace beer or head for a picturesque *winstub* – wine bar – and tuck into a steaming dish of choucroute – sauerkraut with smoked pork – and a huge slice of *kugelhof* cake, all washed down with a glass of fruity Sylvaner or Riesling wine.

• Bas-Rhin (67)   • Haut-Rhin (68)

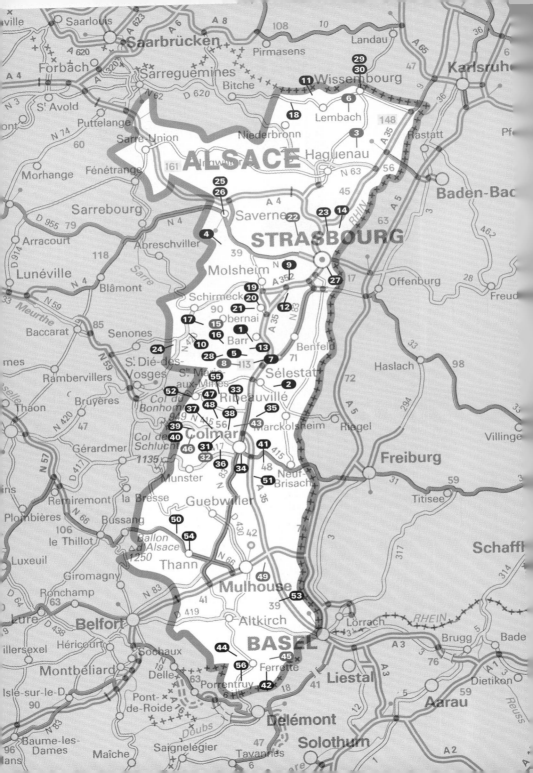

 ZINCKHOTEL
M. Zinck

13 rue de la Marne
67140 Andlau
Tel. 03 88 08 27 30
Fax 03 88 08 42 50
zinck.hotel@wanadoo.fr
www.zinckhotel.com

Open all year • 18 rooms with bath/WC or shower/WC and television • €59 to €95; breakfast €8 • No restaurant • Terrace, park, private car park. No dogs admitted

 LES PRÉS D'ONDINE
M. Dalibert

5 route de Baldenheim
Rathsamhausen-le-Haut
67600 Baldenheim
Tel. 03 88 58 04 60
Fax 03 88 58 04 61
message@presdondine.com
www.presdondine.com

Open all year • 12 rooms, on 2 levels, with bath/WC and television, 1 with disabled access • €78 to €130, breakfast €10 • Table d'hôte evenings only for guests (closed Sun and Wed); menu €30 • Garden, private car park. No dogs allowed in restaurant • Fitness room, library

  Relaxing in the flower-decked garden and fruit orchards on a summer's day.

A building in the tanners' quarter in the 16C, a mill until 1830, a hosier's shop and now a hotel complete with a contemporary wing - if the walls of the Zinckhotel could speak, what tales they would tell! The old millwheel still takes pride of place in the breakfast room, reminding visitors of the building's past. However guests are often even more surprised by the unusual decorative themes of the rooms ranging from "English" to "Zen" and "The Arabian Nights".

 The pastoral charm of this riverside setting on the banks of the Ill.

This former forest house built in the early 20C near the river has been treated to a recent makeover. Its bright colourful façade invites visitors to venture through the garden gate. Inside, you will be delighted first by the sitting room-library and then by the trim restaurant with its attractive woodwork and tasty table d'hôte. Carefully-chosen furniture, warm colours, matching fabrics and knick-knacks give the rooms an elegant flavour.

Access : D500, exit 13 mittelbergheim

Access : 5km eastbound of Sélestat on the D 21

 KRUMEICH
M. Krumeich

23 rue des Potiers
67660 Betschdorf
Tel. 03 88 54 40 56
Fax 03 88 54 40 56

Open all year • 3 rooms • €48 to €53, breakfast included
• No table d'hôte • Garden, car park. No dogs allowed
• Pottery courses

 AU CHASSEUR
M. Gass

7 rue de l'Eglise
67440 Birkenwald
Tel. 03 88 70 61 32
Fax 03 88 70 66 02
hotel.au-chasseur @ wanadoo.fr
chasseurbirkenwald.com

Closed in Jan • 22 rooms with bath/WC or shower/WC
and television • €60 to €115; breakfast €12; half board
available • Non-smoking restaurant closed Mon and Tue
and Thu lunchtimes; menus €15 (weekday lunchtimes) to
€65 • Terrace, garden, car park. No dogs allowed in
rooms • Heated, indoor swimming pool, sauna, Jacuzzi

 **The warm welcome from the owner,
who is also a potter.**

Situated in the heart of a village renowned for its
stoneware pottery, this large property provides clean,
quiet rooms decorated with elegant period furniture –
including beautiful wardrobes – and a lovely shaded
flower garden. The owner, the proud descendant of a
long line of potters, organises introductory pottery
courses all year long.

 **Taking the time to enjoy the covered
heated swimming pool, sauna, Jacuzzi
and solarium.**

This family-run hostelry, hidden behind an inviting
flower-decked façade, dominates the village of Birkenwald, guaranteeing nights of peaceful slumber to even
the lightest sleepers. The rooms are comfortable,
pleasant and extremely well kept; a few command a
view over the Vosges mountains. The owner takes
pleasure in concocting tasty dishes which are a happy
blend of classical and regional cooking, served in a
dining room whose multicoloured wainscoting is the
work of a local artist.

Access : 15 km north-east of Haguenau, towards
Wissembourg on the D 263 then the D 243

Access : In the centre of the village between Saverne
and Mosheim

BLIENSCHWILLER - 67650

CLEEBOURG - 67160

5 WINZENBERG
Mme Dresch

58 route des vins
67650 Blienschwiller
Tel. 03 88 92 62 77
Fax 03 88 92 45 22
winzenberg@visit-alsace.com
www.winzenberg.com

Closed 3 Jan to 18 Feb • 13 rooms all with bath/WC or shower/WC and television • €41 to €48; breakfast €6 • No restaurant • Private car park. Dogs not admitted

6 KLEIN
Mme Klein

59 rue Principale
67160 Cleebourg
Tel. 03 88 94 50 95
Fax 03 88 94 50 95
annejp.klein@laposte.net

www.chez.com/cleebourg

Open all year • 4 rooms • €40, breakfast included, half board available • Table d'hôte €12 (evening only) • Garden, car park. Credit cards not accepted

 Ideally located in a village along the Wine Route.

A little village surrounded by vineyards provides the backdrop to this former wine-grower's house, now restored and transformed into a hotel. Although not exactly enormous, the rooms are pleasantly appointed with colourfully painted furniture and some have sloping ceilings while others boast balconies. The current owners, also wine-growers, enjoy taking guests on a guided tour of the cellar, finishing up with a tasting session.

 The lovingly preserved, authentic Alsatian décor.

This 18C-19C Alsatian house in the heart of an acclaimed wine-growing village could well prove irresistible: there's no mistaking the true Alsatian style. The peaceful rooms, all on the ground floor, are decorated with pristine antique furniture; wood is the predominant feature of the dining room which serves typical regional cuisine. Guests can relax in the pretty garden to the rear.

Access : In the main street of the village

Access : 7km south-west of Wissembourg on the D 7, in the centre of the village

7 LE VIGNOBLE
M. Boulanger

1 rue de l'Église
67650 Dambach-la-Ville
Tel. 03 88 92 43 75
Fax 03 88 92 62 21

Closed from 24 Jun to 8 Jul and 24 Dec to 15 Mar
• 7 rooms, one of which has disabled access, most have bath/WC, all have television • €46 to €53; breakfast €6 • No restaurant • Private car park. No dogs allowed

8 LA ROMANCE
M. Geiger

17 route de Neuve-Église
67220 Dieffenbach-au-Val
Tel. 03 88 85 67 09
Fax 03 88 57 61 58
corinne@la-romance.net
www.la-romance.net

Open all year • 6 rooms, one of which is split-level, two have sitting rooms • €75 to €85, breakfast included • No table d'hôte • Garden, car park. Credit cards not accepted, no dogs allowed • Sauna and spa

 Walking along the Dambach wine path.

This hotel's architecture is characteristic of the modest wine-growers houses dotted along the Wine Route. A narrow façade facing onto the street, only the upper residential storey of which has the traditional half-timbering, and a ground floor devoted to grape pressing equipment and the cellar. The peaceful rooms have retained their oak beams and the bells of the neighbouring church remain considerably silent during the night. Family breakfast room.

 The modern comfort of this pretty regional residence.

Although rather difficult to find, this snug house is so comfortable that, once over the threshold, you may not want to leave! Warm welcome and spotless interior. The well-appointed, tastefully decorated rooms are named after flowers and trees and two of them overlook the valley. Add to this a warm welcome, spotless housekeeping and a garden on the edge of the forest which is the perfect spot for breakfasts in the summertime.

Access : In the centre of the village

Access : 12km north-west of Sélestat on the N 59 and the D 424, towards Villé

9 PÈRE BENOIT
M. Massé

34 route de Strasbourg
67960 Entzheim
Tel. 03 88 68 98 00
Fax 03 88 68 64 56
hotel.perebenoit@wanadoo.fr
www.hotel-pere-benoit.com

Closed from 2 to 22 Aug and from 20 Dec to 5 Jan
• 60 rooms on 2 floors, 4 of which have disabled access, all have bath/WC and television • €58 to €72; breakfast €7 • Air-conditioned restaurant; menu €18 to €24 • Terrace, garden. Private car park • Fitness room, sun deck

10 JULIEN
M. Goetz

12 route Nationale
67130 Fouday
Tel. 03 88 97 30 09
Fax 03 88 97 36 73
hoteljulien@wanadoo.fr
www.hoteljulien.com

Closed Jan and Mon • 44 rooms, 8 of which are split-level, all have bath/WC or shower/WC and television • €70 to €115, breakfast €10; half board available • Menus €18 (weekdays) to €35 • Terrace, garden, indoor swimming pool, car park. No dogs allowed in restaurant • Aquatic leisure centre. Organised tours of Alsace

A farmhouse full of character near Strasbourg airport.

Behind the half-timbered, red façade of this genuine 18C Alsatian farmhouse, a range of dining choices reveals a real love of good food. Take your pick from a family dining room, the adorable balcony-cum-terrace installed under a wooden gallery, a snug "winstub" – literally a "wine room", with paintings, wood panelling and earthenware stove – or a vaulted cellar serving local tartes flambées. Snug rooms, most overlooking a peaceful flowered courtyard.

The scenic valley view with the hotel's footbridge in the foreground.

Even though the street façade with its copper-roofed overhang may strike visitors as unusual, it is nothing in comparison to the breathtaking sight of the garden side simply overflowing with flowers. In just a few years this family-run establishment has evolved immensely and the rooms reflect this renovation, ranging from comfortable to luxurious. Another of the establishment's appeals is its delicious regional cuisine.

Access : 12 km from Strasbourg on the A 35 (exit no 8), then take the D 400 and D 392

Access : On leaving the village drive towards Schirmeck

GIMBELHOF - 67510

INNENHEIM - 67880

11 GIMBELHOF
M. Gunder

67510 Gimbelhof
Tel. 03 88 94 43 58
Fax 03 88 94 23 30
info @ gimbelhof.com
www.gimbelhof.com

Closed 15 Nov to 26 Dec and during the February holidays • 9 rooms, most of which have shower/WC • €35 to €67; breakfast €6; half board available • Restaurant closed Mon and Tue; menus €11 (weekdays) to €28 • Car park

12 AU CEP DE VIGNE
M. Schaal

5 route de Barr
67880 Innenheim
Tel. 03 88 95 75 45
Fax 03 88 95 79 73
www.aucepdevigne.com

Closed from 15 to 28 Feb, 1 to 15 July, Sun evening (except the hotel) and Mon • 37 rooms, one of which has disabled access, all have bath/WC or shower/WC and television • €44 to €64; breakfast €7.50; half-board available • Menus €15 to €40 • Garden, car park

 The ruins and caves of Fleckenstein Castle.

 Hospitality in the old French tradition.

A narrow forest road leads to this unassuming family inn hidden away in the dense woodland of Northern Vosges. The countrified rooms and dining room are simply furnished but there is no better starting point for nature lovers, walkers and history enthusiasts to explore the surrounding countryside. A footpath lined with fir trees winds its way past four ancient fortresses, along the Franco-German border affording superb views over the Palatinate countryside.

The steep eaves, impressive half-timbered façades and wooden balconies are in keeping with the consistently high hotel standards and attention to detail shown by the Schall family, owners of this traditional establishment since 1902. The rooms vary from functional and light to rustic and a little dark; ask for one of the quieter ones overlooking the garden. Cosy dining room with dark wood panelling and carved ceiling.

Access : Leave Lembach on the D 3, after 3.5km take a right onto the D 925, then the forest road on the right

Access : Between Strasbourg and Obernai, in the village

13 ARNOLD
M. Arnold

98 route des vins
67140 Itterswiller
Tel. 03 88 85 50 58
Fax 03 88 85 55 54
arnold-hotel @ wanadoo.fr
www.hotel-arnold.com

Closed 25 and 26 Dec • 30 rooms, 10 of which in a separate wing, 1 with disabled access; all have bath/WC or shower/WC and television • €89 to €111 (€77 to €99 low season), breakfast €10, half board available • Menus from €23 (weekdays) to €46 • Terrace, garden, car park

14 AU MOULIN
Mme Wolff et Mme Dametti

3 impasse du Moulin
67610 La Wantzenau
Tel. 03 88 59 22 22
Fax 03 88 59 22 00
moulin-wantzenau @ wanadoo.fr
www.moulin-wantzenau.com

Closed from 24 Dec to 2 Jan • 20 rooms and 1 split-level on four levels with lift, with bath/WC or shower/WC and television • €68 to €85, breakfast €11, half board available • Air-conditioned restaurant closed 7 to 28 Jul, 27 Dec to 8 Jan, Sun and public holidays; menus €20 to €28 • Terrace, garden, private car park • Nearby: golf, tennis, horse riding, fitness

Filling up our shopping basket from the regional produce boutique.

The Arnold Hotel epitomises Alsace from its vineyard landscape to its spruce half-timbered façades and smart, immaculately cared-for interior. Recent renovations have added to guests' well-being without detracting from the regional character of its three buildings. The comfortable welcoming rooms overlook either the picturesque village or the vineyards. As for the winstub, its typical local décor and regional cuisine are an invitation to sample its excellent fare.

Charm and tranquillity just a few minutes from Strasbourg.

This former mill on the banks of a branch of the Ill enjoys a superbly quiet countryside setting. Pastel-coloured striped wallpaper, matching hangings, exposed beams and light-coloured wooden furniture give the welcoming rooms an incredibly cosy feel. The sitting room with its fireplace is equally inviting and is the setting for delicious breakfasts of carefully selected country fare. The restaurant opposite the Moulin is run by the same family.

Access : In the heart of the village, south of Obernai

Access : 12km north-east of Strasburg on the D 468

15 CHAMBRE D'HÔTE TILLY'S INN
M. et Mme Hazemann

28 rue Principale
67140 Le Hohwald
Tel. 03 88 08 30 17
Fax 03 88 08 30 17

Open all year • 3 rooms • €55 to €60 (€50 to €55 in low season); breakfast €8 • Table d'hôte €22 (evenings only and by reservation) • Car park. Credit cards not accepted, no dogs allowed

16 LA PETITE AUBERGE
M. Hubrecht

6 rue Principale
67140 Le Hohwald
Tel. 03 88 08 33 05
Fax 03 88 08 34 62
hrpetiteauberge@aol.com
www.lapetiteauberge-hohwald.com

Closed 1 to 5 Feb, Tue lunchtime and Wed • 7 rooms with bath/WC and television • €58; breakfast €7; half board available • Non-smoking restaurant; menus €14.50 to €25.50 • Terrace, car park

The conspicuous, brightly coloured decoration.

The bright red façade decorated with naive paintings makes it impossible to miss this guesthouse. The interior decoration is just as colourful, beginning with the breakfast room, painted in vivid hues and further embellished by a 19C piano and a wooden horse from a merry-go-round. The rooms, some of which are lined in wood, are less ostentatious and the two suites are extremely spacious. Warm, friendly welcome.

The split-level rooms are wonderfully spacious.

The accommodation wing of La Petite Auberge is located behind a long brand-new wooden façade. The rooms are most pleasant: 36m² in size, a private terrace, tastefully decorated with light wooden furniture, functional bathrooms and a sleeping area upstairs under the timber-framed roof. Meals are served in a more traditionally-inspired house with a choice of classical cuisine in the restaurant or regional dishes in the Caveau le Relais.

Access : In the village

Access : In the heart of the village

17 **AUBERGE METZGER**
M. Metzger

55 rue Principale
67130 Natzwiller
Tel. 03 88 97 02 42
Fax 03 88 97 93 59
auberge.metzger@wanadoo.fr
www.hotel-aubergemetzger.com

Closed Sun evening and Mon from 3 to 24 Jan, 21 June to 4 July • 16 rooms all with bath/WC or shower/WC and television • €59 to €73; breakfast €9, half board available • Menus €13 (weekdays) to €53 • Garden

18 **AU CHEVAL BLANC**
M. Zinck

11 rue Principale
67510 Niedersteinbach
Tel. 03 88 09 55 31
Fax 03 88 09 50 24
contact@hotel-cheval-blanc.fr
www.hotel-cheval-blanc.fr

Closed 24 Jan to 3 Mar, fortnight in late Jun and a fortnight early Dec • 25 rooms, 3 of which are suites, with bath/WC or shower/WC and television • €49 to €68; breakfast €8; half board available • Menus €18 (weekdays) to €52 • Terrace, garden. • Outdoor swimming pool, tennis, children's play area

 The lush green garden filled with flowers.

Set in the heart of a peaceful village in the midst of Alsace's green countryside, everything about this appealing country inn conjures up an image of peace and quiet. The rooms are tastefully and individually decorated in a modern decorative style which provides the backdrop to period and contemporary furniture. Appetising, liberally-served regional cuisine is served in a welcoming dining room or in the shade of a pleasant terrace.

 The owners' gracious welcome.

An impressive traditional country inn set in the midst of a land of medieval fortresses dating from the Holy Roman Empire. Most of the slightly old-fashioned, but comfortable and well-kept rooms overlook wooded vales; ask for one which doesn't face the street. Tuck into generously served regional dishes served in cosy, regional dining rooms, modelled after the "winstub" wine-bar. Half-timbered reading room. Former German leader and keen gastronome, Helmut Kohl, is said to be a regular!

Access : In the upper reaches of the village

Access : 8 km north-west of Lembach on the D 3, towards Bitche

19 **COLOMBIER**
M. Baly

6/8 rue Dietrich
67210 Obernai
Tel. 03 88 47 63 33
Fax 03 88 47 63 39
info @ hotel.colombier.com
www.hotel.colombier.com

Open all year • 44 air-conditioned rooms with bathrooms and television; 2 have disabled access • €72 to €98; breakfast €9 • No restaurant • Garage

Leave your car in the hotel garage and discover the charm of Obernai on foot.

The Colombier is proof that regional architecture and contemporary interior design can coexist happily. The flower-decked façade, which fits so perfectly into the lovely Alsace city, hides a surprising interior which is a mixture of designer furniture, modern light fittings, metal structures, half-timbered walls and bare beams. Most of the rooms are spacious and a few boast a balcony overlooking the street.

Access : In the heart of the village

20 **LES JARDINS D'ADALRIC**
Mme Bossert

19 rue du Maréchal-Koening
67210 Obernai
Tel. 03 88 47 64 47
Fax 03 88 49 91 80
jardins.adalric @ wanadoo.fr
www.jardins-adalric.com

Closed Sun evening from Jan to Apr • 46 rooms with bath/WC or shower/WC and television, 6 are non-smoking and 2 have disabled access • €59 to €82 (€49 to €72 low season), breakfast €10 • No restaurant • Park, private car park. Credit cards accepted except Diners • Swimming pool

Lazing by the swimming pool overlooking the garden and stream on a summer's day.

This immense building, which dates from 1991, is located in a quiet residential neighbourhood. The interior is full of charm, further enhanced by recent restoration work which has spruced up the cosy sitting room-bar, pretty yellow-walled breakfast room and inviting bedrooms, some of which overlook the garden and pool. The exposed rafters of the rooms on the top floor lend them a slightly romantic appeal.

Access : East of Obernai on the D 426 towards Strasburg, first right then left before the River Ehn

 21 À L'AMI FRITZ
M. Fritz

8 rue des Châteaux
67530 Ottrott-le-Haut
Tel. 03 88 95 80 81
Fax 03 88 95 84 85
ami-fritz@wanadoo.fr
www.amifritz.com

Closed from 18 Jan to 4 Feb and one week in Feb
• 22 rooms with bath/WC or shower/WC and television,
half are air-conditioned and 1 has disabled access • €67
to €97; breakfast €11; half board available • Restaurant
closed Wed; menus €21 to €59 • Terrace, park, private
car park, garage

 **Sipping the red wine of Ottrot while
digging into one of the chef's tasty
dishes.**

The hotel's name, taken from a novel by Erckmann-
Chatrian, also refers to the owner of this trim Alsace
house located on the heights of the village. Personalised,
cosily comfortable, impeccably-kept and stunningly
quiet bedrooms set the scene of the establishment. The
chef's tasty regional fare is served in a pleasant dining
room or in a picturesque winstub. The annex (Le Chant
des Oiseaux), located 500m away in the heart of the
countryside, is home to simply furnished small rooms.

 22 LA MAISON DU CHARRON
Mme Gass

15 rue Principale
67370 Pfettisheim
Tel. 03 88 69 60 35
Fax 03 88 69 85 45
mdc67@free.fr
 www.maisonducharron.com

Open all year • 5 rooms, 2 are split-level and 2 are gîtes
• €43 to €51, breakfast included • No table d'hôte
• Garden. Credit cards not accepted, dogs not allowed

 **The personalised decoration of each
room.**

The owners of these two 1858 houses enthusiastically
took a hand in their renovation. The master-carpenter
husband undertook the individual decoration of the
rooms, each of which takes its inspiration from a
different type of tree - birch, maple, larch, among others
- while his wife, a gifted seamstress, decorated the
house with her patchworks. The small garden is very
pleasant in the summer and the horses are always
popular with children.

Access : In the centre of the village 4km to the west
of Obernai on D 426

Access : 13km north-west of Strasbourg on the D 31

 23 AIGLE D'OR
Mme Jung

5 rue de la Wantzenau
67116 Reichstett
Tel. 03 88 20 07 87
Fax 03 88 81 83 75
info @ aigledor.com
www.aigledor.com

Closed from 25 Dec to 2 Jan and 5 to 21 Aug • 17 rooms with bath/WC or shower/WC and television • €62 to €99, breakfast €9 • No restaurant • Car park • Nearby: walks along the banks of the canal from the Marne to the Rhine

 A deliciously sophisticated small family establishment.

The attractive white, half-timbered façade of the Aigle d'Or Hotel stands near the church of this picturesque market town near Strasbourg. Original stained-glass windows flood the hall with light and the breakfast room, in the basement, is most appealing. Upstairs, wrought-iron or Louis XVI-style furniture, wainscoting and warm fabrics more than make up for the small size of the bedrooms.

Access : 7km northbound of Strasburg on the D 468 and D 37, or via the A4 and the D 63, near the village church

 24 LA BELLE VUE
Mme Boulanger

36 rue Principale
67420 Saulxures
Tel. 03 88 97 60 23
Fax 03 88 47 23 71
labellevue @ wanadoo.fr
www.la-belle-vue.com

Closed from 17 Feb to 2 Mar, 27 Jun to 7 Jul and 25 Oct to 9 Nov • 11 rooms, 7 split-level, on 2 levels with lift, with shower/WC and television • €76 to €110, breakfast €10.50, half board available • Restaurant closed Tue and Wed, non-smoking room; menus €19 to €50 • Terrace, car park • Tennis

 The delightful interior decoration, an intelligent mix of old and new.

This village inn founded in the 19C and run by the same family for five generations has evolved admirably over the decades. The present-day accommodation features modern, spacious fittings and personalised decoration with bright woodwork, original paintings and brightly-coloured curtains; the split-level rooms have a pleasant sitting room. The inventive cuisine is served in a non-smoking restaurant which sports exposed timber-work and contemporary frescoes.

Access : In the village between Saales and St-Blaise-la-Roche

 25 **LE CLOS DE LA GARENNE**
Mme Schmitt

88 route du Haut-Barr
67700 Saverne
Tel. 03 88 71 20 41
Fax 03 88 02 08 86
clos.garenne@wanadoo.fr
www.closdelagarenne.fr.st

Open all year • 14 rooms with bath/WC or shower/WC and television • €46 to €84, breakfast €8; half board available • Menus €14 to €60 • Car park, park

 26 **EUROPE**
M. Kuhry

7 rue de la Gare
67700 Saverne
Tel. 03 88 71 12 07
Fax 03 88 71 11 43
info@hotel-europe-fr.com
www.hotel-europe-fr.com

Closed 18 to 31 Dec • 28 rooms, 20 of which have shower/WC, 8 have bath/WC, all have television • €61 to €120, breakfast €9 • No restaurant • Garage, public car park nearby • Visits to the nearby Château des Rohan

 The landscaped gardens.

This early 20C family residence is peacefully located on the edge of a forest of fir trees. It is impossible to resist the temptation to snuggle up in the individually decorated rooms furnished in a tasteful period or country style. The all-wood, snug dining room is reminiscent of an old mountain inn. The terrace overlooks a landscaped park on a hillside.

 The individual decoration of each room.

Within easy reach of the station and the castle on the banks of the canal which links the Marne to the Rhine, this family-owned business has recently been partly refurbished. In keeping with the hotel's namesake, each spacious room features a different European style: the choice includes "Scandinavian", "French", "English" and "contemporary". A delightful sitting room decorated with frescoes and an Art Nouveau-style breakfast room. Private garage and car-park opposite.

Access : From place des Dragons take the road to Haut Barr Castle

Access : Near the railway station

ALSACE

STRASBOURG - 67000   **VILLÉ - 67220**

27 **DIANA-DAUPHINE**
M. Baly

30 rue de la 1er Armée
67000 Strasbourg
Tel. 03 88 36 26 61
Fax 03 88 35 50 07
info @ hotel-diana-dauphine.com
www.hotel-diana-dauphine.com

Closed from 24 Dec to 2 Jan • 45 rooms, 41 have bath/WC, 4 have shower/WC and all have television • €94 (€78 low season), breakfast €9 • No restaurant • Garage

28 **LA BONNE FRANQUETTE**
M. Schreiber

6 place du Marché
67220 Villé
Tel. 03 88 57 14 25
Fax 03 88 57 08 15
bonne-franquette @ wanadoo.fr

Closed from 15 Feb to 8 Mar, 28 June to 5 July and 25 Oct to 8 Nov • 10 rooms, 2 non-smoking, all with bath/WC or shower/WC and television • €48 to €53; breakfast €7, half board available • Restaurant closed Sat lunchtime, Sun evening and Mon, menus €8 to €52

 Comfortable bedrooms and sitting rooms.

Within walking distance of the Place de l'Étoile, this hotel provides impeccable rooms whose decoration is loosely based on Louis XV and Louis XVI styles. A distinctly contemporary style has been adopted for the sitting room which overlooks a pleasant breakfast room and leads into the lobby. Excellent soundproofing means that the traffic in the busy street and the nearby trams do not spoil the establishment's calm. Useful private garage.

 Being so close to the Regional Park of the Ballons des Vosges.

The white façade, hidden by flowers during the summer, invites you to venture inside this aptly named country inn, which roughly translates as "A good, simple meal". The owner's kindness and friendly welcome immediately make it clear that he has his guests' welfare at heart. Unpretentious, practical and spotlessly clean rooms. The restaurant - a favourite with the locals, which is always a good sign - has a basement and an upper room, both serving traditional fare.

Access : Near the town centre, towards Place du Marechal De Lattre-de-Tassigny

Access : In the town centre

29 **HOSTELLERIE DU CYGNE**
M. et Mme Kientz

3 rue du Sel
67160 Wissembourg
Tel. 03 88 94 00 16
Fax 03 88 54 38 28
hostellerie-cygne @ wanadoo.fr

Closed from 18 Feb to 4 Mar, from 30 Jun to 15 Jul, from 10 to 25 Nov and Wed • 16 rooms in two adjacent houses, with bath/WC or shower/WC, all have television • €49 to €70; breakfast €7; half board available • Restaurant closed Thu lunchtime and Sun evening; menus €25 (weekdays) to €60 • Terrace. No dogs allowed in rooms

 The Salt House (1448) and its amazing roof.

This inn's two buildings, one of which was built in the late 14C and the other in 1535, typify the style of this well-preserved small town, where over 70 of the houses date from before 1700. The bedrooms, somewhat old-fashioned but still comfortable, are ideal for an overnight halt. The restaurant's two dining rooms are lit by stained-glass windows; the cosiest has recently been embellished with a lovely marquetry ceiling. A terrace in the courtyard overlooks a handsome half-timbered façade.

Access : In the town centre, next to the town hall

30 **AU MOULIN DE LA WALK**
M. Schmidt

2 rue de la Walk
67160 Wissembourg
Tel. 03 88 94 06 44
Fax 03 88 54 38 03
info @ moulin-walk.com
www.moulin-walk.com

Closed from 3 to 24 Jan and from 13 to 30 Jun • 25 rooms, one of which has disabled access, with bath/WC or shower/WC and television • €47 to €60; breakfast €7; half board available • Menus €29 to €39 • Terrace, garden, car park. No dogs allowed in rooms

 A slice or two of raisin cake - the famous "kugelhof" - at breakfast time.

This cluster of buildings built on the foundations of an old mill, whose well-preserved wheel is still in working order, stands on the banks of the Lauter on the outskirts of the town. Most of the rooms have been refurbished with modern fittings and brand new bathrooms. Tasty, traditional fare is served in a cosy, wainscoted dining room and a pretty flower-decked terrace.

Access : Out of the town centre, on the banks of the Lauter

31 **AUX ARMES DE FRANCE**
M. Gaertner

1 Grand' Rue
68770 Ammerschwihr
Tel. 03 89 47 10 12
Fax 03 89 47 38 12
aux.armes.de.france@wanadoo.fr
www.aux-armes-de-france.com

Closed Wed and Thu • 10 rooms with bath/WC and television • €65 to €80; breakfast €12 • Menus €18 to €93 • Garden, private car park • Located in the heart of the Alsace vineyards. Golf 1km away

32 **MAISON THOMAS**
Famille Thomas

41 Grand'Rue
68770 Ammerschwihr
Tel. 03 89 78 23 90
Fax 03 89 47 18 90
thomas.guy@free.fr
 www.maisonthomas.com

Open all year • 4 rooms with a kitchenette • €43 to €46, breakfast included • No table d'hôte • Garden, car park. Credit cards not accepted • Sauna

Good taste abounds in this warm Alsatian inn.

Numerous famous chefs have learnt their craft in this handsome house rebuilt after the air raids of the Second World War. Its long culinary tradition dates back to the Thirties, when the grandmother of the present chef ruled the kitchen. Spacious rooms and a bourgeois-style dining room where mouth-watering dishes are served under the watchful eye of ancestors' portraits. Definitely worth tasting!

Extremely well-appointed rooms.

This former wine-grower's house – painted an unmissable turquoise – stands in the most picturesque part of the village. Each of the spacious, well-equipped rooms carries a name and all have kitchenettes. The well thought-out garden has something for everyone: a shaded corner for afternoon naps, bower, barbecue, swings, table-tennis and boules, not forgetting the view over the vineyards. The house also boasts a sauna and keep-fit equipment.

Access : At the entrance to the town centre

Access : In the village

33 CHEZ NORBERT
M. Moeller

9 Grand'Rue
68750 Bergheim
Tel. 03 89 73 31 15
Fax 03 89 73 60 65
labacchante@wanadoo.fr

Closed from 4 to 9 Jan, 20 Feb to 19 Mar and 1 to 8 Jul
• 12 rooms and 1 suite, some split-level, most have bath/WC, all have television • €69; breakfast €10; half board available • Restaurant closed Wed lunchtime, Thu and Fri lunchtime; menus €26 (weekdays) to €48 • Terrace, courtyard, private car park

34 TURENNE
Mme Helmlinger

10 route de Bâle
68000 Colmar
Tel. 03 89 21 58 58
Fax 03 89 41 27 64
helmlinger@turenne.com
www.turenne.com

Open all year • 85 rooms, 42 of which are non-smoking, all have bath/WC or shower/WC, air-conditioning and television • €59 to €68; breakfast €8 • No restaurant • Garage

 Home-made cakes and jams for breakfast.

The cachet of this group of wine-growers' farms is undeniable. The colourful, half-timbered façades (14C) vie for pride of place with the other picturesque houses of this town on the Alsace Wine Route. Some of the contemporary, practical rooms are located under the eaves; avoid those overlooking the road, which are noisier. Good country fare served in a typically Alsatian restaurant or on a pleasant terrace, bedecked with geraniums in the summer.

 A convenient distance from the old town.

Conveniently located two minutes away from the picturesque Little Venice district, you can't miss the distinctive pink and yellow façade of this large house. Spacious, refurbished double rooms some of which have traditional regional furniture. Smaller, single rooms, equally well-kept and soundproofed, are also available. Breakfasts are served in a typically Alsatian dining room. Wainscoted sitting room and bar, heaven-sent private garage and friendly family welcome.

Access : On the main street in the centre of the village

Access : Coming from the railway station, head for the A 35 motorway and turn left at the Elf petrol station

35 **LES HIRONDELLES**
M. et Mme Muller

33 rue du 25-Janvier
68970 Illhaeusern
Tel. 03 89 71 83 76
Fax 03 89 71 86 40
hotelleshirondelles @ wanadoo.fr
www.hotelleshirondelles.com

Closed 30 Jan to 4 Mar and 23 May to 6 Jul • 19 rooms, most have shower/WC, all have television • €68 to €72, breakfast included • No restaurant • Garden, private car park • Outdoor swimming pool

The swallows, which really do make the summer.

Rustic painted furniture and oak beams set the tone of the relatively soberly-decorated rooms which overlook a flowered inner courtyard or a picture-book landscape of kitchen gardens. The recent swimming pool, complete with teak sun-deck and air-conditioning in the adjacent accommodation building makes the hotel very pleasant during the hot summer months.

Access : In the centre of the village

36 **À L'AGNEAU**
M. et Mme Mann-Meyer

16 Grand'Rue
68230 Katzenthal
Tel. 03 89 80 90 25
Fax 03 89 27 59 58
hotel-restaurant.agneau @ wanadoo.fr
www.hotelrestaurantagneau.fr

Closed from 10 Jan to 10 Feb, 29 Jun to 7 Jul and from 15 to 24 Nov, 24 to 26 Dec, Wed, Thu lunchtime from Jul to early Oct • 12 rooms and 1 suite (2-6 people), 2 of which are in a separate wing, with shower/WC and some with television • €43 to €55, breakfast €9, half board available • Menus €16 (weekdays) to €43 • Private car park. • Wine tasting

The tour of the family's wine business.

The creamy façade and blue shutters of this house in the heart of a wine-growing town catch the eye of all who pass. The almost monastical rooms are spotlessly kept and some enjoy a view over the vineyard. Two newer annexe rooms, added in 1998, are a touch more spacious and up-to-date. The menu features excellent Alsatian dishes, complete with wine from the estate. The young husband and wife team are known for their warm welcome.

Access : In the centre of the village

 37 **L'ARBRE VERT**
Famille Kieny-Wittner

1 rue Haute du Rempart
68240 Kaysersberg
Tel. 03 89 47 11 51
Fax 03 89 78 13 40
arbrevertbellepromenade @ wanadoo.fr
http://perso.wanadoo.fr/
arbrevertbellepromenade

Closed from 1 to 31 Jan • 20 rooms with bath/WC or shower/WC and television, 14 in a separate wing • €59 to €72 (€57 to €62 low season), breakfast €7.20; half board available • Restaurant (non-smoking only) closed Mon; menus €23 to €42

 38 **HOSTELLERIE SCHWENDI**
M. et Mme Schillé

2 place Schwendi
68240 Kientzheim
Tel. 03 89 47 30 50
Fax 03 89 49 04 49
hotel-schwendi @ wanadoo.fr
www.hotel-schwendi.com

Hotel closed from 24 Dec to 15 Mar (except by reservation) • 17 rooms all with bath/WC and television, 9 with air-conditioning • €65 to €78; breakfast €8; half board available • Restaurant closed Wed and Thu lunchtime and from 24 Dec to 15 Mar; menus €22 to €52 • Terrace, private car park

 A walk round this tiny Alsatian town rich in points of interest.

The birthplace of the humanitarian Dr Schweitzer, the most famous inhabitant of Kayserberg, stands side by side this hostelry comprised of two Alsace houses located on either side of a square of greenery. The low-key countrified rooms and the restaurant, renowned for its regional-inspired classical cuisine, are located in the main house. The other, called the Belle Promenade, offers more spacious, pleasant accommodation, furnished in particular with pieces painted by the lady of the house.

 The delightful welcome of the hotel owners-cum-winegrowers.

An old well, around which the terrace is laid in the summer, stands in the paved courtyard of this 17C inn with its elegant, pale yellow facade. Guests are accommodated in renovated rooms with original timber ceilings. A likeable blend of classical Louis XIII chairs and bare stone walls adds a cosy combination of rustic and bourgeois to the dining room, where wholesome country cooking is served with delightful home-made wines.

Access : 6km westbound of Colmar in the centre of the village

Access : 3km to the east of Kaysersberg on the D 28

ALSACE

 39 LES ALISIERS
M. et Mme Degouy

Lieu-dit Faudé
68650 Lapoutroie
Tel. 03 89 47 52 82
Fax 03 89 47 22 38
jacques.degouy@wanadoo.fr
www.alisiers.com

Closed 6 Jan to 5 Feb, 25 Jun to 1 Jul (except hotel), 21 to 25 Dec, Mon, Tue and Wed lunchtime • 18 rooms, one of which has disabled access and 5 are non-smoking. Rooms have bath/WC or shower/WC • €50 to €122; breakfast €9; half board available • Non-smoking restaurant; menus €15 to €46 • Terrace, garden, car park

 The kindness of the staff and the owners.

All the windows of this extended farmhouse built in 1819 overlook the pleasant, rolling countryside of the Béhine Valley, whether it be from the snug and countrified or more contemporary rooms; you can choose your favourite on the hotel's website. The veranda restaurant shares the same great view; generous helpings of regional cooking, with an accent on local produce, are served in the non-smoking dining room. Pleasant garden overlooking the village of Lapoutroie.

Access : In the upper reaches of the village, 3km to the south-west on a minor road

 40 DU FAUDÉ
M. et Mme Baldinger

28 rue du Général-Dufieux
68650 Lapoutroie
Tel. 03 89 47 50 35
Fax 03 89 47 24 82
info@faude.com
www.faude.com

Closed from 27 Feb to 16 Mar and from 4 to 29 Nov • 31 rooms, 2 of which are suites, with bath/WC or shower/WC, all have television • €60 to €90; breakfast €13; half board available • Restaurant closed Tue and Wed; menus €15 to €65, children's menu €10 • Garden, terrace, private car park • Indoor swimming pool, fitness room, hammam, jacuzzi, skiing

 A riverside country garden.

The Baldinger family has run this traditional country inn for over 40 years and have certainly learnt a thing or two about making their guests feel at home. Well-soundproofed bedrooms are spacious and comfortable. The restaurant staff, dressed in traditional Alsatian costume, serve tasty, locally sourced food whose continued popularity is due to the chef's ability to move with the times, introducing lighter dishes and vegetarian meals. Attractive indoor swimming pool and a fitness room.

Access : In the centre of the village

  41 À LA VIGNE
M. Bauer

5 Grande-Rue
68280 Logelheim
Tel. 03 89 20 99 60
Fax 03 89 20 99 69
restaurant.alavigne@calixo.net
www.reperes.com/la-vigne

Closed from 23 Jun to 10 Jul and from 23 Dec to 8 Jan
• 9 rooms with bath/WC or shower/WC and television
• €50 to €68; breakfast €6; half board available
• Restaurant closed Sat lunchtime, Sun and Mon evening; menus €20 (weekdays) to €27 • A few parking spaces. No dogs allowed in rooms

 The simple, friendly atmosphere.

An attractive village house with a redbrick façade and a totally renovated interior. Only 10min from Colmar, this tranquil hotel is an excellent choice for an overnight stop. The tastefully decorated rooms are pleasant and spotless. Wood is the predominant feature of the family dining room which offers a menu of French classics, while the bar serves the region's famous tartes flambées – light pizzas on an extra-thin crust – by the warmth of an earthenware stove.

Access : To the south-east of Colmar, on the D 13 then the D 45

  42 AUBERGE ET HOSTELLERIE PAYSANNE
Mme Guérinol

1 rue de Wolschwiller
68480 Lutter
Tel. 03 89 40 71 67
Fax 03 89 07 33 38
aubergepaysanne2@wanadoo.fr
www.auberge-hostellerie-paysanne.com

Closed for 3 weeks in February, 1 to 15 Jul • 16 rooms at the Auberge and 9 in the separate wing (L'Hostellerie) 200m away. Rooms have bath/WC or shower/WC, all have television • €48 to €68, breakfast €7, half board available • Restaurant closed Tue lunchtime out of season and Mon; menus from €9 (weekday lunchtimes) to €38 • Terrace, garden, car park

The picturesque, unspoilt landscapes of the Sundgau.

This establishment does offer its own modern accommodation, but most people prefer the annexe, 200m away: a 1618 farmhouse typical of the Sundgau region, which was actually taken apart brick by brick and rebuilt here, a short distance from the Swiss border. Some of the rooms, of varying quality it must be said, have oak beamed ceilings, and a pretty flowered garden leads out towards the fields. Check-in at the main inn and sample the regional specialities and seasonal game in its dining room.

Access : Leave Ferrette south-east bound on the D 23, at Sondersdorf take the D 21B, then at Raedersdorf go back onto the D 23

 43 DOMAINE DU BOUXHOF
M. et Mme Edel

 Rue du Bouxhof
68630 Mittelwihr
Tel. 03 89 47 93 67
Fax 03 89 47 84 82

Closed Jan • 3 rooms with television and fridge • €50, breakfast included • No table d'hôte • Garden, car park. Credit cards not accepted, dogs not allowed

 Staying in a wine-growing property and trying a glass – it would be impolite to refuse!

This 17C castle flanked with square towers seems to rise out of a sea of vines. Guests can choose between two types of accommodation: modern, spotless rooms or very well-equipped cottages; those with a balcony overlooking the vineyards are the most attractive. The superb breakfast room is housed in a 15C chapel. Don't pass up a chance to visit the cellar and its oak vats where the estate's wine is made, finishing with a wine-tasting session.

Access : In the upper part of the village, on the wine-growing estate

 44 AUX DEUX CLEFS
Mme Enderlin

 218 rue Hennin Blenner
68480 Moernach
Tel. 03 89 40 80 56
Fax 03 89 08 10 47
 auxdeuxclefs@wanadoo.fr

Closed for two weeks in February, one week early Nov, one week in Jul and Thu • 7 rooms with shower/WC, almost all have television • €41 to €47 (€40 low season) ; breakfast €6; half board available • Restaurant closed Wed evening and Thu; menus €22 (weekdays) to €46. Daily set menu €9.50 • Garden, car park, garage

 An afternoon nap in the pretty tree-lined garden.

A handsome half-timbered and gabled country house, characteristic of the Sundgau; look for its attractive wrought-iron sign of two crossed keys. Taste the local delicacy, fried carp, in the welcoming wood-panelled dining room, tastefully decorated with paintings. Comfortable, inviting rooms, which are being progressively renovated, occupy a wing which dates from the Sixties.

Access : At Vieux-Ferrette leave the D432 for the D 473 which goes through Koestlach and Moernach

45 MOULIN DE HUTTINGUE
M. Thomas Antoine

68480 Oltingue
Tel. 03 89 40 72 91
Fax 03 89 07 31 01

Closed in Jan and Feb • 4 rooms • €54 to €74, breakfast included • Car park, garden, terrace. Credit cards not accepted, no dogs allowed

46 FERME DU BUSSET
Mme Batôt

33 rue du Busset
68370 Orbey
Tel. 03 89 71 22 17
Fax 03 89 71 22 17
fabienne.batot@wanadoo.fr
www.fermedubusset.com

Closed 23 to 26 and 29 to 31 Dec • 6 rooms • €46, breakfast included • No table d'hôte • Garden, car park. Credit cards not accepted, no dogs allowed

The decorative features which bear witness to the mill's long history.

The Franco-Swiss border is only a short distance from this 17C wheat mill on the banks of the Ill, which is little more than a stream here. The rooms, all upstairs, are quite simply appointed on the whole. The superb loft under the eaves has been fitted with a useful kitchenette. Breakfast is served in a dining room complete with magnificent wooden pillars or on the terrace when the weather permits.

The panoramic view over the Orbey Valley.

A steep road winds its way up to this farmhouse, which still breeds its own poultry and sheep, high on a lush green plateau at an altitude of 600m. Choose from self-catering cottages or bed and breakfast rooms: the latter are lined in wood and while not enormous are very well-kept and quiet. Before leaving, make sure you stock up on cheese, cooked meats and home-made jams.

Access : 1.5km south of Oltingue on the D 21e

Access : 1km to the east of Orbey on a minor road

  47 L'ORIEL
Mme Wendel

  48 LE SARMENT D'OR
M. et Mme Merckling

3 rue des Écuries-Seigneuriales
68340 Riquewihr
Tel. 03 89 49 03 13
Fax 03 89 47 92 87
info @ hotel-oriel.com
www.hotel-oriel.com

4 rue du Cerf
68340 Riquewihr
Tel. 03 89 86 02 86
Fax 03 89 47 99 23
info @ riquewihr-sarment-dor.com
www.riquewihr-sarment-dor.com

Open all year • 22 rooms, 3 of which are split-level, with shower/WC or bath/WC, all have television • €65 to €98; breakfast €10 • No restaurant • Shaded terrace

Closed from 3 Jan to 2 Feb, from 27 Jun to 5 Jul • 9 rooms, 2 of which are split-level, most have bath/WC, all have television • €60 to €80; breakfast €8 • Restaurant closed Sun evening, Mon and Tue lunchtime; menus €20 to €55 • No dogs allowed in rooms

 Breakfast served in the inner courtyard in summertime.

 The owners' attentive welcome.

The frontage of this 16C country home is adorned with a handsome two-storey oriel window and an amusing wrought-iron sign; the delightful maze of corridors and staircases bear witness to the house's old age. The rooms, in the progress of being renovated, are decorated in a variety of styles, ranging from rustic to more modern – families generally prefer one of the split-level rooms.

The Sarment d'Or – or golden vine – has put down its roots in a quiet street lined with handsome 16C houses. A spiral staircase leads up to the cosy, modern bedrooms. The snug, warm dining rooms are characteristic of Alsatian interior decoration with pine panelling and dark beams lit up by the crackling flames of a welcoming log fire.

Access : From the town hall take Rue du Général de Gaulle then the first street on the right

Access : From the town hall square, drive to the end of Rue du Général de Gaulle and turn left (pedestrian street)

49 LE CLOS DU MÛRIER
Mme Volpatti

42 Grande-Rue
68170 Rixheim
Tel. 03 89 54 14 81
Fax 03 89 64 47 08

Open all year • 5 rooms with kitchenettes, bathrooms with separate WC • €59; breakfast €7 • No table d'hôte • Garden, car park. No dogs allowed

50 AUBERGE DU MEHRBÄCHEL
M. et Mme Kornacker

Route de Geishouse
68550 Saint-Amarin
Tel. 03 89 82 60 68
Fax 03 89 82 66 05
sarlkornacker@wanadoo.fr

Closed for one week early Nov, Mon evening, Thu evening and Fri all day • 23 rooms located in 2 buildings, with bath/WC or shower/WC • €53 to €55; breakfast €9; half board available • Air-conditioned restaurant; menus €16 (weekdays) to €45 • Car park. No dogs allowed • Ideal for resting and walking

The spacious, comfortable rooms.

This venerable 16C Alsatian house has been tastefully renovated. Old beams blend well with a modern décor and each bedroom has its own kitchenette. On the leisure side, the house has a pleasant walled courtyard and the owners are happy to lend bicycles to guests.

Toasting your toes by the warm stove after a hard day's trekking.

This old farmhouse built on the edge of a forest of fir trees, so characteristic of the Vosges scenery, has been in the family since 1886. Half the simple but spacious and well-kept rooms have balconies and most of them overlook the wonderful Rossberg mountain range. Game and regional dishes are served in the air-conditioned dining room, its walls are adorned with hunting trophies. A hiking trail runs past the inn, ideal for walkers!

Access : 6km eastbound from Mulhouse, drive towards Basle, in the centre of Rixheim

Access : Between Thann and Bussang, drive for 4km on the Mehrbächel road

ALSACE

51 AU MOULIN
M. et Mme Woeffle

Route d'Herrlisheim
68127 Sainte-Croix-en-Plaine
Tel. 03 89 49 31 20
Fax 03 89 49 23 11

Open from 1 Apr to 3 Nov • 17 rooms with bath/WC, almost all have television • €40 to €80; breakfast €9 • Menus from €15 to €25 • Garden, car park • Small museum about Alsace in the inner courtyard

52 AUX MINES D'ARGENT
Mme Willmann

8 rue du Docteur-Weisgerber
68160 Sainte-Marie-aux-Mines
Tel. 03 89 58 55 75
Fax 03 89 58 65 49

Open all year • 9 rooms with shower/WC and television • €38 to €55; breakfast €6; half board available • Menus €10 to €32 • Terrace

 Lingering over breakfast in the enchanting flowered courtyard.

With its flowered courtyard and half-timbered buildings, this former flour-mill, built in 1880, represents a haven of peace and quiet, just a short distance from an interchange on the A35! The sizeable rooms are practical and tastefully decorated with cane furniture. Some overlook the peaks of the Vosges, while others look down on the plain; all are wonderfully quiet. Interesting mini-museum on the Alsace of yesteryear.

 The busy atmosphere surrounding the famous Mineral, Gem And Fossil Show (June).

The mullioned windows of the façade testify to the old age of this house, said to have been built in 1596 by a miner who would appear to have struck it rich! The original spiral staircase leads up to the rooms, graced with large windows and furniture dating from 1900 or thereabouts. The family dining room, in the "winstub" style, is embellished with wood carvings which depict the miners' lives: the seam at Ste Marie was mined from the 9C to the 18C.

Access : 10km southbound from Colmar on the D 201, then at Sainte-Croix-en-Plaine take the D 1

Access : In the centre, in the street parallel to the main road (where the town hall is)

 53 **AUBERGE ST-LAURENT**
M. et Mme Arbeit

 1 rue Fontaine
68510 Sierentz
Tel. 03 89 81 52 81
Fax 03 89 81 67 08
info @ auberge-saintlaurent.fr
www.auberge-saintlaurent.fr

Closed Mon and Tue and fortnight in Mar and fortnight
in Aug • 10 rooms upstairs, all are air-conditioned with
bathrooms and television • €100 to €120, breakfast €13,
half board available • Menus €39 to €70 • Terrace, car
park

 54 **LE MOSCHENROSS**
M. Geyer

 42 rue du Général-de-Gaulle
68800 Thann
Tel. 03 89 37 00 86
Fax 03 89 37 52 81
info @ le-moschenross.com
 www.le-moschenross.com

• 23 rooms, one of which has disabled access, most have
shower/WC, some have bath/WC, all have television
• €38 to €52; breakfast €7; half board available • Menus
€9 to €46 • Terrace, private car park

 **Deliciously classical home cooking
spiced up with a touch of modernity.**

A stopover in this former staging inn is a treat for the
eyes, soul and palate! It is impossible not to give in to
the infectious good humour of the owners' charming
welcome. The decoration of the spruce bedrooms evokes
the ancestors of the Arbeit family: Sophie the baker,
Marie the grandmother, Gustave the labourer and
others, and is full of charming details. The restaurant,
furnished in soft colours, has a collection of cockerels,
knick-knacks and paintings, and a lovely terrace.

 **The path winding through the
vineyards up the Rangen.**

Close to the post office and opposite the station, this
neat, ochre-red fronted 1839 hotel has been renovated
from top to bottom. The small, modern rooms are
practical and well soundproofed: ask for one commanding views over the steep slopes of the famous
Rangen vineyards. The spacious dining room is
decorated in a hybrid contemporary-bourgeois style.
Charming service.

Access : On the way through the village

Access : In the village

  55 AUBERGE LA MEUNIÈRE
M. et Mme Dumoulin

30 rue Sainte-Anne
68590 Thannenkirch
Tel. 03 89 73 10 47
Fax 03 89 73 12 31
info @ aubergelameuniere.com
www.aubergelameuniere.com

Open from 21 Mar to 19 Dec • 25 rooms at the rear of
the building. Rooms have bath/WC or shower/WC, all
have television • €56 to €79; breakfast €7; half-board
available • Restaurant closed Mon-Wed lunchtimes;
menus €17 (weekdays) to €36 • Terrace, car park, garage
• Sauna, fitness room, table-tennis, billiards

  56 AU CERF
M. Koller

76 rue Principale
68480 Winkel
Tel. 03 89 40 85 05
Fax 03 89 08 11 10
g.koller @ tiscali.fr

Closed from 7 to 28 Feb • 6 rooms upstairs with
bath/WC, some have television • €47 to €50 (€42 to €47
low season); breakfast €7; half board available • Menus
€10 to €25 • No dogs allowed • Hiking

 **The restful view of the forest, from
some of the bathrooms!**

The imposing flowered façade of this inn conceals a host
of attractions. Almost all the rooms are rear-facing –
avoid those overlooking the street – with a view of the
Bergenbach Valley and the towers of Haut-Koenigs-
bourg Castle, which film buffs may recognise as
the location of Jean Renoir's anti-war masterpiece
"La Grande Illusion". The restaurant is decorated in a
delightful rustic style and the terrace opens out onto the
splendid Vosges scenery.

 **The family atmosphere behind these
red walls.**

The smart red frontage of this inn near the Swiss border
cannot be missed. The rather bare rooms are tiled and
furnished practically; nearly all have been recently
renovated and the proverbial Swiss obsession with
cleanliness has clearly made it over the border here.
Family dining rooms in an up-to-date "winstub" style.
Bring a rucksack and walking stick and explore the
beautiful Sundgau region and the source of the Ill along
countless footpaths.

Access : Between Ribeauvillé and Sélestat, in a
village very near Haut-Koenisbourg

Access : In the centre of the village

AQUITAINE

Friendly Aquitaine has welcomed mankind since prehistoric times. Its varied mosaic of landscapes is as distinctive as its inhabitants' dedication to hospitality, invariably spiced with a generous sprinkling of forthright rural humour. No stay in Aquitaine would be complete without visiting at least one of Bordeaux' justly famous châteaux and vineyards. Afterwards head for the "Silver Coast", prized by surfers and rugby fans alike, and sample delicious Basque gâteau, have a drink in a tapas bar or even take ringside seats for a bullfight! This rugged yet sunny land between the Pyrenees and the Atlantic has always been fiercely proud of its identity and the inhabitants of the Basque country still celebrate their time-honoured traditions in truly vigorous style. If you spend a little time in one these sleepy Basque villages, all of which sport the region's colours, red and green, you will be astounded by the ease with which they suddenly burst into spirited song and games.

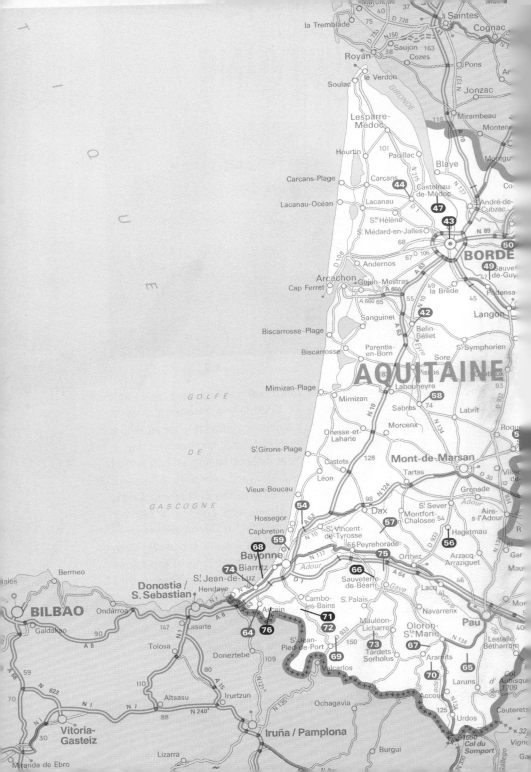

1 CÔTÉ RIVAGE
Mme De Roton-Couderc

Au bourg
24150 Badefols-sur-Dordogne
Tel. 05 53 23 65 00
Fax 05 53 22 56 01
coterivage@online.fr

Open 30 Apr to mid-Oct, closed Sun • 7 air-conditioned rooms • €55 to €90; breakfast €9; half board available • Menu €20 to €29 • Terrace, garden. Dogs not allowed in restaurant

2 LE RELAIS DE LAVERGNE
Mme Pillebout

« La Vergne »
24150 Bayac
Tel. 05 53 57 83 16
Fax 05 53 57 83 16
relaisdelavergne@wanadoo.fr

• 4 rooms upstairs, one suite has disabled access, all have bathrooms • €58, breakfast included • Table d'hôte €20 • Park, terrace, car park. Credit cards not accepted, no dogs allowed in restaurant • Outdoor swimming pool

Cutting through the garden to walk along the banks of the Dordogne.

The tranquillity of this handsome 17C manor house.

This welcoming, restored house is located between the presbytery and a fishermen's house, a few steps from the Dordogne River. Spotless walls, colourful curtains, antique furniture and air-conditioning make the rooms very pleasant. The bar and sitting room are decorated with old advertising gadgets, while beams, bare stone walls and wrought iron furniture set the contemporary tone of the dining room which leads into a pleasant terrace. Fresh, local produce and a fine wine menu of local vintages.

The peaceful appeal of this house is such that guests often wish they had planned to stay longer. The attentive welcome of the two hostesses, the tranquil atmosphere and mouth-watering smells wafting from the kitchen never fail to enchant. Light, airy bedrooms combine the charm of yesteryear with modern-day comforts. The spacious restaurant and inner courtyard provide a perfect setting for elegant dining.

Access : On the banks of the Dordogne

Access : 10km to the south-east of Lanquais, on the Beaumont road

 3 L'ANCIENNE BOULANGERIE
M. Chapelle

Le Bourg
24340 Beaussac
Tel. 05 53 56 56 51
Fax 05 53 56 56 59
katerine.chapelle-welffens @ wanadoo.fr

Open all year • 3 rooms with shower/WC • €49, breakfast included • No table d'hôte • Garden, car park. Credit cards not accepted • Swimming pool, fishing and hiking nearby

 4 LA FLAMBÉE
M. Dupouts

153 avenue Pasteur
24100 Bergerac
Tel. 05 53 57 52 33
Fax 05 53 61 07 57
laflambée @ wanadoo.fr

Closed 24 to 30 Dec and February holidays • 21 rooms, 7 of which are in a separate wing. Rooms have bath/WC, some have shower/WC, all have television • €55 to €83 (€43 to €68 low season); breakfast €8; half board €60 to €70 (€60 to €62 low season) • Restaurant closed Mon, Sat lunchtime, Sun evening; menus €16 to €31 • Terrace, park, car park • Swimming pool, tennis

 Wake up to the enticing smell of freshly baked bread.

As the name suggests, this large square townhouse in the upper part of the town used to be a bakers' shop; the old bread oven can still be seen in the dining room. White-wood furniture, beautiful wardrobes and old photos adorn the tranquil rooms. A wealth of information about the region can be gleaned from the sitting room's bookshelves and guests can relax in the pretty little garden.

 A tennis match and swim in the pool, or a quiet glass of Bergerac for the less energetic!

This pleasant old country home on the doorsteps of the tobacco capital of France has been recently renovated. The rooms, practical and spacious with a personal touch, are named after one of the surrounding vineyards; those in the annexe are more simply decorated but have private terraces overlooking the flowered grounds. The stylish dining rooms feature cosy armchairs, wrought-iron furniture, oak beams, log fires and a veranda.

Access : Between Mareuil and Nontron, a few kilometres north of the D 708

Access : Leave Bergerac on the N 21 towards Périgueux: after 3km, the hotel is on the right

BOURDEILLES - 24130   **BRANTÔME - 24310**

5 HOSTELLERIE LES GRIFFONS
M. et Mme Lebrun

Le bourg
24310 Bourdeilles
Tel. 05 53 45 45 35
Fax 05 53 45 45 20
griffons @ griffons.fr
www.griffons.fr

Open from 9 Apr to 15 Oct, closed Mon and Fri lunchtimes Jul-Aug, lunchtimes except weekends and national holidays from Sep to Jun • 10 rooms with bath/WC or shower/WC and television • €80 to €96 (€80 to €90 low season), breakfast €9, half board available • Non-smoking restaurant; menus €21.70 to €40 • Terrace, car park

 A visit to the two castles of Bourdeilles.

This 16C mansion, at the foot of a medieval and a Renaissance castle, stands on the banks of the River Dronne close to its picturesque old bridge. Exposed stonework and beams, antiques and curios help to give the rooms a rustic feel; those on the first floor boast decorative fireplaces, while the rafters upstairs under the eaves add a distinctly romantic flavour. The stylish dining room opens out onto a pleasant terrace overlooking the river.

Access : In the centre of the village between the château and the river

6 LES HABRANS
M. Falcoz

Les Habrans
24310 Brantôme
Tel. 05 53 05 58 84
Fax 05 53 05 58 84

Closed from 30 Oct to 1 May • 5 rooms, 4 of which are on the first floor • €55 to €60, breakfast included • No table d'hôte • Terrace, garden. Credit cards not accepted

 Boating down the Dronne.

The riverside setting of this unpretentious little house is without question its main asset. The simple rooms are tastefully decorated; those on the first floor under the eaves have sloped ceilings and windows overlooking the river. When the weather is fine, guests can tuck into breakfast on the delightful terrace.

Access : In the lane opposite the gendarmerie (police station)

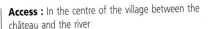

BRANTÔME - 24310 **CAMPAGNE - 24260**

7 LA MAISON FLEURIE
M. et Mme Robinson

54 rue Gambetta
24310 Brantôme
Tel. 05 53 35 17 04
Fax 05 53 05 16 58
info @ maisonfleurie.net
www.maisonfleurie.net

Closed 14 Feb to 1 Mar • 5 non-smoking rooms • €60 to €85, breakfast included • No table d'hôte • Credit cards not accepted, no dogs allowed • Outdoor swimming pool

8 HÔTEL DU CHÂTEAU
Mme Petit

Le bourg
24260 Campagne
Tel. 05 53 07 23 50
Fax 05 53 03 93 69
hotduchateau @ aol.com

Open from Apr to 15 Oct • 16 rooms with bath/WC or shower/WC, all with television • €45 to €60; breakfast €7; half board available • Menus €18 to €45 • Terrace, car park. No dogs allowed in rooms

Staying in the heart of the hometown of the 16C court chronicler Brantôme.

This 19C property, in the shadow of the elegant Romanesque belfry of the abbey, boasts a number of attractions: a convenient town centre location, exemplary welcome, excellent value for money and above all, its charming, comfortable rooms. Whenever the weather permits, generous breakfasts are served in the flowered courtyard and the small swimming pool is always appreciated during the hot weather.

The simple authenticity of this family home.

A handsome country house in the midst of an enchanting Périgordian hamlet. The charming, old-fashioned rooms are spacious, comfortable and well kept, and stay cool even in the height of summer thanks to their thick stone walls. From the windows of the dining room, diners can see Campagne Castle while they sample the chef's carefully prepared regional cooking. Pleasant, shaded terrace, decked in flowers in the summer.

Access : In the town centre

Access : Leave Le Bugue south-east bound on the D 703 and drive for 4km

9 LA GUÉRINIÈRE
M. et Mme Demassougne

« Baccas »
24250 Cénac-et-Saint-Julien
Tel. 05 53 29 91 97
Fax 05 53 30 23 89
contact @ la-gueriniere-dordogne.com
www.la-gueriniere-dordogne.com

Closed from 2 Nov to 1 Apr • 5 rooms upstairs and 2 gîtes
• €75 to €90, breakfast included • Table d'hôte €21
• Terrace, park, car park. Credit cards not accepted, no
dogs allowed • Outdoor swimming pool, tennis, bicycles,
golf

10 CHÂTEAU DE LA BORIE-SAULNIER
M. et Mme Duseau

24530 Champagnac-de-Belair
Tel. 05 53 54 22 99
Fax 05 53 08 53 78
chateau-de-la-borie-saulnier @ wanadoo.fr
www.perso.wanadoo.fr/chateaudelaborie
saulnier

Closed in Jan • 5 rooms • €75 to €79, breakfast included
• No table d'hôte • Park, car park. Credit cards not
accepted, no dogs allowed • Outdoor swimming pool

 Sampling the tasty meals made with fresh farm produce.

This 18C manor farm, extensively remodelled over the
centuries, is reminiscent of a charterhouse. Each of the
extremely spacious rooms - with bare stone walls, period
furniture and tasteful fabrics - is named after a flower.
Cats, dogs and farmyard animals enjoy the run of the
extensive grounds, to the invariable delight of children.

 The tennis courts, free for guests.

The owners of this fortified medieval château have been
lovingly renovating their property, which once ruled the
whole Dronne Valley, for some twenty years. The towers
and crenellated walls, complete with firing positions, are
carefully preserved and the interior has been sensitively
redecorated. Each room features a different colour
– turquoise, yellow, green, grey and blue – and
commands a lovely view over the park. The breakfast
room is simply beautiful.

Access : On the D 46 road to Gourdon

Access : 6km to the north-east of Brantôme on the
D 75 and then the D 83

 11 LES LANDETTES
M. Stocklouser

24260 Journiac
Tel. 05 53 54 35 19
Fax 05 53 54 35 19

Open all year • 2 rooms on garden level, with bathrooms • €50, breakfast included • No table d'hôte • Credit cards not accepted, no dogs allowed • Outdoor swimming pool

12 LES VIGNES DE CHALUSSET
M. Senee et Mme Chedeville

24630 Jumilhac-le-Grand
Tel. 05 53 52 38 25
msenee @ free.fr

Open from Apr to Oct • 5 air-conditioned rooms, 1 of which has disabled access • €42, breakfast included, half board available • Table d'hôte €15 (evenings only) • Terrace, park, car park. Credit cards not accepted, no dogs admitted in restaurant • Outdoor swimming pool

 The scenery of the Vézère Valley.

The setting of this wonderfully renovated 1850 Périgordian farmhouse couldn't be more rural. The bedrooms, fitted-out in the outhouses, make up in charm what they lack in dimensions, with pastel shades, white tiled floors, colourful fabrics and old furniture; all overlook the swimming pool. The shade of a giant lime-tree makes the inner courtyard very pleasant in the summer.

 Riders and horses can be sure of a warm welcome.

This old barn turned into a bed and breakfast is a successful blend of old and new. Oak beams and bare stone walls add character to the spacious, air-conditioned rooms and those on the ground floor have been adapted for disabled guests. The delicious home cooking, an excellent opportunity to try a local Périgordian recipe, is served on the communal table in the dining room or in the inner courtyard during the summer.

Access : 13km westbound from La Madeleine

Access : 4km from Jumilhac-le-Grand, towards St-Yrieix

 13 AUBERGE LA PLUME D'OIE
M. et Mme Walker

24250 La Roque-Gageac
Tel. 05 53 29 57 05
Fax 05 53 31 04 81
laplumedoie @ wanadoo.fr
www.hotels-restau-dordogne.org

Closed from 20 Nov to 20 Dec and mid-Jan to late Feb;
Sun evening, Mon and Tue lunchtime • 4 non-smoking
rooms upstairs, reserved mainly for the restaurant clients,
with bath/WC and television • €70 to €80; breakfast €12
• Menus €36 to €56

 14 LA BELLE ÉTOILE
Famille Ongaro

Le bourg
24250 La Roque-Gageac
Tel. 05 53 29 51 44
Fax 05 53 29 45 63
hotel.belle-etoile @ wanadoo.fr

Open from late Mar to early Nov • 15 rooms with
bath/WC and television • €50 to €75; breakfast €8; half
board available • Menus €23 to €37 • Terrace, garage.
No dogs allowed in rooms • Canoeing, swimming, fishing

 **The picturesque site
of La Roque-Gageac.**

This old residence, built on the flanks of the cliff, stands
in the heart of the idyllic medieval town. A spiral
staircase leads up to a few refreshingly cool bedrooms
decorated with pastel fabrics. The pretty dining room
features light wooden beams, painted straw-bottomed
chairs and bare stone walls. Diners can enjoy a view
of the picturesque "gabarres" and canoes floating down
the Dordogne. Imaginative menu.

 **Floating down the Dordogne in a
"gabarre".**

This fine old creamy-coloured stone house perched on
the cliff commands a wonderful view over the peaceful
meanders of the Dordogne. The bedrooms have been
painted white and most are furnished in a period style.
The typical Périgordian repertoire, served in two
pleasant dining rooms, or in the summer, under a trellis,
will tempt even the most refined of palates. Numerous
nearby leisure activities, including canoeing, swimming
and fishing.

Access : In the village, on the banks of the
Dordogne

Access : On the D 703, between the cliff and the
river

15 DOMAINE DE LA MARMETTE
Mme Ossedat

« La Crabe »
24150 Lanquais
Tel. 05 53 24 99 13
Fax 05 53 24 11 48
george.ossedat@wanadoo.fr

Closed 1 Jan to 1 Apr • 5 rooms on garden level • €56 to €65, breakfast included, half board available • Table d'hôte €23 by reservation and evenings only • Garden, terrace, car park. Credit cards not accepted, no dogs allowed • Outdoor swimming pool

 Back to basics in a land of open fields.

This 16C farm and outbuildings dotted with lawns and countless clumps of flowers is almost a little hamlet in itself. The former loose-boxes have been turned into bedrooms on the ground floor and each one is decorated with a personalised fabric, chest of drawers and a wrought-iron bed. A sitting room, library and dining room-conservatory are located in the main house. A kitchen is also available for use by guests.

16 MAISON DE LA FORÊT
M. Swainson

Pas de l'Eyraud
24130 Laveyssière
Tel. 05 53 82 84 50
Fax 05 53 82 84 51
info@aubergerac.com
www.aubergerac.com

Closed 24 to 26 Dec • 5 rooms with bathrooms • €65 (€55 low season), breakfast €6 • No table d'hôte • Park, garden, car park. Credit cards not accepted, no dogs allowed • Outdoor swimming pool

 Staying just 10min away from Bergerac without suffering the hordes of tourists.

This welcoming white house stands in its own extensive grounds, surrounded by forest. Run by a delightful English couple, the establishment offers colourful rooms under the eaves, on the small side but all with views of the countryside. The prettiest rooms are to the rear of the house. Breakfast is served on the terrace in fine weather.

Access : Take the Faux road then turn left towards Bournaz after leaving town and continue for 200m

Access : 14km northbound from Bergerac on the D 709, then take a minor road

 17 MAISON OLÉA
Mme Nardou

 La Combe-de-Leygue
24260 Le Bugue
Tel. 05 53 08 48 93
Fax 05 53 08 48 93
info @ olea-dordogne.com
www.olea-dordogne.com

Open all year • 5 rooms, all with bath/WC or shower/WC
• €60 to €75 (€50 to €65 low season); breakfast included
• Garden, car park. Credit cards not accepted • Heated
outdoor swimming pool

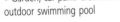 **Lazing about on terraces of the
rooms, overlooking the swimming
pool and valley.**

Though recently built, this house has faithfully upheld
the style and tradition of local architecture. South-
facing, it overlooks a superb overflow swimming pool
with the Vézère Valley in the distance. On the ground
floor you will be met with Moorish touches, murals,
red-brick floor tiles and an amazing veranda-cum-winter
garden. The immense rooms upstairs feature immaculate walls, pedestal tables draped in lace, antique
furniture and exquisite bedding. Blissfully calm!

Access : 5km to the east of Le Bugue on the D 703,
towards Sarlat-la-Canéda and then a minor road on
the left

 18 HOSTELLERIE DU PASSEUR
M. Brun

 Place de la Mairie
24620 Les Eyzies-de-Tayac
Tel. 05 53 06 97 13
Fax 05 53 06 91 63
hostellerie-du-passeur @ perigord.com
www.hostellerie-du-passeur.com

Open early Mar to early Nov • 19 rooms on 3 floors, most
have shower/WC, some have bath/WC, all have television • €62 to €100; breakfast €8; half board available
• Restaurant closed Mon and Tue lunchtimes (low
season); menus €23 to €45 • Terrace, car park • A short
distance from the Prehistory Museum

 **The home-made foie gras which can
be bought in the hotel or from its
website.**

This handsome stone house covered in Virginia creeper
stands in the heart of the Périgord capital, known for
its prehistoric heritage. The stylish, cheerful rooms all
sport bright colours; some overlook the cliffs dotted with
oak trees. Diners can choose from a traditional dining
room complete with an attractive stone fireplace, a
bright conservatory or a country terrace under lime-trees
facing the Vézère, in all of which guests can relax and
savour the hotel's renowned regional dishes.

Access : In the town centre, not far from the Vézère

19 **LE MOULIN DE LA BEUNE**
M. Soulié

2 rue du Moulin-Bas
24620 Les Eyzies-de-Tayac
Tel. 05 53 06 94 33
Fax 05 53 06 98 06
contact @ moulindelabeune.com
moulindelabeune.com

Open from Apr to Oct • 20 rooms with bath/WC or shower/WC, all have television • €58 to €67; breakfast €7; half board available • Restaurant closed on Tue, Wed and Sat lunchtimes; menus €22 to €45 • Terrace, garden, car park.

20 **LE PANORAMIQUE**
M. et Mme Spadi

Beune
24620 Les Eyzies-de-Tayac
Tel. 05 53 06 98 82
Fax 05 53 05 24 04

Open all year • 4 rooms • €28 to €36, breakfast €5 • No table d'hôte • Park, car park. Credit cards not accepted • Swimming pool

 Talking into the early hours of the morning on the riverside terrace.

The attractive stone walls of this former seed and sawmill now house a charming hotel-restaurant. All the pleasant, tastefully decorated rooms enjoy peace and quiet and the stylish wood-panelled dining room commands views of the wonderfully preserved paddle wheel and the garden and river. The setting, on the banks of the Beune, is quite idyllic in fine weather.

 An unmatchable view of the village and site of Eyzies-de-Tayac.

One hectare of parkland protects these three regional-style houses, which dominate the "prehistoric capital", from the outside world. The rooms are deliberately understated in spirit but most pleasing, and two boast wonderful panoramic terraces. On your way to the breakfast room under the veranda, look out for the collection of coffee and pepper mills picked up by the delightful owners over the years. Two gîtes are also available.

Access : In the town centre, off the road on the banks of the Beune

Access : 4km south-east of Eyzies-de-Tayac on the D47, towards Sarlat, then take the Saint-Cyprien road

21 LE PIGEONNIER DE PICANDINE
M. Lacourt

La Picandine
24350 Lisle
Tel. 05 53 03 41 93
Fax 05 53 03 28 43
picandine @ aol.com
www.picandine.com

Closed 15 Nov to 15 Feb • 5 rooms with shower or bath • €50; breakfast included; half board available • Table d'hôte €19 • Terrace, car park. Credit cards not accepted, no dogs allowed • Outdoor swimming pool

22 LA GRANDE MARQUE
Mme Cockcroft

24440 Marnac
Tel. 05 53 31 61 63
grande.marque @ perigord.com
www.lgmfrance.com

Open all year • 5 rooms with bathrooms • €65 to €75, breakfast €5.50 • Table d'hôte €32 • Terrace, park, car park. Credit cards not accepted, no dogs allowed • Outdoor swimming pool

 The sweeping view over the Périgord countryside.

This lovely 17C farmhouse is graced with two-hundred-year-old chestnut trees in the inner courtyard. Stone walls and wood beams set the tone for the bedrooms in the main wing, while two suites in the renovated barn are well suited to families. It's an ideal place to unwind: snuggle up with a good book in the cosy sitting room-library or treat yourself to a game of billiards.

 Strolling round the magnificent ten-acre parkland.

This wonderful 17C Périgord estate commands a sumptuous view of the Dordogne Valley and the quaint, riverside village of Siorac-en-Périgord. The rooms under the eaves have recently been treated to a simple, tasteful facelift. The estate boasts a wide range of leisure activities including a fitness room, sauna and tennis court.

Access : From Lisle, take D 1 towards Périgueux, then take the third turning on the right

Access : 9km to the north-east on the D 703, take the road to Sarlat and then turn right

 23 HÔTEL DES BORIES
M. et Mme Dalbavie

Le bourg
24620 Marquay
Tel. 05 53 29 67 02
Fax 05 53 29 64 15
hotel.des.bories@wanadoo.fr
 www.membres.lycos.fr/hoteldesbories/

Open from 1 Apr to 2 Nov • 30 rooms, 20 of which are in a separate wing, 5 have private terraces, all have bath/WC or shower/WC and television • €33 to €61, breakfast €8; half board available • Restaurant closed Sat lunchtimes; menus €15 to €38 • Terrace, garden, car park • 2 outdoor swimming pools

 24 CHÂTEAU DAME DE FONROQUE
Mme Fried

Fonroque
24230 Montcaret
Tel. 05 53 58 65 83
Fax 05 53 58 60 04
brigittefried@wanadoo.fr

Closed from Dec to 15 Feb • 5 rooms with bathrooms and 2 gîtes • €65, breakfast €6; half board available • Table d'hôte €21 (Mon to Sat) • Terrace, park, car park • Outdoor swimming pool

 Peace and quiet guaranteed.

Despite the name, you won't have to sleep in a "borie", one of the somewhat Spartan dry-stone huts that abound in the region. The accommodation in this family home may not be luxurious, but it is well equipped with modern comforts. Some rooms also have a terrace where you can take breakfast, and the most stylish of all has a superb stone fireplace and wooden beams. Relax in the swimming pool overlooking the countryside.

 Visiting the Gallo-Roman ruins at Montcaret.

The talented proprietor of this 16C fortified manor house successfully runs both a wine business and a bed and breakfast establishment. The comfortable, often spacious rooms are decorated with stylish, old furniture and all overlook the parkland and its hundred-year-old trees. You will adore the wholesome, country cooking.

Access : On leaving Sarlat-la-Canéda, drive towards Les Eyzies-de-Tayac and follow the D 6 on the right

Access : In the Fonroque Park

25 CHRISTINE ET MAURICE BIRON
M. et Mme Biron

Le Domaine du Petit-Houx "Brégou"
24300 Nontron
Tel. 05 53 60 78 82
Fax 05 53 60 78 81
layourte @ wanadoo.fr
www.perigord.com/lepetithoux

Open all year • 3 rooms upstairs, all with bath/WC • €57; breakfast €7 • Table d'hôte €18 • Sitting room, park, car park. Credit cards not accepted, no dogs allowed • Hiking, horse riding, mountain biking

 We most liked **Strolling through the grounds overlooking Périgord's rambling landscape.**

Nearly 10 acres of open fields planted with magnificent mature oaks surround this former smallholding. The barn, sheepfold and main building have been treated to a recent, painstaking makeover, with priority given to retaining distinctive regional features. The main building houses a pleasant sitting room-library, heated in the winter by a fine stone fireplace, and attractive, brightly coloured, comfortable rooms with new bedding, rush matting on the floor and full bathrooms.

Access : 6km to the east of Nontron on the D 707, towards Thiviers and then left onto the D 85 towards Châlus

26 CHAMBRE D'HÔTE LE CLOS-VALLIS
M. Bosio

Croix-d'Alon
24210 Peyrignac
Tel. 05 53 28 95 64
Fax 05 53 28 95 21
br.b @ wanadoo.fr
www.closvallis.fr.fm

Open from Easter to late Oct • 4 non-smoking rooms, 2 of which are upstairs, all have bathrooms • €50; breakfast included • No table d'hôte • Sitting room, garden, car park. Credit cards not accepted, no dogs allowed

 We most liked **The calm of the countryside just a few kilometres outside Sarlat.**

The buildings and outhouses of this carefully restored farmhouse are laid out around a pleasant Périgord-style courtyard. An old barn is now home to light, airy rooms, decorated in a refreshingly simple style with bare stone or white-washed walls, tiles or coconut matting and pine furniture. The sitting room, complete with fireplace, displays the same welcoming simplicity as does the teak-furnished breakfast room. Discreetly cordial welcome.

Access : 4km north-east of Peyrignac on the D47 and D 56, road to Proissans and then a lane to the left

27 **LE BRANCHAT**
M. et Mme Ginioux

Lieu-dit de Branchat
24170 Sagelat
Tel. 05 53 28 98 80
Fax 05 53 28 90 82
lebranchat @ lebranchat.com
www.lebranchat.com

Open Apr to Oct • 6 rooms, all with bath/WC or shower/WC • €63 to €69 (€53 to €63 low season); breakfast included • Table d'hôte €20 to €25 • Children's play area, park, car park. Dogs not admitted • Outdoor swimming pool, ponies

28 **LES GRANGES HAUTES**
M. Fauste

Le Poujol
24590 Saint-Crépin-et-Carlucet
Tel. 05 53 29 35 60
Fax 05 53 28 81 17
fauste @ netcourrier.com
www.les-granges-hautes.fr

Closed 15 Dec to 28 Feb • 5 non-smoking rooms, all have baths or showers • €55 to €76, breakfast €7 • No table d'hôte • Garden, car park. No dogs allowed

The two rooms with a private terrace and a view of the lofty village of Belvès.

The quality of the restoration lavished on the sheepfold, cowshed, barn and farmhouse, now turned into chambres d'hôte, is quite outstanding. White walls and parquet flooring and wooden furniture set the tone. Surrounded by some 12 acres of valleys, woods and hazel trees, you won't have time to count sheep at night! On the leisure side: swimming pool, walks in the park or pony riding.

The sophisticated charm of a French country house.

It is hard to resist the charm of this 18C-19C Périgord country house, surrounded by superb gardens and a salt-water swimming pool. The stylish rooms feature oak beams, warm, sunny colours and immaculate bathrooms. The sitting room, whose central feature is a large fireplace, is the perfect place to relax and read. The charming owners are delighted to recommend interesting places to visit in the region.

Access : 3km south of Belvès on the D 710, towards Fumel and then a minor road on the left

Access : 12km to the north-east of Sarlat towards Brive then Salignac

29 LE MOULIN NEUF
MM. Chappell et Stuart

Paunat
24510 Sainte-Alvère
Tel. 05 53 63 30 18
Fax 05 53 63 30 55
moulin-neuf @ usa.net
www.the-moulin-neuf.com

Closed from 15 to 31 Oct • 6 rooms with bathrooms • €60 to €65, breakfast €10 • No table d'hôte • Terrace, garden. Credit cards not accepted, no dogs allowed

30 LE MANOIR DU GRAND VIGNOBLE
M. Scoty

Le grand vignoble
24140 Saint-Julien-de-Crempse
Tel. 05 53 24 23 18
Fax 05 53 24 20 89
grand.vignoble @ wanadoo.fr
www.manoirdugrandvignoble.com

Open from late Mar to mid-Nov • 44 rooms with bath/WC and television • €82 to €109 (€58 to €79 low season), breakfast €9, half board available • Menus €23 to €44 • Park, car park • Swimming pool, tennis, golf practice, sauna, Jacuzzi, fitness, riding centre, wine tasting lessons

 The laughter of children playing in the estate's pond.

This attractive old mill house is hidden in the heart of a country estate complete with pond. The cosy interior features light colours, roomy sofas and floral print fabrics. The modest-sized rooms are tastefully decorated and located in a beautifully restored old barn. In the summer months, breakfast is served under an arbour and by the fireside in the sitting room in the winter.

 A canter around the estate thanks to the riding school on site.

This 17C manor house enjoys a wonderfully tranquil setting in the midst of over 100 acres of parkland. In the main wing are the reception, sitting room and pleasantly unassuming dining room, where guests are invited to sample regional fare and wines (Bergerac, Pécharmant). A dozen or so rooms, some with four-poster beds, can also be found in this wing. The other wing of the hotel is located in the outbuildings where the extra space has given rise to a more contemporary feel.

Access : Take the D 2 southbound

Access : 16km northbound from Bergerac on the N 21 as far as Campsegret, then left on a minor road towards Saint-Julien-de-Crempset, before Saint-Julien

 31 LA FOMPEYRINIÈRE

 M. et Mme Vandamme

Lapeyronnie
24470 Saint-Pardoux-la-Rivière
Tel. 05 53 56 75 16
Fax 05 53 60 53 30

Open all year • 4 rooms with bath/WC • €40, breakfast included • Table d'hôte €17 (evenings only and by reservation) • Sitting room, garden, car park. Credit cards not accepted, no dogs allowed • Swimming, fishing nearby

32 DOUMARIAS

 M. et Mme Fargeot

24800 Saint-Pierre-de-Côle
Tel. 05 53 62 34 37
Fax 05 53 62 34 37
doumarias @ aol.com

Closed from 30 Sep to 31 Mar • 6 rooms • €58, breakfast included; half-board €43 • Table d'hôte €16 • Garden, car park. No dogs allowed • Outdoor swimming pool

 All the jams are home-made.

Located in the heart of the town, this former farmhouse boasts a pleasant garden and a scenic view of the countryside. Inside, colourful fabrics and rugs set off a tasteful blend of antique and contemporary furniture; modest-sized rooms are stylish and immaculately kept. The master of the house, a former pork butcher, whips up delicious dishes in the kitchen.

 Hooking a fish in the River Côle just a step away.

The leaves and branches of a great lime-tree throw a welcome shadow over the courtyard of this pleasant country property curtained in Virginia creeper, at the foot of the crumbling towers of Bruzac Castle; the charm of the Périgord at its best. The stylish, peaceful rooms are lavishly adorned with period furniture, ornaments and paintings. The swimming pool and garden are most appreciated, as is the staff's friendly welcome.

Access : In the centre of the village

Access : 12km eastbound from Brantôme on the D 78

VILLA DES COURTISSOUS
M. et Mme Dalibard

24210 Saint-Rabier
Tel. 05 53 51 02 26
Fax 05 53 50 73 55
villa.courtissous @ libertysurf.fr
www.bienvenue-montignac.com

Closed from late Nov to Easter • 4 rooms with bathrooms • €74, breakfast included • No table d'hôte • Terrace, garden, car park. Credit cards not accepted, no dogs allowed • Outdoor swimming pool

CHAMBRE D'HÔTE LA CALADE
Mme Hottiaux

Le Bourg
24420 Saint-Vincent-sur-l'Isle
Tel. 05 53 07 87 83
j.hottiaux @ libertysurf.fr

Closed 1 week late Dec • 5 rooms one of which has disabled access, all have bathrooms • €50; breakfast included • No table d'hôte • Garden, car park. Credit cards not accepted, no dogs admitted • Outdoor swimming pool

We most liked
Visiting the nearby Hautefort Castle.

This dignified villa was built in 1800 in the middle of a landscaped garden. The recently renovated, well-proportioned rooms are painted white, adorned with the occasional photo, carefully chosen fabrics and lovingly restored old furniture. The bathrooms are faultless, with all mod-cons to hand. Depending on the season, breakfast is served at the large kitchen table in front of the open fire or on the terrace next to the swimming pool.

We most liked
The warm, simple family welcome.

This farm located on the town's doorstep is said to date back to 1750. The tastefully decorated rooms, located in the main wing and in a restored barn, are furnished with a combination of family heirlooms, antiques and modern pieces. Pastimes include a library complete with piano and board games and swings for the children in the garden under the shade of a superb chestnut tree.

Access : 12km southbound from Hautefort on the D 704

Access : 15km north-east on the N 21 towards Limoges and then right on the D 705

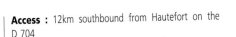

35 **HÔTEL DE LA MADELEINE**
M. Mélot

1 place de la Petite-Rigaudie
24200 Sarlat-la-Canéda
Tel. 05 53 59 10 41
Fax 05 53 31 03 62
hotel.madeleine @ wanadoo.fr
www.hoteldelamadeleine-sarlat.com

Closed 1 Jan to 12 Feb • 39 rooms, 2 of which have disabled access, with bath/WC or shower/WC, all have air-conditioning and television • €73 to €94 (€61 to €74 low season); breakfast €9; half board available • Menus from €26 to €44 • Terrace

36 **HÔTEL DES RÉCOLLETS**
M. Larequie

4 rue Jean-Jacques-Rousseau
24200 Sarlat-la-Canéda
Tel. 05 53 31 36 00
Fax 05 53 30 32 62
contact @ hotel-recollets-sarlat.com
www.hotel-recollets-sarlat.com

Open all year • 18 rooms with bathroom and television • €42 to €62; breakfast €7 • No restaurant • Car park

 Ideally located a step from the centre of historic Sarlat.

Freshly painted sky-blue shutters, restored frontage, stylishly renovated rooms with modern amenities, a brand-new dining room in shades of red and orange and a spacious sitting room decorated with prints and green plants. This fine hotel, said to be the oldest in town, dating from 1840, has just been renovated from top to bottom. Extremely practical garage (at an extra cost).

 The tranquillity of this hotel in the heart of the medieval city.

The cloisters of the Récollets convent, which dates back to the 17C, is now home to a characterful hotel, whose attractive stone walls are covered in wisteria and climbing roses. A narrow staircase leads up to small, well-restored rooms. Each one is different, but all feature the same happy blend of contemporary furniture and original beams and walls. Breakfast is served in a handsome room, where stone prevails, or on a delightful patio. Baggage service available from the public car park.

Access : On a main square at the entrance to the medieval town

Access : In the old town

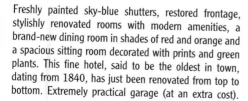

SARLAT-LA-CANÉDA - 24200

SORGES - 24420

37 LE MAS DE CASTEL
Mme Castalian

Sudalissant
24200 Sarlat-la-Caneda
Tel. 05 53 59 02 59
Fax 05 53 28 25 62
castalian @ wanadoo.fr

Open from 30 Mar to 11 Nov • 13 rooms, half of which are on garden level and one has disabled access. Rooms have bath/WC or shower/WC and television • €48 to €66 (€46 to €56 low season); breakfast €6.80 • No restaurant • Garden, car park. No dogs allowed • Outdoor swimming pool

38 CHAMBRE D'HÔTE AU VILLAGE
M. Valentini

Le Bourg
24420 Sorges
Tel. 05 53 05 05 08
Fax 05 53 05 05 08

Closed in Oct • 3 rooms with shower/WC and television • €34, breakfast €5 • No table d'hôte • Terrace, garden. Credit cards not accepted

The enchanting countryside feel of this authentic farmhouse.

Located in the heart of an unspoilt countryside, this farmhouse has been turned into a welcoming hostelry with rustic rooms upstairs or level with the garden (our favourites). A cockerel, the last remaining survivor of the hen house, joyfully serenades guests with a not-too-early morning call. Enjoy the relaxed pace of a traditional Périgord home and take a dip in the swimming pool before breakfast. The nights are so peaceful that you'll even be philosophical about the rooster's morning chorus.

Sampling the "black diamond" that has made Sorges famous.

This tiny village house, probably built in the 15C, is just next door to the Tourist Office and the Truffle Museum, devoted to the local "black diamonds". Bedrooms in a charming rural style feature wooden floorboards, stone walls, wooden ceilings and antique furniture. In the summer, breakfast is served in the lovely inner courtyard under the welcome shade of an enormous lime-tree.

Access : 3km from Sarlat-la-Canéda on the D 704 towards Gourdon, right onto the Canéda road, then take a minor road

Access : In the village

TOURTOIRAC - 24390

VAUNAC - 24800

39 **L'ENCLOS**

M. et Mme Ornsteen

Pragelier
24390 Tourtoirac
Tel. 05 53 51 11 40
Fax 05 53 50 37 21
rornsteen@yahoo.com
www.hotellenclos.com

Closed from Oct to Apr • 5 rooms • €60 to €100, breakfast €9 • Table d'hôte €15 to €30 • Park, car park. Credit cards not accepted • Outdoor swimming pool

40 **FERME DES GUEZOUX**

M. Fouquet

Les Guezoux
24800 Vaunac
Tel. 05 53 62 06 39
Fax 05 53 62 88 74
escargot.perigord@wanadoo.fr
www.escargotduperigord.com

Open all year • 3 rooms • €34 (€30 low season), breakfast €4 • No table d'hôte • Garden, car park

 The unusual complex of seven independent cottages.

You too will fall under the charm of this unusual hamlet of cottages, also a favourite with a number of American film stars! The luxuriously decorated, personalised rooms are dotted around the garden in various outhouses, such as the former chapel, bakery and estate manager's house. Definitively rustic in character, all feature beautiful provençal fabrics. Walnut and fruit trees abound in the beautiful parkland which is well worth a ramble.

 Delicious home-made walnut cake served at breakfast time.

Hidden by dense woodland, this stone farmhouse was restored in 1990 and makes a wonderfully peaceful retreat for anyone hoping to get away from it all. Whitewashed walls, tiled floors and pine furniture paint the picture of the simple, but impeccably kept bedrooms. The genial proprietor loves showing his guests his very own snail farm.

Access : 5km westbound from Hautefort on the D 62, then the D 67

Access : 9km northbound on the RN 21, then take the lane on the right

 41 HOSTELLERIE LES AIGUILLONS
M. Beeuwsaert

 Le Beuil
24320 Saint-Martial-Viveyrols
Tel. 05 53 91 07 55
Fax 05 53 91 00 43
lesaiguillons @ aol.com
www.hostellerielesaiguillons.com

Closed 1 Jan to 15 Apr and 15 Oct to 31 Dec • 8 rooms, one of which has disabled access, all have bath/WC and television • €62 to €107; breakfast included; half board available • Menus €25 to €42 • Terrace, park, car park • Outdoor swimming pool

42 CHAMBRE D'HÔTE M. CLÉMENT
M. et Mme Clément

 1 rue du Stade
33830 Belin-Béliet
Tel. 05 56 88 13 17
maison.clem @ wanadoo.fr

Open all year • 5 rooms • €6, breakfast €6 • No table d'hôte • Park, car park. Credit cards not accepted

 Woods, hills and open fields for as far as the eye can see.

Here you will find total peace and quiet and a place in the sun, disturbed only by the twittering of birds and the occasional distant murmur of country life. Built on the ruins of an old farmhouse, this hotel offers fresh, spacious rooms, a restaurant in hacienda style and a terrace overlooking the grounds, surrounded by countryside. If you find yourself suffering withdrawal symptoms, the traffic jams, pollution and stress of Paris are a mere 500km stone's throw away!

 The refined decoration of this 16C manor house.

This handsome manor house is encircled by grounds, planted with immemorial oaks and many rarer varieties. The interior decoration is sophisticated down to the tiniest details, from the elegant wainscoting in the lobby and the thick oak doors with wrought-iron locks to the parquet floors and marble fireplace in each sitting and dining room. The light, airy bedrooms are equally elegant and most overlook the beautiful parkland. Discreet staff.

Access : 5km to the north-west of Verteillac on the D 1, then right on the D 101, the C 201 and finally a minor road

Access : In the park

 43 **CONTINENTAL**
M. Landereethe

10 rue Montesquieu
33000 Bordeaux
Tel. 05 56 52 66 00
Fax 05 56 52 77 97
continental@hotel-le-continental.com
www.hotel-le-continental.com

Closed 25 Dec to 3 Jan • 51 rooms, 22 of which are air-conditioned, all have bath/WC or shower/WC and television • €71 to €95; breakfast €7 • No restaurant • Car park nearby

44 **DOMAINE DE CARRAT**
M. et Mme Péry

Route de Sainte-Hélène
33480 Castelnau-de-Médoc
Tel. 05 56 58 24 80
Fax 05 56 58 24 80

Closed at Christmas • 3 rooms • €53 to €59, breakfast included • No table d'hôte • Park, car park. Credit cards not accepted

An ideal starting point for exploring Bordeaux on foot.

This 18C town mansion is located on a semi-pedestrian, shopping street in historic Bordeaux. The entrance hall, staircase and glass-ceilinged breakfast room testify to the establishment's stylish history, and though the bedrooms cannot compete for character, a hospitable master of the house makes it a point of pride to see that they are comfortable and well kept. Snug sitting room.

Romance pervades this country estate.

This red-shuttered country seat, built in 1885, nestles in its own grounds, surrounded by 50 acres of woodland. Formerly the stables of the neighbouring castle, it now houses comfortable, quiet bedrooms, graced with family heirlooms. The most pleasant, on the ground floor, open directly onto the lawn. A roaring open fire welcomes guests in the winter, while the summer months ring to the voices of children swimming in the Jalette. Extremely attentive staff.

Access : In the pedestrian area

Access : 1km to the south-west of Castelnau-de-Médoc

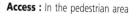

  45 HENRI IV
M. Chalvet de Recy

Place du 8-Mai-1945
33230 Coutras
Tel. 05 57 49 34 34
Fax 05 57 49 20 72
hotel-henriIV.gironde @ wanadoo.fr

Open all year • 14 rooms on 2 floors with bath/WC or shower/WC and television • €49 to €51; breakfast €7 • No restaurant • Garden, car park

  46 LES REMPARTS
M. Povéromo

16 rue du Château
33890 Gensac
Tel. 05 57 47 43 46
Fax 05 57 47 46 76

Closed from 11 Nov to 31 Dec, Sun evening, Mon and Tue lunchtime • 7 rooms, one of which has disabled access; all have bath/WC or shower/WC and television • €60 (€55 low season); breakfast €7.50, half board available • Menus €24 (weekdays) to €40 • Car park, garden

We most liked **The hotel's polished service.**

Coutras rose to fame following a battle fought here in 1587 by Henry of Navarre, the future Henry IV. The 19C mansion with a graceful courtyard-garden to the front now houses a well-kept hotel with pine furnished rooms. Double-glazing efficiently blocks out the rumble of the nearby railway and the attic rooms on the top floor are air-conditioned.

We most liked **The warm, friendly welcome from the whole family.**

Exceptionally well-located, this house stands on the site of the former ramparts, dominating the old village and the surrounding countryside. The 11C presbytery now houses simple but appealing rooms furnished in a rustic style and hung with bright, colourful fabrics. The dining room, which affords a splendid panoramic view of the Durèze Valley, lies on the other side of a delightful little garden.

Access : In the town centre, opposite the railway station

Access : Very close to the church

47 LE PAVILLON DE MARGAUX
Mme Laurent

3 rue Georges-Mandel
33460 Margaux
Tel. 05 57 88 77 54
Fax 05 57 88 77 73
le-pavillon-de-margaux@wanadoo.fr
www.pavillondemargaux.com

Open all year • 14 rooms with bath/WC television, 5 in a separate wing, 10 are air-conditioned • €81 to €110; breakfast €10; half board available • Restaurant closed Tue and Wed from 16 Nov to 31 Mar; menus €12 (weekday lunchtimes) to €51 • Private car park • Surrounded by vineyards

The hotel's remarkable wine cellar.

As you contemplate this entrancing 19C abode on the edge of the vineyards, it is difficult to imagine that it was formerly home to the village school. The shouts and laughter of the playground have given way to sophisticated decoration and a much calmer atmosphere. Each room is named after and decorated in the spirit of a Médoc château; those in the new wing are smaller but just as comfortable as the others. Elegant dining room and veranda overlooking the vineyards.

Access : On the way into the village of Margaux

48 L'ESCAPADE
M. Bolton

La Grâce
33220 Port-Sainte-Foy
Tel. 05 53 24 22 79
Fax 05 53 57 45 05
info@escapade-dordogne.com
www.escapade-dordogne.com

Open from Feb to early Nov; closed Sun evening and Fri in Feb and Mar • 12 rooms with bath/WC or shower/WC and television • €48 to €52; breakfast €7; half board available • Restaurant only open in the evening; menus €18 to €50 (booking necessary) • Terrace, car park. No dogs allowed • Outdoor swimming pool, fitness room, sauna, squash

An active country-break in an unspoilt setting.

This 17C tobacco farm, run by a Franco-English team, boasts impressive leisure installations including a swimming pool, fitness room, squash court and sauna. The countrified rooms all look out over the peaceful, unspoilt countryside. Some also have a view of the foals, mares and stallions of the nearby riding stables. Rustic-style restaurant.

Access : Westbound from Sainte-Foy-la-Grande on the D 936, then a minor road

49 CHÂTEAU DU BROUSTARET
M. et Mme Brunet

Le Broustaret
33410 Rions
Tel. 05 56 62 96 97
Fax 08 26 07 04 44
broustaret @ libertysurf.fr
 www.broustaret.net

Closed from 1 Nov to Easter • 5 rooms with bath/WC • €45 to €50, breakfast included • No table d'hôte • Park, car park. Credit cards not accepted, no dogs allowed

50 CHÂTEAU MEYLET
Mme Favard

La Gomerie
33330 Saint-Émilion
Tel. 05 57 24 68 85
Fax 05 57 24 77 35
château.meylet @ free.fr
www.chateau.meylet.free.fr

Open all year • 4 rooms with bathrooms • €52 to €58, breakfast included • No table d'hôte • Sitting room, garden, car park. Credit cards not accepted

Soaking up the atmosphere of a Bordeaux vineyard.

This stately late-19C manor house on a wine-growing estate enjoys a wonderful position in the heart of the acclaimed Côtes de Bordeaux vineyards. Well-proportioned, tranquil rooms command views over the hills, vineyards and woodland. Guests can prepare their own breakfast in a fitted kitchen. Wine-tasting and visits of the cellars organised on request.

The rustic charm of the rooms.

A five-acre vineyard surrounds this elegant 1789 property. The rooms boast polished parquet floors and lovely 18C furniture inherited by the family or unearthed in the local flea markets. Some bedrooms enjoy a view of the vineyard, while others overlook the garden's magnificent Indian bean tree. Breakfast is served in the conservatory in the winter and under the arbour in the summer.

Access : 6km northbound from Cadillac on the D 11 towards Targon, then take the D 120

Access : 1.5km westbound from Saint-Émilion on the Libourne road (D 243)

SAINT-FERME - 33580

SAINT-HIPPOLYTE - 33330

 51 LE MANOIR DE JAMES
M. et Mme Dubois

Route de Sainte-Colombe
33580 Saint-Ferme
Tel. 05 56 61 69 75
Fax 05 56 61 89 78
midubois2 @ wanadoo.fr
www.manoir-de-james.com

Closed from 1 to 15 Jan • 4 rooms, one is on the ground floor, all have bath/WC • €65, breakfast included • No table d'hôte • Car park. No dogs admitted, credit cards not accepted • Barbecue. Outdoor swimming pool, bicycles, table-tennis, boules, board games

 The manor's unbeatable position in the heart of a sought-after tourist region.

Set in ancient woodland and meadows, this 18C manor makes an ideal base camp for touring the hilly vineyards of the legendary Entre-Deux-Mers region. Period furniture adorns the well-proportioned, quiet rooms, all of which offer wonderful views of the surrounding countryside. The lady of the house, a former tourist guide, is happy to share her valuable insights into the region. Excellent welcome.

Access : 15km eastbound from Sauveterre-de-Guyenne on the D 230 and then the D 139

 52 CHÂTEAU MONLOT CAPET
M.et Mme Rivals

33330 Saint-Hippolyte
Tel. 05 57 74 49 47
Fax 05 57 24 62 33
mussetrivals @ belair-monlot.com
www.belair-monlot.com

Open all year • 6 rooms with bathrooms • €61 to €115, breakfast included • No table d'hôte • Garden, car park

 The personalised decoration of the rooms.

This château, with its chalk façade and lovely tiled roof is typical of the many stately homes of the region. Each room, stylishly furnished with antiques, paintings and old photos, is named after a variety of grape: Merlot, Cabernet, Sauvignon and so on. The vine theme is also prominent in the pleasant breakfast room. The lovely shaded garden is at its most idyllic in summer.

Access : 3km eastbound from St-Émilion, towards Castillon on the D 245

 53 LA LÉZARDIÈRE
M. et Mme Mattei

Boimier-Gabouriaud
33540 Saint-Martin-de-Lerm
Tel. 05 56 71 30 12
Fax 05 56 71 30 12
lalezardiere@free.fr
www.lalezardiere.free.fr

Closed Jan, Feb ● 6 rooms and one gîte with shower/WC or bath/WC ● €60, breakfast included, half-board available ● Table d'hôte €20 ● Garden, car park. Credit cards not accepted ● Outdoor swimming pool, bikes, children's games, pétanque, table tennis

 54 TY-BONI
M. et Mme Boniface

1831 route de Capbreton
40150 Angresse
Tel. 05 58 43 98 75
Fax 05 58 43 98 75
info@ty-boni.com
www.ty-boni.com

Open all year ● 3 rooms ● €70 (€55 low season), breakfast included ● No table d'hôte ● Park, car park. Credit cards not accepted, no dogs allowed ● Outdoor swimming pool

 Lazing by the swimming pool in the immense garden.

 The owners' warm, generous welcome.

A beautifully restored 17C farmhouse enjoying a stunning view over the Dropt Valley. Stone and wood add warmth to the welcoming rooms in the renovated cowsheds. The exposed beams, terracotta tiled floor, huge table and fireplace and original mangers lend the breakfast room a real country character. Ask to see the owner's fine collection of works on the local wines and produce.

Only the chirping of birds and gentle breezes rustling through the pine trees interrupt the peace and quiet of this contemporary house in regional style. The soberly decorated rooms are very pleasant. Guests can cook their own meals in a guest kitchen. The park and swimming pool next to the pond are particularly pleasant during the summer months. An ideal situation within easy reach of the beach and the lively seaside village of Hossegor.

Access : 8km to the south-east of Sauveterre-de-Guyenne on the D 670, the D 230 and then the D 129

Access : 3km eastbound from Hossegor on the D 133

55 LE DOMAINE DE PAGUY
M. et Mme Darzacq

Domaine de Paguy
40240 Betbezer-d'Armagnac
Tel. 05 58 44 81 57
Fax 05 58 44 68 09
albert.darzacq @ wanadoo.fr

Closed Wed from 1 July to 15 Sep • 6 rooms • €40 to €63, breakfast included • Table d'hôte from €16 (weekdays) to €31 • Park, terrace, car park. Credit cards not accepted, dogs not allowed in rooms • Outdoor swimming pool. Guided tours of the Armagnac cellars

56 LES LACS D'HALCO
M. et Mme Demen

Route de Cazalis
40700 Hagetmau
Tel. 05 58 79 30 79
Fax 05 58 79 36 15
contact @ hotel-des-lacs-dhalco.fr
www.hotel-des-lacs-dhalco.com

Open all year • 24 rooms with bath/WC and television, 2 have disabled access • €64 to €98; breakfast €10; half board available • Air-conditioned restaurant with disabled access; menus €25 to €50 • Car park. No dogs allowed in restaurant • Indoor swimming pool, tennis, bicycle rentals

 The tour and commentary of the Armagnac cellars.

This 16C manor house stands in the centre of a vast wine-growing estate overlooking the Douze Valley. Spacious, attractive rooms, partly renovated, open onto the landscaped park and the vineyards, where hens and ducks roam free. Fine local Landes cuisine takes pride of place in the kitchen of this handsome property.

 The resolutely futuristic architecture blends in perfectly with the Landes countryside.

Steel, glass, wood and stone comprise the surprising modern architecture overlooking the lakes and forest. The countless bay windows of this semi-circular construction invite guests to gaze out on the countryside. A spacious hall, contemporary bar and unusual dining room, built on a rotunda which seems to float on the water, are located on the ground-floor. Upstairs, the ample, modern bedrooms are decorated in a pleasantly unfussy style. Covered swimming pool, rowing boats and crazy golf.

Access : 5km to the north-east of Labastide-d'Armagnac on the D 11 then the D 35

Access : 3km south-west of Hagetmau on the Cazalis road

AQUITAINE

 57 CAPCAZAL DE PACHIOU
Mme Dufourcet

 606 route de Pachiou
40350 Mimbaste
Tel. 05 58 55 30 54
Fax 05 58 55 30 54

Open all year • 4 rooms • €48 to €65, breakfast included • Table d'hôte €20 (evening only) • Car park. Credit cards not accepted

 58 LES ARBOUSIERS
Mme Labri

 Le Gaille
40630 Sabres
Tel. 05 58 07 52 52
Fax 05 58 07 52 52
lesarbousiers @ aol.com
www.chambres-landes.com

Open all year • 6 rooms • €49 (€45 low season), breakfast included, half board available • Table d'hôte €18 • Park, car park. Credit cards not accepted, no dogs allowed

The authenticity of the house and the welcome.

This wonderful old house has been in the same family since it was built in the 17C. Its loving restoration has preserved countless traces of its illustrious past, such as a dovecote, bird cage, original panelling and parquet floors. The house exudes history, as the canopied beds, carved fireplaces and old prints illustrate, and this same proud commitment to tradition is in evidence in the kitchen, where duck and goose feature prominently in mouth-watering local dishes.

 The enchanting picture of this half-timbered house.

Set in a clearing in a pine forest, this half-timbered home, typical of the region, never fails to attract admiring glances. The comfortable new rooms are bright and airy. The large bay windows of the restaurant also flood the dining room with light, while diners can enjoy the view of a park which makes no secret of the owner's passion for wildlife and ornithology. What's more, the owner's simple, unaffected welcome is quite irresistible.

Access : 12km south-east of Dax by N 947. Don't take D 16 at Mimbaste junction; continue for 1km and follow the yellow arrow to the right

Access : 7.5km westbound from Sabres on the D 44

59 CHAMBRE D'HÔTE M. LADEUIX
M. et Mme Ladeuix

26 avenue Salvador-Allende
40220 Tarnos
Tel. 05 59 64 13 95
Fax 05 59 64 13 95
heleneladeuix @ hotmail.com
www.enaquitaine.com

Open all year • 5 rooms and one gîte • €65, breakfast included • No table d'hôte • Park, car park. Credit cards not accepted • Outdoor swimming pool

60 CHÂTEAU DES JACOBINS
Mme Bujan

1 ter place des Jacobins
47000 Agen
Tel. 05 53 47 03 31
Fax 05 53 47 02 80
www.chateau-des-jardins.com

Open all year • 15 rooms with bath/WC or shower/WC and television, 13 are air-conditioned • €94 to €103; breakfast €12 to €14 • No restaurant • Park, private car park. No cats allowed, dogs admitted on request

The pleasant surprise of the woodland to the rear of the house.

From the road, it is impossible to imagine that this house covered in wisteria opens onto such a sumptuous park of oak, chestnut, maple, mimosa, banana and pear trees. Most of the rooms are relatively simply decorated, except one which has a distinctly Basque accent. Guests have the use of a laundry room and a kitchen. Children will love the sheep pen, as well as the nearby rabbit and poultry cages.

The pleasantly old-fashioned atmosphere which reigns throughout this characterful abode.

The central location combined with tranquillity is greatly appreciated by the patrons of this private mansion built in 1832. A shady courtyard leads visitors into the establishment. On the ground-floor are two prettily decorated sitting rooms and a handsome staircase which leads up to the bedrooms. Of varying sizes, all are comfortably appointed and decorated individually in a deliciously outmoded style. A perfect antidote to those who abhor hotel chains!

Access : 5km northbound from Bayonne on the N 10

Access : In the town centre near the Jacobins Church

 61 CHÂTEAU DE LA SEIGLAL
M. et Mme Decourty

 47380 Monclar-d'Agenais
Tel. 05 53 41 81 30
decourty-chambres-hotes @ wordonline.fr

Open all year (by reservation) • 5 rooms • €60, breakfast included, half board €96 • Table d'hôte €18 (evening only) • Park, car park. Credit cards not accepted, no dogs allowed • Outdoor swimming pool, table-tennis, table football, football pitch, fishing, walking, cycling

 62 LE DOMAINE DU CAUZE
SCI du Cauze

 47600 Nérac
Tel. 05 53 65 54 44
Fax 05 53 65 54 44
cauze.pope @ wanadoo.fr
www.domaineducauze.com

Closed from 23 Dec to 2 Jan • 4 rooms • €53, breakfast included, half-board available • Table d'hôte €18 to €24 (except Jul-Aug) • Car park. No dogs allowed • Outdoor swimming pool

We most liked **The friendly atmosphere of this 19C castle.**

Hidden by a park planted with ancient trees, this small château built in 1820 is a haven of peace and quiet. The renovated, well-proportioned, comfortable rooms, named after the owner's five sisters, overlook the park and the surrounding meadows. The dining room is a real treasure chest of period furniture, carved hunting scenes and a superb marble and earthenware fireplace. Not to be outdone, the menu boasts produce from the surrounding farms as well as delicious home-made pastries.

We most liked **The tranquillity of this hundred-year-old establishment.**

This superbly restored old farmhouse has it all. First and foremost, an idyllic situation on a hillside with sweeping views of the dense forests of the Landes and the Gers on fine days. Add to this the tranquillity of the tastefully decorated rooms and last, but not least, the meals, served under the arbour in the summer and whipped up with rare enthusiasm by the imaginative owner-chef. Friendly, hospitable hosts.

Access : 6km northbound from Fongrave on the D 238 then the D 667, at the no 25 kilometre marker

Access : 2.5km eastbound from Nérac towards Agen (D 656)

 63 CHÂTEAU CANTET
M. et Mme Raitrie

47250 Samazan
Tel. 05 53 20 60 60
Fax 05 53 89 63 53
jbdelaraitrie@wanadoo.fr

Closed 15 Dec to 15 Jan • 4 rooms with bath or shower and separate WC • €56 to €70, breakfast included • Table d'hôte €23 • Park, car park. Credit cards not accepted, no dogs allowed • Outdoor swimming pool. Children's games room

 64 CHAMBRE D'HÔTE ARRAYOA
M. Ibarburu

Ferme "Arrayoa"
64310 Ascain
Tel. 05 59 54 06 18

Open all year • 4 rooms with bathrooms • €50, breakfast included • No table d'hôte • Living room with a kitchen and library. Credit cards not accepted

 We most liked
The wide range of leisure activities.

An elegant 16C manor house set in well-tended grounds in the heart of the countryside. The bright colour scheme of the rooms sets off a smart but homely interior, with a hint of rustic style. Meals are served in the Louis XIII-style dining room or under the arbour around the pool. The choice of leisure activities is vast: play room, bicycles, lawn croquet, billiards, table-tennis, basketball, pétanque and only 10km away, a golf course and tennis courts.

Access : 10km southbound from Marmande towards Casteljaloux

 We most liked
Getting away from it all without entirely forgoing the social whirl of the Basque coast.

This lovely house seems to have been designed with the good life in mind, from the charming countrified rooms to the tempting home-made foie gras and other delicacies served in the former cowshed. If your waistband feels a little tight, you can try your hand on the establishment's private pelota court or don your walking boots and hike up the Rhune. The superb view is more than worth the effort, but those with fewer calories to burn may prefer to catch the little train from the Col de St Ignace.

Access : 800m from the pelota court

65 MAÏMADE
Mme Augareils

6 place Cazenave
64260 Buzy
Tel. 05 59 21 01 01
Fax 05 59 21 01 01
rolande.augareils @ wanadoo.fr

Closed in Jan • 6 rooms • €48 to €52, breakfast included, half board available • Table d'hôte €16 to €20 • Car park. Credit cards not accepted, no dogs allowed

66 LA BELLE AUBERGE
M. et Mme Vicassiau

64270 Castagnède
Tel. 05 59 38 15 28
Fax 05 59 65 03 57

Closed from 1 to 15 Jun, 20 Dec to 31 Jan, Sun and Mon evenings • 14 rooms with bath/WC or shower/WC, all have television • €37 to €50; breakfast €5.50; half board €40 • Restaurant closed Sun and Mon evenings; menus €12 to €22 • Terrace, garden, car park. No dogs allowed • Outdoor swimming pool

The warm welcome extended by the lady of the house, Rolande, and her staff.

This attractive Béarn farmhouse with its wrought-iron gate, flowered window boxes and courtyard, lies in the heart of the village. Don't stand on ceremony, just sit down with the other guests and Rolande's family at the huge open-air table, which can seat up to 25, and enjoy a wonderful meal, invariably accompanied by a song or two. The rooms are lovingly decorated with old lace and family heirlooms, but, beware, none are heated. 100 % authentic Béarn cooking.

Killing time around the swimming pool.

Nothing could be more welcoming than this family-run establishment nestling in a picturesque hamlet on the fast-flowing Gave d'Oloron river. The bar and two country-style dining rooms, serving generous helpings of hearty, local dishes, are located in the main wing of the old house. The bedrooms, in a later wing, are not luxurious but they are well looked-after and all overlook the spacious garden and unusually-shaped swimming pool.

Access : 4km northbound from Arudy on the D 920

Access : Leave Salies-de-Béarn on the D 17 (towards Peyrehorade), then left onto the D 27 and right onto the D 384

 67 LE CHÂTEAU DE BOUES
Mme Dornon

 64570 Féas
Tel. 05 59 39 95 49
Fax 05 59 39 95 49

Closed from late Sep to Apr • 4 rooms • €59, breakfast included • No table d'hôte • Garden, car park. Credit cards not accepted, no dogs allowed • Outdoor swimming pool

 68 BRIKÉTÉNIA
M. et Mme Ibarboure

142 rue de l'Église
64210 Guéthary
Tel. 05 59 26 51 34
Fax 05 59 54 71 55

Open from 15 Mar to 15 Nov • 21 rooms, 12 of which have balconies, 1 has disabled access, all have bath/WC and television • €65 to €90 (€60 to €80 low season); breakfast €10 • No restaurant • Car park

 The kindness of the hospitable owners.

On the doorstep of Baretous Valley, the pristine walls of this lofty 18C castle dominate the surrounding Béarn countryside. The bedrooms, located in the central wing – the owners occupy the towers – enjoy views of the garden, swimming pool and superb kitchen garden. Breakfast is a lively, friendly affair and guests are made to feel like friends of the family.

 Grab a "makhila" – a traditional Basque walking stick – and explore this seaside resort.

The coaching inn, built in 1680 on the heights of Guéthary, is a fine example of traditional Basque architecture: steep tiled roof, balcony, whitewashed walls, timber frames and red shutters. Perhaps it was the ocean view from some of the rooms that appealed to one Napoleon Bonaparte, an illustrious former guest? Be that as it may, the energetic proprietors are not the sort to rest on their laurels and the inn has recently been renovated from top to toe.

Access : 8km to the south-west of Oloron-Ste-Marie on the D 919

Access : Near the church

ISPOURE - 64220

ISSOR - 64570

 69 FERME ETXEBERRIA

M. Mourguy

64220 Ispoure
Tel. 05 59 37 06 23
Fax 05 59 37 06 23

Open all year • 4 rooms • €44, breakfast included • No table d'hôte • Car park • Tour of the cellars and wine-tasting

 70 LA FERME AUX SANGLIERS

M. Delhay-Cazaurang

Micalet
64570 Issor
Tel. 05 59 34 43 96
Fax 05 59 34 49 56

Open all year • 5 rooms with bathrooms • €37 to €50, breakfast €50 • Table d'hôte €14 • Car park. Credit cards not accepted, no dogs allowed • Tasting and sale of home-made "charcuterie"

Donkey rides through Irouleguy's vineyards.

What better way to really get to know the Basque country than by staying in this attractive farmhouse surrounded by vineyards. The converted barn houses modern, soberly decorated and very pleasant rooms. Guests have the use of a kitchenette, an attractive breakfast room and a conservatory which overlooks the vines. The owners, who also produce wine and raise donkeys, are happy to help guests organise hikes throughout the region.

The stunning view from all the bedrooms.

A narrow road winds its way up to this lovingly restored Béarn farmhouse. You can be sure of a warm, generous welcome, together with comfortable rooms, all of which command sweeping views of the valley and the Pyrenean peaks. The focus is on healthy, local produce and the owner, who breeds animals, adores taking visitors round his boar parks, to the delight of children.

Access : 0.8km to the north-east of Saint-Jean-Pied-de-Port on the D 933

Access : 10km westbound from St-Christau on the D 918 as far as Asasp, then the N 134 and the D 918 towards Arette

 71 HÔTEL DU CHÊNE
Mme Salaberry

 64250 Itxassou
Tel. 05 59 29 75 01
Fax 05 59 29 27 39

Closed in Jan and Feb, on Mon and Tue from Oct to Jun, and on Mon in Jul, Aug and Sep • 16 rooms with bath/WC, some have television • €43 (€41 low season); breakfast €6.50; half-board available • Menus €15 to €38 • Terrace, garden, car park. No dogs allowed in restaurant

 72 SOUBELETA
Mme Régérat

 64250 Itxassou
Tel. 05 59 29 78 64

Open all year • 5 rooms • €46 to €52, breakfast included • No table d'hôte • Garden, car park. Credit cards not accepted, no dogs allowed

 The superb Villa Arnaga, nearby, one-time home to Edmond Rostand, creator of Cyrano de Bergerac.

The doors of this hospitable country inn have been open since 1696. The bedrooms, some of which are graced with marble fireplaces and old Basque furniture, overlook the cherry trees of Itxassou – a sight to behold in the spring! Make sure you sample the famous blackcherry jam under the colourful blue beams of the dining room or in the shade of the sweet-scented wisteria.

 The tranquil mood of this peaceful 17C mansion.

This imposing mansion, built in 1675, certainly makes the most of a lovely spot in the upper part of the village. The generously proportioned rooms, graced with gleaming family antiques, look over meadows and the orchard; two have marble fireplaces. The light, airy sitting room is very pleasant and children will love visiting the cows in the neighbouring dairy farm.

Access : Near the church

Access : In the village, stay on the D 918 until the Nive bridge, then turn right

73 **MAISON ELIXONDOA**
M. et Mme Walther

64120 Pagolle
Tel. 05 59 65 65 34
Fax 05 59 65 72 15
jean.walther @ wanadoo.fr
www.elixondoa.com

Open all year • 4 rooms • €48, breakfast included • Table d'hôte €20 • Garden, car park. Credit cards not accepted

74 **VILLA ARGI-EDER**
M. Basset

Avenue Napoléon III
64500 Saint-Jean-de-Luz
Tel. 05 59 54 81 65
Fax 05 59 54 81 65
villa-argi-eder @ wanadoo.fr

Open all year • 4 rooms • €50, breakfast €5 • No table d'hôte • Terrace, garden, car park. Credit cards not accepted

 The pastoral charm of this remote spot.

Those in need of a serious break should head for this 17C farm, set among open fields, on one of the old pilgrim roads to Santiago de Compostela. The bedrooms, recently fitted-out with all the modern comforts, overlook the surrounding hillsides. Meals are taken in the vast dining room where the exposed stone work and timbers cannot fail to catch the eye. Friendly service.

 Admire the reckless surfers braving the giant waves.

This handsome Basque villa, recently spruced up with a new coat of paint, has something for everyone: tranquillity, a well-tended lawn lined in flowers and a superb location just 100m from the surfing beach. The brand-new spacious bedrooms are an invitation to meditation and those overlooking the garden have private terraces. The bathrooms are neat and well appointed. One of the resort's most pleasant hotels.

Access : 13km westbound from Mauléon-Licharre on the D 918 then the D 302

Access : 5km to the north-east of Saint-Jean-de-Luz on the N 10 towards Biarritz, then take a minor road

SALIES-DE-BÉARN - 64270

SARE - 64310

75 LA CLOSERIE DU GUILHAT
Mme Potiron

Le Guilhat
64270 Salies-de-Béarn
Tel. 05 59 38 08 80
Fax 05 59 38 31 90
guilhat @ club-internet.fr

Open all year • 4 rooms and one gîte • €48 to €54, breakfast included, half board available • Table d'hôte €20 (evenings only except Thu) • Park, car park. Credit cards not accepted, no dogs allowed

76 ARRAYA
M. Fagoaga

64310 Sare
Tel. 05 59 54 20 46
Fax 05 59 54 27 04
hotel @ arraya.com
www.arraya.com

Closed 2 Nov to 27 Mar • 23 rooms, most have bath/WC, some have shower/WC, all have television • €69 to €120; breakfast €9; half board available • Restaurant closed Sun evening and Mon lunchtime (13 Sep to 2 July); menus €21 to €31 • Terrace, garden. No dogs allowed in rooms • Shop with Basque linen and local produce

 Whiling away the evenings on the terrace facing the Pyrenees.

It is difficult to find a fault with such a lovely old country house, especially one with a sumptuous landscaped park and an exquisite terrace overlooking the valley, set against a backdrop of Pyrenean peaks. A bold colour scheme distinguishes the quiet, well-dimensioned rooms, each of which is named after a flower. The mistress of the house makes guests feel truly welcome and dining on the winter veranda or summer terrace is an unforgettable experience.

 Chugging up the Rhune in an old train (1924).

This village, nestling at the foot of the Rhune, is a treasure chest of Basque heritage. In keeping with its historic past, the 17C coaching inn, which formerly welcomed pilgrims of St James, is a fine example of regional interior design with dark timbers, old furniture and colourful fabrics. The surrounding countryside, a former "smugglers' paradise" is now heaven on earth: footpaths criss-cross the region, winding through meadows where the local ponies and sheep graze peacefully.

Access : 4km northbound from Salies towards Puyoo, in the upper reaches of Salies

Access : In the heart of the village, near the main square, next to the pelota court

AUVERGNE

Shh! Auvergne's volcanoes are dormant and have been for many millennia, forming a natural rampart against the inroads of man and ensuring that this beautiful wilderness will never be entirely tamed. If you listen very carefully, you may just make out a distant rumble from Vulcania, where spectacular theme park attractions celebrate the sleeping giants. The region's windswept domes and peaks, sculpted by long-extinguished fires, are now the source of countless mountain springs that cascade down the steep slopes into brooks, rivers and crystal-clear lakes. Renowned for the therapeutic virtues of its waters, the region has long played host to countless well-heeled *curistes*, come to take the waters in its elegant spa resorts. It has to be said that many find it impossible to follow doctor's orders when faced with the enticing aroma of a country stew or a full-bodied Cantal cheese.

- Allier (03)
- Cantal (15)
- Haute-Loire (43)
- Puy-de-Dôme (63)

1 G. H. MONTESPAN-TALLEYRAND
M. Livertout

Place des Thermes
03160 Bourbon-L'Archambault
Tel. 04 70 67 00 24
Fax 04 70 67 12 00
hotelmontespan @ wanadoo.fr
www.hotel-montespan.com

Open from 1 Apr to 20 Oct • 44 rooms, 4 of which have kitchenettes, all have bath/WC or shower/WC and television • €56 to €100; breakfast €10; half board available • Menus €22 (in the week) to €45 • Garage. No dogs allowed • Outdoor swimming pool, fitness room

2 LE CHALET
M. Schweizer

03000 Coulandon
Tel. 04 70 46 00 66
Fax 04 70 44 07 09
hotel-chalet @ cs3i.fr
www.hotel.lechalet.com

Closed from Dec to Jan • 28 rooms, 19 of which are in a separate wing, one has disabled access. Rooms have bath/WC or shower/WC and television • €65 to €80; breakfast €9; half board available • Restaurant "Le Montégut": menus €18 (weekdays) to €39 • Terrace, park, car park • Outdoor swimming pool

 The attractive flowered garden at the foot of a medieval tower.

These historic houses stand next door to the spa centre with the Castle of the Dukes of Bourbon in the background. Practically all the ceilings feature traditional dark-timbered beams, while simple white-stone walls, adorned with elegant fireplaces, light up the cosy, personalised rooms. Talleyrand, and a number of noble ladies, including Mme de Montespan and Mme de Sévigné resided here while taking the waters. A grand old establishment which is definitely a cut above your average spa hotel.

 Generous breakfasts with a distinctly Alpine flavour; the landlord is Swiss.

A cluster of three buildings make up this 10-acre country estate, complete with a large pond for fishing, hundred-year-old parkland and a swimming pool. The rooms are situated in the "chalet", which also houses the reception and in the former stables, while the restaurant is in a more recent building. Savour the pleasure of waking up in the heart of the peaceful Bourbon countryside.

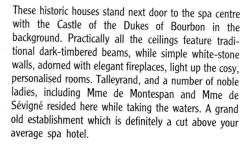

Access : In the centre of the resort, next to the spa

Access : 7km to the south-west of Moulins on the D 945 (towards Souvigny), then right on a minor road

3 DEMEURE D'HAUTERIVE
Mme Lefebvre

03340 La Ferté-Hauterive
Tel. 04 70 43 04 85
Fax 04 70 43 00 62
j.lefebvre @ demeure-hauterive.com
www.demeure-hauterive.com

Open all year • 5 rooms, one of which is on the ground
floor • €70 to €76 (€67 to €73 low season), breakfast
included • Park, car park • Swimming pool, horse-drawn
carriage outings

4 MANOIR LE PLAIX
Mme Raucaz

03320 Pouzy-Mésangy
Tel. 04 70 66 24 06
Fax 04 70 66 25 82
leplaix @ yahoo.fr

Closed 15 Dec to 15 Mar • 4 non-smoking rooms, all have
bathrooms • €40 to €44; breakfast included; half board
available • Table d'hôte €16 (evenings only) • Sitting
room, car park. Credit cards not accepted • Nearby:
tennis, mini golf

 We most liked
**Strolling through the park bedecked
in autumn colours.**

It would be difficult to find a more gracious
establishment than this opulent mansion, built in 1850
in the heart of an 8-acre park. The exquisitely decorated
rooms, particularly those on the ground floor, are
spacious. The house also provides its guests with a wide
range of leisure activities, including billiards, badminton
and table tennis, but the most pleasant of all is a stroll
through parkland dotted with ornamental pools and
follies. Highly friendly atmosphere.

 We most liked
**Walking along the banks of the
Bieudre, which meanders its way
through the immense property.**

This welcoming 16C stronghold stands in the heart of
a working farm. One of the chambres d'hôte is reached
by a handsome spiral staircase. Red-brick floor tiles,
wooden beams, old furniture and stone fireplaces set the
scene for a pleasantly, relaxed stay. In the evenings,
don't miss the chance to sample the delicious local
produce, including the tender Charolais beef raised on
the estate. Depending on the season, you can go
walking, fishing or mushroom picking.

Access : 12km northbound from
St-Pourçain-sur-Sioule on the N 9 then the D 32

Access : Drive for 1.5km to the north-west on a
minor road

 5 L'OMBRE DE GOZINIÈRE
Mme Pamela Line

03350 Theneuille
Tel. 04 70 67 59 17
Fax 04 70 67 59 17
 pamelaline@wanadoo.fr

Open Apr to Sep • 3 rooms • €45; breakfast included
• Table d'hôte €17 (by reservation only) • Sitting room,
garden, car park. Credit cards not accepted • Outdoor
swimming pool

 6 LE CHALET DE LA NEVERDIÈRE
M. et Mme Vrel

Les Ferrons
03160 Ygrande
Tel. 04 70 66 31 67
 Fax 04 70 66 32 64

Open all year • 4 rooms located in a small house 100m
from the farm • €42, breakfast included • Garden, car
park. Credit cards not accepted, no dogs allowed

 Taking a dip in the circular swimming pool set in a garden opening onto the countryside.

The owners of this attractive 17C building, a former outhouse of the neighbouring manor, have every right to be proud of its renovation. It now boasts fetching rooms with sloping ceilings where gingham fabrics, massive beams and rustic-style furniture create a pleasing, countrified atmosphere. Breakfasts and dinners are served in a cosy dining room which leads into a sitting room.

 The gargantuan breakfasts.

This early 20C house with its ochre edged façade and steep roof nestling in the heart of the Bourbon countryside, looks nothing like the chalets the region abounds in, but who cares? Its well-proportioned and well thought-out rooms overlook lush, green countryside. Tronçais Forest, 12km away, is perfect to walk off the extremely generous breakfasts. Very friendly staff.

Access : On the way out of the village on the D 953

Access : 10km to the south-west of Bourbon-l'Archambault on the D 953, then a minor road

7 BEAUSÉJOUR
M. Puech

15340 Calvinet
Tel. 04 71 49 91 68
Fax 04 71 49 98 63
beauséjour.puech @ wanadoo.fr
www.cantal-restaurant-puech.com

Closed from Jan to Apr • 10 rooms with bath/WC or shower/WC, all have television • €58 to €130; breakfast €10; half board available • Menus €25 (weekdays) to €60 (booking recommended) • Private car park

8 AUBERGE DU VIEUX CHÊNE
Mme Moins

34 route des Lacs
15270 Champs-sur-Tarentaine
Tel. 04 71 78 71 64
Fax 04 71 78 70 88
danielle.moins @ wanadoo.fr

Closed 1 Nov to 1 Apr, Sun and Mon out of season • 15 rooms on 2 floors with bathrooms, some have television • €62 to €80 (€50 to €71 low season); breakfast €9; half board available • Restaurant open only in the evenings; menus €23 to €31 • Terrace, garden, car park

An unforgettable dining experience.

A larger than life genius reigns over the kitchens of this traditional Auvergne house in the middle of nowhere. The master chef whips up imaginative recipes based on wholesome local produce in which mushrooms, chestnuts and pork figure prominently. Guests feast on his inspired creations in an elegant brick-coloured dining room-veranda. The rooms, practical rather than charming, are amply compensated for by the quality of the cooking.

The picturesque Artense region, somewhat reminiscent of Scandinavia.

The frontage of this historic 19C farmhouse is almost hidden by Virginia creeper and flowers. The pretty, cosy rooms overlook a pleasant, peaceful garden. Exposed beams, thick stone walls and a huge fireplace add character to the dining room in the converted barn. Relax on the shaded terrace and admire the beautiful countryside of hills and meadows where the owners' horses graze.

Access : On the Figeac road to Aurillac, leave the N 22 at Maurs for the D 19. In the centre of the village

Access : Not far from the centre of the village

 9 AUBERGE DE L'ASPRE
M. Landau

15140 Fontanges
Tel. 04 71 40 75 76
Fax 04 71 40 75 27
auberge.aspre @ worldonline.fr
www.auberge-aspre.com

Closed 17 Nov to 4 Feb and Oct to May Wed evenings and Mon • 8 rooms, one of which has disabled access. All have unusual split-level bathrooms and television • €50; breakfast €8; half board available • Menus €16 to €32 • Terrace, garden, car park • Outdoor swimming pool

 10 DE BARATHE
M. et Mme Breton

15130 Giou-de-Mamou
Tel. 04 71 64 61 72
Fax 04 71 64 85 10
 barathe @ wanadoo.fr

Open all year • 5 rooms • €45, breakfast included • Table d'hôte €12 (evenings only) • Garden, car park. Credit cards not accepted, no dogs allowed

 The tinkling of the cow-bells.

This old farmhouse with its beautiful stone-shingled roof lies in a secluded hamlet of the Aspre Valley not far from the village of Salers. The modern, brightly-coloured bedrooms, each of which has an unusual split-level bathroom, are situated in the old barn. Savour the traditional, tasty Auvergne menu in the rustic-style dining room, the veranda or on the pleasant terrace overlooking the garden.

 The authentic character of this country setting.

If you like the idea of waking to the sound of the cow-bells from the Salers cattle grazing in the lush, green meadows, then make a beeline for this place! Simple yet comfortable rooms, ideal for families. Exposed stonework, old furniture, a fireplace, wood benches and a sink set the scene of the authentic dining room. Meals are, of course, prepared using produce grown and reared on the farm.

Access : 5km southbound from Salers on the D 35

Access : 7km eastbound from Aurillac on the N 122 then the D 58

11 **AUBERGE DU PONT DE LANAU**
M. et Mme Kergoat

Lanau
15260 Neuvéglise
Tel. 04 71 23 57 76
Fax 04 71 23 53 84
aubergedupontdelanau@wanadoo.fr
auberge-du-pont-de-lanau.com

Closed from mid-Dec to Feb; Mon and Tue lunchtime
• 8 rooms on 2 floors, all have bath/WC or shower/WC
• €55 to €60; breakfast €9, half board available • Menus
€25 (weekdays) to €50 (by reservation only) • Terrace,
garden, car park

12 **LAC DES GRAVES**
M. Barbério

Jaulhac
15590 Lascelle
Tel. 04 71 47 94 06
Fax 04 71 47 96 55
lac.des.graves@wanadoo.fr
www.lacdesgraves.com

Open all year • 24 rooms, 5 of which are non-smoking,
2 of which have disabled access; all have bath/WC or
shower/WC and television • €54 to €58 (€40 to €45 low
season); breakfast €6; half board available • Menus €13
to €38 • Private car park, park, terrace • Swimming pool,
fishing in the lake, horse riding

The endless meanders of the River Truyère.

This former coaching house, built in 1821, spans one
of the rare crossing-places over the Truyère. Good, solid
furniture adorns the well-maintained rooms. The typical,
Auvergne-style decoration of the dining room with its
well-worn panelling, exposed beams and huge stone
fireplaces, has been preserved by successive owners over
the years. Guests have the run of a small garden and
a pleasant, shaded terrace.

Ever fancied a spot of fly fishing?

The Canadian-inspired architecture of this hotel blends
in perfectly with the superb landscape of the Jordanne
Valley. Several wood chalets built on the edge of the
lake house brand new rooms, which are both simple and
welcoming, and a panoramic restaurant. Sweeping
views of the water or the Cantal mountains are available
from all the rooms. Horse-lovers will be enchanted by
the riding center in extensive 90 acre grounds.

Access : 4.5km from Chaudes-Aigues on the D 921
(Saint-Flour road)

Access : 25km southbound from Aurillac on the
N 122 and the D 66

LOUBARESSE - 15320

MURAT - 15300

 13 LA PAGNOUNE
Mme et Mlle Coutarel

Valadour
15320 Loubaresse
Tel. 04 71 73 74 69
auberge-lapagnoune @ wanadoo.fr
www.auberge-lapagnoune.com

Closed in Jan and Feb, Sun evening and Mon from 1 Sep to 1 Jul • 7 rooms, 1 with disabled access, all have bathrooms • €50 (€44 low season), breakfast €5.50 • Menus €13 (weekdays) to €18 (Sun and school holidays)

 14 HOSTELLERIE LES BREUILS
M. et Mme Rochès

34 avenue Docteur Mallet
15300 Murat
Tel. 04 71 20 01 25
Fax 04 71 20 33 20
info @ hostellerie-les-breuils.com
www.hostellerie-les-breuils.com

Closed from 2 Nov to early May • 10 rooms, most have bath/WC, some have television • €62 to €78 (€60 to €76 low season); breakfast €7 • No restaurant • Garden, private car park • Indoor swimming pool, sauna, leisure area

 A visit to the Pierre Allègre Farm, a farming museum in the heart of the village.

Farewell calves, cows and pigs! This former farm, built in 1877, is now home to an inviting hostelry whose simplicity and authenticity are irresistible. Exposed beams and rough stone walls, impressive fireplaces, an old grandfather clock, farming tools and rustic furniture grace the country-style dining room, whose cuisine is of course equally regional. The rooms may not be luxurious, but they are comfortable, well kept and fitted out in a similar rustic spirit.

 The friendly, personalised welcome.

All the rooms of this small 19C mansion backing onto the historic town, have recently been treated to a facelift of bright, bold colours and some have retained their Louis XVI furniture. The roomy bathrooms are well fitted-out. Attractive reading room with fireplace and piano. A building to the rear of the garden houses an indoor swimming pool.

Access : 5km southbound from the Viaduc du Garabit on the D909, head towards Charmensac

Access : Outside the ramparts, by the main road

 15 LOU FERRADOU
M. et Mme Balleux

 Caizac
15130 Saint-Étienne-de-Carlat
Tel. 04 71 62 42 37
Fax 04 71 62 42 37
lou.ferradou @ tiscali.fr
www.louferradou.com

Open all year • 5 non-smoking rooms with bathrooms
• €42 to €54; breakfast included; half board available
• Car park, garden, terrace. Credit cards not accepted,
no dogs admitted • Games room

 16 LE GRIOU
M. Troupel

 15800 Saint-Jacques-des-Blats
Tel. 04 71 47 06 25
Fax 04 71 47 00 16
hotel.griou @ wanadoo.fr
 www.hotel-griou.com

Closed 20 Oct to 20 Dec • 16 rooms all with bath/WC
or shower/WC, one has disabled access, some have
television • €40 to €47; breakfast €6, half board available
• Menus €13 to €29 • Car park, garden

 **Dining and breakfasting in the
enchanting garden in fine weather.**

The typically austere Auvergne façade of this old farm
cannot fail to impress. The eye is also drawn to the
recently restored beams, bare stone walls and fireplace
indoors. One of the rooms in the main wing has its own
sitting room and an outhouse is home to two split-level
rooms, all are furnished in a regional style. Large games
room. At mealtimes, sample the vegetables fresh from
the garden and other local delicacies, such as the famous
truffade, a dish of potatoes, cheese, bacon and garlic.

 **Admiring the natural and architectural
wealth of the Regional Volcano Park.**

Built in two stages, the hotel offers guests a choice of
accommodation; recent rooms, furnished in a Louis-
Philippe style or others in more classical vein. All are
quite spotless and most have a balcony. If unsure about
which of the two dining rooms to choose, we recommend
the one with the large bay windows that offers a
delightful view over the village steeple and Cantal
mountains.

Access : Drive for 4km on a minor road

Access : On the way out of the village

 17 LE BAILLIAGE
M. et Mme Gouzon

 Rue Notre-Dame
15140 Salers
Tel. 04 71 40 71 95
Fax 04 71 40 74 90
info@salers-hotel-bailliage.com
www.salers-hotel-bailliage.com

Closed from 15 Nov to 1 Feb • 26 rooms, 4 in a separate wing (La Demeure Jarriges, 300m away), all have bath/WC and television • €48 to €78; breakfast €9; half board available • Menus €14 to €40 • Terrace, garden, garage, car park • Outdoor swimming pool

18 CHAMBRE D'HÔTE M. PRUDENT
M. et Mme Prudent

   Rue des Nobles
15140 Salers
Tel. 04 71 40 75 36
 Fax 04 71 40 75 36

Open all year • 6 rooms with separate entrances • €42, breakfast included • No table d'hôte • Garden

 Strolling past the historic buildings of Salers.

The stone walls of this 1960s farmstead stand in one of the region's most enchanting medieval villages. The spacious, comfortable rooms overlook either the garden, the town or the slopes of the nearby Puy Violent. Soft lighting, cane furniture and red and orange drapes adorn the stylish redecorated restaurant. Gourmets come from miles around to enjoy the cuisine in which the region's famous Salers beef naturally takes pride of place, as does its namesake cheese. Pleasant garden-terrace.

Contemplating the exceptional panorama of the volcanic peaks of the Cantal.

This 17C house is idyllically situated in the heart of the picturesque medieval village of Salers. All the simply decorated yet comfortable rooms have their own private entrance and some command a fine view over the volcanoes. Treat yourself to breakfast in bed or venture downstairs and admire the attractive Auvergne dining room or the wonderful view from the terrace in fine weather. Souvenir shop in the hotel.

Access : At the entrance to the village next to the large car park

Access : In the town centre

 19 LE COUVENT
M. et Mme Belaiche

 Le Bourg
15400 Trizac
Tel. 04 71 78 67 51
Fax 04 71 78 67 51
le-couvent@wanadoo.fr
www.lecouvent.fr

Open from Easter to 31 Oct • 4 rooms with bathrooms • €60 to €70; breakfast €10 • No table d'hôte • Park. Credit cards not accepted, dogs admitted on request

 20 AUBERGE DES MONTAGNES
M. et Mme Combourieu

 15800 Vic-sur-Cère
Tel. 04 71 47 57 01
Fax 04 71 49 63 83
info@auberge-des-montagnes.com
www.auberge-des-montagnes.com

Closed from 12 Oct to 20 Dec • 25 rooms, 10 of which are in a separate wing and one has disabled access. Rooms have bath/WC or shower/WC, some have television • €46 to €50 (€42 to €48 low season); breakfast €7; half board available • Restaurant closed Tue out of season; menus €14 (weekdays) to €23 • Terrace, car park, garage • 2 swimming pools, mountain biking, fishing, horse-drawn rides, cross-country skiing

 Relaxing in the peaceful garden between the former convent and the village's Romanesque church.

Ask your friendly hosts to tell you the long story of this ancient abode and its slightly forbidding façade. You will find it all the easier to appreciate the efforts deployed since 1995 to turn it into a delightful house, whose comforts are now the antithesis of its former monastic vocation. A fine staircase leads up the master bedroom and to three suites, each unique, and all comfortably and tastefully decorated and extremely peaceful.

 Visiting the farm where the film "With a friend like Harry" was shot.

The still waters of a pond reflect this picture-book hotel comprised of a handsome old farmstead with a stone-shingled roof, a more recent house flanked by a tower and a spacious stone terrace. The vast rooms are decorated in a rustic or a contemporary style. Swimming pool, mountain bikes, hiking, horse-drawn carts, fishing, skiing: the extensive range of activities illustrates the owners' get-up-and-go personality. Delicious feasts of Auvergne cooking.

Access : In the centre of the village, on the D678 between Mauriac and Riom-ès-Montagne

Access : At Vic-sur-Cère leave the N 122 (Aurillac-Murat road) and take the D 54 for Pailherols

21 **AUBERGE DE LA TOMETTE**
M. Chausi

15220 Vitrac
Tel. 04 71 64 70 94
Fax 04 71 64 77 11
latomette @ wanadoo.fr
www.auberge-la-tomette.com

Open from 1 Apr to 15 Nov • 15 rooms, one of which
has disabled access; all have bath/WC or shower/WC and
television • €73 to €77 (€63 to €68 low season);
breakfast €9; half board available • Menus €24 to €38
• Private car park, garden, terrace. No dogs admitted in
restaurant • Swimming pool, fitness room

22 **LES CÈDRES BLEUS**
M. et Mme Duverney

Route de la Rivière
43110 Aurec-sur-Loire
Tel. 04 77 35 48 48
Fax 04 77 35 37 04
www.lescedresbleus.com

Closed from 2 to 25 Jan, Sun evening and Mon lunchtime
• 15 rooms, one has disabled access, most have
bath/WC, some have shower/WC, all have television
• €53 to €55; breakfast €8; half board available • Air
conditioned restaurant. Menus €18 (weekdays) to €75
• Terrace, garden, car park.

 **Relaxing in the shade of the cottage
garden filled with flowers.**

Three houses, the oldest of which is 19C, make up this
pleasant inn at the heart of a sleepy village. The modern,
well-kept rooms are equally tranquil and each one is
named after a bird or a flower. The pleasant dining room
features wood panelling, tomettes - local tiles - and a
few pieces of old furniture; it leads out onto a terrace
with a superb view of the countryside. There's also an
indoor swimming pool with roll-away roof, a relaxation
corner, bicycles to rent and a children's play area.

 **Trying your hand at water-skiing on
Lake Grangent.**

Even though the site may lack the giant redwood trees,
grizzly bears and log cabins of America's national parks,
the same spirit reigns in this lakeside spot. The reception
and restaurant are installed in the old family house,
while three modern "chalets" house functional rooms,
all of which overlook the garden and cedars. A well
cared-for flowered terrace adds the final touch to this
pastoral picture of unspoilt countryside.

Access : In the centre of the village

Access : To the south-west of Saint-Étienne on the
D 46, then at Aurec-sur-Loire towards Bas-en-Basset

 23 LA PARAVENT
M. Jourde

43700 Chaspinhac
Tel. 04 71 03 54 75
michel-jourde @ wanadoo.fr

Open all year • 5 rooms • €44 to €48, breakfast included • Table d'hôte €16 • Garden. Credit cards not accepted, no dogs allowed

 24 LA JACQUEROLLE
 Mme Chailly

Rue Marchédial
43160 La Chaise-Dieu
Tel. 04 71 00 07 52
lajacquerolle @ hotmail.com

Open all year • 4 rooms • €55 to €58, breakfast included, half board available • Table d'hôte €22 • Car park. Credit cards not accepted, no dogs allowed

 The warm atmosphere of this handsome early-20C house.

The sterling welcome, constant attention to detail and eagerness to please immediately strike the visitor to this country house, just a few minutes' drive from Le Puy-en-Velay. The rustic-style interior decoration is full of character. Some of the cosy rooms have their own small sitting room and all have a private entrance. In the winter the lady of the house runs patchwork courses.

Going mushrooming for cèps in the surrounding forest.

Entirely built out of local stone, this characterful house stands in the lower part of town. Countless family heirlooms, including a beautiful Louis-Philippe wardrobe and elegant looking mirrors grace the tastefully decorated, predominantly wood interior. A roaring log fire, lit in the dining room's magnificent stone fireplace, takes the chill off the short autumn and winter days.

Access : 10km to the north-east of Le Puy on the D 103 towards Retournac, then take the D 71

Access : In the lower part of town

25 **LE PRIEURÉ**
Mme Pougheon

Le Prieuré
43100 Lamothe
Tel. 04 71 76 44 61
spougheon @ hotmail.com
www.auprieure.com

Open Jul and Aug • 5 rooms, all have bathrooms, 1 has disabled access • €70; breakfast included • No table d'hôte • Garden, car park. Credit cards not accepted, no dogs admitted

26 **MISTOU**
M. et Mme Roux

43500 Pontempeyrat
Tel. 04 77 50 62 46
Fax 04 77 50 66 70
moulin.de.mistou @ wanadoo.fr
www.mistou.fr

Closed Nov to late April • 14 rooms, one with disabled access, one for non-smokers, 4 with spa baths, all with bath/WC or shower/WC. • €95 to €130, breakfast €12; half board available • Restaurant closed lunchtime except Sunday and public hols. Menus €32 to €58 • Park, car park. Dogs not allowed in restaurant • Outdoor swimming pool, fitness room

 The bedroom with the bathroom in the 12C keep.

Enjoy the superb vista over Brioude and the Allier Valley from this lovely old stone abode which dates from the 12C and 18C. Tastefully chosen period furniture, curios and family portraits add character to the establishment, which boasts spacious, individually decorated rooms, a sitting room complete with period fireplace, a large dining room and an old-fashioned kitchen. Take the time to savour the delicious breakfasts and sample the home-made jams.

 Only the babble of the river disturbs the silence.

The poor miller would no doubt be flabbergasted to see how comfortable his former workplace, a simple watermill built on the banks of the Ance around 1730, has become! The peace and quiet reign throughout this welcoming hostelry lost in the countryside, from the sophisticated bedrooms, some of which open onto the grounds, to the elegant dining room whose bay windows overlook the parkland. Attentive staff, a fitness room and a pleasant pool all combine to make your stay unforgettable.

Access : 4km north-east of Brioude, on the D19 towards La Chaise-Dieu

Access : North-east of Craponne-sur-Arzon by D 498; follow signs to St-Etienne

 27 LES REVERS

M. et Mme Chevalier

 43130 Retournac
Tel. 04 71 59 42 81
Fax 04 71 59 42 81
jean-pierre.chevalier6 @ libertysurf.fr
 www.lesrevers.fr.st

Closed from Oct to Apr • 4 rooms • €44, breakfast included • Table d'hôte evenings only and by reservation €16 • Garden, car park. Credit cards not accepted, dogs not allowed

 28 L'HERMINETTE

M. Mathieu

 Bigorre - Les Maziaux
43550 Saint-Front
Tel. 04 71 59 57 58
Fax 04 71 56 34 91
lherminette @ wanadoo.fr

Open all year, bookings necessary out of season • 6 rooms with bathrooms • €66 to €70 (€56 to €60 low season), breakfast included; half board available • Restaurant closed Sun evening and Mon; menus €11 (weekdays) to €20 • Garden, car park. No dogs allowed • Museum of local life nearby

🙂 **The unspoilt countryside of this rural hideaway.**

🙂 **The change of scenery offered by this hamlet.**

Those on a quest for silence, nature and authenticity will swoon at the sight of this extraordinarily secluded spot, wedged in between field and forest. The capacious, well-appointed rooms are furnished with comfortable bedding and all overlook the unspoilt countryside. Two rooms are on split-levels. The owner breeds horses and can organise rides for guests. A perfect hideaway for a relaxed, peaceful break.

An enchanting hamlet of stone farmsteads topped with well-combed thatched roofs forms the backdrop to this typical Auvergne inn. Large, airy bedrooms, two on split-levels, regional-style dining rooms and delicious country cooking at unbeatable prices. If you're interested in finding out more about daily life in years gone by and how thatched roofs are made, stop by the Ecomuseum, and all will be revealed.

Access : 8km to the south-east of Retournac on the D 103, then follow the signs

Access : 5 km to the north-west of Saint-Front on the D 39, then take the lane on the right

29 AUBERGE DE LA VALLÉE
M. et Mme Merle

43340 Saint-Haon
Tel. 04 71 08 20 73
Fax 04 71 08 29 21
aubergevallée43 @ aol.com
www.auberge-de-la-vallee.fr

Closed from 1 Jan to 15 Mar, Sun evening and Mon from Oct to Apr • 10 rooms with bath/WC or shower/WC • €37 to €43; breakfast €7; half board available • Menus €15 to €33 • Terrace • Hiking, river water sports

Diving into the crystal-clear waters of Bouchet Lake at the bottom of a crater.

The legend of the Beast of Gévaudan continues to echo around the narrow gorges of the Allier, although today's walkers and nature-lovers are more enamoured of its peaceful setting than its "gory" past. Rustic furniture and roughcast walls set the tone for the small, beautifully kept rooms of this unpretentious inn. Recently spruced up, the dining room now boasts new light fittings, a stylish wooden ceiling and a bold colour scheme.

Access : Between Le Puy-en-Velay and Pradelles, 10km from the N 88 (west of La Sauvetat)

30 LES GABALES
M. Gauthier

Route du Puy-en-Velay
43170 Saugues
Tel. 04 71 77 86 92
Fax 04 71 77 86 92
pierrelesgabales @ wanadoo.fr
www.lesgabales.com

Closed 1 Dec to late Feb • 5 non-smoking rooms • €45 to €72, breakfast included, half board available • Sitting room, park, car park. Credit cards not accepted, no dogs allowed

Finding out more about the legendary Beast of Gévaudan.

The legend of the Beast of Gévaudan is far from dead as you will find out when you listen to the tales related by the owner of this good-sized 1930s house. His other passion is walking and he is happy to share tips. Once safely back inside the hotel's walls, relax in the cosy sitting room-library; the wood panelling in the dining room is original. In the morning, after a well-earned night's sleep in one of the charmingly "retro" personalised rooms, guests can also enjoy a walk in the park.

Access : On the road from Le Puy-en-Velay

 31 LA TERRASSE
M. Fargier

 Cours Dr. Gervais
43170 Saugues
Tel. 04 71 77 83 10
Fax 04 71 77 63 79
laterrasse-saugues @ wanadoo.fr

Closed 30 Nov to 28 Feb; Sun evening and Mon (out of season) • 9 rooms on two floors, all with bath/WC or shower/WC and television • €55 to €69 (€50 to €69 low season); breakfast €8, half board available • Air-conditioned restaurant: menus €21 (weekdays) to €55 • Garage

 32 ERMITAGE SAINT VINCENT
M. et Mme Boyer

 Place de l'Église
43100 Vieille-Brioude
Tel. 04 71 50 96 47

Closed Dec and Jan (except for groups with reservation)
• 5 rooms with bathrooms • €49, breakfast included
• Table d'hôte €20 (reservation only) • Terrace, garden.
Credit cards not accepted, no dogs admitted

 We most liked **Enjoy the thrill of exploring the home of the legendary Beast of Gévaudan.**

The Fargier family, inhabitants of Saugues since 1795, welcomes guests in a house originally built for the town's solicitor now restored and turned into a hotel. The cleverly renovated rooms are modern and comfortable and most are quite spacious except for two smaller ones. As you sit down in the welcoming half-rustic, half-contemporary dining room with stone fireplace to feast on the chef's traditional fare, make sure you leave room to sample the impressive array of Auvergne cheeses.

We most liked **Enjoy listening to the babble of the river and the birdsong.**

This restored former presbytery overlooks the river, commanding a fine view of the Allier Valley. Indoors, guests are immediately impressed by the proportions of the large hall, adorned with old farming tools, the extensive sitting room-library and the great stone staircase leading up to equally sizeable and comfortable bedrooms, fitted with good quality contemporary furnishings. The kind owner bends over backwards to make your stay as pleasant as possible, whatever your fancy.

Access : In the centre of the village

Access : 4km southbound of Brioude, on the N102 near l'Allier

AUVERGNE

AUBUSSON-D'AUVERGNE - 63120   BEAUREGARD-VENDON - 63460

 33 LE MOULIN DES VERNIÈRES
Mme Hansen

 63120 Aubusson-d'Auvergne
Tel. 04 73 53 53 01
Fax 04 73 53 53 01
www.lemoulindesvernières.com

Closed from 1 Nov to 1 Mar, Sun evening and Mon
• 5 non-smoking rooms • €60 to €70, breakfast included
• Table d'hôte €20 (evenings) • Sitting room, park, car park. No dogs allowed • Outdoor swimming pool

 34 CHAMBRE D'HÔTE MME BEAUJEARD
Mme Beaujeard

 8 rue de la Limagne à Chaptes
63460 Beauregard-Vendon
Tel. 04 73 63 35 62

Closed from 1 Nov to 1 Mar except by reservation
• 3 non-smoking rooms • €58 to €64, breakfast included
• No table d'hôte • Garden. Credit cards not accepted, no dogs allowed

 The chef's inventive recipes using delicious local produce.

It is easy to see why the owner fell in love with this old mill and the artistically laid out garden and cascading stream. The scent of rose and jasmine fills the pretty rooms, named after cottage garden flowers (English rose, Forget-me-not, Poppy). Inside the owner has given free rein to her decorative flair with polished antique furniture, classic black and white photos by Doisneau and naive paintings. The cooking is just as inventive and your host loves rustling up mouth-watering dishes.

 The enchanting, old-fashioned decoration.

This handsome late-18C country seat is the epitome of charm and tranquillity. The tastefully furnished rooms, all non-smoking, are perfect for winding down at the end of the day. The cosy sitting room with its fireplace, lavishly flowered garden in the summer, generous breakfasts, excellent welcome and moderate prices all add to the appeal.

Access : 7km eastbound from Coupière on the D 7 and the D 311

Access : 9km northbound from Riom on the N 144 then the D 122

AUVERGNE

 35 HOSTELLERIE DU BEFFROY
M. Legros

 26 rue Abbé-Blot
63610 Besse-en-Chandesse
Tel. 04 73 79 50 08
Fax 04 73 79 57 87

Closed from 4 Nov to 26 Dec and on Mon and Tue (except evenings in Jul and Aug), Wed lunchtime (Jul-Aug) • 12 rooms with bath/WC or shower/WC and television • €50 to €85; breakfast €10; half board available • Menus from €24 to €60 • Garage. No dogs allowed in restaurant

 36 RÉGENCE
M. et Mme Porte

 31 avenue des États-Unis
63140 Chatelguyon
Tel. 04 73 86 02 60
Fax 04 73 86 02 49
hotel-regence3@wanadoo.fr
www.hotel-regence-central.com

Closed from 1 Oct to 15 Mar; Mon and Sun evening • 26 rooms with bath/WC or shower/WC, some have television • €46 to €48; breakfast €8; half board available • Menus from €16 (weekdays) to €26 • Garden, private car park. No dogs allowed in the restaurant • Free shuttle bus to the spa

The contrast between the medieval city of Besse and the mountain resort of Super-Besse.

This 15C house beside the belfry at the entrance to the town is thought to have housed the old town guards. A few old pieces of furniture add style to the rooms' slightly faded air. In the dining room, the rugs strewn here and there, dark timbered beams, heavy fabrics and straw-bottomed chairs upholstered in tasteful cream hemp further accentuate the house's historic character.

 The architecture of this quaint old resort.

A splendid carved wooden fireplace, well-worn, polished antique furniture and an upright piano contribute to maintaining the delicious 1900s atmosphere of the Régence. The ground floor has however been entirely renovated with a fresh coat of paint, double-glazing and a smart red and gold facelift for the sitting and dining rooms; the bedrooms are next in line. Lush green garden.

Access : In the centre of the medieval village

Access : At the entrance to the resort, on the main road

COLLANGES - 63340　　　　**DAVAYAT - 63200**

37 CHÂTEAU DE COLLANGES
M. et Mme Félus

63340 Collanges
Tel. 04 73 96 47 30
Fax 04 73 96 58 72
chateau-de-collanges @ wanadoo.fr
www.chateaudecollanges.com

Closed from 3 Jan to 10 Feb and 7 Nov to 15 Dec • 6 rooms • €79 to €129, breakfast included • Table d'hôte €38 • Park, car park. No dogs admitted in restaurant • Swimming pool

38 LA MAISON DE LA TREILLE
M. et Mme Honnorat

25 rue de l'Église
63200 Davayat
Tel. 04 73 63 58 20
honnorat.la.treille @ wanadoo.fr
http://honnorat.la.treille.free.fr

Open all year • 4 rooms including one suite, all with bath/WC or shower/WC • €67 to €80, €105 suite for 4 people; breakfast included • No table d'hôte • Park, car park. Credit cards not accepted, no dogs allowed

Strolling leisurely back in time.

Guests are treated like royalty in this castle surrounded by seven acres of parkland. The vaulted ceilings, original parquet floors and superb antique furniture will take you on a voyage through time from the Renaissance to the 18C. Imagine what it was like to be lord or lady of the house as you wake up in a canopied bed draped with rich fabrics, then draw back the curtains on a view of the park. A genuine Gaveau piano and a marquetry-inlaid billiard table add to the castle's sophistication.

Tucking into the jams made with fruit from the orchard at breakfast time.

Italian Neoclassicism clearly inspired this smart bourgeois property built in 1810. A pleasant sitting room with piano and breakfast room, lit by a stone fireplace, make up the ground floor. Guests are accommodated in the orangery, an elegant outhouse which stands in the enchanting garden. The names of the trim, well-tended rooms give guests an idea of each room's decorative style: wheat, birds, grapes and beehive (for four people).

Access : 12km southbound from Issoire, on the A 75, exit Saint-Germain-Lembron

Access : 7km northbound from Riom on the N 144

AUVERGNE

 39 **AUBERGE DE LA FORGE**
M. et Mme Zuk

 Place de l'Église
63160 Glaine-Montaigut
Tel. 04 73 73 41 80
Fax 04 73 73 33 83
a.delaforge @ wanadoo.fr
www.aubergedelaforge.com

Closed from 1 to 20 Sep • 4 rooms with showers/WC
• €39 to €50 (€28 to €39 low season); breakfast €6;
half-board available • Restaurant closed Sun evening and
Tue; menus €15 to €30 • Terrace

 40 **AUBERGE DE FONDAIN**
Mme Demossier

 lieu-dit Fondain
63820 Laqueuille
Tel. 04 73 22 01 35
Fax 04 73 22 06 13
auberge.de.fondain @ wanadoo.fr
www.auberge-fondain.com

Closed for 10 days early Mar, Nov, Sun evening and Mon
• 6 rooms with bath/WC or shower/WC • €66 (€58 low
season); breakfast €8; half board available • Menus €12
(weekdays) to €23 • Terrace, garden, car park • Fitness
room with sauna, hiking, mountain biking, themed walks

 **Wholesome country snacks served all
day long.**

Situated opposite a beautiful Romanesque 11C-12C
church, the village café and forge have been successfully
converted into a pleasant country inn. A smart façade
with pale blue shutters, traditional old walls, simple yet
appealing rooms and a restaurant, with a reconstruction
of the former blacksmith's workshop complete with
hearth, bellows and anvil, serving yummy country
cooking. A renovation which marries authenticity with
intelligence.

 **Signposted footpaths on themes such
as fauna, flora and crater lakes.**

This elegant 19C country house lost among fields and
meadows is said to have belonged to the inventor of
a local blue cheese: Laqueuille. The recently renovated
rooms, named after flowers, combine a light, airy colour
scheme with contrasting dark timbers, discreetly modern
fittings and in some cases, a view of the Banne
d'Ordanche. A fitness room, sauna and a dozen or so
mountain bikes will make sure you work up an appetite
for the tasty Auvergne cooking served in a welcoming
rustic dining room.

Access : Around 5km to the north-east of Billom,
towards Thiers on the D 229 and the D 212

Access : 2km to the north-east of Laqueuille, on the
D 922 then a minor road

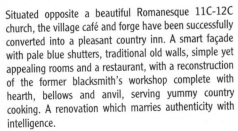

  41 LA CLOSERIE DE MANOU
Mme Larcher

Au Genestoux - BP 30
63240 Le Mont-Dore
Tel. 04 73 65 26 81
Fax 04 73 65 58 34
lacloseriedemanou @ club-internet.fr

Closed from 1 Nov to 1 Mar • 5 non-smoking rooms
• €75, breakfast included • No table d'hôte • Garden,
car park. Credit cards not accepted, no dogs allowed

  42 AUBERGE DE MAZAYES
M. Michy

à Mazayes-Basses
63230 Mazaye
Tel. 04 73 88 93 30
Fax 04 73 88 93 80
www.restolit-auvergne.com

Closed from 13 Dec to 21 Jan, Mon (Oct-Mar) and Tue
lunchtime • 15 rooms, one of which has disabled access,
with shower/WC, all have television • €56 to €65;
breakfast €8; half-board available • Menus €15.50
(weekdays) to €35 • Terrace, car park

😊 *We most liked* **The wealth of information about the region.**

😊 *We most liked* **The farm's ideal situation for exploring the Monts Dôme.**

Nestling in the countryside, this traditional 18C Auvergne house with its stone walls and white shutters is quite enchanting. The decoration of the spacious rooms wavers between modern-uncluttered and snug; all are non-smoking. The sitting and dining rooms, furnished with antiques, provide a wonderful backdrop to the delicious breakfasts. The charm and attention of your hostess will be another reason why you won't want to leave.

This attractive Auvergne farmhouse built out of solid basalt stone is located just near the popular tourist site of the Puy de Dôme (1 465m). Bold colours, carefully chosen fabrics and a few old pieces of furniture adorn the rooms which are a stylish blend of rustic and modern. The stables have been converted into a dining room full of character with a lava stone floor and a low ceiling supported by dark timber rafters. Wholesome regional cooking.

Access : 3km westbound from Mont-Dore on the D 996

Access : South of Pontgibaud, 6km on the D 986, cross the Sioule at St Pierre-le-Chastel and drive to Mazayes

43 CHAMBRE D'HÔTE MME BOISSIÈRE
Mme Boissière

Rue de la Poterne
63114 Montpeyroux
Tel. 04 73 96 69 42
Fax 04 73 96 95 39
jules.boissiere @ wanadoo.fr

Open all year • 5 non-smoking rooms • €48 to €58, breakfast included • No table d'hôte • Car park. Credit cards not accepted

44 LES PRADETS
Edith Grenot

Les Pradets
63114 Montpeyroux
Tel. 04 73 96 63 40
Fax 04 73 96 63 40
grenot @ maison-hotes.com
www.auvergne.maison-hotes.com

Open all year • 3 rooms with bathrooms • €68; breakfast included • No table d'hôte • Sitting room, garden. Credit cards not accepted

We most liked **Exploring this historic village overlooking the Allier River.**

Set at the foot of a 13C keep, this pretty sandstone house is well worth the short climb up the hill from the town car park; there are a few parking spaces in front of the house if needed. Each of the bedrooms boasts its own little extra bonus: terrace, fireplace, canopied bed or jacuzzi bath. After taking refreshments in the vaulted dining room, set off round the narrow lanes and meet the painters and potters who have replaced the wine-growers of yesteryear.

We most liked **Edith Grenot's faultless welcome.**

This delightful house lies in a secluded lane of the picturesque fortified village of Montpeyroux. Relax in the cosy ground floor sitting room strewn with well-used furniture, a piano and books on the Auvergne region. In fine weather, you will no doubt make a beeline for the inner courtyard garden where breakfast is served. Parquet floors, rugs, paintings by local artists and rustic furniture add character to the well-decorated rooms.

Access : 8km to the south-west of Vic-le-Comte on the A 75, exit no 7

Access : In the heart of the village

45 LES GRANGES
Mme Gauthier

Recoleine
63210 Nébouzat
Tel. 04 73 87 10 34
Fax 04 73 87 10 34

gauthier.jocelyne @ free.fr

Closed from 15 Nov to 1 Feb • 3 rooms • €43 to €46, breakfast included, half board available • Table d'hôte €14 • Sitting room. Credit cards not accepted, no dogs allowed

46 DOMAINE DE TERNANT
Mme Piollet

Ternant
63870 Orcines
Tel. 04 73 62 11 20
Fax 04 73 62 29 96
domaine.ternant @ free.fr
www.domaine.ternant.free.fr

Closed from 15 Nov to 15 Mar • 5 non-smoking rooms • €72 to €86, breakfast included • No table d'hôte • Sitting room, park, car park. Credit cards not accepted, no dogs allowed • Tennis, billiard room

We most liked

The pastoral scene just two minutes from the Dôme mountain range.

A warm welcome awaits visitors inside this old barn, beautifully renovated by a farming couple. The comfortable, tasteful rooms all enjoy views of the surrounding countryside. An immense living-sitting room and spacious sofa are most appreciated. Your charming, talkative hostess will be more than happy to point out walks and hikes. Ideal for nature lovers.

We most liked

The sheltered environment of this old building.

This elegant 19C property stands in 25 acres of grounds at the foot of the Dôme mountain range. A profusion of family heirlooms scattered throughout the bedrooms, sitting room, library and games room creates a warm, lived-in feel. The personal touch and taste of the lady of the house, a patchwork artist, can be felt everywhere. Tennis court in the grounds and other sports facilities nearby, including Vulcania, the Regional Volcano Park.

Access : 3km from Randanne on the N 89

Access : 11km north-west of Clermont-Ferrand on the D 941A and the D 90

47 HOSTELLERIE LES HIRONDELLES
M. Amblard

Route de Limoges
63870 Orcines
Tel. 04 73 62 22 43
Fax 04 73 62 19 12
info @ hotel-leshirondelles.com
www.hotel-leshirondelles.com

Closed from 8 Nov to 8 Feb, Sun evening, Mon and Tue lunchtime from Oct to Apr • 18 rooms, one of which has disabled access. Rooms have bath/WC or shower/WC, all have television • €59.50 to €66.50; breakfast €7.40; half-board available • Restaurant closed Mon lunchtime and Tue lunchtime (May, Jun, Sep).Menus €16.20 (weekdays) to €40 • Terrace, car park

The fascinating Monts Dôme.

This old grey-stone family farmstead, recently converted into an inn, nestles at the foot of the Monts Dôme. The rooms situated in the converted barn are practical before all else; those overlooking the street are larger and lighter. The vaulted dining room located in the former cow-shed offers more character; the swallows' nests, from which the inn takes its name, complete the rural picture.

Access : Westbound from Clermont-Ferrand, take the D 941A then the D 941B (Limoges road) to Orcines

48 CHAMBRE D'HÔTE PAUL GEBRILLAT
M. Gebrillat

Chemin de Siorac
63500 Perrier
Tel. 04 73 89 15 02
Fax 04 73 55 08 85
lequota @ club-internet.fr

Closed 1 Dec to 31 Jan • 4 rooms and one suite • €48 to €55, breakfast included • No table d'hôte • Garden, car park. Credit cards not accepted, no dogs allowed

Strolling in the park bounded by the Couze de Pavin River.

This handsome 18C country house is perfect for those wishing to get to know the Dore Mountains a little better. The tastefully decorated rooms marry charm and comfort. As soon as the first rays of sun appear, the breakfast table is laid outdoors under a heated awning which overlooks a delightful inner courtyard; warm sweaters advisable. You host, Paul, is a gold mine of useful tourist tips.

Access : 3km westbound from Issoire on the D 996

49 CHÂTEAU DE VOISSIEUX
M. et Mme Phillips

Saint-Bonnet-d'Orcival
63210 Rochefort-Montagne
Tel. 04 73 65 81 02
Fax 04 73 65 81 27

Closed from Nov to Jan • 3 rooms with bathrooms • €52 to €60, breakfast included • No table d'hôte • Terrace, park, car park. Credit cards not accepted • Mountain biking, horse-riding, swimming, golf, paragliding, hot-air ballooning and skiing nearby

50 CHÂTEAU DE CHARADE
M. et Mme Gaba

63130 Royat
Tel. 04 73 35 91 67
Fax 04 73 29 92 09
gaba @ chateau-de-charade.com
www.chateau-de-charade.com

Closed from early Nov to late Mar • 5 rooms with bathrooms • €72 to €81, breakfast included • No table d'hôte • Park, car park. Credit cards not accepted, no dogs allowed

 Being treated like the lord or lady of the manor in the heart of the Auvergne Regional Park.

Volcanic stone was of course used to build this 13C castle, it was also used to restore it to its present-day state. In the park a 400-year-old lime tree keeps watch over the estate's quiet solitude. You have a choice between two soberly furnished rooms or a more exuberant rococo style in the third. Breakfasts are served in the kitchen by the fireside or on the flowered terrace overlooking the park. It isn't possible to lunch or dine in the castle, but restaurants are hardly in short supply.

 The country house feel of this whimsical castle just two minutes from the regional capital.

This castle which borders the Royat golf course extends a majestic welcome. High ceilings, a stone staircase and the antique furniture in the bedrooms and bathrooms all bear witness to an illustrious past. As for the present, guests are invariably charmed by the appeal of the lady of the house's gracious welcome, the tinkling of the piano playing in the sitting room or the click of billiard balls. If you don't feel like visiting the town, head for the nearby Dôme mountains.

Access : 4km to the north-east of Orcival on the D 27

Access : 6km to the south-west of Royat on the D 941C and the D 5, towards the racing track and golf course

 51 AU PONT DE RAFFINY
M. et Mme Beaudoux

Raffiny
63660 Saint-Anthème
Tel. 04 73 95 49 10
Fax 04 73 95 80 21
hotel.pont.raffiny @ wanadoo.fr
 www.hotel-pont-raffiny.com

Closed from 3 Jan to 25 Feb, Sun evening and Mon (except Jul-Aug) • 13 rooms, 2 of which are small wooden chalets with private gardens. All rooms have bath/WC or shower/WC, some have television • €38 to €44; breakfast €7; half board available • Menus €15 to €30 • Car park • Games room with billiards, hiking, mountain bike rental

 A ride in the panoramic "Livradois-Forez" train.

Two chalets designed for families, complete with kitchenette and private gardens, have recently been added to the hotel's amenities. The bedrooms in the main wing – a former village café – are more simply furnished, even if those on the second floor, lined in wood, do have a certain alpine charm. A rockery fountain lends an amusing touch to the rustic dining room. All in all, we were quite won over by the charm of this country hotel.

Access : Leave Saint-Anthème southbound on the D 261 and drive for 5.5km

 52 CASTEL HÔTEL 1904
M. Mouty

Rue du Castel
63390 Saint-Gervais-d'Auvergne
Tel. 04 73 85 70 42
Fax 04 73 85 84 39
castel.hotel.1904 @ wanadoo.fr
www.castel-hotel-1904.com

Open from Mar to Nov; restaurant closed Mon, Tue and Wed • 17 rooms with bath/WC or shower/WC, all have television • €65 to €75; breakfast €8; half board available • Menus €35 to €55 • Garden, car park. No dogs allowed

 The rather quaint old-fashioned atmosphere.

The carved "1616" over the fireplace bears witness to the age of these walls. This private residence, built for the Marquis of Maintenon, passed into the hands of a religious community in the 19C before it became a coaching inn at the turn of the 20th Century. Beams, creaky floorboards, well-worn furniture, gleaming silver and 1900 statuettes and lights bestow an almost nostalgic feel to this "castel". Sample the excellent home cooking of the Comptoir à Moustaches, a nearby country bistro.

Access : In the centre of the village

53 MONTARLET

M. et Mme Pelletier

Lieu-dit Montarlet
63390 Saint-Gervais-d'Auvergne
Tel. 04 73 85 87 10
Fax 04 73 85 75 79
montarlet @ libertysurf.fr
 www.montarlet-chambresdhotes.com

Closed 1 Jan to 29 Feb • 3 rooms with bathrooms • €44, breakfast included • No table d'hôte • Park, car park. Credit cards not accepted

54 RÉGINA

M. et Mme Vircondelet

63710 Saint-Nectaire
Tel. 04 73 88 54 55
Fax 04 73 88 50 56
regina.st-nectaire @ wanadoo.fr

Open from Easter to 1 Nov • 25 rooms, 6 are in a separate wing, most have shower/WC, some have bath/WC, all have television • €46 to €56 (€40 to €46 low season); breakfast €6; half board available • Menus €16 to €23 • Car park • Heated outdoor swimming pool with sun deck

The enchanting natural site of this farmhouse.

Guests are often in raptures over the charm and tranquillity of this renovated farmhouse in the middle of the countryside. The rooms illustrate how much the owners have their guests' welfare at heart, from the sponge-painted walls and antique furniture gleaned in local flea markets to the matching bed-linen and curtains and roomy bathrooms. The sitting room is graced with a fireplace and floor made out of Volvic stone and the landscaped parkland commands a fine view over the Auvergne mountains.

Cheese-making and tasting!

The tower of this 1904 building makes it easily recognisable in this small spa-resort. The well-soundproofed and recently freshened-up small bed-rooms are soberly furnished; we recommend avoiding those in the other wing. Exposed beams and period wood panelling add character to the dining room. The attractive swimming pool and the vast sun deck are also extremely popular.

Access : 3km westbound from St-Gervais-d'Auvergne on the D 90 towards Espinasse and take the lane on the left

Access : In the lower part of Saint-Nectaire, on the main road

55 LE PARC DE GEOFFROY
M. Brugere

49 avenue du Général-de-Gaulle
63300 Thiers
Tel. 04 73 80 87 00
Fax 04 73 80 87 01
reservation @ parc-de-geoffroy.com
www.parc-de-geoffroy.com

Open all year • 31 rooms on 3 floors. Rooms have bath/WC and television • €67 to €75; breakfast €8; half board available • Menus €11 to €38 • Terrace, garden, car park

56 LES BAUDARTS
Mme Verdier

63500 Varennes-sur-Usson
Tel. 04 73 89 05 51
Fax 04 73 89 05 51

Closed from 1 Oct to 1 May • 3 rooms • €60 to €72, breakfast included • No table d'hôte • Garden, car park. Credit cards not accepted, no dogs allowed

 Enjoying a cutting-edge visit to the House of Cutlery-makers.

A luxurious walled garden protects the residence from the bustle of the nearby busy shopping centre. The comfortable reception and dining rooms decorated with frescoes are housed in a former cutlery workshop. The rooms, located in a quiet, modern wing, are light, airy and practical. The well-provisioned breakfast table provides guests with the energy necessary to embark on the "ascent" of the upper town.

 The unadulterated sophistication of every room.

Tucked away in the countryside, this establishment may not be easy to find, but it is well worth persevering because its dusty pink walls contain a marvel of sophistication, calm and comfort. The superb, spacious rooms are exquisitely decorated in light, warm tones, and the sitting room, lit in the winter by a roaring log fire, is crammed with books.

Access : 5km along the N 89 towards Clermont-Ferrand

Access : On leaving Varennes take the first right (D 123), then turn into the wooded lane at the first bend

BURGUNDY

A visit to Burgundy takes travellers back through time to an era when its mighty Dukes rivalled even the kings of France. Born of an uncompromising desire for perfection, their stately castles and rich abbeys bear witness to a golden age of ostentation and prestige. As we look back now, it is difficult to reproach them for the flamboyance which has made Dijon a world-renowned city of art. And who would dispute Burgundy's claim to the "best wines in Christendom" when one sees how the hordes of today continue to lay siege to the region's cellars, where cool and canny wine-growers guard the secret of their finest vintages? This dedication to time-honoured traditions also rules the region's steadfast homage to the culinary arts, from strong-smelling époisses cheese to ginger-bread dripping with honey. After sinning so extravagantly, you may be tempted to make amends and take a barge trip down the region's canals and rivers to digest in peace amidst the unspoilt countryside.

- Côte-d'Or (21)
- Nièvre (58)
- Saône-et-Loire (71)
- Yonne (89)

AIGNAY-LE-DUC - 21510

ATHÉE - 21130

 1 MANOIR DE TARPERON
M. de Champsavin

Route de Saint-Marc
21510 Aignay-le-Duc
Tel. 03 80 93 83 74
Fax 03 80 93 83 74
manoir-de-tarperon @ wanadoo.fr

Closed from Nov to Mar • 5 rooms with bathrooms • €62, breakfast included • Table d'hôte €20 to €25 • Sitting room, terrace, garden. Credit cards not accepted, no dogs allowed • Stabling, concerts, exhibitions

 2 LES LAURENTIDES
Mme Royer-Cottin

27 rue du Centre
21130 Athée
 Tel. 03 80 31 00 25

Open all year • 4 rooms, 2 of which open onto the garden • €45, breakfast included • Table d'hôte €19, only from Fri to Sun. No dogs allowed in the restaurant • Garden, car park. Credit cards not accepted

 The beautiful "Wind in the Willows" feel to this location.

A unique charm emanates from this manor and its superb riverside setting on the banks of the Coquille. The bedrooms, of varying sizes, are colourfully and tastefully furnished. The sitting room, complete with library, leads onto a pleasant veranda overlooking the garden. Fly fishing enthusiasts are in for a treat with a private stream all of their own. Those otherwise inclined will enjoy boat trips and an excursion to the source of the Seine.

 The personalised decoration of the bedrooms.

This attractive flower-decked farmhouse, built in the heart of the village in 1870, is a perfect marriage of charm and comfort. The rooms in the converted attic reveal the lady of the house's exquisite taste and painting talents; the most pleasant have a view of the magnificent garden. Meals are only served at weekends or on national holidays and bookings are essential. An establishment that has made gracious living its byword.

Access : Take the small road in the direction of Saint-Marc

Access : 6km northbound from Auxonne on the D 24

 3 **GRILLON**
M. et Mme Grillon

21 route de Seurre
21200 Beaune
Tel. 03 80 22 44 25
Fax 03 80 24 94 89
joel.GRILLON @ wanadoo.fr
www.hotel-grillon.fr

Closed from 31 Jan to 3 Mar inclusive • 18 upstairs rooms, most of which have bath/WC and television. Several are non-smoking • €52 to €65; breakfast €8 • No restaurant • Garden, terrace, private car park • Swimming pool

 A haven of greenery close to the Hospices de Beaune.

This spruce pink house with light-green shutters is almost hidden in the summer by a thick curtain of chestnut trees, but we highly recommend venturing past the wrought-iron gate and inside the comfortable 19C mansion. The rooms vary between light and airy or cosy and some feature interesting old pieces of furniture picked up in local antique shops. The vaulted cellar has been turned into a sitting room and bar. Breakfast is served on a pretty flowered terrace.

Access : At the entrance to Beaune, from Seurre (D 973, Dôle road)

 4 **VILLA FLEURIE**
Mme Chartier

19 place Colbert
21200 Beaune
Tel. 03 80 22 66 00
Fax 03 80 22 45 46
la.villa.fleurie @ wanadoo.fr
www.lavillafleurie.fr

Open from 1 Jan to 1 Feb • 10 rooms, most have bath/WC, all have television • €67 to €77; breakfast €8 • No restaurant • Garden, private car park

 The friendly, family atmosphere.

This small 1900 villa is entwined in the sweet-scented branches of an old wisteria bush. It offers three styles of room: contemporary, bourgeois and split-level family on the top floor. Chintz curtains, a fireplace and mouldings give the breakfast room a distinctly English feel, while the deck-chairs on the garden-terrace invite guests to relax and unwind.

Access : Set back from the lane, on a small square near the swimming pool

5 CHAMBRE D'HÔTE MME BAGATELLE
Mme Bagatelle

Rue des Moutons
21320 Châteauneuf
Tel. 03 80 49 21 00
Fax 03 80 49 21 49
jean-michel.bagatelle @ wanadoo.fr

Closed during the February holidays • 4 rooms with shower/WC • €50 to €60, breakfast included • Table d'hôte €23 • Garden, car park. Credit cards not accepted, no dogs allowed

6 HOSTELLERIE DU CHÂTEAU
M. Hartmann

21320 Châteauneuf
Tel. 03 80 49 22 00
Fax 03 80 49 21 27
hdc @ hostellerie-chateauneuf.com
www.hostellerie-chateauneuf.com

Closed from Dec to Feb, Mon and Tue except in Jul and Aug • 17 rooms, 8 of which are in a separate wing (4 are split-level for families) and one has disabled access. Rooms have bath/WC or shower/WC • €45 to €70; breakfast €8; half board available • Menus €23 to €36 • Terrace, garden

Wandering through the narrow streets of this lovely fortified village.

This old stone sheepfold stands in the centre of the medieval village on the banks of the Burgundy Canal. Stone and wood take pride of place in this tastefully decorated house. Guests immediately feel at home in the welcoming bedrooms, one of which has a fireplace, while the split-level rooms are perfectly suited to families.

Contemplating the medieval castle over a refreshing glass of kir.

The fortified town, perched high above France's "motorway to the south", formerly controlled the entire plain below. Today its heavy doors swing open to reveal a pleasant stopping place. The hostelry is just an arrow's distance from the majestic medieval castle which can be seen from the garden. The main building and annex, a 17C house, are home to a few rooms decorated with original old beams and stonework. Warm medieval-style sitting room.

Access : In the village

Access : In the centre of the village next to the castle

 7 CHAMBRE D'HÔTE LES BRUGÈRES
M. et Mme Brugère

7 rue Jean-Jaurès
21160 Couchey
Tel. 03 80 52 13 05
Fax 03 80 52 93 20
brugeref @ aol.com
www.francoisbrugere.com

Closed from Dec to Mar • 4 rooms with shower/WC • €52 to €60, breakfast included • No table d'hôte • Car park. Dogs not allowed

 8 WILSON
Mmes Descaillot et Etievant

1 rue Longvic
21000 Dijon
Tel. 03 80 66 82 50
Fax 03 80 36 41 54
hotelwilson @ wanadoo.fr
www.wilson-hotel.com

Open all year • 27 rooms, 18 of which have bath/WC, 9 have shower/WC, all have television • €70 to €88; breakfast €10 • No restaurant • Garage

Soak up the atmosphere of a wine estate.

This charming 17C establishment, the property of a Marsannay wine-grower, provides a perfect opportunity to get to know more about the region's wine. The attractively restored rooms are decorated with exposed beams and prize finds from the local antique dealers: one bedroom even has a piano. In the winter, roaring log fires light up the breakfast room, hung with tapestries. The cellar is open for visits and wine-tastings.

Snug as a bug in this house of character.

Lovingly and tastefully restored, this 17C coaching inn has now added the bonus of modern comforts to its beautifully preserved Burgundian architecture. The exposed beams and cosy, lived-in feel of the well-soundproofed rooms, laid out round an inner courtyard, never fail to win over guests. Breakfast is served by an open fire in winter.

Access : 2km southbound from Marsannay on the D 122

Access : From the town centre, drive to Place du Théâtre and then along Rue Chabot-Charny

 9 **LES GRANDS CRUS**
Mme Farnier

Rue de Lavaux
21220 Gevrey-Chambertin
Tel. 03 80 34 34 15
Fax 03 80 51 89 07
hotel.lesgrandscrus@ipac.fr
www.hoteldesgrandscrus.com

Open from 1 Mar to 30 Nov • 24 rooms on 2 floors, all have bath/WC and television • €70 to €80; breakfast €10 • No restaurant • Garden, private car park

10 **LA MUSARDE**
M. Ogé

7 rue des Riottes
21121 Hauteville-lès-Dijon
Tel. 03 80 56 22 82
Fax 03 80 56 64 40
hotel.rest.lamusarde@wanadoo.fr

Closed from 20 Dec to 10 Jan • 12 rooms with bath/WC or shower/WC and television • €54 to €61; breakfast €8; half board available • Restaurant closed Sun evening and Mon; menus €17 (weekdays) to €64 • Terrace, garden, car park

 Burgundy's amply justified pride in its wine.

Treat yourself to a night in this village, also known as the kingdom of wine and celebrated by hosts of wine lovers and writers: one of the authors, Gaston Roupnel, even tried his hand at wine-making. The plush bourgeois or rustic-style rooms command fine views over the vineyards. In wintertime, snuggle up in the deep armchairs next to a log fire and wax lyrical over the merits of this or that vintage year. Pleasant flowered garden and summer terrace.

 Unspoilt countryside on the doorstep of Dijon.

Follow the suggestion on the sign – literally "the idler" – and put off a visit to the capital of the Dukes of Burgundy in favour of dawdling in the local countryside. Relax in the welcome shade of the thick branches of cypress, hazelnut and oak trees on the terrace and enjoy the tranquillity of this charming village on the heights of Dijon. A rustic style has been adopted for the family-sized, simply furnished rooms, which all look out over the peaceful garden.

Access : On the corner of Route des Grand Crus and Rue de Lavaux

Access : 6km to the north-west of Dijon, on the N 71 (towards Troyes), then take the D 107 on the right

 11 PARC
M. Oudot

13 rue du Golf
21200 Levernois
Tel. 03 80 24 63 00
Fax 03 80 24 21 19
hotel.le.parc @ wanadoo.fr
www.hotelleparc.fr

Closed from 23 Nov to 22 Jan • 25 rooms, all of which have bath/WC or shower/WC and television • €40 to €89; breakfast €7 • No restaurant • Car park, park. Dogs not allowed

 12 LA SAURA
M. et Mme Berthaud

Route de Beaune
21360 Lusigny-sur-Ouche
Tel. 03 80 20 17 46
Fax 03 80 20 07 73
la-saura @ wanadoo.fr
www.douix.com/la-saura

Open all year • 6 rooms with shower/WC • €60 to €80, breakfast included • No table d'hôte • Garden, car park. Credit cards not accepted • Outdoor swimming pool. Horse-riding, tennis, golf and boating on the canal nearby

 Listening to the wind rustling the leaves of the hundred-year-old trees in the park.

A lovely flowered courtyard separates these two buildings, whose distinctive Burgundy-style façades are covered in Virginia creeper. The eye is drawn to the tall trees standing in the pleasant grounds. A cosy family atmosphere reigns throughout the rooms decorated with old furniture, retro lamps and flowered drapes. All are equally impeccably looked after and those in the second building are slightly larger. Most attentive family welcome.

 The fine collection of contemporary art.

The owner, a painter in his spare time, has acquired a fine collection of contemporary works, including several abstracts which blend in beautifully with the original fireplace, beams and stone floors. The rooms are decorated in a variety of eclectic styles, marrying parquet floor and antiques in one and a wrought-iron bed, terracotta tiles and painted furniture in another; all overlook the terraced garden. An art gallery and a swimming pool have recently been built in the outbuildings.

Access : To the south-east of Beaune 5km along the Verdun-sur-le-Doubs road, D 970 and D 111

Access : 2km southbound from Bligny-sur-Ouche on the D 970

  13 **DOMAINE DU MOULIN AUX MOINES**
M. Hanique

Auxey-Duresses
21190 Meursault
Tel. 03 80 21 60 79
Fax 03 80 21 60 79
contact @ laterrasse.fr
www.laterrasse.fr

Open all year • 3 rooms and 1 gîte at the mill, 3 rooms 500m away at Meursault, all have bathrooms • €70 to €110, breakfast €7 • No table d'hôte • Garden, car park

  14 **LE CLOS**
M. Oudot

22 rue des Gravières
21200 Montagny-lès-Beaune
Tel. 03 80 25 97 98
Fax 03 80 25 94 70
hotelleclos @ wanadoo.fr
www.hotelleclos.com

Closed from 25 Nov to 15 Jan • 19 rooms and 5 suites, 2 rooms have disabled access, with bath/WC or shower/WC and television • €65 to €110 (€60 to €100 low season); breakfast €9 • No restaurant • Car park, park. Dogs not allowed

 Its unique location in the heart of the prestigious Meursault vineyard.

This handsome property surrounded by vineyards once belonged to the Abbey of Cluny. Stone walls, beams, tiled floors and a fireplace add a great deal of cachet to the tastefully-appointed rooms; ask for the one in the mill. The inner courtyard, right on a riverbank, is also very pleasant. A wealth of activities awaits guests, including tastings of the estate's wine and visits to the dovecote and to the small wine-growing museum with an interesting 15C wine press.

 A quiet night's sleep just five minutes from the heart of Beaune, France's prestigious city of wine.

An ancient wine press stands proudly in the centre of the large courtyard of this lovely 18C property, formerly home to wine-growing estate. Entirely restored, it now offers well-proportioned rooms furnished in a rustic style and fitted with good quality linen: rest and relaxation guaranteed.

Access : In the middle of the estate's vineyards

Access : 3 km southbound from Beaune on Avenue Charles-de-Gaulle and the D 113

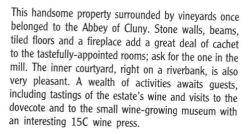

15 AU TEMPS D'AUTREFOIS
M. Pocheron

Place Monge
21340 Nolay
Tel. 03 80 21 76 37
Fax 03 80 21 76 37
noellepocheron@wanadoo.fr
www.terroirs-b.com/gite

Open all year • 4 rooms, one of which is a suite • €60, breakfast included • No table d'hôte

16 CHAMBRE D'HÔTE MME BACCHIERI
Mme Bacchieri

La Forge, bord du Canal de Bourgogne
21500 Rougemont
Tel. 03 80 92 35 99
Fax 03 80 92 35 99

Closed from Christmas to 1 Jan • 3 rooms with bath/WC • €50, breakfast included • No table d'hôte • Car park. Credit cards not accepted • Boating

 The well-preserved charm of yesteryear.

A deliciously faded atmosphere emanates from this attractive 14C half-timbered house, standing on a little square opposite a fountain. The warm, welcoming interior features exposed beams, antique furniture, chequered curtains and tiled floors. The quiet, pretty rooms are adorned with old black and white photos of Nolay. In the summer, breakfast is served on the terrace of the inn, on the opposite side of the square.

 Boating on the untroubled waters of the Burgundy Canal.

This delightful little house on the banks of the Burgundy Canal in the Armançon Valley lives up to its promise of peace and quiet. The welcoming, well-kept rooms are full of character and above all very peaceful; all have a fireplace. The manicured garden near the lock and the bicycle towpath along the banks of the canal further enhance its charm. Lavish breakfasts and gracious welcome.

Access : In the heart of the village

Access : 10km to the north-west of Montbard on the D 905

 17 HOSTELLERIE DE LA TOUR D'AUXOIS
M. Prevost

Square Alexandre-Dumaine
21210 Saulieu
Tel. 03 80 64 36 19
Fax 03 80 64 93 10
jlprevost @ tourdauxois.com
www.tourdauxois.com

Open all year • 35 air-conditioned rooms, 6 of which are split-level and 2 have disabled access. Rooms have bath/WC or shower/WC and television • €78 to €102 (€75 to €98 low season); breakfast €9 • Menus €19 (weekdays) to €34 • Terrace, landscaped garden, garage, private car park • Heated outdoor swimming pool, piano bar

 We most liked The split-level room in the old presbytery.

Formerly very popular, this famous town and stopping point has declined in favour since the motorway diverted much of the traffic off the traditional holiday road. This 17C hostelry nonetheless remains true to its tradition of service and hospitality. The building has been renovated from top to bottom with whitewashed walls, tiled floors, painted furniture and exposed beams in some rooms. The circular dining room overlooks a landscaped garden with a view of the ruins of an old 14C tower.

Access : On the road through the town, next to the 14C tower

18 HÔTEL - BUREAU LES CYMAISES
M. et Mme Faidide

7 rue Renaudot
21140 Semur-en-Auxois
Tel. 03 80 97 21 44
Fax 03 80 97 18 23
hotel.cymaises @ libertysurf.fr
www.hotelcymaises.com

Open all year • 18 rooms, one of which has disabled access, most have bath/WC, some have shower/WC, all have television • €55 to €59; breakfast €7 • No restaurant • Garden, private car park

 We most liked A leisurely stroll on the ramparts of Semur.

The small capital of Auxois is within "cannonball" distance of some of the most noted jewels of Burgundy, including the Abbey of Fontenay, the fortified village of Flavigny and the Gallo-roman excavations at Alésia. A street near the Porte Sauvigny leads to this imposing 18C townhouse. The rooms are well soundproofed and furnished in a practical country style, while a comfortable sitting room plus conservatory makes a perfect setting for breakfast. Pleasant, peaceful garden to the rear.

Access : On a side street in the medieval city

TALANT - 21240

VILLARS-ET-VILLENOTTE - 21140

19 LA BONBONNIÈRE
M. Kreis

24 rue des Orfèvres
21240 Talant
Tel. 03 80 57 31 95
Fax 03 80 57 23 92
labonbonniere @ wanadoo.fr
www.labonbonnierehotel.fr

Open all year • 20 rooms, all of which have bath/WC or shower/WC and television • €65 to €90; breakfast €8 • No restaurant • Private car park. Dogs not allowed

20 LES LANGRONS
Mme Collins Mary

21140 Villars-et-Villenotte
Tel. 03 80 96 65 11
Fax 03 80 97 32 28
langrons @ club-intenet.fr

Expected to close for refurbishment during the year, call beforehand. • 3 rooms upstairs • €55, breakfast included • No table d'hôte • Garden, car park. Credit cards not accepted, no dogs allowed

We most liked **Savouring the tranquillity of this lovely flowered garden just a few kilometres from Dijon.**

This private house transformed into a hotel, almost on the doorstep of a 13C church, stands in a fetching little village overlooking Lake Kir. The interior decoration fully justifies the establishment's name and the pastel colours and stylish furniture definitely lend it a bijou feel. Quiet, spacious rooms, plush bourgeois sitting room and welcoming breakfast room. Even better, the patrons can't do enough to make their guests feel welcome.

We most liked **The welcoming warmth of the old stove after a hard day's exploring.**

This entirely restored farmhouse, situated very close to the picturesque medieval town of Villars, can hardly be said to lack character. A handsome staircase leads up to the whitewashed walls, exposed beams, rugs and matching curtains and bedspreads in the rooms. Lavish breakfasts are served in a rustic dining room with flagstones, heated in the winter by the welcoming embers of an old stove. Mountain bikes can be rented.

Access : In the centre of the village near the church

Access : 5.5km to the north-west of Semur-en-Auxois on the D 954 then the D 9A

 21 **LE VAL D'ARON**
M. Terrier

5 rue des Écoles
58340 Cercy-la-Tour
Tel. 03 86 50 59 66
Fax 03 86 50 04 24
val.aron @ wanadoo.fr
www.hotelrestaurant-aron.com

Closed 15 Dec to 15 Jan, Sat and Sun from Oct to May
• 12 rooms with bath/WC and television; the 4 rooms overlooking the garden have a balcony • €54 to €71 (€54 to €61 low season); breakfast €9; half board available • Menus €18 (weekdays) to €45 • Terrace, garden, car park • Outdoor swimming pool

 22 **LES FORGES**
M. Marcellot

21 rue Saint-Agnan
58200 Cosne-Cours-sur-Loire
Tel. 03 86 28 23 50
Fax 03 86 28 91 60
denis.cathye @ wanadoo.fr

Closed in Jul and Dec • 7 rooms with bath/WC, television and internet access • €45 to €60, breakfast €7 • Air-conditioned restaurant, closed Sun evening and Mon; menus €18 to €60 • No dogs allowed in restaurant

 Whiling away a few hours on the Nivernais Canal.

This 19C mansion formerly housed the local police station before it was turned into a hotel. The attic rooms feature exposed beams and timbers, while those on the ground floor open onto the garden: take your pick when you book – all are spacious and cool. In the winter, meals are served in the rustic dining room with fireplace, and in the summer on a "terrace" under the rafters of a reconstructed farmhouse.

 The discreet charm of this beautifully renovated establishment.

Colour greets the eye right from the lovely green façade of this well-renovated traditional house, encouraging guests to cross its threshold. The small spruce rooms sport yellow and white striped wallpaper, pastel shades and matching fabrics. Ochre takes pride of place in the restaurant, while in the welcoming dining room, burgundy-coloured tablecloths and white mats provide the setting for deliciously up-to-date cuisine.

Access : Midway between Decize and Saint-Honoré-les-Bains

Access : In the town centre

 23 **LE BON LABOUREUR**
M. Boulin

 Quai Romain Mollot
58400 La Charité-sur-Loire
Tel. 03 86 70 22 85
Fax 03 86 70 23 64
lebonlaboureur @ wanadoo.fr
www.lebonlaboureur.com

Open all year • 16 rooms with bath/WC and shower/WC
and television • €40 to €50; breakfast €6 • No restaurant
• Garden. No dogs allowed • Reading room

24 **PERREAU**
M. et Mme Girbal

 8 route d'Avallon
58140 Lormes
Tel. 03 86 22 53 21
Fax 03 86 22 82 15

Closed from 25 Dec to 31 Jan, Sun evening and Mon
from Oct to Apr • 17 rooms, 9 of which are in a separate
wing, have bath/WC or shower/WC, all have television
• €44 to €60; breakfast €6; half board available • Menus
€16 to €32 • Private car park. No dogs allowed • Hiking,
horse-riding and mountain biking

 Killing time in the peaceful garden on a summer's day.

This former coaching inn, complete with a barn formerly
used by bargees, is located on an island on the Loire.
The gracious proprietors take great pleasure in
welcoming their guests in style. All the rooms are
renovated, light and airy and perfectly kept. The
breakfast room with a veranda section overlooking a
charming garden is another high spot of this address.

 The fine views of the Morvan from Lormes and the Mount of Justice.

This traditional hostelry stands on the road through a
picturesque Morvan town. Behind its recently spruced
up façade lie pleasant bedrooms, while those in the
other wing are quieter and more modern. The exposed
stone, dark timbers and stained-glass lights make the
dining room most inviting.

Access : Near the town centre on the Loire on the
D 955 towards Sancerre

Access : In the centre of the village, 29km
southbound from Avallon on the D 944

 25 **CLOS SAINTE-MARIE**
M. et Mme F. Vincent

25 rue du Petit Mouësse
58000 Nevers
Tel. 03 86 71 94 50
Fax 03 86 71 94 69
clos.ste.marie@wanadoo.fr

Closed 24 Dec to 2 Jan • 17 rooms with bath/WC and shower/WC and television, 8 are non-smoking • €66 to €80 (€62 low season) • No restaurant • Garden, car park. No dogs allowed

 26 **VERDUN**
M. et Mme Prat

4 rue de Lourdes
58000 Nevers
Tel. 03 86 61 30 07
Fax 03 86 57 75 61
hotel.de.verdun@wanadoo.fr

 www.hoteldeverdun-nevers.com

Closed from 7 to 23 Aug and 26 Dec to 13 Jan • 21 rooms around a patio or in a separate wing, with bathrooms with or without WC and television, 1 has disabled access • €30 to €52, breakfast €5.50 • No restaurant • No dogs allowed • Two minutes from the historic centre

 Relaxing to the sound of the pools in the hotel's inner courtyard.

Some of the rooms of this hotel near a busy street overlook the road but are well soundproofed to ensure a good night's sleep; most are however laid out around a lush green, peaceful patio whose ornamental pools are home to goldfish. The bedrooms, most of which are spacious, are all excellently looked after and furnished with antiques picked up in local markets; some have been recently renovated.

 Strolling through Roger Salengro Park opposite the hotel.

This town centre hotel has been treated to a well-needed makeover. The determination and commitment of the new owners have transformed the establishment into a very pleasant port of call in this ancient city. Bright colours, new fabrics, modern bedding and renovated bathrooms give the unpretentious bedrooms an inviting appeal. The breakfast buffet is served in a pleasant country-style dining room and, in summer, on a pleasant patio.

Access : 2km from the town centre on the N 81 towards Dijon

Access : In the town centre, opposite the town park

27 L'ORÉE DES VIGNES
Mme Kandin

Croquant
58200 Saint-Père
Tel. 03 86 28 12 50
Fax 03 86 28 12 50
loreedesvignes @ wanadoo.fr
www.loreedesvignes.com

Open all year • 5 non-smoking rooms • €50 to €52, breakfast included; half board available • Table d'hôte €22 (by reservation only) • Terrace, garden, car park. Credit cards not accepted, no dogs allowed

28 LE GRAND HOTEL
M. Monssus

Parc Thermal
71140 Bourbon-Lancy
Tel. 03 85 89 08 87
Fax 03 85 89 32 23
bourbon.thermal @ wanadoo.fr
www.grand-hotel-thermal.com

Open Apr to Oct • 27 rooms with bath/WC or shower/WC, all have television and 8 have a kitchenette • €53 to €75; breakfast €6; half board available • Menus €10 to €31 • Terrace, inner courtyard, park, car park

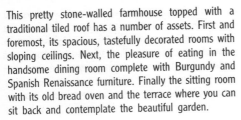

We most liked **The well-stocked information corner in the hall.**

This pretty stone-walled farmhouse topped with a traditional tiled roof has a number of assets. First and foremost, its spacious, tastefully decorated rooms with sloping ceilings. Next, the pleasure of eating in the handsome dining room complete with Burgundy and Spanish Renaissance furniture. Finally the sitting room with its old bread oven and the terrace where you can sit back and contemplate the beautiful garden.

We most liked **A leisurely stroll along the ramparts of this spa town.**

This hotel, a former convent, lies on the edge of the spa centre's woody park. The gradually renovated and spacious rooms feature a variety of functional or more old-fashioned furniture and all benefit from the pervading restful atmosphere. Light floods in through the dining room's large bay windows but on fine days many guests prefer the terrace in the cloisters.

Access : 3.2km eastbound from Cosne-sur-Loire on the D 33 and the D 168

Access : In the town centre, next to the spa and park

BOURBON-LANCY - 71140

BOURGVILAIN - 71520

29 VILLA DU VIEUX PUITS
M. et Mme Perraudin

7 rue de Bel-Air
71140 Bourbon-Lancy
Tel. 03 85 89 04 04
Fax 03 85 89 13 87

Closed from mid-Feb to mid-Mar, Sun evening and Mon • 7 rooms upstairs with bath/WC or shower/WC, all have television • €40 to €50; breakfast €8; half board available • Menus €16 to €45 • Terrace, garden, car park. No dogs allowed in restaurant

30 LE MOULIN DES ARBILLONS
M. et Mme Dubois-Favre

71520 Bourgvilain
Tel. 03 85 50 82 83
Fax 03 85 50 86 32
arbillon@club-internet.fr
www.club-internet.fr/perso/arbillon

Open 15 Apr to 15 Oct 2005 • 5 rooms • €58 to €79, breakfast included • No table d'hôte • Sitting room, terrace, garden, park. Credit cards not accepted, no dogs allowed • Wine cellar, tasting and sales

 The landscaped garden complete with pond.

 The rural setting of this group of 18C, 19C and 20C buildings.

The walls of a former tannery now house this smart country inn. The rooms of variable size are both cosy and modern; those on the garden side are quieter and enjoy a better view. A countrified dining room, pleasant outdoor terrace and a slightly threadbare sitting room, its piano still in good tune, complete the picture of this unpretentious, excellent family establishment where guests can always be sure of a warm welcome.

The 18C mill is flanked by a handsome 19C country house and set in a park which boasts a river and a pond. Beautiful period wardrobes grace the generally well-proportioned rooms, all of which overlook the valley and village. A bold blue and white colour scheme and vaulted ceiling make the smallest room our favourite. Breakfast is served in the 20C orangery which features frescoes, iron furniture and a porcelain stove.

Access : Near to Place d'Aligre and the spa

Access : 8km southbound from Cluny on the D 980 then the D 22

31 MANOIR DE CHAMPVENT
Mme Rullière

Lieu-dit Champvent
71700 Chardonnay
Tel. 03 85 40 50 23
Fax 03 85 40 50 18

Closed from 1 Nov to 1 Mar • 5 rooms • €52 to €58 (€50 to €55 out of season), breakfast included • No table d'hôte • Garden, park, car park. Credit cards not accepted • Art gallery

32 LA POSTE
M. et Mme Doucet

2 avenue de la Libération
71120 Charolles
Tel. 03 85 24 11 32
Fax 03 85 24 05 74
hotel-de-la-liberation-doucet@wanadoo.fr
www.la-poste-hotel.com

Closed Nov, Sun evening and Mon • 14 rooms, 3 of which have a terrace. Rooms have bath/WC and television • €48 to €120; breakfast €8; half board available • Menus €23 (weekdays) to €70 • Terrace, garage

 The regular drama performances.

Venture past the porch and you will discover a lovely stone manor house. The rooms are in the outbuildings and furnished with antiques, still-lifes and abstract works by a family ancestor. A room is set aside for regular drama performances and exhibitions of sculpture. The gardens are equally attractive and children generally love romping through the meadow. Flowered courtyard.

 The festive atmosphere of the cattle markets.

The comfortable bedrooms of this traditional well-kept Burgundian house are equally classical with their chocolate box patterns. Alcove statues, ornaments, period furniture and Charolles porcelain tableware abound in the refined bourgeois décor of the dining room. Burgundy's legendary generosity and hospitality are done full justice in the delicious menu, where the local Charolais beef, of course, has pride of place. Meals are served in the flowered courtyard in fine weather.

Access : 11km to the south-west of Tournus on the D 56 then the D 463

Access : On a street corner, opposite the church in the town centre

BURGUNDY

33 CHÂTEAU DE SALORNAY
M. Guérin

71870 Hurigny
Tel. 03 85 34 25 73
Fax 03 85 20 11 43

Open all year • 4 rooms • €45 to €52 , breakfast included • No table d'hôte • Garden, car park. Credit cards not accepted

 34 MOULIN DE BOURGCHÂTEAU
M. Donatelli

Rue du Guidon
71500 Louhans
Tel. 03 85 75 37 12
Fax 03 85 75 45 11
bourgchateau@netcourrier.com
www.bourgchateau.com

Closed from 1 to 25 Jan and Mon • 19 rooms with bath/WC or shower/WC, all have television • €54 to €85; breakfast €9; half board available • Menus €22 (weekdays) to €50 • Park, car park. No dogs admitted in restaurant • 2 pedalos available, local wines sold

 The sweeping view over Mâcon from the castle terrace.

The towers, thick walls and guard posts of this 11C and 15C castle cannot fail to attract admiring glances. The antique furnished rooms were built along the same grand lines and overlook the fields. The room in the keep has retained its original terracotta flooring and mullioned windows. Not to be outdone, the dining room boasts beams, flagstones and a fireplace. Children are always welcome to visit the barnyard animals in the nearby farm. Two gîtes are also available.

 Relaxing amidst the cogs and gears of the old mill's machinery.

This enchanting 1778 mill spanning the Seille River was in use up until 1973. The modern, immaculate rooms on the upper floors enjoy a wonderful view of the woodland and river. A millstone and its hopper, leftovers from the mill's working days, lend the dining room a great deal of character. Local wines are on sale in one of the outbuildings. Two pedalos are available for the use of guests who fancy a spin on the river.

Access : 6km westbound from Mâcon on the D 82 then a minor road

Access : Leave Louhans towards Chalon on Rue du 11-Nov-1918, then Rue du Guidon, turn right into the lane towards Bourgchâteau

35 CHAMBRE D'HÔTE M. MATHIEU
M. et Mme Mathieu

Sermaize
71600 Poisson
Tel. 03 85 81 06 10
Fax 03 85 81 06 10

Closed from Nov to 15 Mar • 5 rooms with shower/WC
• €48 to €58, breakfast included • Table d'hôte €20
• Garden, parking. Credit cards not accepted

36 HOSTELLERIE BRESSANE
M. et Mme Giot

2 route de Sens
71330 Saint-Germain-du-Bois
Tel. 03 85 72 04 69
Fax 03 85 72 07 75

Open all year • 8 rooms upstairs, some with bath/WC or
shower/WC • €17 to €41; breakfast €13; half board
available • Restaurant closed Sun eve and Mon except Jul
and Aug; menus €11 (weekdays) to €35 • Private car
park

The library's excellent collection of works about the region.

This former 14C hunting lodge with its impressive circular tower and flower-filled courtyard forms a very pleasing picture. An original spiral staircase winds up to a few personalised rooms, two of them have bathrooms in the tower. The suite boasts immense beams, cosy armchairs and walls lined with prints of 19C paintings and old photos by Doisneau. The garden overlooking the open countryside is very pleasant in the summer.

The ecomuseum about the Bresse region in the castle of Pierre-en-Bresse.

This manor house built in the 18C for the Marquis of Scorailles has been an inn since 1815. The somewhat faded allure of the bedrooms is compensated for by the generous sprinkling of well-polished regional furniture. Polished oak floors, dark timber beams and a fireplace adorn the rustic dining room while attractive frescoes lighten the more urban 1900 room. Classic French dishes, plus some local Bresse delicacies, like the famously tender chicken.

Access : 12.5km south-east of Paray-le-Monial on the D 34 then the D 458, towards Saint-Julien-de-Civry

Access : In the centre of the village

37 LA VIOLETTERIE
Mme Chartier

71740 Saint-Maurice-lès-Châteauneuf
Tel. 03 85 26 26 60
Fax 03 85 26 26 60
madeleinechartier@yahoo.fr

Closed from 1 Jan to 15 Mar and 11 Nov to 31 Dec
• 3 rooms, one of which is in the attic, all have bath/WC
• €50, breakfast included • Table d'hôte €18 (evenings only and by reservation only) • Garden, car park. Credit cards not accepted, no dogs allowed

38 AUBERGE DU SAINT-VÉRAN
Mme Leguet

La Roche
71570 Saint-Vérand
Tel. 03 85 23 90 90
Fax 03 85 23 90 91
www-auberge-saint-veran.com

Closed 3 weeks in Jan, and on Mon lunchtime and Tue out of season • 11 rooms with shower/WC and television
• €56 to €68; breakfast €8.50; half-board available
• Menus €21 (weekdays) to €58.50 • Terrace, garden, private car park

The sophisticated 19C ambience.

A wrought-iron gate takes you into the courtyard and garden and a flight of steps leads into this 19C mansion. The former holiday home of architect Roux-Spitz, it is now a hotel with light, airy rooms. Those in the attic with painted furniture have retained their original tiled floors and beams. The elegant wood panelling and the fireplace in the sitting and dining room further add to the establishment's appeal.

Tune your ears to the delightful music of French country life.

The creaking of the millstone and the gears of this old flour mill have given way to the funky beat of dinner concerts in the evening. The magnificent piano, which graces the rustic dining room, bears witness to the lady of the house's passion for music. The dawn chorus is however sung by a company of ducks. As the water gently laps the banks of the Pétry, catch a quick forty winks, before being awakened by the joyful laughter of the village children playing in the nearby river.

Access : 10km to the north-east of Charlieu on the D 487, then the D 987 towards La-Clayette

Access : Leave the N 6 at Crèches-sur-Saône for the D 31 to Saint-Véran

39 LE CHÂTEAU D'ESCOLLES
M. et Mme de Potter

71960 Verzé
Tel. 03 85 33 44 52
Fax 03 85 33 34 80
info @ gite-escolles.com

Open all year • 4 rooms with bathrooms • €70, breakfast included • No table d'hôte • Park, car park. No dogs allowed

40 MAXIME
M. et Mme Leclerc

2 quai de la Marine
89000 Auxerre
Tel. 03 86 52 14 19
Fax 03 86 52 21 70
hotel-maxime @ wanadoo.fr
www.lemaxime.com

Open all year • 25 rooms with bath/WC and television • €75 to €120; breakfast €10; half board available • Terrace, private car park

 The faultless decoration of this elegant house.

Guests are always welcomed warmly to this outbuilding of a 17C castle, standing on the edge of a 12-acre park with a pond and surrounded by vineyards and woodland. The sloping ceilings of the bedrooms add a cosy touch, further enhanced by thick carpets, beams and old furniture. Breakfasts, a chance to feast on home-made jams and fresh fruit juice, are served in a beautiful room graced with a dresser, old kneading machine and wrought-iron light. Delightful terrace.

 Trying to learn how to pronounce "Ausserre" like the locals.

This hotel is in the midst of Auxerre's marine district, surrounded by the barge owners half-timbered houses and the Horse-Drawn Barge Museum. The rooms facing the quay with a view of the Yonne are being gradually renovated, but those to the rear are quieter. The typically Burgundian restaurant and the vaulted bistro have, over the years, become the haunt of Auxerre's successful football team. The sounds of liberally washed-down post match celebrations still echo round the walls.

Access : 2km to the north of Roche-Vineuse by D 85

Access : On the road on the left bank of the Yonne

  41 **NORMANDIE**
M. Ramisse

41 boulevard Vauban
89000 Auxerre
Tel. 03 86 52 57 80
Fax 03 86 51 54 33
reception@hotelnormandie.fr
www.hotelnormandie.fr

Open all year • 47 rooms, most at the rear of the building. All rooms have bath/WC or shower/WC and television, 4 are non-smoking • €57 to €77; breakfast €8 • No restaurant • Terrace, garage • Billiards

  42 **LE PARC DES MARÉCHAUX**
M. et Mme Leclerc

6 avenue Foch
89000 Auxerre
Tel. 03 86 51 43 77
Fax 03 86 51 31 72
contact@hotel-parcmarechaux.com
www.hotel-parcmarechaux.com

Open all year • 25 air-conditioned rooms on 2 levels, all have bath/WC and television • €79 to €110; breakfast €12, half board available • No restaurant but room service available from €18.50 to €29.50 • Terrace, park, car park • Swimming pool

Endless discussions over a game of billiards.

Virginia creeper has covered the pretty redbrick and white stone façade of this comfortable 19C townhouse with a pleasant gravel forecourt where breakfasts are served in the summer. Most of the rooms, which are in the process of being renovated, are situated in a more recent, quieter wing. The rooms are comfortable and some have power showers. Guests' welfare is the prime concern of this pleasant establishment - they even provide room service.

The recently sunk swimming pool which blends into the abundant foliage.

A Parisian judge had this elegant mansion built in 1854 in a style favoured by Napoleon III. When it was converted into a hotel in 1980, the owners were astute enough to retain as much of its original character as possible. The Empire bedrooms are named after Marshals of the French army, while the sitting rooms and breakfast room are reminiscent of Victorian parlours. The superb park and its hundred-year-old trees add a certain hint of romanticism to the mansion.

Access : On the ring-road round town, right at the roundabout coming from the A 6 (Paris) and the N 6 (Sens)

Access : From the A 6 or N 6 turn right at Boulevard Vauban roundabout, then right past the Natural History museum

 43 HOSTELLERIE DES CLOS
M. et Mme Vignaud

 18 rue Jules-Rathier
89800 Chablis
Tel. 03 86 42 10 63
Fax 03 86 42 17 11
host.clos @ wanadoo.fr
www.hostellerie-des-clos.fr

Closed from 20 Dec to 16 Jan • 32 rooms and 4 apartments with bath/WC and television • €60 to €183; breakfast €10; half board available • Menus €35 to €72 • Garden, car park

 44 CHÂTEAU DE RIBOURDIN
M. et Mme Brodard

 89240 Chevannes
Tel. 03 86 41 23 16
Fax 03 86 41 23 16

Open all year • 5 rooms, one of which is on the ground floor and has disabled access • €60 to €70, breakfast included • No table d'hôte • Garden. Credit cards not accepted, no dogs allowed • Outdoor swimming pool

 Savouring a Havana cigar in the smoking room instead of being banished to the garden.

This former hospital, which still has its original 14C chapel, used to own numerous vineyards. The beautiful vaulted cellar bears witness to the house's wine-growing heritage and has a choice of over 30 Chablis. Rich fabrics and modern comforts adorn the recently renovated rooms. The bow windows of the restaurant open onto a patio where drinks are served in the evenings and breakfast in the morning, the cooking is generous and full of flavour and the wine-list is quite simply out of this world!

 The select atmosphere of this wonderful little castle.

The 16C dovecote and castle stand at the foot of the village in the midst of wheat fields. Patience and care lavished over the years have resulted in the beautiful restoration visible today. The 18C barn now houses the bedrooms, each of which is named after a local castle and the spacious breakfast room has a fireplace. The overall look is rustic, mirroring the countryside views from the windows.

Access : In the centre of the village

Access : 9km to the south-west of Auxerre on the N 151 then the D 1, then a minor road

 45 LA MARMOTTE
M. et Mme Lecolle

 2 rue de l'École
89700 Collan
Tel. 03 86 55 26 44
Fax 03 86 55 00 08
lamarmotte.glecolle@wanadoo.fr
www.bonadresse.com/bourgogne/collan.
htm

Open all year • 3 non-smoking rooms with bathrooms
• €43, breakfast included • No table d'hôte • Garden,
car park. Credit cards not accepted, no dogs allowed
• Horse-drawn carriage rides, boating on the Burgundy
canal and fishing nearby

 We most liked
The footpaths through the Chablis vineyards.

This beautiful old stone house lies in the heart of one
of the Yonne's picturesque little villages. All the
personalised rooms are named after a colour chosen for
the interior decoration. The "Blue" room has cane
furniture, while open beams and a wrought-iron
four-poster bed grace the "Pink" room. Breakfast is
served in the winter garden to the tinkling sound of the
fountain.

46 DOMAINE BORGNAT LE COLOMBIER
Mme Borgnat

 1 rue de l'Église
89290 Escolives-Sainte-Camille
Tel. 03 86 53 35 28
Fax 03 86 53 65 00
regine@domaineborgnat.com

Open all year • 5 rooms, 3 of which have shower/WC,
the other 2 have bath/WC • €48 to €50, breakfast
included; half board available • Table d'hôte €22 to €35.
No dogs admitted in restaurant • Garden, car park
• Outdoor swimming pool, tours of the wine cellars

 We most liked
 Visiting the superb cellars.

This fortified 17C farmhouse presides over a superb
wine-growing estate. On the accommodation side,
guests can choose between the simple comfort of B&B
rooms or the self-catering cottage in the former
dovecote. Bistro tables, a piano and a terrace around
the swimming pool set the scene for breakfasts. Meals
are invariably served with a choice of "home-grown"
wines. Don't miss the chance to visit the splendid 12C
and 17C cellars for further tasting sessions.

Access : 7.5km to the north-east of Chablis on the
D 150 then the D 35

Access : 9.5km southbound from Auxerre on the
D 239

LÉZINNES - 89160

LIGNY-LE-CHATEL - 89144

47 CHAMBRE D'HÔTE M. PIEDALLU
M. et Mme Piedallu

5 avenue de la Gare
89160 Lézinnes
 Tel. 03 86 75 68 23

Open all year • 3 rooms • €43, breakfast included • No table d'hôte • Sitting room, garden, car park. Credit cards not accepted, no dogs allowed

48 LE RELAIS SAINT VINCENT
Mme Vuillemin

14 Grande-rue
89144 Ligny-le-Chatel
Tel. 03 86 47 53 38
Fax 03 86 47 54 16
relais.saint.vincent @ libertysurf.fr

Closed from 20 Dec to 2 Jan • 15 rooms in 2 buildings, one room has disabled access, all have bath/WC and television • €42 to €69; breakfast €8; half board available • Menus €13 to €26 • Terrace, inner courtyard, private car park • Ideally located to visit the vineyards and abbeys

The immaculate upkeep of this contemporary house.

This brand-new house has been built in keeping with local styles and even has a square stone tower. The interior is equally pleasing and the spacious, well-appointed rooms with sloping ceilings are furnished with antiques. The breakfast room leads onto a pleasant veranda and guests have the run of a private sitting room for a quiet read.

The Chablis white wines.

Precious historic clues narrate the illustrious past of these 17C walls, formerly the home of the bailiffs of Ligny. The slightly faded rooms are spacious and calm. The Renaissance era of the restaurant is apparent in the monumental fireplace, open beams and old tapestries. When the weather is fine, meals are served in the inner courtyard surrounded by stone walls or traditional timber frames. The magnificent Abbey of Pontigny is 4km away.

Access : 11km to the south-east of Tonnerre on the D 905

Access : Leave Auxerre on the N 77 towards St-Florentin, turn right between Montigny-la-Resle and Pontigny (D 8)

BURGUNDY

L'ISLE-SUR-SEREIN - 89440   **MOLAY - 89310**

 49 **AUBERGE LE POT D'ÉTAIN**
M. et Mme Pechery

24 rue Bouchardat
89440 L'Isle-sur-Serein
Tel. 03 86 33 88 10
Fax 03 86 33 90 93
potdetain @ ipoint.fr
www.potdetain.com

Closed in Feb, the last week of Oct, Sun evening and Mon (except Jul and Aug) and Tue lunchtime • 9 rooms, the most spacious has a fireplace. All rooms have bath/WC or shower/WC and television • €56 to €75; breakfast €8; half board available • Menus €23 (weekdays) to €49 • Terrace, garage

Meals are served in the flowered inner courtyard in the summer.

Who could possibly want to remain stuck to the boiling tarmac of the A6 when the enchanting valley of Serein is so close at hand? Particularly as we've found "the" place that will capture your heart for ever. Nothing quite matches the unparalleled desire to please as that of this 18C coaching inn. Choose your room from the inn's web-site. All display the same faultless style and character as that present in the tasty Burgundian dishes and the fine selection of Chablis vintages.

Access : In the village, on the D 86: leave Avallon north-east bound on the D 957 then left 2km after Montréal

 50 **LE CALOUNIER**
M. et Mme Collin

5 rue de la Fontaine
Hameau de Arton
89310 Molay
Tel. 03 86 82 67 81
Fax 03 86 82 67 81
info @ lecalounier.fr
www.lecalounier.fr

Open all year • 5 non-smoking rooms, 2 of which are on the ground floor and have disabled access. All rooms have bathrooms with WC • €56, breakfast included; half board available • Table d'hôte €22 • Sitting room, library, garden, car park. Credit cards not accepted, no dogs allowed

The cookery courses run by the owner, a cordon-bleu chef.

It is impossible to resist the charm of this lavishly restored Burgundian farm, named after the walnut trees on the estate. The rooms are situated in two wings and are decorated in a hybrid mixture of "colonial" and rustic styles, with bold colour schemes, old furniture picked up in local antique shops and works by local artists. The barn, graced with two large windows, is home to the dining and sitting rooms. Local produce has pride of place on the dining table.

Access : 8km northbound from Noyers on the D 86, and then a minor road

51 AUBERGE DES BRIZARDS
M. Besancenot

Les Brizards
89630 Quarré-les-Tombes
Tel. 03 86 32 20 12
Fax 03 86 32 27 40
lesbrizards@free.fr
www.aubergedesbrizards.com

Closed from 5 Jan to 15 Feb and on Mon and Tue • 20 rooms, 7 of which are in the annex, most have bath/WC, some have television • €39 to €115; breakfast €9; half-board available • Menus €23 (weekdays) to €46 • Terrace, garden, park, car park • Tennis, ponds

52 LES VIEILLES FONTAINES
M. et Mme Moine

89270 Sacy
Tel. 03 86 81 51 62
Fax 03 86 81 54 86
lesvieillesfontaines@tiscali.fr
http://lesvieillesfontaines.free.fr

Closed in Jan • 5 rooms • €45, breakfast included • No table d'hôte • Garden, car park

 The forest path leading to the Abbey of Pierre qui Vire.

The position of this inn in the heart of the Morvan region would be hard to beat, surrounded by lakes, ponds, forests, unspoilt countryside and utter peace and quiet. A group of outbuildings, including two dolls' houses hidden in the park, make up the hotel; most of the snug rooms have been freshly renovated. The sophisticated restaurant, overlooking the flowered garden, serves generous country cooking. Ideal for nature lovers who enjoy the good things in life.

 Putting your feet up with a good book in the magnificent vaulted cellar-sitting room.

This delightful stone house in the heart of an old Burgundy village used to belong to a local wine-grower. The simple but comfortable rooms have parquet floors. The sitting room and kitchen, fitted out in the old vaulted wine cellar, are definitely worth a look. Meals are served in the owners' dining room, graced with a fireplace and a beautiful wrought-iron light, or on the covered terrace, weather permitting.

Access : South-east of Quarré-les-Tombes, 10km on the D 55 and the D 355, after Moulin Colas and Trinquelin

Access : 10km eastbound from Vermenton on the D 11

 53 LE HARAS DE KENMARE
Mmes O'Sullivan

19 route du Morvan. Le Meix
89630 Saint-Germain-des-Champs
Tel. 03 86 34 27 63
Fax 03 86 34 24 91
kenmare89 @ aol.com
www.harasdekenmare.com

Open all year • 5 rooms with bathrooms • €52, breakfast included • Table d'hôte €20 to €28 (by reservation only) • Sitting room, terrace, garden, car park.

 54 LE MOULIN DE LA FORGE
M. et Mme Gagnot

89350 Tannerre-en-Puisaye
Tel. 03 86 45 40 25
renegagnot @ aol.com

Open all year • 5 rooms, 3 of which are on the ground floor, all have bath/WC • €52, breakfast included • No table d'hôte • Terrace, garden, car park. Credit cards not accepted • Outdoor swimming pool

 The easy-going, lived-in feel of this family estate.

The pride and joy of this 19C home is the tapestry adorning the entrance, a copy of a medieval piece entitled Offering of the Heart. The establishment which endeavours to make guests feel totally at home more than lives up to the tapestry's message. Each of the personalised bedrooms is named after one of the region's illustrious sons and daughters (Vauban, Colette, Lamartine, Vincenot and the story-teller Marie Noël) and decorated appropriately. The family's stud farm is just next door.

 Fishing in the estate's river.

It is impossible not to admire the careful restoration of this 14C mill. The wheel has been rebuilt and the old sawmill turned into a pleasing rustic room with a kitchenette for the sole use of guests. Bare beams and 1930s furniture grace the comfortable rooms. Venture out into the landscaped parkland and explore the river, waterfall and pond teeming with fish.

Access : 10km southbound from Avallon on the D 944, the D 10 then the D 75

Access : 11km to the north-east of Saint-Fargeau on the D 18 then the D 160

 55 LE MOULIN DE LA COUDRE
M. et Mme Vaury

La Coudre
89290 Venoy
Tel. 03 86 40 23 79
Fax 03 86 40 23 55
moulin89 @ wanadoo.fr
www.moulin-de-la-coudre.com

Open all year • 14 rooms, 5 of which are in a house at the other side of the garden. Rooms have bath/WC or shower/WC and television • €60 to €80 (€57 to €76 low season); breakfast €9; half board available • Restaurant closed Sun eve and Mon; menus €20 to €62 • Terrace, garden, car park

 The peace and quiet just a giant's step from a slip-road off the A6 motorway.

The gardener-handyman clearly has his work cut out here amid the pools full of croaking frogs, borders of primroses and pansies and well-tended paths. This 19C mill on the banks of the Sinotte is perfect for a relaxing night's sleep on your journey southwards. The countrified rooms are a haven of peace and quiet and, in the summer, meals are served in the shade of dense foliage. Staff will happily give the lovingly restored millwheel a spin if so requested, to the delight of young and old alike.

Access : Leave Auxerre on the N 65 towards Chablis, turn left past the A 6 (Auxerre-Sud interchange)

 56 LE MOULINOT
M. et Mme Wootton

Route d'Auxerre - RN 6
89270 Vermenton
Tel. 03 86 81 60 42
Fax 03 86 81 52 21
lemoulinot @ aol.com
www.moulinot.com

Closed 20 Dec to 10 Jan • 6 rooms with bathrooms • €55 to €80, breakfast included • No table d'hôte • Garden, park, car park. Credit cards not accepted. No dogs allowed • Outdoor swimming pool

 The wealth of water activities.

Guests have to cross a narrow bridge over the rapid waters of the Cure to reach the idyllic site of this 18C mill. A fine wood staircase leads up to pretty, spacious rooms each of which is individually decorated. Cane furniture, beams, fireplaces and reproduction Impressionist paintings adorn the dining and sitting rooms overlooking the pond. Swimming, fishing, canoeing and mountain biking are just a few of the countless outdoor activities close at hand and the port is just five minutes away.

Access : Take the small private bridge spanning the Cure

57 **LES AQUARELLES**
Mme Basseporte

Fontette, 6 ruelle des Grands Prés
89450 Vézelay
Tel. 03 86 33 34 35
Fax 03 86 33 29 82

Closed from 1 Jan to 15 Mar, 12 Nov to 5 Dec; Tue and Wed • 10 rooms, one of which has disabled access, most have bath/WC • €46 to €52; breakfast €6; half board available • Menu à la carte €12 to €34 • Terrace, car park. No dogs allowed in restaurant

58 **CABALUS,**
L'ANCIENNE HÔTELLERIE DE L'ABBAYE

Albert Schmidij

Rue Saint-Pierre
89450 Vézelay
Tel. 03 86 33 20 66
Fax 03 86 33 38 03
contact @ cabalus.com
www.cabalus.com

Closed Mon and Tue • 4 rooms • €42 to €56, breakfast €9 • Table d'hôte €9 to €19 • Terrace

 The path winding its way through the fields to Vézelay.

When this old farmstead was turned into a hotel, the owners were determined to preserve its original character and cachet. The stables now house a sitting room, while the oak furnished bedrooms have been installed in the former hayloft. Meals are served on two enormous farm tables. In the summertime, Mrs Basseporte insists that dinner be taken outside to benefit from the warmth of the beautiful old limestone walls.

 The art gallery exhibiting contemporary pottery, sculpture and paintings.

The magic of this inn and its amazing location just 100yds from the basilica lend it a quite unique charm. It was built as the hostelry of the Abbey of Vézelay and its magnificent 12C vaulted room is now home to a tea-room and an art gallery. The extremely well-proportioned and comfortable rooms are imaginatively decorated. Generous breakfasts are served on an enchanting terrace shaded by a scent-laden wisteria.

Access : 5km eastbound from Vézelay on the D 957 (Avallon road)

Access : Near the abbey

 59 CRISPOL
Mme Schori

 Fontette
89450 Vézelay
Tel. 03 86 33 26 25
Fax 03 86 33 33 10

Closed Mon and Tue lunchtime • 12 rooms in a separate wing, one of which has disabled access. All rooms have bath/WC and television • €71 to €115; breakfast €9; half board available • Menus €20 to €48 • Terrace, garden, car park.

 60 LA PALOMBIÈRE
M. Danguy

 Place du Champ-de-Foire
89450 Vézelay
Tel. 03 86 33 28 50
Fax 03 86 32 35 61
lapalomberie-host@wanadoo.fr

Closed from Jan to mid-Feb and Mon • 10 rooms with bathrooms • €55 to €78, breakfast €9 • No table d'hôte • Garden, car park

 We most liked **The impeccable upkeep of this establishment.**

A number of surprises await visitors inside the thick stone walls of this building in the heart of a hamlet. Firstly, the unexpected contemporary style of the rooms' decoration with sharp corners, lacquered ceilings and works by the owner-artist. Next, the peaceful garden sheltered from the hairpin bend in the road. Finally, the elegant restaurant which surveys the Cure Valley, with the hilltop basilica in the background.

We most liked **The pleasant blend of styles and periods.**

Situated in the lower part of town, this elegant 18C mansion swamped in Virginia creeper is not lacking in character. The spacious, snug rooms feature an eclectic mixture of styles and periods ranging from Louis XIII, Louis XIV and Empire to satin bedspreads and "retro" bathrooms. Breakfasts, which are lavishly accompanied with home-made jams, are served on the veranda which opens onto the surrounding countryside. The flowered garden is at its best in full bloom in early summer.

Access : Leave Vézelay on the D 957 towards Avallon and drive 5km; the hotel is on the roadside

Access : In the lower part of town

  61 LE RELAIS SAINT BENOÎT
M. et Mme Roche

89130 Villiers-Saint-Benoît
Tel. 03 86 45 73 42
Fax 03 86 45 77 90
micheline.roche @ wanadoo.fr
www.relais-saintbenoit.fr

Closed from 3 to 16 Feb, from 25 to 30 Dec and on Sun evening and Mon • 6 rooms with shower/WC and television • €41 to €60; breakfast €7.50; half-board available • Menus €18 to €36 • Terrace, garden • Second-hand/antique "shop" at the bottom of the garden

  62 AUBERGE LE VOUTENAY
M. et Mme Poirier

89270 Voutenay-sur-Cure
Tel. 03 86 33 51 92
Fax 03 86 33 51 91
auberge.voutenay @ wanadoo.fr
www.monsite.wanadoo.fr/auberge.
voutenay

Closed first three weeks of Jan, third week of Jun and of Nov and on Sun eve, Mon and Tue • 8 rooms with bath/WC, and a suite opening onto the garden • €45 to €62; breakfast €7; half board available • Menus €23 to €52 (limited seating so it is necessary to book) • Garden, car park. No dogs allowed

Picking up bargains in the back room of this hotel-cum-restaurant-cum-antique shop.

Those who have read Colette, a local author born in the nearby town of St Sauveur, will immediately recognise Claudine's surroundings. Indeed the village even boasts an Art and History Museum just a step from the hotel to further steep yourself in local traditions. The hotel features renovated rooms, a sandstone collection from the region in the restaurant and a tiny shaded terrace. A country inn which lives up to the best local traditions.

The mountain bikes and canoes available for use by guests.

The inn's canine mascot, Lafayette, happily does the honours of this handsome 18C mansion which is little by little undergoing a facelift. The bedrooms are being renovated, a spacious 45sq metre flat has just been installed and the restaurant boasts a handsome fireplace with a carved wooden mantelpiece. The slightly unruly walled garden planted with hundred-year-old trees and extending down as far as the River Cure, is sheer bliss. A hiking path runs alongside the establishment.

Access : Leave the Auxerre-Saint-Fargeau road (N 965) at Toucy to take the D 950 for 8.5km

Access : On the N 6 from Auxerre to Avallon

BRITTANY

Brittany – Breizh to its inhabitants – is a region of harsh granite coastlines, dense, mysterious forests and pretty ports tightly packed with brightly painted fishing boats. Its charm lies in its brisk sea breeze, its incredibly varied landscapes, its countless legends and the people themselves, born, so they say, with a drop of salt water in their blood. Proud of the customs and language handed down from distant Celtic ancestors, today's Bretons nurture their identity throughout the year with a calendar of events, in which modern-day bards and minstrels exalt their folklore and traditions. Of course, such devotion to culture requires plenty of good, wholesome nourishment: sweet and savoury pancakes, thick slices of *kouign-aman* (pronounced "queen-aman") dripping in caramelised sugar and salted butter and mugs of cold cider. However, Brittany's gastronomic reputation extends far beyond such tasty titbits and gourmets can feast on the oysters, lobster, crab and other seafood delicacies for which this rocky peninsula is renowned.

- Côte-d'Armor (22)
- Finistère (29)
- Ille-et-Vilaine (35)
- Morbihan (56)

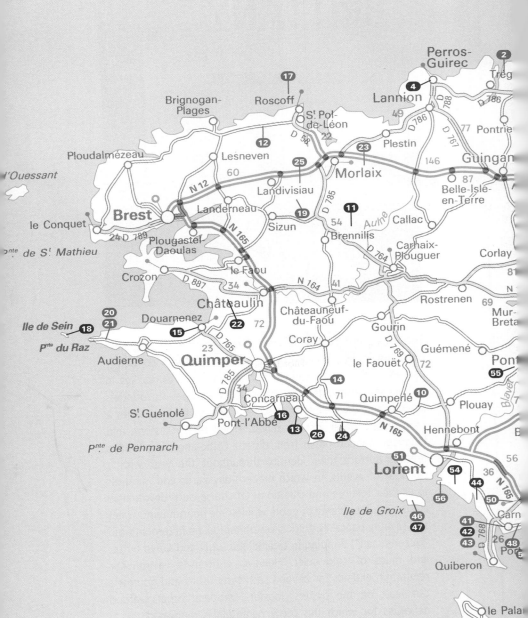

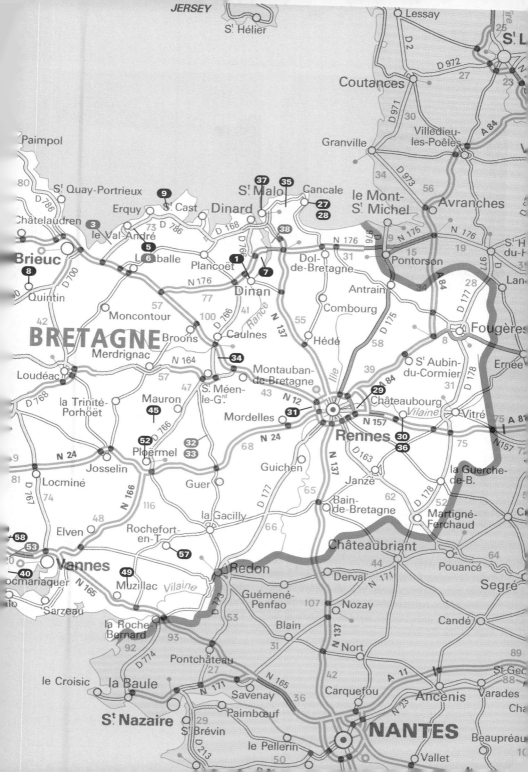

 1 ARVOR
M. Renault

5 rue A. Pavie
22100 Dinan
Tel. 02 96 39 21 22
Fax 02 96 39 83 09
hote-arvor@wanadoo.fr
www.hotel-arvor-dinan.com

Closed Jan • 24 rooms, one of which has disabled access, all have bath/WC or shower/WC and television • €47 to €100; breakfast €6 • No restaurant • Private car park

 2 MANOIR DE TROÉZEL VRAS
M. et Mme Maynier

22610 Kerbors
Tel. 02 96 22 89 68
Fax 02 96 22 90 56
troezel.vras@free.fr
http://troezel.vras.free.fr

Closed 20 Oct to 1 Apr • 6 rooms • €63 (€57 low season), breakfast included • Table d'hôte €19 (except Sun) • Garden, car park. Credit cards not accepted, no dogs allowed

 Dinan's streets lined with lovely old half-timbered houses.

Guests are often struck by the amazing contrast between the old 18C walls of this former convent and the distinctly modern flavour of the bedrooms. A handsome Renaissance porchway leads into the reception and functional, well-equipped identical rooms. A few parking spaces near a ruined chapel are most welcome in the heart of the old town.

 The numerous walking and biking opportunities.

This pretty 17C manor house surrounded by rambling peaceful countryside has everything the travel-weary visitor could wish for. Terracotta tiled floors, apricot painted walls, antique wardrobes and prints of local landscapes adorn the bedrooms. The equally agreeable dining room features white-painted beams and a stone fireplace. Depending on the season, meals are served in the garden or near a log fire: seafood is a speciality all year round.

Access : In the old town almost opposite the theatre

Access : 9km to the north-east of Tréguier on the Paimpol road towards Pleumeur-Gautier, then Kerbors

 3 LE MANOIR DE LA VILLE GOURIO
M. et Mme Guihot

22400 Morieux
Tel. 02 96 32 72 60
Fax 02 96 32 75 68
golf @ lacriniere.fr
www.lacriniere.fr

Closed late Dec • 5 rooms with bath/WC and television • €58 to €107; breakfast €9 • Table d'hôte €11 • Sitting room, terrace, garden, park, car park. No dogs allowed in rooms

  4 LE MANOIR DU SPHINX
M. et Mme Le Verge

67 chemin de la Messe
22700 Perros-Guirec
Tel. 02 96 23 25 42
Fax 02 96 91 26 13
lemanoirdusphinx @ wanadoo.fr

Closed from 16 Jan to 24 Feb • 20 rooms with bathrooms and television, 1 has disabled access • €107 to €122; breakfast €9; half board available • Restaurant closed Sun evening from 1 Oct to 1 Apr, Mon and Fri lunchtimes except national holidays; menus €29.50 (weekdays) to €50 • Garden, car park. No dogs admitted • Beach, water sports and fishing nearby

 Taking a golf lesson with a pro.

This 17C Brittany manor house overlooks a 9-hole golf course surrounded by trees which are almost as old as the house. The rustic rooms upstairs all overlook the garden, fairways and ponds. On the ground floor, guests have the run of a reading room, a billiards table and a breakfast room where a fire takes the chill out of those brisk autumn mornings. The former stables house a bar, restaurant, night club and the clubhouse – ask here for expert tips and private coaching.

Gazing at the sea and Seven Isles archipelago.

This Sphinx, which resembles a pretty hundred-year-old sea view villa, will not speak in riddles as you explore its snug, welcoming bar, with a hint of British style; its attractive dining room lined with bay windows and furnished with Empire style chairs; and its elegant rooms. Decorated in an English country style, all the rooms enjoy a sea view and some have bow windows.

Access : 11km southbound from Val-André on the D 786 and the D 34

Access : On the outskirts of the centre, on Trestrignel Beach

 5 GRAND HÔTEL DU VAL ANDRÉ
M. Crété

 80 rue Amiral-Charner
22370 Pléneuf-Val-André
Tel. 02 96 72 20 56
Fax 02 96 63 00 24
accueil @ grand-hotel-val-andre.fr
www.grand-hotel-val-andre.fr

Closed in Jan • 39 rooms, 2 of which have disabled access, 36 have bath/WC and 3 have shower/WC • €75.80 to €86.10 (€72 to €82 low season); breakfast €9; half board available • Menus €35 (weekdays) to €70 • Private car park. Dogs not allowed in restaurant • Tennis, horse-riding and water sports nearby

 6 VILLA MARGUERITE
M. et Mme Campion-Levive

 34 rue des Garennes
22370 Pléneuf-Val-André
Tel. 02 96 72 85 88
Fax 02 96 72 85 88

Open Apr to Sep (by reservation in low season) • 4 rooms on 2 floors, 3 of which have a sea-facing balcony • €57 to €63, breakfast included • No table d'hôte • Garden. Credit cards not accepted, no dogs allowed

 The idyllic situation on the edge of a white sandy beach.

The faded charm of the grand seaside hotels of yesteryear can still be felt in this stone and brick edifice built in 1895. Rest assured, however, most of the rooms have been recently renovated with cane furniture and brand new bathrooms, while light coloured walls contrast beautifully with navy blue carpets and bedspreads. Those overlooking the sea are well-nigh perfect. Panoramic dining room and a terrace planted with hundred-year-old pine trees.

 Strolling along the pedestrian coast path alongside Val-André beach.

This pretty villa, quite in keeping with the architectural style of this quaint 19C seaside resort, enjoys a fine view over the Bay of St-Brieuc. Sea-lovers will adore the rooms, most of which have sea-facing balconies. All are decorated in a sober yet fetching style with floorboards, colourful walls and two have four-poster beds. Peaceful nights guaranteed thanks to the large garden surrounding the house. Note the interesting antique furniture which adorns the breakfast room.

Access : Along the seafront

Access : 300m from the town centre, on the sea front

7 MANOIR DE RIGOURDAINE
M. Van Valenberg

Route de Langrolay
22490 Plouër-sur-Rance
Tel. 02 96 86 89 96
Fax 02 96 86 92 46
hotel.rigourdaine@wanadoo.fr
www.hotel-rigourdaine.fr

Closed from 11 Nov to 2 Apr • 19 rooms, 5 of which are split-level, 2 have disabled access. Rooms have bath/WC or shower/WC and television • €66 to €82 (€58 to €74 low season); breakfast €7 • No restaurant • Park, private car park. No dogs allowed • Games room with billiards, private fishing

8 COMMERCE
M. Gourdin

2 rue Rochonen
22800 Quintin
Tel. 02 96 74 94 67
Fax 02 96 74 00 94

Closed from 1 to 4 Jan, 22 to 28 Mar and 23 to 29 Aug and on Mon, Fri eve and Sun eve (except by reservation) • 11 rooms, all have shower/WC and television; non-smokers only • €51 to €57 (€47 to €53 low season); breakfast €7; half board available • Menus €14 (week-days) to €39

 The countless paths around the Rance estuary.

A narrow lane leads up to this picturesque farmstead, which is almost as old as the River Rance itself. Its secluded position overlooking the estuary ensures guests a peaceful night's sleep, awakened only by the calls of the seagulls overhead. Good old country furniture and brightly coloured fabrics grace the bedrooms, while old beams, bare stone walls and a gigantic family table adorn the breakfast room. Full of character.

Walking along the banks of the Gouët.

The origins of this impressive granite house covered in Virginia creeper have been traced back to the 18C. The modern, personalised rooms have been recently renovated and each is named after an appetising spice or condiment, such as Fleur de sel, paprika or cinnamon. A beautiful period fireplace with a carved wooden mantelpiece is the centrepiece of the rustic wainscoted dining room.

Access : 3km northbound from Plouer-sur-Rance on the D 12 towards Langrolay, then right at a private road

Access : In the centre of the village, on the D 790 between Saint-Brieuc and Rostrenen

  9 MANOIR SAINT-MICHEL
M. et Mme Fournel-Besnier

La Carquois
22240 Sables-d'Or-les-Pins
Tel. 02 96 41 48 87
Fax 02 96 41 41 55
manoir-st-michel@fournel.de
www.fournel.de

Open late Mar to early Nov • 20 rooms on 2 floors, all have bath/WC or shower/WC and television • €43 to €106 (€38 to €90 low season), breakfast €7 • No restaurant • Car park, garden • Fishing in the lake

  10 CHÂTEAU DE KERLAREC
M. et Mme Bellin

Kerlarec
29300 Arzano
Tel. 02 98 71 75 06
Fax 02 98 71 74 55
château-de-kerlarec@wanadoo.fr
www.chateaux-France.com

Closed 25 Dec to 2 Jan • 6 rooms • €78 to €110, breakfast included • No table d'hôte • Sitting room, park, car park. Credit cards not accepted • Outdoor swimming pool, tennis, exhibitions. 18-hole golf course and horse-riding nearby

In fine weather, breakfast overlooking the garden with the ocean in the background.

What better spot for a romantic stay than this 16C and 17C manor? The little lane leading up to the property is quickly forgotten as you are greeted by the lovely stone walls of the building and the immense garden and pond.You may even catch a glimpse of the breathtaking Sables-d'Or-les-Pins beach. An old-fashioned charm pervades the rooms which are appointed with splendid old wardrobes and furnished in a variety of styles ranging from rustic to Louis XIII and Louis XV. Attentive staff.

The well-preserved Second Empire style.

It is easy to see why the current owners fell in love with this 1830 mansion set in a park complete with ornamental pool. The Second Empire reigns supreme amid the period frescoes, antique furniture and objets d'art gleaned from local antique shops and flea markets or brought back from voyages overseas. Relax in the peace and quiet of the spacious, individually decorated bedrooms. Don't leave without a look at the Jeanne d'Arc room.

Access : 1.5km eastbound on the D 34

Access : 6km eastbound from Quimperlé on the D 765 Lorient road, and left onto the Arzano road (D 22)

 11 LA FERME DE PORZ KLOZ
M. et Mme Berthou

Trédudon-le-Moine
29690 Berrien
Tel. 02 98 99 61 65
Fax 02 98 99 67 36
porzkloz @ wanadoo.fr

Open Mar to Nov • 5 rooms and 1 suite with bath/WC
• €45 to €100 (€39 to €90 out of season); breakfast €7
• Restaurant by reservation only: €20 • Car park. Credit cards not accepted. No dogs allowed • Horse-riding, swimming pool, tennis and golf nearby

 12 COS-MILIN
Mme Moysan

29233 Cléder
Tel. 02 98 69 42 16
Fax 02 98 69 42 16

Open all year • 3 non-smoking rooms, all have bathrooms • €50, breakfast included • No table d'hôte • Sitting room, garden, car park. Credit cards not accepted, no dogs allowed

 Finding out more about Brittany's less well-known hinterland.

Time seems to have stood still in this cluster of 17C farmhouses, formerly outbuildings of the Abbey of Releq, where only the best locally-grown produce is good enough for the dinner table. The bedrooms, decorated with family heirlooms, are particularly delightful and most are large enough to sleep entire families. Admire the photos relating aspects of daily life in 19C Brittany in the reception.

 Traditional Breton favourites at breakfast.

The seaside and coastal footpaths are not far from this stone-built house with slate roof. Individually decorated bedrooms combine old and new in an imaginative blend and, on the ground floor, the elegant sitting and breakfast rooms are furnished in the same eclectic style. Tuck into a delicious spread of pancakes, "far", a local rum and raisin flan and other traditional Breton delicacies at breakfast, before relaxing on a deck chair in the flowered garden.

Access : 11km to north-west of Huelgoat on the D 14, take the Berrien road and the D 42 on the left

Access : 3km northbound from Saint-Pol-de Léon, take the D 10 and at Lléder follow signs to "les plages"

13 KER MOOR
M. Violant

Plage des Sables-Blancs
29900 Concarneau
Tel. 02 98 97 02 96
Fax 02 98 97 84 04
kermoor @ lespiedsdansleau.com

Open all year • 12 rooms • €70 to €150; breakfast €12
• No restaurant • Car park. No dogs allowed

14 LE MANOIR DE COAT CANTON
M. et Mme Simon

Grandbois
29140 Rosporden
 Tel. 02 98 66 31 24

Open all year • 4 rooms, 2 of which are on the ground
floor, all have bathrooms • €40 to €45, breakfast
included • No table d'hôte • Sitting room, car park.
Credit cards not accepted, no dogs allowed • Horse-
riding in the grounds

 A sweeping view of the ocean.

This delightfully situated 1900 villa is located right on
the white sandy beach overlooking the ocean. The
distinctly maritime décor of the interior decoration
features white-painted wood lined walls, nautical prints
and photos and model boats. All the rooms overlook the
sea and three have a terrace. Totally unforgettable!

 **Going hacking around the lush, green
Breton countryside.**

The construction of this pleasing manor house full of
character took place from the 13C to the 17C. The
rooms, located in a converted farmhouse, are decorated
in a variety of styles, including medieval, Breton and
English. The antique furnished breakfast room is very
pleasant. The owners, who also run a riding stable
nearby, will be only too happy to introduce you to the
joys of riding.

Access : Northbound, towards the Forêt-Fouesnant

Access : 13km north-east of Concarneau on the
Pont-l'Abbé road (D 783), and right on the Rosporden
road (D 70)

15 AUBERGE DE KERVEOC'H
M. et Mme Chacun

42 route de Kerveoc'h
29100 Douarnenez
Tel. 02 98 92 07 58
Fax 02 98 92 03 58
auberge.de-kerveoch@worldonline.fr
www.auberge-kerveoch.com

Open all year • 14 rooms, 10 of which are in a separate wing, all have bath/WC or shower/WC and television • €54 to €70 (€45 to €60 low season); breakfast €7; half board available • Menus €18 to €22 • Terrace, car park. No dogs allowed in restaurant

16 LA POINTE DU CAP COZ
M. et Mme Le Torc'h

153 avenue de la Pointe - Cap Coz
29170 Fouesnant
Tel. 02 98 56 01 63
Fax 02 98 56 53 20
bienvenue@hotel-capcoz.com
www.hotel-capcoz.com

Closed 1 Jan to 10 Feb; Sun evening and Mon lunchtime from 15 Sep to 15 Jun and Wed • 16 rooms with bath/WC or shower/WC and television • €62 to €88; breakfast €8 • Menus €20.50 to €41 (non-smokers only, disabled access) • Terrace. No dogs admitted • Billiards; nearby: golf, beach, water sports

 The owners' warm welcome.

The inn of Kerveoc'h was a farm and a riding stables before becoming a hotel; guests can now enjoy the peace and quiet of the Breton countryside whilst being on the doorstep of a host of local sights. These include the Museum Port of Douarnenez, Locronan's medieval square and the breathtaking view of the sharp rocks battered by the waves. The simple, yet spacious rooms are located in a spruce white house and all have been treated to new bedding. Dining in the former stables is not to be missed.

 The site which is quite as exotic as other more far-flung destinations.

The hotel is built on a stretch of sandy beach bounded on one side by the ocean and on the other by a small bay whose waters are crystal-clear. The rooms are low-key and discreet, as if to do full justice to the beauty of the coast. All are peaceful and some enjoy terraces from which to contemplate the superb vista. Both dining rooms, recently renovated and non-smoking only, specialise in fresh local produce mainly from the sea. Enchanting sitting room-bar.

Access : 4km from Douarnenez on the Quimper road

Access : 2.5km south-east from Fouesnant on minor road

ÎLE-DE-BATZ - 29253

ÎLE-DE-SEIN - 29990

 17 TI VA ZADOU
M. et Mme Prigent

 Le bourg
29253 Île-de-Batz
Tel. 02 98 61 76 98
Fax 02 98 61 76 98

Closed from 15 Nov to 1 Feb • 4 rooms on 2 floors, all have bathrooms, except for one family room with a bathroom on the landing • €55, breakfast included • No table d'hôte • Sitting room. Credit cards not accepted, no dogs allowed

 18 AR-MEN
M. Fouquet-Portais

 Route du Phare
29990 Île-de-Sein
Tel. 02 98 70 90 77
Fax 02 98 70 93 25
hotel.armen@wanadoo.fr
www.hotel-armen.com

Closed 10 to 25 Jan and 27 Sep to 19 Oct • 10 rooms with sea view, all have shower/WC • €50 to €65, breakfast €7, half board available • Restaurant closed Sun evening and Wed (in season), menus from €18 to €24 • Sitting room-library

 Cycling around on the lanes of this tiny island village.

A sense of humour and a love of life set the tone in this blue-shuttered residence, whose name means "house of my fathers" in Breton. Old and new mingle happily in the cosy, welcoming bedrooms and all have a splendid view of the port, the cluster of islets and the mainland. Family heirlooms take pride of place in the sitting and breakfast rooms, both with fireplace. Bicycles can be rented nearby.

 Tasting the charm of island life.

Forget the hurly-burly of urban life for a few days and head for the island of Sein! After a short crossing, pass through the village and head towards the lighthouse to reach the imposing pink façade of this house. The modestly-sized, relatively simple rooms are painted bright colours and all enjoy a sea view. The meals are equally simple and rich in sea flavours; try the island's speciality, lobster stew. Sitting room-cum-library with fireplace and friendly welcome.

 **Access :** Near the harbour

Access : On the way out of the village towards the lighthouse

 19 TY-DREUX

Mme Martin

29410 Loc-Eguiner-Saint-Thégonnec
Tel. 02 98 78 08 21
Fax 02 98 78 01 69
ty-dreux @ club-internet.fr

Open all year • 7 rooms with shower/WC • €45,
breakfast included • Table d'hôte €18 • Garden. Credit
cards not accepted, no dogs allowed

 20 AN TIEZ BIHAN

M. et Mme Ganne

Kerhuret
29770 Plogoff
Tel. 02 98 70 34 85

Open all year • 4 rooms • €38, breakfast included • Table
d'hôte €18 by reservation (except Wed and Sun) • Car
park, garden. Credit cards not accepted

It is worthwhile remembering that home-made cider is pretty potent!

The name of this dairy farm, more than worth a trip, in the heart of the countryside means "weaver's house" in testimony to its textile heritage. Period furniture, a huge 18C granite fireplace and a permanent exhibition of costumes belonging to former generations set the scene for this establishment which upholds local traditions. Modern canopied beds add character to the renovated rooms. Meals are a chance to sample the succulently prepared farm-grown produce.

Tucking into homemade pancakes and jams at breakfast time.

A recent restoration has breathed a new lease of life into this old farmhouse, whose new owners wisely chose to retain the original proportions and materials. Several little houses, formerly stables and barns, are now home to simply furnished rooms and a gîte is also available. The main building houses the dining room where you can sample delicious local seafood. Hikers will enjoy the chance to set off along the coast path as far as the Pointe du Raz.

Access : 3.5km to the south-east of Guimiliau on the Plouneour-Menez road (D 111)

Access : 2.5km along the D 784 towards the Pointe du Raz

21 DE LESCOFF
M. et Mme Le Corre

29 rue des Hirondelles - Lieu-dit "Lescoff"
29770 Plogoff
Tel. 02 98 70 38 24

Open all year • 3 rooms with bath/WC • €40 (€38 low season), breakfast included • No table d'hôte • Car park, garden, terrace. Credit cards not accepted

22 PORZ-MORVAN
M. Nicolas

Route de Lescuz
29550 Plomodiern
Tel. 02 98 81 53 23
Fax 02 98 81 28 61
christian.nicolas19@wanadoo.fr

Closed 10 Jan to late Feb • 12 rooms, 4 upstairs, 8 are in a separate wing. All have bath/WC or shower/WC and television • €46 to €50; breakfast €6 • Crêperie in an old barn • Terrace, garden with pond, car park • Tennis

 A bracing walk along the cliffs to the Pointe du Raz during rough weather.

The little town of Lescoff is home to the last cluster of houses before you reach the unspoilt, windswept site of the Pointe du Raz. Laid out around a little courtyard, the buildings of this former working farm offer a highly inviting picture. The rooms make up in charm what they may lack in size with rustic furniture and bare stone or white roughcast walls. Guests have the use of a practical kitchenette in the breakfast room with a sloping ceiling on the first floor.

 Feasting on pancakes!

Those in search of peace and quiet will adore this delightful stone farmhouse built in 1830 just next door – as the seagull flies – from the famous viewpoint of Ménez-Hom (330 m), which overlooks the region. Most of the gradually-renovated rooms are on the garden level in the former cow-shed. The barn has been converted into a friendly crêperie where the old rafters and timbers have been preserved. Large garden with pond and warm welcome guaranteed.

Access : 300m from the Pointe du Raz car park

Access : 3km eastbound from Plomodiern on a minor road

23 MANOIR DE LANLEYA
M. Marrec

Au bourg de Lanleya
29610 Plouigneau
Tel. 02 98 79 94 15
Fax 02 98 79 94 15
manoir.lanleya @ libertysurf
www.multimania.com/lanleya

Open all year • 5 non-smoking rooms with shower/WC
• €61, breakfast included • No table d'hôte • Garden,
car park. Credit cards not accepted, no dogs allowed

24 LE MOULIN DE ROSMADEC
M. et Mme Sébilleau

29930 Pont-Aven
Tel. 02 98 06 00 22
Fax 02 98 06 18 00

Closed during the February holidays, from 14 to 30 Oct,
Sun evening out of season and Wed • 4 rooms in a
separate wing with bath/WC and television • €80 to
€100; breakfast €9 • Menus €28 to €70; limited seating
so book in advance

The manor's legend, related by the lord of the house.

The quality of the restoration is such that it is difficult
to believe that this 16C manor house and its adjoining
18C malouinière were saved from ruin in the nick of
time. The stunning interior features Breton furniture, old
beams, slate floors, exposed stone walls, a beautiful
spiral staircase, pink granite fireplace and rich fabrics.
The Louis XV room is particularly splendid, but the
others, which are smaller, display the same exquisite
taste. Lovely riverside garden.

Breakfasting on the delightful veranda overlooking the river.

This bucolic mill was built in 1456. According to a local
proverb, "Pont Aven, a town of standing, boasts fourteen
mills and fifteen houses". The town no doubt owes at
least part of its celebrity to the millers who settled by
its fast-flowing river, but the town's renowned pancakes
and the painters who endowed it with worldwide
posterity, also played their part. The traditional Breton
restaurant is decorated with artwork from the local
school. Spacious, modern bedrooms.

Access : 5km to the south-east of Morlaix on the
D 712, then take the D 64 towards Lanmeur

Access : In the town centre, near the bridge

BRITTANY

25 AR PRESBITAL KOZ
Mme Prigent

18 rue Lividic
29410 Saint-Thégonnec
Tel. 02 98 79 45 62
Fax 02 98 79 48 47
andre.prigent @ wanadoo.fr

Open all year • 6 rooms on 2 floors, 4 of which have bath/WC, the other 2 have shower/WC • €44 to €47, breakfast included • Table d'hôte €17 (evenings only) • Garden, car park. Credit cards not accepted, no dogs allowed

26 AUBERGE LES GRANDES ROCHES
M. Raday

Les Grandes-Roches
29910 Trégunc
Tel. 02 98 97 62 97
Fax 02 98 50 29 19
hrlesgrandesroches @ club-internet.fr
www.hotel-lesgrandesroches.com

Closed from 20 Dec 2004 to 1 Feb 2005 • 17 rooms located in several houses and cottages, all have bath/WC or shower/WC • €75 to €130; breakfast €12; half board available • Menus €41 • Park with dolmen and standing stone, car park. No dogs allowed

The nearby "enclos paroissiaux".

This former 18C presbytery, hidden by a curtain of cypress trees, is home to comfortable, well-dimensioned rooms, each of which is decorated in a different colour and furnished with antiques. The largest has a fireplace. Admire the collection of ducks from all over the world in the smoking and sitting rooms. In the summer, wander round the garden and vegetable plot or rent a bicycle (from the hotel) and venture further afield.

The 100 % "Breizh" - Breton - character of this establishment.

This delightful hamlet of old farms and two-hundred-year-old cottages nestles in the semi wilderness of five acres of parkland where a giant dolmen and sacred menhir still stand. The stylish, tastefully decorated and regularly refurbished rooms resound to the immense silence all around. The restaurant boasts all the authentic character of traditional Breton houses with huge fireplaces and thick stone walls.

Access : Near the Saint Bernadette Retirement Home

Access : 0.6km to the north-east of Trégunc on a minor road

CANCALE - 35260

 27 LE CHATELLIER
Mme Lescarmure

Route de Saint-Malo
35260 Cancale
Tel. 02 99 89 81 84
Fax 02 99 89 61 69
hotelchatel @ aol.com
www.hotellechatellier.com

Open all year • 13 rooms, one of which has disabled access, with bath/WC or shower/WC and television • €43 to €71; breakfast €8 • No restaurant • Garden, car park

 28 LA POINTE DU GROUIN
Mme Simon

À la Pointe-du-Grouin
35260 Cancale
Tel. 02 99 89 60 55
Fax 02 99 89 92 22
hotel-pointe-du-grouin @ wanadoo.fr
www.hotelpointedugrouin.com

Open all year • 16 rooms on 2 floors with bath/WC or shower/WC, all have television • €78 to €98; breakfast €8; half board available • Restaurant closed Tue and Thu lunchtime in low season; menus €20 to €61 • Car park. • 400m from the beach

 The untamed landscape of the rocky Pointe du Grouin just a stone's throw away.

This comfortable stone house, a former farm turned into a hotel, makes an ideal base camp to explore the region in fine weather and get away from the bustling seaside resort. Four rooms are brand new; the others are relatively generously sized, decorated in a rustic style and spotlessly clean. A log fire heats the sitting room during the cold winter nights.

 Venturing onto the outcrop at sunset.

In the summer, things can get a bit frantic here. What's more, the iconic landmark of the Pointe du Grouin is also the starting point of the famous Route du Rhum sailing race which takes place every four years (2006). Come sunset, however, the view from this stone house, perched on a cliff in a far corner of Brittany, is breathtaking. The cosy, comfortable rooms and panoramic restaurant all enjoy a splendid vista over the Island of Landes, sanctuary to countless seabirds, and St Michel Bay.

Access : 2km westbound on the D 355 towards Saint-Malo

Access : 5km northbound from Cancale on the D 201

 **29** GERMINAL
M. et Mme Goualin

 9 cours de la Vilaine
35510 Cesson-Sévigné
Tel. 02 99 83 11 01
Fax 02 99 83 45 16
le-germinal @ wanadoo.fr
www.legerminal.com

Closed during the Christmas school holidays • 20 rooms on 3 floors, all have bath/WC and television • €68; breakfast €10 • Restaurant closed Sun (except summer) and Mon; menus €17 to €45 • Terrace, car park.

 We most liked
The terrace overlooking the river.

An unusual spot, to say the least: this 19C mill stands on an islet of the River Vilaine. Another little island has a car park and guests reach the hotel over a footbridge. The new owners are determined to add a new lease of life to their establishment and both the restaurant and the rooms are being renovated. The views and idyllic location are gradually re-establishing this unique building as one of the unexpected delights of the Rennes area.

  30 AR MILIN'
M. Burel

30 rue de Paris
35220 Châteaubourg
Tel. 02 99 00 30 91
Fax 02 99 00 37 56
resa.armilin @ wanadoo.fr
www.armilin.com

Closed 1 to 4 Jan • 32 rooms in the Moulin and Résidence du Parc, with bath and shower/WC and television • €83 (€77 low season); breakfast €11, half board available • Menus €26.50 to €42 • Park and arboretum, terrace, car park • Tennis court

 We most liked
The superb 12.5-acre park complete with arboretum and sculptures.

Welcome to Ar Milin', an inviting flour mill built in the 19C on the banks of the Vilaine. The building is home to two restaurants: a comfortable dining room with exposed rafters and a veranda overlooking the river, and a pleasantly contemporary-style bistro. A few rooms full of character are available in the mill, but the majority of the accommodation is located in a pavilion surrounded by greenery which is calmer and more modern in spirit.

Access : 6km eastbound from Rennes, on a small island in the Vilaine

Access : 16km west of Rennes on the N157, Châteaubourg exit, 900m from the exit in the heart of the village

LE RHEU - 35650

PAIMPONT - 35380

31 MANOIR DU PLESSIS
M. Desmots

Route de Lorient
35650 Le Rheu
Tel. 02 99 14 79 79
Fax 02 99 14 69 60
info@manoirduplessis.fr
www.manoirduplessis.fr

Closed 1 to 3 Jan and 15 to 28 Feb • 5 rooms with bath/WC and television • €95; breakfast €9 • Menus €16 (weekday lunchtimes) to €37 • Terrace, park, car park. No dogs allowted in rooms • Billiards rooms

32 LA CORNE DE CERF
Mme Morvan

Le Cannée
35380 Paimpont
Tel. 02 99 07 84 19

Closed in Jan • 3 rooms, one of which is on the ground floor, with bathroom • €50, breakfast included • No table d'hôte • Sitting room, library, garden. Credit cards not accepted, no dogs allowed

Indulge in a game of billiards before sitting down to the chef's tasty cooking.

A six-acre park protects this lovely old manor house from the busy Lorient road. The manor is well known for its excellent up-to-date cooking, stylish dining rooms, with parquet floors, wainscoting, fireplaces and Louis XVI-style furniture and its lush green terrace. The spacious bedrooms, all of which overlook the park, are equally worthy of praise and equipped with all the modern comforts in a pleasantly old-fashioned style.

The epitome of sophistication.

This lovely old home is hidden deep in the heart of the forest of Brocéliande, a land steeped in legends of wizards and magic. A profusion of paintings, tapestries and painted furniture set the tone for the tasteful, elegant interior decoration. The light, airy rooms open onto a delightful, well cared-for garden. There is absolutely no shortage of leisure activities in the vicinity including many footpaths, and water sports on the village lake.

Access : 6km westbound of Rennes on the Lorient road

Access : 2km southbound from Paimpont on the D 71

BRITTANY

 33 LE MANOIR DE LA RUISSELÉE
Mme Hermenier

Lieu-dit la Ruisselée
35380 Paimpont
Tel. 02 99 06 85 94

Open all year • 3 rooms • €50, breakfast included • No table d'hôte • Sitting room, garden, car park. Credit cards not accepted

 34 RELAIS DE LA RANCE
M. Guitton-Chevrier

6 rue de Rennes
35290 Quedillac
Tel. 02 99 06 20 20
Fax 02 99 06 24 01
relaisdelarance @ 21s.fr

Closed from 20 Dec to 20 Jan, Fri and Sun evenings • 13 rooms with bath/WC and shower/WC and television • €45 to €60; breakfast €9; half board available • Menus from €19 to €66 • Car park

 Merlin gathered his herbs in these forests and moors.

This attractive 1769 manor house lies next to the ruins of an abandoned farmhouse and is on the doorstep of the forest of Brocéliande, birthplace of Merlin, whom everyone knows was Breton and not Cornish at all! The rooms are comfortable and tastefully decorated; some have original parquet floors. Breakfasts are served in front of a roaring log fire in the winter and in the garden during the summer months.

 The faultless welcome extended by the Guitton family since 1946.

This house has quietly and steadfastly remained true to its founding spirit, to the delight of its regulars who grow in number each year. What lures them back time after time? The pleasant family atmosphere that reigns throughout this regional-style residence, the tasty traditional cuisine supplemented by local produce and the recently renovated, comfortable rooms, each of which is personalised and equipped with a modern bathroom.

Access : A short distance from Brocéliande forest

Access : On the edge of the département, between Rennes and Saint-Brieuc, on the N 12 and D 220, in the centre of the village

 35 AUBERGE DE LA MOTTE JEAN
Mme Simon

35350 Saint-Coulomb
Tel. 02 99 89 41 99
Fax 02 99 89 92 22
hotel-pointe-du-grouin@wanadoo.fr
www.hotelpointedugrouin.com

Open all year • 11 rooms located in 2 modern buildings. Rooms have bath/WC or shower/WC, all have television • €78 to €130 (€65 to €110 low season); breakfast €7; half board available • Menus €20 to €61 • Garden, car park. No dogs allowed in rooms • Duck pond

 Breakfasts are served by the fireside in winter and opposite the garden in summer.

The headlands, bluffs and capes carved by the ocean and the island of Guesclin, whose fort belongs to singer-songwriter Léo Ferré, are just two minutes away from this secluded farmhouse which dates from 1707. The good taste of the lady of the house can be seen in the cosy style and old furniture in the rooms, particularly those in the former stables. Gardeners will adore the rose bushes in the beautiful garden "à la française".

 36 PEN'ROC
M. Froc

La Peinière
35220 Châteaubourg
Tel. 02 99 00 33 02
Fax 02 99 62 30 89
hotellerie@penroc.fr
www.penroc.fr

Closed from 22 Dec to 7 Jan • 29 air-conditioned rooms with bath/WC or shower/WC, all have television • €101 to €183, (€78 to €170 low season); breakfast €11; half board available • One non-smoking room; menus €20 (weekdays) to €64 • Shaded terrace, garden, car park. No dogs allowed in restaurant • Swimming pool, fitness room, sauna

 The peaceful Brittany countryside.

It is difficult to picture Pen'Roc as it was when it was just a farm because so much has clearly changed. The peace and quiet of the countryside still remain as does the nearby chapel (pilgrimages), but today creature comforts are clearly the priority. A few of the colourful, modern rooms are decorated with Asian-inspired or antique furnishings and some bathrooms have a spa bath or massage showers. Traditional-modern cuisine is served in a string of small rooms and on a pleasant terrace.

Access : On leaving Cancale, take the D 355 towards Saint-Malo

Access : 23km west of Rennes on the N157, Châteaubourg exit, then take the D33 to Saint-Didier and the D105 towards Saint-Jean-sur-Vilaine

37 QUIC-EN-GROIGNE
Mme Roualec

8 rue d'Estrées
35400 Saint-Malo
Tel. 02 99 20 22 20
Fax 02 99 20 22 30
rozenn.roualec@wanadoo.fr
www.quic-en-groigne.com

Closed 7 to 21 Jan • 15 rooms on 2 levels, all have bath/WC or shower/WC and television • €57 to €63 (€52 to €57 low season); breakfast €6 • No restaurant • Garage. No dogs allowed

38 LES MOUETTES
Mme Rouvrais

17 Grande-Rue
35430 Saint-Suliac
Tel. 02 99 58 30 41
Fax 02 99 58 39 41
 contact@les-mouettes-saint-suliac.com

Open all year • 5 rooms, one of which has disabled access, all have bathrooms • €41 to €46, breakfast included • No table d'hôte • Garden. Credit cards not accepted, no dogs allowed

 The peace and quiet of this hotel located in the heart of St Malo.

The name, taken from the tower next to the castle, is a reminder of Anne of Brittany's haughty reply to the townspeople of St Malo who took a very poor view of the ramparts erected round their town. The duchess dismissed them with the words: "Grumble as you will ('qui qu'en groigne'), so I decide". The hotel is in an old stone house near the beaches. The rooms are modern and gradually being redone. Breakfasts can be taken in the cane-furnished veranda or the pleasant garden.

 The sincerity of the warm welcome.

Formerly the village grocery store and pork butchers, this stone house built in 1870 stands on the main road leading to the banks of the River Rance. Today it features snug rooms painted in pastel colours and decorated with old paintings and furniture picked up in second-hand antique shops. One of the rooms is equipped for disabled guests. The breakfast room, complete with library, as well as the small garden in the rear, are both very pleasant.

Access : In the old town, take Rue de Toulouse from Porte Saint-Louis, at the end turn right twice

Access : In the heart of the village

39 LES CHAUMIÈRES DE CAHIRE
Mme Rault

Hameau de Cahire
56400 Auray
Tel. 02 97 57 97 26

Closed from 15 Dec to late Jan • 3 rooms with shower/WC • €60 to €65, breakfast included • No table d'hôte • Garden, car park. Credit cards not accepted, no dogs allowed • Tennis and horse-riding nearby

 The manicured lawns and flowerbeds.

Three instantly likeable 17C cottages stand clustered together in a listed hamlet. Beautiful antiques and contemporary works of art adorn the sophisticated, well-dimensioned rooms. Two are in the converted press-house, another is in the old bakery and the last is in the main wing. Fortifying breakfasts are served in the wonderful kitchen before an open fire.

Access : 7km on the Vannes road, Plougoumelen exit, then drive towards Cahire

40 GAVRINIS
M. et Mme Justum

Toulbroch
56870 Baden
Tel. 02 97 57 00 82
Fax 02 97 57 09 47
gavrinis@wanadoo.fr
www.gavrinis.com

Closed from 9 Jan to 13 Feb, Sat lunchtime, Mon lunchtime (in season), Sun evening and Mon (out of season) • 18 rooms, 4 non-smoking, with bath/WC or shower/WC and television • €72 to €86, breakfast €11, half board available • Restaurant closed Mon; menus €18 to €65 • Terrace, garden, car park • Nearby: mountain biking and walking, fishing, sailing

 A perfect HQ to explore the Gulf of Morbihan and its islands.

The classical neo-Breton architecture of this house and garden is home to a highly welcoming family establishment. A few of the comfortable, exquisitely kept rooms boast a small balcony. But for many guests, the real draw is the establishment's cooking: the owner, assisted by his son, tirelessly scours the region for good local produce which he lovingly transforms into dishes which reveal a mouth-watering blend of traditional and regional.

Access : From Baden, head towards Vannes as far as the hamlet of Toulbroch

 41 L'ALCYONE
Mme Balsan

 Impasse de Beaumer - Carnac-plage
56340 Carnac
Tel. 02 97 52 78 11

Closed fortnight in Nov • 5 rooms with bathrooms • €55
to €59, breakfast included • No table d'hôte • Sitting
room, garden, car park. Credit cards not accepted

 42 AUBERGE LE RÂTELIER
M. et Mme Bouvart

 4 chemin du Douet
56340 Carnac
Tel. 02 97 52 05 04
Fax 02 97 52 76 11
bouvart@infonie.fr
www.le-ratelier.com

Closed from 5 Jan to 5 Feb, Tue and Wed out of season
• 8 rooms, some have shower/WC and television • €46
to €55 (€38 to €43 low season); breakfast €7; half board
available • Menus €17 to €40 • Courtyard, car park

 Scrumptious breakfasts.

Whitewashed walls, parquet floors and tasteful fabrics
await behind the creeper-clad façade of this 1870
farmhouse. The soft, inviting sofas in the sitting room
and the deck chairs in the garden overlooking the fields
make it impossible not to take things easy. The sea and
menhirs are within easy reach, as is one of the most
beautiful beaches of the bay of Carnac.

 **The superb view of Carnac's famous
menhirs without risking wrack and
ruin!**

This stone farmhouse on a quiet side street of the old
village was built by a soldier returning from Napoleon's
Grande Armée, or so the story goes. Its granite façade,
swamped by Virginia creeper, hides a welcoming,
country interior: the unfussy rustic charm of the
bedrooms makes up for their small size. The beams and
manger in the former cow-shed, converted into a dining
room, are original and the pretty flowered fabrics add
a cheerful touch.

Access : On leaving Carnac Plage drive towards
Trinité-sur-Mer

Access : In the old village, a short distance from the
church

43 TY ME MAMM
Mme Daniel

56340 Carnac
Tel. 02 97 52 45 87

Open all year • 4 rooms, one of which is on the ground floor • €45, breakfast included • No table d'hôte • Garden, car park. Credit cards not accepted

44 LE TRIANON
Mme Guezel

14 rue du Général-Leclerc
56410 Étel
Tel. 02 97 55 32 41
Fax 02 97 55 44 71
hotel.letrianon@wanadoo.fr
www.hotel-le-trianon.com

Closed in Jan; Mon and Sat lunchtimes and Sun eve from Nov to Mar • 20 rooms with bath/WC or shower/WC and television • €58 to €80 (€48 to €60 low season); breakfast €9; half board available • Menus €20 to €45 • Garden, car park

Your hosts' hospitality and spontaneity.

Off the beaten track, this handsome farmhouse, built in 1900 and entirely restored, stands in a large garden, bordered by a pond on one side. Each of the immaculate rooms, named after one of Carnac's beaches, is decorated in a mixture of rustic and modern styles. Breakfast time by the side of the huge granite fireplace is always pleasant. Guests have the use of a fridge and a microwave.

The awe-inspiring sight of the Barre d'Étel during bad weather.

Don't be put off by the somewhat ordinary façade of this building in the heart of the little fishing port, the interior has a few surprises up its sleeve. The bedrooms, decorated in a chocolate-box style, vary in size and comfort; some still have original hip baths – ask for one in the villa at the end of the peaceful garden. Attractive rustic and homely dining room and very warm welcome.

Access : 5km northbound from Carnac on the D 768 and then the Quelvezin road (C 202)

Access : In the centre of the village, near the church

45 RELAIS DU PORHOËT
M. et Mme Courtel

11 place de l'Église
56490 Guilliers
Tel. 02 97 74 40 17
Fax 02 97 74 45 65
aurelaisduporhoet @ wanadoo.fr
www.aurelaisduporhoet.com

Closed from 1 to 22 Jan, 1 to 8 Oct, 1 to 8 Jul, Sun evening and Mon (out of season) • 12 rooms with bath/WC or shower/WC and television • €32 to €45; breakfast €6; half board available • Menus €10 (weekdays) to €36 • Garden, private car park. No dogs allowed

We most liked **The delightful young owners so in love with their region.**

Let's not beat about the bush: this handsome country inn, adorned with flowers in the summer, is a very special place. Peaceful nights of refreshing sleep in rustic-style bedrooms more than large enough to swing a cat and delicious, generous helpings of good local recipes served in a pretty dining room complete with a huge fireplace. Children can romp to their heart's content in the garden.

Access : In the centre of the village, opposite the church

46 LA GREK
M. et Mme Le Touze

3 place du Leurhé
56590 Île de Groix
Tel. 02 97 86 89 85
Fax 02 97 86 58 28
groe @ infonie.fr
www.groix.com

Closed in Feb • 4 non-smoking rooms, with bath/WC • €50 (€38 low season), breakfast included • No table d'hôte • Sitting room, garden, car park. Credit cards not accepted, no dogs allowed

We most liked **Hoping a storm would blow up and cut us off for days.**

The name of this Art Deco-style property, formerly the home of a tuna boat owner, is the nickname given to the inhabitants of this windswept island. Restored in 1993 and 1997, the hotel has retained its appealing insular charm. One of the best things about the elegant, comfortable bedrooms is the enormous bathrooms. Antique furniture adorns the sitting rooms, one of which has a fine collection of old coffee pots. Laze about in the large walled garden.

Access : In the village

47 **LA MARINE**
Mme Hubert

7 rue du Général-de-Gaulle
56590 Île de Groix
Tel. 02 97 86 80 05
Fax 02 97 86 56 37
hotel.dela.marine @ wanadoo.fr
www.hoteldelamarine.com

Closed in Jan, Sun evening and Mon out of season except in the school holidays • 22 rooms with bath/WC or shower with or without WC • €42 to €86 (€36 to €76 low season); breakfast €8; half board available • Menus €16 to €25 • Terrace, garden

48 **STIREN AR MOR**
M. et Mme Hans

1 clos du Poulbert
56470 La Trinité-sur-Mer
Tel. 02 97 30 15 28
Fax 02 97 30 15 28
danchant @ libertysurf.fr
www.stiren-ar-mor.fr.st

Open from Easter to 15 Nov • 4 rooms with bath/WC or shower/WC and television • €45 to €60, breakfast included • No table d'hôte • Car park, terrace. Credit cards not accepted, no dogs allowed

Sailing round the island on an old pirate ship.

The short walk from the landing stage to the main town is enough to work up a healthy appetite and ensure you do full justice to the hearty, varied dishes rustled up in the kitchen of this plush bourgeois 19C home. Don't worry about the calories, the best way to explore the Island of Groix is on foot or by bicycle! Simple, spotless rooms, a terrace shaded by tall pine trees and a walled garden will make you wish you had planned to stay longer...

Parking the car and setting off for the beach and coastal paths on foot.

This modern Breton-style house and garden is ideally located near the beach in a quiet residential neighbourhood. The blue, salmon, yellow and green rooms are all comfortable, recently fitted out and furnished in a rustic or more classical style. The largest are on the first floor and have their own sitting room, but those on the second floor with sloping ceilings and beams are just as appealing. Family heirlooms and knick-knacks brighten up the ground floor.

Access : In the town, 5min walk from the port

Access : 300m from the beach

49 MANOIR DE BODREVAN
M. et Mme Rüfenacht

56190 Noyal-Muzillac
Tel. 02 97 45 62 26
Fax 02 97 45 61 40

Closed 7 Jan to 1 Apr and 2 Nov to 20 Dec • 6 rooms, 1 of which has disabled access; all have bath/WC or shower/WC and television • €70 to €94 (€65 to €82 low season), breakfast €10, half board available • Menus €21 (evenings only) • Private car park, garden. No dogs allowed in restaurant

50 CHAMBRE D'HÔTE M. MALHERBE
M. et Mme Malherbe

Kerimel
56400 Ploemel
Tel. 02 97 56 84 72
Fax 02 97 56 84 72
elisabeth.malherbe@wanadoo.fr
http://kerimel.free.fr

Closed 15 Nov to 1 Feb • 4 non-smoking rooms, with bathrooms and television • €65 to €70, breakfast included • No table d'hôte • Garden, car park. Credit cards not accepted, no dogs allowed

 The delightful flower garden noted for its roses.

If in need of a break from the stress of urban life, this former 16C hunting lodge set in the heart of Brittany's peaceful countryside, will suit you to a T. The "prestige boarding house" atmosphere announced on the sign outside the manor is more than amply justified. An eclectic taste in interior decoration, bordering on the baroque at times, sets the tone for the spacious rooms. Only house guests are invited to partake of the appetising set menu.

 The enveloping warmth of the wood stove after a day in the open air.

This cluster of 17C cottages laid out around a large lawn complete with flower-beds is definitely worth a photo or two. Inside, the stylish renovation of the attic rooms with period furniture, comfortable bedding and well-fitted bathrooms leaves nothing to be desired. Tuck into the profusion of Breton delicacies at breakfast time (croissants, "far", pancakes, home-made jams), served in front of the huge granite fireplace in winter. Guests also have the run of a pleasant sitting room and library.

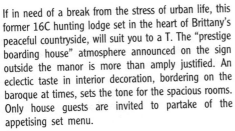

Access : 2km north-east on the D 153 and a minor road

Access : 8km northbound from Carnac on the D 119

PLOEMEUR - 56270   PLOËRMEL - 56800

51 LIBEURTHEU
M. et Mme Le Lostec-Demaret

23 rue de l'Anse de Stole
56270 Ploemeur
Tel. 02 97 82 86 22
Fax 02 97 82 86 22

Open all year • 3 rooms with bath/WC and television
• €44 (€40 low season), breakfast included • No table
d'hôte • Car park, garden, terrace, sitting room. Credit
cards not accepted

52 LE THY
M. et Mme Dinael

19 rue de la Gare
56800 Ploërmel
Tel. 02 97 74 05 21
Fax 02 97 74 02 97
hotel@le-thy.com
www.le-thy.com

Open all year • 7 rooms with bath/WC or shower/WC
and television • €50 to €60; breakfast €5 • No restaurant
but the bar serves sandwiches • Small car park. No dogs
allowed • Concerts and theatre at weekends

**An invigorating walk along the
coastal path past beaches and cliffs.**

Ideally situated, this modern Breton-style house lies
within close reach of the beach of Stole cove, the
marshes of Pen-Palud and the picturesque fishing port
of Lomener. A collection of regional furniture, gleaned
locally and restored by the owner, graces the sitting and
breakfast rooms. Each of the three comfortable, if not
enormous, rooms bears a name in keeping with the
region: shell, boat and lighthouse. A perfect example of
the delightfully quaint atmosphere of many French
seaside resorts.

**The 3km-long path lined
with 220 species of hydrangea
on the banks of the lac au Duc.**

This unusual hotel has absolutely nothing in common
with your run-of-the-mill establishments. As the
web-site proudly proclaims, the imaginative rooms are
named after and decorated in the style of artists from
all periods: "Tapies", "Hopper", "Bonnard", "Hugo
Pratt", "Klimt", "Van Gogh" and a "Flemish artist's
studio". A cabaret room, decorated with three hundred
drawers, stages "rock" concerts at the weekends.
Trendy, personalised and immaculate – definitely worth
a visit!

Access : 50m from Anse de Stole beach

Access : In the town centre

 53 FERME DE GUERLAN
M. Le Douaran

 Guerlan
56400 Plougoumelen
Tel. 02 97 57 65 50
Fax 02 97 57 65 50
ledouaran@aol.com

 www.bedbreak.com/guerlan

Closed from 1 Jan to 29 Feb • 5 rooms, one of which is
a family room and one has disabled access • €36 to €50,
breakfast included • No table d'hôte • Sitting room,
garden, car park. Credit cards not accepted

54 HÔTEL DE KERLON
M. et Mme Coeffic

 56680 Plouhinec
Tel. 02 97 36 77 03
Fax 02 97 85 81 14
hotel-de-kerlon@wanadoo.fr
www.auberge-de-kerlon.com

Hotel open from late Mar to early Nov • 16 rooms, some
of which have bath/WC, the others have shower/WC, all
have television • €50 to €59; breakfast €7; half board
available • Restaurant open in the evening only; menus
€16 • Garden, car park. No dogs allowed

 **The rapturous smiles of toddlers
visiting the farm.**

This impressive 18C country seat makes an ideal base
for exploring the Gulf of Morbihan. The spotless rooms
are a happy marriage of old and new. One is designed
for families and another for disabled guests. A fireplace
graces the enormous dining room and guests have the
use of a kitchen and a shaded garden. The owners are
very happy to show you round the farm.

**The spectacle of the sea crashing
against the Ria d'Étel.**

This stone-built 19C farmstead, cradled in a peaceful
Morbihan hamlet, commands a wonderful view of the
Ria d'Étel. The bedrooms are somewhat outdated and
hardly enormous but very well cared for and at
delightfully reasonable prices. All overlook the peaceful,
flowered garden. Traces of the establishment's farming
past can be seen in the restaurant, which serves
home-reared poultry and lamb. The sea is just 10min
away.

Access : 12km westbound from Vannes on the
N 165, then take a minor road towards Plougoumelen

Access : 1.5km to the north-east of Plouhinec, on
the D 158 then a minor road

QUELVEN - 56310

RIANTEC - 56670

 55 **AUBERGE DE QUELVEN**
SCI de la Lande

 À la Chapelle
56310 Quelven
Tel. 02 97 27 77 50
Fax 02 97 27 77 50

Closed on Wed • 7 rooms have shower/WC and television • €43 to €48; breakfast €6 • No restaurant, but there is a crêperie: prices are around €10 to €16 • Car park

 56 **LA CHAUMIÈRE DE KERVASSAL**
M. et Mme Watine

 Lieu-dit Kervassal
56670 Riantec
Tel. 02 97 33 58 66
Fax 02 97 33 58 66
gonzague.watine@wanadoo.fr
http://pro.wanadoo.fr/chaumiere.kervassal

Open all year • 3 non-smoking rooms under the eaves with bathrooms • €64, breakfast included • No table d'hôte • Sitting room, garden, car park. Credit cards not accepted, no dogs allowed • Beach nearby

 "Napoléonville" or Pontivy: a geometric town laid out by the Emperor himself.

The long granite façade of this inn is in the heart of this secluded hamlet in the Morbihan countryside. Practical, spotless bedrooms, some of which overlook the pretty 16C chapel and a traditional-style crêperie full of character with stone walls and a beautiful old fireplace. A very pleasant establishment noted for its warm welcome.

 The faultless taste of this delightful home.

It is difficult not to fall head over heels in love with this beautifully restored 17C cottage. It has everything from an impeccable thatched roof, exposed beams and stone walls, period furniture and tasteful fabrics down to abundant bouquets of flowers. Inside and out it is a delight for the eyes. The tranquil bedrooms have high ceilings and ultra-modern bathrooms. Exquisite breakfasts are served in the garden in the summer.

Access : 10km to the south-west of Pontivy on the Plouay road. Opposite the chapel

Access : 8km eastbound from Port-Louis on the D 781, then the D 33, Merlevenez road

 57   LE PÉLICAN
M. Nays

Place des Halles
56220 Rochefort-en-Terre
Tel. 02 97 43 38 48
Fax 02 97 43 42 01

Closed from 18 Jan to 18 Feb and Mon • 7 rooms with bath/WC or shower/WC and television • €53 to €63; breakfast €7; half board available • Menus €17 (lunchtime weekdays) to €36

 58   L'AUBERGE
M. et Mme Larvoir

56 route de Vannes
56400 Sainte-Anne-d'Auray
Tel. 02 97 57 61 55
Fax 02 97 57 69 10
auberge-jl-larvoir@wanadoo.fr
www.auberge-larvoir.com

Closed from 24 Feb to 13 Mar, from mid-Nov to mid-Dec, Tue (except Jul-Aug) and Wed • 6 rooms with bath/WC or shower/WC, all have television • €44 to €50 (€38 to €45 low season); breakfast €7; half board available • Air-conditioned restaurant; menus from €20 (weekdays) to €67 • Car park

 A picturesque site worthy of a watercolour or, for the less artistic among us, a photo!

A charming Breton town is home to this delightful 16C-18C house whose window-boxes are adorned with brightly coloured geraniums in the summer. The spruce, modern rooms are decorated with modern furniture, with one exception, which boasts an old wardrobe and bed. The high rafters of the dining room add a rustic air, further enhanced by a handsome fireplace.

 The pilgrimages or "pardons" of Saint Ann are a sight to behold.

The impressive basilica, the house of Nicolazic and the pilgrimages in honour of Saint Ann, the patron saint of Brittany, offer an authentic insight into Breton tradition at is most fervent and picturesque. This spruce, flower-decked inn offers modern rooms in bright fabrics, decorated with regional or Art Deco-style furniture. Admire the elegant Quimper tableware as you eat in the traditionally-furnished Breton dining room, which is clearly, and justifiably, proud of its local produce.

Access : On the main square, next to the town hall and tourist office

Access : At the entrance to the village, on the main street

59 CHAMBRE D'HÔTE MADAME GOUZER

Mme Gouzer

17 route de Quéhan (C 203)
56470 Saint-Philibert
Tel. 02 97 55 17 78
Fax 02 97 30 04 11
fgouzer @ club-internet.fr
http://chrisgouzer.free.fr

Open all year • 3 rooms • €50 to €65, breakfast included
• No table d'hôte • Garden, car park. Credit cards not
accepted

We most liked

**The sweeping view over the River
Crach and the oyster beds.**

Lovers of seafood, oysters in particular, and Brittany in
general will adore this place. This charming oyster
farmhouse enjoys an exceptional situation, in the midst
of pine trees, overlooking the River Crach and opposite
the busy port of Trinité sur Mer. Guests are always
welcomed warmly. The light, airy rooms all command
a view of this fascinating coastal scenery. Two rooms
are equipped with a kitchenette and the largest also
boasts a balcony.

Access : 2km on the Auray road, turn left at the first
set of traffic lights (after Kérisper bridge)

CENTRE AND UPPER LOIRE VALLEY

Sleeping Beauty is said to slumber still within the thick walls of one of the Loire's fairy-tale castles, like Chambord, Azay-le-Rideau or Chenonceau. A list of the region's architectural wonders and glorious gardens would be endless; but its treasures are shown to full effect in a season of 'son et lumière' shows depicting the fabled deeds of brave and courtly knights and the thwarted love of fair demoiselles. The landscape has inspired any number of writers, from Pierre de Ronsard, "the Prince of Poets", to Balzac and Georges Sand. All succumbed to the charm of this valley of kings, without forgetting to give the game-rich woodlands their due. To savour the region's two-fold talent for storytelling and culinary arts, first tuck into a delicious chicken stew, then curl up by the fireside to hear your hosts' age-old local legends.

- Cher (18)
- Eure-et-Loir (28)
- Indre (36)
- Indre-et-Loire (37)
- Loir-et-Cher (41)
- Loiret (45)

 1 CHÂTEAU DE BEL AIR
M. et Mme Maginiau

Lieu-dit le Grand-Chemin
18340 Arcay
Tel. 02 48 25 36 72
Fax 02 48 25 36 72

Open all year • 6 rooms with bath/WC • €45, breakfast included • No table d'hôte • Park, car park. Credit cards not accepted

 2 LE MOULIN DE CHAMÉRON
MM. et Mmes Rommel et Mérilleau

18210 Bannegon
Tel. 02 48 61 83 80
Fax 02 48 61 84 92
moulindechameron @ wanadoo.fr
www.moulindechameron.fr.st

Closed from 15 Nov to 28 Feb and Mon out of season • 13 rooms located in 2 small buildings, with bath/WC or shower/WC, all have television • €65 to €88; breakfast €10 • Restaurant closed Mon and Tue lunchtime; menus €23 to €46 • Terrace, garden, car park • Swimming pool, small museum of milling

 We most liked
Unbeatable value for money.

This 19C castle stands in a 10-acre parkland whose trees and grounds afford calm and comfort. Most of the large rooms are furnished in a Louis XVI style. One also features a private sitting room with fireplace, while another connects with a room which can accommodate two child-sized beds. The stately dining room, complete with monumental fireplace, is equally characterful. Bicycle rentals and golf practice in the grounds.

 We most liked
You might not believe us but paying your bill amid the machinery of the old mill is a pleasure!

Nature lovers are in for a real treat! For starters, there is the monastical peace and quiet that emanates from the two cottages in which the somewhat antiquated bourgeois rooms are located. Then there's the mill lost in the midst of fields and which is now a pleasant rustic restaurant, with a wheel in working order. And finally, the utterly rural setting of the terrace and the sound of webbed feet splashing about in the duck pond.

Access : 11km northbound from Châteauneuf on the D 73

Access : Leave Bannegon on the D 76, then drive along a minor road, 3km in all

 3 DOMAINE DE L'ERMITAGE
M. et Mme De La Farge

L'Ermitage
18500 Berry-Bouy
Tel. 02 48 26 87 46
Fax 02 48 26 03 28
domaine-ermitage@wanadoo.fr

Closed 20 to 31 Dec • 5 rooms with bathrooms • €55 to €58, breakfast included • No table d'hôte • Car park. Credit cards not accepted, no dogs allowed

 4 LA SOLOGNOTE
M. et Mme De Passos

34 Grande-Rue
18410 Brinon-sur-Sauldre
Tel. 02 48 58 50 29
Fax 02 48 58 56 00
lasolognote@wanadoo.fr
www.lasolognote.com

Closed from 21 Feb to 9 Mar • 13 rooms with bath/WC or shower/WC and television • €58 to €78; breakfast €10; half board available • Air-conditioned restaurant; menus €26 to €45 (from Jul to Sep, open Tue and Wed evenings) • Garden, car park. No dogs allowed in rooms

We most liked **The tranquillity of the park disturbed only by the twittering of birds.**

This handsome property, formerly the priory of the Abbey of Saint Sulpice of Bourges, owes its name to a hermit who stayed here for a while. The nearby paper mill dates back to 1495. Nowadays, the quite large, tastefully decorated rooms are situated in two buildings, each as quiet as the next. Take a pleasant stroll through the grounds and admire the ancient trees.

We most liked **A glimpse of village life in France.**

Anyone who has read Alain-Fournier will instantly recognise the inimitable soul of this old country village full of French character and charm. The unpretentious hotel stands in the main street where it blends in perfectly with the other redbrick houses. Cosy or more contemporary rooms are laid out around a delightful courtyard-garden. The red floor tiles, stained glass and period furniture are all synonymous with local styles and the fine porcelain bears the hallmark of Gien.

Access : 6km to the north-west of Bourges on the D 60

Access : Leave the N 20 at Lamotte-Beuvron onto the D 923

CHÂTEAUMEILLANT - 18370   **SAINT-THIBAULT - 18300**

 5 **AUBERGE DU PIET À TERRE**
M. Finet et Mme Piet

21 rue du Château
18370 Châteaumeillant
Tel. 02 48 61 41 74
Fax 02 48 61 41 88
TFINET @ wanadoo.fr
http://le.piet.a.terre.free.fr

Open from Mar to 11 Nov, closed Sun evening, Mon and Tue lunchtime (except Jul-Aug) • 5 rooms with bath/WC or shower/WC, all have television • €46 to €74; breakfast €12 • Air-conditioned restaurant; menus €35 (weekdays) to €88; limited seating, booking necessary • No dogs allowed

 6   **HÔTEL DE LA LOIRE**
M. Harison

2 quai de la Loire
18300 Saint-Thibault
Tel. 02 48 78 22 22
Fax 02 48 78 22 29
hotel-de-la-loire @ hotmail.com
www.hotel-de-la-loire.com

Closed from 20 Dec to 5 Jan • 10 rooms, one of which with disabled access, with bath/WC or shower/WC and television • €65 to €85; breakfast €7 • No restaurant • Car park

The parents' suite with a proper child's room.

Hear ye, hear ye, good folk! Here is a pleasant inn where every weary traveller should rest awhile! Entrust your faithful steed to the groom, have no fear, the stables, sorry the car park, is next door to the mounted constabulary, and rest your tired feet in this country haven. The rooms are as pretty as a picture and the tavern replete with good victuals to tickle even the finest palate. The chef's devotion has won the establishment a well-earned Michelin star.

Curling up in a chair overlooking the Loire with one of Georges Simenon's novels.

Georges Simenon, the creator of Inspector Maigret, stayed in this hotel on the banks of the Loire several times and in fact, the famous Belgian author wrote two novels here. Ask if you can sleep in the room he stayed in the 1930s: you will not be disappointed by its lovely, faintly dated, period style. The other rooms illustrate quite different themes, including Africa, Provence, Louis XV, etc, but all reveal the same inimitable charm and modern comfort.

Access : Next to the gendarmerie (police station)

Access : In the heart of the village on the riverfront

 7 VILLEMENARD
M. et Mme Gréaud

18500 Vignoux-sur-Barangeon
Tel. 02 48 51 53 40
Fax 02 48 51 58 77
villemenard @ wanadoo.fr

Open all year • 6 rooms • €44 to €55, breakfast included • No table d'hôte • Park, terrace, car park. Credit cards not accepted, no dogs allowed • River and pond on the property. Billiards room

8 LE PRIEURÉ
Famille Ribail

2 route de Saint-Laurent
18500 Vignoux-sur-Barangeon
Tel. 02 48 51 58 80
Fax 02 48 51 56 01
prieurehotel @ wanadoo.fr
www.leprieurehotel.com

Open all year • 7 rooms upstairs with shower/WC and television • €54 to €66 (€49 to €60 low season); breakfast €6.50; half board available • Menus €26 (weekdays) to €64. Restaurant closed Tue and Wed except public hols. • Terrace, garden, car park • Outdoor swimming pool

We most liked **An afternoon stroll through ancient woodland.**

The lane, lined with ponds, crosses a river before entering this wonderful 19C country house which is still the hub of a thriving agricultural business. The interior decoration is particularly worthy of note: beautiful azulejos tiles grace the entrance and dining room, weapons and prints adorn the staircase and a superb varnished wooden bar stands in the billiards room. All the well-dimensioned, quiet rooms overlook the peaceful Berry countryside.

We most liked **A religious devotion to guests' welfare.**

Built in 1860 for the village priest, the ogival windows immediately evoke this priory's religious roots. The establishment's former spiritual vocation has given way to a more down-to-earth, but equally committed desire for hospitality. The intimate, bright rooms are named after flowers. Traditional dishes and flavourful Berry wines are consumed with gusto on the pleasant terrace. Connoisseurs will immediately recognise the beautiful tableware as Foëcy porcelain!

Access : 6km northbound from Méhun on the D 79 towards Vouzeron

Access : Set back from the lane, on the D 30 (towards Neuvy-sur-Barangeon), near the church

 9 LA FERME DU CHÂTEAU
M. et Mme Vasseur

 Lévesville
28300 Bailleau-l'Évêque
Tel. 02 37 22 97 02
Fax 02 37 22 97 02

Open all year • 3 rooms • €50 to €55, breakfast included
• Table d'hôte €16 • Garden, car park. Credit cards not
accepted, no dogs allowed

 10 CHÂTEAU DE JONVILLIERS
M. et Mme Thompson

 17 rue L.-Petit-Jonvilliers
28320 Écrosnes
Tel. 02 37 31 41 26
Fax 02 37 31 56 74
info @ chateaudejonvilliers.com
www.chateaudejonvilliers.com

Closed in Jan • 5 rooms with shower/WC, non-smokers
only • €60 to €70, breakfast included • No table d'hôte
• Garden, car park. No dogs allowed

 **The overwhelming peace and quiet of
this country spot.**

A pretty manor farm laid out around a spacious inner
courtyard next door to a small castle. The good-sized
rooms are cheerful, well equipped and all are peaceful.
The simple, unaffected welcome, reasonable prices,
pretty garden and its location only 15km from Chartres
are among the most noteworthy of this establishment's
many charms.

 **The sheer elegance of this majestic
property.**

A pleasant drive leads up to this elegant 18C castle
which stands in private grounds next to thick woodland.
Peace and quiet reign in all the spacious, tastefully
decorated rooms. Delicious and generous helpings of
breakfast fare are served in a huge antique furnished
dining room. Note that the establishment is entirely
non-smoking.

Access : 8km to the north-west of Chartres on the
N 154 then the D 134

Access : 4km to the north-east of Gallardon on the
D 32

 11 LE MOULIN DES PLANCHES
Mme Maï

 28270 Montigny-sur-Avre
Tel. 02 37 48 25 97
Fax 02 37 48 35 63
moulin.des.planches@wanadoo.fr
www.moulin-des-planches.fr

Closed in Jan, Sun evening and Mon • 18 rooms, most have bath/WC, all have television • €49 to €99; breakfast €9 • Menus €26 (weekdays) to €55 • Terrace, park, car park. No dogs allowed in rooms • Board games, billiards

  12 L'AULNAYE
M. et Mme Dumas

 Route d'Alençon
28400 Nogent-le-Rotrou
Tel. 02 37 52 02 11
http://laulnaye-accueil-France.com

Open all year • 3 rooms with bath/shower and WC • €58 to €59, breakfast included • No table d'hôte • Park, car park. Credit cards not accepted, no dogs allowed

We most liked **The total seclusion of this riverside mill.**

However hard you listen, the only sounds you will hear are those of the countryside, but those who know the embattled history of the borderlands between France and Normandy may think they can still make out the distant echo of battle cries over the river. Nowadays the mill is a perfect haven of tranquillity, to which is added the pleasure of rooms decorated in period furniture and overlooking the river or the park. Beams, red floor tiles and open brickwork further enhance the rustic ambience.

We most liked **The tranquillity of the park so close to the town centre.**

The main appeal of this almost Victorian-looking 19C mansion is its priceless position in the heart of a park full of countless species of trees and plants. The plush interior decoration is also worthy of note: a handsome wooden staircase leads up to the rooms, all of which boast parquet floors, period furniture and marble fireplaces. Delicious breakfasts are served in the wainscoted dining room in winter and in the delightful wrought-iron conservatory in the summer.

Access : 1km to the north-east on the D 102 (towards Tillières-sur-Avre)

Access : 3.5km westbound from Nogent-le Rotrou towards Alençon

13 LES CHANDELLES
M. et Mme Simon

19 rue des Sablons, village les Chandelles
28130 Villiers-le-Morhier
Tel. 02 37 82 71 59
Fax 02 37 82 71 59
info@chandelles-golf.com
www.chandelles-golf.com

Open all year • 5 non-smoking rooms with bath/WC and television • €60 to €80, breakfast included • No table d'hôte • Garden, car park. No dogs allowed

14 MANOIR DE BOISVILLERS
M. et Mme Fournal

11 rue du Moulin-de-Bord
36200 Argenton-sur-Creuse
Tel. 02 54 24 13 88
Fax 02 54 24 27 83
manoir.de.boisvilliers@wanadoo.fr
www.manoir-de-boisvilliers.com

Closed from 26 Dec to 17 Jan • 16 rooms located in 2 buildings, all have bath/WC or shower/WC and television • €56 to €102 (€55 to €94 low season); breakfast €8 • No restaurant • Garden, private car park. No dogs allowed • Outdoor swimming pool

 We most liked
A wealth of leisure activities so close at hand.

An impressive wooden porch leads into this renovated 1840 farmhouse set in grounds where horses graze peacefully. The barn has been converted into a guest wing which features bold colour schemes and excellent bathrooms. Interesting old furniture picked up from antique dealers and flea markets adds character to the breakfast room. On the leisure side, you can choose between golf and horse-riding (the owner's twin passions – he is a golf pro) or try your hand at fishing.

 We most liked
Diving into the pool after a hot day's sight-seeing.

The Boisvilliers went into exile during the Revolution, but their manor house in old Argenton continues to honour their memory. Cheerful Jouy tapestries and antique furniture set the tone in the main wing which overlooks the valley, while the other wing is more modern. All the hotel's bedrooms have been lovingly renovated by the current owners, but the sitting room is resolutely modern with luxurious designer sofas, high-tech TV and striking modern works of art. Delightful garden.

Access : 8km northbound from Maintenon on the D 116, towards Coulomb

Access : In the town centre, drive towards Gargilesse, turn right at Rue Paul Bert, left at Rue d'Orion then a sharp right

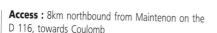

15 ● CHÂTEAU DE BOUESSE
M. et Mme Lorry

36200 Bouesse
Tel. 02 54 25 12 20
Fax 02 54 25 12 30
château.bouesse @ wanadoo.frf
www.chateau-bouesse.de

Closed Jan-Mar, Oct-Dec and Mon, Tue in April
● 12 rooms, all with WC/bath, 6 with television ● €85 to
€100, breakfast €10; half-board available ● Menus €28
to €35 ● Terrace, park, car park

16 ● LE PORTAIL
Mme Boyer

Rue Émile-Surun
36170 Saint-Benoît-du-Sault
Tel. 02 54 47 57 20
Fax 02 54 47 57 20

Open all year ● 3 rooms, one of which is a studio ● €42
to €54, breakfast included ● No table d'hôte ● Credit
cards not accepted, no dogs allowed

We most liked The bedroom in the dungeon and raftered ceiling.

Joan of Arc, Charles VII, Louis XI and Charles VIII are just a few of the famous names to have stayed in this small fortified 13C castle. Today the charm of yesteryear can still be felt in the spacious bedrooms, some medieval-style with four-poster beds and fireplaces, others with a more intimate appeal, and in the elegant restaurant which boasts a 15C fresco on the ceiling and a lovely terrace overlooking the garden à la française. Wouldn't it be easy to get used to a life of luxury?

We most liked Wandering around the historic medieval city.

A fortified gate, carved stone cross and spiral staircase bear witness to the venerable age of this beautiful 14C-15C former property of the Knights Templar. Character and authenticity emanate from the old beams and medieval or Renaissance inspired furniture in the bedrooms and apartment. The breakfast room is equally appealing and the lady of the house's gracious welcome is quite faultless.

Access : In the centre of the village, 11km from Argenton-sur-Creuse by N 20

Access : In the medieval city

 17 MONTGARNI
M. et Mme Labaurie

 36230 Sarzay
Tel. 02 54 31 31 05
Fax 02 54 31 30 10

Open all year • 5 rooms • €43, breakfast included;
half-board available • Table d'hôte €17 • Park, car park.
No dogs allowed • Outdoor swimming pool. Farm-grown
produce

 18 LE BLASON
M. Varin

 11 place Richelieu
37400 Amboise
Tel. 02 47 23 22 41
Fax 02 47 57 56 18
leblason@wanadoo.fr
www.leblason.fr

Closed from 10 Jan to 10 Feb • 26 rooms, 2 of which
have disabled access, all have shower/WC and television
• €49 to €54; breakfast €6 • Terrace, garage

 **The gourmet owner-chef's inspired
culinary talents.**

This farming couple have been extending their friendly
hospitality to guests in search of tranquillity and the
good things in life for over 15 years. The rooms in the
19C mansion, half-hidden by greenery, are extremely
comfortable. Only 100 % local produce crosses the
threshold of the kitchen to become healthy, mouth-
watering dishes. If you feel like some gentle exercise,
the immense parkland which extends into the unspoilt
Berry countryside offers some great walks.

 The easy-going atmosphere.

Leonardo da Vinci ended his days in this town, now
home to a family inn offering appealing attic rooms with
a dash of local character. If you're feeling downhearted,
ask for one of the rooms facing the street, which
overlook the "Rue Joyeuse". A discreetly rustic atmosphere reigns in the dining room and the terrace-
veranda in the rear courtyard, where good home cooking
can be savoured.

Access : 1.5km southbound from Sarzay on the
D 41 towards Chassignolles

Access : On a square in the town centre

19 LE CLOS PHILLIPA
Mme de Drezigue

10-12 rue de Pineau
37190 Azay-le-Rideau
Tel. 02 47 45 26 49
Fax 02 47 45 31 46
le.clos-philippa@wanadoo.fr
http://le-clos-philippa.monsite.wanadoo.fr

Open all year • 5 rooms with bathrooms • €58 to €88, breakfast included • Table d'hôte €27 (evenings only) • Sitting room, garden, car park. No dogs admitted

20 DE BIENCOURT
Mme Marioton

7 rue Balzac
37190 Azay-le-Rideau
Tel. 02 47 45 20 75
Fax 02 47 45 91 73
biencourt@infonie.fr
www.hotelbiencourt.com

Open from 1 Mar to 15 Nov • 16 rooms located in the main building and the old school, with bath/WC or shower/WC, some have television • €37 to €52, breakfast €7 • No restaurant • Inner courtyard. No dogs allowed

The exceptional situation of this pleasant mansion.

The priceless location, in the heart of the town two minutes walk from the castle, explains much of the appeal of this pleasant 18C mansion. Spacious, well laid-out rooms are embellished with interesting antique pieces. The large sitting room is very friendly. The delightful garden, where breakfast is served in fine weather, is just next door to the castle grounds. Ask about wine tastings of local vintages.

Being on the doorstep of a famous castle and parkland.

This elegant 18C property is tucked away in a semi-pedestrian street which leads to one of France's most beautiful Renaissance castles. Space and rustic furniture characterise the rooms, which have sloping ceilings on the top floor. A number of rooms decorated in Directoire style are also available in a building in the rear of the courtyard. Attractive cane-furnished sitting room, comfortable 19C-style dining room with a winter garden conservatory where breakfast is served.

Access : In the town centre

Access : In the town centre (near the post office), on the semi-pedestrian street leading to the castle

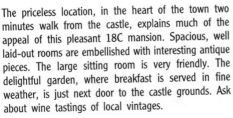

 21 LE CHEVAL BLANC
M. et Mme Blériot

Place de l'Église
37150 Bléré
Tel. 02 47 30 30 14
Fax 02 47 23 52 80
le.cheval.blanc.blere @ wanadoo.fr
www.lechevalblancblere.com

Closed from Jan to mid-Feb, Sun evening, Fri lunchtime
and Mon • 12 rooms with bath/WC or shower/WC and
television • €58 to €90; breakfast €9; half board available
• Air-conditioned restaurant; menus €20 (weekdays) to
€58 • Terrace, garden, private car park • Outdoor
swimming pool

 **Wine and dine among the lush foliage
of the inner courtyard.**

Built in the 17C opposite the parish church, this
townhouse was converted into an inn in the 19C. The
view from the rooms of the restful inner garden
compensates for their rather outdated appearance.
Meals are served in two elegant dining rooms – the one
with the fireplace has most character – or on the
delightful flowered courtyard-terrace. The chef has made
it a point of honour to uphold French culinary traditions.

Access : In the town centre, in the pedestrian
quarter near the church

 22 LE FLEURAY
M. et Mme Newington

37530 Cangey
Tel. 02 47 56 09 25
Fax 02 47 56 93 97
lefleurayhotel @ wanadoo.fr
www.lefleurayhotel.com

Closed from 21 Jan to 2 Feb and 3 to 14 Nov • 14 rooms
with bath/WC or shower/WC and television, 6 with
disabled access • €78 to €110 (€72 to €98 low season),
breakfast €10, half board available • Non-smoking
restaurant open only in evenings and by reservation;
menus €28 to €38 • Terrace, garden, garage • Heated
swimming pool

 **Sauntering round the garden between
fruit trees and the small pond.**

The charm of the countryside, unmitigated peace and
quiet and a matchless welcome explain the appeal of
this beautifully restored farmhouse. Guests can choose
between the comfortably cosy rooms in the main wing
or those in the barn, which are more spacious and which
open out directly onto the handsome swimming pool.
The dining room aims for a Country Chic style and in
summer, meals are served on a lovely terrace
overlooking the countryside. The only drawback is
having to say goodbye!

Access : 15km northbound from Amboise on the
D 31 and D11 as far as Cangey and then the D 74
between Fleuray and Dame-Marie-des-Bois

23 LE CLOS DU PETIT MARRAY
M. et Mme Plantin

37310 Chambourg-sur-Indre
Tel. 02 47 92 50 67
Fax 02 47 92 50 67
serge.plantin@wanadoo.fr
www.opencom.fr/petitmarray

Open all year • 4 rooms with bathrooms • €60, breakfast
included • Table d'hôte €25 (evenings only and by
reservation) • Garden, car park. Credit cards not
accepted, no dogs allowed in restaurant • Play area and
fishing for children

24 DIDEROT
M. et Mme Dutheil

4 rue Buffon - 7 rue Diderot
37500 Chinon
Tel. 02 47 93 18 87
Fax 02 47 93 37 10
hoteldiderot@hoteldiderot.com
www.hoteldiderot.com

Open all year • 27 rooms, 1 with disabled access, all have
bath/WC or shower/WC, some have television • €50 to
€71; breakfast €7 • No restaurant • Inner courtyard,
private car park. No dogs allowed

We most liked

Walking along the banks of the Indre.

Children will enjoy fishing in the pond in the grounds
of this handsome 19C farmhouse in the heart of the
countryside. Names evocative of well-being and freedom
have been given to each of the generously-sized and
tastefully decorated rooms. A library and the nearby
forest will keep you busy throughout your stay.

We most liked

**Home-made lavender jam made with
home-grown lavender!**

Olive, banana, lemon, mandarin and medlar trees form
a spectacularly exotic curtain of greenery to this 18C
hotel acquired in the 1970s by the Cypriot owner. A
classical accent is being given to the gradually renovated
rooms, the quietest overlooking the courtyard. Home-
made jams figure prominently on the breakfast table,
served next to a crackling log fire in winter or out on
the terrace whenever the weather permits.

Access : 5km northbound from Loches on the
N 143, towards Tours

Access : A short distance from the town centre, on
a quiet street between Place Jeanne d'Arc and Rue
Diderot

CINQ-MARS-LA-PILE - 37130

CIVRAY-DE-TOURAINE - 37150

 25 LA MEULIÈRE

M. et Mme Manier

10 rue de la Gare
37130 Cinq-Mars-la-Pile
Tel. 02 47 96 53 63
Fax 02 47 96 53 63
cgmanier-lameuliere @ planetes.com
www.lameuliere.free.fr

Open all year • 3 rooms with bathrooms • €42 to €50, breakfast included • No table d'hôte • Garden, car park. Credit cards not accepted, no dogs allowed

26 CHAMBRE D'HÔTE LA MARMITTIÈRE

M. et Mme Boblet

22 Vallée-de-Mesvres
37150 Civray-de-Touraine
Tel. 02 47 23 51 04
marmittiere @ libertysurf.fr
http://perso.libertysurf.fr/marmittiere

Open from 16 Mar to 14 Nov • 3 non-smoking rooms • €55, breakfast included • Table d'hôte €22 (closed Sat-Sun and by reservation only) • Terrace, garden, car park. Credit cards not accepted, no dogs allowed

We most liked
The tranquillity of this establishment within walking distance of the station.

The uncontested bonus of this handsome 19C mansion is its situation close to the station without any of the noise or fuss you might expect. A fine wooden staircase takes you up to colourful, well-soundproofed rooms furnished with antiques. A comfortable dining room provides the backdrop to breakfasts. In the summer, deck chairs can be found in the garden for a quiet afternoon nap.

We most liked
Breakfasts and dinners are prepared with 100 % organic produce.

The breakfast room and table d'hôte are located in a 17C wine-growers home, while the rooms have been fitted out in an early 20C stone villa. The interior decoration, although contemporary and highly colourful, blends in wonderfully with the old walls. To wind up this enticing picture, take a stroll round the garden and be ready to encounter some of its residents – the estate's donkeys and chickens – roaming freely.

Access : Near the railway station

Access : 4km westbound of Chenonceaux on the D 40 then a minor road

CONTINVOIR - 37340

GENILLÉ - 37460

27 LA BUTTE DE L'ÉPINE
M. Bodet

37340 Continvoir
Tel. 02 47 96 62 25
Fax 02 47 96 07 36

Closed from 15 Dec to 15 Jan • 3 rooms, one of which is upstairs • €57, breakfast included • No table d'hôte • Park. Credit cards not accepted, no dogs allowed

28 LE MOULIN DE LA ROCHE
Mme Mieville

37460 Genillé
Tel. 02 47 59 56 58
Fax 02 47 59 59 62
clive.mieville @ wanadoo.fr
www.moulin.de.la.roche.com

Closed in winter • 4 non-smoking rooms • €60 to €65, breakfast included • No table d'hôte • Garden, parking. Credit cards not accepted, no dogs allowed

 We most liked **The amazing care taken to restore this period house to its former glory.**

The owners have spent years faithfully restoring this delightful residence of 16C-17C origins using only authentic materials. The sitting-breakfast room is imaginatively strewn with period furniture and features a huge fireplace. The spotless rooms are genuine boudoirs, the most romantic of which is upstairs. Well-tended flower-beds grace the park behind the house.

 We most liked **A lazy afternoon's fishing or "déjeuner sur l'herbe" in a beautiful rural setting.**

Feast your eyes on this picture of paradise! The old water mill smothered in Virginia creeper stands on the banks of the somewhat fickle River Indrois. The oldest sections date from the 17C and 18C as can be seen from the original beams and terracotta floor tiles. The rooms are endowed with the charm of an English cottage, down to the ubiquitous tea and coffee making facilities; all overlook the garden and river. A snug sitting room is lined with books, antiques and lit by a log fire in winter.

Access : 2km eastbound from Gizeux on the D 15

Access : 10km to the north-east of Loches on the D 31 and the D 764, Montrichard road

HUISMES - 37420

LANGEAIS - 37130

 29 LA PILLETERIE
Mme Prunier

37420 Huismes
Tel. 02 47 95 58 07
Fax 02 47 95 58 07

Open all year • 4 rooms • €55 to €60, breakfast included
• No table d'hôte • Garden, car park. Credit cards not
accepted, no dogs allowed • Nearby: Châteaux of Azay
le Rideau, Villandry

30 ERRARD-HOSTEN
M. et Mme Errard

2 rue Gambetta
37130 Langeais
Tel. 02 47 96 82 12
Fax 02 47 96 56 72
info @ errard.com
www.errard.com

Closed Dec, Jan, Mon and Tue lunchtime and Sun
evening from Oct to Apr • 10 rooms with bath/WC and
television • €65 to €92; breakfast €12 • Menus €28 to
€47 • Terrace, garage

 **The convenient situation near the
castles of Azay and Villandry.**

If in dire need of a break from the stress of urban life,
this 19C farm in the middle of the countryside is just
what the doctor ordered. Original red floor tiles add
character to the rustic rooms, the quietest of which are
located in an independent cottage. Young children adore
the sheep, geese and other farmyard animals all of
whom happily cohabit in a single pen. Relaxed and
friendly hosts will make you feel at home the moment
you arrive.

 **The gargantuan hospitality of this
provincial inn.**

This hostelry is surrounded by some of Touraine's most
beautiful castles and within walking distance of
Langeais. Guests can choose between plush 19C or
contemporary rooms, but those overlooking the street
are noisier, even though the traffic can hardly be called
"busy" after nightfall. Any doubts you may still have that
you are in the birthplace of Rabelais' Gargantua, epic
trencherman, will immediately vanish at the sight of the
Brobdingnagian dishes liberally washed down with Loire
wines.

Access : 6km northbound from Chinon on the D 16

Access : In the town centre, opposite the tourist
office

LIGRÉ - 37500

NAZELLES-NÉGRON - 37530

 31 LA MILAUDIÈRE
M. et Mme Marolleau

5 rue St-Martin
37500 Ligré
Tel. 02 47 98 37 53
Fax 02 47 98 37 52
milaudiere @ club-internet.fr
www.milaudiere.com

Open all year • 4 rooms, one of which is on the ground floor and 3 are upstairs • €43 to €60, breakfast included • No table d'hôte • Car park. Credit cards not accepted, no dogs allowed

 32 CHÂTEAU DE NAZELLES
M. et Mme Fructus

16 rue Tue-la-Soif
37530 Nazelles-Négron
Tel. 02 47 30 53 79
Fax 02 47 30 53 79
info @ chateau-nazelles.com
www.chateau-nazelles.com

Open all year except Christmas and New Year • 3 rooms • €90 to €105, breakfast included • Table d'hôte (by reservation in summer) €23 • Garden, car park. No dogs admitted • Outdoor swimming pool

 The owners' exquisite charm and hospitality.

The walls of this original old 18C house are built out of "tuffeau", a soft local chalk. The owners dug in and undertook the majority of the restoration work themselves and can rightly be proud of the result. The rooms under the eaves are extremely pleasant and those on the ground floor with their old tiled floors, net curtains and rustic furniture are full of character. The breakfast room which boasts an old bread oven is also something of an eye-opener.

 Taking a well-earned rest in the sitting room complete with billiards table and fireplace.

There's no point in attempting to withstand the charm of this 16C castle built on a hillside by the architect of Chenonceau. The rooms on the first floor are a fine example of how well old can be married with new; all overlook the valley and the Château d'Amboise, those in the independent wing have old floor tiles, beams and terracotta tiled showers. The highlight has however got to be the swimming pool, sunk into the rock and the terraced garden.

Access : 8km to the south-east of Chinon, towards Île-Bouchard on the D 749, then take the D 29

Access : 3km northbound from Négron on the D 5

33 DOMAINE DE BEAUSÉJOUR
M. et Mme Chauveau

37220 Panzoult
Tel. 02 47 58 64 64
Fax 02 47 95 27 13
info@domainedebeausejour.com
www.domaine.de.beausejour.com

Open all year • 3 rooms • €70 to €84 (€61 to €77 low season), breakfast included • No table d'hôte • Car park. Credit cards not accepted, no dogs allowed • Outdoor swimming pool

34 LE LOGIS DE LA PAQUERAIE
M. et Mme Binet

La Paqueraie
37320 Saint-Branchs
Tel. 02 47 26 31 51
Fax 02 47 26 39 15
monique.binet@wanadoo.fr
http://perso.wanadoo.fr/lapaqueraie/

Open all year • 4 rooms with bathrooms and one gîte • €79, breakfast included, half board available • Table d'hôte €25 • Garden, car park. Credit cards not accepted • Outdoor swimming pool. Fishing, hiking, tennis, 18-hole golf course and riding nearby

We most liked
Relaxing on a genuine wine-growing estate in Gargantua's homeland: in vino veritas!

This delightful house was built in 1978 from old materials gleaned in the region, some said to be three centuries old! The slate floors of the carefully decorated rooms contrast beautifully with the choice antique furniture. The superb view over Rabelais' beloved Chinon vineyards bodes well for a pleasant stay; those who so desire can taste some of the estate's best vintages in the company of the proprietress.

We most liked
The delightful landscaped garden and swimming pool.

The traditional regional architectural style, rampant curtain of Virginia creeper and the venerable old oaks in the park all combine to lend this recently built house a much older feel! The rooms display an excellent blend of practicality, comfort and sophistication. Mirrors, antiques and an original fireplace grace the sitting room. At mealtimes, you will sample classic French cooking made with local produce. If still not convinced, the peace and quiet of the grounds are bound to win you over.

Access : 5km to north-west of Bouchard on the D 757, then drive towards Chinon on the D 21

Access : On leaving Cormery (coming from Tours) take the D 32 and turn right after the level-crossing

35 LES PERCE-NEIGE
Mme Chemin et M. Laguette

13 rue Anatole-France
37210 Vernou-sur-Brenne
Tel. 02 47 52 10 04
Fax 02 47 52 19 08
perceneige @ perceneige.com
www.perceneige.com

Closed Nov • 5 rooms, mainly with bath/WC or shower/WC • €45 to €60; breakfast €5 • No table d'hôte • Terrace, shaded garden, private car park

36 DOMAINE DES BIDAUDIÈRES
Mme Suzanne

rue du Peu-Morier
37210 Vouvray
Tel. 02 47 52 66 85
Fax 02 47 52 62 17
resa @ bidaudieres.com
www.bidaudieres.com

Open all year • 6 rooms • €110 to €130; breakfast included • No table d'hôte • Park, car park. Credit cards not accepted, no dogs admitted • Swimming pool

 The peaceful village encircled by the vineyards of Vouvray.

This modest 19C mansion formerly served as the offices of the solicitor of Vernou. An "old world" aura still pervades the rooms, which vary in comfort: book one which overlooks the spacious gardens and the old well. Local Loire dishes and wines are served in two elegant dining rooms and on the terrace to a backdrop of greenery and flowers.

 Playing at being lord - or lady - of the manor in this sumptuous estate.

It would be difficult to imagine a more idyllic place for a romantic getaway than this lovely 18C château with panoramic terrace set in over 30 acres of parkland and surrounded by vineyards. However the welcoming owners are not content to rest on the laurels of this spellbinding setting and have superbly restored the interior of this prestigious abode. The different styles of the spacious comfortable rooms are all equally appealing and certain to entice you back time and time again!

Access : In the centre of the village, 4km eastbound from Vouvray (D 46)

Access : 3km eastbound of Vouvray on the D 46 towards Château-Renault, between Vouvray and Vernou-sur-Brenne

 37 MANOIR DE LA SALLE DU ROC
M. Jean Boussard

69 route de Vierzon
41400 Bourré
Tel. 02 54 32 73 54
Fax 02 54 32 47 09
boussard.patricia @ wanadoo.fr
www.manoirdelasalleduroc.monsite.
wanadoo.fr

Open all year • 4 rooms • €70 to €110, breakfast included • No table d'hôte • Park, car park. American Express not accepted, no dogs admitted • Tennis

 38 LA FARGE
M. de Grangeneuve

41600 Chaumont-sur-Tharonne
Tel. 02 54 88 52 06
Fax 02 54 88 51 36
sylvie.lansier @ wanadoo.fr

• 4 rooms with bath/WC • €60 to €75, breakfast included • No table d'hôte • Swimming pool. Credit cards not accepted, no dogs allowed

 Luxury, calm and voluptuousness, a stone's throw from the troglodyte village of Bourré.

A handsome tree-lined drive leads up to this pretty manor built against a rock face. The eye is naturally drawn to the welcoming façade, but also to the lovely park surrounding it, whose features include pools, old stone staircases, clipped boxwood hedges, statues, flowerbeds and over 500 rosebushes. The charm of the interior also greets the eye, whether in the ground-floor sitting rooms and the lovely library or upstairs in the comfortably furnished, plush bedrooms.

 The surrounding forest, full of surprises and adventure.

This 16C and 19C traditional farmhouse hidden deep in the forest makes a fine picture with its half-timbered brick walls and turret. The rooms are located in three buildings. The most pleasant boasts old beams and fabric lined walls, the others' main claim to fame is their size and all are decorated with sturdy country furniture. The swimming pool, shaded garden and nearby riding stables also make this farm a perfect place from which to explore the secrets of the Sologne.

Access : 2km northbound of Montrichard on the D 62

Access : 4km to the north-east of Chaumont towards Vouzon on a minor road

 39 LA RABOULLIÈRE
Mme Thimonnier

Chemin de Marçon
41700 Contres
Tel. 02 54 79 05 14
Fax 02 54 79 59 39
raboullière @ wanadoo.fr
www.laraboullere.com

Open all year • 6 rooms, one of which is upstairs • €59
to €107, breakfast included • No table d'hôte • Sitting
room, park, car park. Credit cards not accepted

 40 LE BÉGUINAGE
M. et Mme Deloison

41700 Cour-Cheverny
Tel. 02 54 79 29 92
Fax 02 54 79 94 59
le.beguinage @ wanadoo.fr
www.multimania.com/beguinage

Open all year • 6 rooms, 4 of which are in a separate wing
• €50 to €95, breakfast included • No table d'hôte • Park,
car park • Hot-air ballooning, golf, hiking

 We most liked **The sophisticated decorative flair.**

The half-timbered walls of this Sologne farmhouse look
so authentic it is hard to believe they were entirely built
from materials found in neighbouring farms. The
sumptuously furnished rooms all have exposed beams.
Breakfasts are served by the fireside in winter and in
the garden in summer. The gentle countryside is perfect
for long country rambles.

 We most liked **Flying over the Loire châteaux in a
hot-air balloon.**

The manicured park and pond are not the only treasures
of this stone property covered in Virginia creeper.
Parquet or tiled floors, exposed beams, fireplaces,
king-size beds and generous dimensions all grace the
sophisticated bedrooms: with the smallest measuring
20sq m, this is truly "the great indoors". For a quite
matchless view of some of France's architectural gems,
forget the cost and treat yourself to a flight over the
Loire châteaux in a hot-air balloon piloted by the
proprietor.

Access : 10km southbound from Cheverny on the
D 102, then a minor road

Access : In a park

LA FERTÉ-IMBAULT - 41300

LA VILLE-AUX-CLERCS - 41160

 41 **AUBERGE À LA TÊTE DE LARD**
M. Benni

13 place des Tilleuls
41300 La Ferté-Imbault
Tel. 02 54 96 22 32
Fax 02 54 96 06 22
www.aubergealatetedelard.com

Closed from 20 Jan to 11 Feb, 10 to 20 Sep, Sun evening
• 11 rooms with bath/WC or shower/WC, all have television • €43 to €72; breakfast €7; half board available • Air-conditioned restaurant; menus €16 (weekdays) to €48 • Terrace, car park. No dogs allowed in rooms

 42 **LE MANOIR DE LA FORÊT**
M. et Mme Redon

Fort Girard
41160 La Ville-aux-Clercs
Tel. 02 54 80 62 83
Fax 02 54 80 66 03
manoirdelaforet @ wanadoo.fr
www.manoirdelaforet.fr

Open all year; • 18 rooms on 2 floors, all have bath/WC or shower/WC and television • €51 to €75; breakfast €9; half board available • Restaurant closed Sun evening and Mon from Oct to Easter, menus €27 to €48 • Terrace, park, car park

 The typically local activities.

A private fishing domain on the banks of the Sauldre and a boat at your disposal, miles of mountain-bike trails and cycles to rent from the hotel, not to mention the regular hunting days (kennels available): surely something takes your fancy? After a day in the open air, this Sologne inn offers comfortable modern rooms and a pleasantly countrified dining room with a shady terrace which serves home-made cooking only!

 The suite with a terrace overlooking the park (sadly the most expensive!).

This redbrick and stone hunting lodge was built in the heart of the countryside on the edge of the forest of Fréteval. The slightly faded rooms are furnished with antiques and all overlook the immense 8-acre park. The tall French windows of the stately dining room are thrown open to the terrace and flowered garden. Two sitting rooms, also furnished with antiques, are perfect for a quiet after-dinner drink or coffee.

Access : On the village square

Access : 1.5km eastbound on a minor road

43 CHAMBRE D'HÔTE PEYRON-GAUBERT
M. et Mme Peyron-Gaubert

Carrefour de l'Ormeau
41170 Mondoubleau
Tel. 02 54 80 93 76
Fax 02 54 80 93 76
i.peyron1 @ tiscali.fr
www.carrefour-de-lormeau.com

Open all year • 5 rooms with bathrooms • €42 to €47, breakfast included • Table d'hôte €21 (evening only, by reservation only) • Garden, car park. Credit cards not accepted, no dogs allowed • Exhibition and concert room

44 HÔTEL DE L'ÉCOLE
M. et Mme Preteseille

12 route de Montrichard
41400 Pontlevoy
Tel. 02 54 32 50 30
Fax 02 54 32 33 58

Closed from 16 Feb to 16 Mar, from 16 Nov to 11 Dec, Sun evening and Mon (except Jul-Aug and national holidays) • 11 rooms with bath/WC or shower/WC, some have television • €50 to €69; breakfast €9; half board available • Menus €19 to €50 • Terrace, garden, private car park. No dogs allowed

This one-off address, also a cabinetmaker's workshop.

The least you can say about this 17C redbrick house is that it is unusual, home to both a B&B establishment and exhibition hall for the cabinetmaker-owner's imaginative furniture. The rooms, of varying sizes, house some of the finished articles; simple, elegant waxed furniture made out of elm, ash and acacia wood. Concerts are sometimes held on the top floor. The garden to the rear is also very pleasant.

The delightful flowered garden and murmuring fountain.

You'll immediately reach for your camera when you catch sight of this adorable house covered in variegated vine and surrounded by masses of brightly coloured geraniums. A distinctly old-fashioned feel in the rooms is compensated for by their size and spotless upkeep. Tables are prettily laid out in one of two rustic dining rooms or on the pleasing shaded terrace. What better invitation to enjoy finely judged dishes which make the most of local produce!

Access : In the town

Access : In the town centre, on the D 764 between Montrichard and Blois

 45 LA VILLA MÉDICIS
M. et Mme Cabin-Saint-Marcel

1 rue Médicis, Macé
41000 Saint-Denis-sur-Loire
Tel. 02 54 74 46 38
Fax 02 54 78 20 27
www.lavillamedicis.fr

Open all year (reservations only in winter) • 6 rooms • €68 to €98, breakfast included • Table d'hôte €18 to €32 (by reservation) • Park, car park. Credit cards not accepted, no dogs allowed

 46 MANOIR DE BEL AIR
M. Abel

1 route d'Orléans
41500 Saint-Dyé-sur-Loire
Tel. 02 54 81 60 10
Fax 02 54 81 65 34
manoirbelair @ free.fr
www.manoirbelair.com

Closed 15 Jan to 20 Feb • 43 rooms located in 3 wings, with bath/WC (3 shower/WC) and television • €60 to €89 (€54 to €75 low season); breakfast €7; half board available • Menus €22 to €45 • Inner courtyard, park, private car park. Dogs not allowed in restaurant

 The exuberant foliage all around.

Once a spa hotel, this 1852 building is named after Marie de Médici who used to take the waters in the park. Some of the beautifully laid-out rooms command a view of the park. Tea and coffee making facilities can be used by guests in the pretty sitting room. If the sun is shining, take breakfast outside, then set out on a stroll or try your hand at kayaking, golf or riding nearby.

 Ambling down the old towpath which skirts the hotel.

A wine merchant and governor of Guadeloupe was among the proprietors of this elegant 17C manor house made out of "tuffeau", the chalky local stone. Most of the rooms have been renovated as has the restaurant which features a fine stone fireplace and regional furniture. All command fine views of the Loire. Pleasant leafy park.

Access : 4km to the north-east of Blois on the N 152, towards Orléans

Access : 15km from Blois towards Orléans, on the D 951 bordering the Loire

 47 LE PRIEURÉ DE LA CHAISE
Mme Duret-Therizols

8 rue du Prieuré - Lieu-dit la Chaise
41400 Saint-Georges-sur-Cher
Tel. 02 54 32 59 77
Fax 02 54 32 69 49
prieuredelachaise @ yahoo.fr
http://www.prieuredelachaise.com

Open all year • 4 non-smoking rooms • €60 to €115, breakfast included • No table d'hôte • Garden, car park, park. Credit cards not accepted, no dogs allowed • Open-air swimming pool

 48 LES ATELLERIES
Mme Quintin

41300 Selles-Saint-Denis
Tel. 02 54 96 13 84
Fax 02 54 96 13 78
caroline.quintin @ wanadoo.fr
www.lesatelleries.com

Closed during Feb school holidays • 4 rooms with bath/WC • €50, breakfast included • No table d'hôte • Sitting room, park. Credit cards not accepted, enquire about their rules on dogs

 Tasting the estate's wines.

A chance to stay in this former priory built in the heart of a wine-growing estate should not be missed. Next door to a magnificent 13C chapel (Mass is still celebrated here once a year), the 16C manor and its rooms are all equally elegant: soft stone walls, red-brick tiles, beams, fireplace and antique furniture and tapestries. The 17C outhouses have been converted into a wine-growing museum which you will come upon as you stroll around the tree-lined grounds.

 The beautiful Sologne countryside surrounding this farm.

Set in a 150-acre estate of woodland, moors and ponds, this old Sologne farm is sure to appeal to small-game hunters. Dog kennels are available and guests can go out hunting for the day with locals who know all the best coverts. As for the accommodation, the rooms are soberly decorated and well kept, two are installed in the former bakery where the old bread oven is still visible. Bicycles can be rented from the estate.

Access : 2km southbound of St-Georges-sur-Cher on the D 27A

Access : 16km to the north-east of Romorantin-Lanthenay on the D 123 between Selles-Saint-Denis and Marcilly

THÉSÉE - 41140

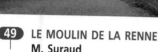 **49** LE MOULIN DE LA RENNE
M. Suraud

11 Route de Vierzon
41140 Thésée
Tel. 02 54 71 41 56
Fax 02 54 71 75 09
contact @ moulindelarenne.com
www.moulindelarenne.com

Closed from mid-Jan to mid-Mar, Sun evening, Mon and Tue lunchtime (high season) • 15 rooms on 2 floors, almost all have bath/WC or shower/WC • €26 to €51; breakfast €8; half board available • Menus €16 (weekdays) to €39 • Terrace, garden, car park • Children's play area

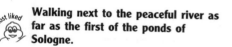 **Walking next to the peaceful river as far as the first of the ponds of Sologne.**

Once upon a time, there lived an old mill surrounded by a shaded garden through which passed the River Renne. Nearly all the simply decorated rooms have been renovated mirroring the dining room's bright, bold colours. An aquarium, a fireplace and children's games are most appreciated in the spacious sitting room, while the terrace on the banks of the millpond adds the finishing touch.

50 BELVÉDÈRE
M. Massicard

192 rue Jules Ferry
45200 Amilly
Tel. 02 38 85 41 09
Fax 02 38 98 75 63
h.belvedere @ wanadoo.fr
http://perso.wanadoo.fr/hbelvedere

Closed 1 to 2 Jan • 24 rooms (12 non-smoking) with bath/WC or shower/WC and television • €49, €39 Sat and Sun (from 15 Nov to 8 May) • No restaurant • Private car park, garages, garden. No dogs allowed in breakfast room

 The calm which prevails in this family-run establishment.

Trees and flowers abound in the garden which takes visitors into the house hidden in a quiet neighbourhood on the outskirts of Montargis. Its countrified charm is enhanced by the rooms, which while they are not enormous, are stylishly and individually decorated with colourful wallpaper, pretty fabrics, antique furniture, knickknacks and potted plants. Non-smoking rooms are available for those that wish (enquire on booking).

Access : Between Montrichard and Noyers-sur-Cher on the D 176, on the banks of the Renne

Access : 4km southbound of Montargis, on the D 943 towards Auxerre, then follow Centre Ville, opposite the school

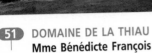

51 DOMAINE DE LA THIAU
Mme Bénédicte François

Route de Gien
45250 Briare
Tel. 02 38 38 20 92
Fax 02 38 38 06 20
lathiau @ club-internet.fr
http://perso.club-internet.fr/lathiau

Open all year • 4 non-smoking rooms upstairs • €46 to 59, breakfast included, half board available • No table d'hôte • Garden, car park. Credit cards not accepted • Tennis, bicycle rentals.

52 LA FERME DU GRAND CHESNOY
M. et Mme Chevalier

45260 Chailly-en-Gâtinais
Tel. 02 38 96 27 67
Fax 02 38 96 27 67
bclechesnoy @ yahoo.fr

Closed from 1 Dec to 31 Mar • 4 non-smoking rooms with bathrooms • €60, breakfast included • No table d'hôte • Sitting room, garden, car park. Credit cards not accepted. No dogs allowed in rooms • Tennis, billiards

The private lane through the estate that leads down to the banks of the Loire.

It is impossible not to miss the ancient old trees, one of which is over two hundred years old, that have taken root in the extensive grounds around this graceful 18C house. The rooms have a pleasantly old-fashioned appeal with flowered wallpaper and period-style patterns on the walls and family heirlooms and antiques picked up in the region. Tennis courts, table tennis and bicycle rentals on the estate.

The country spirit of the decoration.

This immense two-hundred-acre estate of woodland, fields and ponds surrounds an immense property built on the banks of the Orléans Canal. Luckily, the owners retained the original parquet floors, family heirlooms, antiques and tapestries in the rooms installed in the 1896 tower. The extremely generously-sized bathrooms are very well fitted-out. A charming dovecote, tennis courts and countless footpaths into the immense forest complete the picture.

Access : 300m from the Loire

Access : 8.5km northbound from Lorris on the D 44, take the Bellegarde road and then the minor road on the right

 53 LES COURTILS
Mme Meunier

 Rue de l'Avé
45430 Chécy
Tel. 02 38 91 32 02
Fax 02 38 91 48 20
les-courtils @ wanadoo.fr
www.france-bonjour.com/les-courtils/

Open all year • 4 rooms with bathrooms • €50, breakfast included • No table d'hôte • Garden. Credit cards not accepted, no dogs allowed

54 LA VIEILLE FORÊT
Mme Ravenel

 Route de Jouy-le-Potier
45240 La Ferté-Saint-Aubin
Tel. 02 38 76 57 20
Fax 02 38 64 82 80
www.vieilleforetra @ aol.com

Closed during the February school holidays • 2 rooms • €46, breakfast included • No table d'hôte • Sitting room, garden, car park. Credit cards not accepted, no dogs allowed

 The owners' loving care and attention is visible in every tiniest detail.

The moment you cross the threshold, you begin to feel at home! The view of the Loire is quite exceptional and the interior decoration rises to the challenge. Flowered fabrics, a tasteful blend of beiges and creams, antique and modern furniture, tiled floors. Each room is named after a local plant – let's see whether you can match the English to the French: "Bitter Apple", "Morning Glory", "Honeysuckle" and "Nasturtium". The friezes in the bathrooms were hand-stencilled.

 The beautiful Sologne scenery surrounding this handsome 20-acre property.

This brick farmhouse, which stands at the end of a forest path frequented by deer, is equally popular with families, walkers, anglers (there's a pond) and those who've had enough of towns in general, at least for a little while. The converted stables are now home to mainly modern looking rooms, with one exception, which has a beautiful tiled floor and fireplace.

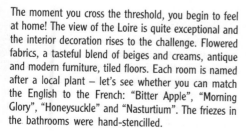

Access : 10km eastbound from Orléans on the N 460

Access : 5.5km to the north-west of Ferté-Saint-Aubin on the D 18, and take the lane on the right

MARIGNY-LES-USAGES - 45760

NEVOY - 45500

55 LES USSES
M. Marin

145 rue du Courtasaule
45760 Marigny-les-Usages
Tel. 02 38 75 14 77
Fax 02 38 75 90 65
kris.marin @ wanadoo.fr
www.france-bonjour.com/marigny

Closed from 20 to 29 Dec • 3 rooms with bath/WC, television and telephone • €55, breakfast included • No table d'hôte • Garden, car park. Credit cards not accepted, no dogs allowed • Children's play area, badminton court, mountain biking

56 LE DOMAINE DE SAINTE-BARBE
Mme Le Lay

45500 Nevoy
Tel. 02 38 67 59 53
Fax 02 38 67 28 96
annielelay @ aol.com
www.france-bonjour.com/sainte-barbe/

Closed from 20 Dec to 6 Jan • 4 rooms, 3 of which have bathrooms, and one gîte 25m from the house • €60, breakfast included • No table d'hôte • Garden, car park. Credit cards not accepted, no dogs allowed • Outdoor swimming pool, jacuzzi, tennis

The encroaching silence of the Forest of Orléans.

After two years of titanic work, this modest 1850 farmhouse has been brought back to life. The beautiful stone walls are inviting and the interior makes you want to stay forever. Period furniture graces the bedrooms, equipped with excellent bathrooms. Breakfast is served in the old stables, complete with manger. The silence of the vast garden is interrupted only by the leaves rustling in the dense forest.

The easy-going personality of the hospitable lady of the house.

This house is imbued with the charm of homes which have belonged to the same family for generations. A few decorative touches from the lady of the house have lent the interior chintz fabrics, tiled floors, ornaments and old furniture. The rooms, some of which have a canopied bed, overlook the garden. Breakfast is served on the terrace overlooking fields and woods in the summer. For those who can't tear themselves away, there's also an independent self-catering holiday cottage.

Access : 12km to the north-east of Orléans, towards Pithiviers on the N 152

Access : 4km north-east of Gien towards Lorris, after the level-crossing take the second road on the left and follow the signs

 57 VILLA HÔTEL
M. et Mme Petit

 Z. A. Le Clair Ruisseau
45500 Poilly-sur-Loire
Tel. 02 38 38 27 03
Fax 02 38 27 03 43

Open all year • 24 rooms with shower/WC and television, 2 rooms have disabled access, 10 rooms are non-smoking • €32, breakfast €5, half board available • Restaurant closed Fri, Sat and Sun, day before national holidays and national holidays, evenings only; menus €11 to €14 • Car park

 58 LE RELAIS SAINT-JACQUES
SCI Trépigneuse

 35 rue de la Mairie
45310 Tournoisis
Tel. 02 38 80 87 03
Fax 02 38 80 82 04

Closed during the February holidays, Sun evening and Mon • 5 rooms upstairs with bath/WC or just bath, and television • €41; breakfast €6; half board available • Menus €16 (weekdays) to €25 • Private car park

 A visit to the delightful museums of Gien, one devoted to porcelain, the other to hunting.

Book your room well in advance because this hotel is often full. Its success can be explained by its quiet neighbourhood location, friendly welcome, modern comforts and immaculate upkeep, though the delightful rooms are not exactly enormous. In the kitchen, the lady of the house rustles up a different main dish every evening and starters and desserts are available from a buffet. Gien porcelain plates adorn the restaurant walls.

 An unostentatious yet authentic interior.

This ancient coaching inn has been a stopping point for St James pilgrims and less devoted travellers since the 16C. The magnificent fretwork of original old oak beams in some of the rooms adds the touch of character so distinctive of old houses. The exposed brick or stone walls, tiled floors or flagstones, fireplace and bread oven of the sitting and dining rooms are equally warm and welcoming. The former "coaching room" is now a banquet hall.

Access : 2km south-west of Gien on the D 940 towards Bourges

Access : In the village, between Orléans and Châteaudun

CHAMPAGNE-ARDENNE

It is easy to spot visitors bound for Champagne-Ardenne by the sparkle in their eyes and a sudden, irrepressible delight when they finally come face to face with mile upon mile of vineyards: in their minds' eye, they are already uncorking a bottle of the famous delicacy which was known as "devil's wine" before a monk discovered the secret of Champagne's divine bubbles. As they continue their voyage, the beautiful cathedral of Reims rises up before them and they remember the delicious taste of its sweet pink biscuits delicately dipped in a glass of demi-sec. At Troyes, their eyes drink in the sight of tiny lanes lined with half-timbered houses while their palate thrills to the flavour of andouillettes, the local chitterling sausages. After such indulgence, our pilgrims welcome the sanctuary of the dense Ardennes forests, bordered by the meandering Meuse. But far from fasting and penitence, this woodland retreat offers a host of undreamt-of delights: the graceful flight of the crane over an unruffled lake or the prospect of sampling the famous Ardennes wild boar.

- Ardennes (08)
- Aube (10)
- Marne (51)
- Haute-Marne (52)

1 CHÂTEAU DE CHÂTEL
M. et Mme Huet

08250 Châtel-Chéhéry
Tel. 03 24 30 78 54
Fax 03 24 30 25 51
jacques.huet @ wanadoo.fr

Closed Sun evenings • 3 rooms • €75 (€65 low season), breakfast included; half board available • Table d'hôte €20 to €25 • Park, car park. Credit cards not accepted, no dogs allowed • Outdoor swimming pool

2 LA COUR DES PRÉS
Mme Avril

08290 Rumigny
Tel. 03 24 35 52 66
Fax 03 24 35 52 66

Closed from Nov to Mar • 2 rooms • €65 to €70, breakfast included • No table d'hôte • Park, car park. Credit cards not accepted, no dogs allowed • Castle visits (except Tue), dinner-concerts in the summer

A glass of champagne is offered to guests on the "Gastronomic" package.

This 18C hillside castle and park dominating the Aire Valley has charm in abundance. Despite major renovation work, numerous traces of the apartments' former glorious days are still visible, including a superb staircase, huge fireplaces and period furniture. All the well-dimensioned rooms have excellent bathrooms. A wide choice of leisure activities is also available with swimming pool, tennis courts on request and walking or cycling trails.

The lady of the house's spontaneity and warmth.

It would be difficult to find somewhere more authentic than this moated stronghold, built in 1546 by the provost of Rumigny. The present owner, a direct descendant, is clearly proud of her roots and only too happy to relate her family's history. The wood panelling and period furniture in the rooms are original, as is the magnificent dining room in what was formerly the guard room. Stroll round the park and admire the ancestral beeches.

Access : 9km to the north-west of Varennes-en-Argonne on the D 38A and then the D 42

Access : On the D 877, entering the village from the east, on the corner of the D 27

BOURGUIGNONS - 10110

BRÉVONNES - 10220

 3 CAPITAINERIE DE SAINT-VALLIER
M. et Mme Gradelet

 Rue du Pont
10110 Bourguignons
Tel. 03 25 29 84 43

Open all year • 4 rooms • €38 to €56, breakfast included • No table d'hôte • Garden, terrace, car park. Credit cards not accepted, no dogs allowed

 4 AU VIEUX LOGIS
M. et Mme Baudesson

 1 rue de Piney
10220 Brévonnes
Tel. 03 25 46 30 17
Fax 03 25 46 37 20
logisbrevonnes@wanadoo.fr
www.auvieuxlogis.com

Closed from 21 Feb to 16 Mar, Sun eve and Mon • 5 rooms with shower/WC and television • €40 to €45; breakfast €6.50; half board available • Menus €15 (weekdays) to €37 • Terrace, garden, private car park • At the edge of the regional park of Forêt d'Orient

 The artistic salon atmosphere around the breakfast table.

Once seen, it is impossible to forget this old lock house. The current lady of the house, a keen art and culture enthusiast, adores receiving artists and scholars of all sorts and regularly organises exhibitions and concerts. The personalised rooms overlook the Seine. Old porcelain adorns the breakfast room, while the bread-oven room is now the home of the master of the house's egg-painting workshop! The large, well-tended garden masks the noise of the nearby road.

 140km of signposted footpaths through the Forêt d'Orient.

Fishing, water sports, or just walking along the shore: the lakes of Orient and Temple, names which recall the medieval religious orders who once owned the land, offer a wide range of activities. Right on the doorstep stands this recently spruced up "old abode", whose delightfully old-fashioned interior preserves the charm of times past. Country furniture, ornaments and flowered paper set the scene for this unostentatious and unpretentious establishment with a singularly friendly atmosphere.

Access : 3km northbound from Bar-sur-Seine on the N 71

Access : To the north-east of Troyes, drive 25km on the D 960, then at Piney take the D11

 5 FERME DE LA GLOIRE DIEU
M. Ruelle

 10250 Courteron
Tel. 03 25 38 20 67
Fax 03 25 38 21 78

Closed in Jan • 3 rooms • €36, breakfast included • Park, terrace, car park. Credit cards not accepted

 6 LE PRIEURÉ
M. et Mme Berthelin

 1 place de l'Église
 10260 Fouchères
Tel. 03 25 40 98 09
Fax 03 25 40 98 09

Open all year • 5 rooms in one of the priory towers, all have bathrooms • €38 to €48, breakfast included • No table d'hôte • Garden, car park. Credit cards not accepted

 We most liked

The delicious farm-grown produce which can be tasted there and/or taken home.

The sign "Farm to the Glory of God" rather gives the game away, even before you've had a chance to glimpse the fascinating architectural remains of the 13C monastery. This immense 16C fortified farm nestles at the foot of a valley; its pretty, well-kept rooms still have their original exposed stone walls. The profusion of patés, cooked meats and poultry, fresh from the farm, will entice even the most delicate of palates. Warm, friendly and very reasonably priced.

 We most liked

Canadian-style breakfasts.

This former priory now manages a thriving farming business from the top of its haughty 11C towers and Renaissance-style wings. Patience and love were lavished on the building to restore it to its current splendid state. The substantial, quiet rooms are decorated with 18C and 19C regional furniture and two boast fireplaces typical of the region. Children are most welcome: one room can sleep up to four. The exuberant hosts, formerly residents of Quebec, make guests feel totally at home.

Access : 10km eastbound from Riceys on the D 70 then the N 71

Access : 10km to the north-west of Bar-sur-Seine on the N 71

CHAMPAGNE ARDENNE

 7 LES COLOMBAGES CHAMPENOIS
Mme Jeanne

33 rue du Haut
10270 Laubressel
Tel. 03 25 80 27 37
Fax 03 25 80 80 67

Open all year • 6 rooms with shower/WC • €40, breakfast included • No table d'hôte • Garden, car park. Credit cards not accepted, no dogs allowed • Outdoor swimming pool

 8 LA BOURSAULTIÈRE
Mme De Coninck

44 rue de la Duchesse-d'Uzès
51480 Boursault
Tel. 03 26 58 47 76
Fax 03 26 58 47 76

Open all year • 4 rooms • €58, breakfast included • No table d'hôte • Garden, car park. Credit cards not accepted

 We most liked **Gazing over the meadows stretching over the horizon.**

Although built only 10 years ago from old materials gleaned from neighbouring ruins, these two enchanting half-timbered houses look as if they've always been here. The ingenious owner has even managed to rebuild a dovecote! The stylish rooms are a tasteful mixture of old beams and modern furniture. The kitchen serves mainly farm-grown produce.

 We most liked **The mammoth breakfasts, liberally served with smiles.**

Bordered by Champagne vineyards on all sides, this attractive stone house provides enchanting rooms lined with medieval or Renaissance-style printed fabrics. The luxurious bathrooms are lightened by beautiful Italian tiles. As soon as the sun shines, you will appreciate the refreshing cool of the paved courtyard, strewn with succulent green plants. Exemplary welcome.

Access : 7km to the north-east of Lusigny-sur-Barse on the N 19 and then the D 186

Access : 9km westbound from Épernay on the N 3 and then the D 222

9 LA FAMILLE GUY CHARBAUT
M. et Mme Charbaut

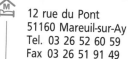

12 rue du Pont
51160 Mareuil-sur-Ay
Tel. 03 26 52 60 59
Fax 03 26 51 91 49
champagne.guy.charbaut @ wanadoo.fr
www.champagne-guy-charbaut.com

Open all year • 6 rooms with bath/WC • €65, breakfast included • Table d'hôte €40 (Mon-Sat evenings) • Car park • Visits to the family's vineyards and the wine cellars

10 LA GROSSE HAIE
M. et Mme Songy

Chemin de Saint-Pierre
51510 Matougues
Tel. 03 26 70 97 12
Fax 03 26 70 12 42

 songy.chambre @ wanadoo.fr

Closed 24 and 25 Dec • 3 non-smoking rooms upstairs • €45, breakfast included • Table d'hôte €18 to €27 (closed Sun) • Garden, park, car park. Credit cards not accepted, no dogs allowed • Farm visits

 The tour of the family estate's vineyard, cellars and grape presses.

Wine growers from father to son since 1930, the Charbauts bend over backwards to make your stay as pleasant as possible in their beautiful old house. They relish taking guests round the grape presses and cellars and introducing them to some of the best white and rosé vintage champagnes. All the airy, spacious rooms have their own sitting room and are decorated with period furniture. In the evenings, dinner is served in the superb wine cellar where the champagne, of course, flows freely!

 Breathing in the rich, evocative scents of the orchard.

A stone's throw from a farm which rears splendid Charolais cattle, this hospitable house knows how to tempt its guests into the out-of-doors. The children can romp unfettered in the orchard and the strawberries, artichokes and other cottage-garden delights are just waiting to be plucked, and, it comes as no surprise to discover, figure prominently on the menu. Pink, white and blue adorn the simply decorated rooms and the traffic on the nearby road will have almost disappeared by nightfall.

Access : In the wine estate

Access : 12km westbound from Châlons-en-Champagne on the D 3, towards Épernay

11 **CRYSTAL**
Mme Jantet

86 place Drouet-d'Erlon
51100 Reims
Tel. 03 26 88 44 44
Fax 03 26 47 49 28
hotelcrystal @ wanadoo.fr
www.hotel-crystal.fr

Closed 24 Dec lunchtime to 5 Jan morning • 31 rooms, 23 of which have shower/WC, 8 have bath/WC, all have television • €48 to €67; breakfast €8 • No restaurant • Garden

12 **GRAND HÔTEL CONTINENTAL**
M. Delvaux

93 place Drouet-d'Erlon
51100 Reims
Tel. 03 26 40 39 35
Fax 03 26 47 51 12
grand-hotel-continental @ wanadoo.fr
www.grandhotelcontinental.com

Closed from 23 Dec to 9 Jan • 50 rooms with bath/WC or shower/WC and television • €56 to €155; breakfast €11 • No restaurant • Public car park nearby • Visit to cellars and vineyards, museum pass

We most liked **The fully original lift shaft.**

This 1920s house provides a welcome and unexpected haven of greenery and calm in the heart of busy Reims, sheltered from the bustle of Place Drouet-d'Erlon by a curtain of buildings. The rooms have recently been treated to good quality furniture and new bedding and the bathrooms are spruce and practical. In the summer, breakfast is served in the charming flowered courtyard-garden.

We most liked **The sheer luxury of this Belle Époque establishment.**

The late-19C walls of the Grand Hotel Continental stand on a pedestrian square right in the heart of the town. A variety of styles can be found in the rooms, which have been renovated; those on the top floor with sloping ceilings are more modern in character. The quietest rooms overlook Boulevard du Général-Leclerc. Plush, stylish sitting room with moulded ceilings, period light fixtures and wrought-iron banisters.

Access : In the town centre near the railway station

Access : In the town centre

 13 UNIVERS
M. Bombaron

41 boulevard Foch
51100 Reims
Tel. 03 26 88 68 08
Fax 03 26 40 95 61
contact @ hotel-univers-reims.com
www.hotel-univers-reims.com

Open all year • 42 rooms, 36 of which have bath/WC, 6 have shower/WC, all have television • €75 to €82 (€68 to €74 low season); breakfast €10; half board available • Menus €16 (weekdays) to €30 • Public car park nearby

 14 CHAMBRE D'HÔTE DELONG
M. et Mme Delong

24 rue des Tilleuls
51390 Saint-Euphraise-et-Clairizet
Tel. 03 26 49 20 86
Fax 03 26 49 24 90
jdscom @ wanadoo.fr

Open all year • 4 rooms, with baths and separate WC • €56, breakfast included • No table d'hôte • Sitting room, car park. No dogs allowed • Visits to the wine cellar and press. Hiking, mountain biking

 Sipping a glass of champagne at the hotel bar.

The Art Deco origins of this corner building built in 1932 opposite Colbert Square are betrayed by a number of architectural features. Excellent soundproofing, king size beds, wifi internet access, burr walnut furniture and beautiful bathrooms: the comfortable rooms are regularly spruced up. The stylish lounge-bar is snug and cosy and the restaurant is panelled in dark wood.

 Opening a bottle of champagne after visiting the estate's cellars.

This former cowshed has stylishly been given a new lease of life in the heart of a thriving family wine business. Exposed stone walls, beams and rafters add character while good quality bedding and furniture and pleasant bathrooms add comfort to the rooms. The equally attractive breakfast room boasts brick walls and a huge country dining table. The owner, a descendant of a long line of "vignerons", happily does the honours of his cellar and grape press.

Access : Near the railway station, opposite Colbert Gardens

Access : In the heart of the village

15 AU BROCHET DU LAC
M. Gringuillard

15-17 Grande-Rue
51290 Saint-Rémy-en-Bouzemont
Tel. 03 26 72 51 06
Fax 03 26 73 06 95
info @ au-brochet-du-lac.com
www.au-brochet-du-lac.com

Closed from Christmas to New Year • 5 rooms • €42, breakfast included, half board available • Table d'hôte €17 • Sitting room, terrace, car park. No dogs allowed in restaurant • Mountain bike rental and canoeing

16 LE CHEVAL BLANC
M. et Mme Chevalier

4 rue de l'Estres
52200 Langres
Tel. 03 25 87 07 00
Fax 03 25 87 23 13
info @ hotel-langres.com
www.hotel-langres.com

Closed from 15 to 30 Nov • 22 rooms, 11 of which are in a separate wing and one has disabled access. All have bath/WC or shower/WC and television • €62 to €80; breakfast €9; half-board available • Restaurant closed Wed lunchtime; menus €24 to €69 • Garage.

Awaiting the arrival of the migratory birds over the nearby Lake Der.

This enchanting wood-framed house is the ideal spot to explore Lake Der-Chantecoq and try some of its countless leisure activities – boating, water-skiing, fishing, swimming. The house is very well-equipped and rents out mountain bikes and canoes. Pristine bedrooms are decorated with good country furnishings and wood features prominently in the red-tiled living room where a roaring fire is most welcome in winter.

A past which dates back to 834.

First an abbey, then a parish church, the White Horse became an inn during the Revolution and its walls could date from any time between the 9C to the 16C. One thing is sure though, they provide excellent natural soundproofing! The rooms in the "Diderot pavilion", a stone house opposite the main hotel, have been recently renovated and their vaulted ceilings and arches are full of character. Paintings and contemporary light fittings set the scene for the restaurant.

Access : 6km westbound from Arrigny on the D 57 and the D 58, in the centre of the village and not far from the lake

Access : In the town centre

  17 L'ORANGERIE
M. et Mme Trinquesse

Place Adrien-Guillaume
52190 Prangey
Tel. 03 25 87 54 85

Open all year • 3 rooms • €55 to €60, breakfast included
• No table d'hôte • Credit cards not accepted, no dogs
allowed

The graceful feminine touch.

Gentility and the romantic reign supreme in this
ivy-covered house, next door to the castle and church
in a pleasantly secluded village, set in Champagne's
unspoilt countryside. Charm fills the bright, cosy rooms,
one of which, decorated in shades of blue, commands
a view of the stately abode and its 12C tower. Best of
all, though, is the lady of the house's exquisite welcome.

Access : 16km southbound from Langres on the
N 74 and then the D 26

CORSICA

Corsica catches the eye like a jewel glinting in the bright Mediterranean sun. Its citadels perched up high on the island's rocky flanks will amply reward you for your perseverance and courage as you embark upon the twisting mountain roads. Enjoy spectacular views and breathe in the fragrance of wild rosemary as you slowly make your way up the rugged, maquis-covered mountains. The sudden sight of a secluded chapel, the discovery of a timeless village or an encounter with a herd of mountain sheep are just a few of the prizes that travellers to the Île de Beauté take home in their memories. Corsicans are as proud of their natural heritage as they are of their history and traditions. Years of experience have taught them how to revive the weary traveller with platters piled high with cooked meats, cheese and home-made pastries. After exploring the island's wild interior, you will probably be ready to plunge into the clear turquoise waters and recharge your solar batteries as you bask on the warm sand of a deserted bay.

- Corse-du-Sud (2A)
- Haute-Corse (2B)

 MARE E MONTI
M. et Mme Renucci

20225 Feliceto
Tel. 04 95 63 02 00
Fax 04 95 63 02 01

Closed from 1 Jan to 1 Apr and 1 Nov to 31 Dec • 16 rooms with bath/WC or shower/WC • €114 (€57 to €92 low season); breakfast €7 • No restaurant • Car park. No dogs allowed • Swimming pool

 A MARTINELLA
Mme Corteggiani

Route du Port
20245 Galéria
Tel. 04 95 62 00 44

Closed from Nov to Feb • 5 rooms on the first floor with private terraces • €52, breakfast €6 • No table d'hôte • Garden, car park. Credit cards not accepted, no dogs allowed • Beach and the Scandola Nature Reserve nearby

The sweet scent of Corsica's wild flowers wafting over the sun-drenched terrace.

Exquisitely set between sea and mountains ("mare e monti" in Corsican), this is one of the rare "American palaces" of Balagne, of which there are many more around the coast of Cap Corse. After striking it rich in sugar cane, this family's ancestors returned from Puerto Rico in the 19C to build this elegant blue-shuttered white house. Character overflows from the slightly monastic rooms offset with brass beds, red floor tiles, fireplaces, etc. Delightful little chapel and exuberant garden.

 Exploring the under-water treasures of the Nature Reserve of Scandola.

An unpretentious, excellently kept place, to which you should add the priceless location just 150m from a large pebble beach and the nature reserve of Scandola. It is easy to see why the place is so popular. The simple rooms all have their own private terrace, while the tranquillity of the garden and the owner's genuinely warm welcome all contribute to its charm.

Access : 20km southbound from Île-Rousse

Access : 150m from the beach

CORSICA

3 **FUNTANA MARINA**
M. et Mme Khaldi

Route de Monticello
20220 - L'Île-Rousse
Tel. 04 95 60 16 12
Fax 04 95 60 35 44
hotel-funtana-marina@wanadoo.fr
www.hotel-funtana.com

• 29 rooms with bath or shower • €84 to €90 (€50 to €61 low season); breakfast €9 • No restaurant • Car park. No dogs allowed • Outdoor swimming pool

4 **LI FUNDALI**
M. et Mme Gabelle-Crescioni

Spergane
20228 Luri
Tel. 04 95 35 06 15

Closed from Nov to Mar • 16 rooms • €40 to €45, breakfast included, half board available • Table d'hôte €13 • Terrace, garden, car park. Credit cards not accepted, no dogs allowed

 The site dominating the harbour of Île Rousse.

The narrow mountain lane that leads up to this recent house hidden by luxuriant vegetation is worth taking, if only to enjoy the super view of the sea and the harbour of Île Rousse. Comfortable renovated rooms all have matching bathrooms, but it's the panoramic swimming pool and your hosts' wonderful welcome that make this place so memorable.

 The owners' boundless hospitality.

This charming house, drenched in sunshine and encircled by foliage, nestles in a hollow (fundali) of the lush green valley of Luri. After trekking along the countless paths around the estate, you will happily return to a simple, yet immaculate room for a well-earned rest. Afterwards you can sit down around the large communal table and sample the delicious family recipes, under your host's attentive eye.

Access : In the upper part of Île-Rousse, 1km drive

Access : In the valley

  5 **SANTA MARIA**
M. et Mme Ettori

Place de l'Église
20113 Olmeto
Tel. 04 95 74 65 59
Fax 04 95 74 60 33
ettorinathalie @ aol.com
www.hotel-restaurant-santa-maria.com

Closed in Nov and Dec • 12 rooms with shower/WC and television • €53 to €55 (€40 to €53 low season); breakfast €6; half board available • Menus €16 (only lunchtime) to €23 • Terrace

  6 **LA CASA MUSICALE**
M. et Mme Casalonga

Fondu di u paese
20220 Pigna
Tel. 04 95 61 77 31
Fax 04 95 61 74 28
infos @ casa-musicale.org
www.casa-musicale.org

Closed from 7 Jan to 10 Feb and Mon from Nov to Mar • 7 rooms with bath/WC or shower/WC • €61 to €93 (€46 to €70 low season); breakfast €6; half-board available • À la carte €25 to €40 • No dogs allowed • Live music (Corsican polyphonic concerts)

Realising how out of place the word "stress" seems on the Island of Beauty.

This old granite house which stands opposite the church has been gazing down on the Gulf of Valinco for over a century. A steep staircase leads up to practical, well-kept rooms, rather lacking in charm however. The vaulted dining room, the only remains of an old oil mill, is pleasant enough, but the highlight of the establishment has got to be the wonderful flowered terrace where you can sample Mimi's delicious cooking.

The "Terza" room with its tiny sun terrace reached by a ladder!

Keep it under your hat! This priceless gem can only be reached on foot through the lanes of its delightful high-perched village laden with the scent of bougainvillaea. The frescoes on the walls of the rooms are a work of art in themselves and all overlook the sea or Corsica's mountainous slopes. The restaurant can be found in a converted olive oil press and the idyllic terrace and concert room are regularly the scene of lively traditional Corsican musical evenings.

Access : In the centre of the village, 8km northbound from Propriano on the N 196

Access : Drive from Île-Rousse towards Calvi on the N 197, after 2km turn left onto the D 151 (8km); park on the square (pedestrian village)

7 **A TRAMULA**
M. Giovanetti

20259 Pioggiola
Tel. 04 95 61 93 54

Open all year • 8 rooms • €52 to €70; breakfast €7 • No restaurant • Park, car park. Credit cards not accepted

8 **PIAGGIOLA**
M. et Mme Paolini

20166 Porticcio
Tel. 04 95 24 23 79

Closed from late Jan to 15 Apr • 6 rooms • €62, breakfast included • Table d'hôte €20 • Car park. Credit cards not accepted, no dogs allowed • Swimming pool

The warm welcome from the native Corsican owner who loves to talk about his country.

The bedrooms on the first floor of this handsome stone-built house all display the same tasteful blend of salmon-coloured walls, terracotta floor tiles, new furniture and modern bathrooms. The bar and sitting room, heated by a stove and fireplace, are most welcoming. Pull on your walking boots and hike round the grounds on the slopes of the mountainside. The honey, lavishly served at breakfast time, is made by the owner himself.

The convenient location just a few minutes from the island's most beautiful beaches.

A warm welcome, innate sense of hospitality and tasty home-cooking are just a few of the many attractions of this neat granite house cradled in the heart of superb grounds. Admire the sweeping view of the Gulf of Valinco or the forest from the windows. The rooms are furnished with fine wardrobes. If you can tear yourself away from the beach, venture out into the grounds which are rich in surprises.

Access : 1.9km westbound from Olmi-Cappella towards Tartagine forest

Access : 13km to the south-east of Agosta beach on the D 255A (towards Pietrosella), then right on the D 255

 9 CHÂTEAU CAGNINACCI
Famille Cagninacci

20200 San-Martino-di-Lota
Tel. 06 78 29 03 94
Fax 06 76 43 01 44

Closed from 1 Oct to 14 May • 4 rooms overlooking the island of Elba • €79 to €83 (€70 to €73 low season), breakfast included • No table d'hôte • Terrace. Credit cards not accepted, no dogs allowed

 10 LA CORNICHE
M. Anziani

20200 San-Martino-di-Lota
Tel. 04 95 31 40 98
Fax 04 95 32 37 69
info @ hotel-lacorniche.com
www.hotel-lacorniche.com

Closed in Jan • 19 rooms with bath/WC and television • €69 to €99 (€50 to €62 low season); breakfast €8; half board available • Restaurant closed Mon and Tue lunchtime; menus €25 to €46 • Terrace, car park • Outdoor swimming pool

 **The utter peace and quiet of this spot hidden in greenery.**

This lovely 17C Capuchin convent, remodelled in the 19C style of a Tuscan villa, is built on a steep mountain hillside. Tastefully renovated, it offers spacious rooms furnished with antiques, and immaculate bathrooms. Wherever you look, you are met with the superb view of the island of Elba and the sea. Taking breakfast on the terrace surrounded by greenery and warmed by the sun's first rays is a moment of sheer bliss.

The swimming pool on the flanks of the mountain, sheltered by a chestnut grove.

The shaded terrace of this establishment perched up high above Bastia is a feast for the eyes. Look out and savour the view of the two-storey bell tower and the houses of the old village cut into the rock face in sharp contrast with the deep blue water stretching out in the background. The practical rooms are gradually being individualised with terracotta tiles and hand-painted walls; they too command a view of the sea. The restaurant is known and appreciated for its excellent Corsican menu.

Access : 10km to the north-west of Bastia on the D 80 (towards Cap Corse), then the D 131 at Pietranera

Access : 13km northbound from Bastia on the D 80, then turn left on the D 131

  11 DOMAINE DE CROCCANO
M. et Mme Perrier

Route de Granace
20100 Sartène
Tel. 04 95 77 11 37
christian.perrier @ wanadoo.fr
www.corsenature.com

Closed in Dec • 4 non-smoking rooms • €72 (€60 low season), breakfast included, half board available • Restaurant for half board guests only • Terrace, park, car park. No dogs allowed • Horse-riding on the estate

12 A SPELUNCA
Mme Princivalle

Place de l'Église
20226 Speloncato
Tel. 04 95 61 50 38
Fax 04 95 61 53 14
hotel.a.spelunca @ wanadoo.fr

Closed from 1 Nov to 31 Mar • 17 rooms • €60 to €70 (€50 to €60 low season); breakfast €6 • No restaurant • Terrace

 We most liked **Waking up to the sight of horses cantering through the maquis.**

Travellers in search of nature, silence and peace and quiet will fall in love with this solid granite house peeping out from behind a wilderness of cork oaks and olive trees. Beautiful old stone walls and terracotta floor tiles add style to the snug, cosy rooms. The simply adorable owners will share their love of horses with you as they take you out riding round the Corsican shrub permeated by the scent of wild rosemary.

We most liked **The sweeping view of the region of upper Balagne.**

The stately architectural masterpiece you see before you is none other than the former palace of Cardinal Savelli, Minister of Police to Pope Pius IX. The vast halls, sitting rooms rich in period furniture, old light fixtures and turret still remain from its glorious past. The discreetly luxurious bedrooms are bathed in an aura of gentility; three command an enchanting view of the valley and village. Highly recommended.

Access : 3.5km to the north-east of Sartène on the D 148

Access : In the heart of the village

13 **L'AIGLON**
M. Quilichini

20124 Zonza
Tel. 04 95 78 67 79
Fax 04 95 78 63 62
info @ aiglonhotel.com
www.aiglonhotel.com

Closed Mon out of season • 10 rooms • €51 to €70;
breakfast €7; half board available • Menus €15.50 to €25
• Terrace, car park

The regularly organised Corsican musical evenings.

This venerable granite house standing in the heart of
the village has committed itself to upholding the soul
of Corsica. Much love and time has been poured into
the stylish interior decoration where collections of old
objects such as coffee grinders and irons are proudly
displayed. Each of the small but delightful rooms is
decorated in a different colour and two have sloping
ceilings. The restaurant takes you on a gastronomic tour
of Corsica's many local specialities.

Access : In the heart of the village

FRANCHE-COMTÉ

Once upon a time in a land called Franche-Comté... So begin many of France's tales and legends, inspired by the secret wilderness of this secluded region on the Swiss border. The Jura's peaks and dales are clad in a dark cloak of fragrant conifers, casting its magic charm over unwitting explorers of the range's grottoes and gorges. The spell is also woven by a multitude of torrents, waterfalls and deep, mysterious lakes, their dark blue waters reflecting the surrounding hills. The nimble fingers of local woodworkers transform its wood into clocks, toys and pipes which will delight anyone with a love of fine craftsmanship. Hungry travellers will be only too happy to give in to temptation and savour the rich hazelnut tang of Comté cheese, made to a recipe passed down through the generations. But beware, the delicate aroma of smoked and salted meats, in which you can almost taste the pine and juniper, together with the tempting bouquet of the region's subtle, fruity wines may well lure you back for more.

- Doubs (25)
- Jura (39)
- Haute-Saône (70)
- Ter.-de-Belfort (90)

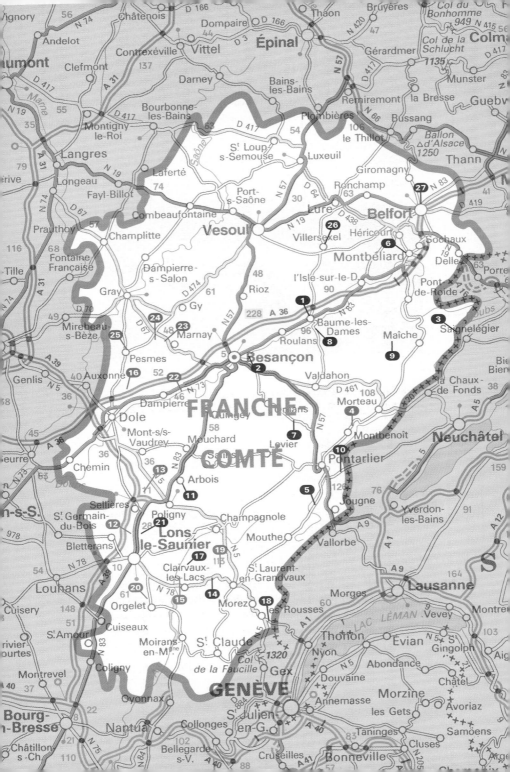

 HOSTELLERIE DU CHÂTEAU D'AS
MM. Patrick et Laurent Cachot

24 rue du Château-Gaillard
25110 Baume-les-Dames
Tel. 03 81 84 00 66
Fax 03 81 84 39 67
chateau.das @ wanadoo.fr
www.château-das.fr

Closed from 24 Jan to 7 Feb, from 21 Nov to 4 Dec, Sun evening and Mon • 6 rooms with bath/WC or shower/WC and television • €54 to €71; breakfast €9; half board available • Menus €19 to €68 • Terrace, car park

 A L'HÔTEL DES TROIS ÎLES
M. Thierry

1 rue des vergers
25220 Chalezeule
Tel. 03 81 61 00 66
Fax 03 81 61 73 09
hotel.3iles @ wanadoo.fr
www.hoteldes3iles.com

Closed from 26 Dec to 6 Jan • 17 rooms, all with bath/WC or shower/WC and television • €46 to €63; breakfast €7; half board available • Menus €16 (evenings) • Terrace, car park, no dogs allowed in the restaurant

You either love or hate the local cheese speciality: Cancoillotte!

This comfortable house, which would blend in perfectly in any number of German or Swiss towns, was built on the heights of this little town in the 1930s. The light, airy and well-equipped rooms have recently been treated to a facelift. The dining room has however retained the grandeur of its bygone days with original light fixtures and grandfather clock. Classic cuisine.

The tranquillity of this village nestling on the right bank of the Doubs.

Guests inevitably fall in love with the peaceful, pastoral setting of this large house with its steep roofline. The rooms are not really spacious but are well renovated and adorned with pleasantly rustic looking furniture. In the kitchen, the chef rustles up a new set menu every day solely for the benefit of his hotel guests. The dining room is equally appealing with its large bay windows, massive pine beams and gaily coloured tablecloths.

Access : In the upper part of town, on the outskirts

Access : 4km north-east of Besançon, in the heart of the village

3 **TAILLARD**
M. Taillard

3 route de la Corniche
25470 Goumois
Tel. 03 81 44 20 75
Fax 03 81 44 26 15
hotel.taillard@wanadoo.fr
www.hoteltaillard.com

Open from Apr to Oct • 21 rooms, 1 with disabled access, all have bath/WC or shower/WC and television • €58 to €85, breakfast €10, half board available • Restaurant closed Wed except evening from Apr to Sep and Mon lunchtime out of season; menus €28.50 to €52 • Terrace, garden, car park • Reading room, open-air swimming pool, fitness room

 An enchanting traditional hostelry nestled in greenery.

The Taillard family has been perfecting the art of hospitality since 1874 within the walls of this lovely hotel overlooking the Doubs Valley. The rooms in the annex, larger and more comfortable, are often preferred to those in the main wing which are due for a spot of sprucing up. In the predominantly warm wood finishings of the restaurant, classical dishes are spiced up with regional accents and accompanied by a fine wine list. Look out for the paintings by the master of the house.

4 **LE CRÊT L'AGNEAU**
M. et Mme Jacquet-Pierroulet

Les auberges
25650 La Longeville
Tel. 03 81 38 12 51
lecret.lagneau@wanadoo.fr
www.lecret-lagneau.com

Closed from 1 to 31 Jul • 7 rooms • €72 to €84, breakfast included • Table d'hôte €21 to €23 • Car park. Credit cards not accepted, no dogs allowed • From Christmas to late March snowshoe trekking and cross-country skiing possible

The countless excursions organised by the owner, a cross-country ski instructor.

This superb 17C farmhouse, tucked away between fir trees and meadows has been offering accommodation and sustenance to all those "in the know" for over twenty years. Wood prevails in the cosy bedrooms. However the main reason for its lasting success is two-fold: first the generous helpings of locally-sourced food cooked by the lady of the house, and second the variety of outings on foot, mountain bikes, snowshoes or skis organised by the owner.

Access : Overlooking the village

Access : 5.5km northbound from Montbenoît on the D 131, until you reach La Longeville-Auberge

5 LE BON ACCUEIL
M. et Mme Faivre

Rue de la Source
25160 Malbuisson
Tel. 03 81 69 30 58
Fax 03 81 69 37 60
lebonaccueilfaivre@wanadoo.fr

Closed 11 to 19 Apr, 24 Oct to 2 Nov, 12 Dec to 11 Jan and Sun evening, Mon and Tue lunchtime • 12 rooms, most of which have shower/WC, some have bath/WC, all have television • €45 to €70; breakfast €8; half board available • Menus €26 to €46 • Garden, garage, car park. No dogs allowed

6 LA BALANCE
M. et Mme Receveur

40 rue de Belfort
25200 Montbéliard
Tel. 03 81 96 77 41
Fax 03 81 91 47 16
hotelbalance@wanadoo.fr
www.hotel-la-balance.com

Closed at Christmas • 44 rooms with bath/WC and television; 2 rooms have disabled access and 5 are non-smoking • €75 to €100; breakfast €9; half board available • Menus €14 to €22 • Terrace, private car park

 The breakfast table laden with brioche, jams, home-made yoghurt and fresh fruit juice.

On the edge of a forest of fir trees, this manicured, hospitable village inn is the sort of place you want to tell your friends about. Immaculate, modern, spacious rooms. Beautiful spruce wood rafters, brightly coloured blinds and large windows overlooking the forest set the scene for the recently extended dining room. The cherry on the cake is without doubt the deliciously inventive cooking.

 The Peugeot Adventure Museum.

At the foot of the castle, this 16C abode was the HQ of one of France's best-known Second World War generals, Marshal De Lattre de Tassigny. A beautiful old wooden staircase leads up to renovated, practical rooms of varying sizes. The warm old-fashioned style and light-wood panelling of the dining room is still visible. We loved the veranda where breakfast is served.

Access : In the village, on a bend by the side of the road

Access : In the main shopping street, at the foot of the castle

 7 **LA CASCADE**
M. et Mme Savonet

4 route des Gorges-de-Noailles
25920 Mouthier-Haute-Pierre
Tel. 03 81 60 95 30
Fax 03 81 60 94 55
hotellacascade@wanadoo.fr

Closed from 1 Jan to 13 Mar • 19 rooms, one of which
has disabled access, most have bath/WC, some have
shower/WC, all have television • €49 to €63; breakfast
€8; half board available • Restaurant non-smoking only;
menus €20 to €43 • Car park. No dogs allowed • Trout
fishing and canoeing on the Loue

 8 **L'AUBERGE DES MOULINS**
M. et Mme Porru

Route de Pontarlier
25110 Pont-les-Moulins
Tel. 03 81 84 09 99
Fax 03 81 84 04 44
auberge.desmoulins@wanadoo.fr

Closed from 22 Dec to 20 Jan, Fri, Sat lunchtime and Sun
evenings from Sep to Jun (except holidays) • 14 rooms
with bath/WC or shower/WC, all have television • €50;
breakfast €7; half board available • Menus €17 (weekdays) to €20 • Park, car park • Private fishing

 **Canoeing down the beautiful gorges
of the River Loue.**

The valley of the Loue is what you will see when you
throw open the windows of the recently spruced-up
rooms of this traditional old hostelry. Excellent family
cooking is served in a non-smoking atmosphere, while
huge bay windows provide guests with a restful view
of the green landscape.

**The wealth of magnificent natural
sites: grottoes, nature reserves and
unforgettable views.**

Jura is renowned for its excellent trout and this place
is bound to appeal to those bitten by the fishing bug:
the country house stands in a park which boasts its very
own private stream. Back at the hotel, relax in rooms
of varying sizes and styles and dream of the one that
got away. A cosy restaurant serves tasty regional dishes.

Access : On the main road, in the centre of the
village

Access : Southbound from Baume-les-Dames, drive
for 6km on the D 50

 9 LE MOULIN
M. et Mme Malavaux

Le Moulin du Milieu
Route de Consolation
25380 Vaucluse
Tel. 03 81 44 35 18

Closed from 15 Oct to 1 Mar and Wed • 6 rooms, all have bath/WC or shower/WC and television • €42 to €65; breakfast €7; half board available • Menus €18 to €30 • Garden, car park. No dogs allowed in restaurant • Private fishing

 10 AUBERGE LE TILLAU
M. Parent

Le Mont-des-Verrières
25300 Verrières-de-Joux
Tel. 03 81 69 46 72
Fax 03 81 69 49 20
luc.parent@wanadoo.fr
 www.letillau.com

Closed from 15 Nov to 15 Dec, April school holidays, Sun evening and Mon • 11 rooms • €38 to €52; breakfast €7; half board available • Menus €14 to €34 • Sitting room, terrace • Sauna, games room, hiking and mountain biking

The spectacular natural site of the Cirque de Consolation.

This unusual 1930s villa, complete with turret and a colonnaded terrace, was built by a miller from the valley. Subsequent owners have lovingly preserved the superb Art Deco decoration – including a Le Corbusier chaise longue in the hall which would be the envy of any collector. The windows of the dining room open onto a shaded garden which leads down to the banks of the Dessoubre.

Toast your toes in front of a roaring log fire after a day in the open air.

This enchanting mountain inn, 1 200m up, is ideal to clear your lungs of urban pollution as you breathe in the crisp, fresh scent of meadows and fir trees. The rooms are appealingly decorated in a Jura mountain spirit and you can relax in the reading room or soothe your muscles in the sauna. The mountain air is guaranteed to work up a healthy appetite for the profusion of local delicacies, including cooked meats and cheeses, sometimes accompanied by more eclectic creations.

Access : From Montbéliard leave the D 437 at St-Hippolyte, take the D 39 and at Pont Neuf turn left towards Consolation

Access : 7km eastbound from La Cluse-et-Mijoux on the D 67bis and a minor road

ARBOIS - 39600

ARLAY - 39140

 11 MESSAGERIES
M. et Mme Ricoux

 2 rue de Courcelles
39600 Arbois
Tel. 03 84 66 15 45
Fax 03 84 37 41 09
hotel.lesmessageries@wanadoo.fr
 www.hoteldesmessageries.com

Closed in Dec, Jan and Wed (low season from 11am to 5pm) • 26 rooms with bath or shower, 8 do not have WC in the room, most have television • €30 to €59; breakfast €7 • No restaurant • Arbois wine tasting and the Pasteur museum nearby

  12 LE JARDIN DE MISETTE
M. et Mme Petit

Rue Honoré-Chapuis
39140 Arlay
Tel. 03 84 85 15 72
jardindemisette@aol.com

Open all year • 4 rooms with shower and separate WC • €45, breakfast included • Table d'hôte €20 (including wine) (except Sun) • Landscaped garden. Credit cards not accepted • Bread oven, regional library

 Tasting the local vintages in the numerous wine cellars dotted round the village.

Wine lovers should make a point of stopping at Arbois, highlight of Jura's vineyards, a delightful village off the beaten track simply bursting with treasures. This former ivy-covered coaching inn offers modest comfort, at equally modest prices, which is all the more appreciated if you are there during the Biou procession, a traditional "grape parade" that takes place in early September. Book one of the rooms at the back which have bathrooms.

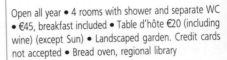 **The delicious meals prepared by the gourmet couple.**

A wine-grower's home on the banks of the Seille. The rooms are comfortable, well decorated and, above all, as quiet as the river itself. The "Chabotte" room in the little house at the end of the garden has the most character. A piano, fireplace and well-lined bookshelves will make you want to linger in the sitting room, particularly if the owner, a very decent singer and musician, steps in and plays a few notes on his accordion.

Access : In the town centre

Access : 12km westbound from Château-Chalon on the D 5 until Voiteur, then the D 120, in the heart of the village

13 LA FERME DU CHÂTEAU
Association E. de Villeneuve-Bargemont

Rue de la Poste
39800 Bersaillin
Tel. 03 84 25 91 31
Fax 03 84 25 93 62

Closed in Jan • 9 rooms, one of which has disabled access • €58 to €60, breakfast €8 • No table d'hôte • Car park • Painting exhibitions, concerts in the summer

14 L'ALPAGE
M. Lerch

1 chemin de la Madone
39130 Bonlieu
Tel. 03 84 25 57 53
Fax 03 84 25 50 74
reservation @ alpage-hotel.com
www.alpage-hotel.com

Closed from 15 Nov to 15 Dec, Mon and Tue lunchtime except during the school holidays • 9 rooms • €53 to €60; breakfast €8; half board available • Menus €22 (weekdays) to €35 • Terrace, car park. No dogs allowed in rooms

Just two minutes from Jura's vineyards and the "Route du Comté".

Many of the original features of this admirably restored 18C farmhouse have been preserved, including the wonderful vaults and columns of the main chamber, where exhibitions and concerts are held in the summer. The sober, yet elegant bedrooms command a view of the countryside and one has been specially equipped for disabled guests. Guests also have the use of a well-equipped kitchen.

The sweeping view over the entire valley of lakes.

A narrow road winds up to this delightful chalet built in the upper reaches of Bonlieu. The valley of lakes and its wooded hillsides are visible from almost all the comfortable bedrooms. Plants and immense bay windows bathe the dining room in dappled light and the sheltered terrace also commands the same sweeping view. Tasty local dishes.

Access : 9km westbound from Poligny on the N 83 and then the D 22

Access : On the N 78 drive towards Saint-Laurent-en-Grandvaux

15 CHAMBRE D'HÔTE MME DEVENAT
Mme Devenat

17 rue du Vieux-Lavoir
39130 Charezier
Tel. 03 84 48 35 79

Open all year • 4 rooms • €35, breakfast included; half board available • Table d'hôte €10 (evenings only from Mon to Sat) • Garden, car park. Credit cards not accepted, no dogs admitted in restaurant

16 À LA THUILERIE DES FONTAINES
M. et Mme Meunier

2 rue des Fontaines
39700 Châtenois
Tel. 03 84 70 51 79
Fax 03 84 70 57 79
michel.meunier2@wanadoo.fr

Open all year • 4 rooms • €40, breakfast included • No table d'hôte • Terrace, park, car park. Credit cards not accepted, no dogs allowed • Outdoor swimming pool

 **The wide range of regional delicacies on offer.**

Guests immediately feel at home in this large, welcoming family house cradled in a tiny village halfway between Clairvaux les Lacs and Lake Chalain. The rooms in the little house near the thicket are more independent and a handsome wooden staircase leads up to the others in the main house. The memory of the delicious local specialities, a different one each day, will have you planning your return trip the moment you arrive home.

 Pick your owners' brains about their beloved region.

Hospitality and attention to detail are the hallmarks of this 18C country house located between the extensive Serre forest and the lower Doubs valley. A flight of stone stairs leads up to well-cared for, very "comfy" and totally peaceful rooms. Stroll round the attractive park or laze on the deck chairs round the swimming pool near the old stables.

Access : 13km to the south-west of Lake Chalain on the D 27

Access : 7.5km to the north-east of Dole on the N 73 towards Besançon, then take the D 10 and the D 79 to Châtenois

17 LE COMTOIS
M. Menozzi

806 route des 3 lacs
39130 Doucier
Tel. 03 84 25 71 21
Fax 03 84 25 71 21

 restaurant.comtois@wanadoo.fr

Closed from 19 Dec to 13 Feb, Tue evening, Wed and Sun evening • 8 rooms with showers, some have WC • €40 to €50, breakfast included; half board available • Menus €19 to €58 • Terrace

18 ARBEZ FRANCO-SUISSE
M. Arbez

La Cure
39220 Les Rousses
Tel. 03 84 60 02 20
Fax 03 84 60 08 59
hotelarbez@netgde.com
www.hotelarbez.fr.st

Open all year • 10 rooms, half are in France and half are in Switzerland. Rooms have bath/WC or shower/WC, all have television • €55 to €59 (€55 low season); breakfast €7; half board available • Menus €13 to €35 • Car park. No dogs allowed in restaurant

 The wonderful footpath to Hérisson Falls just a few kilometres away.

Le Comtois offers an ideal introduction to this fascinating region. The heart of a remote Jura village is home to this spruce auberge offering a few rooms and above all a menu worthy of the most demanding traveller. A warm neo-rustic setting provides the backdrop to delicious recipes with a modern slant prepared with a strong focus on local products. The owner, who is also President of Jura's Association of Wine Waiters, will wax lyrical about wine and food for as long as you'll listen...

Testing your balance on the "commando course" at nearby Fort Rousses!

Make sure you take your passport when you go to the bathroom and also remember to decide which half of you will sleep in Switzerland and which in France! This Swiss-French inn, quite literally on the border, offers modern rooms lined in pine and has a choice of classic restaurant fare or quick brasserie snacks and dishes, all within easy reach of alpine ski slopes, cross-country ski trails, snowshoe paths and Rousses Lake. Is there anything else to declare?

Access : In the centre of the village, opposite the post office

Access : On the Swiss border, to the south-east of Rousses, drive 2.5km on the N 5 (towards Geneva)

19   LES CINQ LACS
M. et Mme Colombato

66 route des Lacs
39130 Le Frasnois
Tel. 03 84 25 51 32
Fax 03 84 25 51 32
pcolomba @ club-internet.fr
http://auberge.5.lacs.free.fr

Open all year (by reservation) • 5 non-smoking rooms, one of which has disabled access. 2 chalets have been converted into gîtes • €48, breakfast included; half board available • Table d'hôte €16 • Terrace. Credit cards not accepted, no dogs allowed • Excursions around the lakes

 The owners' useful tips about the area.

Hikers have held this old Jura farmstead in great esteem ever since it opened; it nestles in the heart of a lush green landscape of lakes, waterfalls and forest. The comfortable rooms were individually decorated by the lady of the house and each is named after one of the region's innumerable lakes. Don't miss the opportunity to taste the many local specialities on the dining table, served before a roaring fire in winter or on the sheltered terrace in the summer.

Access : 3.5km northbound from Illay on the D 75

20   LA BARATTE
M. et Mme Chalet

39270 Présilly
Tel. 03 84 35 55 18
Fax 03 84 25 43 49
labaratte @ free.fr
www.labaratte.fr

Open all year • 4 rooms • €52, breakfast included, half board available • Table d'hôte €19 • Car park. Credit cards not accepted, no dogs allowed

 The happy marriage of modern comfort and rustic charm.

This village house stands within a stone's throw of the impressive dam of Vouglans. The imaginative restoration has endowed it with all the modern comforts whilst preserving numerous traces of its old age, such as the fine flagstone floor in the dining room where you will savour tasty local dishes. The rustic flavour of the bedrooms contrasts admirably with a few modern touches. Stabling for horses.

Access : 5km northbound from Orgelet on the D 52 then the D 175

21   HOSTELLERIE SAINT-GERMAIN
M. et Mme Bertin

39210 Saint-Germain-les-Arlay
Tel. 03 84 44 60 91
Fax 03 84 44 63 64

Open all year • 8 rooms, most have bath/WC, some have shower/WC, all have television • €50 to €70; breakfast €6; half board available • Menus €18 to €34 • Terrace, car park

22   LE CHÂTEAU DE SALANS
M. Guillemin

39700 Salans
Tel. 03 84 71 16 55
Fax 03 84 79 41 54

Open all year • 4 rooms with bathrooms • €95, breakfast included • No table d'hôte • Park, car park. Credit cards not accepted, no dogs allowed

 The mouth-watering "pâté en croute" – a sort of pork pie!

Should you want to find out more about this region's rich store of traditions and legends, the Hostellerie St Germain, right in the heart of Jura's vineyards, is the ideal place to start. A refreshing night's sleep in the spotless rooms will leave you eager to begin exploring, and after a hard day's touring, you will be able to tuck into the delicious traditional recipes served in one of three vaulted dining rooms, complete with exposed beams and stonework.

 Throwing open the shutters of your bedroom onto acres of parkland.

This magnificent 17C château was built in the midst of 7 acres of parkland. Its peaceful, beautiful setting was greatly appreciated by famous figures, such as Charles Nodier and Montalembert. Modern-day visitors will find it more comfortable than did their predecessors, but the aristocratic soul of the castle can still be felt in the lovely ground-floor sitting rooms and in the bedrooms, furnished in Louis XVI and Directoire style and with lovely red-and-white tiled bathrooms.

Access : At the crossroads in the centre of the village, opposite the church

Access : 5km northbound of Courtefontaine on a minor road

23 CHAMBRE D'HÔTE LES ÉGRIGNES
Mme Lego-Deiber

Le Château - Route d'Hugier
70150 Cult
Tel. 03 84 31 92 06
Fax 03 84 31 92 06
lesegrignes@wanadoo.fr
www.les-egrignes.com

Open all year • 3 non-smoking rooms, all with bath/WC • €70, breakfast included • Table d'hôte €25 (evening only by reservation) • Sitting room, park, car park. Credit cards not accepted, no dogs allowed

24 LES PÉTUNIAS
M. et Mme Knab

70150 Hugier

  Tel. 03 84 31 58 30

Closed Dec and Jan • 4 rooms • €40 to €45, breakfast included • No table d'hôte • Terrace, car park. Credit cards not accepted, no dogs allowed

 Forget about your diet and do justice to the lady of the house's delicious cooking.

This 19C mansion stands proudly in grounds lined with trees and flowers. A tasteful, well-thought out interior restoration has enhanced the original moulded ceilings, stucco work, staircase and trompe-l'oeil marble. Louis-Philippe, Directoire and Napoleon III furniture graces the elegant rooms all of which enjoy the same pastoral view. In the dining room, note the lovely old porcelain stove which dates from 1805.

 Sipping a glass of Alsatian wine in the charming company of your hosts.

This impressive 18C farmstead, hidden by Virginia creeper, lies in the lower valley of the River Ognon, renowned for its fishing, canoeing and kayaking. The establishment's name betrays the current owners' lifelong passion for gardening. Family heirlooms adorn the comfortable, well-kept rooms. A pleasant swimming pool, a veranda strewn with plants and games and a barbecue in the garden will ensure that your stay is full of fun.

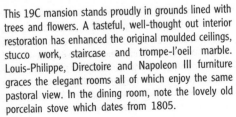

Access : 4 km to the north-east of Marnay

Access : 7km to the north-west of Marnay on the D 67, then the D 228, on the way out of the village

 25 LA MAISON ROYALE
M. Hoyet

70140 Pesmes
Tel. 03 84 31 23 23
Fax 03 84 31 23 23

Closed from 15 Oct to 15 Mar • 7 rooms • €65 to €70, breakfast included • No table d'hôte • Garden, car park. Credit cards not accepted, no dogs allowed • Library, billiards, organ, art exhibitions and cultural events

26 LA TERRASSE
Mme Routhier

Route de Lure
70110 Villersexel
Tel. 03 84 20 52 11
 Fax 03 84 20 56 90

Closed from 18 Dec to 2 Jan, Sun and Fri evenings out of season • 13 rooms with bath/WC or shower/WC, all have television • €40 to €49; breakfast €6; half board available • Menus €12 to €28 • Terrace, garden, car park • Bicycle rentals, table tennis, boules

Living like royalty without blowing the family fortune!

The quality of the restoration and the sheer beauty of this superb 15C stronghold always draw gasps of admiration. The hospitable owners have filled this aptly named establishment with objects from their countless trips around the world. Most of the highly individualised rooms enjoy an exceptional view over the village rooftops and the countryside. Relax in style with a game of billiards, play a few notes on the organ and if the weather is fine, take time to enjoy the pretty flowered garden.

The old sand quarries now filled with water and the venue for many water sports.

Anglers hold this country inn on the banks of the Ognon, a stream renowned for its fishing, in high esteem. The rooms of varying sizes have recently been treated to a facelift, as has the dining room overlooking the garden. In the summer the dense foliage of the huge trees clothes the terrace in a welcome cool shade. Relaxing and restful.

Access : In the town centre, near a service station

Access : On leaving the village drive towards Lure

27 **VAUBAN**

M. Lorange

4 rue du Magasin
90000 Belfort
Tel. 03 84 21 59 37
Fax 03 84 21 41 67
hotel.vauban @ wanadoo.fr
www–hotel–vauban.com

Closed from Christmas to New Year, February holidays
and Sun • 14 rooms with bath/WC or shower/WC, all
have television • €69 to €73; breakfast €8 • No
restaurant • Garden. No dogs allowed

The easy-going family atmosphere.

You will feel more like a friend of the family than a
paying guest behind the colourful façade of this inviting
hotel where hundreds of paintings by the owner and his
artist friends adorn the walls. The rooms, gradually
being renovated, are pretty and well soundproofed; ask
for one in the rear from which you will enjoy a view
of the pretty flowered garden stretching down to the
banks of the Savoureuse.

Access : Near the tourist office, on the street
running alongside the Savoureuse

ILE-DE-FRANCE AND PARIS

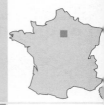

Historic Paris, the City of Light, is the first name to spring to mind at the mention of the île de France. The slender outline of the Eiffel Tower dominates France's chic and cosmopolitan capital, where former royal palaces are brazenly adorned with glass pyramids, railway stations become museums and close-set alleyways of bohemian houses lead off broad, plane-planted boulevards. Paris is a never-ending kaleidoscope of contrasts: the sleepy village side street decked in flowers and the bustle of the big department stores; the artists' studios of Montmartre and the crowded cafés where screen celebrities sit side by side with star-struck fans; a view of Paris by night from a bateau-mouche and the whirlwind glitz of a cabaret. But the fertile land along the Seine is not content to stay in the shadows of France's illustrious first city; the region is also home to secluded châteaux set in formal gardens, the magic of Disneyland and the turn-of-the-century gaiety of the summer cafés along the banks of the Marne. And who could forget the sheer splendour of Versailles, home to the 'most beautiful palace in the world'?

- Seine (Paris) (75)
- Seine-et-Marne (77)
- Yvelines (78)
- Essonne (91)
- Hauts-de-Seine (92)
- Seine-Saint-Denis (93)
- Val-de-Marne (94)
- Val-d'Oise (95)

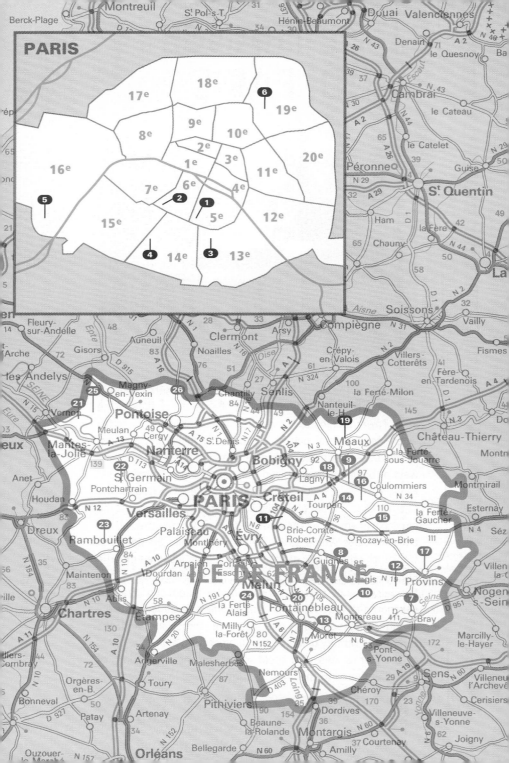

 1 PIERRE NICOLE
M. Dayot

39 rue Pierre-Nicole
75005 Paris
Tel. 01 43 54 76 86
Fax 01 43 54 22 45
hotelpierre-nicole @ voila.fr

Open all year • 33 rooms, most have bath/WC or shower/WC, all have television • €70 to €90; breakfast €6 • No restaurant • No dogs allowed

 2 SÈVRES-AZUR
M. Baguès

22 rue de l'Abbé-Grégoire
75006 Paris
Tel. 01 45 48 84 07
Fax 01 42 84 01 55
sevres.azur @ wanadoo.fr
www.sevres-azur.com

Open all year • 31 rooms with bath/WC or shower/WC and television • €80 to €120; breakfast €8 • No restaurant

 We most liked
Ambling round the deliciously romantic Jardin de Luxembourg.

This hotel, in a handsome Haussmann building, pays homage to a controversial 17C theologian of Paris's Port-Royal Abbey. Many more recent celebrities, such as novelist Gabriel García Márquez and Patrick Modiano have stayed in these compact, practical and well-kept rooms, which maybe lack a little Parisian chic. The comparative calm of this side street, close to the busy restaurants of the Boulevard Montparnasse, should ensure a good night's sleep.

 We most liked
The unusual chapel of the Miraculous Medal on Rue du Bac.

A 19C stone building near the smart Bon Marché department store: well-soundproofed rooms, some of which have brass beds, are decked out with colourful fabrics. Plants adorn the light breakfast room. The preferential rates in the nearby car park for hotel guests are a definite bonus.

Access : Coming from Bd du Montparnasse, continue onto Bd de Port-Royal and take the third street on the left

Access : Go up Rue de Vaugirard and take the second left past Bd du Montparnasse

3 RESIDENCE VERT GALANT
M. et Mme Laborde

43 rue Croulebarbe
75013 Paris
Tel. 01 44 08 83 50
Fax 01 44 08 83 69

Open all year • 15 rooms, 11 of which have bath/WC,
4 have shower/WC, all have television • €90; breakfast
€7 • Menus €18 to €30 • No dogs allowed in rooms

4 APOLLON MONTPARNASSE
M. Prigent

91 rue de l'Ouest
75014 Paris
Tel. 01 43 95 62 00
Fax 01 43 95 62 10
apollonm @ wanadoo.fr
www.apollon-montparnasse.com

Open all year • 33 rooms, 22 of which have shower/WC,
11 have bath/WC, all have television • €79 to €89;
breakfast €7 • No restaurant • Nearby car park • Near
Montparnasse railway station and close to bars and
cinemas

 **The village ambience, just two
minutes from the Place d'Italie.**

This hotel in the Gobelins area is welcome proof that
it is still possible to find quiet accommodation in the
heart of Paris at a reasonable price. All the functional,
neatly kept rooms are sheltered by a restful curtain of
greenery. Depending on the weather, breakfast is served
in the small garden lined by vines or in a winter-garden
dining room. The owners of the Vert Galant also run
the cheerful Basque restaurant next door.

 **A pleasant welcome in the heart of
Montparnasse.**

This small hotel is ideally placed for those intending to
spend a few days in the French capital, close to the
Montparnasse railway station and Air France's shuttle
buses, the Rue de la Gaîté and cinemas for evenings
out and Ricardo Bofill's amazing architectural feats. The
bedrooms, in fairness, are more practical than charming,
but look all the better for their recent makeover. Vaulted
breakfast room.

Access : From Place d'Italie, go along Avenue des
Gobelins and turn left

Access : From Place de Catalogne go along Rue du
Château and turn right

5 BOILEAU
M. Fabrice Royer

81 rue Boileau
75016 Paris
Tel. 01 42 88 83 74
Fax 01 45 27 62 98
boileau@noos.fr
www.hotel-boileau.com

Open all year • 31 rooms with bath/WC or shower/WC and television, 1 of which has disabled access • €77 to €83 (€65 to €69 low season); breakfast €8 • No restaurant

6 HOTEL LAUMIÈRE
Mme Desprat

4 rue Petit
75019 Paris
Tel. 01 42 06 10 77
Fax 01 42 06 72 50
le-laumiere@wanadoo.fr
www.hotel-lelaumiere.com

Open all year • 54 rooms with bath/WC or shower/WC and television • €51 to €69; breakfast €7 • No restaurant

 The cheerful welcome from Oscar, the hotel parrot.

Situated in a smart street of what used to be the "village of Auteuil" until 1860, a distinctly un-Parisian atmosphere continues to reign in this hotel. Paintings and ornaments picked up in antique shops relate tales from Brittany and North Africa, the owner's twin passions. The statues in alcoves and wainscoting in the lobby lend it a resolutely classical air. Ask for one of the renovated Eastern-styled rooms. Breakfast is served in a room flooded with sunlight overlooking a flowered patio.

 A (well-needed) breath of fresh air in the picturesque Buttes Chaumont Park.

This charming small hotel, run by the same family since 1931, makes up for its distance from Paris' main monuments with a whole host of other advantages: the attractive modern flavour of the renovated interior, a leafy corner where breakfast is served on sunny days and the nearby Laumière métro station. If you prefer more space and calm, book one of the rooms overlooking the cheerful garden.

Access : From Place Porte de Saint-Cloud take Rue Michel-Ange, then first right and second left

Access : From Place de Stalingrad take Av J Jaurès, turn right into Rue A Carrel, take the second on the left and the second on the right

7 LA FERME DE TOUSSACQ
Mme Colas

Hameau de Toussacq
77480 Bray-sur-Seine
Tel. 01 64 01 82 90
Fax 01 64 01 82 61
toussacq @ terre-net.fr
www.hameau-de-toussacq.com

Open all year • 5 non-smoking rooms with bathrooms
• €48, breakfast included • Table d'hôte €13 to €15 (only
by reservation) • Garden, park, car park. Credit cards not
accepted • Chapel and dovecote visits

 The country atmosphere on the banks of the Seine.

Don't be put off by the somewhat forbidding aspect of
this 17C farmhouse: you will, in any case, be sleeping
in the castle outbuildings, whose loving restoration has
taken more than 25 years. Bedrooms are simply styled
with sloping ceilings and the breakfast room is a
pleasant blend of rustic and modern. A fountain, chapel
and dovecote together with a few sheep can be seen
in the park. Appetising home cooking with a sprinkling
of home-grown produce.

Access : 20km southbound from Provins on the
Nogent-sur-Seine road (N 19), then the D 78 and the
D 411

8 LA FERME DU COUVENT
M. et Mme Legrand

Rue de la Chapelle Gauthier
77720 Bréau
Tel. 01 64 38 75 15
Fax 01 64 38 75 15
ferme.couvent @ wanadoo.fr
www.lafermeducouvent.fr

Open all year • 13 rooms • €50, breakfast included
• Table d'hôte €17 to €18 (weekdays, by reservation
only) • Garden, park. Credit cards not accepted • Tennis,
hot-air ballooning

 Flying over the Brie region in a hot-air balloon.

What better place to relax than this handsome 18C
farmhouse planted in the middle of nearly 20 acres of
parkland in the countryside. Attractive modern furniture
graces the bedrooms, freshly painted in shades of cream
with sloping ceilings. If you fancy something different,
climb aboard the experienced owners' multicoloured
hot-air balloon for a proper bird's eye view of the Brie
region.

Access : 14.5km eastbound from Vaux-le-Vicomte on
the Provins road (D 408) and then the D 227 on the
left

9 LA HÉRISSONIÈRE
M. Bordessoule et M. Besselieure

4 rue du Barrois
77580 Crécy-la-Chapelle
Tel. 01 64 63 00 72
Fax 01 64 63 09 06
laherissoniere@free.fr

Closed from 3 Jan to 28 Feb and 15 Nov to 15 Dec • 5 rooms • €60, breakfast included • Table d'hôte €20 to €35 (evenings only) • Garden. Credit cards not accepted

10 FERME DE LA RECETTE
Famille Dufour

Au hameau d'Échou
77830 Échouboulains
Tel. 01 64 31 81 09
Fax 01 64 31 89 42
fermedelarecette@aol.com
www.aubergeetfermeauberge.com

Closed during the February holidays • 7 rooms with bath/WC and television • €48, breakfast included • Table d'hôte €17 to €30 • 17C dovecote. No dogs allowed in rooms

The riverside location.

This delightful 18C manor house enjoys a wonderful position on the banks of the Morin in a pretty village, which was once home to the artist Corot. Wood panelling, old oak beams and family heirlooms are lovingly maintained. The elegant, comfortable bedrooms all overlook the river and the one with the balcony is particularly appealing. Dining under the pergola in the summer is an enchanting experience.

The farmer-owner's friendly, genuine welcome.

The origins of this farm, formerly the property of the Cistercian abbey of Preuilly, have been traced back to the 12C. It now houses cosy rooms with snug, inviting duvets. Meals are served in a dining room where stone and wood feature prominently. Remember to reserve one of the tables near the windows so that you can enjoy the view of the pond, meadows and contented grazing cows.

Access : Near the church square

Access : 11km to the north of Montereau-Fault-Yonne on the N 105 Melun road then on the D 107 at Valence-en-Brie

 11 HÔTEL DU GOLF
M. Moatti

Ferme des Hyverneaux
77150 Lésigny
Tel. 01 60 02 25 26
Fax 01 60 02 03 84
reservation @ parisgolfhotel.com
www.parisgolfhotel.com

Open all year • 48 rooms, 2 of which have disabled access, all have bath/WC and television • €65 to €95 (€65 to €85 low season); breakfast €10 • Private car park • Golf course

 12 CHAMBRE D'HÔTE M. DORMION
M. et Mme Dormion

2 rue des Glycines
77650 Lizines
Tel. 01 60 67 32 56
Fax 01 60 67 32 56

Open all year • 5 non-smoking rooms, all are in the attic with kitchenettes • €43, breakfast included • No table d'hôte • Garden, park. Credit cards not accepted

 The excellent soundproofing which masks the noise of Paris' busy outer ring road.

The remains of a 12C abbey can still be seen in this hotel, where the addition of huge skylights and glass walls add a light, modern touch. The practical rooms and timbered restaurant command a view of an 18-hole golf course of nearly 250 acres. The terrace of the clubhouse is practically on the green.

 The immaculate bedrooms.

This three-century-old building, still a working farm, has offered accommodation and sustenance to visitors for over a decade. The spotless rooms with sloping ceilings are decorated with rustic furniture and each one has its own kitchenette. An old barn has been converted into a light, airy breakfast room with an enormous bay window. Venture out of doors and admire the lawn and orchard in the garden.

Access : Drive to Lésigny on the "Francilienne" or on the A 4 (exit no 19), then head for the golf course

Access : 15km to the south-west of Provins on the N 19 and the D 209

13 CHAMBRE D'HÔTE M. GICQUEL
M. et Mme Gicquel

 46 rue René-Montgermont
77690 Montigny-sur-Loing
Tel. 01 64 45 87 92

Open all year • 2 rooms • €46, breakfast included • No table d'hôte • Credit cards not accepted

14 BELLEVUE
M. et Mme Galpin

 77610 Neufmoutiers-en-Brie
Tel. 01 64 07 11 05
Fax 01 64 07 19 27
bellevue @ fr.st
www.bellevue.fr.st

Open all year • 7 rooms, 5 of which are in a separate wing, all have bath/WC and television • €55 to €74, breakfast included • No table d'hôte • Garden, car park

 Exploring the twisting lanes of this tiny picturesque village.

A traditional paved courtyard stands in the foreground of these former stables converted into a B&B. Exposed beams and old wardrobes add character to the rooms under the eaves, all of which are wonderfully quiet. When you go down to breakfast, don't forget to look up and admire the ceiling hung with wicker baskets. Excellently situated to explore the Loing Valley.

 The elegant setting of this 19C manor house.

Don't be put off by the sight of the surrounding residential suburbia, because the garden of this fine 19C manor house commands a view of open fields which stretch as far as the eye can see. All the split-level bedrooms have a few personal touches. Two lodges with private garden and deck chairs are the most pleasant. A superb dining room with beams, old flagstones and a beautiful wood table set an elegant tone for mealtimes.

Access : 7km to the south-west of Moret-sur-Loing on the D 104

Access : 10km south of Disneyland-Paris, on the A 4 take exit no 13, the D 231 then the D 96

ORMEAUX - 77540

POMMEUSE - 77515

 15 LA FERME DU VIEUX CHÂTEAU
Mme Maegerlein

Chemin du Pont-Levis
77540 Ormeaux
Tel. 06 78 02 25 17
BandB77 @ wanadoo.fr
www.chambres-table-hotes.com

Open all year by reservation • 4 non-smoking rooms
• €48 to €65, breakfast included • Table d'hôte €13 to
€55 • Garden, car park. Credit cards not accepted, no
dogs allowed in rooms

 16 LE MOULIN DE POMMEUSE
M. et Mme Thomas

32 avenue du Général-Herne
77515 Pommeuse
Tel. 01 64 75 29 45
Fax 01 64 75 29 45
info @ le-moulin-de-pommeuse.com
www.le-moulin-de-pommeuse.com

Open all year • 6 non-smoking rooms • €58, breakfast
included • Table d'hôte €20-25 • Park, car park. No dogs
allowed • Watermill (dating back to the 14C)

Guests and their horses are received warmly.

The "old castle" is no longer visible, but the exquisitely
restored 18C farmhouse is guaranteed to satisfy even
the most demanding visitor. The owners' decorative flair
has combined rich materials and period furniture with
collections of old tools and popular arts. The bathrooms
of the cosy rooms are all fitted with power showers. The
high ceilinged lounge is graced with a huge Louis XIII
fireplace. You are welcome to try your hand at carriage
riding in the company of the farm's mare, Ivoire.

 As soon as you've crossed the threshold, you'll start to feel at home.

The lady of the house certainly knows how to receive
her guests in style, offering them a drink on arrival, the
traditional sprig of lily of the valley on May 1 and gifts
at Christmas. The setting of the 14C water mill is quite
delightful, as are the rooms, which have suitably
agricultural names such as Sowing, Harvesting, Thresh-
ing. Relax in the small sitting room in the old machine
room or in the park which hides its very own island!

Access : In the town

Access : 5km westbound from Coulommiers on the
N 34, then a minor road

17 FERME DU CHATEL
M. Lebel

5 rue de la Chapelle-Saint-Jean
77160 Provins
Tel. 01 64 00 10 73
Fax 01 64 00 10 99

fermeduchatel @ wanadoo.fr

Open all year • 5 non-smoking rooms, all have bathrooms
• €44 to €46, breakfast included • No table d'hôte
• Garden, car park. No dogs allowed

18 LES HAUTS DE MONTGUILLON
M. et Mme Legendre

22 rue de Saint-Quentin
Hameau de Montguillon
77860 Saint-Germain-sur-Morin
Tel. 01 60 04 45 53
Fax 01 60 42 28 59
chantal.legendre @ wanadoo.fr

Open all year • 3 rooms, 2 of which are upstairs, all have
bathrooms • €60, breakfast included • Garden, car park.
Credit cards not accepted • Disneyland Paris nearby

"Wasting" time in the orchard garden.

This old house, built and rebuilt from the 12C to the
18C, enjoys a superb position in the heart of the
medieval town. The bedrooms, under exposed rafters,
are peaceful and spotless with well-equipped bathrooms. Breakfast is served in a rustic dining room full
of character; afterwards head for the huge garden and
wander between the fruit trees.

Access : In the medieval city

The cheerful decoration.

This lovingly restored farmhouse is conveniently located
near Disneyland-Paris. A tasteful contrast of pastel
shades and dark timbered beams prevails in the
bedrooms which have large beds, old wardrobes and
chest of drawers picked up in second-hand shops and
brand new bathrooms. This creative mixture of old and
new continues in the rest of the establishment,
particularly in the hall with its old bread oven. The
shaded, well-manicured garden is the place to be on
sunny days.

Access : Southbound from St-Germain sur Morin, in
the upper part of Montguillon

  19 **AUBERGE DU CHEVAL BLANC**
Mme Cousin

55 rue Victor-Clairet
77910 Varreddes
Tel. 01 64 33 18 03
Fax 01 60 23 29 68
r.cousin2 @ libertysurf.fr
www.auberge-cheval-blanc.fr

Closed from 1 to 24 Aug, Sun evening, Mon and Tue lunchtime • 8 rooms with bath/WC and television • €76 to €95; breakfast €9 • Menus €33 to €49 • Garden, private car park

  20 **LA FERME DE VOSVES**
Mme Lemarchand

155 rue de Boissise
77190 Vosves
Tel. 01 64 39 22 28
Fax 01 64 79 17 26
contact @ fermedevosves.com
www.fermedevosves.com

Closed from 21 Dec to 3 Jan • 3 rooms • €50 to €65, breakfast included • No table d'hôte • Garden, car park. Credit cards not accepted, no dogs allowed

The terrace decked in flowers and shaded by trees.

This former staging inn houses recently redone "chocolate-box" bedrooms featuring designer fabrics, pine and wrought-iron furniture and teak-floored bathrooms. In the plush dining room hung with still-lifes, the accent is on creativity and healthy local produce. Don't even think about leaving without tasting the inimitable Brie de Meaux cheese!

The simple, unpretentious welcome and setting.

This green-shuttered old farmhouse is bordered by two attractive gardens full of fruit trees and flowers and complete with a well. The unostentatious, tranquil bedrooms, spread throughout the buildings and the warm, unaffected welcome from the lady of the house are reason enough to stay, but the sitting room with piano and dining room with fireplace and watercolours by the owner are also delightful.

Access : On the main road in the village

Access : 10km northbound from Barbizon on the N 7 and the D 372, then take Rue de la Gare

 **LE PRIEURÉ MAÏALEN**
M. et Mme Lévi

 4 allée du Jamboree
78840 Moisson
Tel. 01 34 79 37 20
Fax 01 34 79 37 58
blevi@free.fr

Open all year • 3 rooms with bathrooms • €59, breakfast included; half board available • Table d'hôte €21 (only by reservation) • Garden, car park. Credit cards not accepted, no dogs allowed • Outdoor swimming pool. Golf, horse-riding, tennis and leisure park nearby

 LA FAUCONNERIE DU ROY
M. et Mme Oger

 1 rue de l'Ormoir
78124 Montainville
Tel. 01 34 75 17 24
oger@lafauconnerie.com
www.lafauconnerie.com

Closed from 24 to 25 Dec • 2 rooms and one gîte • €75 to €80, breakfast included • No table d'hôte • Car park. Credit cards not accepted, no dogs allowed • Outdoor swimming pool

 A spin in one of the owner's vintage cars.

A former 16C priory is an excellent place to spend a night in the heart of this village so dear to Monet. Time and care have clearly been lavished on the interior and each room is a delight to behold. The "Boat" room contains an 18C model sailing boat, "Scheherazade" is steeped in mystery and "Provence" bathed in bright, cheerful colours. Antique furniture, ornaments and a collection of LPs add a personal touch to the sitting room and the flowered garden is perfect to relax in.

The history behind these beautifully preserved buildings.

History and character meet your eye wherever you turn in this falconry built in 1680 for Louis XIV. Everything is authentic from the original wooden carved staircase and doors, tiled floors and period furniture down to the piano in the breakfast room. Excellent mattresses, canopy and four-poster beds and good quality bathrooms have been chosen for the bedrooms. Swimming pool, children's play area in the park and bicycle rental available.

Access : 3km to the south-east of Roche-Guyon

Access : 6km eastbound from Thoiry on the D 45, take the Maule road and turn right

23 LE CHÂTEAU
M. Le Bret

2 rue de l'Église
78125 Poigny-la-Forêt
Tel. 01 34 84 73 42
Fax 01 34 34 74 38
lemanoirdepoigny@wanadoo.fr

Open all year • 6 rooms, one of which is a family room
• €60 to €68, breakfast included • No table d'hôte
• Garden, car park. No dogs allowed

24 CHAMBRE D'HÔTE MONSIEUR LENOIR
M. Lenoir

9 rue du Souvenir
91490 Moigny-sur-École
Tel. 01 64 98 47 84
lenoir@aol.com
www.compagnie-des-clos.com

Open all year • 4 rooms, one of which is on the ground
floor • €55 to €60, breakfast included • Table d'hôte €16
• Garden. Credit cards not accepted

 The exquisite decoration of this 19C abode.

Magical! Words fail us when describing this sumptuous 19C castle, laden with furniture and objects brought back from all over the world. The resulting mixture of styles and periods is both bewildering and enchanting. Each of the rooms is styled on a different theme: "Morocco", "Indonesia", "Louis XIII" and even "Coca-Cola". The garden full of ducks, ganders, dogs and horses has a distinctly Noah's Ark air about it. Definitely worth making a beeline for!

 The sheltered landscaped garden.

High walls protect this handsome stone house and its beautifully laid-out garden from prying eyes. The tastefully decorated rooms are totally tranquil and the one on split-levels is very practical for families. If you listen quietly you may still hear the clucking of the former inhabitants of the breakfast room, where the chicken roosts can still be seen. A pleasant stay and cordial welcome assured.

Access : 8km to the north-west of Rambouillet on the D 936 then the D 107

Access : 3.5km northbound from Milly-la-Forêt

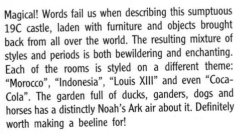

 25 CHAMBRE D'HÔTE LE SAINT-DENIS
Mme Pernelle

1 rue des Cabarets
95510 Chérence
Tel. 01 34 78 15 02

Open all year (by reservation) • 5 rooms with bathrooms • €58 to €62; breakfast included • No table d'hôte • Garden, car park. Credit cards not accepted, no dogs allowed

 26 CHAMBRE D'HÔTE MONSIEUR DELALEU
M. Delaleu

131 rue du Maréchal-Foch
95620 Parmain
Tel. 01 34 73 02 92
Fax 01 34 08 80 76
ladelaleu @ minitel.net

Open all year • 4 rooms • €49, breakfast included • No table d'hôte • Garden, car park. Credit cards not accepted, no dogs allowed

 The lavish breakfasts.

This appealing stone house in the lovely medieval village of Chérence was formerly a traditional hotel-restaurant. It was turned into a B&B establishment in 1996, offering simple, compact rooms in all shapes and sizes. The ground floor, full of nooks and crannies, houses the dining and sitting room complete with fireplace. Spending or wasting time in the delightful garden is definitely a high point. Faultless welcome.

 The unusual bathrooms.

By the time you have opened your suitcase, you will feel that you have come home. Each of the spacious, colourful rooms is named after a playing card; Spade, Heart, Diamond and Club. However the highly unusual bathrooms, all are different, are what guests always rave about. Children are in heaven over the vaulted cellar turned into a games room, the mini football pitch and the visit to the working farm.

Access : 4km to the north-east of Roche-Guyon on the D 100

Access : 1km westbound from Isle-Adam on the D 64

LANGUEDOC-ROUSSILLON

Languedoc-Roussillon is home to a diverse collage of landscape and culture: the feverish rhythm of its festivals, the dizzying beauty of the Tarn Gorges, the haughty splendour of the Pyrenees, the bewitching spell of its caves and stone statues, the seclusion of its clifftop Cathar citadels which witnessed one of the bloodiest chapters of France's history, the heady perfumes of its sunburnt garrigue, the nonchalance of the pink flamingos on its long salt flats, the splendour of Carcassonne's ramparts, the ornamental exuberance of Catalan altarpieces, the quietly flowing waters of the Midi Canal and the harsh majesty of the Cévennes mountains. Taking in so many contrasts is likely to exhaust more than a few explorers, but effective remedies are close at hand: a steaming plate of *aligot* – mashed potato, garlic and cheese – and a simmering cassoulet, the famously rich combination of duck, sausage, beans and herbs, followed by a delectable slice of Roquefort cheese, all washed down with a glass of ruby-red wine.

- Aude (11)
- Gard (30)
- Hérault (34)
- Lozère (48)
- Pyrénées-Orientales (66)

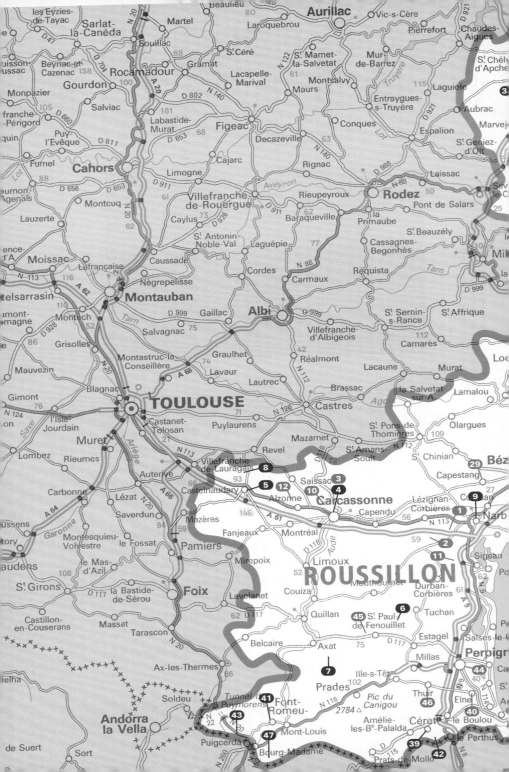

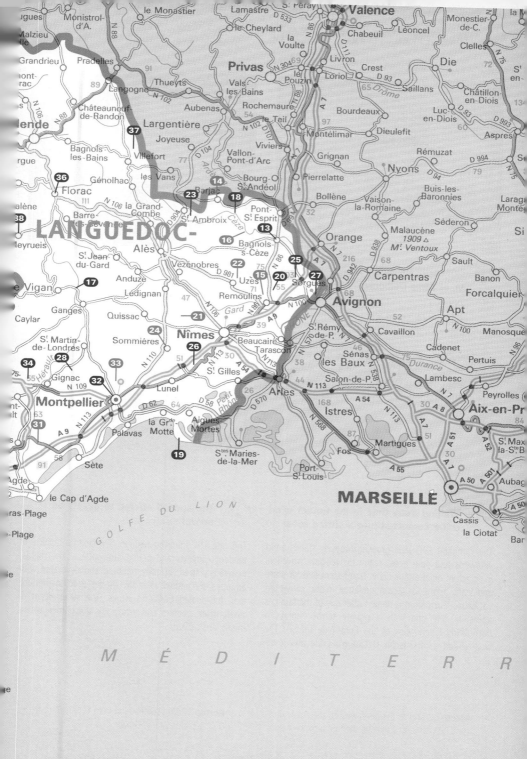

 1 DOMAINE DE SAINT-JEAN
M. et Mme Delbourg

11200 Bizanet
Tel. 04 68 45 17 31
Fax 04 68 45 17 31

Open all year • 4 upstairs rooms, all have bathrooms
• €55 to €65, breakfast included • No table d'hôte
• Garden. Credit cards not accepted, no dogs allowed

 2 LA BASTIDE DES CORBIÈRES
M. et Mme Camel

17 rue de la Révolution
11200 Boutenac
Tel. 04 68 27 20 61
Fax 04 68 27 62 71
bastide.corbières @ wanadoo.fr
www.bastide-corbieres.com

Closed from 15 Jan to 15 Feb and 15 to 30 Nov • 5 rooms
with bath/WC • €79 to €84 (€70 to €75 low season),
breakfast included • Table d'hôte €29 (evenings only
except Tue and Fri) • Terrace, garden. No dogs allowed
• Reading room, table-tennis, mountain bike rental

 Whiling away time in the former wine cellar converted into a sitting room.

This rambling 19C wine-growing property stands amid vineyards and pine trees, ready to welcome travellers in search of quiet authenticity. Hand-stencilled furniture and walls adorn the accommodation in the converted vat house: each room is named after one of the family's ancestors; the one with a private terrace enjoys a particularly lovely view of the Fontfroide massif. The well-tended garden is Mr Delbourg's pride and joy.

 The apéritif offered to guests on arrival.

This late 19C mansion features a wonderful mixture of modern comforts and period atmosphere. The rooms, generously sized, brightly coloured and decorated with antiques are named after the grapes used to produce rich, full-bodied Corbières wines. The sweet scent of roses, irises, peonies and acacia fills the garden where meals are served.

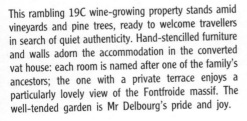

Access : 2.5km to the north-west of the abbey on the D 613 towards Lagrasse, then on a minor road

Access : 7.5km southbound from Lézignan on the D 61 towards Luc-sur-Orbieu

 3 LA MAISON SUR LA COLLINE

Mme Galinier

Lieu-dit Sainte-Croix
11000 Carcassonne
Tel. 04 68 47 57 94
Fax 04 68 47 57 94
contact @ lamaisonsurlacolline.com
www.lamaisonsurlacolline.com

Closed from 1 Dec to Feb • 6 rooms with bathrooms and television • €65 to €85, breakfast included • Table d'hôte €27 (evenings only by reservation) • Garden, car park. Credit cards not accepted • Outdoor swimming pool

4 MONTSÉGUR

M. Faugeras

27 allée d'léna
11000 Carcassonne
Tel. 04 68 25 31 41
Fax 04 68 47 13 22
info @ hotelmontsegur.com
www.hotelmontsegur.com

Closed from 20 Dec to 1 Feb • 21 rooms on 3 floors, all have air-conditioning, bath/WC or shower/WC and television • €70 to €92 (€67 to €88 low season); breakfast €9; half board available • Menus €22 to €40 • Private car park

As soon as you hear the chirping of the cicadas you know you're in the south.

The unforgettable tour of the historic city ramparts.

Broom, cypress trees, thyme and wild mint lend a wonderfully relaxing atmosphere to this hillside farmstead overlooking the historic city of Carcassonne. Old red floor tiles, antiques and knick-knacks adorn the spacious rooms. Each has its own colour scheme, beige, blue, yellow – the "white" room has a private garden. Breakfast is served by the pool in the summer.

A late-19C mansion on the doorstep of the lower town. An undeniable faded charm emanates from these gradually spruced-up rooms filled with the scent of beeswax. Herringbone parquet floors, "retro" lights and a marble fireplace are among the features of the classic period sitting room. The breakfast room is graced with a beautiful old dresser.

Access : 1km southbound from the historic town on the Sainte-Croix road

Access : From Castelnaudary on the N 113 (Av du Prés F Roosevelt), turn right at Artigues Bridge

5 HÔTEL DU CANAL
M. Brajeux et Mme Geli

2 ter avenue Arnaut-Vidal
11400 Castelnaudary
Tel. 04 68 94 05 05
Fax 04 68 94 05 06
hotelducanal @ wanadoo.fr
www.hotelducanal.com

Open all year • 38 rooms, 2 have disabled access. All have bath/WC, television and broadband internet access €5/night • €48 to €59 breakfast €6 to €9 • No restaurant • Garden, car park • Billiards room

6 AUBERGE DE CUCUGNAN
M. Villa

2 place de la Fontaine
11350 Cucugnan
Tel. 04 68 45 40 84
Fax 04 68 45 01 52

Closed Jan to 15 Mar and Wed • 6 air-conditioned rooms with bath/WC or shower/WC and television • €43 to €50, breakfast €6.50, half board available • Restaurant closed Wed, menus €16 to €40 • Terrace, car park

 Stepping out of the hotel onto the banks of the Canal du Midi.

These handsome ochre walls housed a quicklime factory back in the 19C. The quiet if ordinary rooms overlook the garden or the canal and in the summer, you will want to linger over breakfast for hours as you gaze at the canal's quietly flowing waters. It would be a crime to leave town without sampling its world-renowned cassoulet!

 Exploring the narrow, winding roads that border the lovely Corbières vineyards.

For several years now the reputation of this inn, nestled in a picturesque village of the Corbières, has been steadily growing thanks to the quality of its country cooking, served in a converted barn and at deliciously reasonable prices. Guests can now also enjoy the prospect of getting to know the region better by booking (recommended) one of the inn's recently fitted-out comfortable rooms whose immaculate walls are set off by wrought-iron furniture and bright fabrics.

Access : Towards Pamiers on the banks of the Midi canal

Access : In a lane in the heart of the village

  7 ## HOSTELLERIE DU GRAND DUC
M. et Mme Bruchet

2 route de Boucheville
11140 Gincla
Tel. 04 68 20 55 02
Fax 04 68 20 61 22
host-du-grand-duc@ataraxie.fr
www.host-du-grand-duc.com

Closed from 3 Nov to 1 Apr • 12 rooms, 3 of which are in a separate wing, all have bath/WC or shower/WC and television • €60 to €67; breakfast €8; half board available • Restaurant closed on Wed lunchtime except in Jul and Aug; menus €28 to €58 • Terrace, garden, garage, private car park • Ideal for exploring the upper Aude Valley

8 ## HOST. DU CHÂTEAU DE LA POMARÈDE
M. Garcia

Place du Château
11400 La Pomarède
Tel. 04 68 60 49 69
Fax 04 68 60 49 71

Closed 12 to 25 Mar, 11 Nov to 4 Dec, Sun evening out of season and Mon and Tue all year • 6 rooms with bath/WC and television • €75 to €160; breakfast €12; half board available • Menus €16 (weekdays) to €70 • Terrace, car park

We most liked **Candle-lit dining overlooking the garden and its ornamental pool.**

This grand old mansion built in 1780 stand proudly in one of Cathar country's many remote villages, perfect for long walks in the nearby forest. The accommodation may be a tad old-fashioned, but certainly can't be faulted for character; a second wing has just been finished with three delightful rooms. An elegant rustic dining room opens onto a terrace shaded by a thick canopy of lime trees.

We most liked **Wouldn't it be easy to get used to living in luxury?**

An enthusiastic young couple are at the head of this wonderful establishment tucked away in a hamlet of the Montagne Noire. The outbuildings of a medieval fortress have recently been converted into a likeable hostelry: tastefully decorated rooms, an elegant dining room with exposed timbers and wrought-iron furniture, a terrace overlooking the valley and, above all, the mouth-watering, confident and inventive cuisine, which earned it a Michelin star, no less, in 2002.

Access : At Lapradelle, leave the D 117 (Quillan to Perpignan road) and take the D 22 alongside the Bouizane

Access : Set back from the D 624 from Castelnaudary to Revel

 9 LA RÉSIDENCE
La Résidence SA

 6 rue du 1er-Mai
11100 Narbonne
Tel. 04 68 32 19 41
Fax 04 68 65 51 82

Closed from 15 Jan to 15 Feb • 25 rooms on 2 floors with bath/WC or shower/WC and television • €68 to €96; breakfast €8 • No restaurant • Small garage • Near the historic centre

 10 CHÂTEAU LE LIET
M. Meynier

 11610 Pennautier
Tel. 04 68 11 19 19
Fax 04 68 47 05 22
claudemeynier@aol.com

Closed from Nov to Feb • 6 rooms with bath/WC • €54 to €69, breakfast included • No table d'hôte • Garden, park, car park. No dogs allowed • Outdoor swimming pool, tennis, mountain biking

 Stepping back in time to the turn of the 20C.

This gracious late-19C residence was converted into a hotel in the 1950s: the atmosphere of old provincial France can still be felt in its lovingly preserved decoration. Some of the rooms overlook the Archbishops' Palace and the cathedral. The hotel has enjoyed the patronage of a whole host of famous politicians, sportsmen and artists, as a peep inside the Visitor's Book will reveal.

 Lording it for a weekend.

The impressive stone walls and lofty turrets of this 19C castle are encircled by wood and parkland rich in flora and fauna, including peacocks, hares, pheasants and, to the delight of children, ponies. The immaculately decorated rooms and suites all enjoy views of this abundant countryside and some have a balcony. Magnificent breakfast room opening onto the grounds.

Access : Take the Narbonne-Sud exit and head for the town centre, cross the Robine canal, turn right at Rue Jean-Jaurès and then the 2nd left

Access : 9km to the north-west of Carcassonne on the N 113 then the D 203

11 DOMAINE DE LA PIERRE CHAUDE
M. et Mme Pasternack

Les Campets
11490 Portel-des-Corbières
Tel. 04 68 48 89 79
Fax 04 68 48 14 03
lescampets@aol.com
www.lapierrechaude.com

Closed from 1 Jan to 15 Feb • 4 rooms with bath/WC
• €69 to €78; breakfast included • No table d'hôte.
Aperitifs served free of charge • Terrace, garden, car
park. Credit cards not accepted, no dogs admitted

12 ABBAYE DE VILLELONGUE
M. Eloffe

11170 Saint-Martin-le-Vieil
Tel. 04 68 76 92 58
Fax 04 68 76 92 58

Closed 10 days in Nov and 10 days at Christmas
• 4 rooms • €60, breakfast included • No table d'hôte
• Car park, park, garden. Credit cards not accepted, no
dogs admitted • Guided and non-guided visits of the
abbey daily

We most liked **Everything!**

This 18C former wine and spirit house nestled in a
hamlet amid vineyards and pinewoods, was beautifully
restored in 1960 by a pupil of the architect Gaudi. Since
then, constant improvements have turned the estate into
a pleasant getaway with splendid bedrooms (terracotta
tiles, wrought iron, worn wooden furniture, warm
fabrics, etc.), a lovely Andalusian-style patio-cum-sitting
room, a terrace shaded by fig trees and a garden rich
with the sweet scents of southern France. Unforgettable!

We most liked **Quietly meditating in the abbey
gardens, before or after the throngs
of daily visitors.**

Stand still and drink in the silence and solemnity of the
former Cistercian abbey built in the 12C. Be reassured,
however, the comfort on offer is far from monastic and
old furniture, canopy beds and private bathrooms now
set the scene in the rooms. All the rooms gaze down
on the lovely cloisters and garden, where breakfast is
served in the summer. In the winter, they are served
in the monks' storeroom, restored in 1998.

Access : In a place known as Les Campets, 6km
from the Wildlife Park on the D 611 A towards
Durban-Corbières

Access : 5km to the north-west on the D 64

 13 ### CHÂTEAU DU VAL DE CÈZE
M. Vanneville

69 route d'Avignon
30200 Bagnols-sur-Cèze
Tel. 04 66 89 61 26
Fax 04 66 89 97 37
hotelvaldeceze @ sud-provence.com
www.sud-provence.com

Closed 1 to 5 Jan, Sat and Sun from Oct to Mar
• 22 air-conditioned rooms with bath/WC and television,
broad-band internet access in rooms, 1 with disabled
access • €100 to €123 (€98 low season), breakfast €10
• No restaurant • Park, private car park • Swimming pool,
tennis

 14 ### LA SÉRÉNITÉ
Mme L'Helgoualch

Place de la Mairie
30430 Barjac
Tel. 04 66 24 54 63
Fax 04 66 24 54 63

Closed from Dec to Easter • 3 rooms with bath/WC or
shower/WC • €70 to €115, breakfast included • No table
d'hôte • Terrace. Credit cards not accepted, no dogs
allowed

 **Gazing up at the hundred-year-old
trees in the park.**

This graceful 17C dwelling set in a 15-acre park was
formerly a hunting lodge. At present, the main wing is
home to the reception, sitting room and seminar rooms.
The bedrooms are located in pavilions dotted around the
estate. Tiled floors, wrought-iron or painted wooden
furniture, bright regional fabrics and whitewashed walls
all depict the demure Provençal tone that prevails
throughout. All boast a private terrace.

 **Snuggling up in the book-lined
bedroom or in front of the fire.**

Fragrant lavender and beeswax greet you as you cross
the threshold of this 17C country home. Afterwards,
feast your eyes on the sophisticated good taste of the
ochre-coloured walls, hand-stencilled friezes, rich fabrics, antiques and ornaments picked up by the antique
dealer-owner and on the personalised rooms decorated
with fine linen and lace. Settle down and relax as you
savour the delicious breakfasts served by the fireside or
on the flowered terrace in the summer.

Access : 1km south-east of Bagnols-sur-Cèze on the
Avignon road

Access : 6km westbound from Aven d'Orgnac on
the D 317 and then the D 176

 15 VIC

M. Vic

 16 LA TONNELLE

M. et Mme Rigaud

Mas de Raffin
30210 Castillon-du-Gard
Tel. 04 66 37 13 28
Fax 04 66 37 62 55
m.v.castillon @ net-up.com
www.chambresdhotes-vic.com

Place des Marronniers
30200 La Roque-sur-Cèze
Tel. 04 66 82 79 37
Fax 04 66 82 79 37
latonnelle30 @ aol.com

Open all year • 5 rooms • €70 to €80, breakfast included
• No table d'hôte • Garden, car park. Credit cards not
accepted • Outdoor swimming pool

Open all year • 6 rooms • €72, breakfast included • No
table d'hôte • No dogs allowed

 The happy marriage of old and new.

 Row, row, row your boat, gently down the Cèze!

It would be difficult to find a more idyllic spot for this former wine-growing farm set amidst the unspoilt landscape of fragrant scrub, vines and hundred-year-old olive trees. Red and yellow features predominantly in the bright rooms where modern amenities blend in wonderfully with old stones and antique furniture; some are vaulted while others are split-level. Savour breakfast served under the refreshing shade of a mulberry tree.

Merrily, merrily, merrily, merrily, life is but a dream! The infectious good humour of the owner is impossible to resist as she guides you round her lovely country house that can't be missed on the way into the village. Each of the sober, immaculate rooms is named after a flower. In the summer, treat yourself to breakfast in the shade of an arbour while you gaze down on the village and its girdle of cypress trees.

Access : 4km to the north-east of Pont-du-Gard on the D 19 and then the D 228

Access : 17km to the north-west of Bagnols-sur-Cèze on the N 86 then the D 298 towards Barjac, and the D 166

17 CHÂTEAU DU REY
Mme Cazalis de Fondouce

Le Rey
30570 Le Vigan
Tel. 04 67 82 40 06
Fax 04 67 82 47 79
abeura @ neuf.fr
www.château-du-rey.com

Closed in Jan and Feb • 13 rooms, all have bath/WC and television • €70 to €97; breakfast €8; half board available • Restaurant closed on Sun evening and Mon except in Jul and Aug; menus €25 to €55 • Terrace, riverside park, car park • Outdoor swimming pool, private fishing

18 LA MAGNANERIE DE BERNAS
M. et Mme Keller

Le Hameau de Bernas
30630 Montclus
Tel. 04 66 82 37 36
Fax 04 66 82 37 41
lamagnanerie @ wanadoo.fr
www.magnanerie-de-bernas.com

Open from Easter to 28 Oct • 15 rooms, one of which has disabled access, all have bath/WC and television • €65 to €120; breakfast €10; half board available • Restaurant closed Tue, Wed in Mar, Apr and Oct; menus €20 to €40 • Terrace, garden, car park • Outdoor swimming pool

 Eight centuries of family history.

This lovely 13C fortress, remodelled by the tireless Viollet-le-Duc, Napoleon's architect, has been in the same family for over eight centuries! The rooms, some with fireplace, are furnished with elegant period furniture. The former sheep pen is now the dining room and its vaulted ceiling makes it pleasantly cool in summer. The view from the terrace extends over the immense parkland and river, much prized by anglers.

 Treasure hunting in this 13C Knights Templar stronghold.

Patrick and Katrin, a young Swiss couple with energy to spare, have recently finished their patient, flawless restoration of this medieval former command post. Beautiful stone walls, exposed beams and rich, warm fabrics adorn the tasteful rooms, most of which look down over the Cèze valley. Character abounds in the vaulted dining room, but the highlight is perhaps the shaded courtyard-terrace and south-facing garden, designed by a professional landscape gardener, none other than Patrick himself.

Access : 5km eastbound on the D 999 (towards Ganges), turn left just before Pont d'Hérault

Access : Between Barjac and Bagnols-sur-Cèze, then 2km eastbound from Monclus

 19 **RELAIS DE L'OUSTAU CAMARGUEN**
M. Daweritz

3 route des Marines
30240 Port-Camargue
Tel. 04 66 51 51 65
Fax 04 66 53 06 65
oustaucamarguen @ wanadoo.fr
www.chateauxhotels.com/camarguen

Open from 19 Mar to 1 Nov • 39 air-conditioned rooms, most on ground-floor, with bath/WC or shower/WC and television • €100 to €147; breakfast €11; half board available • Air-conditioned restaurant, open 2 May to late Sep, closed Wed; menus €27 to €31 (evening only) • Terrace, garden, private car park • Outdoor swimming pool

 Winding down in the peaceful atmosphere of this small mas.

This recently-built hotel has adopted a traditional Camargue style as its name suggests. All the rooms are spacious and on the ground-floor and some have small, flower-decked terraces overlooking the pleasant garden. The tasteful interior decoration was clearly inspired by neighbouring Provence. A country style with exposed beams in the restaurant, a pleasant pool-side terrace and a select traditional menu comprise the establishment's other appeals.

Access : On Route des Marines

---

 20 **L'ARCEAU**
M. et Mme Brunel

1 rue de l'Arceau
30210 Saint-Hilaire-d'Ozilhan
Tel. 04 66 37 34 45
Fax 04 66 37 33 90
patricia.brunel2 @ wanadoo.fr
www.multimania.com/arceau

Closed from 20 Nov to 15 Feb, Sun evening, Tue lunchtime, and Mon from 1 Oct to Easter • 25 rooms with bath/WC or shower/WC, all have television • €50 to €60; breakfast €8; half board available • Menus €22.50 (weekdays) to €61. Dogs not allowed in restaurant • Terrace, private car park

 The sweet-scented garrigue.

Before the sun has risen to its zenith, leave the sizzling A9 motorway and head straight for the shelter of this welcoming mas and its cool terrace just two minutes drive away. The fragrant odours of the scrub surrounding the village seep into every nook and cranny of its thick dry-stone walls. Even better, it is within easy reach of one of the marvels of Roman architecture, the Pont du Gard aqueduct. When you book, ask for one of the renovated rooms whose stone and beams are visible.

Access : 4.5km to the north-east of Remoulins on the D 792

 21 ## LA MAZADE
Mme Couston

Dans le village
30730 Saint-Mamert-du-Gard
Tel. 04 66 81 17 56
Fax 04 66 81 17 56
www.bbfrance.com/couston.html

Open all year • 3 rooms with bathrooms • €53 to €60, breakfast included • Table d'hôte €20 (by reservation) • Garden, car park. Credit cards not accepted, no dogs allowed

Mrs Couston's highly personal approach to interior decoration.

This beautiful country mas, set in the heart of a sleepy village, reveals the talents of its owner's flair for interior decoration. An almost staggering collection of antique and contemporary furniture, rugs and modern and folk art blends surprisingly well in the plant-filled rooms: the result is truly unique. All the rooms overlook the garden and arbour, where dinner is served in the long summer evenings.

Access : 17km westbound from Nîmes on the D 999 and then the D 1

 22 ## LE MAS DU CAROUBIER
Mme Charpentier

684 route de Vallabrix
30700 Saint-Quentin-la-Poterie
Tel. 04 66 22 12 72
Fax 04 66 22 12 72
contact @ mas-caroubier.com
www.mas-caroubier.com

Closed in Jan • 4 rooms, non-smokers only • €70 to €80, breakfast included • No table d'hôte • Garden. Credit cards not accepted, no dogs allowed • Outdoor swimming pool

A secret hideaway.

The traditional ochre walls and sky-blue shutters of this 18C mas suddenly appear when you reach the end of a country lane. Inside, the guests' welfare is clearly the only thing that counts, from the gracious greeting and rooms filled with old furniture to the delicious home-made jams at breakfast time. Outside, the turquoise water of the swimming pool and quiet garden encourage you to idle away long summer afternoons, unless of course you would prefer to do a pottery, painting or cookery course.

Access : 5km to the north-east of Saint-Quentin-la-Poterie on the D 982 and then the D 5

 23 | **LA BASTIDE DES SENTEURS**
M. Subileau

30500 Saint-Victor-de-Malcap
Tel. 04 66 60 24 45
Fax 04 66 60 26 10
subileau @ bastide-senteurs.com
www.bastide-senteurs.com

Open from Apr to Oct • 9 rooms, one of which has disabled access, all have bath/WC and television • €60 to €75; breakfast €8, half board available • Menus €25 to €75 • Private car park, terrace • Swimming pool

 24 | **MAS FONTCLAIRE**
Mme Labbé

8 rue Émile-Jamais
30250 Sommières
Tel. 04 66 77 78 69
Fax 04 66 77 78 69

Open all year • 3 rooms • €67 to €80, breakfast included • No table d'hôte • Garden, car park. Credit cards not accepted • Outdoor swimming pool

 Choosing which local wine to drink with the chef's cuisine.

This 19C stronghold is built against the walls of a delightful village dominated by the shadow of a medieval castle. The fully renovated abode offers pleasant, colourful rooms decked out in antique and wrought iron furniture. Some enjoy a fine view of the Cèze Valley and all are equally tranquil. Gourmets will love sitting down in the stylish Southern-flavoured dining room or on the terrace opening onto the overflow swimming pool.

 Speech may be silver, but silence is golden!

Imagine waking up to blue, cloudless skies and tucking into delicious home-made jams and freshly squeezed orange juice, served on the patio in the summer or by the fireside in winter. You only need to put one foot over the threshold of this former wine-grower's house to know you're in for a treat. The three rooms in the converted outbuildings are decorated in different styles: Provençal, modern and Louis XVI. The quality of the silence is such that you may even find yourself whispering!

Access : In the village

Access : In the village

 25 LE PONT DU ROY
M. Schorgere

 Route de Nîmes - D 976
30126 Tavel
Tel. 04 66 50 22 03
Fax 04 66 50 10 14
contact@hotelpontduroy.fr
www.hotelpontduroy.fr

Open from 25 Mar to 30 Sep • 14 air-conditioned rooms with bath/WC or shower/WC and television • €69 to €73 (€57 to €61 low season); breakfast €7; half board available • Menus €23 to €43 (evenings only) • Terrace, garden, private car park. No dogs allowed in restaurant • Outdoor swimming pool, pétanque, play area

 26 LA PASSIFLORE
M. et Mme Booth

 1 rue Neuve
30310 Vergèze
Tel. 04 66 35 00 00
Fax 04 66 35 09 21

Open all year; • 11 rooms, all have bath/WC or shower/WC, and air conditioning • €43 to €62; breakfast €7; half board available • Restaurant closed from 2 Oct to 30 Mar, Sun and Mon; menus (evenings only) €26 • Terrace, private car park. No dogs allowed in restaurant

 Never make the mistake of thinking that pétanque is "just a game"!

You can always dive into the swimming pool for a refreshing dip if things get too hot on the pétanque ground! Built in the style of a Provençal mas, this house was turned into a hotel in 1986. The pastel coloured rooms overlook either the shaded garden or the legendary vineyards of Tavel. A fresh country look prevails in the restaurant and in the summer tables are laid outside on the terrace. The self-taught owner-chef rustles up regional dishes depending on what he finds in the market.

 Treat yourself to one of Mr Mayle's tales of life in Provence as you relax in this picturesque mas.

At last you can find out if Peter Mayle's humorous accounts are true! This 18C mas in the heart of a pretty village is run by an English couple, Mr and Mrs Booth. They have clearly taken their adoptive land to heart as the Provençal decoration of the restaurant and breakfast room testifies, even though a snug sitting room is perfect for teas. Small, well-maintained, quiet rooms overlook a lush green inner courtyard or a small garden.

Access : 3km to the south-east of Tavel, on the D 4 then the D 976 (Roquemaure-Remoulins road)

Access : Between Nîmes and Lunel, leave the N 113 for Codognan and follow the D 104 to Vergèze

 27 L'ATELIER
M. et Mme Burret

5 rue de la Foire
30400 Villeneuve-lès-Avignon
Tel. 04 90 25 01 84
Fax 04 90 25 80 06
hotel-latelier @ libertysurf.fr
www.hoteldelatelier.com

Closed from 3 Jan to 19 Feb • 23 rooms, all have bath/WC or shower/WC and television • €56 to €91 (€46 to €71 low season); breakfast €8 • No restaurant • Garden, garage • Exhibition of painting and sculpture, tea room

 The view of Avignon from the patio and tiny terrace.

This 16C "workshop" in the heart of a picturesque town has just been creatively redesigned by a film set decorator. Tasteful ornaments, antique furniture, rush matting, elegant bathrooms, exposed beams, fireplaces and a lovely staircase are combined in this masterful renovation which has retained the character of the abode's ancestral walls. Mediterranean-style breakfast room, exhibitions of painting and sculpture.

Access : In the old town

 28 AUBERGE DE SAUGRAS
M. et Mme Aurelle

Domaine Saugras
34380 Argelliers
Tel. 04 67 55 08 71
Fax 04 67 55 04 65
auberge.saugras @ wanadoo.fr

Closed from 9 to 25 Aug, 20 Dec to 20 Jan, Mon lunchtime in Jul-Aug, Tue except evening in Jul-Aug and Wed • 7 air-conditioned rooms, with bath/WC and television • €40 to €85, breakfast €8, half board available • Menus €18 to €50 • Terrace, car park • Swimming pool

Feeling like you've left the everyday world behind - even though Montpellier is close by.

Finding your way to the inn is something of a treasure hunt, but once there, your efforts will be more than rewarded. The bare stone walls of this old mas which dates back to the 12C are splendidly isolated and surrounded by sweet-smelling garrigue and wooded hills. The appetising local fare, served in a rustic dining room or on the panoramic terrace, also tempts visitors to return. Finally, lovers of peaceful nights will appreciate the recently renovated comfortable bedrooms.

Access : 21km southbound of St-Martin-de-Londres on the D 32, D 127 and D 127 E

 29 ## LA BASTIDE VIEILLE
M. et Mme Fouissac

La Bastide Vieille
34310 Capestang
Tel. 04 67 93 46 23
Fax 04 67 93 46 56

Closed from 1 Nov to 1 Mar • 3 rooms • €51, breakfast included • Terrace, garden, car park. Credit cards not accepted, no dogs allowed

30   ## LE BARRY DU GRAND CHEMIN
M. et Mme Clarissac

88 faubourg Saint-Martin
34520 Le Caylar
Tel. 04 67 44 50 19
Fax 04 67 44 52 36

Open all year • 5 rooms • €50, breakfast included, half board available • Table d'hôte €18 • Car park. Credit cards not accepted, no dogs allowed

 Whether by bicycle, carriage or barge (on request), the Canal du Midi is a joy to explore.

These old walls flanked by a 12C tower lie amid vineyards in a totally secluded spot, well off the beaten track. The spacious rooms installed in the former outbuildings are decorated with appealing Provençal prints and colours. The dining table is in the former bread-making room. On the leisure side, get to grips with a good book in the delightful sitting room-library or in the small garden.

 The secretive, silent countryside – the "causse" – surrounding this stone farmstead.

Built in 1850, the immaculate stone walls of this house stand at the foot of the strange, tormented Roc Castel in the heart of the unspoilt Larzac limestone plateau. The ground floor rooms are quiet and very well-maintained if not vast. Tuck into the delicious chargrilled fare cooked over an open fire in the delightful vaulted dining room, which remains refreshingly cool in the height of summer.

Access : 13km westbound from Béziers, Castres road on the D 39

Access : In the village

31 CHAMBRE D'HÔTE MONSIEUR GENER
M. et Mme Gener

34 avenue Pierre-Sirven
34530 Montagnac
Tel. 04 67 24 03 21
Fax 04 67 24 03 21

Open all year • 4 rooms with shower/WC, all air-conditioned • €45, breakfast included • No table d'hôte • Terrace, garden, car park. Credit cards not accepted

 32 PARC
Mme Jacquin

8 rue Achille-Bège
34000 Montpellier
Tel. 04 67 41 16 49
Fax 04 67 54 10 05
hotelduparc@ifrance.com
www.hotelduparc-montpellier.com

Open all year • 19 rooms, most have shower/WC, some have bath/WC or shower without WC, all have air-conditioning and television • €48 to €72 breakfast €9 • No restaurant • Car park

 Pézenas and its wealth of craft stalls within easy reach.

In 1750, the buildings laid out around the well-sheltered, spacious inner courtyard belonged to the mounted constabulary. Nowadays, the stables have been converted into large, calm, well-appointed rooms, in some of which the old oak partitions between the loose-boxes can still be seen. In the summer, breakfast is served on a pleasant upstairs terrace.

 Being treated like a regular.

Despite the fact that the park has been sold off, the noble walls of this 18C mansion are as smart as ever and the plush bourgeois rooms are being gradually and tastefully renovated. The regulars of this establishment, located in a quiet side street, appreciate its calm just two minutes away from the town centre and the nearest tram stop; they generally leave their cars in the private car park in the courtyard. In the summer, breakfast is sometimes served on the terrace.

Access : 6.5km to the north-west of Pézenas on the N 9 then the N 113

Access : Drive up Rue Proudhon (towards the zoo), and at the ECAT, take a left at Rue Turgot

 33 DOMAINE DE SAINT-CLÉMENT
Mme Bernabe Calista

34980 Saint-Clément-de-Rivière
Tel. 04 67 66 70 89
Fax 04 67 84 07 96
calista.bernabe@wanadoo.fr
www.ledomainesc.com

Closed from Dec to Feb • 5 rooms with bathrooms • €66 to €76, breakfast €7 • No table d'hôte • Sitting room, garden, car park. Credit cards not accepted, no dogs allowed • Outdoor swimming pool

 34 OSTALARIA CARDABELA
M. et Mme Pugh

10 place de la Fontaine
34725 Saint-Saturnin-de-Lucian
Tel. 04 67 88 62 62
Fax 04 67 88 62 82
ostalaria.cardabela@wanadoo.fr

Closed from 1 Jan to 10 Mar and 31 Oct to 31 Dec • 7 rooms on 2 floors with bath/WC • €65 to €90; breakfast €10 • No restaurant at the hotel, but the owners also run Le Mimosa at St-Guiraud • No dogs allowed

 Faultlessly decorated and oozing with character.

This beautiful 18C mansion only 10min from the heart of busy Montpellier is a haven of peace and quiet. The immense rooms, furnished with antiques and paintings and equally enormous bathrooms, overlook the park or the swimming pool. A string of sitting rooms, decorated with red floor tiles and hung with eye-catching contemporary art, comprises the ground floor. Don't miss the library complete with fireplace and the hand-painted azulejos tiles in the patio.

 Ostalaria's authenticity.

The only clue that this delightful village house is a hotel is the tiny sign almost absentmindedly posted outside. The recently spruced up rooms have plenty of style with brightly coloured quilts, elegant lights and Provençal furniture blending in perfectly with the lovely exposed stone walls, polished floor tiles, well-worn beams and original fireplaces. Some overlook the quite exquisite little square of St-Saturnin. Breakfast is served on a large friendly dining table. Delightful.

Access : 10km northbound from Montpellier on the D 17 then the D 112

Access : On the village square near the church

35 **GRAND HÔTEL PROUHÈZE**
M. et Mme Roudgé

2 route du Languedoc
48130 Aumont-Aubrac
Tel. 04 66 42 80 07
Fax 04 66 42 87 78
prouheze@prouheze.com
www.prouheze.com

Closed from 1 Dec 31 Jan • 24 rooms with bath/WC and television • €67 to €90; breakfast €10, half board available • Menus €33 to €58; at the Compostelle (bistro) €18 to €27. Restaurant closed Sun evening, Mon (lunchtime only Jul and Aug) and Tue lunchtime • Terrace, car park

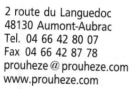

Mr and Mrs Prouhèze's spontaneity and warmth.

This traditional hostelry was founded in 1891 by the current owners' great-grandmother. Snug rooms are decorated with painted wood or Louis Philippe-style furniture. Brightly coloured fabrics are a recent addition to the main dining room which specialises in large helpings of good regional cooking. A country bistro caters to pilgrims on the way to St James of Compostela who pass by on the GR footpath through the village. Chinaware and home-made preserves on sale.

Access : In the village, opposite the railway station

36 **LA LOZERETTE**
Mme Agulhon

48400 Cocurès
Tel. 04 66 45 06 04
Fax 04 66 45 12 93
lalozerette@wanadoo.fr

Open from Easter to 1 Nov • 21 rooms, one of which has disabled access, all have bath/WC or shower/WC and television • €52 to €72 (€50 to €70 low season); breakfast €8; half-board available • Restaurant closed Tue and Wed lunchtime; Tue lunchtime only in Jul-Aug. Menus €15 (weekdays) to €23 • Car park, garden

Oleander bushes planted in the lovely glazed Anduze vases in the garden.

This inn is both a hamlet on the doorstep of the National Park of Cévennes and a genuine family home because the young owner was born here and the auberge was opened by her grandmother. Feast your eyes on the renovated rooms with matching bedspreads, lace curtains and flowered balconies overlooking the village and the countryside. Admire the carved ceiling in the "country chic" dining room. The extensive wine-list is further proof of the owner-sommelier's many talents.

Access : 5.5km to the north-east of Florac on the N 106, then right onto the D 998

37 AUBERGE RÉGORDANE
M. Nogier

48800 La Garde-Guérin
Tel. 04 66 46 82 88
Fax 04 66 46 90 29
pierre.nogier @ free.fr
www.regordane.com

Closed from 1 Jan to 26 Mar and 2 Oct to 31 Dec
• 15 rooms with bath/WC or shower/WC, some have
television • €49 to €60; breakfast €8; half board available
• Menus €17 to €32 • Terrace in an inner courtyard

 The head-spinning view of the gorges of Chassezac from the village.

This fortified village was founded by the bishops of
Mende along the old Roman road linking Auvergne with
the Languedoc in an effort to eradicate highway robbery.
An order of knights from La Garde Guérin were entrusted
with the task of escorting voyagers. The stronghold of
one of these knights is now a characterful inn with small
rooms and mullioned windows, a restaurant with vaulted
ceiling and a beautiful terrace-courtyard of granite
flagstones.

Access : In the heart of the village

38 LE SAINT-SAUVEUR
M. Bourguet

Place Jean-Séquier
48150 Meyrueis
Tel. 04 66 45 62 12
Fax 04 66 45 65 94
saint-sauveur @ demeures.de.lozere.com
 www.demeures-de-lozere.com

Open from 25 Mar to 15 Nov • 10 rooms, all have
bath/WC and television • €39 to €44 (€37 to €42 low
season); breakfast €6; half board available • Menus €15
to €30 • Terrace

 The stone terrace shaded by a lovely old sycamore tree.

This elegant 18C mansion, full of character and very
reasonably priced, stands in the heart of a region that
abounds in magnificent natural sites: Aven Armand,
Dargilan Cave and the Gorges de La Jonte. Well-
appointed rooms are decorated with cherry wood
furniture and well protected by double-glazing. Both
dining rooms have been entirely refurbished.

Access : In the town centre

 39 LES ARCADES
M. Astrou

1 place Picasso
66400 Céret
Tel. 04 68 87 12 30
Fax 04 68 87 49 44
hotelarcades.ceret@wanadoo.fr

 www.hotelarcades-ceret.com

Open all year • 30 rooms, on 4 levels with lift, with bath/WC or shower/WC, 7 are air-conditioned and 12 have a kitchenette • €42 to €57; breakfast €7 • No restaurant • Garage. No dogs admitted

 40 CAN OLIBA
M. Boisard et Mme Le Corre

24 rue de la Paix
66200 Elne
Tel. 04 68 22 11 09
elna@club-internet.fr
www.can-oliba.com

Open all year • 6 non-smoking rooms with bath/WC • €60, breakfast included • Table d'hôte €22 (by reservation and evenings only) • Garden. Credit cards not accepted, no dogs allowed • Swimming pool

 The superb collections of Céret's Museum of Modern Art are definitely worth a visit.

To reach the entrance to this well-located establishment opposite the ramparts of the small Catalan town, guests must cross a large café terrace shaded by colourful parasols and plane trees. Admire the paintings, posters and lithographs in tribute to painters of the Céret School in the hall, staircase and corridors on your way up to your room. The excellent upkeep, dark country furniture and comfortable family atmosphere all contribute to the hotel's appeal.

 The owner's experience as interior decorator can be seen everywhere.

Visitors inevitably fall head over heels in love with this attractive 17C Catalan abode not far from the cathedral. A fine stone staircase and delightful sitting room strewn with antique furniture immediately set the tone and visitors cannot help but be spellbound. In the unusual rooms, the colours, furniture, curios and paintings vie with each other to incite guests to return and try them all... Don't miss the tiny walled garden complete with swimming pool. Irresistible!

Access : In the heart of the town near the archaeological museum

Access : In the historic centre of the town, near Sainte-Eulalie Cathedral

41 **Y SEM BÉ**
M. et Mme Blanche

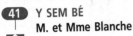

5 rue des Écureuils
66120 Font-Romeu
Tel. 04 68 30 00 54
Fax 04 68 30 25 42
www.hotel-ysembe.com

Closed from 7 Nov to 3 Dec • 22 rooms with bath/WC or shower/WC and television, 2 have kitchenettes • €33 to €80 (€30 to €60 low season); breakfast €7, half board available • Menus from €12 to €20 • Terrace, small garden • Skiing and mountain walks, fishing

We most liked **The south-facing aspect, to catch as many of the sun's warm rays as possible.**

This 1950s wood and stone chalet lies in a quiet, residential quarter of the mountain resort. The establishment spares no effort to make guests feel at home in its modest rooms with balconies in the process of being renovated, all of which is not surprising given its name – Y Sem Bé roughly translates as "At home" in Catalan!

Access : Take Avenue d'Espagne (towards Toulouse, Andorre) and turn right on Rue des Écureuils

42 **HOSTAL DELS TRABUCAYRES**
M. Davesne

66480 Las Illas
Tel. 04 68 83 07 56
Fax 04 68 83 07 56

Closed from 6 Jan to 15 Mar, from 25 to 30 Oct, Tue and Wed out of season • 5 rooms upstairs, 3 of which have a terrace • €28 to €32; breakfast €5; half board available • Menus €12 (weekdays) to €41 • Terrace, car park. No dogs allowed in the rooms • Walking

We most liked **Long walks in the silent forest of cork oaks surrounding the hotel.**

Don't give up! The winding hairpin bends of this tiny mountain road may seem endless but your efforts will be repaid tenfold. This tiny hamlet in the middle of nowhere is home to an old inn which provided accommodation to the exiled officers of Spain's Republican Army in 1936. Admire the view from the simple but pleasant rooms. The restaurant in a converted barn serves typically Catalan dishes.

Access : Take the D 618 between Céret and Le Boulou; at Maureillas take the D 13 and drive south-west for 11km

 43 **AUBERGE CATALANE**
Mme Ernst

10 avenue du Puymorens
66760 Latour-de-Carol
Tel. 04 68 04 80 66
Fax 04 68 04 95 25
auberge-catalane @ club-internet.fr
www.auberge-catalane.fr

Closed fortnight in May, from 12 Nov to 20 Dec, Sun evening and Mon except during school holidays • 10 rooms with shower/WC and television • €52 (€48 low season); breakfast €6; half board available • Menus €15 to €31 • Terrace, car park

 44 **DOMAINE DU MAS BOLUIX**
M. et Mme Ceilles

chemin du Pou de les Colobres
66100 Perpignan
Tel. 04 68 08 17 70
Fax 04 68 08 17 71
www.domaine-de-boluix.com

Open all year • 7 rooms with bath/WC • €73, breakfast included • No table d'hôte • Terrace, garden, car park. Credit cards not accepted, no dogs allowed • Swimming pool and tennis nearby

 Taking a ride on the little canary-yellow train through the picturesque Cerdagne region.

This inn, built in 1929, returned to the family when the original owner's grandchildren bought it back a few years ago and today the great-grandson, Benoît, presides over the kitchens. The rooms have been renovated and modernised, but the original Art Deco-inspired furniture has been retained; some bedrooms have balconies overlooking the village rooftops. Dining room-veranda.

 The secluded situation on the doorstep of Perpignan.

An easy-going atmosphere reigns throughout this 18C mas set in the midst of Cabestany's vineyards and orchards. Restored in 1998, the interior is comfortable, roomy and spotlessly clean. Each of the personalised rooms, whose immaculate walls are hung with bright regional fabrics, is named after a famous Catalan: Dali, Rigaud, Maillol, Picasso, Casals. The sweeping view over Roussillon, the coast and that emblem of Catalonia, the mighty Canigou mountain, is definitely worth a trip.

Access : On the main road of the village (N 20) between Bourg-Madame and the Puymorens Pass

Access : 5km southbound from Perpignan towards Argelès

LANGUEDOC ROUSSILLON

45 DOMAINE DE COUSSÈRES
Joo et Ann Maes

Domaine de Coussères
66220 Prugnanes
Tel. 04 68 59 23 55
Fax 04 68 59 23 55
www.cousseres.com

Open from 16 Mar to 31 Oct • 6 rooms • €68; breakfast included • Table d'hôte €23 (evenings only) • Car park, park. No dogs allowed • Swimming pool

46 CASA DEL ARTE
Mme Toubert

Mas Petit
66300 Thuir
Tel. 04 68 53 44 78
Fax 04 68 53 44 78
casadelarte@wanadoo.fr
www.casadelarte.fr.fm

Open all year • 6 rooms • €75 to €100 (€70 to €95 low season), breakfast included • Meals €22 • Sitting room, garden, car park • Outdoor swimming pool, sun deck

Basking in the silence disturbed only by the twittering of birds.

The setting will take your breath away: perched on a hillock surrounded by vineyards, this superb fortified house dominates the impressive landscape of mountains and sweet-scented scrub. The spacious, tastefully and individually decorated rooms and the welcoming dining room and massive table within all live up to expectations. A lovely garden, swimming pool and maze of terraces around the house enhance the matchless calm and tranquillity of this spot.

The arty feel to the individually decorated rooms.

The owner-painter has converted this 11C and 14C mas into a real art gallery. The walls of the often well proportioned rooms and bathrooms are covered in colourful paintings; the one devoted to ancient Rome is particularly lovely. Works by local artists adorn the walls of the sitting room, whose centrepiece is a medieval fireplace. The sun deck overlooking the swimming pool, the hundred-year-old oaks in the park and the small bamboo grove invite guests to take life easy.

Access : 5km to the north-west of Saint-Paul-de-Fenouillet on the D 117 and D 20

Access : 17km westbound from Perpignan, towards Thuir and Ille-sur-Têt

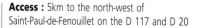

 47 **AUBERGE LES ÉCUREUILS**
M. et Mme Laffitte

 66340 Valcebollère
Tel. 04 68 04 52 03
Fax 04 68 04 52 34
auberge-ecureuils@wanadoo.fr

Closed from 5 to 20 May and 15 Oct to 20 Dec
• 15 rooms with bath/WC, some have television • €70
to €95; breakfast €9 to €11; half board available • Menus
€18 (weekdays) to €45 • Terrace, fitness room • Cross-
country skiing, snowshoe trekking. Hiking, mushrooming, fishing

Whether it be smuggler's footpaths or secluded fishing spots, the owner is a treasure-trove of tips.

Only twenty-or-so souls still live in this half-abandoned
village, perched at an altitude of 1 500m on a dead-end
road in the remote Pyrenees. Should you decide to join
them for a day or so, you won't regret it! The genuine
warmth and solicitude of the owners of this former 18C
sheep-fold, full of character, are quite captivating.
Comfortable rooms, with bathrooms done out in Spanish
marble, and an elegant rustic dining room complete the
picture.

Access : 9km to the south-east of Bourg-Madame on
the D 70, then at Osséja take the D 30

LIMOUSIN

Life in Limousin is lived as it should be: tired Parisians in need of greenery flock here to taste the simple joys of country life, breathe in the bracing air of its high plateaux, stroll along the banks of rivers alive with fish and wander through its woodlands in search of mushrooms and chestnuts. The sight of peaceful cattle grazing in utter contentment or lambs frolicking in the meadows in spring is enough to rejuvenate even the most jaded city-dweller. By late October, the forests are swathed in a cloak of autumn colours and the ground becomes a soft carpet of russet leaves. A perfect backdrop to the granite walls and soft sandstone façades of sleepy hamlets and peaceful cities, where ancestral crafts, such as Limoges porcelain and Aubusson tapestries, combine a love of tradition with a whole-hearted desire to embrace the best in contemporary art. The food is as wholesome as the region: savoury bacon soup, steaming Limousin stew and, as any proud local will tell you, the most tender, succulent beef in the world.

- Corrèze (19)
- Creuse (23)
- Haute-Vienne (87)

 1 LA TOUR
M. Lachaud

Place de l'Église
19190 Aubazine
Tel. 05 55 25 71 17
Fax 05 55 84 61 83

Closed 2 to 24 Jan • 19 rooms with bath/WC or shower/WC and television • €48; breakfast €6; half board available • Menus €15 (weekdays) to €35

 2 LA MAISON
M. Henriet

11 rue de la Gendarmerie
19120 Beaulieu-sur-Dordogne
Tel. 05 55 91 24 97
Fax 05 55 91 51 27

Closed from Oct to Mar • 6 rooms, 4 overlooking a patio, all have bath/WC • €52 to €62, breakfast included • No table d'hôte • Credit cards not accepted, no dogs allowed • Terraced garden, outdoor swimming pool

We most liked **Amble alongside the pretty Canal des Moines dug in the 12C.**

On the village square, opposite the Cistercian Abbey stand two characterful houses, the older one flanked by the tower from which the hotel takes its name. Bright wallpaper livens up the bedrooms, while the main dining room and smaller rooms for families or business lunches feature a rustic flavour in keeping with the array of regional delicacies on the menu. Apéritifs and after-dinner coffee are served on the terrace.

We most liked **More hacienda than country farmhouse.**

The arcades, ruddy ochre walls and profusion of hydrangeas, rose bushes and lemon trees in the patio are more reminiscent of an exotic hacienda than a French country farmhouse: all becomes clear when you learn that this astonishing 19C house was built by one of Napoleon's generals, homesick for Mexico. The adorable, unusually named rooms – "The Bride", "The Indians", "The Caricatures" – are quite unique; two overlook the sumptuous hanging garden and swimming pool.

Access : On the main square in the village, opposite the abbey

Access : In the village

LIMOUSIN

 3 **LEMANOIR DE BEAULIEU**
M. et Mme Bessière

 4 place du Champ-de-Mars
19120 Beaulieu-sur-Dordogne
Tel. 05 55 91 01 34
Fax 05 55 91 23 57

Closed from 3 Jan to 4 Mar • 20 rooms with bath/WC or shower/WC, some have television • €45 to €52; breakfast €6.50; half board €42 to €50 • Menus €16 (weekdays) to €35 • Terrace, private car park

 4 **LA RAZE**
Mme Tatien

19500 Collonges-la-Rouge
Tel. 05 55 25 48 16
domainedelaraze@yahoo.fr
http://chambrelaraze.free.fr

Open all year • 5 rooms • €65 to €70, breakfast included, dogs not allowed • No table d'hôte • Car park, garden. Credit cards not accepted

Take a compass to explore the labyrinth of narrow lanes in the historic town.

The central location of this sturdy hotel, founded in 1912 by Amélie Fournié, does full justice to its name. When booking, ask for one of the renovated rooms. The house's excellent reputation is also due to the generous helpings of wholesome country cooking served in an agreeable rustic dining room or on the terrace where you can enjoy the warm breeze.

 Throw open your windows and feast your eyes on the countryside.

This 18C farmstead lies just 800m outside the crimson sandstone village: serenity reigns, broken only by the high-pitched calls of the peacock in the mating season. The lady of the house's artistic talents can be admired in the hand-stencilled patterns on the walls of the comfortable bedrooms. The breakfast room, adorned with family furniture and heirlooms and the park "à l'anglaise" overflowing with fruit trees and roses, are magnificent.

Access : On the main square in the centre of the village

Access : 5.5km to the south-west of Collonges on the D 38 and the D 19, then follow the La Raze signs

DONZENAC - 19270

NAVES - 19460

 5 LE RELAIS DU BAS LIMOUSIN
M. et Mme Delavier

 Sadroc
19270 Donzenac
Tel. 05 55 84 52 06
Fax 05 55 84 51 41
relais-du-bas-limousin @ wanadoo.fr
 www.relaisbaslimousin.fr

Closed from 9 to 16 Jan, 23 to 29 Feb and 1 to 14 Nov
• 22 rooms with bath/WC or shower/WC and television
• €38 to €63; breakfast €7; half board available
• Restaurant closed Sun evening except Jul-Aug and Mon
lunchtime; menus €16 (weekdays) to €47 • Terrace,
garden, garage, car park • Outdoor swimming pool

 6 CHEZ MONSIEUR ET MADAME PERROT
M. et Mme Perrot

 Gourdinot
19460 Naves
Tel. 05 55 27 08 93
brunhild.perrot @ wanadoo.fr
 www.hotes-naves-correze.com

Open all year • 3 rooms upstairs, one of which has a
loggia • €36 to €40, breakfast included, half board
available • Table d'hôte €14 • Car park. Credit cards not
accepted, no dogs allowed

 **A visit to the disused slate quarries –
if you're not afraid of heights!**

This solid construction inspired by regional styles dates
from the 1960s and was clearly built to last a few
centuries. The stylish personalised rooms have matching
fabrics, bedspreads and lampshades and those facing
the rear look out over a peaceful Limousin landscape.
Welcoming family dining rooms, a veranda flooded with
light and a terrace opening onto the garden complete
with swimming pool and play area.

 **The sense of being right in the middle
of nowhere.**

This old Corrèze farmhouse built out of rough-hewn
stone and nestling in a wooded valley is ideal for touring
the region: Millevaches – literally "Thousand cows"
plateau, Lake Seilhac and Uzerche. Soak up the peaceful
atmosphere of the cosy bedrooms and relax by the
fireside in the company of your lively young hosts. In
the morning, you will awake to the enticing smell of
fresh-baked bread, steaming coffee and a breakfast
table piled high with a profusion of home-made
gingerbreads and preserves.

Access : 6km on the D 920 towards Uzerche

Access : 5km northbound from Naves on the N 20,
then take a minor road

7 À LA TABLE DE LA BERGÈRE
Mme Verlhac

Belveyre
19600 Nespouls
 Tel. 05 55 85 82 58

Open all year • 5 rooms • €28 to €38, breakfast included, half board available • Table d'hôte €14 • Garden, car park. Credit cards not accepted, no dogs allowed

8 LES VOYAGEURS
M. et Mme Chaumeil

Place de la Mairie
19320 Saint-Martin-la-Méanne
Tel. 05 55 29 11 53
Fax 05 55 29 27 70
info @ hotellesvoyageurs.com
 www.hotellesvoyageurs.com

Open from mid-Feb to mid-Nov; closed Sun evening and Mon out of season • 8 rooms upstairs with bath/WC or shower/WC, some have television • €39 to €50; breakfast €6; half board available • Menus €15 to €24 • Terrace, garden, car park • Private pond for anglers

 If this farm wins any more awards, it may well run out of space to display them.

This sturdily built farmstead in the midst of oaks, meadows and dry stone huts is very well placed to explore the region's wealth of tourist sights. The rooms, furnished with family heirlooms, are very inviting, particularly those on the second floor, while the flavourful regional cooking, friendly atmosphere and Madame's ability to make you feel at home are unparalleled.

 The lady of the house's warm greeting.

This establishment, which has been run by the same family for five generations, is ideal to get away from it all and take things easy. Within its solid stone walls, built in 1853, you'll find simple, but well cared-for bedrooms. Admire the wood carving in the rustic dining room, if you can tear yourself away from the traditional cuisine prepared by the chef-owner for a minute. After lunch or dinner, venture out into the garden as far as the pond and watch the carp and pike.

Access : 15km southbound from Brive towards Nespouls, then take the D 19 and the D 920

Access : On a square in the centre of the village

 9 LA MAISON DES CHANOINES
M. et Mme Cheyroux

Chemin de l'Église
19500 Turenne
Tel. 05 55 85 93 43
Fax 05 55 85 93 43
www.maison-des-chanoines.com

Open from Easter to late Sep • 6 rooms located in 2 buildings, with bath/WC or shower/WC • €60 to €85; breakfast €9; half-board available • Air-conditioned restaurant; evenings only except Wed (Jun), Sun and national holidays; menus €30 (by reservation) • Terrace. No dogs allowed in rooms

 10 CHAMBRE D'HÔTE M. DUMONTANT
M. et Mme Dumontant

Les Vergnes
23200 Saint-Pardoux-le-Neuf
Tel. 05 55 66 23 74
Fax 05 55 67 74 16
sylvie.dumontant @ freesbee.fr
www.lesvergnes.com

Closed from late Oct to early Apr • 6 rooms with bathrooms and separate WC • €55 to €77, breakfast included; half-board available • Table d'hôte €15 to €23 • Terrace, car park. Credit cards not accepted • Fishing

 The terrace overlooking a manicured herb garden.

It is well worth venturing past the handsome late Gothic-style door and into this lovely 16C house built in the heart of a picturesque village. There is as much character inside as out, with the vaulted dining room, fireplace and spiral staircase climbing up to the rooms, which are furnished with the results of forays to local antiques dealers. At mealtimes, roll up your sleeves and dig into the chef's creative recipes prepared with the best local produce. Limited seating only.

 Fishing in the nearby pond.

If in desperate need of a break from city life, your prayers will be answered in this 18C farmhouse, set in the heart of the countryside and surrounded by a prosperous working farm, only 7km from the tapestry capital of France. All the spacious, fully renovated rooms overlook the pond and nearby woodland. Original exposed stone walls and a huge fireplace add character to the dining room.

Access : In the centre of the village, 16km south of Brive-la-Gaillarde

Access : 7km eastbound from Aubusson on the N 141

LIMOUSIN

11 LE MOULIN DE MARSAGUET
M. Gizardin

87500 Coussac-Bonneval
Tel. 05 55 75 28 29
Fax 05 55 75 28 29

 www.tourismorama-moulindemarsaguet.com

Closed from 30 Sep to 15 Apr and Sun • 3 rooms • €35 to €40, breakfast included • Table d'hôte €17 • Garden, terrace, car park. Credit cards not accepted, no dogs allowed • Cookery courses. Fishing, boating and swimming

12 MANOIR HENRI IV
M. Broussac

D 220
87250 La Croix-du-Breuil
Tel. 05 55 76 00 56
Fax 05 55 76 14 14
manoirhenriiv @ tele2.fr

Closed Mon from Oct to May and Sun evening all year • 11 rooms on 2 floors, with bath/WC or shower/WC, all have television • €45 to €58; breakfast €6 • Menus €15 (weekdays) to €42 • Terrace, garden, car park

 We most liked **Finding out how tasty farm delicacies are made.**

The hospitality of this farming family will make you want to return to their rambling 18C farmstead and its immense 30-acre fishpond. Anglers will love catching pike while the others can go swimming or boating. The light, airy rooms are simply decorated and every evening brings an excellent opportunity to wine and dine on the succulent home-made delicacies in lively company.

 We most liked **Walls steeped in history, a stone's throw from a motorway junction.**

This fortified 16C farmstead, flanked by a pretty turret, does full honour to its namesake and former royal guest who used to hunt in the area. The rustic, well-kept rooms are smaller and less airy under the eaves. Countrified dining rooms with exposed beams and an interesting collection of farming implements on the walls; one has a lovely fireplace.

Access : 3.6km northbound from Coussac on the D 17 towards La Roche-l'Abeille, then take the D 57

Access : 3km northbound from Bessines-sur-Gartempe

SAINT-PRIEST-TAURION - 87480

SAINT-VICTURNIEN - 87420

13 LE RELAIS DU TAURION
M. Roger

2 chemin des Contamines
87480 Saint-Priest-Taurion
Tel. 05 55 39 70 14
Fax 05 55 39 67 63

Closed from 15 Dec to 15 Jan • 8 rooms with bath/WC or shower/WC, almost all have television • €48 to €70; breakfast €9; half board available • Restaurant closed Sun evening and Mon; menus €19 (weekdays) to €33 • Terrace, garden, car park • Swimming, fishing, canoeing nearby

14 DOMAINE DU LOUBIER
M. et Mme Dauriac

Lieu-dit « Le Petit-Loubier »
87420 Saint-Victurnien
Tel. 05 55 03 29 22

Closed from Dec to Jan • 4 rooms with bathrooms, one room has disabled access • €48, breakfast included • No table d'hôte • Park, car park. Credit cards not accepted • Fishing, canoeing, swimming, horse-riding and tennis nearby

The delightful owners.

This grand hundred-year-old mansion covered in Virginia creeper is home to immaculate little rooms, some of which have old marble fireplaces. Old beams and rustic furniture add charm to the sitting room. In the fine weather, tables are laid amid the luxuriant foliage of the flowered garden. Traditional cuisine.

The allure of this estate will linger in your memory for years.

A park planted with lindens, oaks, chestnuts, giant thujas and a superb monkey puzzle tree is the setting for this gracious 18C-19C country residence. Well-dimensioned rooms, tastefully decorated by the owner-antique dealer.

Access : 11km to the north-east of Limoges on the D 29

Access : 5km southbound from Oradour-sur-Glane on the D 9, take the D 3, then the dead-end road on the right

15 SAINT-ÉLOI
Mme Ashton

66 avenue Saint-Éloi
87110 Solignac
Tel. 05 55 00 44 52
Fax 05 55 00 55 56
lesaint.eloi @ wanadoo.fr
www.lesainteloi.fr

Closed in Jan, from 1 to 10 Sep, 1st week Nov, Mon, Sat lunchtime and Sun evening • 15 rooms with bath/WC and television, one room has disabled access • €44 to €61; breakfast €7 to €10; half board available • Menus €20 (weekdays) to €39 • Terrace • Tea room with painting and sculpture exhibitions

16 LA POMME DE PIN
M. Mounier

Étang de Tricherie
87140 Thouron
Tel. 05 55 53 43 43
Fax 05 55 53 35 33

Closed during the February holidays, in Sep, Mon and Tue lunchtime • 7 rooms with bath/WC and television • €48 to €65; breakfast €6, half board available • Menus €24 (weekdays) to €37 • Terrace, garden. No dogs allowed in rooms

 The blessed union of medieval and modern.

Opposite the abbey founded by St Éloi, this half-timbered house in local stone welcomes guests in a spirit of peace and quiet. Spacious, well-soundproofed rooms are adorned with bright sunny fabrics and paintings. From his stained-glass window, good King Dagobert's treasurer, the patron saint of goldsmiths, gazes benignly down on diners as they savour the owner's flavourful cooking in a 12C dining room complete with granite fireplace.

 Feast your eyes on a landscape of ponds, lakes and forest.

All the quiet, spacious rooms in the former spinning mill enjoy a view of the river, while the old mill on the banks of the millpond houses two dining rooms. The first offers an authentically rustic setting with rough stone walls and a huge fireplace where meat is roasted; the second is airier and overlooks the wonderful Limousin countryside.

Access : 10km southbound from Limoges on the D 704 (towards St-Yrieix), then right on the D 32

Access : Northbound from Limoges on the A 20, drive until exit no 26, then take the D 5 towards Nantiat

LORRAINE

If you are planning a trip to Lorraine and want to do justice to the region's wealth of wonderful sights, make sure you pack your walking boots. However, before you set off for the distant reaches of its lofty slopes, pause for a moment in Nancy and take in its splendid artistic heritage, without forgetting to admire the lights of Metz. You can then move on through a string of tiny spa resorts, renowned for the slimming properties of their water, and the famous centres of craftsmanship which produce the legendary Baccarat crystal, enamels of Longwy and porcelain of Lunéville, before you reach the poignant silence of the dormant mines and quarries at Domrémy and Colombey. The deep lakes, thick forests and wild animals of the Vosges Regional Park will keep you entranced as you make your way down through the gentle hillsides, dotted with plum-laden orchards. Stop for a little 'light' refreshment in a *marcairerie*, one of the region's old farm-inns, and sample the famous quiches and tarts, before finishing with a slab of pungent Munster cheese or a kirsch-flavoured dessert for the sweet-toothed among us.

- Meurthe-et-Moselle (54)
- Meuse (55)
- Moselle (57)
- Vosges (88)

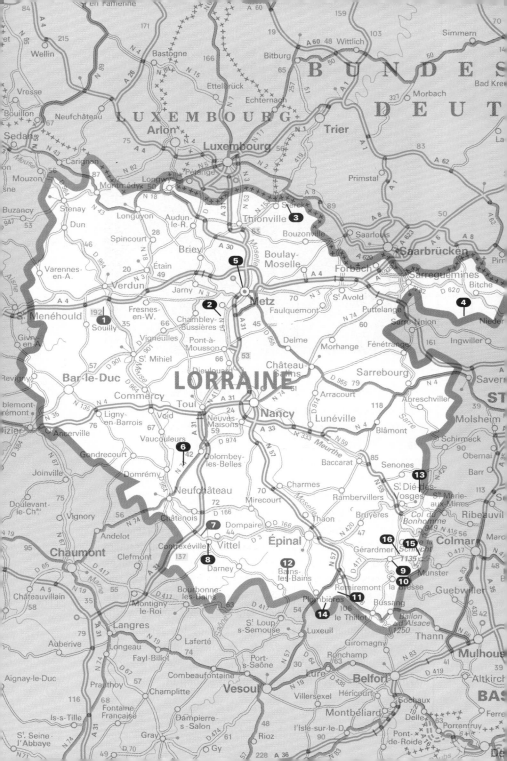

ViaMichelin

LET VIAMICHELIN PDA SOFTWARE GUIDE YOU THROUGHOUT YOUR EUROPEAN JOURNEYS

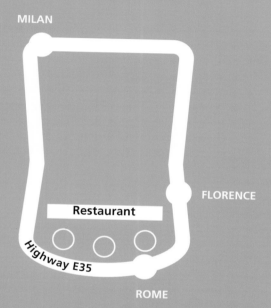

MILAN

Restaurant

FLORENCE

Highway E35

ROME

*PDA must be connected to a GPS receiver

With PDA software from ViaMichelin, complimented by Michelin maps and The MICHELIN® Guide, you can display a map of your route, be guided by vocal instructions* and, with just a few simple clicks, find hotel and restaurant recommendations.

For more information, go to: www.ViaMichelin.com

Wherever you're going, go ViaMichelin

☐ a. ✗✗ **A comfortable restaurant ?**

☐ b. ❀ **A very good restaurant in its category ?**

☐ c. 😊 **Good food at moderate prices ?**

Can't decide?

Then immerse yourself in the Michelin Guide!

In this collection the Michelin inspectors recommend and describe more than 45,000 hotels and restaurants across Europe ranging from new 'Bib Gourmand' 😊 bistros to luxury 3 star ❀❀❀ restaurants. There are also 300 maps and 1600 town plans to help you find each establishment.

Discover the pleasure of travel with the Michelin Guide.

 ① CHÂTEAU DE LABESSIÈRE
M. Eichenauer

9 rue du Four
55320 Ancemont
Tel. 03 29 85 70 21
Fax 03 29 87 61 60
rene.eichenauer@wanadoo.fr
www.labessiere.com

Closed at Christmas and 1 Jan • 4 rooms • €70, breakfast included; half-board available • Table d'hôte €25 • Garden, car park. Credit cards not accepted, no dogs allowed • Outdoor swimming pool

 ② HOSTELLERIE DU LION D'OR
M. Erman

105 rue du Commerce
57680 Gorze
Tel. 03 87 52 00 90
Fax 03 87 52 09 62

Closed Sun evening and Mon • 15 rooms located in 2 buildings, with bath/WC or shower/WC, all have television • €48 to €55; breakfast €8; half board available • Menus €25 (lunchtime weekdays) to €57 • Terrace, garden, car park • Children's play area

 We most liked
A mite outdated but full of charm.

Midway between Argonne and the Côtes de Meuse, this unassuming 18C castle makes an ideal base camp to explore the region. Pastel wallpaper, canopied beds and old furniture all add to rather than detract from the rooms' appeal. The same pleasantly outmoded atmosphere prevails in the sitting room, remarkably well stocked with guides, brochures and works on the Meuse. The table d'hôte, open every evening, shaded garden and attractive outdoor swimming pool further enhance the establishment's allure.

 We most liked
The dense foliage shading the terrace.

Run by the same family for over fifty years, this 19C coaching inn has moved with the times without losing sight of its roots. The rooms have been gradually updated and we recommend those opening onto the lovely patio with a trout aquarium and splendid rafters. Back in the restaurant, a huge stone fireplace, fine enough to grace any castle banquet hall, holds its own among the distinctly contemporary-style furniture.

Access : 15km southbound from Verdun on the D 34 (Saint-Mihiel road)

Access : On the main road: to the south-west of Metz, on the D 6, then at Ancy-sur-Moselle turn right

MANDEREN - 57480

MEISENTHAL - 57960

 3 AU RELAIS DU CHÂTEAU DE MENSBERG
M. Schneider

15 rue du Château
57480 Manderen
Tel. 03 82 83 73 16
Fax 03 82 83 23 37
aurelaismensberg @ aol.com

Closed 26 Dec 2004 to 19 Jan 2005 • 13 rooms, one of which has disabled access, almost all have shower/WC (2 have bath/WC), all have television • €60 (€51 low season); breakfast €7; half board available • Restaurant closed Tue; menus €19 to €44 • Terrace, garden, car park

 4 AUBERGE DES MÉSANGES
M. et Mme Walter

2 rue du Tiseur
57960 Meisenthal
Tel. 03 87 96 92 28
Fax 03 87 96 99 14
hotel-restaurant.auberge-mesanges
@ wanadoo.fr
www.aubergedesmesanges.com

Closed from 12 to 28 Feb and from 23 to 27 Dec • 22 rooms with shower/WC, half of the rooms have television • €45 to €51 (€32 to €44 low season); breakfast €7; half board available • Restaurant closed Sun evening and Mon; menus €10 (weekdays) to €20 • Terrace, car park

 The castle forms a handsome backdrop to a wide variety of performances.

"Malbrouck" was the name the French soldiers gave to one of their most redoutable enemies, the Duke of Marlborough. The duke set up his HQ here at Mensberg (also called Marlborough) Castle in 1705 but was unable to do battle, giving rise to a nursery rhyme still sung today. Three rooms overlook the beautifully restored castle. In addition to a rustic dining room graced by a huge stone fireplace, the inn has two split-level sitting rooms and a quiet terrace in the rear.

 Need to get back in touch with the things that really matter?

This inn, on the edge of the Nature Reserve of the Northern Vosges, is ideally located in calm surroundings and close to a whole range of leisure pursuits, including walking, golf, museums and castles. Good-sized, practically-equipped rooms in excellent order. Meals are served in a dining room whose uncluttered rustic style perfectly complements the simple, regional fare.

Access : From Sierck-les-Bains take the N 153 northbound for 2km, then at Apach turn right on the D 64

Access : Near the centre of the village

 5 LA CATHÉDRALE
M. Hocine

 25 place de la Chambre
57000 Metz
Tel. 03 87 75 00 02
Fax 03 87 75 40 75
hotelcathedrale-metz@wanadoo.fr
www.hotelcathedrale-metz.fr

Open all year • 20 rooms on 3 floors, most have bath/WC, some have shower/WC, all have television • €68 to €95; breakfast €11 • No restaurant

6 LE RELAIS ROSE
M. Loëffler

 24 rue de Neufchâteau
88300 Autreville
Tel. 03 83 52 04 98
Fax 03 83 52 06 03

Open all year • 16 rooms located in 3 buildings, most have bath/WC or shower/WC, all have television, some are non-smoking • €45 to €75; breakfast €8; half board available • Menus €12 to €30 • Terrace, garden, garage, car park

 The splendid view of St Étienne Cathedral from most of the rooms.

The passing of time seems to have left no traces on the fine façade of this former coaching inn, which first opened its doors in 1627. Inside, however, the owners have really gone to town: individually styled rooms are adorned with wrought-iron furniture, bright fabrics or old pieces of furniture picked up in auctions and antique shops. The timber frames, fireplaces and parquet all bear witness to the establishment's four-hundred-year commitment to hostelry.

 The whole family bends over backwards to please its guests.

A prayer-stool, a handsome wardrobe, a well-worn leather armchair, an unusual patchwork of wallpapers from every age and era, some adorned with wonderfully garish flowers: the list is endless and the result a higgledy-piggledy mixture which proudly refuses to toe the line to any theme or age, and will strike a chord with your secret nonconformist side! For all their casually eclectic style, the renovated rooms are most appealing and the restaurant tables are laid with elegant china from Limoges.

Access : In the town centre, near Saint-Étienne Cathedral

Access : In the village, on the N 74 between Colombey-les-Belles and Neufchâteau

LORRAINE

 7 CHAMBRES D'HÔTES M. BRETON
M. Breton

74 rue des Récollets
88140 Bulgnéville
Tel. 03 29 09 21 72
Fax 03 29 09 21 72
benoit.breton@wanadoo.fr

Open all year, in winter by reservation only • 4 rooms
• €68, breakfast included • No table d'hôte • Garden,
car park. Credit cards not accepted

 8 LA SOUVERAINE
M. Paris

Parc Thermal
88140 Contrexéville
Tel. 03 29 08 09 59
Fax 03 29 08 16 39
contact@hotel-souveraine.com
www.hotel-souveraine.com

Open all year • 31 rooms, half overlook the park, all have
bath/WC or shower/WC and television • €35 to €85;
breakfast €9; half board available • Car park

 A faultlessly decorated country home.

This unostentatious country house dating from 1720 was
entirely redecorated by the owner-antique dealer. The
result invites the admiration of everyone who sees it:
spacious, comfortable rooms decorated with a tasteful
blend of period furniture and modern décor. The
sandstone bathrooms are particularly lovely and the
garden behind the house is also worthy of note.

 **The branches laden with crows do
have a slightly Hitchcockian air to
them.**

Contrexéville was "the" place to take the waters at the
height of the Belle Époque. The glass awning and friezes
which embellish the graceful pink and white façade of
this elegant home, leave one in no doubt about its
allegiance to a former illustrious guest, the Grand
Duchess Vladimir, aunt of Czar Nicholas II. Marble
fireplaces, moulded ceilings and brass beds continue to
grace the recently renovated bedrooms, some of which
overlook the resort park.

Access : 7.5km westbound from Contrexéville on the
D 164

Access : In the spa resort

 9 LE CHALET DU LAC
M. Vallcaneras

 10 JAMAGNE
Famille Jeanselme

97 chemin de la Droite du Lac
88400 Gérardmer
Tel. 03 29 63 38 76
Fax 03 29 60 91 63

Closed from 1 to 31 Oct • 11 rooms, 4 of which are in a separate chalet, with shower/WC and television • €56 breakfast €8; half board available • Menus €20 to €40 • Garden, car park • Table-tennis

2 boulevard Jamagne
88400 Gérardmer
Tel. 03 29 63 36 86
Fax 03 29 60 05 87
hotel.jamagne@wanadoo.fr
www.jamagne.com

Closed from 6 Mar to 25 Mar and from 13 Nov to 23 Dec • 48 rooms with bath/WC or shower/WC, all have television • €70 to €90 (€55 to €85 low season); breakfast €10; half board available • Menus €13 to €40 • Terrace, private car park. No dogs allowed in restaurant • Indoor swimming pool, fitness room, sauna, hammam, jacuzzi, hiking, water sports

 Time seems to stand still on the shores of the lake.

This trim, traditional Vosges chalet built in 1866 is one of the few holiday homes of this sort, so popular round Lake Gérardmer in the 19C, to have made it through to the present day. The sober, immaculate rooms are sometimes furnished with family heirlooms; ask for a renovated room. Alsace tableware and cut-crystal glasses adorn the tables in the "winstub" styled restaurant with a sweeping view. The garden tumbles down to the lake and it is a real pleasure to wander round its paths.

 Upholding traditions since 1905.

It is impossible to miss this impressive building on a street corner. Its owners endeavour to cater to families, offering several partitioned rooms, and to those with fewer family worries, with a cosy bar and sitting rooms. Guests eager to sample the region's delicious recipes can head for two lovely dining rooms, while those who have come for the region's sporting pursuits will not be disappointed by the hotel's excellent keep-fit facilities, indoor swimming pool and the countless forest paths.

Access : On the Épinal road, 1km to the west, opposite the lake

Access : In the town centre

LORRAINE

GIRMONT-VAL-D'AJOL - 88340

LA CHAPELLE-AUX-BOIS - 88240

 11 AUBERGE DE LA VIGOTTE
M. et Mme Bouguerne

 88340 Girmont-Val-d'Ajol
Tel. 03 29 61 06 32
Fax 03 29 61 07 88
courrier@lavigotte.com
www.lavigotte.com

Open all year • 18 rooms and 1 suite, most have bath/WC, some have shower/WC • €55 to €65; breakfast €6; half board available • Restaurant closed Tue and Wed; menus €25 to €38 • Terrace, garden, car park. No dogs allowed • Tennis, fishing and swimming in private ponds, play area, hiking, cross-country skiing

12 LES GRANDS PRÉS
Mme Chassard

 9 les Grands-Prés
88240 La Chapelle-aux-Bois
Tel. 03 29 36 31 00
 Fax 03 29 36 31 00

Open all year • 3 rooms and 2 gîtes • €40, breakfast included; half board available • Table d'hôte €14 • Sitting room, garden, car park. Credit cards not accepted, no dogs allowed

We most liked **It is impossible to find a fault with this Vosgian inn.**

A quick glimpse at the web site of the "via gotta" – "way of springs" – will give you an idea of the new owners' energetic, up-to-date approach since buying the inn in 2000. In no time at all, this old farmhouse, perched at a height of 700m in a forest of fir trees and ponds, has become a very pleasant and popular hostelry thanks to its delightful rooms and "country chic" restaurant. The chef's inventive recipes are a feast for the eyes as well as the mouth.

We most liked **Fishing in the garden.**

This immense 19C house encircled by lush green countryside lies just a few minutes from the spa resort of Bains-les-Bains. Spotless, soberly styled rooms overlook a garden through which a fishing stream gurgles and babbles. Home-grown vegetables from the cottage garden and fresh poultry and rabbit reared on the premises are among the specialities on the dinner table.

Access : Between the Ajol Valley and Remiremont (D 23), at Faymon take the D 83 for 5km

Access : 3.5km to the south-east of Bains-les-Bains towards Saint-Loup, then take a minor road

 **AUBERGE DU SPITZEMBERG**
M. et Mme Fleury

88490 La Petite-Fosse
Tel. 03 29 51 20 46
Fax 03 29 51 10 12

Closed Mon • 10 rooms upstairs with bath/WC or shower/WC, some have television • €46 to €61; breakfast €7; half board available • Menus €18 (weekdays) to €25 • Garden, garage, car park • Mini-golf and walks in the forest

 LA RÉSIDENCE
Mme Bongeot

5 rue des Mousses
88340 Le Val-d'Ajol
Tel. 03 29 30 68 52
Fax 03 29 66 53 00
contact@la-residence.com
www.la-residence.com

Closed from 26 Nov to 26 Dec • 49 rooms located in 3 buildings with bath/WC or shower/WC and television • €58 to €85; breakfast €9; half board available • Restaurant closed Sun eve from 1 Nov to 30 Apr except national and school holidays; menus €17 (weekdays) to €50 • Park, car park • Swimming pool with a retractable roof, tennis

 Swathed in a curtain of greenery.

Step inside this haven of tranquillity in the remote forest of the Vosges and forget your troubles for a while. The comfortable rooms are pleasantly homely and welcoming and the tasty, unfussy cooking, made with rigorously selected regional produce, is served in a rustic dining room. All you have to decide now is which direction to head off for your long walk in the country. No need to leave that trail of breadcrumbs, though; all the paths are well signposted.

 Waking up to a dawn chorus.

Contemporary and Louis XV rooms are spread over three buildings backing onto the forest which make up the Residence: a 19C country house, an "orangery" which can be reached by a glass-covered gallery, and a former coaching inn, 50m away. A fireplace is the centrepiece of a light, airy dining room. As for leisure, the hotel offers a swimming pool with removable roof, tennis courts and a mature wooded park for pre-dinner strolls.

Access : 3.5km from Provenchères-sur-Fave on the D 45, then take a forest road

Access : On leaving the village take the lane leading to Hamanxard

15 LE VAL JOLI
M. et Mme Laruelle

12 bis Le Village
88230 Le Valtin
Tel. 03 29 60 91 37
Fax 03 29 60 81 73
le-val-joli @ wanadoo.fr
www.levaljoli.com

Closed from 11 Nov-31 Dec, Sun evening, Mon lunchtime (except public holidays, Mon evening and Tue lunchtime (except school holidays) • 7 rooms, one has disabled access, most have bath/WC, all have television • €70 to €150; breakfast €10; half board €64 to €104 • Restaurant closed Mon lunchtime; menus €18 (weekdays) to €60 • Terrace, garden, car park • Tennis, hiking

 That sound, unlike anything else you have ever heard, is that of a rutting buck!

This appealing country inn almost on the doorstep of the superb Route des Crêtes (Peak Road) has a number of renovated rooms; and all the accommodation overlooks the dense pine forests and mountains. A strong emphasis is given to local produce on the menu and meals are served in the rustic dining room – yes, the 19C carved wooden ceiling is original – or in the more modern veranda. The owner-mayor is a mine of helpful tips about the "panoramic path" around the village, dotted with viewpoints.

Access : In the village, drive along the D 23 from Fraize to the Schlucht Pass

16 LE COLLET
M. et Mme Lapôtre

Col de la Schlucht
88400 Xonrupt-Longemer
Tel. 03 29 60 09 57
Fax 03 29 60 08 77
hotcollet @ aol.com
www.chalethotel-lecollet.com

Closed from 10 to 24 Apr and from 13 Nov to 11 Dec • 25 rooms, all have bath/WC or shower/WC and television • €69 to €85; breakfast €9; half board available • Restaurant closed Wed lunchtime and Thu; menus €15 (lunchtime weekdays) to €26 • Terrace, car park. No dogs allowed in restaurant • Skiing and hiking trails nearby

 A perfect base camp to explore the breathtaking Route des Crêtes (Peak Route).

The walls of this hotel chalet, lost in a forest of fir trees, make it impossible to guess what is inside. For the hospitable owners, entertaining guests does not simply mean providing a cheerful mountain décor with pretty fabrics and painted furniture or a deliciously tempting regional menu: it is above all, a state of mind. Their attention to detail can be felt in the smell of warm brioche in the morning, the wealth of useful tips for walkers or the magic shows for children.

Access : 2km from the Schlucht Pass on the Gérardmer road, by the D 417

MIDI-PYRÉNÉES

Lourdes may be famous as the site of miracles, but some would say that the whole of the Midi-Pyrénées has been uniquely blessed. The region is home to a rich and varied plant and animal life, with the remoter parts of the Pyrenees still supporting a population of brown bears. A great rampart guarding the border with Spain, these breathtaking mountains are riven by spectacularly deep clefts and are drained by rushing torrents. At sunset, the towers of medieval cities and fortresses glow in the evening light; forbidding Cathar castles are stained a bloody red, Albi and its famous fortified cathedral turn crimson while Toulouse is veiled in dusty pink. Deep beneath the surface of the earth at Lascaux and elsewhere are equally extraordinary sights, the vivid cave-paintings of our gifted prehistoric ancestors. To this list of regional marvels must be added the bounteous lands along the River Garonne, a fertile land famous for its cereal crops, vegetables fruit and wine, which has given rise to a host of culinary traditions; it would be a crime to leave without sampling a sumptuous cassoulet, confit de canard or foie gras.

- Ariège (09)
- Aveyron (12)
- Haute-Garonne (31)
- Gers (32)
- Lot (46)
- Hautes-Pyrénées (65)
- Tarn (81)
- Tarn-et-Garonne (82)

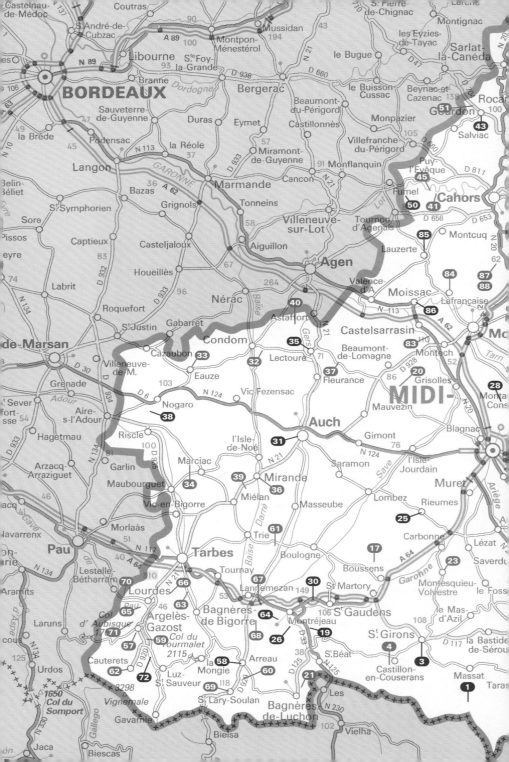

MIDI PYRÉNÉES

 1 LES OUSSAILLÈS
Mme Charrue

09140 Aulus-les-Bains
Tel. 05 61 96 03 68
Fax 05 61 96 03 70
jcharrue@free.fr

Open all year • 12 rooms on two floors, with bath/WC or shower/WC and television • €47 to €53; breakfast €6.50, half board available • Menus €10 to €23 • Terrace, garden, garage. No dogs allowed

 2 AUBERGE LES MYRTILLES
M. et Mme Blazy

Col des Marrous - 09000 Foix
Tel. 05 61 65 16 46
Fax 05 61 65 16 46
aubergelesmyrtilles@wanadoo.fr
http://perso.wanadoo.fr/auberge.
les.myrtilles

Closed from 1 Jan to 6 Feb, 31 Oct to 31 Dec, Mon, Tue and Wed lunchtime (low season) • 7 rooms, 2 of which have a terrace. 5 rooms have shower/WC, 2 have bath/WC, all have television • €60 to €75; breakfast €7; half board available • Menus €16 (weekdays) to €22 • Terrace, garden, car park. No dogs allowed in restaurant • Swimming pool, sauna, jacuzzi

 So friendly, you'll think you're at home.

This 1920s stone house is flanked by a turret. The bedrooms overlooking the garden, by far the most pleasant, enjoy a lovely view of the flourishing green valley. Even better, you can ask for breakfast to be served on your own private balcony. In fine weather, the welcoming restaurant opens onto a shaded terrace.

 The two rooms recently renovated in an alpine spirit.

Dig into a piece of blueberry pie, choose a vintage Bordeaux from the wine-list, dive into the swimming pool, walk along the signposted footpath through a beech forest, gaze down on Arget Valley from the terrace, listen to the bucks rutting or just soak up the priceless serenity. Shake them all up and voilà: a delicious "sport and leisure" cocktail! You can of course simply do absolutely nothing from dawn until dusk!

Access : In the heart of the village, 33km to the south-east of Saint Girons

Access : 19km westbound from Foix on the D 17

 3 EYCHENNE
Famille Bordeau

 8 avenue Paul-Laffont
09200 Saint-Girons
Tel. 05 61 04 04 50
Fax 05 61 96 07 20
eychen@club-internet.fr

Closed from 1 Dec to 31 Jan, Sun evening and Mon from Nov to Mar (except during holidays) • 43 rooms, all have bath/WC or shower/WC and television • €50 to €180 (€40 to €160 low season); breakfast €9; half board available • Menus €25 to €53 • Private car park • Swimming pool

 4 MAISON DE LA GRANDE OURSE
Mme Matulova

 09800 Salsein
Tel. 05 61 96 16 51

Open weekends in winter • 3 rooms, one of which is independent. One room has a shower and 2 have a private sitting room and bathroom • €45, breakfast included • Table d'hôte €15 • Car park. Credit cards not accepted

 The banks of the Salat shaded by a long line of plane trees - how beautifully, typically French!

The Bordeau family has been running this coaching inn for seven generations. This lasting dedication probably explains the quality of the welcome and the deliciously old-fashioned atmosphere that reigns throughout the establishment. The stamp of a family business can be felt everywhere from the scent of beeswax in the bedrooms or the tad outdated wallpaper down to the lovely "retro" lamps. Classic cuisine and full-bodied wines from south-western France take pride of place on the table.

 The sophistication of this mountain dwelling.

This old village house has been beautifully restored. The rooms are tastefully decorated and the one under the eaves boasts a bathroom with a magnificent claw-footed bathtub and an enormous aquarium. Breakfast and meals are taken in the delightful flagstoned kitchen decorated with old furniture. Highly recommended.

Access : Leave Bd du Général de Gaulle to take Av d'Aulot, then Rue F. Arnaud and turn right

Access : 3km westbound from Castillon-en-Couserans

 5 ## HÔTEL - RESTAURANT LA DÔMERIE
Mme David

12470 Aubrac
Tel. 05 65 44 28 42
Fax 05 65 44 21 47
david.mc@wanadoo.fr
www.hoteldomerie.com

Closed from mid-Nov 2004 to mid-Feb 2005 • 28 rooms on 2 floors with bath/WC or shower/WC, some have television • €48 to €76; breakfast €9; half board available • Restaurant closed Wed, Thu and Fri lunchtimes (low season); menus €19 to €38 • Garden, car park • Walking

 6 ## HÔTEL DU VIEUX PONT
Mmes Fagegaltier

12390 Belcastel
Tel. 05 65 64 52 29
Fax 05 65 64 44 32
hotel-du-vieux-pont@wanadoo.fr
www.hotelbelcastel.com

Closed from 1 Jan to 15 Mar, Sun evening, Mon and Tue lunchtime • 7 rooms in a converted barn, one of which has disabled access, all have bath/WC and television • €73 to €87; breakfast €11; half board available • Menus €26 (weekdays) to €75 • Car park

 Don't miss your chance to taste a real "aligot" – mashed potato with garlic and local cheese!

Aubrac is justly renowned for its exceptional wild flora, sprawling fields dotted with peacefully grazing light-brown cows and "burons", or cowherds' huts, its vast beech forests and its old Roman road. Countless footpaths criss-cross the region and the owner is more than happy to advise and point you in the right direction! His large house, built in 1870 out of local basalt, offers well-maintained rooms with sturdy farmhouse furniture and a timbered dining room in pale wood.

 The village of Belcastel, voted one of the most beautiful in Aveyron.

Two old stone houses stand on either side of the beautiful 15C arched bridge which spans the River Aveyron. The hotel, on the left bank, is home to small rooms with parquet floors, most of which overlook the river. In the summer, breakfast is served in the garden. The restaurant, on the right bank, is an elegant blend of rustic and modern styles; its gourmet dishes do full justice to the excellent local produce and have earned the house "star" status in the Michelin Red Guide since 1991.

Access : In the centre of the village

Access : In the heart of the village, opposite the old bridge

 7 À LA ROUTE D'ARGENT
M. Catusse

 La Rotonde
12340 Bozouls
Tel. 05 65 44 92 27
Fax 05 65 48 81 40
 yves.catusse @ wanadoo.fr

Closed in Jan, Feb, Sun evening and Mon except evening in Jul-Aug • 21 rooms with bath/WC or shower/WC and television, 6 in a separate wing, 1 with disabled access • €40 to €56, breakfast €6, half board available • Air-conditioned restaurant; menus €15 (weekdays) to €35 • Car park, garage • Outdoor swimming pool

 Tasty traditional fare lovingly prepared by the owner-chef.

The unassuming façade of this family hostelry hides a contemporary interior. Unpolished metal, modern light fixtures, warm woodwork and light fabrics set the scene in the lobby and restaurant. The bar-sitting room lit by a veranda window is equally unusual in style with a fresco and map of the region engraved on a sheet of glass. The rooms are cheerful and comfortable; those in the annex are more spacious with balconies overlooking a small garden.

 8 AUBERGE DU FEL
Mme Albespy

 Le Fel
12140 Entraygues-sur-Truyère
Tel. 05 65 44 52 30
Fax 05 65 48 64 96
info @ auberge-du-fel.com

Open from 3 Apr to 3 Nov • 10 rooms with bath/WC or shower/WC and television, 1 with disabled access • €50 to €59, breakfast €7, half board available • Restaurant closed lunchtimes except Sat, Sun, national and school holidays; menus €18 to €38 • Terrace, garden

 This hamlet overlooking the Lot Valley feels like the middle of nowhere.

This stone house, veiled in Virginia creeper and nestling in a peaceful hamlet, is perfect for those in search of ultimate quiet. The owner however takes nothing for granted and is devoted to the upkeep of her inn, from the pretty personalised bedrooms, each named after a vine, to the delicious dining room, part of which overlooks the Lot Valley. Pounti, charcuterie, truffade and other local dishes are just a few of the delicacies you can taste, all washed down with a Fel wine perhaps.

Access : On the way into Bozouls, at the crossroads between the D 988 and the D 920

Access : 10km westbound of Entraygues-sur-Truyère, take the D 107, turn right on the D 573

 9 AUBERGE SAINT-FLEURET
Mme Moreau

 19 rue François d'Estaing
12190 Estaing
Tel. 05 64 44 01 44
Fax 05 65 44 72 19
auberge.st.fleuret @ wanadoo.fr

Open from 15 Mar to 15 Nov, closed Sun evening and
Mon out of season • 14 rooms with shower/WC, some
have a television • €46 to €50 (€41 to €43 low season);
breakfast €7, half board available • Menus €17 to €50
• Garden, garage

 **Savouring the full-flavoured cuisine in
front of the fire or overlooking the
garden depending on the season.**

"A good meal and a good night's sleep" is the
self-declared motto of this welcoming inn, a staging post
in its former life. The rooms may not be enormous, but
are renovated, colourful and well soundproofed, with a
view either of the village or the garden. Don't forget
to book a table in the restaurant. The chef gets up before
dawn to select the best produce of the season which
he skilfully assembles into a host of tasty regional dishes.

Access : In the heart of the village

---

 10 CHÂTEAU DE GISSAC
Mme Wolkowitzky

 12360 Gissac
Tel. 05 65 98 14 60
Fax 05 65 98 14 61
château.gissac @ wanadoo.fr
www.chateau.gissac.com

Open all year • 31 rooms with bath/WC or shower/WC
and television; 2 have disabled access • €61 to €72,
breakfast €8, half board available • Closed Sun evening,
Mon and Tue lunchtime from mid-Mar to mid-Jun and
mid-Sep to mid-Dec; menus €23 (weekdays) to €35
• Terrace, garden, car park. No dogs allowed in rooms
• Heated swimming pool

 **In the summer, book a seat at
the Festival of Religious Music in
Sylvanès Abbey 4km away.**

Peaceful nights of slumber are guaranteed in this
charming 16C and 18C château which lies in a secluded
hamlet. A splendid stone and wrought-iron staircase
leads up to bedrooms, where a decorous contemporary
style has been adopted. The restaurant is more
characterful, thanks to a lovely vaulted ceiling, under
which traditional cuisine takes pride of place. A small
garden à la française and a swimming pool (heated from
May to September) complete the estate's facilities.

Access : Between Albi and Millau on the D999; at
Saint-Affrique take the D7, at Lapeyre the D92
towards Gissac

11 GRAND HÔTEL AUGUY
Famille Muylaert-Auguy

2 allée de l'Amicale
12210 Laguiole
Tel. 05 65 44 31 11
Fax 05 65 51 50 81
grand.hotel-auguy@wanadoo.fr
www.chateauxhotels.com/auguy

Closed 7 Nov to 20 Mar, Sun evening, Tue lunchtime and Mon except in the summer • 22 rooms with bath/WC or shower/WC and television • €65 to €90 (€55 to €70 low season); breakfast €10; half board available • Menus €28 to €50 • Garage • Visits to the Laguiole cutlery workshops nearby

12 CHÂTEAU DE CREISSELS
M. et Mme Austruy

Route de Saint-Affrique - Creissels
12100 Millau
Tel. 05 65 60 16 59
Fax 05 65 61 24 63
www.château-de-creissels.com

Closed Jan and Feb • 30 rooms, 2 of which have disabled access, 12 are in the old castle. Most rooms have bath/WC, some have shower/WC, all have television • €58 to €84; breakfast €9; half board available • Restaurant closed Sun evening and Mon lunchtime; menus €23 to €48 • Terrace, garden, car park

 Choosing a 100 % authentic Laguiole folding knife in the workshop.

This traditional house is surprisingly dynamic and forward-looking. Book one of the renovated rooms which are smart and modern with balconies overlooking the countryside. The tables of the warm and comfortable wood-lined dining room are laid with Laguiole cutlery, all the better to dig into the sumptuous, well-judged cooking. This is the work of the granddaughter of the Grand Hotel's founder and has earned the restaurant a star in the Michelin Red Guide.

 View of the village and valley.

Chequered parquet floors, wainscoting, a marble fireplace and period furniture: the "Bishop's Room" in the medieval castle can hardly be said to lack character. The others, more everyday, are located in the 1970s wing and have balconies. A vaulted 12C hall houses the restaurant. On fine days, tables are laid outdoors under the arcades of a gallery overlooking the village rooftops.

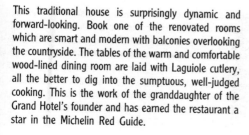

Access : In the town centre

Access : In a small village above Millau, on the road to Albi

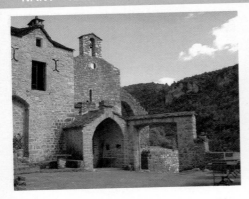

13 L'HERMITAGE SAINT-PIERRE
M. et Mme Macq

Lieu-dit Saint-Pierre-de-Revens
12230 Nant
Tel. 05 65 62 27 99
madeleine.macq@wanadoo.fr
http://hermitage.st.pierre.site.voila.fr

Open all year • 5 rooms • €79, breakfast included • Table d'hôte €25 by reservation (from 1 Oct to 15 Apr) • Credit cards not accepted, no dogs allowed • Swimming in the river nearby

 The laughter of the children swimming in the crystal-clear waters of the Dourbie.

You can't blame the owners for falling head over heels with this spot steeped in history which was originally a chapel (10C and 11C), then a Knights Templar post and a parish church. Now a B&B establishment, it offers beautifully decorated rooms whose heritage can still be seen in any number of details, such as the stone vaults, period furniture, four-poster beds or a 17C altarpiece. The garden at the foothills of the Causse Noir and on the banks of the Dourbie is equally delightful.

Access : 11km to the north-west of Nant towards Millau on the D 991

14 HOSTELLERIE DE FONTANGES
M. Charrié

Route de Conques
12000 Rodez
Tel. 05 65 77 76 00
Fax 05 65 42 82 29
fontanges-hotel@wanadoo.fr
www.hostellerie-fontanges.com

Open all year • 48 rooms, 4 of which are suites, most have bath/WC, some have shower/WC, all have television • €59 to €148; breakfast €10; half board available • Menus €24 (weekdays) to €70 • Terrace, park, car park • Outdoor swimming pool, tennis

 The rare feeling of true authenticity in this castle.

More of a castle than a house, it was built in the 16C and 17C by a draper from Rodez. Parquet floors and period furniture grace the bedrooms, most of which have just been treated to a well-deserved facelift. A huge fireplace and hunting trophies lend the breakfast room a lordly air, while the exposed beams of the dining room set the scene perfectly for traditional country fare. A municipal golf course is just a few swings away.

Access : 3.5km northbound from Rodez on the D 901 (towards Marcillac-Vallon)

15 MIDI-PAPILLON
M. et Mme Papillon

12230 Saint-Jean-du-Bruel
Tel. 05 65 62 26 04
Fax 05 65 62 12 97

Open from 26 Mar to 11 Nov • 18 rooms with bath/WC, some have shower/WC • €32 to €58; breakfast €5; half board available • Menus €13 (weekdays) to €37 • Garden, car park, garage • Outdoor swimming pool

16 CARAYON
M. Carayon

Place du Fort
12380 Saint-Sernin-sur-Rance
Tel. 05 65 98 19 19
Fax 05 65 99 69 26
carayon.hotel @ wanadoo.fr
www.hotel-carayon.com

Closed Sun evening, Mon and Tue lunchtime (except national holidays and Jul-Aug) • 60 rooms, 4 of which with disabled access, with bath/WC or shower/WC and television • €41 to €89; breakfast €8, half board available • Menus €14 to €54 • Garage, private car park, park, terrace • Tennis, mini-golf, keep-fit rooms, sauna, swimming pools

A hotel committed to upholding country traditions.

Ten pigs fatted up each year by a local farmer, a full-time gardener supplying fresh fruit and vegetables to the kitchen table, a farmyard full of barn animals and mushrooms picked by shepherds: ever since 1850, the Papillon family has been a perfect illustration of the fierce local desire to remain close to its roots. Personalised bedrooms, without the modern distraction of television, and a restaurant which overlooks the Dourbie and its lovely 15C arched bridge.

The countless leisure activities dotted around the tree-lined park.

Since 1876, this coaching inn has been the hub of this peaceful Aveyron village standing on the banks of the Rance. The Carayon family has been perfecting the art of receiving guests here for four generations. You will sleep either in the original building, a more recent wing or in one of the little houses in the park. The rooms are comfortable and practically fitted out; we recommend those opening onto the woodland. The spacious dining room leads onto a terrace overlooking the open fields.

Access : In the village, on the D 999, next to the stone bridge

Access : In the heart of the village

17 LE POUPAT
Mme Marnay

Route de Bachas
31420 Alan
Tel. 05 61 98 98 14
Fax 05 61 98 71 45

 michelle.bechard @ wanadoo.fr

Open all year • 3 rooms with bath/WC • €42, breakfast included • Table d'hôte €15 • Play area, park, garden, car park • Swimming pool, horses

 Riding round the countryside on one of the three horses available to guests.

This sprawling 16C building, nestling within extensive parkland lost in the countryside, is ideal for weary travellers in need of a peaceful night's rest. On the ground-floor, the sitting and dining rooms boast impressive period fireplaces and are furnished with Louis XV-style pieces. Upstairs, bare beams, rustic furniture, colourful walls and knickknacks adorn the sober rooms. Guests appreciate the pleasant homely atmosphere.

Access : 1km from Alan on the Bachas road

---

18 LA PRADASSE
M. et Mme Antoine

39 chemin de Toulouse
31450 Ayguesvives
Tel. 05 61 81 55 96
Fax 05 61 81 89 76
contact @ lapradasse.com
www.lapradasse.com

Open all year • 5 rooms with bath/WC or shower/WC, 1 with disabled access • €55 to €65; breakfast included • Table d'hôte €25 • Park, car park. No dogs allowed • Swimming pool

 The exquisite interior decoration is worthy of the cover of any Home and Garden magazine.

The brochure of La Pradasse mentions "characterful rooms set in a haven of peace and quiet". Which is totally misleading, because the reality is much better! The superbly restored, early-19C house boasts rooms, each more charming than the last, to such an extent that you will want to try them all. Light floods into the dining-sitting room through an enormous glass window and outside an extensive park, flower garden, vegetable plot and swimming pool are just waiting to be discovered.

Access : 15km south-east of Toulouse on the N113, then the D16 for 1.1km

 19 HOSTELLERIE DE L'ARISTOU
M. Géraud

Route de Sauveterre
31510 Barbazan
Tel. 05 61 88 30 67
Fax 05 61 95 55 66

Closed from 1 Dec to 13 Feb, Sun evening and Mon from 1 Sep to 30 Apr • 6 rooms, 2 of which are non-smoking, most have bath/WC, all have television • €52 to €58; breakfast €7; half board available • Restaurant closed from Mon lunchtime to Thu lunchtime from 18 Jul to 11 Aug; menus €19 to €37 • Terrace, garden, private car park. No dogs allowed

  20 CHÂTEAU DE SÉGUENVILLE
M. Lareng

Séguenville
31480 Cabanac-Séguenville
Tel. 05 62 13 42 67
Fax 05 62 13 42 68
info @ chateau-de-seguenville.com
www.chateau-de-seguenville.com

Closed from 15 Dec to 15 Jan • 5 rooms with bath/WC or shower/WC • €95 to €110, breakfast included • Table d'hôte €20 • Park, car park. Credit cards not accepted, no dogs admitted • Swimming pool

 The view from the windows is so pretty you will wish you could paint.

This farm, dating from 1832, has been converted into a smartly-kept country inn with apple-green shutters. Painted or antique furniture adorns the rooms, some of which have canopied beds. The dining rooms display the owners' eclectic tastes with 70s-style ornaments alongside classic oil paintings and delightfully outdated floral wallpaper; tables are laid in the inner garden-courtyard when the sun comes out.

 Exploring the park and its hundred-year-old trees with the Pyrenees in the background.

The origins of this château, set in a secluded park, date back to 1271, but its current architecture bears more resemblance to the 19C because it was rebuilt after the French Revolution. The guestrooms, reached by a lovely staircase, are full of charm with old parquet floors or tiles, handsome fireplaces, antique furniture, bright colours, curios and immaculate bathrooms. On the ground-floor, two inviting sitting rooms add to the establishment's appeal.

Access : To the south-west of Saint-Gaudens, on the outskirts of the village

Access : 5km from Cox on the D 1 north-west of l'Isle-Jourdain

 21 LE POUJASTOU
M. Cottereau

Rue du Sabotier
31110 Juzet-de-Luchon
Tel. 05 61 94 32 88
Fax 05 61 94 32 76
info @ lepoujastou.com
www.lepoujastou.com

Open all year • 5 rooms upstairs, all have bath/WC or shower/WC • €45; breakfast included; half board available • Table d'hôte €8 to €15 (picnic lunches) • Terrace, garden, car park. Credit cards not accepted, no dogs allowed

 22 CHAMBRE D'HÔTE BIGOT
M. Pinel

Lieu-dit Bigot
31450 Montesquieu-Lauragais
Tel. 05 61 27 02 83
Fax 05 61 27 02 83
joseph.pinel @ libertysurf.fr

Closed for one week in February • 5 rooms, one of which has a jacuzzi • €45 to €60, breakfast included; half board available • Table d'hôte €15 to €20 • Sitting room, terrace, car park. Credit cards not accepted, no dogs allowed • Outdoor swimming pool

 Your host, an alpine guide, organises snowshoe excursions in winter and mountain biking in summer.

This large south-facing house, which commands fine views of the Luchonnais peaks, began life as the village's concert hall in the 18C. Stylishly renovated, it now offers brand new ochre-coloured bedrooms, some sizeable, others more compact. A warm sitting room lined with works on the region's fauna and flora and a Pyrenean-style dining room are on the ground floor. A terrace, garden and finely-flavoured home cooking round off the picture of an excellent establishment.

 The marriage of old and new.

You won't be disappointed by the comfort of this fully renovated 17C farmhouse. Beautiful old furniture, in the family for donkey's years or picked up in local antique shops, graces the rooms, one of which has a jacuzzi bathtub. The old beams, brick walls and original mangers of the former stables add character to the breakfast room. The huge covered terrace is very pleasant in fine weather.

Access : Near the church

Access : 5km to the north-east on the D 11, take the lane on the left after the A 61, towards Villenouvelle

 23 LA HALTE DU TEMPS
Mme Garcin

72 rue Mage
31310 Montesquieu-Volvestre
Tel. 05 61 97 56 10
Fax 05 61 90 49 03
lahaltedutemps @ free.fr

Open all year • 5 rooms with bathrooms • €54 to €62, breakfast included, half board available • Table d'hôte €20 • Garden. Credit cards not accepted • Outdoor swimming pool

 24 HÔTELLERIE DU LAC
M. Maréchal

Avenue Pierre-Paul Riquet
31250 Saint-Ferréol
Tel. 05 62 18 70 80
Fax 05 62 18 71 13
contact @ hotellerie-du-lac.com
www.hotellerie-du-lac.com

Open all year • 25 rooms, 4 of which are split-level (with kitchenettes), one has disabled access, all have bath/WC and television • €62; breakfast €8; half board available • Menu €14 to €35 • Terrace, garden, car park. No dogs allowed • Heated outdoor swimming pool

Madame's exceptional story-telling talents.

Cross the charming inner courtyard to reach this elegant 17C mansion in the heart of town: the façade may not seem inspiring but the fully original staircases, floors and furniture make it well worth a stay. Superb, exquisitely decorated bedrooms with alcove bathrooms. The lovely dining room with a huge fireplace is quite the equal of the delicious cuisine.

The view of the lake from the striking terraced swimming pool

If the locals are to be believed, Saint Ferréol, the local patron saint, continues to watch over the tranquillity of this elegant lakeside house surrounded by greenery. A masterful renovation has left the original character of the place intact: most of the rooms share a splendid view of the lake with the exquisite swimming pool. When it comes to relaxing, the warm sitting room-bar, sauna, fitness room and quaint garden are also worthy of mention. Classic dishes on a traditional menu.

Access : In the town centre

Access : Overlooking the lake, 3km to the south-east of Revel on the D 629

 25 **AUBERGE LES PALMIERS**
M. Vallès

 13 place du Foirail
31370 Rieumes
Tel. 05 61 91 81 01
Fax 05 61 91 56 36
infos @ auberge-lespalmiers.com
www.auberge-lespalmiers.com

Closed at Easter, early Sep and at Christmas • 7 rooms, one of which has disabled access, with bath/WC or shower/WC and television • €56 to €58; breakfast €7, half board available • Air-conditioned restaurant closed Sun evening and Mon; menus €10 (weekdays) to €35 • Garden, terrace. Dogs not allowed in rooms

 26 **HÔTEL DU COMMINGES**
Mme Alaphilippe

 Place de la Basilique
31510 Saint-Bertrand-de-Comminges
Tel. 05 61 88 31 43
 Fax 05 61 94 98 22

Open from Apr to Oct. Closed from 31 Oct to 31 Mar • 14 rooms, most have bath/WC or showers, with or without WC • €30 to €50, breakfast €6 • No restaurant • Small car park. No dogs allowed

 The friendly, down-to-earth owners.

Several palm trees adorn the garden behind this picturesque inn. Built in the 19C, it was recently extended, and borders the pretty village square. The spacious, comfortable rooms feature a happy marriage of rustic furniture, parquet floors and contemporary touches. Fancy a snack or a full three-course meal? Sit down under the beams in the dining room and build up your strength with generous helpings of traditional cuisine.

 The peace and quiet of a convent.

Overlooking the forecourt of the fascinating Cathédrale Ste-Marie, this hotel was once a convent and it cannot be faulted for its peace and quiet, particularly in the summer, when the square is entirely free of cars. The guests' quarters and rooms are all fitted with handsome country furniture. During the long summer months, a pleasant terrace is laid under an arbour behind the main building. Run by the same family for three generations, it is a place you will remember.

Access : In the heart of the village

Access : In the centre of the village, opposite the cathedral

27 **AUBERGE DU POIDS PUBLIC**
M. Taffarello

Rue St-Roch
31540 Saint-Félix-Lauragais
Tel. 05 62 18 85 00
Fax 05 62 18 85 05
poidspublic @ wanadoo.fr
www.auberge-du-poidspublic.com

Closed from 25 Oct to 1 Nov and Sun evening (except hotel in Jul-Aug) • 9 rooms and 1 suite with bath/WC or shower/WC and television, 4 are air-conditioned • €60 to €95, breakfast €11, half board available • Menus €27 to €65 • Terrace, garage

 The unusual and historic public weighing-scales next door to this charming inn.

This inn is the talk of the town and the region! Some vaunt the quality of the cooking which is a creative blend of classical cuisine and local produce, while others sing the praises of the country-style restaurant with its pleasant terrace overlooking the countryside. Finally, the comfortable, low-key rooms have been gradually renovated and are immaculately cared for. All in all, this attractive village inn is a treat, as much for the eye as for the palate.

Access : In the village

28 **VILLA LES PINS**
Mme Daigre

Route de Bouloc
31340 Vacquiers
Tel. 05 61 84 96 04
Fax 05 61 84 28 54
www.villa-les-pins.com

Open all year • 15 rooms with bath/WC or shower/WC and television • €55 to €60, breakfast €7 • Restaurant closed Sun evening, Mon and Tue lunchtime (except national holidays); menus €15 to €30 • Car park, terrace, garden

 Summer evenings on the charming terrace overlooking the park.

To the north of busy Toulouse, this pleasant halt is beautifully quiet. A pine forest surrounds this extensive villa with a pleasant guesthouse atmosphere. The rooms, more spacious on the first floor, have a plush bourgeois flavour created by antique furniture, chandeliers and thick curtains. The same ambience extends to the dining room and its impressive fireplace.

Access : 2km westbound on the D 30

 29 CHÂTEAU DES VARENNES

M. et Mme Mericq

31450 Varennes
Tel. 05 61 81 69 24
Fax 05 61 81 69 24
j.mericq@wanadoo.fr

Open all year • 5 rooms with bath/WC • €75 to €125, breakfast €5 • Table d'hôte €30 to €35 • Terrace, garden, park, car park. Credit cards not accepted • Outdoor swimming pool. Tennis and horse-riding nearby

30 HOSTELLERIE DES CÈDRES

M. Taffarello

31800 Villeneuve-de-Rivière
Tel. 05 61 89 36 00
Fax 05 61 88 31 04
information@hotel-descedres.com
www.hotel-descedres.com

Open all year. • 22 rooms located in the main building and in a separate wing in the garden, all have bath/WC or shower/WC and television • €50 to €80; breakfast €10; half board available • Restaurant closed Sun evening and Mon lunchtime (low season) and Mon and Tue lunchtimes (high season); menus €22 to €52 • Terrace, garden, car park • Outdoor swimming pool

 The view of the slopes of Lauragais from the swimming pool.

 The white-calf market at St Gaudens.

The magic begins from the moment you set foot in the park of this 16C castle next to the church. Push open the iron gate, venture into the wonderful courtyard and through a heavy wooden door into the main pink brick building, where you will find yourself gazing up at a double flight of stairs. Superbly exotic colours adorn the "Bédouin" room on the ground floor and those upstairs are equally elegant and opulent. The sitting rooms and vaulted cellars add the finishing touch.

This 16C monastery, bought by the Montespan family in the 17C, and its old doors, mullioned windows and stone staircases still bear witness to its glorious past. The watchful eye of the Marquise of Montespan, mistress of none other than the Sun King himself, gazes benevolently down as you sit in the recently refurbished dining room. Thick stone walls protect the traditional rooms from the hot summer sun. Magnificent old cedars, the hotel's namesake, stretch their branches in the garden.

Access : 15km westbound from Saint-Félix on the Toulouse road (D 2)

Access : 5km westbound from Saint-Gaudens on the N 117

31 HOTEL DE FRANCE
M. Garreau

Place de la Libération
32000 Auch
Tel. 05 62 61 71 71
Fax 05 62 61 71 81
roland.garreau @ wanadoo.fr

Open all year • 29 rooms, 22 of which are air-conditioned, all have bath/WC or shower/WC and television • €78 to €146; breakfast €10; half board available • Air-conditioned restaurant, closed Sun evening; menus €25 (weekdays) to €68

32 AU VIEUX PRESSOIR
M. Martin

Saint-Fort
32100 Caussens
Tel. 05 62 68 21 32
Fax 05 62 68 21 32
auvieuxpressoir @ wanadoo.fr

Closed for a fortnight in February during the school holidays • 3 rooms • €48, breakfast included, half board available • Meals at l'Auberge: €15 to €25 • Terrace, garden, park, car park. No dogs allowed in rooms • Outdoor swimming pool, jacuzzi

Shopping for local produce in a vaulted cellar.

An old coaching inn with a classical façade houses spacious, more or less personalised rooms, which it is planned to spruce up in the near future, but you can bet your last euro that the room where the film "Le Bonheur est dans le pré" was shot will retain its rococo style. Tasty robust Gascony cuisine is served in a lovely old restaurant which is happy to let the latest fashions pass it by.

The lively atmosphere at the weekends.

This lovely old 17C stone house commands a fine view over the vineyards, countryside and the flocks of ducks reared on the property. The rooms, furnished with old pieces, are comfortable and well looked after. The family suite in the attic has been thoughtfully equipped with a games room and a VHS recorder. Farm produce takes pride of place on the dinner table and connoisseurs in search of fine foie gras will not be disappointed.

Access : In the town centre

Access : 11km from Caussens on the D 7 and take a lane on the right

MIDI PYRÉNÉES

EAUZE - 32800   **JUILLAC - 32230**

 33 CHAMBRE D'HÔTE HOURCAZET
M. Lejeunne

Hourcazet
32800 Eauze
Tel. 05 62 09 99 53
Fax 05 62 09 99 53
claude.lejeunne @ mageos.com

Open all year (out of season by reservation) • 4 rooms
• €55 to €60, breakfast included • No table d'hôte
• Terrace, park, car park. Credit cards not accepted

 34 AU CHÂTEAU
M. et Mme de Rességuier

32230 Juillac
Tel. 05 62 09 37 93
deresseguier @ marciac.net

Closed for one week in October • 3 rooms with
bathrooms • €50, breakfast included • Table d'hôte €16
• Terrace, garden, park, car park. Credit cards not
accepted, no dogs allowed • Fishing

 We most liked
Soaking up the vineyard ambience.

An air of tranquillity reigns in these two houses standing
side by side in the midst of Armagnac's vineyards. The
rooms are tastefully decorated with beautiful fabrics and
furniture and equipped with fine bathrooms. The largest
are under the massive beams up in the converted attic,
the other two open directly onto the garden. Meals are
served in a traditionally decorated dining room or on
one of two terraces. Forty winks can be had in the
garden complete with pond.

 We most liked **Lie on your back and gaze up into
the branches of the ancient trees.**

Fie, fair visitor! What you see is no castle, but an 18C
charterhouse, now the headquarters of a thriving
farming business. The rooms, in a separate wing, are
vast and tastefully decorated and the bathrooms boast
all the modern comforts. As you would expect, a
generously spread table d'hôte showcases the wealth of
produce grown and reared on the farm. Bicycling,
walking and fishing feature among the possible leisure
activities, and the owner and mayor of Juillac is a
wonderful source of advice.

Access : 7km westbound from Eauze on the D 926,
then the Barbotan road and a lane on the right

Access : 5km westbound from Marciac, towards
Juillac on the D 255

35 DE BASTARD
M. et Mme Arnaud

Rue Lagrange
32700 Lectoure
Tel. 05 62 68 82 44
Fax 05 62 68 76 81
hoteldebastard@wanadoo.fr

Closed from 20 Dec to 1 Feb, Sun evening, Mon and Tue lunchtime • 29 rooms on 2 floors, all have bath/WC or shower/WC and television • €45 to €68; breakfast €10; half board available • Menus €15 (weekdays) to €56 • Terrace, garden, garage • Outdoor swimming pool. Bar-lounge

36 AU PRÉSIDENT
M. Piquemil

32300 Mirande
Tel. 05 62 66 64 06
Fax 05 62 66 64 06
jacques.piquemil@wanadoo.fr
www.chez.com/aupresident

Open all year • 4 rooms, 2 of which are on garden level, with bathrooms • €50, breakfast included • No table d'hôte • Terrace, garden, car park. Credit cards not accepted, no dogs allowed • Billiards, play area

One for all and all for one.

Your quest for a harbour in Gascony is over! Despite its name, the pedigree of this 18C house is flawless. Elegance and opulence reign throughout. Progressively renovated rooms, a string of sophisticated sitting and dining rooms with parquet floors, moulded ceilings and fireplaces, a pleasant garden terrace, a cottage with a sitting room-bar for lovers of good cigars and Armagnac and succulent cooking worthy of the most demanding musketeers among you.

Trying your luck on the billiards table in the elegant sitting room.

This lovely abode flanked with turrets belonged to the president of Mirande's law courts during the first half of the 20C, hence its name. The bedrooms with sloping ceilings all have brand new bathrooms. Those on the ground floor are enormous and adorned with family heirlooms. In the winter, breakfast is served by the fireside in the huge dining room and in a sheltered courtyard in the summer. Pretty garden.

Access : From Agen, follow rue d'Alsace-Lorraine, turn left at the post office, then right on rue Subervie, then left again

Access : 3km northbound from Mirande on the N 21 route d'Auch

 37 LA GARLANDE
M. et Mme Cournot

Place de la Mairie
32380 Saint-Clar
Tel. 05 62 66 47 31
Fax 05 62 66 47 70
nicole.cournot @ wanadoo.fr

Closed from 1 Jan to 12 Mar and 13 Nov to 31 Dec
• 3 rooms with bathrooms • €51 to €62, breakfast
included • No table d'hôte • Garden. Credit cards not
accepted, no dogs allowed

 38 AUBERGE DU BERGERAYRE
Mme Sarran

32110 Saint-Martin-d'Armagnac
Tel. 05 62 09 08 72
Fax 05 62 09 09 74
pierrette-sarran @ wanadoo.fr

Closed Tue, Wed and Feb • 12 rooms located in 2
buildings, all are on the ground floor. Rooms have
bath/WC or shower/WC and television • €47 to €64;
breakfast €10; half board available • Restaurant (closed
Tue and Wed) is only for half board guests; menus €20
to €34 • Terrace, garden, car park

 Harmony abounds in all the rooms.

Standing firmly four-square on its arcades, this
beautiful, rambling house with an ochre façade is in the
heart of the village opposite a 16C hall. The rooms,
decorated with tapestries and well-polished antiques,
have retained their original parquet or tiled floors. The
bathrooms have been renovated. The reading room and
walled herb garden are perfect places to relax. Guests
have the use of a summer kitchen.

 **Taste a slice of Gascony pastis (pie),
flamed with Armagnac!**

If words such as foie gras, magret, cèps, Armagnac,
tradition, farm or family fail to bring to a gleam to your
eye, then read no further. Otherwise make a beeline for
this little corner of Gascony where country life still has
meaning and take a seat in one of the three rustic dining
rooms, or on the terrace overlooking the famous
Armagnac vineyards. As for accommodation, you can
choose a welcoming rural style or a modern atmosphere
and a private terrace.

Access : Opposite the covered market

Access : 8km to the south-west of Nogaro on the
D 25, then take a minor road

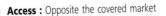

39 **DOMAINE DE LORAN**
M. et Mme Nédellec

32300 Saint-Maur
Tel. 05 62 66 51 55
Fax 05 62 66 78 58

Open from 30 Apr to 30 Oct (by reservation the rest of the year) • 2 rooms and 2 suites with bathrooms • €45 to €50, breakfast included • No table d'hôte • Park, car park. Credit cards not accepted • Billiards

40 **CHAMBRES D'HÔTES LE SABATHÉ**
M. et Mme Barreteau

Le Sabathé
32700 Saint-Mézard
Tel. 05 62 28 84 26

Open all year • 4 rooms • €41, breakfast included; half board available • Table d'hôte €10 to €15 • Terrace, car park. Credit cards not accepted

Fishing in the lake hidden in the park.

Two towers, a long colonnade of plane trees and parkland graced with huge old trees make this Gascony farm look more like a castle. A lovely wooden staircase will take you up to the spacious rooms fitted out with old furniture; the two suites are particularly worth a look. The immense dining room on the ground floor with dark wainscoting is furnished with lovely antiques. Fishing, billiards and table-tennis will keep you amused for hours.

Take refuge in this sanctuary of meditation.

Tai Chi sessions are organised every morning in this unaffected, almost monastic abode. The old farm on the doorstep of the town aims to provide sanctuary to those in search of a place for meditation. The rooms, spread throughout the outbuildings, are all fully independent. Depending on the weather, meals are served by the fireside in the dining room or on a tiny walled terrace in front of the main hall, overlooking the chapel of Notre-Dame-d'Esclaux.

Access : From the N 21 take the long lane that leads to the Domaine de Loran

Access : 12km northbound on the D 36

41 MARLIAC
Mme Stroobant

46140 Bélaye
Tel. 05 65 36 95 50
Fax 05 65 31 99 04

Closed from early Nov to late Mar • 5 rooms • €60 to €66, breakfast included • Table d'hôte €15 to €17 • Park, car park. Credit cards not accepted, no dogs allowed • Swimming pool

42 LE PONT D'OR
M. et Mme Bonnaud

2 avenue Jean-Jaurès
46100 Figeac
Tel. 05 65 50 95 00
Fax 05 65 50 95 39
contact@hotelpontdor.com
www.hotelpontdor.com

Open all year • 35 rooms on three levels, all with bathrooms, television and air-conditioning; 2 have disabled access and 7 are non-smoking • €75 to €96; breakfast €10; half board available • Menus €11.50 to €15 • Lift, terrace, garden, car park • Billiards, overflow swimming pool, fitness room with sauna

 Close your eyes and listen to the sound of silence.

A long, winding lane leads to this 18C farmhouse, a haven of peace and quiet in the midst of over 10 acres of woods and fields. You will want to unpack your cases and spend time in the tastefully decorated utterly calm rooms; two of which are on split levels. The breakfast room has preserved its beams, stonework and the old oven. Engaging welcome.

 The Champollion Museum, located in the birthplace of the famous Egyptologist.

This welcoming stone house, ideally located on the banks of the Célé at the foot of a medieval bridge, reopened in 2001 after major renovation work. A yellow and orange colour scheme, contemporary furniture, new bedding and immaculate bathrooms characterise the rooms, some of which have a balcony. In addition the hotel boasts a fitness room, and a swimming pool on the roof of the house. In summer, breakfast is served on the riverside terrace.

Access : 15km westbound from Luzech on the D 8 and the D 50

Access : On the way into the historic centre, near the medieval bridge

43 DOMAINE DU BERTHIOL
M. Mays

Route de Cahors
46300 Gourdon
Tel. 05 65 41 33 33
Fax 05 65 41 14 52
domaine-du-berthiol@wanadoo.fr
www.hotelperigord.com

Open from 1 Apr to 31 Dec • 29 rooms with bath/WC or shower/WC and television • €76 to €93 (out of season €67 to €79); breakfast €11; half board available • Air-conditioned restaurant; menus €17 (weekdays) to €24 • Park, car park. No dogs allowed in rooms • Outdoor swimming pool, tennis

44 MOULIN DE FRESQUET
M. et Mme Ramelot

46500 Gramat
Tel. 05 65 38 70 60
Fax 05 65 33 60 13
moulindefresquet@ifrance.com
www.moulindefresquet.com

Closed from 1 Nov to 1 Apr • 5 non-smoking rooms with bathrooms • €57 to €76, breakfast included • Table d'hôte €21 • Park, car park. Credit cards not accepted, no dogs allowed

 Lush green countryside.

On the outskirts of the town in the middle of a beautifully maintained park, this impressive country house offers identical rooms with fully equipped bathrooms. Tennis courts, swimming pool and children's play area. The contemporary dining room opens onto the pleasant greenery. The menu shows a marked preference for local produce. Immense banquet hall in another wing.

 Wining and dining by candlelight on Périgord's succulent fare.

The good life at its best! This authentic 17C water mill stands in an idyllic rural spot, just 800m from the centre of Gramat. Lovely furniture and tapestries, exposed stonework and beams and a profusion of good books set the scene for the interior. Most of the comfortable, elegant rooms have a view of the enchanting shaded garden and the stream, much prized by fishermen. Gracious hosts and wonderful food.

Access : 1km eastbound from Gourdon on the D 704

Access : On the way into Gramat

 45 CHÂTEAU DE LA COSTE
M. Coppé

46700 Grézels
Tel. 05 65 21 38 28
Fax 05 65 21 38 28
gervais.coppe @ wanadoo.fr

Open in Jul and Aug • 3 rooms • €75 to €105, breakfast included • No table d'hôte • Credit cards not accepted, no dogs allowed

 46 LA TERRASSE
M. Amalric

Le Bourg
46120 Lacapelle-Marival
Tel. 05 65 40 80 07
Fax 05 65 40 99 45
hotel-restaurant-la-terrasse @ wanadoo.fr

Closed 2 Jan to 1 Mar, Sun evening, Mon except evenings in summer, Tue lunchtime • 13 rooms, all have bath/WC or shower/WC and television • €45 to €65; breakfast €7; half board available • Menus €18 (weekdays) to €35 • Garden • Fishing

We most liked **The Cahors Wine Museum within the walls of this fortified castle.**

If you're passing through, this medieval fortress dominating the Lot Valley is definitely worth a visit. Character abounds in the rooms which have been given evocative names such as "Study of the setting sun", "Lookout tower" and "Squire's abode" – all are furnished with lovely period pieces. In addition, the striking dining room commands an exceptional view. Don't leave without visiting the Wine Museum.

 We most liked **Forty winks in the flower garden.**

The hotel is next door to the massive square keep, flanked by the towers of the castle of Lacapelle. Practical, recently renovated rooms and a light, airy veranda-dining room whose bay windows overlook the pretty garden on the banks of a stream, with the Francès Valley in the background. Park and private fishing 2km away.

Access : 16km westbound from Luzech on the D 8

Access : Near the castle

 47 CHÂTEAU DE GAMOT
M. et Mme Belières

46130 Loubressac
Tel. 05 65 10 92 03
Fax 01 48 83 01 91
annie-belieres@wanadoo.fr
www.domaine-de-gamot.com

Closed in Oct and Apr • 7 rooms, some have bathrooms
• €45 to €60, breakfast included • No table d'hôte
• Garden, car park. Credit cards not accepted, no dogs
allowed

 48 LES TILLEULS
Mme Ménassol

46160 Marcilhac-sur-Célé
Tel. 05 65 40 62 68
Fax 05 65 40 74 01
michelle.menassol@wanadoo.fr
www.les-tilleuls.fr.st

Closed from 16 Nov to 16 Dec • 4 rooms • €40 to €42,
breakfast included • No table d'hôte • Park, car park.
Credit cards not accepted

 **Conveniently located near Quercy's
main tourist attractions.**

The allure of this rambling 17C stately home and its
pastoral setting opposite the castle of Castelnau never
fails to weave its magic spell. The comfortable rooms
are well proportioned. Guests who visit in June and
September enjoy the run of the owners' private
swimming pool. Other leisure activities in the vicinity
include a 9-hole golf course, tennis courts and
horse-riding.

 Meeting the enchanting owner.

Cradled in the heart of the village, this 19C stately home
owes its success to the lady of the house's efforts to
make guests feel truly welcome: she is always well
informed about life in the region and is happy to suggest
local activities. The rooms are comfortable and unfussy
and the breakfasts copious to say the least: prepare to
delve into a memorable array of up to 50 home-made
jams. The garden, complete with barbecue and
hammock, is slightly unruly and instantly likeable.

Access : 5km westbound from St-Céré on the D 673
and the D 30

Access : In the village

  49 LA COUR AU TILLEUL
Mme Bazin

Avenue du Capitani
46600 Martel
Tel. 05 65 37 34 08

Open all year • 3 rooms with shower/WC • €55 (€50 low season), breakfast included • No table d'hôte • Credit cards not accepted

  50 HOSTELLERIE LE VERT
M. Philippe

Lieu-dit Le-Vert
46700 Mauroux
Tel. 05 65 36 51 36
Fax 05 65 36 56 84
hotellevert @ aol.com
www.hotellevert.com

Closed from 1 Nov to 31 Mar • 7 rooms with bath/WC or shower/WC and television • €55 to €110 (€55 to €90 low season; breakfast €9; half board available • Restaurant closed Thu; menus €42 • Terrace, garden, car park. No dogs allowed in rooms • Outdoor swimming pool. Bicycle and mountain bike rental in the summer

 A bright, well cared-for interior behind very old walls.

The walls of this enchanting stone house bedecked in flowers date back to the 12C no less! A great deal of time has clearly been lavished on the decoration of the tranquil, spacious rooms which are located to the rear of the house. Depending on the season, breakfast is served in the brightly coloured blue and orange dining room or in the inner courtyard under the shade of a linden tree. The welcome is as friendly as you could wish.

 Signposted footpaths weaving in and out of vineyards and old farms.

An ideal opportunity to get back to grass roots! This former wine estate, which lies in the remote countryside, is surrounded by a garden planted with cedar trees and a timeless silence. The hotel does its utmost to welcome you in style with its character-filled dining room with exposed beams, stonework and old furniture and personalised rooms in the same vein. The most unusual room is in the converted pantry with a lovely stone vaulted ceiling and tiny windows to keep it cool in the summer.

Access : In the village

Access : In the countryside, 12km to the south-west of Puy-L'Évêque on the D 8 then the D 5

 51 CHAMBRE D'HÔTE DU SYNDIC

M. et Mme Capy

Le Syndic
46300 Payrignac
Tel. 05 65 41 15 70
Fax 05 65 41 15 70
info@internet46.fr

Closed 1 to 15 Oct • 6 rooms, 4 of which air-conditioned, with bathrooms and hair-driers • €50 to €55, breakfast included • No table d'hôte • Park, car park. Credit cards not accepted, no dogs allowed

 52 LE BEAU SITE

M. Menot

Cité Médiévale
46500 Rocamadour
Tel. 05 65 33 63 08
Fax 05 65 33 65 23
hotel@bw-beausite.com
www.bw.beausite.com

Closed from 15 Nov to 20 Dec and 1 Jan to 7 Feb • 39 rooms located in 2 buildings on each side of the street. Rooms have bath/WC or shower/WC and television, 21 are air-conditioned • €63 to €95; breakfast €10; half board available • Menus €23 to €49 • Terrace, garage, car park (access by a pedestrian road)

 Madame Capy's enthusiastic welcome.

This impressive regional-style bourgeois home dominates the Germaine Valley. Its countryside location guarantees nights of sweet dreams in the spacious, comfortable rooms; some of which are up under the eaves. When the weather cools down, a roaring fire is lit in the sitting and dining rooms.

 The mountain village of Rocamadour – words fail us!

Old beams blackened by the centuries, a massive wooden staircase, stone walls and beautiful worn flagstones: the hall of this 15C bastion in the heart of the city is definitely worth a look. The rooms in the wing, of variable sizes, are more up-to-date and enjoy a fine view. The elegant restaurant-veranda and its flowered terrace overlook the Alzou canyon. 2km from the hotel, a swimming pool has been sunk in a lovely park of oak trees.

Access : 6km to the north-west of Gourdon on the D 704, towards Sarlat-la-Canéda then a minor road on the left

Access : Main road of the medieval city (pedestrian road) between Porte Salmon and Porte du Figuier

53 DOMAINE DE LA RHUE
M. Jooris

La Rhue
46500 Rocamadour
Tel. 05 65 33 71 50
Fax 05 65 33 72 48
domainedelarhue@wanadoo.fr
www.domainedelarhue.com

Open from 26 Mar to 22 Oct • 14 rooms, most with bath/WC, some with shower/WC; all are air-conditioned and have television • €65 to €125 (€65 to €90 low season), breakfast €8 • No restaurant • Car park, garden. No dogs allowed • Swimming pool

Walking to Rocamadour (45min walk) along the path out of the estate.

Lost in the countryside, this delightful hotel has been built in former stables (1863) amid almost 100 acres of grounds. The ground floor, graced with flagstones, fireplace, beams, half-timbering and old and modern furnishings, houses the reception, sitting and breakfast rooms. The tastefully decorated and well-fitted rooms illustrate the owners' flair for marrying old with new. Add to this idyllic picture a swimming pool and wonderful tranquillity. So, get your diary out and book right away!

Access : 6km eastbound on the D 673, N140, then a minor road

54 LE TROUBADOUR
M. Menot

Route de Brive
46500 Rocamadour
Tel. 05 65 33 70 27
Fax 05 65 33 71 99
troubadour@rocamadour.com

Open from 15 Feb to 15 Nov • 10 rooms with bath/WC or shower/WC and television • €70 to €85 (€60 to €85 low season); breakfast €9, half board available • Air-conditioned restaurant; menus €23 to €35 (evenings only) • Car park, garden, terrace • Swimming pool, billiards

Lazing around the swimming pool after a hard day's sightseeing.

A handsome flowered and tree-lined garden protects the peace and quiet of this tastefully renovated old farmhouse. Forget the size of the rooms and admire the rustic furniture and floorboards of the pristine bedrooms. Some enjoy a view of the swimming pool with the countryside in the distance. The restaurant, which is only open out of season, doesn't believe in fussy, elaborate cuisine. Friendly, family welcome.

Access : 2.5km to the north-east on the D 673

55 LES VIEILLES TOURS
M. Brousse

Lieu-dit Lafage
46500 Rocamadour
Tel. 05 65 33 68 01
Fax 05 65 33 68 59
les.vieillestours@wanadoo.fr
www.chateauxhotels.com/vieillestours

Closed from 1 Jan to 26 Mar and 16 Nov to 31 Dec • 17 rooms located in 2 buildings, almost all are on garden level, with bath/WC and television • €60 to €110; breakfast €12; half board available • Menus €25 (weekdays) to €61 • Terrace, garden, car park • Outdoor swimming pool

Sleeping in a 13C falconry!

The construction of this secluded hunting lodge took place over several centuries from the 13C to the 17C. Most of the rooms in the outhouses open directly onto the garden and enjoy a splendid view of the countryside. Diners can choose between a welcoming country-style restaurant and a quiet, shaded terrace to sample a sophisticated regional repertoire.

56 LES MOYNES
M. et Mme Le Cerf-Arets

Les Moynes de Saint-Simon
46320 Saint-Simon
Tel. 05 65 40 48 90
Fax 05 65 40 48 90
les.moynes@free.fr
http://les.moynes.free.fr

Open from 16 Mar to 14 Nov • 5 rooms, one of which has disabled access, with bath/WC or shower/WC and television • €50 to €60 ; breakfast included; half board available • Table d'hôte €19 • Terrace, car park, park. Credit cards not accepted • Open-air swimming pool, table-tennis, mountain biking

A guided tour of the duck farm in the company of the owner.

This recently renovated Quercy house, which dates back to 1885, is located in a nearly 30-acre working farm. Bright colours, timber beams and stone walls, new parquet flooring and well-fitted bathrooms depict the snug rooms, all with names which reflect the region. Breakfasts and dinners are served in a delightful dining room complete with old mangers and a fireplace big enough to sit in.

Access : 4km westbound from Rocamadour on the D 673 towards Payrac, then take a minor road

Access : 7km north-west of Assier on the D 11 and D 25, towards Flaujac

MIDI PYRÉNÉES

 57 CHAMBRE D'HÔTE MADAME VERMEIL
Mme Vermeil

3 rue du Château
65400 Arcizans-Avant
Tel. 05 62 97 55 96
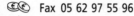 Fax 05 62 97 55 96

Open all year • 3 rooms • €43, breakfast included • No table d'hôte • Credit cards not accepted, no dogs allowed

 58 ANGLETERRE
Mme Aubiban

Route de Luchon
65240 Arreau
Tel. 05 62 98 63 30
Fax 05 62 98 69 66
hotel-angleterre@oreka.com
www.hotel-angleterre-arreau.com

Closed Mon and Tue lunchtime from 1 Jan to 30 Mar (open Sat-Sun and school holidays) • 20 rooms with bath/WC or shower/WC and television • €56 to €84 (€48 to €67 low season); breakfast €7, half board available • Menus €19 to €38 • Car park, garden. No dogs allowed • Heated swimming pool

 A panoramic wide-screen view of the valley.

This handsome 19C house boasts a wealth of attractions. Wood prevails in the attic rooms – walls, floors and furniture – which afford a fine view of the valley or the mountains. Guests have the run of a kitchen, a pleasant garden and a dining room with a relief map of the Pyrenees: plan your next expedition over a coffee and feel free to ask for advice from the owner, a mountain guide who speaks from experience.

 The friendly welcome and the family atmosphere.

A little village typical of the Aure Valley is the site of this former coaching inn. All the rooms have been recently renovated. The stylish dining room sports country furniture, old utensils dotted about here and there and bright, contemporary colours. Meals are also served in the veranda facing the garden where a swimming pool and play area will keep the children busy.

Access : 5km southbound from Argèles on the D10, then on the D13.

Access : On leaving Arreau, take the D 618 towards Luchon

59 ETH BÉRYÈ PETIT

M. et Mme Vielle

15 route de Vielle
65400 Beaucens
Tel. 05 62 97 90 02
Fax 05 62 97 90 02
contact @ beryepetit.com
www.beryepetit.com

Open all year • 3 rooms with bathrooms • €45 to €54, breakfast included • Table d'hôte €15 • Credit cards not accepted, no dogs allowed

60 LA COUETTE DE BIÉOU

Mme Moreilhon

65170 Camparan
Tel. 05 62 39 41 10
Fax 05 62 39 41 10

Open all year • 3 rooms • €40, breakfast included • No table d'hôte • Car park. Credit cards not accepted, no dogs allowed

 The lady of the house's gracious welcome.

This country house, whose name means "little orchard" in Occitan, was built in 1790 in the purest traditions of regional architecture. Tastefully decorated rooms overlook the Lavedan and the Pyrenean peaks, the one upstairs is the most spacious and leads out onto a balcony which runs along the entire length of the façade. There are two others under the eaves. Breakfast is always a delight by the fireside or on the terrace.

 Stupendous view of the valley and the Pyrenean peaks.

Right in the heart of town, this attractive stone farm with flower-decked balconies commands a matchless view of the valley and the Pyrenees. Wood sets the tone in the cosy rooms which enjoy exceptional views, one of which overlooks Saint-Lary-Soulan. The hospitable owners are both genial souls and if you're lucky, you'll be able to see how the local "gâteau à la broche" is made, even lending a welcome helping hand in the four hours of spit-roasting in front of the fire.

Access : 8.5km to the south-east of Argelès on the D 100, then take a minor road

Access : 4km northbound, on the Arreau road and then turn right

 61 CHAMBRE D'HÔTE LE MOULIN D'ARIES

M. Dorit Weimer

 À Aries-Espenan
65230 Castelnau-Magnoac
Tel. 05 62 39 81 85
Fax 05 62 39 81 82
moulindaries@aol.com
www.poterie.fr

Open from 15 May to 31 Dec • 5 rooms with bathrooms and separate WC • €56, breakfast included • Table d'hôte €18 to €23 (evenings) • Reading room. No dogs allowed in restaurant

 62 GRANGE SAINT-JEAN

M. Igau

 Quartier Calypso
65110 Cauterets
Tel. 05 62 92 58 58
Fax 05 62 92 58 58
igau.brigitte@wanadoo.fr

Closed from 15 May to 15 Jun and 30 Sep to 1 Dec • 2 rooms • €60 to €70, breakfast included • No table d'hôte • Terrace, garden, car park. Credit cards not accepted, no dogs allowed

 Open the door and breathe in the perfume of yesteryear.

Time and care have clearly been lavished over the restoration of this 14C mill next door to an attractive manor whose stylish interior reveals original wood floors, an ancient staircase and latched doors. White prevails in the spacious rooms with king-size beds and well-equipped bathrooms. In the mill are a reading and television room and a small bar, all set against the backdrop of the old millstones. Forget about your diet and treat yourself to Gascony's delicacies!

 Stretching out in the warmth after a day in the open air.

The blue and yellow walls of this old wood barn never fail to catch the eye. A mountain flavour has been given to the beautifully restored interior in the form of wood-lined walls, occasionally breached by stone, warm colours and family furniture. The rooms are very peaceful and one has a private terrace. Children adore romping about the garden and immense meadow at an altitude of 900m, in sight of the Pyrenees.

Access : 4km to the south-east of Castelnau-Magnoac on the D 623 towards Boulogne, then turn right towards Aries-Espenan

Access : On the Lourdes road

63 MAISON BURRET
M. Cazaux

67 le Cap-de-la-Vielle
65200 Montgaillard
Tel. 05 62 91 54 29
Fax 05 62 91 52 42

 jecazaux @ tiscali.fr

Open all year • 3 rooms, one of which is a suite • €40 to €50, breakfast included • Table d'hôte €16 • Garden, car park. Credit cards not accepted, no dogs allowed

64 LE RELAIS DU CASTERA
M. Latour

Place du calvaire
65150 - Nestier
Tel. 05 62 39 77 37
Fax 05 62 39 77 29

 sarl.sergelatour @ wanadoo.fr

Closed from 1 to 8 Jun, 3 to 21 Jan, Sun evening, Mon, Tue evening (out of season) • 7 rooms upstairs, all have shower/WC, some have television • €40 to €60; breakfast €7; half board available • Menus €17 (weekdays) to €42 • Terrace. No dogs allowed

 Authentic and delightfully anachronistic.

Countless original architectural features are still visible in this lovely farmhouse, dating from 1791, such as the dovecote, bakery, stables, cowshed, handsome carved staircase and collection of old agricultural machinery. The comfortable rooms have been decorated with some fine antique pieces and in the winter a fire is lit in the one on the ground floor. Meals are served in a friendly dining room.

 The delicious cassoulet simmering on the stove

The village in the Comminges region is dominated by Mount Arès and its unusual calvary of twelve shrines on the slope. The inn offers recently renovated rooms in an up-to-date style and a welcoming restaurant renowned for its generous traditional cooking which makes the most of local ingredients. The almost sophisticated rustic interior makes it a pleasant stopping place near the attractive walled town of Montréjeau.

Access : 5km northbound from Pouzac on the D 935

Access : Westbound from Montréjeau, take the D 638 then the D 938 as far as Saint-Laurent-de-Neste and turn left

 65 LES ROCAILLES
M. Fanlou

65100 Omex
Tel. 05 62 94 46 19
Fax 05 62 94 33 35
muriellefanlou @ aol.com
www.lesrocailles.com

Closed from 1 Nov to Easter • 3 rooms • €65, breakfast included • Garden, car park. Credit cards not accepted, no dogs allowed • Outdoor swimming pool

 66 LE MOULIN D'ORINCLES
Mme Grimbert

Passage du Moulin
65380 Orincles
Tel. 05 62 45 40 65
Fax 05 62 45 60 50
moulindo @ free.fr

Closed from 30 Oct to 31 Jan • 3 rooms and one gîte • €56, breakfast included • Table d'hôte €18 • Garden, car park. Credit cards not accepted • Spa, jacuzzi

 The discreet luxury of this snug little nest.

It is impossible not to be won over by the charm of this small stone house with comfortably modern rooms. One of the rooms, named "The Seamstress" by the owner and former wardrobe mistress of the Paris Opera House, is home to an old sewing machine and a mannequin; it also has a private terrace. Those under the eaves are air-conditioned and command a fine view of the valley. A fireplace and old furniture set the scene in the dining room and the flowered garden and swimming pool are most welcome.

 The murmur of the stream running through the property.

This recently restored cereal mill has nonetheless retained its soul. You can admire the impressive millstones and other mechanical components which are still visible in the sitting and dining rooms. The bedrooms' names – "corn", "wheat" and "barley" – bear proud witness to the mill's past, and exposed beams, hand-stencilled motifs, old furniture and ochre colour-scheme further add to their appeal. The stream running through the courtyard, also home to a kitchen garden, completes the picture.

Access : 4.5km to the south-west of Lourdes on the D 13 then the D 213

Access : 3km to the north-west of Loucrup on the D 937 then the D 407

 67 DOMAINE DE JEAN-PIERRE
Mme Colombier

20 route de Villeneuve
65300 Pinas
Tel. 05 62 98 15 08
Fax 05 62 98 15 08
marie@domainedejeanpierre.com
www.domainedejeanpierre.com

Open all year, by reservation only in winter • 3 rooms upstairs • €48, breakfast included • No table d'hôte • Park. Credit cards not accepted • Tennis and golf nearby

 68 DOMAINE VÉGA
M. et Mme Mun

65250 Saint-Arroman
Tel. 05 62 98 96 77
Fax 05 62 98 96 77

Closed from Nov to Easter • 5 rooms with bath/WC or shower/WC • €55, breakfast included, half board available • Table d'hôte €18 to €22 • Park, car park. Credit cards not accepted, no dogs allowed • Swimming pool

 Long walks in the country.

This handsome house covered in Virginia creeper stands at an altitude of 600m on the plateau of Lannemezan, looking south towards the Pyrenees. Old furniture and pretty fabrics adorn the spacious, quiet rooms, all of which overlook the beautifully cared-for grounds. The distant notes of a piano being played in the sitting room can sometimes be heard. In the summer, breakfast is served on the terrace. Simple, cordial welcome.

 Lovely landscaped garden and grounds.

Originally built in the 16C, this manor house was the property of a Russian prince in the Belle Époque and a Buddhist centre in the 1970s. Now a B&B, it offers pleasant rooms named after flowers, with unusual carved headboards. All overlook the cedars, giant thuja and linden trees in the park and the countryside beyond. In the kitchen, the chef prepares imaginative recipes based on regional produce.

Access : 200m eastbound from the town on the D158

Access : 11km northbound from Sarrancolin on the D 929 then the D 26

69 LA FERME DE SOULAN
M. et Mme Amelot

Soulan
65170 Saint-Lary-Soulan
Tel. 05 62 98 43 21
Fax 05 62 98 43 21
fermedesoulan @ tiscali.fr
www.fermedesoulan.free.fr

Open all year • 4 rooms with bathrooms and television
• €80, breakfast included, half board available • Menus
€21 (evening only, including beverages) • Garden
• Sauna, hammam

70 LE GRAND CÈDRE
M. Peters

6 rue du Barry
65270 Saint-Pé-de-Bigorre
Tel. 05 62 41 82 04
Fax 05 62 41 85 89
chp @ grandcedre.com
www.grandcedre.com

Open all year • 4 rooms with bathrooms • €60, breakfast
included • Table d'hôte €22 • Terrace, park, car park.
Credit cards not accepted

The superb view overlooking the Aure valley from this mountain village at an altitude of 1280m.

Utter peace and quiet and pure mountain air (no smoking please!) pervade this old farmhouse located in the heart of a high-perched village whose name means sun in the local dialect. The buildings, set around a paved courtyard, are home to a ground-floor rustically-decorated dining room with a fireplace and two comfortable bedrooms with exposed beams and wainscoting. Upstairs are two other rooms with sloping ceilings and a panoramic sitting room with a south-facing bay window.

Botanical walks in the park.

This 17C country seat owes its name to the three-hundred-year-old cedar planted in the centre of the park, which casts a welcome shade over a few garden chairs. Each of the personalised rooms, linked by an outdoor gallery, is in a different style: Art Deco, Louis-Philippe, Henry II and Louis XV. The music room and piano, the classical dining room, the greenhouse with orchids, geraniums and cacti and the delightful cottage garden are a delight for the eyes.

Access : North-west of St-Lary-Soulan; go to Vieille-Aure, then turn left onto the D 123

Access : In the village

 71 LE BELVÉDÈRE
Mme Crampe

6 rue de l'Église
65400 Salles
Tel. 05 62 97 23 68
Fax 05 62 97 23 68
www.argeles-pyrenees.com

Closed in Nov • 3 rooms with shower/WC • €60, breakfast included; half board available • Table d'hôte €14 (evenings only except Sun) • Park, car park. Credit cards not accepted, no dogs allowed • Excursions to the mountains, swimming pool

 72 LA GRANGE AUX MARMOTTES
M. et Mme Senac

Au village
65120 Viscos
Tel. 05 62 92 91 13
Fax 05 62 92 93 75
hotel@grangeauxmarmottes.com
www.grangeauxmarmottes.com

Closed from 20 Nov to 20 Dec • 6 rooms with bath/WC or shower/WC and television • €60 to €72 (€55 to €67 low season); breakfast €10; half board available • Menus €19 (weekdays) to €40 • Terrace, garden • Outdoor swimming pool

 The enchanting perspective from this 18C abode.

The sweeping view of the valleys of Luz, Cauterets and Arrens with the Pyrenean peaks in the distance from this handsome manor house does full justice to its name. The rooms under the eaves are modern in flavour while those on the first floor are decorated with lovely old furniture and a fireplace; all enjoy the same view. In the winter, meals are served by the fireside and in the summer under an arbour.

 Heaven for sleepyheads and marmots.

The region is so untamed and rich in spectacular natural sights that you will spend all your days out exploring until the mountain cows come home! This old stone barn, with its cosy rooms and perfect peace and quiet are just what you need when your head finally does touch the pillow. The sun will already be high in the sky before you're ready to get up and feast your eyes on the sumptuous view of the valley, hemmed in all sides by peaks and summits.

Access : 12.5km southbound from Lourdes on the N 21 then the D 102

Access : To the north-west of Luz-Saint-Sauveur towards Pierrefitte-Nestalas

73 **GEORGE V**
Mme Selles

29 avenue du Maréchal-Joffre
81000 Albi
Tel. 05 63 54 24 16
Fax 05 63 49 90 78
info @ hotelgeorgev.com
 www.hotelgeorgev.com

Open all year • 9 rooms, all have showers with or without WC, television, some have fireplaces • €33 to €44; breakfast €6 • No restaurant • Shaded inner courtyard

74 **LA MÉTAIRIE NEUVE**
M. Tournier

Bout-du-Pont-de-L'Arn
81660 Pont-de-Larn
Tel. 05 63 97 73 50
Fax 05 63 61 94 75
metairieneuve @ wanadoo.fr
www.metairieneuve.com

Closed from 15 Dec to 25 Jan • 14 rooms, most have bath/WC, some have shower/WC, all have television • €69 to €80; breakfast €9; half board available • Restaurant closed Sat lunchtime (all year) and Sun evening and Mon (Oct to Easter); menus €23 to €32 • Terrace, garden, car park • Outdoor swimming pool

Basking in the first rays of morning sunshine.

Although not as luxurious as its famous Parisian namesake, this establishment is fully worthy of notice and most definitely less expensive than your average palace! The recently spruced up, spacious rooms are quiet despite the nearby railway station and decorated in pastel shades with good quality furniture; some have fireplaces. In the rear, a small shaded courtyard is perfect for open-air breakfasts.

After a refreshing night's sleep, dig into a delicious breakfast.

We recommend booking one of the rooms recently renovated in a "country chic" style, which are not without character, overlooking the garden of this 18C family farmhouse converted into an inn in the 1980s. There are two pleasantly decorated rustic indoor dining rooms, but most guests prefer the rafters of the old barn which is now a delightful summer terrace.

Access : On one of the roads that leads to the railway station

Access : 2km eastbound from Mazamet: leave on the N 112 towards Saint-Pons and turn left at La Richarde

75 **LE CASTEL DE BURLATS**
M. et Mme Dauphin

8 place du 8-Mai-1945
81100 Burlats
Tel. 05 63 35 29 20
Fax 05 63 51 14 69
www.lecasteldeburlats.fr.st

Closed from 1 to 15 Mar • 10 non-smoking rooms, all have bath/WC or shower/WC and television • €61 to €100; breakfast €10 • Menus €20 • Park with garden, private car park • Billiard room, reading room, hiking trails nearby

76 **EUROPE**
MM. Loiseau et Vialar

5 rue Victor-Hugo
81100 Castres
Tel. 05 63 59 00 33
Fax 05 63 59 21 38
hotelrenaissanceeurope@wanadoo.fr
www.hotelrenaissance.fr

Open all year • 38 rooms, all have bath/WC or shower/WC and television • €60 to €80 (€50 to €70 low season); breakfast €8; half board available • Menus €10 from Mon to Sat • Patio • Piano bar on Fri and Sat

We most liked
Savouring a whisky in the Renaissance salon.

You cannot miss this lovely 14C and 16C "castel" at the entrance to this medieval village in the gorges of the Agout. Spacious rooms, individually decorated with furniture picked up in antique shops, overlook a park where Mother Nature appears to have been given a free rein. Try your hand at billiards or catch up on the region's art and history in the Renaissance room complete with fireplace, wainscoting and beams. Even if it's your first stay, you will be greeted like a friend of the family.

We most liked
The unusual interior decoration.

Right in the heart of the historic town of Castres, these three 17C houses linked by a patio have been embellished with a lovely hotchpotch of objets trouvés, sculpture, paintings of cherubs and plants. The owners' originality and flair is also visible in the rooms' brick walls, timbers and open-plan bathrooms. The sitting rooms double as dining rooms and there is live music at the weekends.

Access : 9km to the north-east of Castres on the D 89, then take the D 58 that runs along the Agout

Access : In the town centre, in a quiet street that links Bd des Lices and Place Jean-Jaurès

77 **LA RENAISSANCE**
M. Vialar

17 rue Victor-Hugo
81100 Castres
Tel. 05 63 59 30 42
Fax 05 63 72 11 57
hotel.renaissance.europe @ wanadoo.fr
www.hotelrenaissance.fr

Open all year • 20 rooms with bath/WC and television
• €60 to €80 (€50 to €70 low season); breakfast €8; half
board available • Menus €10 (except Sun)

78 **AURIFAT**
Mme Wanklyn

81170 Cordes-sur-Ciel
Tel. 05 63 56 07 03
Fax 05 63 56 07 03
aurifat @ wanadoo.fr
www.aurifat.com

Closed from mid-Dec to mid-Feb • 4 non-smoking rooms
• €70 (€62 low season), breakfast included • No table
d'hôte • Garden, car park. Credit cards not accepted, no
dogs allowed • Outdoor swimming pool

**Peaceful nights in the heart of the
historic town.**

This 17C half-timbered brick house offers accommodation in a few rooms whose charm it is impossible to resist. Elegant canopied beds and a beautiful choice of furniture elegantly marrying periods and styles. An inviting bar and sitting rooms adorned with old furniture and objets d'art further contribute to making you feel at home: settle in for the evening and discuss and compare different approaches to interior decoration!

A magical place steeped in history.

The superb restoration of this 13C half-timbered brick watchtower is most impressive. Its name, which means "path of gold" was inspired by the Aurosse stream which runs down below. All the cane-furnished rooms have a balcony overlooking the fields and valley. Make sure you have a peep in the suite in the 17C dovecote. The terraced gardens are also worth exploring. The tower's situation, just a few minutes walk from the medieval heart of Cordes, is one of its greatest assets.

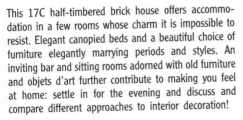

Access : In the town centre, between Boulevard des Lices and Place Jean Jaurès, in the pedestrian area

Access : 800m from the city on the St-Jean road

 79 HOSTELLERIE DU VIEUX CORDES
M. et Mme Thuriès

 Haut de la Cité
81170 Cordes-sur-Ciel
Tel. 05 63 53 79 20
Fax 05 63 56 02 47
vieux.cordes @ thuries.fr
www.thuries.fr

Closed in Jan • 20 rooms at the Hostellerie, some have a view over the valley, 8 are in a separate wing: La Cité. All rooms have bath/WC or shower/WC and television • €48 to €72; breakfast €9; half board available • Menus €15 to €33 (no restaurant in the separate wing) • Shaded terrace

 Exploring the countless secrets of the medieval city of Cordes.

The tasteful bedrooms might lack the character of the main building, an old monastery with an original spiral staircase, but they do allow visitors to explore and enjoy the heart of this medieval Gothic town, "the city of a hundred arches". The windows overlook the valley of Cérou and command picturesque views of the tiny paved streets or of the old wisteria whose perfume lingers on the exquisite patio terrace. Salmon and duck take pride of place on the menu.

Access : In the town centre, between the covered market and the church

 80 MAISON BAKEA
M. et Mme Aguirre

 28 Le Planol
81170 Cordes-sur-Ciel
Tel. 05 63 56 29 54
Fax 05 63 56 29 54
maison bakea @ tiscali.fr
www.maisonbakea.chez.tiscali.fr

Open all year • 5 rooms • €55 to €75; breakfast included • No table d'hôte • Credit cards accepted in high season, no dogs allowed

 A serene atmosphere reigns throughout this establishment run by two opera singers.

This beautiful 13C house blends perfectly into the picturesque medieval town. A delightfully restored inner courtyard enhances the appeal of the covered passages, brickwork and timbers. Bright colours, antique furniture, stained-glass windows, bare flagstones and beams set the tone for the personalised bedrooms, each of which has a modern bathroom. The terrace overlooking the hilly countryside is impossible to resist. A dream come true!

Access : 800m from Cordes on the Planol in the medieval city

  81 DEMEURE DE FLORE

M. Di Bari

106 route Nationale
81240 Lacabarède
Tel. 05 63 98 32 32
Fax 05 63 98 47 56
demeure.de.flore@hotelrama.com
www.hotelrama.com

Closed from 5 Jan to 3 Feb and Mon out of season • 10 rooms (3 in a detached house) and one suite, one of which has disabled access, with bath/WC and television • €79 to €90; breakfast €10; half board available • Menus €25 to €33 • Terrace, garden, private car park. No dogs allowed • Outdoor swimming pool

  82 LA RANQUIÈRE

M. et Mme Lecoutre

La Ranquière
81240 Rouairoux
Tel. 05 63 98 87 50
ranquiere@aol.com

Open all year • 4 rooms with bath/WC or shower/WC • €60 to €65 (€50 to €55 low season), breakfast included • Table d'hôte €18 by reservation • Terrace, garden, park, car park. Credit cards not accepted, dogs not allowed • Swimming pool

We most liked **Wandering around the delightfully unruly garden.**

From the moment you set foot (or wheel) on the drive lined by majestic linden trees, you will fall under the spell of this charming manor-villa, built back in 1882. The rooms are decorated with elegant Louis XVI furniture and three open directly onto the swimming pool with the Montagne Noire in the background. The meals demonstrate a distinctly Italian-Provençal influence but the establishment also serves an excellent cup of tea – even by British standards!

We most liked **This smart trim farmhouse would be at home in any interior decorating magazine.**

Blue, yellow, green or pink - which room of this splendid 17C farmhouse set on a 5-acre estate will you be lucky enough to sleep in? Whatever the colour, they are all brimming with charm and delightfully appointed with bare beams, polished red tiles, worn wooden doors, colourful fabrics and antique furniture. The warm welcome, inviting garden and orchard, handsome pool and terrace overlooking the Montagne Noire all add to the appeal of this maison d'hôte.

Access : In Lacabarède, leave the N 112 and drive along a lane bordered with lime trees

Access : At Lacabarède take the D52 towards Rouairoux, 800m further on turn left towards La Ranquière

 83 MAISON DES CHEVALIERS
M. et Mme Choux

 Place de la Mairie
82700 Escatalens
Tel. 05 63 68 71 23
Fax 05 63 30 25 90
claude.choux@wanadoo.fr
www.maisondeschevaliers.com

Open all year • 6 rooms with bathrooms • €70, breakfast included; half board available • Table d'hôte €20 to €25 • Terrace, garden, park, car park. Credit cards not accepted • Outdoor swimming pool

 84 LE PLATANE
Mme Horf

 Coques-Lunel
82130 Lafrançaise
Tel. 05 63 65 92 18
Fax 05 63 65 88 18

Open all year • 4 rooms • €60 to €65, breakfast included. half board available • Table d'hôte €20 • Garden, car park. Credit cards not accepted • Outdoor swimming pool, horse-riding

 The imaginative cooking of the lady of the house, originally from southern Portugal.

Good taste and a certain daring distinguish the restoration of this lovely 18C manor house. Warm, sunny colours adorn the immense rooms complete with four-poster beds and period furniture, while the bathrooms boast superb old bathtubs and washbasins in Portuguese marble. A games room and a music room have been installed in the outbuildings. Shaded by a two-hundred-year-old chestnut tree, the courtyard is delightful.

 The quintessence of comfort.

This lovely brick country house, flanked by stables and a dovecote, dates from 1904. Comfort was clearly high on the priority list of the restoration and the rooms are spacious and decorated in a modern or Neo-rustic style. Sunbathe around the oval swimming pool or head for the shade of the park's magnificent old planes, lindens and weeping willows. Horse-riding and bicycling available for those in need of more exercise.

Access : 14km eastbound from Montauban on the N 113

Access : 10km eastbound from Moissac on the D 927, the D 2 and then the D 68

85 LE QUERCY
M. Bacou

Faubourg d'Auriac
82110 Lauzerte
Tel. 05 63 94 66 36

Fax 05 63 39 06 56

Open all year • 10 rooms, 4 have a view over the countryside, with bath/WC or shower/WC • €32 to €42; breakfast €6; half board available • Restaurant closed Mon and Sun evening (low season); menus €17 to €41 • Small car park

86 LE MOULIN DE MOISSAC
M. Barthélémy

Esplanade du Moulin
82200 Moissac
Tel. 05 63 32 88 99
Fax 05 63 32 02 08
hotel@lemoulindemoissac.com
www.lemoulindemoissac.com

Closed Sat lunchtime and Sun all day • 35 air-conditioned rooms with bath/WC and television, lift, 2 with disabled access, 26 non-smoking rooms • €48 to €80; breakfast €7.50 • Air-conditioned restaurant; menus €22 (week-days) to €35 • Private car park • In the heart of the historic centre

 Following in the footsteps of the pilgrims on the road to St James of Compostela.

The GR65 footpath runs alongside this late 19C house in the heart of a village, perched high on an outcrop, whose lovely timber framed medieval houses nestle around a pretty covered square. The small rooms have been fully renovated and four, in the rear of the house, overlook the valley of the Barguelonne. The restaurant has also been tastefully and simply redone. Very friendly.

 Gazing at the Tarn from the windows of this lovely mill before visiting the former abbey of Moissac.

After a former vocation as a flour mill, this establishment is now devoted to the well-being of its guests. The origins of the mill, anchored on the right bank of the Tarn, date back to 1474. Countless transformations and several fortunes later, a serious rejuvenation programme has endowed the impressive building with great charm, from the comfortable theme rooms (country, alpine or seafaring) to the cosy piano-bar and delightful restaurant with a contemporary bistro atmosphere.

Access : In the heart of the medieval village reached by the D 953, between Montcuq and Valence-d'Agen

Access : From the A62 motorway, take exit 9 towards Moissac Centre, turn right after Napoléon Bridge

87 LE BARRY
M. Bankes et M. Jaross

Faubourg Saint-Roch
82270 Montpezat-de-Quercy
Tel. 05 63 02 05 50
Fax 05 63 02 03 07
lebarry-montpezat@wanadoo.fr

Closed from 24 to 26 Dec • 5 rooms • €67 (€63 low season), breakfast included; half board available • Table d'hôte €23 • Garden. Credit cards not accepted, no dogs allowed • Outdoor swimming pool

88 DOMAINE DE LAFON
M. et Mme Perrone

Pech de Lafon
82270 Montpezat-de-Quercy
Tel. 05 63 02 05 09
Fax 05 63 27 60 69
micheline.perrone
@domainedelafon.com
www.domainedelafon.com

Closed first fortnight of Mar, second fortnight of Nov and Christmas • 3 rooms with bathrooms • €72 (€65 low season), breakfast included; half board available • Table d'hôte €22 (evenings by reservation) • Terrace, garden, car park. Credit cards not accepted, no dogs allowed

Forget your worldly cares in this undisturbed setting.

Built on the outskirts of the medieval town close to the collegiate church, this handsome village property commands an exceptional view of the valley and the hillsides. The pleasant rooms are tastefully decorated and one opens directly onto the delightful garden complete with swimming pool. The stylish sitting room is lined with books. A perfect country retreat.

Taking a course in trompe l'œil painting.

Perched on a green hillside, this 19C square manor house enjoys a sweeping view of the surrounding countryside. Admire the immense rooms decorated by the owner, an artist and a former theatre set designer. The "Indian" is cloaked in oriental fabrics, marble and architectural trompe-l'œil scenes, azulejos tiles adorn the "Parrots" and "Baldaquin" features a pretty yellow and grey foliage pattern. Not to be missed!

Access : In the village

Access : 2km on the D 20 towards Molières, then turn left towards Mirabel for 2km

89 LA RÉSIDENCE
M. et Mme Weijers

 37 rue Droite
82140 Saint-Antonin-Noble-Val
Tel. 05 63 67 37 56
Fax 05 63 67 37 56
info@laresidence-france.com
www.laresidence-France.com

Open all year • 5 non-smoking rooms overlooking the garden or the terrace, all have bath/WC • €65 to €78, breakfast included; half-board available • Table d'hôte €22 (evening only) • Garden. Credit cards not accepted, no dogs allowed

 Idyllically situated in the heart of the medieval village.

The different cultures and backgrounds of the Franco-British husband and wife team that runs this 18C manor house are reflected in its interior decoration. Most of the spacious, tastefully decorated rooms overlook the Roc d'Anglars; book the one with a private terrace if possible. In the summer, linger in the beautiful garden, unless of course you would prefer the more energetic appeal of the nearby climbing centre.

Access : In the heart of the medieval village

NORD-PAS-DE-CALAIS

This region of northern France has everything to warm the soul. According to a local saying, "the hearts of the men of the north are warm enough to thaw the coldest climate." Just watch these northerners as they throw themselves body and soul into the traditional 'Dance of the Giants', re-enacted everywhere in countless fairs, fêtes and carnivals. Several tons of chips and mussels – and who knows how many litres of beer! – are needed to sustain thousands of stall-holders and over one million visitors to Lille's annual Grande Braderie, just one of many huge street markets. The influence of Flanders can be seen not only in the names of many of the towns and inhabitants and the wealth of Gothic architectural treasures, but also in filling local dishes such as *carbonade* of beef, braised in amber beer, and *potjevleesch*, a chicken or rabbit stew with potatoes. Slender belfries, neat rows of former miners' houses and the distant outline of windmills further remind visitors that they are on the border of Belgium, or, as a glance over the Channel on a sunny day will prove, just a pebble's throw from the white cliffs of Dover!

Nord (59)

Pas-de-Calais (62)

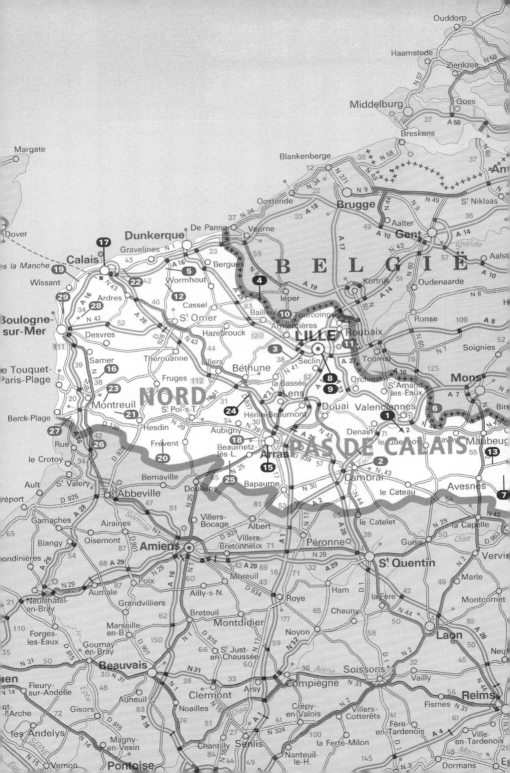

 1 LA GENTILHOMMIÈRE
Mme Fournier

2 place de l'Église
59269 Artres
Tel. 03 27 28 18 80
Fax 03 27 28 18 81
la.gentilhommiere@wanadoo.fr

Closed from 2 to 25 Aug, Sun evenings and evenings of public holidays • 10 rooms with bath/WC and television • €80; breakfast €10 • Menus €22 (weekdays) to €36 • Garden, private car park • Horse-riding treks (by reservation), hiking, mountain biking, horse-drawn carriage rides

 2 FERME DE BONAVIS
Mme Delcambre

59266 Banteux
Tel. 03 27 78 55 08
Fax 03 27 78 55 08
delcambre-gitesdefrance@club-internet.fr

Open all year • 3 rooms with bathrooms • €46 to €60, breakfast included • No table d'hôte • Credit cards not accepted, no dogs allowed

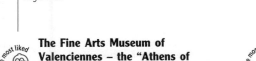 **The Fine Arts Museum of Valenciennes – the "Athens of the North".**

This redbrick farmstead on the doorstep of Valenciennes was built in 1746: its surprisingly airy, well-proportioned rooms overlook a quiet inner courtyard or the manicured garden. Sample delicious regional dishes in the light restaurant installed in the converted cow-shed, complete with vaulted ceiling and old mangers. The hotel can arrange horse-riding excursions and outings in a horse-drawn carriage if you book ahead.

 Children adore exploring the ins and outs of this working farm.

You can't help but be impressed by the handsome scale of this former coaching inn, turned into a farm at the end of the Second World War. High ceilings and parquet floors set the scene for the well-decorated and well-soundproofed rooms. Countless leisure activities on the farm or nearby, including boules, table-tennis, table-football, cycling and walking trails; gliding and aerodrome 9km away.

Access : Southbound from Valenciennes on the D 958 (towards Le Cateau), take a left on the D 400 after Famars

Access : 11km southbound from Cambrai on the N 44

 3 CHEZ JULIE
M. et Mme Tilmant

8 rue Radinghem
59134 Beaucamps-Ligny
Tel. 03 20 50 33 82
Fax 03 20 50 34 35
ctilmant @ wanadoo.fr
http://perso.wanadoo.fr/chezjulie

Open all year • 3 rooms with shower/WC and telephone • €44, breakfast included • No table d'hôte • Sitting room, car park. Credit cards not accepted, no dogs allowed

 4 AUBERGE DU VERT MONT
M. et Mme Ladeyn-Dubrulle

13-18 rue du Mont-Noir
59299 Boeschepe
Tel. 03 28 49 41 26
Fax 03 28 49 48 58
aubergevertmont @ aol.com

Closed Mon and Tue lunchtimes out of season • 7 rooms • €73 to €80 (€65 to €75 out of season); breakfast €7; half board available • Menus €23 to €33 • Terrace, garden • Children's play area, animal park

 Simple and unaffected.

Guests immediately feel at home and welcome in this comfy farmstead, built in Flanders brick on the threshold of a village near Lille. Pastel shades of yellow or beige adorn the immaculate rooms, two of which are upstairs under the eaves. A piano, wood stove, two traditional Flemish games and pleasant light wooden furniture adorn the breakfast room. Stretch out in inviting deep armchairs in the sitting room.

 The pleasant country feel to the dining room.

This trim redbrick inn perched on the heights of the village is a welcome surprise. Pretty, well-appointed rooms overlook the valley, while those upstairs, the most pleasant, have amusing porthole windows and sloping ceilings. Meals are served in a country dining room adorned with old farm tools and objects such as clogs, kegs and wooden wheels. A children's play area and small animal park will appeal to younger visitors.

Access : 12km westbound from Lille on the A 25, exit no 7, then take the road to Radinghem (D 62)

Access : 9km northbound from Bailleul on the D 10

BOURBOURG - 59630

JENLAIN - 59144

 5 LE WITHOF
Mme Battais

Chemin du Château
59630 Bourbourg
Tel. 03 28 22 16 17
Fax 03 28 62 38 88

Open all year • 5 non-smoking rooms with bathrooms
• €50, breakfast included • Table d'hôte €17 • Garden,
car park. No dogs allowed

 6 CHÂTEAU D'EN HAUT
M. Demarcq

59144 Jenlain
Tel. 03 27 49 71 80
Fax 03 27 35 90 17
chateaudenhaut@fr.st
www.chateaudenhaut.fr.st

Open all year • 6 rooms with bathrooms • €50 to €72,
breakfast included • No table d'hôte • Park, car park.
Credit cards not accepted, no dogs allowed

 **The magnificent architecture
of this 16C farm.**

This fortified 16C farmhouse seems to float on its moat
which, combined with its turrets and an imposing
entrance reminiscent of a drawbridge, gives it the allure
of a full-blown castle. This stately atmosphere extends
through handsome doors into spacious bedrooms, all
with immense bathrooms. On sunny days, breakfast is
served in the courtyard. Excellent value for money.

 **A castle literally crammed with
antiques.**

A long paved drive leads up to this magnificent 18C
château and dovecote, set in the middle of pleasant
parkland. The remarkable interior, rich in marquetry,
antiques and period paintings is certainly worthy of the
grand approach and is beautifully cared for by the
charming hosts. Four-poster beds adorn the comfortable
bedrooms and guests have the run of a light, airy
breakfast room, library and even a small chapel.

Access : 14km to the south-west of Dunkirk on the
A 16 towards Calais (exit no 23)

Access : 6km to the south-east of Valenciennes on
the D 934 and the D 59

 CHÂTEAU DE LA MOTTE
Mme Plateau

 59740 Liessies
Tel. 03 27 61 81 94
Fax 03 27 61 83 57
contact @ chateaudelamotte.fr
www.chateaudelamotte.fr

Closed from 20 Dec to 10 Feb and Sun evening and Mon lunchtime • 9 rooms in 2 wings, most have bath/WC, some have shower/WC, all have television • €64; breakfast €8; half board available • Menus €20 (week-days) to €70 • Park, car park • Mountain-bike rental, walking and hiking at Val Joli Lake 5km away

 BRUEGHEL
Mme Lhermie

 3-5 parvis Saint-Maurice
59000 Lille
Tel. 03 20 06 06 69
Fax 03 20 63 25 27
hotel.brueghel @ wanadoo.fr
www.hotel-brueghel.com

Open all year • 65 rooms with bath/WC or shower/WC, all have television • €71 to €79; breakfast €8 • No restaurant • Public car park nearby

 Sampling a little slice of the very, er,... "robust" local Boulette d'Avesnes cheese.

This delightful pink-brick edifice was built in the 18C on the edge of the forest of l'Abbé Val Joly for the Benedictine brotherhood of Liessies; the monks may have gone, but the peace and quiet remains. The wide bay windows of the restaurant, reminiscent of an orangery, overlook a leafy park and the rooms, furnished with rustic or period pieces, and the bathrooms have just been treated to a new lease of life. Guests can look forward to exploring the paths of the Avesnes Nature Reserve.

 The lively historic centre of Lille and its convivial atmosphere.

This unpretentious establishment is rarely empty and it's not hard to see why. There's the typically Flemish first impression of its redbrick and chalk-white façade, then its pleasing old-fashioned interior with dark wainscoting and a period lift shaft in wood and wrought-iron, not to mention the fresh, pastel-coloured rooms, most of which overlook the Gothic church of St Maurice. Best of all is its practical location in the heart of Lille, just two minutes from the Grand'Place.

Access : Leave Liessies southbound on the D 133 or the D 963 and take the minor road to Motte

Access : Opposite St Maurice Church

 9 PAIX
PAIX
M. et Mme Trénaux

46 bis rue de Paris
59000 Lille
Tel. 03 20 54 63 93
Fax 03 20 63 98 97
hotelpaixlille @ aol.com
www.hotel-la-paix.com

Open all year • 35 rooms with bath/WC or shower/WC, all have television • €80 to €93; breakfast €9 • No restaurant • Public car park nearby • Well located: near the Grand'Place, theatre and opera house

 10 LA FERME BLANCHE
LA FERME BLANCHE
Mme Delaval

Rue Pasteur
59840 Lompret
Tel. 03 20 92 99 12
Fax 03 20 54 29 82
 dadeleval @ nordnet.fr

Closed for a fortnight in August • 3 rooms with bath/WC • €43 to €48, breakfast included • No table d'hôte • Park, car park. Credit cards not accepted. €2 supplement for dogs • Outdoor swimming pool

 The arty feel to this reasonably priced hotel.

The delightfully askew frontage of the Hôtel de la Paix, which in fact dates back to 1782, hides a collection of 250 reproduction works of art worthy of an art gallery. The rooms, corridors and staircases each has its own "old master", exhibited on yellow, dusty pink or light green walls. This "Who's Who" of fine art is curated by the owner, whose own creations can be admired on the walls of the breakfast room. A friendly establishment which has earned itself a loyal clientele.

 Cycling around the countryside.

A stony lane leads to this pretty farm whose whitewashed buildings form a rectangle behind the large iron gate, watched over by the vigilant eye of a security camera. The old barn has been converted into simple, comfortable rooms; one of which features a lovely mixture of crimson, pink and white. The exposed beams and pastel shades in the breakfast room are also very pleasant. A small swimming pool lies in the inner courtyard.

Access : In the town centre, near the Grand'Place and the opera house

Access : 7km to the north-west of Lille exit no 6, then take the lane on the right

 ABRI DU PASSANT
M. Renart

 14 rue Vauban
59100 Roubaix
Tel. 03 20 11 07 62
Fax 03 20 11 07 62
jean-françois.renart @ wanadoo.fr

Closed in Aug • 5 rooms with bathrooms • €44, breakfast included, half board available • Table d'hôte €11 (evening only) • Garden. Credit cards not accepted

 CHÂTEAU DE SAINT-PIERRE-BROUCK
M. et Mme Duvivier

287 route de la Bistade
59630 Saint-Pierre-Brouck
Tel. 03 28 27 50 05
Fax 03 28 27 50 05
nduvivier @ nordnet.fr
www.lechateau.net

Open all year by reservation • 5 non-smoking rooms • €65, breakfast included • Table d'hôte €22 • Park, car park. Credit cards not accepted, no dogs allowed

 Contemporary works of art adorn the whole house.

You will not be disappointed by the restful mood of this late-19C property next door to Barbieux park. Many original architectural features, such as the tiled mosaic floor in the hall, impressive high ceilings and lovely light wood staircase, still reveal an almost Victorian love of discreet home comforts. The bedrooms and bathrooms are all generously proportioned. The sitting and dining room provide the setting for an exhibition of works of art by a young local painter.

 Cosily comfortable.

Nestling in a five-acre park, this impressive château built in 1905 is home to richly furnished rooms complete with moulded ceilings and marble fireplaces, and named after flowers. Make sure you taste the mistress of the house's tasty Flemish-flavoured cooking, served in the plush dining room or in the lovely winter garden-cum-conservatory overlooking the countryside.

Access : To the south-west of town, near the park

Access : 8km northbound from Éperlecques National Forest, on the D 1

  13 HÔTEL DU MARQUAIS
Mmes Carrié et Guinot

  14 LA VILLA MARIANI
Mme Mariani

65 rue du Général-de-Gaulle
59216 Sars-Poteries
Tel. 03 27 61 62 72
Fax 03 27 57 47 35
hoteldumarquais@aol.com
www.hoteldumarquais.com

5 Grand'Place
59740 Solre-le-Château
Tel. 03 27 61 65 30
Fax 03 27 61 63 38
mariani59@aol.com

Closed from 15 Dec to 1 Mar • 11 rooms with bath/WC or shower/WC • €48; breakfast €6 • No restaurant • Garden, car park • Tennis

Open all year • 3 rooms • €45 to €50, breakfast included • No table d'hôte • Garden. Credit cards not accepted, no dogs allowed • Bicycles available for guests

 Picking out a treasure in the stone pottery workshops of Sars, still in working order.

 Regular contemporary art exhibitions.

Painted brick walls and old furniture grace the bedrooms of this former farmhouse, converted into a hotel. Depending on the weather, breakfast is served on the large communal table in the hall or on the terrace overlooking the garden. Guests can choose between tennis or a visit to the Museum-Workshop of Glass in the rambling house of the former director of the glassworks.

This impressive 19C mansion built on the ruins of an old fortified castle has charm to spare. Comfortable, elegant rooms survey the peace and quiet of the garden, the shelves in the sitting room are well stocked with books on the region and the walls are frequently adorned with exhibitions of contemporary art, the lady of the house's passion. The house lends bicycles to explore the region.

Access : On the main road through town, on the outskirts

Access : In the centre of the village

ARRAS - 62000

BEUSSENT - 62170

 15 LES 3 LUPPARS
M. Libouton

 49 Grand'Place
62000 Arras
Tel. 03 21 60 02 03
Fax 03 21 24 24 80
contact.3luppars@wanadoo.fr

Open all year • 42 rooms, one of which has disabled access, all have shower/WC and television • €60 to €65; breakfast €7 • No restaurant • Sauna

 16 LA HAUTE CHAMBRE
M. Barsby

 124 route d'Hucqueliers
Hameau le Ménage
62170 Beussent
Tel. 03 21 90 91 92
Fax 03 21 86 38 24

Closed from 1 to 15 Sep and from 15 Dec to 15 Jan • 5 rooms upstairs • €80, breakfast included • No table d'hôte • Garden, park, car park. Credit cards not accepted, no dogs allowed • Visit of the owner's art studio

 Strolling underneath the arcades of the magnificent Grand'Place.

We must admit that the simple, practical accommodation is nothing special in itself and the quieter rooms to the rear don't overlook the square. But surely this is a small price to pay for the luxury of staying in the oldest house in Arras. Built in 1467, its lovely Gothic façade, richly worked with gables, watchtower and ogival windows, fully deserves its place on the meticulously restored Grand'Place, one of the marvels of Flemish architecture.

 A delightful 19C manor nestling behind a curtain of greenery.

Sumptuous! If we only had one word to describe this mid-19C country house and its idyllic park, that would be it. A collection of the sculptor-owner's works is dotted around the grounds. The comfortable, exquisitely furnished rooms are a feast for the eyes and the breakfasts generous enough to satisfy the most demanding appetites. Exploring the park, home to some 300 animals, is always a hit with children.

Access : In the town centre, on the Grand'Place

Access : 10km northbound from Montreuil on the N 1 then the D 127

 17   **MEURICE**
M. et Mme Cossart

5 rue Edmond-Roche
62100 Calais
Tel. 03 21 34 57 03
Fax 03 21 34 14 71
meurice @ hotel-meurice.fr
www.hotel-meurice.fr

Open all year • 41 rooms on 3 floors, most of which have bath/WC, some have shower/WC, all have television • €79 to €130; breakfast €12; half board available • Restaurant closed Sat lunchtime; menus €12 (weekdays) to €70 • Garage

 18   **LE CLOS GRINCOURT**
Mme Annie Senlis

18 rue du Château
62161 Duisans
Tel. 03 21 48 68 33
Fax 03 21 48 68 33
patrick.senlis @ wanadoo.fr

Closed from Nov to Mar, except by reservation • 1 room and 1 suite (non-smoking) • €49, breakfast included • No table d'hôte • Park, car park. Credit cards not accepted, no dogs allowed

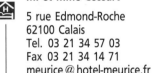 **The Lace Museum next door to the hotel.**

Although a coaching inn had stood here since before the Revolution, its old walls were unable to survive the air raids of the Second World War. Rebuilt in a style reminiscent of a miniature palace, this period-piece has the evocative look of a 1950s film set. Crystal chandeliers, a fireplace and antique furniture adorn the vast classical hall, the rooms have a charmingly old-fashioned feel and the restaurant has kept its period-style wood panelling.

 The Clos believes in pampering its guests.

As you drive up the paved lane to this delightful manor house, get ready to be coddled and indulged. A lovely white spiral staircase leads up to rooms, more akin to suites, all of which overlook the park, which becomes a carpet of daffodils in the spring. Family photos adorn the walls of this lovely building begun in the reign of Louis XIV but only finished in the Second Empire.

Access : Behind the Lace Museum, in a small quiet street, near Rue Royale and Richelieu Park

Access : 9km westbound from Arras on the N 39

 19 LA GRAND'MAISON
M. Boutroy

Hameau de la Haute-Escalles
62179 Escalles
Tel. 03 21 85 27 75
Fax 03 21 85 27 75
www.lagrandmaison.chez.tiscali.fr

Open all year • 6 rooms, 4 of which have bath/WC and television, the other 2 have shower/WC • €45 to €55, breakfast included • No table d'hôte • Garden, car park. Credit cards not accepted, no dogs allowed

 20 LE MOULIN
M. et Mme Legrand

16 rue de Saint-Pol
62770 Fillièvres
Tel. 03 21 41 13 20
Fax 03 21 04 32 41
aufildeleau @ free.fr
http://aufildeleau.free.fr

Open all year • 5 non-smoking rooms with bathrooms • €48 to €51, breakfast included • Table d'hôte €17 (weekdays) to €22 • Garden, park, car park. Credit cards not accepted, no dogs allowed • Fishing, canoeing, mountain bike rental

 Poised between land and sea.

Wedged between two headlands and almost in sight of the white cliffs of Dover, this lovely 18C flower-decked farm has a spacious inner courtyard whose centrepiece is a dovecote. The spacious rooms overflow with antiques, the "prestige" rooms are the most comfortable. Children can romp to their heart's content in their very own play area and in the garden, which is home to a few animals. Walking, mountain biking and windsurfing less than 2km away.

 The idyllic country setting of this mill.

This 18C mill, which boasts its original wheel and mechanism, lies on the road of the Field of the Cloth of Gold, where François I and Henry VIII's diplomatic summit once indulged their shared passion for power politics and full-blown pageantry. The well-restored mill is home to spacious rooms furnished with old pieces, where only the murmur of the Canche flowing beneath the windows will disturb the quiet. Magnificent park with two ponds, one for fishing.

Access : 2km eastbound from Cap-Blanc-Nez on the D 243

Access : 7km to the south-east of Vieil-Hesdin on the D 340

 21 LA COMMANDERIE
Mme Flament

 Allée des Templiers
62990 Loison-sur-Créquoise
Tel. 03 21 86 49 87

Closed in Feb • 3 non-smoking rooms • €62 to €70, breakfast included • No table d'hôte • Garden, car park. Credit cards not accepted, no dogs allowed

 22 LE MANOIR DU MELDICK
M. et Mme Houzet

 2528 avenue du Général-de-Gaulle
Le Fort-Vert
62730 Marck
Tel. 03 21 85 74 34
Fax 03 21 85 74 34
jeandaniele.houzet @ free.fr

Open all year • 5 rooms • €58, breakfast included • No table d'hôte • Car park. Credit cards not accepted, no dogs allowed

 The atmosphere, dripping with character and history.

The wonderful architecture of this former Knights' Templar command post, said to date back to the 12C, has been beautifully restored. Each of the refined rooms is named after one of the family's ancestors: Alice, Maria, Mancienne and Tantise. An agreeable clutter of old objects adorns the ground floor including pewter pots, a classically-French zinc bar and a set of forge bellows turned into a coffee table. The gurgling waters of the Créquoise add to the appeal of the park.

 The owners' attentive care.

So close to the port of Calais and yet so far, this lovingly restored manor house is a little gem of a find. Each of the spacious, individually decorated rooms is named after a flower: "Daisy", "Cornflower", "Rose" and "Poppy" – "Hyacinth" has a king-sized bed. All are equipped with coffee and tea making facilities and biscuits. Even better than home!

Access : Take the long drive near the river

Access : 6km eastbound from Calais on the D 940 and the D 119

 23 MANOIR FRANCIS
Mme Leroy

1 rue de l'Église
62170 Marles-sur-Canche
Tel. 03 21 81 38 80
Fax 03 21 81 38 56

Open all year • 3 rooms with bath/WC • €50 to €60, breakfast included • No table d'hôte • Garden. Credit cards not accepted, no dogs allowed

 24 LES TOURTERELLES
M. et Mme Verbrugge

374 rue Nationale
62290 Noeux-les-Mines
Tel. 03 21 61 65 65
Fax 03 21 61 65 75
les.tourterelles@wanadoo.fr
www.lestourterelles.fr

Open all year • 22 rooms on 3 floors, with bath/WC or shower/WC and television • €50 to €75; breakfast €8; half board available • Menus €20 to €50 • Terrace, garden, private car park. No dogs allowed • Loisinord Park nearby: year-round skiing, water sports

 The lady of the house's attention to detail.

You have to go under the immense porch and through the garden, home to a host of farmyard animals, to reach this 17C fortified farmhouse. We loved the interior, particularly the ground floor with its lovely chalk vaults upheld by diagonal beams. Old furniture, a private sitting room and unusual bathrooms complement the spacious rooms. The terrace under the shade of an apple tree is enchanting.

 Skiing down the slag heap ski slope of Loisinord!

This redbrick house was the headquarters a coal mining company over a century ago. The modest rooms are more than compensated for by the elegant restaurant installed in the muted atmosphere of the former boardroom with dark wainscoting, marble fireplace and Louis XVI cane chairs. Terrace in the garden in fine weather.

Access : 5.5km to the south-east of Montreuil-sur-Mer on the D 113

Access : Between Arras and Béthune, by the main road going through the town

 25 CHÂTEAU DE SAULTY
Mme Dalle

 82 rue de la Gare
62158 Saulty
Tel. 03 21 48 24 76
Fax 03 21 48 18 32
chateaudesaulty@nordnet.fr

Closed in Jan • 5 rooms with bathrooms • €50, breakfast included • No table d'hôte • Park, car park. Credit cards not accepted, no dogs allowed

  26 LE PRIEURÉ
M. Delbecque

 Impasse de l'Église
62180 Tigny-Noyelle
Tel. 03 21 86 04 38
Fax 03 21 81 39 95
r.delbecque@wanadoo.fr
www.leprieure-tigny.com

Open all year • 5 rooms with bath/WC and television • €60 to €88, breakfast included • Table d'hôte €25 • Garden, park

 A glass of home-grown apple or pear juice at breakfast time.

This splendid castle, built in 1835, lies opposite a superb park and a fruit orchard. The rooms, of varying sizes, have parquet floors and are decorated with old or pine furniture; all have a decorative marble fireplace. An assortment of home-made jams and fruit juices are served at breakfast in the ancestral dining room. Library and table-tennis.

 Stylish interior decoration.

The owner-antique dealer has lovingly restored his pretty turquoise-shuttered house, set in a small park. The rooms are stylish and feature exposed beams and antiques; the split-level room is most praiseworthy, as is the suite with sitting room and fireplace. The breakfast room and the superb regional fireplace are also worth a look. Golfers will adore the prospect of trying out the 36-hole golf course of Nampont, only 3km away.

Access : 19km to the south-west of Arras towards Doullens on the N 25

Access : Behind the church

 27 LA CHAUMIÈRE
Mme Terrien

19 rue du Bihen
62180 Verton
Tel. 03 21 84 27 10
genevieve.terrien@free.fr
www.alachaumiere.com

Open all year • 4 non-smoking rooms, 2 are on the ground floor and 2 are upstairs • €46 to €53, breakfast included • No table d'hôte • Garden, car park. Credit cards not accepted, no dogs allowed

 28 LA FERME DU VERT
M. Bernard

62720 Wierre-Effroy
Tel. 03 21 87 67 00
Fax 03 21 83 22 62
ferme.du.vert@wanadoo.fr
www.fermeduvert.com

Closed from 15 Dec to 20 Jan • 16 rooms with shower/WC • €57 to €117; breakfast €9; half board available • Menus €22 to €39 • Garden, park, car park

We most liked
The charm of a doll's house.

This quaint cottage with its thatched roof and flowered garden is just 4km from the sea. An atmosphere of refined elegance and warmth pervades the place. Each of the non-smoking rooms has its own individual personality. Stay for a few days and you'll notice that breakfast is served on different tableware each morning, thanks to the lady of the house's wonderful collection. Golf nearby.

We most liked
Visiting the cheese-makers, also run by your hosts.

A perfect invitation to get back to grass roots. You won't be disappointed by the comfortable, quiet rooms, decorated simply and tastefully; the largest are full of amusing nooks and crannies. Sample the delicious home cooking made with local produce. Before leaving, make sure you stop by the next door cheese-makers and stock up on fresh and matured cheeses.

Access : 4km eastbound from Berck on the D 303

Access : 10km to the north-east of Boulogne on the N 42 and the D 234

29 LA GOÉLETTE

Mme Avot

13 Digue de Mer
62930 Wimereux
Tel. 03 21 32 62 44
Fax 03 21 33 77 54
lagoelette@nordnet.fr
www.lagoelette.com

Open all year • 4 rooms with bath/WC • €61 to €110
(€61 to €90 low season), breakfast included • No table
d'hôte • Credit cards not accepted, no dogs allowed

**Gulping down the fresh sea air
when you open your shutters
in the morning.**

Who could resist the charm of this 1900 villa so well
located on the dyke-promenade of Wimereux? The
perfectly restored interior has remained authentic and
the rooms now reveal their original harmonious shades,
moulded ceilings and warm sea-faring pine furniture.
The Blue and Yellow rooms offer a wonderful view of
the sea, while the others overlook the inner garden. Ask
your hosts for walking tips.

Access : On the seafront

NORMANDY

Hormandy, the muse of poets and artists from the world over, offers an ever-changing vision of rural pleasures. Take a bracing walk along the miles of coastline and admire her string of elegant seaside resorts. You will be left breathless when you first catch sight of Mont Saint-Michel rising from the sands or look down over Étretat's chalky cliffs into the sea crashing on the rocks below. It is impossible not to be moved by the memory of the men who died on Normandy's beaches in June 1944 or to be captivated by the cottage-garden charm of Guernsey and Jersey. Further inland, acres of neat'hedge-lined fields meet the eye, home to thoroughbred horses and herds of dairy cows. Breathe in the scent of the apple orchards in spring and admire the half-timbered cottages and smart manor houses, before wandering down to the Seine, following its meanders past medieval cities, daunting castles and venerable abbeys. No description would be complete, however, without Normandy's culinary classics: fresh fish and seafood, creamy, ivory-white Camembert, cider and, last but not least, the famous oak-aged apple brandy, Calvados.

- Calvados (14)
- Eure (27)
- Manche (50)
- Orne (61)
- Seine-Maritime (76)

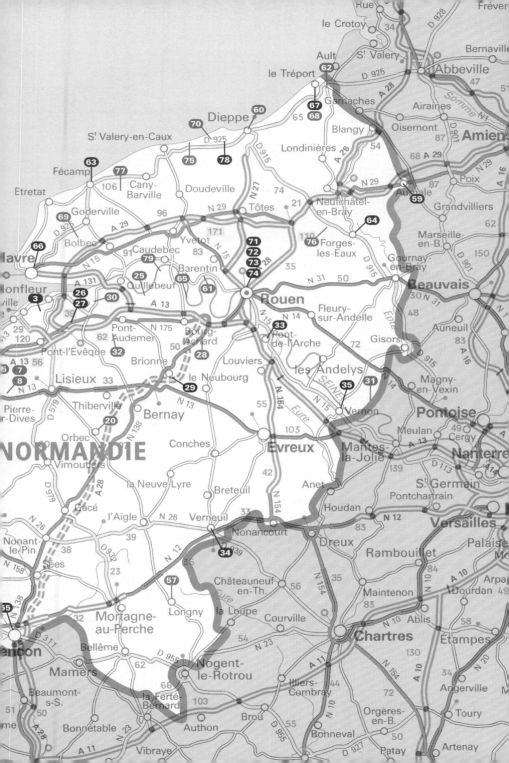

 1 **LA MARINE**
M. Durand

1 quai du Canada
14117 Arromanches-les-Bains
Tel. 02 31 22 34 19
Fax 02 31 22 98 80
hotel.de.la.marine@wanadoo.fr
www.hotel-de-la-marine.fr

Closed from 1 Jan to 11 Feb and 7 Nov to 31 Dec
• 28 rooms with bath/WC or shower/WC and television
• €61 to €87; breakfast €8; half board available • Menus
€19 to €49 • Car park

 2 **FERME LE PETIT VAL**
M. Gérard Lesage

24 rue du Camp-Romain
14480 Banville
Tel. 02 31 37 92 18
Fax 02 31 37 92 18

Closed from 1 Nov until the spring holidays • 5 rooms,
2 of which are on the ground floor and 3 are upstairs,
all have bathrooms • €47 to €53, breakfast included • No
table d'hôte • Garden, car park. Credit cards not
accepted, no dogs allowed

 **Imagine the Allied Forces landing on
D-Day.**

The discreet, practical rooms of this rambling white hotel
resemble the cabins of a luxury liner. Taking pride of
place on the menu are lobster – choose your own in
the tank – fish and shellfish, served in the turquoise
dining room and bar-brasserie. All the windows overlook
the Channel and the horizon out of which the Allied
forces emerged, before landing at dawn on "the longest
day", 6th June 1944.

 **Watch the cows grazing
in the meadows.**

This characteristic farmhouse, thought to date from the
17C, is ideal to get back to grass roots. Its snug, quietly
elegant rooms are spread over two wings around a
central courtyard. Family heirlooms adorn the pleasant
breakfast room. In the summer, the flowered garden is
particularly inviting.

Access : At the port

Access : In the town

 AUBERGE DE LA SOURCE
M. et Mme Legeay

14600 Barneville-la-Bertran
Tel. 02 31 89 25 02
Fax 02 31 89 44 40

Closed from 15 Nov to 15 Feb • 16 rooms with bath/WC and television • €64 to €108, breakfast €7 • No restaurant • Garden, private car park. No dogs allowed

 HOSTELLERIE DU MOULIN DU PRÉ
Mme Holtz

Route de Gonneville-en-Auge
14860 Bavent
Tel. 02 31 78 83 68
Fax 02 31 78 21 05

Closed 1 to 15 Mar, Oct, Sun evening, Mon (except from 15 Jul to 15 Aug and national holidays) and Tue lunchtime • 10 rooms upstairs, with shower with or without WC • €45 to €60; breakfast €7 • Menus €35 to €47 • Garage. No dogs allowed in rooms • Park

Waking to the sound of bird song.

A half-timbered farm and a redbrick house laid out around a delightful flowered garden with a pool filled with trout and sturgeon: the perfect picture of a welcoming country inn. The rooms echo with the sounds of this country haven and are equipped with modern bathrooms. Breakfast is served by the fireside in winter and under the apple trees in the summer.

Peace and quiet guaranteed.

Just a few kilometres from the sea, this old half-timbered farmhouse and its outbuildings lie in the middle of the countryside in grounds complete with a duck pond. The rooms are modest and a little on the dark side but very well kept, even though the old hip baths do make showers something of an acrobatic feat. Lovely rustic dining room with lace tablecloths, dressers and a huge fireplace for delicious chargrilled meats.

Access : 6km southbound from Honfleur on the D 62A, turn right at the entrance to Équemauville (D 62), then left (D 279)

Access : Leave Cabourg on the D 513 towards Caen, and after Varaville turn right on the D 95 towards Gonneville-en-Auge

NORMANDY

 5 D'ARGOUGES
M. et Mme Ropartz

 21 rue Saint-Patrice
14400 Bayeux
Tel. 02 31 92 88 86
Fax 02 31 92 69 16
dargouges@aol.com

Closed from 24 to 25 Dec • 28 rooms, most have bath/WC, some have shower/WC, all have television • €68 to €100 (€52 to €84 low season); breakfast €8 • No restaurant • Garden, garage, car park. No dogs allowed

 6 LE COTTAGE
Mme Rival

 24 avenue du Général-Leclerc
14390 Cabourg
Tel. 02 31 91 65 61
Fax 02 31 28 78 82
www.hotellecottage.com

Closed 15 Nov to 15 Dec • 14 rooms on 2 floors, with bath/WC or shower/WC and television • €64 to €89 (€64 to €86 low season); breakfast €7.50 • No restaurant • Garden • Gym, sauna

 **A quiet garden in the heart of the town.**

It is more than worthwhile venturing past the rather austere façade of this 18C house to catch a glimpse of the lovely garden in the rear. The house's glorious past can still be seen in the intricate patterns of the parquet floors, old doors and worn beams in some of the rooms. A number of the most spacious bedrooms are perfect for families: new bedding, fabrics and wallpaper are on the agenda for the bedrooms.

As pretty as a picture.

This lovely 1900 half-timbered cottage lies at the rear of a pretty garden. A staircase winds its way up to snug rooms, all of which are individually decorated and regularly smartened up. Those on the upper floor are the least roomy. Family breakfast room, billiards and a small fitness room. Home from home!

Access : In the road running from the town centre to the N 13, Cherbourg road

Access : Opposite the church, on the avenue that extends from the D 514, from Ouistreham

 ## MANOIR DE CANTEPIE
Mme Gherrak

 Le Cadran
14340 Cambremer
Tel. 02 31 62 87 27
Fax 02 31 62 87 27

Closed from 15 Nov to 1 Mar • 3 rooms upstairs, with bathrooms • €60, breakfast included • No table d'hôte • Sitting room, garden, park, car park. Credit cards not accepted, no dogs allowed

 ## LES MARRONNIERS
M. et Mme Darondel

 Les Marronniers
14340 Cambremer
Tel. 02 31 63 08 28
Fax 02 31 63 92 54
chantal.darondel@wanadoo.fr
www.les-marronniers.com

Open all year • 5 rooms • €45 to €55, breakfast included • No table d'hôte • Park. Credit cards not accepted, no dogs allowed

Normandy at its best!

This splendid early 17C manor house will weave its magic spell the minute you set foot within its elegant, tasteful walls. A superb oak staircase takes you up to immense, well-appointed rooms; the old-fashioned bathrooms are particularly stunning. Family heirlooms grace the sitting room and the flowered grounds are clearly the work of a devoted gardener. Not to be missed!

Time and care have clearly been lavished over the rooms.

This pleasant 17C edifice set in the middle of a flowered park enjoys a lovely view over the Dive Valley, with the sea in the distance. Each of the personalised rooms has been named after a goddess: "Venus", is full of light, "Diane" is smaller but much more romantic. Tuck into the ample breakfasts served on a pretty patio.

Access : 11km westbound from Lisieux on the N 13 then the D 50

Access : 5km on a by-road

9 LA FERME DE LA RANÇONNIÈRE
Mme Vereecke

Route d'Arromanches-les-Bains
14480 Crépon
Tel. 02 31 22 21 73
Fax 02 31 22 98 39
hotel @ ranconniere.com

Open all year • 35 rooms, 1 of which has disabled access, with bath/WC or shower/WC and television. In the separate wing: La Ferme de Mathan, suites are €120 • €50 to €160; breakfast €10; half board available • Menus €15 (weekdays) to €40 • Garden, car park

10 LE MANOIR DE CRÉPON
Mme Poisson

14480 Crépon
Tel. 02 31 22 21 27
Fax 02 31 22 88 80
manoirdecrepon @ wanadoo.fr

Closed from 10 Jan to 10 Feb • 4 rooms with bath/WC • €75, breakfast included • No table d'hôte • Garden, car park • Mountain biking

A stay in these farms is like reading a page of a history book.

High ceilings upheld by worn beams, vaults, monumental fireplaces, exposed stone walls and flagstones are just some of the original decorative features of this 13C fortified farmhouse. The furniture and ornaments showcased in the rooms were found in local second-hand and antique shops. For a few euros extra, treat yourself to the luxury of added space and calm in the 18C Ferme de Mathan just 800m away.

A faultlessly decorated home.

Towering trees grace an immense park surrounding this 18C manor house whose blood-red façade is characteristic of the region. Once inside the well-dimensioned, comfortable rooms, the owner-antique dealer's flair is visible in the beautiful choice of furniture. On cold winter days, a log fire burns in the breakfast room, formerly the kitchen. Bicycles rented on the estate.

Access : Westbound from Bayeux, take the D 12 towards Douvres-la-Délivrande for 12km, turn left onto the D 65

Access : In the village

 11 CHÂTEAU DE DAMPIERRE
M. Jouvin

Le Château
14350 Dampierre
Tel. 02 31 67 31 81
Fax 02 31 67 02 06
www.chateau-de-dampierre.com

Open all year • 5 rooms with a view of the dovecote
• €65 to €95, breakfast included • No table d'hôte
• Receptions organised

 12 CHAMBRE D'HÔTE DE FALAISE
M. de Rooij

1 rue du Sergent-Goubin
14700 Falaise
Tel. 02 31 40 95 86
Fax 02 31 40 95 86
padero@wanadoo.fr
www.bandbfalaise.com

Closed from 22 Nov to 22 Feb • 5 non-smoking rooms
with bath/WC and television • €85 to €120, breakfast
included • No table d'hôte • Terrace, garden, car park.
No dogs allowed • Sitting room-library, swimming pool,
boules

 The sight of the impressive corner watchtowers at the end of the drive invariably takes one's breath away.

In the heart of the Normandy countryside on the borders of Calvados and Manche, this splendid 16C manor house, is the work of François Gabriel who also built the château of Carrouges. The rooms are more functional than you might expect in a castle, and are comfortably equipped and well cared for. They look down onto the deep moat, former Henry IV-style gatehouse and superbly restored pigeon coop, whose 2200 nesting alcoves bear witness to the prestige of the lords of Dampierre.

 Lazing about on the high-perched terrace.

This handsome 18C house, near St-Gervais Church, whose garden and swimming pool are flanked by the town ramparts, boasts a stunning view over the Falaise countryside. The interior decoration is a happy marriage of old and new. Relax in the sitting room and well-stocked library, enjoy the parquet-floored rooms adorned with contemporary paintings and savour the quiet luminosity of the breakfast room. Boules and a barbecue by the riverside.

Access : 9km from Thorigny-sur-Vire on the D 13, then right on the D 53

Access : Near the town centre, 400m from the church

FORMIGNY - 14710

GÉFOSSE-FONTENAY - 14230

 13 LA FERME DU MOUCHEL

Mme Lenourichel

Lieu-dit Le Mouchel
14710 Formigny
Tel. 02 31 22 53 79
Fax 02 31 21 56 55
odile.lenourichel @ liberty.surf.fr

Open all year • 4 rooms with bathrooms, some non-smoking • €44, breakfast included • No table d'hôte • Garden, car park. Credit cards not accepted • Near the D-Day Landing Beaches

 14 MANOIR DE L'HERMEREL

M. et Mme Lemarié

14230 Géfosse-Fontenay
Tel. 02 31 22 64 12
Fax 02 31 22 76 37
lemariehermerel @ aol.com

Closed from 15 Nov to 15 Mar • 4 rooms with bathrooms • €60, breakfast included • No table d'hôte • Car park. No dogs allowed

We most liked **The spontaneity and quality of Odile's welcome.**

This inviting manor farmhouse which dates back to the 16C stands at the end of a tiny country lane. Three delightful rooms are located upstairs in the main wing, while another room complete with an adjoining small room, is situated in the wing next door, on the ground-floor of which breakfast is served. The welcoming owners, who also raise dairy cows, might even introduce you to the pleasures of milking if you're lucky!

We most liked **A guided visit of the manor and the farm.**

Surrounded by meadows, this 17C fortified manor-farm with its proud aspect, handsome porch, regular lines and elegant dovecote could easily pass for a castle. The rooms in the manor are a subtle blend of comfort and charm. The sitting room in a 15C Gothic chapel is supremely restful and your hosts' unaffected welcome quite captivating.

Access : Leave the Carentan-Bayeux N 13 road at Formigny on the D 517, turn right, then left onto a minor road

Access : 8km northbound from Isigny on the D 514 then take the D 200 to Osmanville

 15 FERME DES GLYCINES
M. et Mme Exmelin

 14510 Gonneville-sur-Mer
Tel. 02 31 28 01 15

Closed from Jan to Mar, Nov to late Dec and Mon to Thu in low season • 3 rooms • €48, breakfast included • No table d'hôte • Garden, car park. Credit cards not accepted, no dogs allowed

 16 1900
M. et Mme Lemarie

 17 rue des Bains
14510 Houlgate
Tel. 02 31 28 77 77
Fax 02 31 28 08 07
www.hotel-1900.fr

Closed from 6 Jan to 6 Feb and from 15 Nov to 3 Dec • 16 rooms, all have bath/WC or shower/WC and television • €65 to €99 (€42 to €99 low season); breakfast €8 to €89 half board available • Menus €11 (weekdays) to €45 • Reading room

 "Old Macdonald had a farm!"

Children love the horses, sheep, hens and ducks who live in the grounds of this timber-framed farm which dates from 1780 and is surrounded by over 40 acres of orchards and park. The colour schemes render the rooms most pleasant and one has a private terrace. Farm produce features prominently on the breakfast table, served by the fireside in winter. Delightful garden.

 Exploring Houlgate's rich architectural pageant.

Ornate villas, Anglo-Norman manor houses, Alpine chalets: this adorable resort on the Norman coast is a delight for anyone intrigued by seaside architecture. The hotel is located in Houlgate's high street and offers rooms redecorated in a Belle Époque chocolate-box style; all are well-soundproofed. Painted ceilings, frosted windows, knick-knacks and a bar found in an antique shop set the scene for the distinctly "retro" bistro.

Access : 7km eastbound from Dives-sur-Mer on the D 45 and a minor road

Access : On the main road of the resort

 17 MANOIR DE MATHAN
M. et Mme de Mathan

14310 Longvillers
Tel. 02 31 77 10 37
Fax 02 31 77 49 13
 mathan.normandie @ caramail.com

Open from late Mar to 15 Nov • 4 rooms on 3 levels with bathrooms for non-smokers • €43 to €50, breakfast included • No table d'hôte • Garden-orchard, car park. Credit cards not accepted, no dogs allowed • Horse riding 500m away.

 18 LA NOUVELLE FRANCE
Mme Godey

Lieu-dit La Nouvelle France
14310 Longvillers
Tel. 02 31 77 63 36
Fax 02 31 77 63 36
courrier @ la-nouvelle-france.com
 www.la-nouvelle-france.com

Open all year • 3 rooms on ground-floor and 2 in another wing, with bath/WC • €40, breakfast included • Table d'hôte closed Sun; menu €16 • Terrace, garden. Credit cards not accepted, no dogs allowed • Swings, table-tennis.

 The owners' faultless hospitality.

Half-way between Aunay-sur-Odon and Villers-Bocage, surrounded by fields and orchards, an imposing manor farmhouse founded in the 15C but reworked several times. A spiral staircase with its own entrance leads up to a sitting room, a small kitchen and three fine rooms all of which are most comfortable. A courtyard shaded by a chestnut tree is lined with barns and outhouses for farm equipment. The former bakery now houses a delightful gîte. Riding centre nearby.

 This little gem is Normandy through and through – but keep it to yourself.

On the edge of a country lane in a little grove stands a delightful stone farmhouse behind a former barn, now home to three bright, cheery rooms and a sitting room. Sober, tasteful interior decoration, a restful garden, a drive lined with birch trees and superb country views from the moment you wake up. Delicious breakfasts and a 100 % Norman table d'hôte served in the owners' home.

Access : 3km northbound of Aunay-sur-Odon on the D 6, half-way from Longvillers

Access : 4km northbound of Aunay-sur-Odon on the D 6, then D 216 towards Longvillers

 19 L'ANCIENNE ÉCOLE
M. Darthenay

 Route d'Arromanches
14960 Meuvaines
Tel. 02 31 22 39 59
Fax 02 31 22 39 11
françoise.georges@ancienne-ecole.net
 www.ancienne-ecole.net

Closed end Dec • 3 rooms with bath/WC • €45, breakfast included; half board available • Table d'hôte €20 (evenings only) • Terrace, car park. No dogs allowed

 20 LE MANOIR DE L'ENGAGISTE
Mme Dubois

 15 rue de Reny
14290 Orbec
Tel. 02 31 32 57 22
Fax 02 31 32 55 58

Open all year • 5 rooms • €75 to €82 (€70 to €75 low season), breakfast included • No table d'hôte • Disabled access. Garden

Betwixt land and sea.

As the name suggests, this building which dates from 1741 was formerly the village school. Now a B&B establishment, it offers rustic rooms under the eaves, all of which overlook the countryside. Regional specialities feature prominently on the table, set by the fireside in the pleasant dining room. Nearby are the D-Day Landing beaches and the delightful inland villages of Bessin.

 An immaculately decorated half-timbered manor house.

Right in the heart of town, this beautifully restored 16C mansion is definitely worth staying a day or two. You will want to snuggle up in the thoughtfully decorated bedrooms with terracotta tiled floors, wood panelling and old tapestries. In the winter, a huge fire burns in the exquisite sitting room whose centrepiece is a mezzanine with exhibitions of paintings and sculpture. An old carriage takes pride of place in the vast inner courtyard. Not to be missed!

Access : 8km to the south-east of Arromanches on the D 65

Access : In the heart of the town

NORMANDY

 21 LE CLOS FLEURI
Mme Weidner

 Hameau Lefèvre
14450 Saint-Pierre-du-Mont
Tel. 02 31 22 96 22
Fax 02 31 22 96 22

Open all year • 3 rooms with bathrooms • €46, breakfast included • Table d'hôte €23 • Garden, car park. Credit cards not accepted, no dogs allowed

 22 LE MOULIN DE HARD
Mme Fichot

 Lieu-dit Le Moulin-de-Hard
14400 Subles
Tel. 02 31 21 37 17
www.gites-de-france-calvados.fr

Open all year • 3 non-smoking rooms • €70 to €85, breakfast included • No table d'hôte • Garden, car park. Credit cards not accepted, no dogs allowed • Fishing in the Drône.

 A garden large enough to accommodate everyone.

No sooner have you settled in than you will feel as if you've always lived in this comfortable house. Old furniture embellishes the spacious, cosy rooms and the family cooking never fails to draw a compliment or two. The enormous garden is big enough to be able to host boisterous children's games, more sedate naps for the less energetic and barbecue lunches for everyone. Even better, you're only a little way from the sea. What more could you want?

 The care taken with the indoor and outdoor fittings.

This handsome 18C watermill stands deep in the country in a landscaped garden through which runs the Drôme, a little river where anglers can savour the pleasure of catching gudgeon in the private fishing waters. Modern fittings add comfort to the rooms which combine old and new decorative elements in the same style found in the communal rooms. Snug sitting room with fireplace and generous breakfasts served in a bright, panoramic kitchen-cum-dining-room.

Access : 2.5km to the south-east of Pointe du Hoc on the road to Vierville

Access : 6km south-west of Bayeux on the D 572, then D 99 left after Subles

23 LE GRAND FUMICHON
M. et Mme Duyck

14400 Vaux-sur-Aure
Tel. 02 31 21 78 51
Fax 02 31 21 78 51
duyckja@wanadoo.fr

Open all year • 4 rooms, one of which is in a separate house • €40, breakfast included • No table d'hôte • Car park. Credit cards not accepted, no dogs allowed • Fresh produce made with Furnichon orchard apples

24 CHÂTEAU DE VOUILLY
M. et Mme Hamel

14230 Vouilly-Église
Tel. 02 31 22 08 59
Fax 02 31 22 90 58
château.vouilly@wanadoo.fr
www.chateau-vouilly.com

Closed from Dec to Feb • 5 rooms with bathrooms • €65 to €75, breakfast included • No table d'hôte • Garden, car park. No dogs allowed

 An apple a day keeps the doctor away!

A former outbuilding of the abbey of Longues-sur-mer, this fortified farmstead with square courtyard, porch and press is clearly proud of its early 17C origins. Today it is a working dairy and cider farm and also offers simple, rustic rooms overlooking the orchard. The quietest is in a small independent house. Before leaving, stock up on farm-grown cider, Calvados – apple brandy – apple juice and preserves.

 A step back in time.

This 18C château surrounded by a moat and carefully tended gardens was commandeered as the American press HQ during the landings in June 1944. Beautifully restored by the owner himself, the rooms are spacious and comfortable and some have old furniture. On the ground floor, guests have the run of a string of impressive sitting rooms, one of which doubles as a breakfast room, with lovely old two-tone tiled floors.

Access : 3km northbound from Bayeux on the D 104

Access : 8km to the south-east of Isigny on the D 5

25 LES SOURCES BLEUES
M. et Mme Laurent

Route du Vieux-Port
27500 Aizier
Tel. 02 32 57 26 68
Fax 02 32 57 42 25

Open all year • 4 non-smoking rooms on 2 floors, with baths, showers and separate WC • €51 to €63, breakfast included • Table d'hôte €18 (evening only) • Sitting room, garden, car park. Credit cards not accepted

26 HÔTEL DE LA POSTE
M. et Mme Bosquer

60 rue Constant-Fouché
27210 Beuzeville
Tel. 02 32 20 32 32
Fax 02 32 42 11 01
www.le-relais-de-poste.com

Open from 18 Mar to 6 Nov • 15 rooms with bath/WC or shower/WC, some have television • €45 to €63; breakfast €7; half board available • Restaurant closed Sun evening late Sep to Jun, Tue lunchtime and Thu; menus €19 (weekdays) to €36 • Terrace, garden, private car park. No dogs allowed in rooms

Exploring the wooded park on the banks of the Seine.

Nestled in a delightfully untrammelled park, this lovely Norman house built in 1854 enjoys a wonderful view over the Seine and the boats plying their course to and from Le Havre. Wood, old tiles and parquet floors prevail in the welcoming interior. The rooms are comfortably uncluttered and the most pleasant have sloping ceilings. On the leisure side, you can choose from tennis, horse-riding and canoeing.

You must try the lady of the house's chocolate and potato cake!

A spacious, flowered garden lies hidden behind the stone and brick walls of this coaching inn which first opened in 1854. A wooden staircase climbs up the three floors where the small, simply furnished rooms are located. The appealing dining room is in the former village café which still boasts its original bar. Don't miss the chance to sample the scrumptious result of Madame's highly individual approach to cooking.

Access : 5km northbound from Bourneville on the D 139

Access : On the main road in the centre of the village, opposite the town hall

394

27 PETIT CASTEL
M. Martin

32 rue Constant-Fouché
27210 Beuzeville
Tel. 02 32 57 76 08
Fax 02 32 42 25 70
auberge-du-cochon-dor@wanadoo.fr
www.le-cochon-dor.fr

Closed from 15 Dec to 15 Jan • 16 rooms with bath/WC
and television • €44 to €54; breakfast €7, half board
available • Menus €14 to €40 • Private car park, garden.
No dogs allowed

28 CHÂTEAU DE BOSCHERVILLE
M. et Mme du Plouy

27520 Bourgtheroulde-Infreville
Tel. 02 35 87 62 12
Fax 02 35 87 62 12

Open all year • 5 rooms • €50, breakfast included • No
table d'hôte • Sitting room, park, car park. Credit cards
not accepted

 The quiet rooms facing the flowered garden.

Guests arriving at the Petit Castel may have to announce
themselves at the nearby Auberge du Cochon d'Or, also
run by the Martin family. In the time it takes to drop
off your cases, you will already feel at home in this large
house in the centre of the village. Tasteful mural fabrics,
white-leaded wooden furniture, recent bedding, spotless
premises further will reinforce your pleasant first
impression. Some rooms overlook the pleasant flowered
garden, where breakfast is served in fine weather.

 "By the work, one knows the workman", Jean de La Fontaine (1621-95)

This delightful 18C château, set in a park of venerable
old oaks, was built on the ruins of the one-time home
to France's best known writer of fables. Today it houses
light, airy rooms which marry comfort and good taste
and an elegant sitting room complete with its original
decorative woodwork. The breakfast table is piled high
with succulent local farm produce and the welcoming
owners are a mine of information about the region.

Access : In the heart of the village

Access : 10km to the north-east of Bec-Hellouin on
the N 138, the D 80 and the D 38

 29 L'AUBERGE DU VIEUX DONJON
M. et Mme Chauvigny

 19 rue de la Soie
27800 Brionne
Tel. 02 32 44 80 62
Fax 02 32 45 83 23
auberge.vieuxdonjon@wanadoo.fr
www.auberge-vieux-donjon.com

Closed 9 Feb to 18 Mar, 19 to 26 Aug, 13 Oct to 4 Nov,
Sun (Oct to late Jun) and Thu evenings and Mon
• 7 rooms with bath/WC or shower/WC and television
• €47 to €53; breakfast €7; half board available • Menus
€13 (weekdays) to €23 • Terrace, private car park

 30 LE VIEUX PRESSOIR
Mme Anfrey

 Hameau le Clos-Potier
27210 Conteville
Tel. 02 32 57 60 79
Fax 02 32 57 60 79

Open all year • 5 rooms with bathrooms • €55, breakfast
included • No table d'hôte • Car park. Credit cards not
accepted, no dogs allowed

 "Trou normand"? a) A hole in Normandy, b) A mid-dinner drink, c) Authentically Norman.

The blue timbers and chequered decoration of this 18C
Norman house, its view of the ruined 11C keep and its
shady patio terrace make up for the modest comfort of
the rooms. Old porcelain, gleaming copper, worn tiles
and dark-timbered beams set the scene for the
characteristically rustic dining room, which would not
seem out of place in a short story by Maupassant!
Shaded patio terrace. This is the place to try the famous
"trou normand", a brisk, mid-meal shot of Calvados, the
local apple brandy.

 Delightfully old-fashioned.

Lovers of calm and authenticity will immediately fall
head over heels for this attractive 18C timber-framed
farm set in the midst of Normandy's green fields. The
picture-perfect interior features a wealth of 19C and 20C
objects and furniture picked up in second-hand and
antique shops. Rooms which make up in charm what
they lack in size, a garden that can hardly be seen for
flowers, ducks paddling on the pond and a three-
hundred-year-old press add the finishing touches to this
rural landscape.

Access : Opposite the market square

Access : 13.5km from Honfleur on the Pont-Audemer
road (D 580), then take the D 312 on the left

 31 CHAMBRE D'HÔTE M. STEKELORUM

M. et Mme Stekelorum

 24 rue du Moulin
27630 Fourges
Tel. 02 32 52 12 51
Fax 02 32 52 13 12
www.giverny.org.hotels/stekelorum

Closed from 1 Nov to 1 Mar • 3 non-smoking rooms, 2 of which are upstairs • €49, breakfast included • No table d'hôte • Garden, car park. Credit cards not accepted, no dogs allowed

 32 LE PRIEURÉ DES FONTAINES

M. et Mme Decarsin

 Route de Lisieux
27500 Les Préaux
Tel. 02 32 56 07 78
Fax 02 32 57 45 83
jacques.decarsin@wanadoo.fr
www.prieure-des-fontaines.fr

Open all year • 5 non-smoking rooms, with bathrooms and telephone • €80 to €130, breakfast included • No table d'hôte • Sitting room, garden, car park. Credit cards not accepted, no dogs allowed • Mountain biking, table-tennis

 Less than 10km from Claude Monet's house and gardens in Giverny.

This old farmhouse stands close to the old mill of Fourges, whose picturesque site has prompted more than one budding Monet to reach for palette and canvas. The rooms are located in a separate wing, two are in the former attic and all feature a rustic flavour, which also extends to the raftered breakfast room, old bread oven, family heirlooms and the beautifully landscaped garden. We wished we could stay for ever!

 Bicycling in the nearby forest.

This 17C priory cradled in the valley of La Risles has been so well restored, you would be forgiven for thinking that it's new. The well-dimensioned, comfortable rooms are graced with old furniture, beams and tiled floors; all are non-smoking and equipped with telephones. A sitting room with fireplace, hall with piano and lovely garden are perfect to relax in.

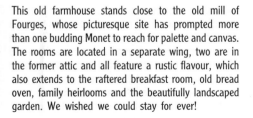

Access : In the town

Access : 5km to the south-west of Pont-Audemer on the D 139

NORMANDY

  33 LA TOUR
M. Hélouard

 41 quai Foch
27340 Pont-de-l'Arche
Tel. 02 35 23 00 99
Fax 02 35 23 46 22
hotel-de-la-tour@wanadoo.fr
www.hoteldelatour.net

Open all year • 18 non-smoking rooms with bath/WC or shower/WC and television • €58, breakfast €6 • No restaurant • Garden. No dogs allowed

  34 HÔTEL DU SAUMON
M. Simon

 89 place de la Madeleine
27130 Verneuil-sur-Avre
Tel. 02 32 32 02 36
Fax 02 32 37 55 80
hotel.saumon@wanadoo.fr
www.hoteldusaumon.fr

Closed from 1 to 10 Jan, 19 to 31 Dec and Sun evenings from Nov to Mar • 29 rooms located in the main building on the street and in 2 separate wings in the courtyard, all have bath/WC or shower/WC and television • €42 to €62; breakfast €7 • Menus €11 (weekdays) to €26 • Courtyard

Walking between the Seine and the Eure Rivers.

In the shade of the church and opposite the Eure, two semi-detached houses have been turned into a hotel. The elegant, personalised rooms are stylishly furnished and tastefully decorated in bright colours; those on the second floor have sloping ceilings. In the summer, breakfasts are served on the terrace, nestling up against the old town ramparts and leading into the garden.

Verneuil's streets lined with half-timbered façades and smart townhouses.

This elegant late-18C coaching inn stands in the heart of this pretty town, opposite the church of La Madeleine flanked by a 56m-high tower, an ideal starting point for a tour of the countryside which inspired Dorothy Sayers' short story "The Bibulous Business of a Matter of Taste". The rooms of varying sizes are in the main and side wings, around a flower-filled courtyard; ask for one of the renovated rooms and sample the house speciality, salmon, in the tasteful restaurant.

Access : In the town centre

Access : On the main square, near the church

 35 HÔTEL D'ÉVREUX
M. Elbaze

 11 place d'Évreux
27200 Vernon
Tel. 02 32 21 16 12
Fax 02 32 21 32 73
hotel.evreux@wanadoo.fr
www.hoteldevreux.fr

Open all year; restaurant closed Sun except on national holidays • 12 rooms upstairs with bath/WC or shower/WC and television • €38 to €59 (€33 to €54 low season); breakfast €6 • Restaurant Le Relais Normand: menus €21 to €27 • Terrace, private car park

 36 LA CROIX D'OR
M. Bertheaume

83 rue de la Constitution
50300 Avranches
Tel. 02 33 58 04 88
Fax 02 33 58 06 95

Closed in Jan, 15 Oct to 1 Apr and Sun evenings • 27 rooms located in several buildings around a courtyard. Rooms have bath/WC or shower/WC and television • €57 to €67; breakfast €8, half board available • Menus €16 (weekdays) to €50 • Garden, private car park

 Two kilometres from Claude Monet's lovely house and exquisite garden.

The rooms of this half-timbered 17C house – former home of the Count of Évreux and later a coaching inn – have recently been renovated. Exposed beams, timber-framed walls, hunting trophies and a stone fireplace set the rustic scene for the dining room. In fine weather, tables are laid in the inner courtyard. An excellent wine-list includes a grand cru or two.

 Daydreaming in the delightful garden.

This 17C coaching inn stands near the Patton Memorial which commemorates the "Avranches Breakthrough". Its half-timbered façade borders a pretty garden planted with apple trees and hydrangeas. Quiet rooms, some of which have been renovated. A countrified dining room whose collections of gleaming clocks, well-worn wardrobes, porcelain and copper pots, exposed beams and stonework would almost be worthy of a museum.

Access : In the town centre, opposite the post office

Access : From the Mont-Saint-Michel, at Place du Général Patton, turn left onto Rue de la Constitution towards the town centre

 37 LE CONQUÉRANT
M. et Mme Delomenede

 16/18 rue Saint-Thomas-Becket
50760 Barfleur
Tel. 02 33 54 00 82
Fax 02 33 54 65 25

Open from 15 Mar to 15 Nov • 13 rooms, some have bath/WC, or shower with or without WC, and television • €35 to €82; breakfast €6 to €10 • No restaurant, but there is a crêperie open in the evening for hotel guests; menus €14 to €25 • Garden, small private car park. No dogs allowed

 38 LES ISLES
M. de Mello

9 boulevard Maritime
50270 Barneville-Carteret
Tel. 02 33 04 90 76
Fax 02 33 94 53 83
hotel-des-isles@wanadoo.fr
www.hoteldesisles.fr

Closed from Jan to 13 Feb • 34 rooms with television, some are non-smoking • €55 to €75, breakfast €10, half board available • Menus €15 to €45 • Terrace, garden, patio • Reading room

 Drinking in the atmosphere of this tiny fishing harbour in a quayside café.

This handsome 17C granite house is just two minutes from the port: back in 1066, its shipyard built the vessel which carried William the Conqueror to the shores of England and victory. Twisting corridors, proof of the house's long past, lead to rustic, immaculate rooms, some of which boast beautiful Norman wardrobes. Breakfasts and supper banquets of sweet and savoury pancakes are served outdoors in the garden.

 In fine weather, the eye can see as far as Alderney, Guernsey, Herm, Sark and Jersey.

This seaside villa, opposite the Channel Islands, is perfect for a bracing holiday break. There are plans to give the rooms, already spruced up in 2004, something of a makeover, and to add a patio, while the communal parts of the house will retain their nautical flavour. Pleasant bar, reading room and panoramic breakfast room where a superb buffet is served. A number of paintings by Brazilian artists dotted about the place add a touch of exoticism.

Access : In the street at right-angles to the seaside, between the harbour and Rue de la Poste

Access : Overlooking the beach

39 VILLAGE GROUCHY
M. Sebire

11 rue du Vieux-Lavoir
50560 Blainville-sur-Mer
Tel. 02 33 47 20 31
Fax 02 33 47 20 31
 jr.sebire@free.fr

Closed from 1 Jan to 1 Mar • 5 rooms • €37, breakfast included • No table d'hôte • Garden, car park. Credit cards not accepted, no dogs allowed

40 BEL AIR
M. et Mme Morel

2 rue du Château
50340 Flamanville
Tel. 02 33 04 48 00
Fax 02 33 04 49 56
hotelbelair@aol.com
www.hotelbelair.biz

Closed from 20 Dec to 31 Jan • 12 rooms, 6 of which are for non-smokers, all have bath/WC or shower/WC and television • €65 to €100 (€55 to €70 low season); breakfast €10 • No restaurant • Garden, car park. No dogs allowed • Piano bar

The rustic modern flavour of this fishermen's house.

Village Grouchy is the name of an old fishing village that formerly stood here. Nowadays the granite walls of this old fishermen's house offer spacious rooms lined in wood from floor to ceiling. In the morning, take a seat on the wooden benches around a large table and toast yourself by the fireside. Summer kitchen in the immense garden in the rear. Warm and welcoming.

The excisemen's cliff path.

The windows of the cosy rooms overlook the neat fields of the Cotentin ("little coast") region of north-western Normandy. The breakfast room is set in a light, airy conservatory, the old-fashioned lounge-bar has a marble fireplace and piano; palm trees adorn the lovely garden. All this awaits you in the thick granite walls of this house, formerly the home of the steward of the castle farms, just a few fields from the beaches overlooking the Atlantic.

Access : 2km northbound from Agon-Coutainville on the D 72

Access : By the D 4 that goes through the village, near the château

NORMANDY

 41 LA MAISON DE FOURMI
M. et Mme Roulland

25 rue de Rauville
50760 Gatteville-le-Phare
Tel. 02 33 43 78 74
Fax 02 33 43 78 74
raymonde.roulland @ free.fr
www.raymonde.roulland.free.fr

Closed for one month in low season • 5 rooms, 3 with disabled access, some are non-smoking • €65 to €100, breakfast included • No table d'hôte • Terrace, garden, car park. Credit cards not accepted, dogs on request

 42 CHÂTEAU DE LA ROQUE
M. et Mme Delisle

50180 Hébécrevon
Tel. 02 33 57 33 20
Fax 02 33 57 51 20
mireille.delisle @ wanadoo.fr
www.chateau-de-la-roque.fr

Closed in Jan • 15 rooms with bath/WC and television • €77 to €82, breakfast included; half board €64 • Menu €23 (evenings only) • Sitting room, park, car park. No dogs allowed • Tennis, fishing, mountain biking. Golf, horse-riding and swimming pool nearby

 The contrast between the exotic accommodation and 100 % Norman landscape.

Sari, Bengal, Indochina, Savannah and Ocean are the decorative themes chosen by the welcoming "explorer-ant" (fourmi means ant!) for the five guestrooms in her lovely old house hidden in the heart of a traditional hamlet. The first two rooms, worthy of an Indian prince, are located in the annex and have their own entrance. A welcoming breakfast room in the main wing features old tiles, a granite fireplace, ethnic artefacts and souvenirs from the owner's travels.

 Walking, riding or bicycling – the choice is yours.

This 16C and 17C edifice rises up at the end of a handsome drive lined with poplar trees, set in the green hillsides of the Terrette Valley. The rooms, lined in fabric, are decorated with lovely old furniture and the bathrooms are immaculate. Succulent home cooking showcases excellent farm-fresh ingredients. In the grounds, two ponds and a keep-fit track through the woods will keep you busy.

Access : 4km north-west of Barfleur on the D 116

Access : 7.5km westbound from Saint-Lô, towards Lessay (D 900)

 43 LE MOULIN DE LA BUTTE
Mme Rabasté

11 rue du Moulin-de-la-Butte
50170 Huisnes-sur-Mer
Tel. 02 33 58 52 62
Fax 03 33 58 52 62
beatrice.rabaste@club-internet.fr
www.bedandbreakfastineurope.com/
lemoulindelabutte

Open all year • 5 rooms on 2 levels, with bath/WC and television,1 with disabled access • €35, breakfast included • No table d'hôte • Terrace. Credit cards not accepted, no dogs allowed • Bicycles available for guests free of charge

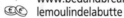 **44** LE LOGIS
M. et Mme Fillâtre

50520 Juvigny-le-Tertre
Tel. 02 33 59 38 20
Fax 02 33 59 38 20
 fillatre.claude@wanadoo.fr

Closed from 15 Nov to 15 Mar • 3 rooms • €38 to €42, breakfast included, half board available • Table d'hôte €14 (evenings only) • Car park. Credit cards not accepted, no dogs allowed in dining room

 Recharging your batteries in this splendid landscape.

Located at the gates of this traditional village in the bay of Mont-Saint-Michel, this recent villa offers quiet accommodation in spacious rooms decorated in a personalised, low-key style; all enjoy the stunning prospect of the famous abbey and rocky island. Breakfast is served in the panoramic sitting room. The owners and staff extend a warm welcome and tourist tips to guests, when they aren't caring for their immaculate and very functional establishment. Guests can borrow bicycles.

 What is so wonderful about France is that you can taste everything!

Old stones and good local produce are the hallmark of this 17C farm. The rooms in the former dovecote are contemporary in style while the one in the main wing, with granite fireplace and beams carved with the royal fleur-de-lys insignia, has more character. Tennis courts and water sports nearby. The farm organises visits and tasting sessions, so save space in the boot to stock up on farm produce, cider and home-made preserves.

Access : Between Avranches and Mont-St-Michel (D 275), head for Huisnes-sur-Mer, then the German Military Cemetery, then turn left on a minor road

Access : 12km westbound from Mortain on the D 977 and the D 5, then take the D 55 towards Saint-Hilaire

  45 LE QUESNOT
M. Germanicus

3 rue du Mont-César
50660 Montchaton
Tel. 02 33 45 05 88

Closed from 15 Nov to Easter • 3 rooms • €42, breakfast included • No table d'hôte • Garden, car park. Credit cards not accepted, no dogs allowed

  46 MANOIR DE LA CROIX
Mme Wagner

50530 Montviron
Tel. 02 33 60 68 30
Fax 02 33 60 69 21
contact@manoirdelacroix.com
www.manoirdelacroix.com

Open all year • 2 rooms and 2 suites (non-smoking only) • €60 (rooms), €77 (suite), breakfast included • No table d'hôte • Garden, car park. Credit cards not accepted, no dogs allowed

 Cradled in a leafy nest of flowers.

Built out of local stone, this 18C house is surrounded by a curtain of foliage and flowers. All the stylish, well-kept rooms are upstairs. On the ground floor is a vast country living-room for the sole use of guests. From the terrace and small garden, you will be able to see the village church perched on an outcrop. Extremely friendly and welcoming.

 Gulp down the fresh air – inside and out of this non-smoking establishment.

If your lungs have had enough of urban pollution, head for this bubble of atmospheric purity. This 19C Anglo-Norman-style manor house overlooks a lovely garden, home to palms and other rare trees. The Empire and Louis-Philippe suites are immense and adorned with antiques, the other rooms and bathrooms are invariably spotless. The breakfast table is laden with cooked meats, cheeses and home-made jams and preserves.

Access : 6.5km to the south-west of Coutances on the D 20 then the D 72

Access : 8km to the north-west of Avranches towards Granville (D 973), then the D 41 (1km after Montviron)

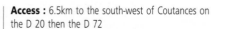

 47 LA FOSSARDIÈRE
M. Fossard

 Hameau de la Fosse
50440 Omonville-la-Petite
Tel. 02 33 52 19 83
 Fax 02 33 52 73 49

Closed from 15 Nov to 15 Mar • 10 rooms located in the hamlet, 9 have bath/WC, one has shower/WC • €40 to €63; breakfast €8 • No restaurant • Car park • Sauna, thalassotherapy, pond with picnic terrace

 48 LA FERME DE CABOURG
Mme Marie

 50760 Réville
Tel. 02 33 54 48 42
 Fax 02 33 54 48 42

Open all year • 3 rooms • €40 to €45, breakfast included • No table d'hôte • Garden, car park. Credit cards not accepted, no dogs allowed

 Nothing could be more pastoral than this hamlet.

This hamlet-cum-hotel is on the doorstep of Omonville, the last resting place of Jacques Prévert, poet-screenwriter and counter-cultural icon. The rooms, which vary in size and comfort, are spread over several sandstone houses. Breakfast is served in the hamlet's former bakery. Young and old always find plenty to do in or around the private pond, 300m away, whether rowing, picnicking or simply making daisy chains.

 Perfectly located, just 150m from the beach.

A lovely drive lined in poplar trees leads up to this 15C fortified farm just two minutes from the Saire Valley and the seaside. The white walls of the rooms are dotted with the occasional block of granite and mullioned windows, loopholes and arrow slits, now glazed, you'll be glad to hear. Toast your toes in front of the roaring log fire lit in the sitting room in winter after trekking round the region's countless marvels of Romanesque architecture. Charming welcome.

Access : Near Cap de la Hague, between Saint-Germain-des-Vaux and Omonville-la-Rogue

Access : 3.5km northbound from Saint-Vaast on the D 1

NORMANDY

49 MANOIR DE LA FÉVRERIE
Mme Caillet

4 route d'Arville
50760 Sainte-Geneviève
Tel. 02 33 54 33 53
Fax 02 33 22 12 50
caillet.manoirlafevrerie@wanadoo.fr

Open all year • 3 rooms • €58 to €68, breakfast included
• No table d'hôte • Sitting room, car park. Credit cards
not accepted, no dogs allowed

50 FERME MUSÉE DU COTENTIN
Mme Guillotte

1 chemin de Beauvais
50480 Sainte-Mère-Église
Tel. 02 33 95 40 20
Fax 02 33 95 40 24
musee.sainte-mere@wanadoo.fr

Closed in Dec and Jan • 4 rooms • €36 to €40, breakfast
included • No table d'hôte • Car park • Visit to the
museum

 A matchless attention to detail.

The sea and Barfleur's picturesque harbour are only
three kilometres from this charming 16C and 17C manor
house. The snug bedrooms, reached by a granite
staircase, were undoubtedly the work of a romantic at
heart, as the pastel wallpaper, old furniture and striped
or floral fabrics confirm. Breakfasts, served by the
fireside in winter, are a feast for the eyes and the palate.
We defy you to resist the temptation to curl up in the
soft, inviting sofas and deep armchairs in the sitting
room.

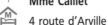 **Spend a night in a museum!**

This farm-museum offers guests the chance to get a real
feel for life on the land. The rooms of this 17C and 18C
stone farmhouse are an integral part of the museum and
their decoration, pastel shades and furniture – including
four-poster or alcove beds – is characteristic of the
region. Guests can also visit the press, the granite tower
where the apples were crushed, the collection of ploughs
and the bakery. Highly unusual and well worth a look.

Access : 3km westbound from Barfleur on the D 25
and the D 525 Sainte-Geneviève road

Access : Northbound exit out of Sainte-Mère-Église,
on the Valognes road

 51 FRANCE ET FUCHSIAS
Famille Brix

20 rue du Maréchal-Foch
50550 Saint-Vaast-la-Hougue
Tel. 02 33 54 42 26
Fax 02 33 43 46 79
 france-fuchsias @ wanadoo.fr

Closed from 3 Jan to 24 Feb, Mon and Tue lunchtime (except Jul-Aug), Tue in Mar, Nov and Dec • 38 rooms with bath/WC or shower/WC and television • €30 to €100; breakfast €8 to €9; half board available • Air-conditioned restaurant, menus €25 to €48 • Terrace, garden • In August mini recitals of chamber music

 52 MANOIR DE BELLAUNEY
Mme Allix-Desfauteaux

11 route de Quettehou
50700 Tamerville
Tel. 02 33 40 10 62
Fax 02 33 40 10 62
bellauney @ wanadoo.fr

Closed from 1 Nov to Easter • 3 rooms upstairs • €50 to €70, breakfast included • No table d'hôte • Garden, car park. Credit cards not accepted, no dogs allowed

 That inimitable feminine touch in the design of the bedrooms.

The façade, adorned with magnificent hundred-year-old fuchsias, of this old coaching inn hides the house's masterpiece, an extraordinary walled garden home to palms, mimosa, eucalyptus, banana trees and other exotic specimens. Who said that the Cotentin's "micro-climate" was a myth? In the summer, regional dishes are served in the midst of this lush green setting. Four rooms have been recently added, two on the ground-floor; those in the annex are more spacious than those in the main wing.

 History oozes from every crevice of this old manor house.

This 16C manor house, flanked by a tower and three handsome Romanesque arches is set in a lovely, tended mature garden. An impressive staircase leads up to the individually decorated rooms, each of which evokes a significant period in the domain's history. "Medieval" on the ground floor, "Louis XV" and "19C Norman" upstairs. The original wainscoting in the breakfast room adds the final touch to this historic abode.

Access : In the town centre, not far from the port

Access : 3km to the north-east of Valognes towards Quettehou

 53 MANOIR SAINT-JEAN
M. et Mme Guérard

 Le hameau Saint-Jean
50110 Tourlaville
Tel. 02 33 22 00 86

Open all year • 3 non-smoking rooms • €46 to €51, breakfast included • No table d'hôte • Car park. Credit cards not accepted, no dogs allowed

54 MANOIR DE L'ACHERIE
M. Cahu

 L'Acherie - Ste-Cécile
50800 Villedieu-les-Poêles
Tel. 02 33 51 13 87
Fax 02 33 51 33 69
manoir@manoir-acherie.fr
 www.manoir-acherie.fr

Closed 8 to 23 Feb, 2 to 17 Nov, Sun evening from 14 Oct to Easter and Mon, except evenings in Jul-Aug • 15 rooms located in 3 buildings around a courtyard, one has disabled access, all have bath/WC or shower/WC and television • €43 to €59; breakfast €7; half board available • Menus €16 to €35 • Garden, car park. No dogs allowed • Play area

 It would be difficult to find a more amiable ambassador for the region.

This warm, welcoming 18C manor lies on the edge of the park of the Château des Ravalets. The view from the windows over Trottebec, Cherbourg and the coast is quite superb. The immaculate rooms are adorned with family heirlooms, as are the sitting rooms. Your graceful hostess could talk until the cows come home about her region's immense natural and cultural heritage.

The peace and quiet of Normandy.

The practical, well-kept rooms have less character than the spot itself, which is comprised of a manor built in 1660, a small 18C chapel and a beautifully manicured flower garden. The restaurant serves copious regional dishes and chargrilled specialities and is extremely popular with locals who come from far and near – always a good sign. Shop selling local produce.

Access : 1km past the castle on the D 322, then head for the "centre aéré" (play centre) and the Brix road

Access : 3.5km eastbound from Villedieu-les-Poêles on the D 554

 55 LE GRAND CERF
M. Bouvet

21 rue Saint-Blaise
61000 Alençon
Tel. 02 33 26 00 51
Fax 02 33 26 63 07
legrandcerf-alencon@wanadoo.fr
www.hotelgrandcerf-61.com

Closed Sun • 22 rooms, all have bath/WC or shower/WC and television • €56 to €59; breakfast €7; half board available • Restaurant closed Sun; menus €14 to €25 • Terrace

 56 L'ERMITAGE
M. Planché

24 boulevard Paul-Chalvet
61140 Bagnoles-de-l'Orne
Tel. 02 33 37 96 22
Fax 02 33 38 59 22
 ermitagemc@aol.com

Closed from Nov to late Mar • 38 rooms with bath/WC or shower/WC and television • €39 to €68, breakfast €8 • No restaurant • Garage. Car park, garden.

 Whether made out of wrought-iron or threads as fine as human hair, lace is everywhere.

The ornate wrought-iron adorning the façade of this hotel, built in 1843, has withstood the passing of time and lives up to Alençon's reputation as the capital of lace. The hotel has recently been treated to a facelift, but the hall is still adorned with the establishment's namesake, a stag's head and the restaurant and most of the rooms have retained their original dimensions and moulded ceilings. In the summer, meals are served in a delightful inner walled courtyard.

 Discovering the villas and tree-lined gardens of the resort's Belle Époque district.

This stylish property was built in 1886 in the Belle Époque style, typical of this smart Bagnoles neighbourhood. Soberly, rustic furnishings garnish the rooms, all of which have balconies, as does the breakfast room, overlooking the quiet garden. The cosy sitting room is adorned with a fresco. The charming owner adores pampering and cosseting her guests.

Access : From Place du Général de Gaulle, drive towards the town centre, the hotel is on the right past the préfecture

Access : In the Belle Époque neighbourhood

NORMANDY

57 L'ORANGERIE
M. et Mme Desailly

9 rue du Docteur-Vivares
61290 Longny-au-Perche
Tel. 02 33 25 11 78
Fax 02 33 73 67 19
desailly-fondeur@tele2.fr
http://lorangerie.free.fr

Open all year • 3 rooms with bath/WC • €45, breakfast included • Table d'hôte (only by reservation) €13 • Sitting room, garden. Credit cards not accepted, no dogs allowed

Settle down for a quiet evening in front of the fire after a day in the open air.

This attractive former orangery is now home to three lovely rooms, each of which is named after a wild flower: honeysuckle, buttercup and bluebell; the last of these is perfect for families. A large sitting room is ideal for long autumn evenings, grilling chestnuts or sizzling mushrooms over a crackling log fire. Ducks and fish have taken up residence in an old wash house hidden in the garden.

Access : In the village

---

58 SAINT-PIERRE
M. et Mme Delaunay

6 rue de la Libération
61150 Rânes
Tel. 02 33 39 75 14
Fax 02 33 35 49 23
info@hotelsaintpierreranes.com
www.hotelsaintpierreranes.com

Open all year • 12 rooms with bath/WC or shower/WC and television • €45 to €60; breakfast €7, half board available • Restaurant closed Fri evening; menus €13 to €35 • Terrace

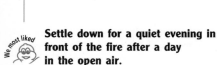

The pleasant family welcome of this village inn.

Two minutes from an old castle now a gendarmerie, this stone-built house stands in the centre of the village. Parquet flooring, stylish wallpaper, exquisite wardrobes and rustic furniture adorn the appealing little rooms which are exceedingly reasonably priced. You will also appreciate the warm dining room; as well as the other traditional recipes made with local produce, make sure you sample the chef's speciality: tripe.

Access : In the centre of the village near the main square

59 **VILLA DES HOUX**
M. Mauconduit

6 av. du Général-de-Gaulle
76390 Aumale
Tel. 02 35 93 93 30
Fax 02 35 93 03 94
lavilladeshoux@wanadoo.fr
www.villa-des-houx.com

Closed Jan, Sun evening and Mon lunchtime from Oct to Mar • 22 rooms, 2 have disabled access, with bath/WC or shower/WC and television • €58 to €72 (€56 to €69 low season); breakfast €6,50, half board available • Menus €20 (weekdays) to €48 • Private car park, garden.

60 **CHAMBRE D'HÔTE LA VILLA-FLORIDA**
M. et Mme Noël

24 chemin du Golf
76200 Dieppe
Tel. 02 35 84 40 37
Fax 01 58 16 45 17
villa-florida@wanadoo.fr
www.lavillaflorida.com

Open all year • 4 rooms, one with mezzanine, with bath/WC or shower/WC • €66, breakfast included • No table d'hôte • Garden, car park. Credit cards not accepted

Tucking into the tasty home cooking on the terrace overlooking the garden.

This handsome half-timbered house used to be the village police station, but the cooking, comfort and welcome have improved since then! The generously proportioned rustically furnished rooms, tasty traditional cuisine enriched by delicious dishes of local produce and the charming dining room will all want to make you come back. The lovingly tended garden full of flowers adds to the villa's charm.

The faultlessly kind welcome.

This imaginatively designed slate covered house nestles in a delightful garden that opens onto the Dieppe golf course. Serenity and light fill the handsome interior proportions. Sober, contemporary rooms, each with a small private terrace, ensure total peace and quiet for all. Breakfasts are taken in the sitting room or garden, depending on the weather.

Access : Near the town centre, not far from the N 29

Access : 2km eastbound of Dieppe, towards Pourville on the D 75, before the Gulf

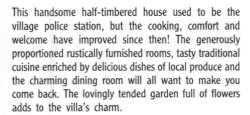

NORMANDY

61 LE PANORAMA

M. et Mme Lemercier

282 chemin du Panorama
76480 Duclair
Tel. 02 35 37 68 84
Fax 02 35 37 68 84

Open all year • 5 rooms • €50, breakfast included • No table d'hôte • Garden, car park. Credit cards not accepted, no dogs allowed

62 MANOIR DE BEAUMONT

Mme Demarquet

Route de Beaumont
76260 Eu
Tel. 02 35 50 91 91
cd@fnac.net
www.chez.com/demarquet

Open all year • 3 rooms • €47, breakfast included • No table d'hôte • Garden, car park. Credit cards not accepted

 **An exceptional view of the Seine.**

This 1930s villa built in the upper part of town lives up to its name, thanks to its idyllic view of the meanders of the Seine down below. The rooms are colourful and attractive; those under the eaves are perhaps the most inviting. The panoramic breakfast room and its tiny sitting room and fireplace are most appreciated, as is the delightful terraced garden.

 Guests are offered a welcome drink on arrival.

On the edge of the forest, this former hunting lodge of the château of Eu enjoys a matchless view of the valley. The comfortable, tastefully decorated rooms overlook the park and the countryside; the family room has been thoughtfully equipped with a kitchenette. Relax in the sitting room and library and delve into the numerous books – in French and English – on the area. Bicycles and horse loose-boxes are also available for guests and their four-legged companions.

Access : Take the chemin du Catel and turn left

Access : 2km eastbound from Eu on the D 49 towards Eu forest

 63 LA FERME DE LA CHAPELLE
M. Buchy

Côte de la Vierge
76400 Fécamp
Tel. 02 35 10 12 12
Fax 02 35 10 12 13
fermedelachapelle@wanadoo.fr
www.fermedelachapelle.fr

Closed from 2 to 21 Jan • 22 rooms, 5 of which are self-contained with kitchenettes, 2 have disabled access, all have bath/WC and television • €60 to €66; breakfast €8; half board available • Restaurant closed on Mon lunchtime; menu €15 to €29 • Garden, car park • Outdoor swimming pool

 64 AUBERGE DU BEAU LIEU
M. et Mme Ramelet

Route de Paris - Le Fossé
76440 Forges-les-Eaux
Tel. 02 35 90 50 36
Fax 02 35 90 35 98
aubeaulieu@aol.com

 www.trucsdechef.com

Closed from 19 Jan to 12 Feb, in Sep and Mon evening and Tue • 3 rooms, with bath/WC and television • €39 to €55; breakfast €6 to €11 • Menus €17 (weekdays) to €50 • Terrace, garden, car park

 The Museum of Newfoundland Fishermen in Fécamp.

This old farm next door to a fishermen's chapel enjoys a wonderful position on the cliff, surveying the Channel and the port of Fécamp, from where French fishing sloops once set sail for the icy waters of Newfoundland. Inside the hotel can hardly be called luxurious, but it offers simple rooms, decorated with pine furniture and roughcast walls, laid out around a large square courtyard. We'll happily exchange luxury for authenticity any day!

 What could be more symbolic of Normandy than apple trees and dairy cows?

Two minutes from the tiny spa-resort of Forges, this attractive country inn is home to cosy rooms which open directly onto the garden and a snug rustic restaurant complete with beams and a stone fireplace. The tableware is a reminder of the town's illustrious porcelain industry. The warmth of your hosts' welcome is such that you will even forget you're in a hotel.

Access : From the town centre, drive towards Dieppe along the harbour, then left towards Notre-Dame du-Salut

Access : 2km on the D 915, towards Gournay

65 LE RELAIS DE L'ABBAYE

M. et Mme Chatel

798 rue du Quesney
76480 Jumièges
Tel. 02 35 37 24 98
Fax 02 35 37 24 98

Open all year • 4 rooms • €33 to €38, breakfast included
• No table d'hôte • Garden, car park. Credit cards not
accepted, no dogs allowed

66 VENT D'OUEST

M. Lassarat

4 rue Caligny
76600 Le Havre
Tel. 02 35 42 50 69
Fax 02 35 42 58 00
contact @ ventdouest.fr
www.ventdouest.fr

Open all year • 35 rooms, all have bath/WC or
shower/WC and television • €80 to €120; breakfast €9
• No restaurant (room service available) • Tea room

 **Roman Polanski's "Tess" could well
have been shot near here!**

Nestling in the shadow of the famous abbey, this pretty
Norman slate-roofed house has everything you could
wish for in a B&B establishment. A sophisticated rustic
interior with beams, timbers, enormous fireplace,
ornaments and antique plates. The rooms under the
eaves upstairs are the most pleasant and the bathrooms
merit a special prize. In the summer, breakfast is served
in the garden.

 **Visiting the port of Le Havre in a
launch.**

Betwixt land and sea, the "Westerly" is a haven of charm
in the heart of Le Havre's Modern Quarter designed by
20C architect Auguste Perret. A stone's throw from the
harbour, the interior decoration has a distinctly briny
flavour. The guest-rooms, on the other hand, are more
adventurous and guests can choose between "country",
"meditation" or "mountain" rooms, among others.
Knick-knacks, snug quilts and a host of tiny details make
all the difference.

Access : Near the abbey

Access : Drive along Quai Colbert past Vauban
docks, turn right at Quai George V (Commerce docks)
and continue straight on as far as St Joseph's Church

67 GOLF HÔTEL
Evergreen SARL

102 route de Dieppe
76470 Le Tréport
Tel. 02 27 28 01 52
Fax 02 27 28 01 51
evergreen2@wanadoo.fr
www.treport-hotels.com

Closed Christmas weekend • 10 non-smoking rooms, all have television • €45 to €65 (€42 to €65 low season); breakfast €7 • No restaurant • Park, car park. No dogs allowed

68 LE PRIEURÉ SAINTE-CROIX
M. et Mme Carton

76470 Le Tréport
Tel. 02 35 86 14 77
Fax 02 35 86 14 77
carton.nicole@wanadoo.fr
http://prieuresaintecroix.free.fr

Open all year • 5 rooms with bathrooms • €45 to €57, breakfast included • No table d'hôte • Garden, car park. Credit cards not accepted, no dogs allowed

Extremely well-equipped rooms.

In front of the entrance to Tréport's campsite, turn left onto the tree-lined drive which will take you up to this lovely late-19C half-timbered property set in the grounds of an immense park. All the non-smoking rooms are generously sized, well-equipped and personalised; all have a fridge. Friendly and excellent value for money.

Listening to the silence all around.

This farmhouse built in the reign of Louis-Philippe was formerly part of the castle of Eu's estate and is still a working cattle-farm. All the rooms, located in a separate wing, have been decorated in the same spirit with parquet floors, period furniture and recent bathrooms. The breakfast area, although entirely revamped, has retained its rustic appeal. Take a seat under the hundred-year-old flowering cherry trees in the garden.

Access : Near Tréport campsite

Access : 2km eastbound from Tréport on the D 925 (Abbeville-Dieppe road)

MANNEVILLE-LA-GOUPIL - 76110 **QUIBERVILLE - 76860**

69 CHAMBRE D'HÔTE FERME D'ÉCOSSE
M. et Mme Loisel

1216 route des jonquilles
76110 Manneville-la-Goupil
Tel. 02 35 27 77 21
Fax 02 35 27 77 21
loisel.nicole @ wanadoo.fr
http://ferme-ecosse.site-voila.fr

Open all year • 2 rooms upstairs • €49, breakfast
included; half board available • Table d'hôte €21
(evening only and by reservation, closed Sun) • Garden,
car park. Credit cards not accepted, no dogs allowed

70 LES VERGERS
M. Auclert

Rue des Vergers
76860 Quiberville
Tel. 02 35 83 16 10
Fax 02 35 83 36 46
christianaucler @ aol.com

Closed from Nov to Feb • 3 rooms with bath/WC • €60,
breakfast included • No table d'hôte • Garden, car park.
No dogs allowed

 **Delicious farm produce takes pride of
place in the tasty home cooking.**

The eye is immediately drawn to the fetching red-brick
façade of this handsome 18C mansion. The establishment's rooms are comfortable and soberly decorated.
Musically-minded guests have the use of a piano, while
others will enjoy strolling through the garden and
vegetable plot past the henhouse and sheepfold and
children inevitably fall for the adorable donkeys. Try a
glass of homemade cider as an aperitif before dinner.

 **A beautifully decorated period
residence.**

Guests can be sure of a pleasant welcome in this early
20C property. The spacious, comfortable rooms show a
distinct preference for a discreetly classical opulence with
pastel shades, floral fabrics and period furniture. Guests
can relax in the lovely landscaped garden. Within easy
reach of the sea, it is ideally situated to explore the
region.

Access : 4.5km on the D 10

Access : 7km eastbound from Veules-les-Roses on
the D 68 then the D 75

71 **DANDY**
Mme Renouard

93 rue Cauchoise
76000 Rouen
Tel. 02 35 07 32 00
Fax 02 35 15 48 82
contact @ hotels-rouen.net
www.hotels-rouen.net

Closed from 25 Dec to 5 Jan • 18 rooms with bath/WC and television • €76 to €99; breakfast €9 • No restaurant • Garage • Tea room, piano bar (hotel guests only)

72 **DIEPPE**
M. Guéret

Place B.-Tissot
76000 Rouen
Tel. 02 35 71 96 00
Fax 02 35 89 65 21
hotel.dieppe @ wanadoo.fr
www.bestwestern.fr

Open all year • 41 rooms, 8 of which are non-smoking, all have bath/WC or shower/WC and television • €92 to €105; breakfast €10; half board available • Air-conditioned restaurant; menus €14 to €36

The lady of the house delights in introducing guests to the many facets of vintage Calvados.

Bathtubs with swan-shaped taps, well-padded beds, Louis XV-style furniture and classical paintings adorn the outrageously dandified rooms that you will either love or hate! Despite the hotel's position on the doorstep of historic Rouen and in the heart of the busy Rue du Gros Horloge, you will sleep soundly and peacefully. Plans are afoot to open a 100 % Norman-flavoured piano bar in the hotel.

Treat yourself to a tipple of well-aged Calvados in the snug bar.

The portraits on the walls are a reminder that the Guéret family has been at the helm of the Dieppe Hotel since 1880. The well-soundproofed, fully refurbished rooms are all equipped with wi-fi and period furniture. The roasting spit, which takes pride of place in the elegant dining room, sets the tone for a menu of local dishes including the restaurant's speciality, duck Rouennais.

Access : Near the town centre in the pedestrian quarter, on the street linking Place Cauchoise to Place du Vieux Marché

Access : Opposite the railway station

 73 LE VIEUX CARRÉ
M. Beaumont

 74 HÔTEL DE LA CATHÉDRALE
M. Delaunay

34 rue Ganterie
76000 Rouen
Tel. 02 35 71 67 70
Fax 02 35 71 19 17
vieux-carre@mcom.fr

12 rue Saint-Romain
76000 Rouen
Tel. 02 35 71 57 95
Fax 02 35 70 15 54
arttra@wanadoo.fr
www.hotel-de-la-cathedrale.fr

Open all year • 13 rooms, one of which has disabled access, with bath/WC or shower/WC and television • €54 to €58; breakfast €7 • Menus €12 to €18

Open all year • 26 rooms with bath/WC or shower/WC, all have television • €59 to €85, breakfast €7.50 • No restaurant

 We most liked **There was nothing we didn't love!**

 We most liked **Breakfasting on the delightful patio which doubles as a tearoom in the afternoons.**

The handsome walls of this house built in 1715, in the company of other august façades of the same vintage, line a street which is typical of Rouen and makes an ideal base camp from which to explore this "museum town". The interior is equally faultless and the rooms are decorated with frescoes and old wardrobes straight out of a boarding school dorm. The sitting room is snug and welcoming and the hotel boasts a courtyard terrace where mouth-watering pastries and a few choice dishes are served.

This enchanting 17C establishment, located on one of Rouen's most beautiful old streets just a two minute walk from the cathedral, is proof that it is still possible to find good, well-priced accommodation in the heart of a tourist neighbourhood. Period furniture of varying styles, half-timbered walls, brightly coloured wallpaper and knick knacks set the scene of this pleasantly old-fashioned hotel. An immense fireplace takes pride of place in the breakfast room with its raftered ceiling.

Access : In the heart of the old town, between the Palais de Justice and the Musée des Beaux Arts

Access : In the heart of the old town

 75 CHAMBRE D'HÔTE MADAME GENTY
Mme Genty

Hameau de Ramouville
76740 Saint-Aubin-sur-Mer
Tel. 02 35 83 47 05
gisele.genty@wanadoo.fr
http://gisele.genty.free.fr

Open all year • 5 rooms, 2 of which are on the ground floor and 3 are in the attic • €47 to €50, breakfast included • No table d'hôte • Garden, car park. Credit cards not accepted

 76 FERME DE BRAY
M. et Mme Perrier

76440 Sommery
Tel. 02 35 90 57 27
 ferme.de.bray@wanadoo.fr

Open all year • 5 rooms with bathrooms • €44, breakfast included • No table d'hôte • Garden, car park. Credit cards not accepted, no dogs allowed • Farm visits, fishing

 Waking up to the enticing aroma of oven-fresh bread.

After a masterful restoration this 18C regional farmstead is back in its prime. The thatched roof may have disappeared, but the lovely half-timbered walls were rescued and well-worn tiles and a fireplace adorn the rustic, warm sitting room. The rooms echo this rustic spirit and three are under the eaves. In the morning, the delicious smell of bread, freshly baked in the old oven, will entice you down to breakfast.

Access : 4km northbound from Bourg-Dun then drive towards Quiberville

 The farm continues to uphold local rural traditions.

The land has been farmed by the same family for 18 generations and their 17C and 18C farmhouse, which doubles as a museum and a B&B, is simply astounding. Rural through and through, the furniture and the simplicity of the interior decoration echo this country spirit: each of the rooms, lightened by striped wallpaper, has its own fireplace. Activities abound on the farm, including a visit to the press, mill, dairy parlour, dovecote, not to mention exhibitions and fishing in the pond.

Access : 10km to the north-east of Forges-les-Eaux on the D 915

  77 LE CLOS DU VIVIER
Mme Cachera

4 chemin du Vivier
76540 Valmont
Tel. 02 35 29 90 95
Fax 02 35 27 44 49
dc@le-clos-du-vivier.com
www.le-clos-du-vivier.com

Open all year • 3 rooms • €80, breakfast included • No table d'hôte • Garden, car park. Credit cards not accepted, no dogs allowed in restaurant

  78 LA TERRASSE
M. et Mme Delafontaine

Route de Vasterival
76119 Varengeville-sur-Mer
Tel. 02 35 85 12 54
Fax 02 35 85 11 70
francois.delafontaine@wanadoo.fr
www.hotel-restaurant-la-terrasse.com

Open from 15 Mar to 15 Oct • 22 rooms with bath/WC or shower/WC • €47 to €52; breakfast €9; half board available • Menus €18 (weekdays) to €30 • Garden, car park. No dogs allowed in restaurant • Tennis

 Breakfasting by the garden where ducks, swans, chickens and peacocks roam free.

This large 17C cottage, hidden deep in the countryside, was formerly an outbuilding of the Château de Valmont. Over the years, the current owners have tirelessly transformed it into a pleasant getaway where they take great pleasure in welcoming guests. Exposed beams, bare stonework and fireplaces make interesting architectural features in the sitting rooms. The appealing "cottage" atmosphere of the rooms has been wisely preserved.

 The family donkey grazing in the meadow alongside the path leading down to the beach.

At the end of a pretty little lane flanked by fir trees, stands an early-20C brick house, which is the family home of the current owners. Nothing opulent or ostentatious deflects from the establishment's quiet charm: the TV has been thankfully banned from the calm rooms, enhanced by colourful fabrics and tartan carpets. Half of the bedrooms enjoy a sea view. Panoramic restaurant and a shaded garden.

Access : 2km eastbound of Valmont on the D 150 towards Ourville

Access : 3km to the north-west on the D 75, then take the small minor road lined by fir trees

79 MANOIR DU PLESSIS

M. et Mme Laurent

1175 route de Coudebec
76940 Vatteville-la-Rue
Tel. 02 35 95 79 79
Fax 02 35 95 79 77
aplvatteville@free.fr

Open all year • 4 rooms with bathrooms • €48 to €53,
breakfast included, half board available • Table d'hôte
€20 to €39 • Garden, car park. No dogs allowed

The country flavour of this fine old manor house.

This Napoleonic brick manor-house topped by two high
chimney stacks is worth a pause, if only to savour its
quiet atmosphere. The rooms with bathrooms boast
parquet floors and lovely antique furniture and are full
of character; the others are more sober. The rustic dining
room, decorated by dark wainscoting and the billiards
table in the sitting room further add to the establishment's appeal. If you can tear yourselves away, do you
fancy a spot of hunting, or brushing up on your artistic
skills?

Access : 1km northbound from Vatteville-la-Rue

PAYS DE LA LOIRE

First there is the peaceful valley of the Loire, the "Garden of France", renowned for its peaceful ambience, enchanting views, sumptuous manor houses and castles, magnificent floral gardens, lavish orchards, fields of vegetables and acre upon acre of vineyards. Tuck into a slab of rillettes pâté liberally spread on a crunchy baguette, a steaming platter of eels or a slice of goat's cheese while you savour a glass of light Loire wine. Continue westwards towards the sea to Nantes, once a port of entrance for enticing spices brought back from the New World: this is the home of the famous dry Muscadet. Further south, the Vendée still echoes to the cries of the Royalists' tragic last stand. Explore the secrets of its salt marshes, relax in its seaside resorts or head for the spectacular attractions of the Puy du Fou amusement park. Simple, country fare is not lacking, so make sure you taste a delicious dish of *mojettes* (white beans), a piping-hot plate of *chaudrée* (fish stew) or a mouth-watering slice of fresh brioche.

- Loire-Atlantique (44)
- Maine-et-Loire (49)
- Mayenne (53)
- Sarthe (72)
- Vendée (85)

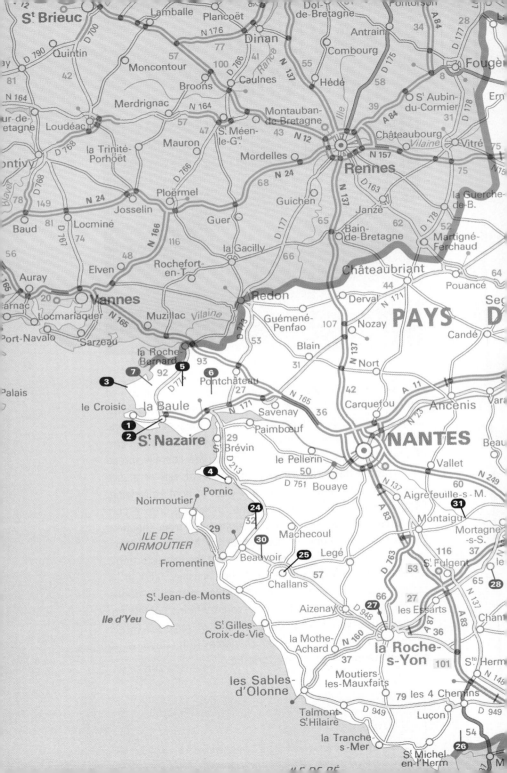

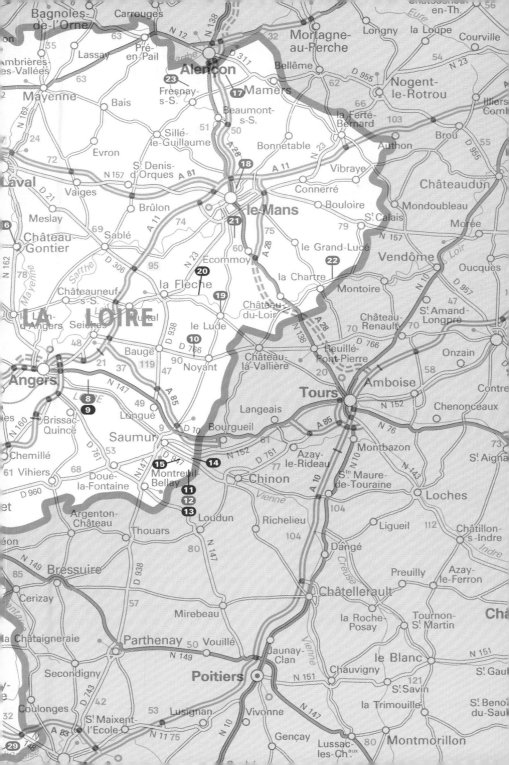

 1 HOSTELLERIE DU BOIS
M. et Mme Lethuillier

65 avenue Lajarrige
44500 La Baule
Tel. 02 40 60 24 78
Fax 02 40 42 05 88
hostellerie-du-bois@wanadoo.fr
www.hostellerie-du-bois.com

Closed from 15 Nov to 15 Mar • 15 rooms on 2 floors, overlooking the garden or the street, all have bath/WC or shower/WC and television • €70 (€60 low season); breakfast €7; half board available • Restaurant closed Sat, menus €20 to €23 (evenings only) • Terrace, garden

 2 LE MARINI
M. Le Boudec

22 avenue Georges-Clemenceau
44500 La Baule
Tel. 02 40 60 23 29
Fax 02 40 11 16 98
interhotelmarini@wanadoo.fr
www.lemarinihotel.com

Open all year • 33 rooms with bath/WC, all have television • €61 to €82 (€52 to €71 low season); breakfast €8 • Half board guests only, €21 • Garage • Indoor swimming pool with jacuzzi

 La Baule les Pins provides a welcome break from the concrete jungle along the coast.

Poised between the ocean and Parc des Dryades, this 1920s seaside hotel has a distinctive green and white half-timbered façade. The well-travelled owners have carefully preserved its pleasantly old-fashioned flavour as a showcase for the countless ornaments and pieces of furniture brought back from their travels in the Far East. The small garden in the back is simply delightful.

 The globetrotter spirit of this hotel.

Whether on a serious excursion throughout France or simply in search of a mooring spot to visit the region, you're bound to warm to the discreet ambience and the well thought-out attention to detail of this hotel. Off the beaten seaside track, it boasts a covered swimming pool and jacuzzi, a welcoming sitting room-bar with cosy armchairs, a reading corner and trim, practical bedrooms equipped with comfortable bedding. Breakfast and dinner are served around the pool.

Access : In the La Baule-les-Pins quarter: at Place des Palmiers head for the railway station

Access : In the town centre

3 POSTE
M. Malnoé

26 rue de la Plage
44420 Piriac-sur-Mer
Tel. 02 40 23 50 90
Fax 02 40 23 68 96

 hoteldelaposte.piriac@wanadoo.fr

Open from Easter to 1 Nov • 15 rooms on 2 floors with bath/WC or showers with or without WC, some have television • €40 to €60; breakfast €6.50; half board available • Restaurant closed Mon; menus €10 to €34.50 (except from 1 Apr to 1 Nov)

4 RELAIS SAINT-GILLES
M. et Mme Robineau

7 rue Fernand-de-Mun
44210 Pornic
Tel. 02 40 82 02 25
www.relaissaintgilles.com

Open all year • 25 rooms with bath/WC and television • €58 to €67 (€48 to €55 low season); breakfast €7 • No restaurant • Terrace

The footpath to the Pointe du Castelli.

This appealing 1930s villa lies in the heart of a tiny fishing port surrounded by picturesque 17C houses. Its spacious, well-appointed rooms are looked after by the owner, for whom the term "clean enough to eat off the kitchen floor" is clearly not an empty remark! The family dining room is lit by immense arcades and in the summer, tables are laid outdoors.

A castle set in foliage, sandy beaches and a picture-postcard harbour: what more could you wish for?

This mid-19C coaching inn can be found on a quiet side street of this seaside resort. Two wings stand on either side of a terrace shaded by an arbour of climbing vines. Inside are regularly spruced up rooms with fresh wallpaper and paintwork, some with old furniture, and a plush bourgeois dining room. Your host, a former merchant navy officer, can point you towards a whole host of beautiful footpaths.

Access : In the centre of the village, on the main road opposite the chemist

Access : In the upper part of town, on a quiet street above the castle

5 LES CHAUMIÈRES DU LAC
M. Logodin

Route d'Herbignac
44110 Saint-Lyphard
Tel. 02 40 91 32 32
Fax 02 40 91 30 33
jclogodin @ leschaumieresdulac.com
www.leschaumieresdulac.com

Closed from 15 Dec to 15 Jan • 20 rooms, 2 of which
have disabled access, all have bath/WC and television
• €65 to €90 (€55 to €75 low season); breakfast €9; half
board available • Auberge Les Typhas: closed Tue and
Wed lunchtime in low season; menus €18 (weekdays) to
€45 • Garden, car park • Swimming in a small lake

**France's best chefs and gourmets only
use Guérande's "fleur de sel" – find
out why.**

This recently built hamlet of cottages right in the heart
of the Brière Nature Reserve may not be the epitome
of authenticity, but it is definitely an excellent way of
finding out more about the region's salt marshes. The
appeal is further enhanced by the tasteful yellow and
white restaurant, pretty terrace and stylish bedrooms
with canopy beds. All the more so once you've caught
a glimpse of what the inside of a local cottage really
looked like, at the reconstructed cottages in Kerhinet.

Access : Outside the village, by the minor road,
opposite the lake

6 TY GWENN
M. Collard

25 Île-d'Errand
44550 Saint-Malo-de-Guersac
Tel. 02 40 91 15 04

Closed from 1 Oct to 1 Apr • 4 non-smoking rooms, all
have shower/WC, television and a small fridge • €52,
breakfast included • Table d'hôte €20 (evening only)
• Sitting room, garden, car park. Credit cards not
accepted, no dogs allowed • Outdoor swimming pool,
billiards. Sailing, golf, horse-riding and fishing nearby

**Barge excursions along the canals of
the Brière (on request).**

The whitewashed walls, thatched roof and the leaded
windows framed with curtains of this adorable cottage
may well find you hunting for your camera. Inside, the
romantic, snug rooms are equally appealing. In the
sitting room you will be met with a sophisticated picture
of exposed beams, a fireplace, lovely fabrics and a
billiards table. Guests – non-smokers only – have the
run of a delightful garden and swimming pool.

Access : 3km from Saint-Malo, straight on after the
church

7 KERVENEL
M. Brasselet

D 252 - Le Pigeon-Blanc
44350 Saint-Molf
Tel. 02 40 42 50 38
Fax 02 40 42 50 55
ybrasselet @ aol.com
www.loire-atlantique-tourisme-com

Open from Apr to Sep • 3 rooms with bath/WC • €60, breakfast included • No table d'hôte • Car park, sitting room. Credit cards not accepted, no dogs allowed • Bicycle rentals.

8 LE GRAND TALON
Mme Guervilly

3 route des Chapelles
49800 Andard
Tel. 02 41 80 42 85
Fax 02 41 80 42 85

Open all year • 3 rooms • €46 to €63, breakfast included • No table d'hôte • Park, car park. Credit cards not accepted

 Lounging in the garden in fine weather.

This former farmhouse restored in the 1970s borders on the Brière Regional Park. A lovely granite façade hides spacious rooms named after the style in which they are furnished: Louis XVI, Louis XVIII and contemporary. Tasteful bed linen, comfortable bathrooms and the tranquillity of the site all contribute to making your stay a pleasant one.

Mrs Guervilly does her utmost to make your stay as pleasant as possible.

The graceful façade of this elegant 18C abode, covered in russet-red leaves in autumn, overlooks a square courtyard just two minutes from Angers. The peaceful bedrooms are tastefully decorated. If you're lucky with the weather, you can breakfast and picnic in the garden under a parasol.

Access : 2.5km on the D 33 towards La Turballe

Access : 11km eastbound from Angers on the N 147, towards Saumur then take the D 113

PAYS DE LA LOIRE

ANGERS - 49100   **AUVERSE - 49490**

 9 HÔTEL DU MAIL
M. et Mme Dupuis

8 rue des Ursules
49100 Angers
Tel. 02 41 25 05 25
Fax 02 41 86 91 20
hoteldumailangers@yahoo.fr
www.destination-anjou.com

Closed Sun and national holidays from 12pm to 6.30pm • 26 rooms on 2 floors, most have bath/WC, the others have shower/WC, all have television • €51 to €63; breakfast €8 • No restaurant • Private car park in the inner courtyard

 10 DOMAINE DE LA BRÉGELLERIE
M. et Mme Sohn

Route de Chigne
49490 Auverse
Tel. 02 41 82 11 69
Fax 02 41 82 11 87
isabellesohn@wanadoo.fr
http://la.bregellerie.free.fr

Open all year • 5 non-smoking rooms, 4 of which are upstairs, all have bathrooms • €55 to €70, breakfast included • No table d'hôte • Garden, car park. Credit cards not accepted • Outdoor swimming pool, fishing in the pond

 Angers is famed for its mild climate and a tradition of gracious living.

This discreet hotel standing in a side street of the historic town was an Ursuline convent in the 17C, before becoming a guesthouse and now boutique hotel. It takes a bit of finding but your efforts will be amply rewarded by the personalised, beautifully decorated rooms awaiting you. The breakfast room is decorated in a classic bourgeois style and guests can also venture onto a lovely mini-terrace in the inner courtyard. Definitely worth mailing home about!

 "The Loire" bedroom.

After a full-scale renovation this old farmstead has been elevated to the rank of inn. The names of the individually decorated rooms located in a recent wing reveal their one-off themes: "Forest", "Vines", "Fields", "Pond" and "The Loire", whose curious boat-shaped bathtub is worth a special mention. A breakfast room, elegantly understated, a pool table, a large summer swimming pool in the garden and a pond – fishing possible – add the finishing touches.

Access : In a quiet street behind the town hall

Access : 14.5km to the south-west on the D 767, Noyant road and the D 79 on the right

11 LA CROIX BLANCHE
M. Jean

7 place des Plantagenêts
49590 Fontevraud-l'Abbaye
Tel. 02 41 51 71 11
Fax 02 41 38 15 38
la_croix_blanche @ hotmail.com
www.fontevraud.net

Closed from 17 to 30 Nov, Sun evening and Mon from Nov to Mar • 25 rooms with bath/WC or shower/WC, all have television • €69 to €121; breakfast €9; half board available • Menus €18 to €52 • Terrace, private car park • Boules, table-tennis, bicycles lent

12 DOMAINE DE MESTRÉ
M. et Mme Dauge

49590 Fontevraud-l'Abbaye
Tel. 02 41 51 72 32
Fax 02 41 51 71 90
domaine-de-mestre @ wanadoo.fr
www.dauge-fontevraud.com

Closed from 20 Dec to 1 Apr • 12 rooms with bathrooms • €60, breakfast €7 • Table d'hôte €24 (evenings only, Mon-Wed, Fri, Sat) • Park, car park. Credit cards not accepted, no dogs allowed

 Guests can borrow bicycles and explore the countryside.

"It all began in 1696, when Mistress Marie Cohier wedded Master Mathieux Blochon and they opened the hostelry." For over three hundred years, this ancient inn has been welcoming travellers from near and far, come to admire the neighbouring monastery. Many of the renovated bedrooms sport raftered ceilings and period fireplaces. Guests also have the run of a sitting-room and billiards room and have the choice of a traditional restaurant (summer terrace) or a crêperie.

 Lavender, vetiver, olive oil, thyme, cinnamon, nutmeg and rose-scented soaps.

This farm and its old tithe barn, dating back to the 13C, once belonged to the Royal Abbey of Fontevraud: nowadays, it is home to attractive, individually decorated rooms in which it is easy to feel at home. Breakfast and dinner, made with home-grown ingredients, are served in the former chapel. The estate's woods and gardens are home to ancient cedar and lime-trees and a visit to the estate's craft soap factory is always a pleasure.

Access : In the town centre, opposite the entrance to the Abbaye Royale

Access : 1km northbound from Fontevraud on the D 947, towards Montsoreau

PAYS DE LA LOIRE

 13 PRIEURÉ-SAINT-LAZARE
M. Haudebault

 Abbaye Royale de Fontevraud
Rue Saint-Jean-de-l'Hubit
49590 Fontevraud-L'Abbaye
Tel. 02 41 51 73 16
Fax 02 41 51 75 50
contact@hotelfp-fontevraud.com
www.hotelfp-fontevraud.com

Closed from 10 Mar to 13 Nov • 52 rooms, 6 are for non-smokers, with bath/WC or shower/WC, all have television • €50 to €110; breakfast €11; half board available • Restaurant closed Tue and Wed lunchtime; menus €16 (weekdays) to €50 • Garden, private car park. No dogs allowed

 Find sanctuary within the walls of the abbey gardens.

The building was indeed a priory and a lazaret before being turned into a hotel. Although rich in history, its ancient walls have an eternal quality that appears to withstand the wear and tear of time: the almost monastical bedroom-cells provide a haven of peace and quiet for busy urban dwellers and the vaulted breakfast room and restaurant tables around the cloisters further extend this invitation to meditate and take stock.

 14 LE BUSSY
Mme Roi

 4 rue Jeanne-d'Arc
49730 Montsoreau
Tel. 02 41 38 11 11
Fax 02 41 38 18 10
hotel.lebussy@wanadoo.fr

Closed on Tue and Wed in Feb, Mar, Nov and Dec; Wed in Apr and Oct • 12 rooms, all have bath/WC or shower/WC and television • €50 to €65 (€47 to €60 low season); breakfast €8 • No restaurant • Private car park

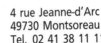 **What better place to curl up with one of Alexander Dumas' novels of romance and action?**

The sign outside this 18C house at the top of the village pays homage to one of Dumas' famous heroes, Bussy d'Amboise, sweetheart of the Dame de Monsoreau. Most of the rooms, furnished in a Louis Philippe style and equipped with brand new bathrooms, survey the castle and the Loire. In the summer, breakfast is served in the flower-decked garden and throughout the rest of the year, in a delightful troglodyte room. Friendly and welcoming.

Access : In the abbey grounds

Access : In the upper part of town behind the castle

15 **DEMEURE DE LA VIGNOLE**
Mme Bartholeyns

3 impasse Marguerite-d'Anjou
49730 Turquant
Tel. 02 41 53 67 00
Fax 02 41 53 67 09
demeure @ demeure-vignole.com
www.demeure-vignole.com

Open from 15 Mar to 15 Nov • 8 rooms, one of which
has disabled access, all have bath/WC and television
• €74 to €102; breakfast €9; half board available
• Menus €26 (evenings only by reservation) • Terrace,
garden, car park. No dogs allowed

16 **LE CHÂTEAU DE MIRVAULT**
M. et Mme d'Ambrières

53200 Château-Gontier
Tel. 02 43 07 10 82
Fax 02 43 07 10 82
château.mirvault @ worldonline.fr

Open all year • 2 rooms • €76 to €80, breakfast included,
10 % discount for 3 nights and more • No table d'hôte
• Park, car park. Credit cards not accepted, no dogs
allowed • Boating

**The troglodyte chamber
where the villagers met in the 12C.**

This exquisite estate only opened its doors as a hotel
in 2000 following several years of major restoration
work under the supervision of the architects of France's
Listed Monuments. The 15C manor house and 17C
outbuildings perched on the cliff have been turned into
individually decorated rooms, where every effort has
been taken to retain their historic decorative features
such as beams, fireplace and bread oven. A terraced
garden commands a wonderful view of the valley.
Admirable.

Friendly family welcome.

This elegant château on the banks of the Mayenne has
been the home of the same family since 1573. The
lavish sitting room is furnished with 18C antiques and
family portraits, a beautiful tapestry hangs on the wall
of the breakfast room and the park is home to warrens
of wild rabbits straight out of "Watership Down". The
rooms are equally ornate and overlook the river where
you can go boating, should you so fancy.

Access : 10km from Saumur on the D 947, in the
heart of the village

Access : Northbound on the N 162, on the Laval
road on the banks of the Mayenne

17 LA GARENCIÈRE
M. et Mme Langlais

72610 Champfleur
Tel. 02 33 31 75 84
Fax 02 33 27 42 09

Closed in Jan • 5 rooms • €46 to €49, breakfast included • Table d'hôte €19 (evening only) • Car park. Credit cards not accepted, no dogs allowed • Indoor swimming pool

18 CHAMBRE D'HÔTE MADAME BORDEAU
Mme Bordeau

Le Monet
72190 Coulaines
Tel. 02 43 82 25 50

Open all year • 4 rooms • €45, breakfast included • No table d'hôte • Garden, car park. Credit cards not accepted, no dogs allowed

 Green fields as far as the eye can see.

At the time of the crusades, this hamlet, a former stronghold of the Knights of la Garencière, was a stopover point for pilgrims on the way to Compostela. Nowadays, the large 19C farmhouse, built on the site of the old pilgrims' refuge, offers quiet, tastefully decorated rooms; the one in an independent cottage is ideal for families. Sample a generous spread of local produce, before taking a dip in the covered swimming pool overlooking the countryside.

 A country atmosphere on the doorstep of Le Mans.

Saved from ruin in the nick of time, this small country house has made a spectacular recovery. Madame clearly spends many hours in her garden. Inside, the original character has been preserved and enhanced by a generous sprinkling of modern comforts. The rooms are not enormous but beautifully furnished; those on the ground floor have exposed beams and the others are under the eaves. A log fire is lit in the winter to take the chill off the morning in the breakfast room.

Access : 6.5km south-east of Alençon towards Mamers and Champfleur (D 19), then continue towards Bourg-le-Roi

Access : 5km northbound from Le Mans, towards Mamers then Ballon on the D 300

19 **CHAMBRE D'HÔTE MADAME PEAN**
Mme Pean

5 Grande-Rue
72800 Le Lude
Tel. 02 43 94 63 36

Closed from Oct to Mar • 3 rooms upstairs • €50, breakfast included • No table d'hôte • Garden. Credit cards not accepted

20 **L'AUBERGE DU PORT DES ROCHES**
M. et Mme Lesiourd

Le Port des Roches
72800 Luché-Pringé
Tel. 02 43 45 44 48

Fax 02 43 45 39 61

Closed in Feb, Sun evening, Mon and Tue lunchtime • 12 rooms with bath/WC or shower/WC, half of them have television • €42 to €52; breakfast €6; half board available • Menus €20 to €42 • Terrace and riverside garden, private car park

Ideally situated, two minutes from the castle.

Who could guess that behind the impressive walls of this handsome 17C property lies such a heavenly garden? Spacious, antique-furnished rooms like these, not to mention the delicious breakfasts, are the makings of a good holiday, but it is the atmosphere that will make you want to return: Madame Pean is so genuinely and clearly delighted to meet her guests that visits might well become an annual event.

Strolling along the banks of the river Loir.

This smart country inn on the banks of the Loir now enjoys a supremely quiet location: it's hard to imagine, that not so long ago, soft local stone was quarried from the surrounding hillsides and loaded onto boats which would be moored in front of the hotel. Light, airy, colourful rooms, a comfortable dining room with a homely feel and a riverside garden-terrace await guests in search of peace and quiet.

Access : In the village

Access : 2.5km eastbound on the D 13 towards Mancigné, then take the D 214

PAYS DE LA LOIRE

21 LE PETIT PONT
Mme Brou

3 rue du Petit-Pont
72230 Moncé-en-Belin
Tel. 02 43 42 03 32
Fax 02 43 42 97 95

Open all year • One room in the house and 5 others in a separate wing • €46 to €56, breakfast included • Table d'hôte €13.50 to €25 • Garden, car park. No dogs allowed

22 CHÂTEAU DE LA VOLONIÈRE
M. Becquelin

49 rue Principale
72340 Poncé-sur-le-Loir
Tel. 02 43 79 68 16
Fax 02 43 79 68 18
chateau-de-la-voloniere @ wanadoo.fr
http://chateaudelavoloniere.free.fr

Closed in Feb • 5 rooms • €60 to €80, breakfast €5 • No table d'hôte • Park, car park • Visits to castles of the Loire

 Your tireless hostess did much of the restoration herself.

Over the years, your energetic hostess has painstakingly restored her lovely house, covered in variegated vine and part of a former working farm. Her efforts have resulted in beautifully appointed, individually decorated rooms (non-smokers only). One of the rooms and a self-catering cottage are in the main building, while the others are in an independent wing. Friendly and welcoming.

 Bohemian and easy-going.

Guests can depend on a perfect welcome when they arrive in this château, next door to the birthplace of the 16C poet, Pierre Ronsard. A bold colour scheme and antiques set the scene for the bedrooms, each of which is decorated on a the theme of a well-known tale: "Bluebeard", "Arabian Nights", "Merlin" and "Romeo and Juliet". The 15C chapel has been turned into the dining room and exhibitions are held in the former troglodyte kitchen.

Access : 11km southbound from Le Mans on the D 147 towards Arnage, then take the D 307

Access : In the village

 23 LE MOULIN DE LINTHE

M. et Mme Rollini

 24 HÔTEL DU MARTINET

Mme Huchet

Route de Sougé-le-Ganelon
72130 Saint-Léonard-des-Bois
Tel. 02 43 33 79 22
Fax 02 43 33 79 22
www.moulindelinthe.com

1 bis place de la Croix-Blanche
85230 Bouin
Tel. 02 51 49 08 94
Fax 02 51 49 83 08
hotel.martinet @ free.fr
www.lemartinet.com

Closed in Jan and Feb • 5 rooms • €60, breakfast
included • No table d'hôte • Terrace, garden, car park.
Credit cards not accepted • Fishing in the River Sarthe

Open all year • 30 rooms, 7 of which are on the ground
floor, with bath/WC or shower/WC and television • €52
to €73; breakfast €7; half board available • Menus €22
to €25 • Garden, car park. No dogs allowed in restaurant
• Outdoor swimming pool, fitness room

 Ever visited an ostrich farm?

 Breathe in the scent of fresh flowers and beeswax.

Get back to grass roots in this three-hundred-year-old
mill surrounded by fields. Anglers can try their luck
tempting the pike in the Sarthe at the bottom of the
garden, others may prefer to visit the nearby ostrich
farm or simply go for long bike rides round the
countryside. Each of the spacious, light rooms is
furnished in a different style: Norman, Louis XVI, 1930s.
The sitting room commands a lovely view of the
millwheel.

The discreet walls of this 18C house hide a whole host
of assets including a quiet garden, a swimming pool and
spotless rooms – those on the ground floor with tiled
floors and cane furniture are the most pleasant. Come
the evening, take your places in the delightful dining
room with its painted woodwork, parquet floor and
marble fireplace. The owner, ever-active and unfailingly
friendly, will often present you with the catch of the day,
brought home by one of her sons and cooked by the
other!

Access : 400m south of the village towards
Sougé-le-Ganelon

Access : In the centre of the village on the D 758,
between Bourgneuf-en-Retz and Beauvoir-sur-Mer

 25 L'ANTIQUITÉ
M. et Mme Belleville

 14 rue Galliéni
85300 Challans
Tel. 02 51 68 02 84
Fax 02 51 35 55 74
antiquitehotel@wanadoo.fr
www.hotelantiquite.com

Open all year • 16 rooms with bath/WC or shower/WC and television • €50 to €76 (€44 to €70 low season), breakfast €6 • No restaurant • Private car park. No dogs allowed • Swimming pool

 26 LA CLOSERAIE
Mme Lagaude

 21 rue de la Paix
85450 Champagné-les-Marais
Tel. 02 51 56 54 54
Fax 02 51 56 55 65
info@closeraie.fr
www.closeraie.fr

Closed 1 to 15 Jan • 5 rooms • €55 to €65 (€49 to €55 low season), breakfast included • Table d'hôte €17 • Garden. No dogs allowed in restaurant • Outdoor swimming pool, bicycle rentals

 The breakfast room which leads into a lovely veranda.

Given the establishment's name, you will not be surprised to learn that this family-run establishment is strewn with antiques picked up in local second-hand shops. Most of the rooms, housed in an imposing white-fronted building, are graced with red-brick tiles, period furniture and old engravings and paintings. A recent wing, with four rather more spacious rooms fitted with brand new bathrooms, has been laid out around the outdoor swimming pool.

 Stocking up on home-made cherry, melon, fig, peach and onion jam.

It is rumoured that this lovely old mid-19C house was once a convent. Now restored, it offers pretty rooms with terracotta tiled floors, beams, antiques and reproductions of Impressionist paintings. All open onto the garden and one even has a fireplace. Plan on doing full justice to the breakfast table, piled high with a head-spinning array of home-cooked goodies. The establishment rents out bicycles and often organises theme weekends (gastronomy, walking, etc).

Access : Near the exhibition hall

Access : 13km southbound from Luçon on the D 50 and the D 949

 LOGIS DE LA COUPERIE
Mme Oliveau

 85000 La Roche-sur-Yon
Tel. 02 51 24 10 18
Fax 02 51 46 05 59

Open all year • 5 rooms, all have bath/WC or shower/WC and television • €74 to €105 (€72 to €78 low season); breakfast €9 • No table d'hôte • Park with cottage garden and pond, car park. Credit cards not accepted, no dogs allowed • Library-sitting room, fishing in pond, bicycles, walking and horse-riding trail

 LA MÉTAIRIE DU BOURG
M. et Mme Retailleau

 85500 Les Herbiers
Tel. 02 51 67 23 97

Open all year • 3 rooms • €50, breakfast included • No table d'hôte • Garden, car park. Credit cards not accepted, no dogs allowed • Working farm (cattle breeding)

 Your hostess' faultless attention to detail.

As soon as your foot crosses the threshold of this delightful country seat, rebuilt after the Revolution, you know you'll never want to leave. Perhaps it is because the lady of the house is so clearly determined to pamper her guests? Perhaps it is the romantic rooms named after fragrant flowers? Or is it the well-tended garden, vegetable plot or pond where swans and ducks paddle? An unforgettable experience.

 Two minutes from the Puy du Fou Theme Park.

This fine old secluded farmhouse is typical of the region with its stone walls and round tiled roof. Still a working cattle farm, it also offers spotless B&B rooms whose generous dimensions include high raftered ceilings. In the sitting room, a conscious effort has been made to maintain a stylish rustic character with tiled floor, exposed beams, old furniture and a fireplace. Copious breakfasts served by the friendly hosts.

Access : 5km eastbound: leave on the D 948 towards Niort, then take a left on the D 80

Access : 5km to the north-east of Herbiers on the D 755, then the D 11 and a minor road

PAYS DE LA LOIRE

 29 CHAMBRE D'HÔTE MADAME BONNET
Mme Bonnet

69 rue de l'Abbaye
85420 Maillezais
Tel. 02 51 87 23 00
Fax 02 51 00 72 44
liliane.bonnet@wanadoo.fr
www.accueilvendee.com

Open all year • 5 rooms with bathrooms • €61 to €63, breakfast included • No table d'hôte • Garden, park, car park. Credit cards not accepted, no dogs allowed • Exhibition of antique tools. Boating available

 30 LE PAS-DE-L'ÎLE
M. Pitaud

Le Pas-de-l'Île
85230 Saint-Gervais
Tel. 02 51 68 78 51
Fax 02 51 68 42 01

Closed from 1 Nov to 15 Mar • 2 rooms on the ground floor • €44, breakfast included • No table d'hôte • Garden, car park. Credit cards not accepted, no dogs allowed

 Boating on the marsh's meandering, and mercifully mosquito-free, irrigation channels.

Ancient yew trees in the park, an orchard and a cottage garden encircle this 19C manor and its orangery. The stylish rooms are pleasant; the one under the eaves has a four-poster bed and the one in the former hen house opens directly onto the park. Boat-lovers will enjoy exploring the marsh's multitude of canals. Before leaving, make sure you take a peek at the collection of old clogs and farming tools.

 Boating in the salt marshes.

This appealing low house is a fine example of the architectural style favoured in the Breton-Vendée marshes. Laid out around a central lawn, each of the rooms, decorated with lovely regional antiques, has its own private entrance. The most recent, under the exposed rafters, were our favourites. Don't miss the chance to sample the mouth-watering foie gras, made from ducks reared on the premises. Countless bicycling and boating opportunities.

Access : Near the abbey

Access : 4km to the south-east of Beauvoir on the D 948, then the D 59 and a minor road

31 LE MANOIR DE LA BARBACANE
M. et Mme Baume

2 place de l'Église
85130 Tiffauges
Tel. 02 51 65 75 59
Fax 02 51 65 71 91
hotelbarbacane @ aol.com
www.hotelbarbacane.com

Closed last week in Dec, mid-Marc; late Sep and Sun from
Oct to Apr • 19 rooms with bath/WC or shower/WC and
television • Menus €72 to €115 (€57 to €95 low season),
breakfast €10 • No restaurant • Garden, garage. No
dogs allowed • Outdoor swimming pool, billiards

The aura of living history.

A visit to Barbacane Castle is like stepping back in time
to the Middle Ages, but the hotel itself, installed in a
19C property, bears a rather striking resemblance to an
English manor house! A countrified atmosphere and
numerous knick-knacks set the scene inside. Plans are
afoot to renovate the rather threadbare rooms, some of
which survey the castle of the sinister Gilles de Rais,
former Lord of Tiffauges, but better known as Blue
Beard...

Access : Half-way between Montaigu and Cholet on
the D 753 in the centre of the village

441

PICARDY

Ready for an action-packed ride over Picardy's fair and historic lands? The birthplace of France itself – the first French king, Clovis, was born in Soissons – Picardy is renowned for its wealthy Cistercian abbeys, splendid Gothic cathedrals, flamboyant town halls, marvellous castles, as well as its poignant reminders of the two World Wars. Those who prefer the pleasures of the countryside can take a boat trip through the floating gardens of Amiens, explore the botanical reserve of Marais de Cessière or observe the thousands of birds in the estuary of the Somme and at the Marquenterre bird sanctuary. Acre upon acre of unspoilt hills, woodland, plateaux, copses, pastures and vineyards welcome you with open arms. Picardy's rich culinary talents have been refined over the centuries and it would be unthinkable to leave without tasting the famous *pré-salé* – lamb fattened on the salt marshes – some smoked eel, duck pâté or a dessert laced with Chantilly cream.

- Aisne (02)
- Oise (60)
- Somme (80)

1 VAL-CHRÉTIEN
M. et Mme Sion

Ancienne abbaye du Val Chrétien
02130 Bruyères-sur-Fère
Tel. 03 23 71 66 71
Fax 03 23 71 66 71
Val.chretien@wanadoo.fr

Open all year • 5 rooms upstairs • €54 to €64, breakfast included, half board available • Table d'hôte €20 • Park. Credit cards not accepted, no dogs allowed • Tennis

2 LA TOQUE BLANCHE
M. et Mme Lequeux

24 avenue Victor-Hugo
02300 Chauny
Tel. 03 23 39 98 98
Fax 03 23 52 32 79
info@toque.blanche.fr
www.toque-blanche.fr

Closed from 2 to 4 Jan, 5 to 18 Feb, 2 to 22 Aug, Sat lunchtime, Sun evening and Mon • 6 rooms on 2 floors with bath/WC or shower/WC, 3 have television, 2 are for non-smokers • €72 to €87; breakfast €12; half board available • Air-conditioned restaurant; menus €31 to €70 • Terrace, park, private car park • Tennis

Exceptional location in the heart of the legendary site of the Tardenois.

This building on the banks of the Ourcq and in the heart of the 12C ruins of the Abbey of Val Chrétien is quite remarkable. The rooms are soberly decorated with one striking exception, which is lined in red velvet and complete with a four-poster bed. On the ground floor are a breakfast room with exposed beams and a library where a fire is lit in winter. The covered tennis court is in an outbuilding.

Duck foie gras is the house speciality.

The Toque Blanche (Chef's hat), a lovely 1920s bourgeois house, not only provides comfortable personalised rooms but also offers cooking renowned for its subtle blends of flavours in either an Art Deco or a more classically-inspired dining room. Don't worry if your waistline seems to have expanded during the meal, you can walk off the extra calories in the immense shaded park.

Access : 8km westbound from Fère-en-Tardenois on the D 310, towards Bruyères-sur-Fère, on a by-road

Access : Near the town centre

CHAMBRE D'HÔTE M. LECLÈRE
M. et Mme Leclère

1 rue de Launay
02330 Connigis
Tel. 03 23 71 90 51
Fax 03 23 71 48 57

Closed from 20 to 31 Dec • 4 rooms • €40 to €48, breakfast included • Table d'hôte €15 • Park, car park. No dogs allowed • Bicycle rentals, hiking trails, trout fishing 200m away

AUBERGE DU VAL DE L'OISE
M. et Mme Trokay

8 rue Albert-Ledent
02580 Étréaupont
Tel. 03 23 97 91 10
Fax 03 23 97 48 92
contact @ clos-du-montvinage.fr
www.clos-du-montvinage.fr

Closed 1 week Dec, 1 week Jan and 15 to 22 August • 20 rooms, one has disabled access, with bath/WC or shower/WC and television • €62 to €103; breakfast €9; half board available • Menus €20 to €38 • Terrace, garden, private car park. No dogs allowed • Billiards room

Walking or bicycling through vineyards.

This husband and wife team of Champagne producers has been painstakingly restoring this 16C farmhouse, once part of the Château de Connigis estate, for over ten years now. Thanks to their efforts, guests are now welcomed into spacious rooms with original parquet floors overlooking a magnificent park alongside the vineyards; the room in the tower, slightly removed from the main wing and decorated in an attractive Flemish style, is the quietest. Children's play area and bicycle rentals.

The honeymoon suite and its four-poster bed!

Driving through the village, the eye is drawn to the intricate pattern of the brick walls of this delightful late-19C mansion. A pleasantly old-fashioned atmosphere extends to the well-dimensioned rooms furnished in a Louis-Philippe style, while a recently opened wing is home to the establishment's brand new restaurant, pleasantly decorated and serving traditional French favourites.

Access : 12km eastbound from Château-Thierry on the N 3 and the D 4

Access : On the N 2, between Vervins and La Capelle, in the village

 5 DOMAINE DES PATRUS
M. et Mme Royol

la Haute Épine
02540 L'Épine-aux-Bois
Tel. 03 23 69 85 85
Fax 03 23 69 30 14
contact@domainedespatrus.com
www.domainedespatrus.com

Closed from Dec to Feb • 5 rooms, 2 of which are in the attic with a small sitting room • €70 to €90, breakfast included • Table d'hôte €28-34 (including wine) • Sitting room, library, park, car park. No dogs allowed • Gallery devoted to La Fontaine. Wine and champagne tasting

 6 FERME DE LA MONTAGNE
M. Ferté

02290 Ressons-le-Long
Tel. 03 23 74 23 71
Fax 03 23 74 24 82
lafermedelamontagne@free.fr
http://www.lafermedelamontagne.free.fr

Closed Jan and Feb • 5 rooms with bathrooms • €50, breakfast included • No table d'hôte • Garden, car park. Credit cards not accepted, no dogs allowed • Billiards and piano

We most liked **The collection of paintings devoted to La Fontaine's fables.**

In addition to the comfort it offers, another reason to stop at this handsome farmhouse is the pleasure of waking up in the morning and gazing out onto the peaceful countryside. The individually decorated rooms are furnished in traditional style; those with sloping ceilings have a little private sitting room. The mezzanine in the library is most attractive. Ask to see the owner's collection of works inspired by La Fontaine's fables; she is a fan and is only too happy to explain them.

We most liked **The sweeping view of the Aisne Valley.**

Built on the edge of the plateau, this old farm of the Abbey of Notre-Dame de Soissons whose foundations date back to the 13C, enjoys a superb view of the Aisne Valley. All the generously-sized rooms have independent access and well-equipped bathrooms. A billiards table and piano adorn the sitting room, which also commands a splendid view of the countryside. Warm and welcoming.

Access : 8km westbound from Montmirail on the D 933, towards Meaux

Access : 8km westbound from Soissons on the N 31 and the D 1160

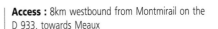

 7 ### AUBERGE LE RELAIS
M. et Mme Berthuit

 2 rue de Paris
02850 Reuilly-Sauvigny
Tel. 03 23 70 35 36
Fax 03 23 70 27 76
auberge.relais.de.reuilly@wanadoo.fr
www.relaisreuilly.com

Closed from 31 Jan to 3 Mar, from 15 Aug to 2 Sep, Tue and Wed • 7 rooms with bath/WC or shower/WC, all are air-conditioned and have television • €70 to €88; breakfast €12 • Air-conditioned restaurant; menus €28 (weekdays) to €73 • Garden, car park. No dogs allowed in rooms

 Limousin veal served with green asparagus in truffle sauce.

The flowered walls of this welcoming roadside-inn invite travellers to pause and stay for a while. The interior decoration reveals a masterful grasp of colour and light: the Provençal or contemporary rooms enjoy a superb view over the Champagne vineyards of the Marne Valley. Not to be outdone, the menu is appetising and up-to-date and served on a terrace-veranda or in the muted atmosphere of the dining room.

Access : In the village by the N 3, between Château-Thierry and Dormans

 8 ### HÔTEL DES CANONNIERS
Mme Michel

 15 rue des Canonniers
02100 Saint-Quentin
Tel. 03 23 62 87 87
Fax 03 23 62 87 86
lescanonniers@aol.com
www.hotel-canonniers.com

Closed from 1 to 15 Aug and Sun evening (except by reservation) • 7 rooms, all of which have equipped kitchenettes, with bath/WC or shower/WC and television • €60 to €105; breakfast €10 • No restaurant • Terrace, garden, private car park • Billiards

Drop by the Lecuyer Museum and admire the portraits by Quentin de La Tour.

Whether you stay for a night or for two weeks, the Canonniers offers superb personalised suites with a kitchenette at wonderfully reasonable prices. This handsome house, built in 1754, provides the service of a hotel and the charm of a maison d'hôte: guests can play billiards or lounge on the terrace opposite the lush green garden. The establishment also caters to businesses and meetings are held in its handsome old reception rooms.

Access : Drive past the town hall, take a left on Rue de la Comédie, past the theatre, turn right

9 MANOIR DE LA SEMOIGNE
M. et Mme Ferry

Chemin de la Ferme
02130 Villers-Agron-Aiguizy
Tel. 03 23 71 60 67
Fax 03 23 69 36 54
xavferry@club-internet.fr
http://manoirdelasemoigne.online.fr

Open all year • 4 rooms with bathrooms • €66 to €84, breakfast included, half board available • Table d'hôte €35 (by reservation only) • Park. Credit cards not accepted, no dogs allowed • Golf

10 LE RÉGENT
M. Brunet

26 rue du Général-Mangin
02600 Villers-Cotterets
Tel. 03 23 96 01 46
Fax 03 23 96 37 57
info@hotel-leregent.com
www.hotel-leregent.com

Open all year • 26 rooms on the front or the back, with bath/WC or shower/WC, all have television • €54 to €74; breakfast €8 • No restaurant • Courtyard, car park

The luxury of an 18-hole golf course right in the grounds.

Golfers will, of course, not be able to resist the prospect of spending a few days in this 18C mansion, whose park and river are home to an attractive golf course. Each of the spacious, quiet bedrooms is named after and decorated in a different colour: beige, blue, yellow, etc. The bathrooms are large and well-equipped. The table d'hôte has laid the accent on wholesome farm produce. If a round of golf doesn't appeal, perhaps tennis or trout fishing will take your fancy.

Remember to bring a copy of The Three Musketeers, written by local boy, Alexander Dumas.

The walls of this elegant 18C mansion, just two minutes from the town, are so smart and spruce they could almost be new. Venture past the porch and say hello to the grey cat – the self-appointed master of the house – before you cross the romantic paved courtyard. Inside, classically decorated rooms in keeping with the architecture await you, some of which should soon be treated to a facelift.

Access : 15km to the south-east of Fère-en-Tardenois

Access : Drive into Villers-Cotterets, the hotel is not far from the town centre, near the post office

  11 LA FERME ANCIENNE DE BELLERIVE
Mme Brunger

492 rue de Bellerive
60170 Cambronne-lès-Ribecourt
Tel. 03 44 75 02 13
Fax 03 44 76 10 34
bellerive@minitel.net
www.bellerive.fr

Open all year • 5 rooms • €50, breakfast included, half board available • Table d'hôte €15 • Garden, car park. Credit cards not accepted, no dogs allowed

  12 RELAIS BRUNEHAUT
M. et Mme Frenel

3 rue de l'Église
60350 Chelles
Tel. 03 44 42 85 05
Fax 03 44 42 83 30

Open all year • 9 rooms, one of which has a kitchenette, all have bath/WC or shower/WC and television • €48 to €55; breakfast €8; half board available • Restaurant closed Mon and Tue lunchtime; menus €23 (weekdays) to €37 • Inner courtyard, garden, private car park. No dogs allowed

 An authentic two-hundred-year-old farmhouse.

This wonderful old farm, poised between canal and river, is a must for anyone who loves tranquillity and authenticity. An old barn houses simple, appealing rooms with white walls, veil curtains and matching bedspreads, in addition to well-appointed bathrooms. The dining room is decorated in appealing rustic tones and the table d'hôte is open for lunch and dinner, serving appetising farm cooking. Lovely garden.

 Disneyland's Sleeping Beauty Castle was partly inspired by that of Pierrefonds.

A stay in this delightful coaching inn, actually two buildings set round a flowered courtyard, is the perfect opportunity to discover Pierrefonds, home to a splendid reconstruction of a medieval Gothic castle masterminded by Napoleon's talented architect, Viollet-le-Duc. The inn's mill, still in working order, houses most of the appealing, rustic rooms, filled with the sound of the gurgling stream nearby. The restaurant serves tasty, traditional cooking.

Access : 7.5km to the south-west of Ourscamps on the N 32 and the D 66

Access : In the centre of the village, 5km eastbound from Pierrefonds on the D 85

CREIL - 60100

GOUVIEUX - 60270

 13 LA FERME DE VAUX
M. et Mme Joly

11 et 19 route de Vaux
60100 Creil
Tel. 03 44 64 77 00
Fax 03 44 26 81 50
joly.eveline@wanadoo.fr

Open all year except Sat lunchtime and Sun evening
• 28 rooms, 10 of which are upstairs, the others are on garden level, all have bath/WC and television • €67; breakfast €8; half board available • Menus €17 to €34 • Car park

 The porcelain of Creil is sought after by collectors from all over the world.

The owners of this old farm take great pleasure in sharing their "art de vivre" with guests. Each of the bedrooms is individually decorated, but the medieval chapel and its far-reaching gastronomic reputation are what attracts gourmets from all over the region. Savour the traditional French cuisine served in a Gothic dining room complete with arched windows and tapestries, or in the other more classical but equally sophisticated dining room. Some temptations are definitely worth giving in to!

Access : On leaving Creil after the crossroads of the N 16/D 120 drive towards Verneuil, on the way into the Vaux Industrial Zone

 14 HOST. DU PAVILLON SAINT-HUBERT
Mme Luck

Avenue de Toutevoie
60270 Gouvieux
Tel. 03 44 57 07 04
Fax 03 44 57 75 42
www.pavillon-sainthubert.com

Closed 15 Jan to 13 Feb, Sun evening and Mon
• 18 rooms, all have bath/WC or shower/WC and television • €50 to €68; breakfast €8; half board available • Menus €25 (weekdays) to €32 • Riverside terrace, garden, car park

 Chocolate lovers should not miss the chance to taste a "Crottin de Chantilly"!

This little gem is hidden at the end of a cul-de-sac, on the banks of the Oise surrounded by acres of peaceful countryside; ask for one of the renovated rooms overlooking the river. In fine weather, let the kids loose in the garden while you linger under the shade of plane trees on the terrace and watch the barges glide gently past. Appetising traditional cuisine.

Access : Leave Chantilly on the D 909 as far as Gouvieux, turn right and at Chaumont take a left into the dead-end road towards the Oise

PICARDY

 15 CHAMBRE D'HÔTE M. BRUANDET
M. et Mme Bruandet

 13 hameau de Bellefontaine
60650 Hannaches
Tel. 03 44 82 46 63
Fax 03 44 82 26 68
bellefontaine@free.fr
 http://bellefontaine.free.fr

Closed in Jan • 3 rooms • €45, breakfast included • Table d'hôte €16 (evening only) • Sitting room, garden. Credit cards not accepted

 16 DOMAINE DU BOIS D'AUCOURT
M. Clément-Bayard

 60350 Pierrefonds
Tel. 03 44 42 80 34
Fax 03 44 42 80 36
bois.d.aucourt@wanadoo.fr
www.boisdaucourt.com

Open all year • 11 rooms with bath/WC • €69 to €107, breakfast €8 • No restaurant • Car park. No dogs allowed • Tennis, walking, mountain biking, horse-riding

The rooms are furnished with unique and quite unusual pieces.

Visitors to this former 19C Picardy farmhouse are often intrigued by both the interior and exterior decoration, all of which is the work of the talented sculptor-owner. Modern furniture adorns the relatively sober rooms, one of which has a mezzanine. The garden is strewn with the owner's metal sculptures, made from salvaged materials such as old farming equipment and everyday scrap. Highly original, to say the least...and most welcoming.

A handsome family property surrounded by foliage.

The peaceful silence of the forest of Compiègne has crept into the walls of this large 19C half-timbered manor house. The rooms, all non-smoking, are decorated individually and all have faultless bathrooms. The only problem is deciding between the "Scottish", "Sevillan", "Tuscan", "Zen" or "Tropical" rooms. Breakfast is served in your hosts' warm, welcoming kitchen.

Access : 5km to the south-west of Gerberoy on the D 930, then the D 104 towards Bellefontaine

Access : 1.6km westbound from Pierrefonds on the D 85

ARGOULES - 80120

CREUSE - 80480

17 ABBAYE DE VALLOIRES
Assocation de Valloires

80120 Argoules
Tel. 03 22 29 62 33
Fax 03 22 29 62 24
contact @ abbaye-valloires.com
www.abbaye-valloires.com

Closed at Christmas and New Year • 18 non-smoking rooms • €52 to €90, breakfast €6 • No table d'hôte • Garden, car park. No dogs allowed • Visits to the abbey, concerts in season

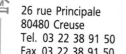

18 LA CHAUMIÈRE
Mme Lemaître

26 rue Principale
80480 Creuse
Tel. 03 22 38 91 50
Fax 03 22 38 91 50
monique.p.lemaitre @ wanadoo.fr

Closed in winter • 2 rooms and one suite • €65 to €92, breakfast included • No table d'hôte • Sitting room, garden, car park. Credit cards not accepted, no dogs allowed

The historic walls of this abbey still offer sanctuary to travellers.

The Abbey of Valloires, a renowned tourist site, also operates a B&B establishment to help preserve and safeguard its rich architectural heritage. Located in a wing rebuilt in the 18C, the rooms, originally the monks' cells, are surprisingly spacious and attractively furnished: all overlook the superb monastery gardens. Who could resist breakfasting in the refectory of the former Cistercian community?

Snuggle up in this appealing Picardy home.

A national forest lies just two minutes from the little village, home to this delightful late-18C regional-style farmhouse. The lady of the house, also an artist, clearly has a flair for interior decoration as is shown by the white-washed walls and lovely regional furnishings in the rooms and the snug breakfast and sitting rooms where a fire roars in a period fireplace in winter. Trees nearly as old the house itself are dotted around the rambling, peaceful garden.

Access : In the abbey

Access : 14km to the south-west of Amiens

PICARDY

  19 CHAMBRE D'HÔTE DU PETIT CHÂTEAU
M. Saguez

2 rue Grimaux
80480 Dury
Tel. 03 22 95 29 52
Fax 03 22 95 29 52
alainsaguez @ libertysurf.fr

Open all year • 4 non-smoking rooms, one of which is on ground level, all have bathrooms • €63, breakfast included • No table d'hôte • Sitting room, garden, park, car park. Credit cards not accepted, no dogs allowed • Horse-drawn carriage rides

  20 LES TOURELLES
M. et Mme Ferreira Da Silva

2 rue Pierre-Guerlain
80550 Le Crotoy
Tel. 03 22 27 16 33
Fax 03 22 27 11 45
lestourelles @ nhgroupe.com
www.lestourelles.com

Closed from 5 to 31 Jan • 27 rooms, most have shower/WC, the others have bath/WC, some have television • €57 to €75; breakfast €8; half board available • Menus €20 to €29 • Unusual children's dormitory

 The appeal of a countryside setting, just a ten-minute drive from the centre of Amiens.

You will soon forget the nearby road when you see the wonderful country setting of this 19C house and are warmly greeted by the convivial owners. The rooms, non-smoking only, are located in a separate wing and are for the most part spacious, but the smallest of them is also the cosiest. The substantial breakfast, taken in the company of your discreet hosts, will set you up for the day.

 The children's "dorm".

The fairy-tale twin turrets of this 19C red and white brick mansion dominate the tiny seaside resort and the "only south-facing beach of the North" (Pierre Guerlain). Most of the rooms, on a contemporary seafaring theme or in a delightfully clean-lined Swedish style, overlook the bay of the Somme. Delicious mounds of fresh fish and seafood will restore the disconsolate spirits of unlucky "shrimpers".

Access : 6km southbound from Amiens on the N 1 towards Beauvais

Access : Overlooking the bay, on the beach road

PORT-LE-GRAND - 80132

QUEND - 80120

21 CHAMBRES D'HÔTES
DU BOIS DE BONANCE
M. et Mme Maillard

Bois-de-Bonance
80132 Port-le-Grand
Tel. 03 22 24 11 97
Fax 03 22 31 72 01
maillard.chambrehote@bonance.com
www.bonance.com

Closed from 12 Nov to 15 Feb • 5 rooms, 2 of which are in a separate wing, with bath/WC • €70, breakfast included • No table d'hôte • Garden • Swimming pool, keep-fit track, table-tennis, children's play area

The charm of a country garden.

You may be amused to learn that the pink walls and narrow Gothic-style windows of this 19C holiday home, in a secluded spot far from the bustle of traffic, are sometimes described as "English"! Whatever, the antique furnished rooms have been decorated with infinite taste; those in the former servants' quarters open directly onto the beautiful garden, brimming with flowers in the summer. In the winter, a cheerful fire adds warmth to the pleasant breakfast room.

Access : 11km eastbound from Saint-Valery-sur-Somme on the D 940, then the D 40 and a minor road

22 AUBERGE LE FIACRE
M. et Mme Masmonteil

6 rue des Pommiers
Hameau de Routhiauville
80120 Quend
Tel. 03 22 23 47 30
Fax 03 22 27 19 80
lefiacre@wanadoo.fr
www.aufiacre.fr

Closed mid-Jan to mid-Feb • 11 rooms, one of which has disabled access and 3 are suites. Most rooms have bath/WC, some have shower/WC and television • €73 to €78; breakfast €12; half board available • Restaurant closed Tue and Wed lunchtimes; menus €19 (weekdays) to €40 • Garden, car park. No dogs allowed in rooms • Golf course 1.5km away

Fancy a quick two-kilometre-run in the dunes?

An old farm has been converted into an appealing inn surrounded in foliage, where the restful, welcoming rooms open onto the lovely garden. In addition, three more modern apartments have recently been created. The restaurant, for its part, has retained a resolutely country style with exposed beams and tiled floors, a perfect setting for its classic repertoire. Character and quality: what more could you want!

Access : Leave the D 940 at Quend, between Berck-sur-Mer and Rue, and take the D 32 towards Fort-Mahon-Plage

 23 LA FERME DU CHÂTEAU DE LA MOTTE
M. et Mme Libert

36 route de Froise
80120 Quend-plage
Tel. 03 22 23 94 48
Fax 03 22 23 97 57
www.edoniaa.com

Open all year • 5 rooms with bath/WC and television
• €62 to €78, breakfast included • No table d'hôte
• Garden, park, car park. No dogs allowed • Outdoor
swimming pool, tennis, table-tennis, fishing, mountain
bike rental, clay pigeon shooting

 24 CHAMBRE D'HÔTE MADAME SERVANT
Mme Servant

117 rue Au-Feurre
80230 Saint-Valery-sur-Somme
Tel. 03 22 60 97 56
Fax 03 22 60 97 56

Closed at Christmas • 4 rooms and 2 suites • €50 to €56,
breakfast included • No table d'hôte • Garden. Credit
cards not accepted, no dogs allowed

 The difficulty is agreeing on what to do!

The perfect "pied-à-terre" to explore the bay of the
Somme: the spacious, comfortable rooms have been
installed on the first floor of an old farmhouse and all
overlook open fields and meadows. Guests have the run
of an immense park with pond, tennis courts and
table-tennis table. Nearby a vast range of paying
activities await those with energy to spare: bicycle and
mountain-bike rentals, fishing, clay pigeon shooting and
hunting. Riders are also welcome.

 **The wonderful view of the unspoilt
bay of the Somme from the Porte
Guillaume.**

This country house and neat garden stand in the upper
part of town, just round the corner from the elegant 12C
Porte Guillaume flanked by two towers. Each of the
rooms has been decorated on a different theme: blue
and white for the sea and sailors, old posters in the
cinema room and shades of green and wrought-iron
furniture in the garden room. The breakfast room is light
and airy and your hosts unfailingly friendly and
welcoming.

Access : 11km to the north-east of Rue on the D
940 then the D 32

Access : In the historic town, near the church and
the town hall

25 LA GRIBANE
M. et Mme Douchet

297 quai Jeanne-d'Arc
80230 Saint-Valery-sur-Somme
Tel. 03 22 60 97 55

Closed in Jan • 4 rooms • €68 to €82, breakfast included • No table d'hôte • Park, car park. Credit cards not accepted, no dogs allowed

26 LE RELAIS GUILLAUME DE NORMANDY
MM. Crimet et Dupré

Quai du Romerel
80230 Saint-Valery-sur-Somme
Tel. 03 22 60 82 36
Fax 03 22 60 81 82
relais-guillaume@wanadoo.fr
www.guillaumedenormandy.com

Closed from 19 Dec to 10 Jan and Tue • 14 rooms, all have bath/WC or shower/WC and television • €50 to €65; breakfast €8; half board available • Air-conditioned restaurant; menus €16 to €42 • Terrace, car park. No dogs allowed in restaurant

The garden has been created in a polder opposite the ramparts.

This 1930 house takes its name from the 18C merchant vessel used to navigate the rivers. The rooms of the main wing, painted in tones of blue, white and beige, overlook the bay; the others are in a pavilion in the middle of the garden. The large bay windows of the breakfast room look out onto the wonderful garden, wedged between the land reclaimed from the sea and the old city walls.

A trip across the bay of the Somme aboard a real steam train.

Take in the lovely Picardy coast from the windows of this elegant manor house facing the bay and on the outskirts of St-Valery-sur-Somme. None of the rooms are enormous, but half face the Channel, where you will sometimes be able to catch a glimpse of seals. The soberly decorated panoramic dining room also enables diners to enjoy the view while sampling the delicious traditional fare rustled up by the chef.

Access : In the historic town, near the beach

Access : On the dike, opposite the bay of the Somme

POITOU-CHARENTES

Illustrious names such as Cognac, Angoulême or La Rochelle all echo through France's history, but there is just as much to appreciate in the here and now. Start your journey lazing on the sandy beaches of its unspoilt coastline where the scent of pine trees mingles with the fresh sea air. A stay in a thalassotherapy resort will revive your flagging spirits, further boosted by a platter of oysters and lightly buttered bread. A bicycle is the best way to discover the region's delightfully unhilly coastal islands as you pedal along quaint little country lanes, lined with tiny blue and white cottages and multico-loured hollyhocks. Back on the mainland, embark on a barge and explore the thousand and one canals of the marshy, and mercifully mosquito-free, "Green Venice". You will have earned yourself a taste of vintage Cognac, or perhaps a glass of the less heady local apéritif, the fruity, ice-cold Pineau. If all this seems just too restful, head for Futuroscope, a theme park devoted to the moving image, and enjoy an action-packed day or two of life in the future.

- Charente (16)
- Charente-Maritime (17)
- Deux-Sèvres (79)
- Vienne (86)

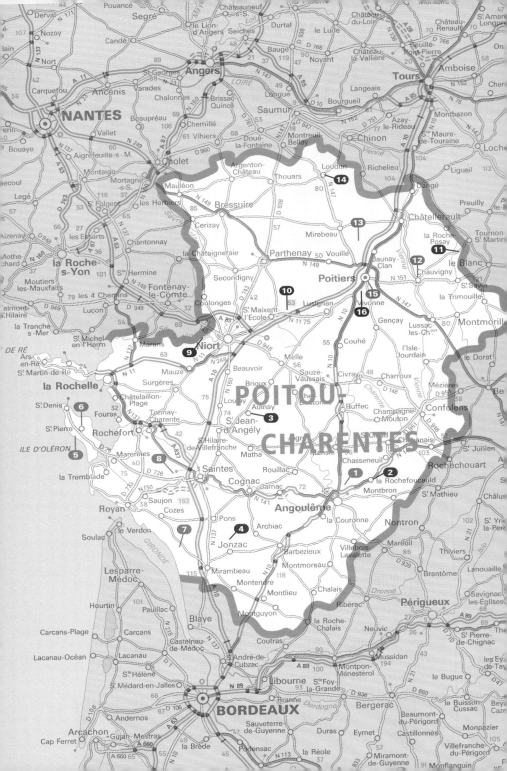

 1 LA TEMPLERIE
M. et Mme Richon

Denat
16430 Champniers
Tel. 05 45 68 49 00
 Fax 05 45 68 91 18

Open all year • 5 rooms, 2 of which are on the ground floor, all have bath/WC • €42, breakfast included • No table d'hôte • Disabled access, garden, car park. No dogs allowed in restaurant • Outdoor swimming pool

 2 LA VIEILLE AUBERGE DE LA CARPE D'OR
M. Ballanger et Mme Moreau

1 rue de Vitrac
16110 La Rochefoucauld
Tel. 05 45 62 02 72
 Fax 05 45 63 01 88

Open all year • 25 rooms, 2 of which have disabled access, all have bath/WC or shower/WC and television • €36 to €48; breakfast €5.50; half board available • Menus €10 (weekdays) to €33 • Private car park 50m away

The windows of this farm have enjoyed the same pastoral view for two hundred years.

Guests are always assured of a warm welcome within this typically regional farmhouse. The rooms, located in the former outbuildings, are colourful and some are furnished with antiques; two open directly onto the garden and the swimming pool. In the winter, a cheerful fire is lit in the immense dining room. The sitting room with a lovely library on a mezzanine particularly caught our fancy.

The atmosphere is so easy-going, you could almost come down to breakfast in your slippers!

A small watchtower adorns the façade of this well-preserved 16C inn. The sweet scent of beeswax greets you in the dining and sitting rooms and reception, which have all kept a distinctly rustic character. Pristine bedrooms are furnished in a variety of styles; some have canopied beds. Breakfast is served in a wainscoted room with a lovely herringbone parquet floor.

Access : 9.5km northbound from Angoulême towards Poitiers on the N 10, then Balzac on the D 105

Access : In the town centre, on a street corner

 3 LE DONJON
M. et Mme Imbach

4 rue des Hivers
17470 Aulnay
Tel. 05 46 33 67 67
Fax 05 46 33 67 64
hotel-du-donjon@wanadoo.fr
www.hoteldudonjon.com

Open all year • 10 rooms, one of which has disabled access, all have bath/WC or shower/WC and television • €61 to €69 (€54 to €61 low season); breakfast €6 • No restaurant

 Long chats around the fire in the sitting room.

The green shuttered façade of this house stands near the Church of St Pierre, a masterpiece of regional Romanesque architecture. The interior of the house has been carefully restored in order to preserve the lovely old beams and gold-coloured limestone walls. Old furniture graces all the rooms and the bedrooms are further brightened by colourful bedspreads and matching curtains; all have modern bathrooms.

Access : In the heart of the village, near the main square

 4 LE VIEUX LOGIS
Mme Brard

3 rue du 8-mai-1945
17500 Clam
Tel. 05 46 70 20 13
Fax 05 46 70 20 64
info@vieuxlogis.com

Closed 9 to 31 Jan, Sun evening and Mon lunchtime (except in season) • 10 ground-floor rooms with bath/WC or shower/WC and television • €48 to €58, breakfast €7, half board available • Air-conditioned restaurant; menus €15 to €34 • Terrace, garden, car park. No dogs allowed in rooms • Outdoor swimming pool, photo exhibitions

 The owners' warm welcome and infectious good nature.

This 'Old Abode' was formerly home to the village's café-grocer's shop. The tiny cup of piping hot espresso on the bar and the shelves laden with tins and jars have since made way for two country-style dining rooms, the walls of which are adorned by photos taken by the master of the house. His cheerful spouse rustles up tasty local dishes. The modern ground-floor building opens onto the garden and the comfortable, pleasant rooms are equipped with terraces.

Access : 6km northbound of Jonzac on the D 142

 5 LES TRÉMIÈRES
Mme Frat

5 route de Saint-Pierre
17310 La Cotinière
Tel. 05 46 47 44 25
www.chambres-lestremieres.com

Open all year • 4 rooms, 2 of which are suites • €43 to €51 (€37 to €45 low season), breakfast €7 • No table d'hôte • Garden, car park. Credit cards not accepted

 6 MADAME MICHELINE DENIEAU
Mme Denieau

20 rue de la Legère, la Menounière
17310 Saint-Pierre-d'Oléron
Tel. 05 46 47 14 34
Fax 05 46 36 03 15
denieau.jean-pierre@wanadoo.fr

Open all year • 5 rooms • €49, breakfast included • No table d'hôte • Garden, car park. Credit cards not accepted

 Just two minutes from the port and its brightly-coloured fishing boats.

This early 20C house with sandy-coloured walls and blue shutters is only a short walk from the port of La Cotinière and its shops. All the rooms and suites are personalised and immaculately cared for. Take things easy in the comfortable leather sofas and armchairs by the fireside in the sitting room. In the summertime, breakfast is served under the chestnut tree.

 Bicycling round the island as you explore its oyster beds and farms.

Oléron wines and the famous Pineau - a fortified aperitif - are still produced on the estate of this stone farmhouse which is a fine example of island architecture. The neat and simple rooms are in the outbuildings; the most recent have old furniture and gaily painted green or blue beams; those with a mezzanine are very popular with families. Guests have the run of a kitchen, complete with an old kneading trough and a fireplace.

Access : 600m from the entrance to the village coming from Maisonneuve

Access : 3km westbound from Saint-Pierre-d'Oléron

463

 7 LE CHÂTEAU DES SALLES
Mme Couillaud

Carrefour D 125 et D 730
17240 Saint-Fort-sur-Gironde
Tel. 05 46 49 95 10
Fax 05 46 49 02 81
chateaudessalles@wanadoo.fr
www.cateaudessalles.com

Closed 15 Oct to Easter • 5 rooms • €100, breakfast €9
• Table d'hôte €34 • Park, garden, car park. Dogs not
allowed • Cognac and Pineau de Charentes on sale

 8 CHAMBRE D'HÔTE M. TROUVÉ
M. et Mme Trouvé

5 rue de l'Église
17810 Saint-Georges-des-Coteaux
Tel. 05 46 92 96 66
Fax 05 46 92 96 66
adtrouve@yahoo.fr

Closed from 15 Nov to 1 Apr • 4 rooms • €47, breakfast
included • No table d'hôte • Garden, car park. Credit
cards not accepted, no dogs allowed • Tennis and
horse-riding centre in the village

 The delicious fare on the table d'hôte lit by candles in the evenings.

 Each bedroom pays light-hearted tribute to a famous author.

The owners of the 15C castle, entirely renovated in the 19C, produce their own Pineau, a delicious aperitif, as well as wines and cognac, which can be bought from the estate. The tastefully furnished, south-facing rooms open onto the garden and its sumptuous magnolia tree; the largest room, under the eaves, displays a happy blend of old and contemporary styles. Lovely old furniture, a piano and a games table grace the sitting room. Candle-lit dining in the evenings.

You will not be disappointed should you decide to spend a night or two in this 18C farmstead, surrounded by a large garden. The cow-shed and barn have been turned into an immense room which serves as a combined lobby, sitting room, library and billiards room. Country furniture adorns the bedrooms, each named after a favourite author – Agatha Christie and Tintin's creator, Hergé, are among them. Make sure you take a look at the old wash house or "bujor".

Access : 7.5km South-east of Mortagne by D 145 and D 125

Access : 9km to the north-west of Saintes towards Rochefort on the N 137 then the D 127

 9 AU MARAIS
Mme Nerrière

46 quai Louis-Hardy
79510 Coulon
Tel. 05 49 35 90 43
Fax 05 49 35 81 98
information @ hotel-aumarais.com
www.hotel-aumarais.com

Closed from 15 Dec to 5 Feb • 18 rooms located in 2 houses, one has disabled access. Rooms have bath/WC or shower/WC, all have television • €70 to €75 (€55 to €65 low season); breakfast €12 • No restaurant

 10 L'ORANGERIE
M. et Mme Drouiteau

 10 route de l'Atlantique
79800 Soudan
Tel. 05 49 06 56 06
Fax 05 49 06 56 10
www.lorangerie-hotel.com

Closed Feb holidays, Sun evening and Wed • 7 rooms, half of which are at the rear, all have bath/WC or shower/WC and television • €34 to €62; breakfast €7; half board available • Menus €15 to €41 • Terrace, garden, car park

 Glide over the waters of "Green Venice".

A perfect place to begin exploring the aquatic maze of what is known as "Green Venice". The pale stone walls and blue shutters of this pair of 19C boatmen's houses face the marsh's landing stage. The modern, cheerful rooms are decorated with bold Provençal fabrics and most give onto the toing-and-froing of the boats. In summer, the area is busy during the day but after nightfall, all becomes peaceful and car-free!

 Lina and Alain's enthusiastic greeting.

This 19C orangery was formerly a wrought-iron workshop. The unpretentious rooms are gradually being renovated; we suggest booking one of those to the rear, which are quieter. The breakfast room is on the veranda and the wine-coloured restaurant overlooks the shaded garden. Just down the road, Bougon is home to five prehistoric tumuli, offering a wonderful opportunity for old and young to travel back in time 5 000 years.

Access : Near the landing stage where boat trips leave

Access : In the centre of the village, on the N 11 from Niort to Poitiers

 11 LE RELAIS DU LYON D'OR
M. Thoreau

 4 rue d'Enfer
86260 Angles-sur-l'Anglin
Tel. 05 49 48 32 53
Fax 05 49 84 02 28
thoreau@lyondor.com
www.lyondor.com

Closed in Dec, Jan and Feb, Tue lunchtime and Mon
• 11 rooms, one of which has disabled access and one
is split-level, all have bath/WC or shower/WC and
television • €65 to €80 (€55 to €70 low season);
breakfast €8; half board available • Restaurant open
7 days/week for guests; menus €23 to €29 • Terrace,
garden, private car park

 Relaxing in the idyllic garden.

In a picturesque village, perched on a rocky outcrop,
this former 15C coaching inn offers personalised rooms
furnished with items picked up in antique shops. The
owners clearly have their guests' physical and cultural
well-being at heart as is shown by the beauty centre
(hammam, massages, etc) and the numerous art courses
organised in the spring and autumn (patina, sponge or
rag painting, plastering, etc).

 12 LA VEAUDEPIERRE
M. de Giafferi

 8 rue du Berry
86300 Chauvigny
Tel. 05 49 46 30 81
Fax 05 49 47 64 12
 laveaudepierre@club-internet.fr

Open all year • 5 rooms • €40 to €47, breakfast included
• No table d'hôte • Garden, car park. Credit cards not
accepted, no dogs allowed

 At the foot of the medieval city.

We were charmed by this superb 18C mansion
dominated by the ruins of the baronial castle. The
interior is particularly rich in wonderful decoration,
including woodwork, period furniture, a lovely stone
staircase and a collection of antique musical instru-
ments. Bedrooms in stylish fabrics all overlook the
walled garden. The hotel is at the foot of steps which
lead to the upper town.

Access : In the centre of the village

Access : From the town hall, take the first left after
the church

 13 CHÂTEAU DE LABAROM
M. et Mme Le Gallais

86380 Cheneché
Tel. 05 49 51 24 22
Fax 05 49 51 47 38
chateau.de.labarom @ wanadoo.fr

Closed from 1 Nov to 30 Mar • 3 rooms • €53.50 to €69, breakfast included • No table d'hôte • Dovecote, park, car park. Credit cards not accepted, no dogs allowed • Outdoor swimming pool

  14 HÔTEL - RESTAURANT DE LA ROUE D'OR
M. Cuvier

1 avenue d'Anjou
86200 Loudun
Tel. 05 49 98 01 23
Fax 05 49 98 85 45

Closed Sun evening and Sat from Oct to mid-Apr • 14 rooms, one of which has disabled access, with bath/WC or shower/WC and television • €43, breakfast €6, half board available • Menus €14 (weekdays) to €35 • Private car park, terrace

 Oh la la! Row upon row of books about the region and all in French!

This 16C and 17C château was built in three hundred acres of parkland. It makes an ideal base camp to explore the region. We loved the well-worn aristocratic feel of the creaky floor boards and old furniture. The spacious rooms are lined in fabric and graced with beautiful antiques: the monumental period fireplace in the breakfast room cannot fail to catch the eye. The owner, who dabbles in art in his spare time, will happily talk you through the rudiments of painting on porcelain.

 Sometimes you may even think you can hear the wheels of the horse-drawn carriages of yesteryear!

The stables still visible in the large courtyard are a constant reminder of the house's former vocation as a coaching inn. The establishment's small rooms are so well soundproofed that you probably won't even notice that it is next door to the ring road. Furnished in a Louis Philippe-style, the rooms are regularly smartened up. A plush, bourgeois dining room provides the setting for tasty traditional cuisine, which displays a distinct preference for local produce.

Access : 15km to the north-west of Futuroscope towards Neuville and Lencloître then the D 15

Access : In the town near Amirault Park

POITOU CHARENTES

 15 CHÂTEAU DE VAUMORET
M. Johnson

Rue du Breuil-Mingot
86000 Poitiers
Tel. 05 49 61 32 11
Fax 05 49 01 04 54
chateau-vaumoret @ tiscali.fr

Open all year • 5 rooms with bath/WC • €54 to €68,
breakfast included • No table d'hôte • Park, car park.
Credit cards not accepted

 16 LE CHALET DE VENISE
M. et Mme Mautret

6 rue du Square
86280 Saint-Benoît
Tel. 05 49 88 45 07
Fax 05 49 52 95 44

Closed during Feb school holidays and last week in Aug
• 12 rooms, one of which has disabled access, with
bath/WC and television • €58; breakfast €7 • Restaurant
closed Sun eve and Mon; menus €19 (weekdays) to €45
• Terrace, garden, car park

 **A countryside setting on the doorstep
of Poitiers.**

Nearly 45 acres of green meadows and woodland
encircle this beautifully restored 17C mansion. The
rooms, in the right wing, boast some fine old furniture,
prints and paintings and all have immaculate bathrooms. Enjoy breakfast in a light, airy room, then borrow
a bike and start exploring.

 **A former Benedictine abbey is the site
for this sleepy village.**

The austere walls conceal a sumptuous interior. The bay
windows of the elegant dining room overlook a riverside
garden and some of the modern, practical rooms have
a balcony. The riverside terrace is quite idyllic in fine
weather, while the meals are imaginative enough to
tempt even the most discerning palates. Heaven for
gourmets!

Access : 10km north-east of Poitiers towards La
Roche-Posay on the D 3, then Sèvres-Anxaumont on
the D 18

Access : In the village, 4km southbound from Poitiers
on the D 88, near the town hall

PROVENCE, ALPS and the FRENCH RIVIERA

As you listen to the fishmongers hawking their wares under its sunny blue skies, you cannot help but fall in love with the infectious, happy-go-lucky spirit of Marseilles. Elsewhere, the steady chirring of the cicadas is interrupted only by the sheep-bells ringing in the hills as the shepherds bring their flocks home at night. The sun rises early over the ochre walls of hilltop villages which keep a careful watch over the fields of lavender below. Venture into the multitude of tiny hinterland villages and slow down to the gentle pace of the villagers as they leave the shade of the lime trees for the refreshingly cool walls of the café. However, come 2pm, you will soon begin to wonder where everyone is. On hot summer afternoons, everyone exercises their God-given right to a nap, from the fashionable beaches of Saint Tropez and seaside cabins of the Camargue to medieval walled cities surrounded by cypresses or a tiny fishing boat off the coast of Toulon. As the sun begins to set, life starts up again and the players of pétanque emerge; join them as they down a glass of pastis, then feast on bubbling *bouillabaisse*.

- Alpes-de-Haute-Provence (04)
- Hautes-Alpes (05)
- Alpes-Maritimes (06)
- Bouches-du-Rhône (13)
- Var (83)
- Vaucluse (84)

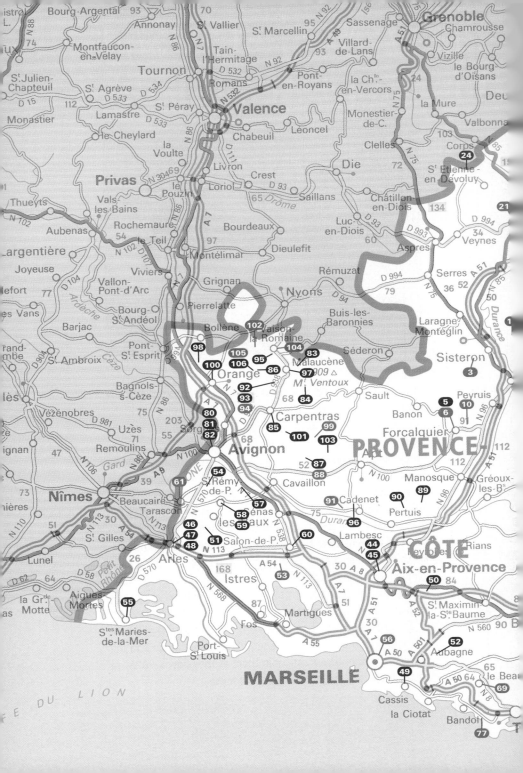

 1   L'AVENUE
M. Génovesi

 Avenue de la Gare
04240 Annot
Tel. 04 92 83 22 07
Fax 04 92 83 33 13
hot.avenue@wanadoo.fr

Closed from Nov to Apr • 11 rooms with shower/WC, all have television • €53 to €56; breakfast €8, half board available • Restaurant closed Wed and Fri lunchtimes; menus €16 (weekdays) to €25 (reservations advised) • No dogs allowed in restaurant

 2   AZTECA
M. Chabre

3 rue François-Arnaud
04400 Barcelonnette
Tel. 04 92 81 46 36
Fax 04 92 81 43 92
www.hotel-azteca.fr.st

Closed from 14 Nov to 5 Dec • 27 rooms, 5 of which are split-level and one has disabled access. Rooms have bath/WC and television • €60 to €95; breakfast €8 to €11 • No restaurant • Private car park, private shuttle bus to the ski resorts • Nearby: swimming pool, tennis, 6-hole golf course, horse-riding, climbing, alpine and white-water sports

 Ambling through the pretty village of Annot and admiring its lanes lined with old houses.

The attractive ochre façade of this regional-style house is impossible to miss as you drive into the village. Excellent soundproofing, practical furnishings and spotless housekeeping are just a few of the appeals of the rooms, all of which sport the warm colours of the south of France. The owner-chef enjoys delving into the region's flavours and scents for his tasty cuisine and the lady of the house is as cheerful as the sunny south itself.

 The fascinating link between this tiny mountain village and Mexico.

A wing has recently been added to this "Mexican" villa built in 1888 by one of the many farmers and craftsmen who left the hills of Ubaye to seek their fortune in the New World, and returned to mark their success in grand style. The hotel's Latin American theme, which may surprise at first but is in fact common throughout the valley, features naive "mural" paintings, an Aztec calendar and arts and crafts from Mexico. We were particularly taken with the three "Mexican" bedrooms.

Access : On the way into the village

Access : Near the post office

 3 MAS DU FIGUIER

M. Levrault

La Fontaine
04200 Bevons
Tel. 04 92 62 81 28
Fax 04 92 62 81 28
mas.du.figuier @ wanadoo.fr
www.guideprovence.com/gites/masdufigier

Closed in Nov, Dec and Jan • 3 rooms with bathrooms • €47 to €65, breakfast included, half board available • Table d'hôte €19 • Park, car park. Credit cards not accepted

 Trekking up to the ridge of the Lure – on donkey-back!

A field of lavender stretches in front of this remote 17C mas – or Provençal farm – which stands at an altitude of 650m opposite the Lure Mountain. A proudly southern flavour prevails in the welcoming rooms, decorated in warm colours with tiled ceilings and exposed beams. We particularly liked the large bathrooms and their Moorish influence. In the winter, the fireside in the sitting room is definitely the cosiest spot in the house.

Access : 18km westbound from Sisteron on the N 85, the D 946 and the D 553

 4 VILLA GAÏA

M. et Mme Martin

24 route de Nice
04000 Digne-les-Bains
Tel. 04 92 31 21 60
Fax 04 92 31 20 12
hotel.gaia @ wanadoo.fr
www.hotelvilla.gaia.fr

Open from Easter to 1 Nov • 10 rooms with bath/WC or shower/WC • €65 to €96; breakfast €8.50, half board available • Restaurant closed 1 to 10 Jul, 28 to 31 Aug and Wed; menus (guests only and evening only) €26 to €32 • Sitting rooms, library, terrace, park, car park. No dogs admitted

 Listen to the wind rustling through the leaves of the ancient trees in the park as you fall asleep.

A relaxed family atmosphere reigns throughout this villa built in 1730, reworked in the early 20C and finally turned into a hotel in 1993. The period furniture, knick knacks, tiles and well-preserved woodwork visible throughout the comfortable rooms, library and sitting rooms bear witness to the villa's past. In the evening, guests of the Villa Gaïa gather in the attractive plush dining room to sample an enticingly simple set menu.

Access : Take the N 85 towards Nice for 2km

5 AUBERGE CHAREMBEAU
M. Berger

Route de Niozelles
04300 Forcalquier
Tel. 04 92 70 91 70
Fax 04 92 70 91 83
contact@charembeau.com
www.charembeau.com

Open from 15 Feb to 15 Nov • 24 rooms, one of which
has disabled access, with bath/WC or shower/WC, all
have television, some have a balcony or terrace • €57 to
€87 (€54 to €82 low season); breakfast €9 • No
restaurant • Park, car park. No dogs allowed • Swimming
pool, tennis, bicycles, horse-riding, mountain-bike rentals

**What better way to explore the region
than by bicycle or on horse-back (on
request)!**

This lovely 18C farmhouse, which lies in a secluded
landscape of hill and dale, enjoys the patronage of
regular, satisfied customers. The lady of the house chose
the Provençal fittings and fixtures in the well-
proportioned bedrooms herself. The house doesn't have
a restaurant but guests are welcome to picnic in the
shaded park and perhaps taste the famous local
goat's-cheese, known as banon.

6 CAMPAGNE « LE PARADIS »
M. Pourcin

04300 Forcalquier
Tel. 04 92 75 37 33
campagneleparadis@wanadoo.fr
www.campagneleparadis.com

Open all year • 4 rooms • €55, breakfast included • No
table d'hôte • Garden, terrace, car park. Credit cards not
accepted, no dogs allowed

**Horses everywhere – the riding
stables are only a horseshoe's throw
away!**

The old horse mangers and photos on the walls of the
vaulted breakfast room bear witness to the establishment's long-standing relations with our four-legged
friends. The old farmhouse nestles at the foot of a
citadel, overlooking the quiet countryside. The immaculate bare walls of the bedrooms in the old barn add
a monastical flavour; two have a mezzanine.

Access : Eastbound from Forcalquier, on the N 100
towards Niozelles for 2.5km, then right on a minor
road

Access : Villeneuve road on the D 16 and the D 216

7 MAISON D'HÔTE DES MÉANS
Mme Millet

Les Méans
04340 Méolans-Revel
Tel. 04 92 81 03 91
Fax 04 92 81 03 91

Closed from Oct to May • 4 rooms and one suite, all have bath/WC • €62 to €95 (€60 to €90 low season), breakfast included • Sitting room, terrace, garden, car park. No dogs allowed

8 LE CLOS DES IRIS
Mlle Dorche-Teissier

Le Pavillon Saint-Michel
04360 Moustiers-Sainte-Marie
Tel. 04 92 74 63 46
Fax 04 92 74 63 59
closdesiris@wanadoo.fr
www.closdesiris.fr

Closed from 1 to 26 Dec • 6 rooms and 2 suites with shower/WC • €65 (€60 low season); breakfast €9 • No restaurant • Garden, terrace

 A glimpse of the typical interior of houses in the valley.

Built when this secluded mountain region still swore allegiance to the counts of Savoy, this 16C farmhouse at an altitude of 1 000m is just the place to get away from it all and catch up on your beauty sleep. The spacious, well-appointed rooms all have lovely bathrooms with earthenware tiles; some also have a balcony. In the winter, a roaring log fire takes the chill off the large vaulted room on the ground floor. In the summertime, meals are often served in the garden, near the old bread oven.

 Cat-napping on a deck chair under the trellis.

We fell head over heels for this blue-shuttered mas surrounded by greenery at the foot of the village. All the garden-level rooms and suites have private terraces equipped with garden tables and deck chairs, protected from the sun by a bower of sweet-scented climbing roses. The bathrooms are tiled with the lovely rustic tiles of Salernes, a famous tile village just a short way down the road to Toulon.

Access : 4km from Martinet on the D 900, Gap road

Access : 400m from the village, on the Chemin de Quinson

9 MONASTÈRE DE SEGRIÈS

M. et Mme Allègre

04360 Moustiers-Sainte-Marie
Tel. 04 92 74 64 32
Fax 04 92 74 64 22
c.allegre @ wanadoo.fr

Closed from Nov to Mar • 5 rooms with bathrooms • €50, breakfast included, half board available • Table d'hôte €18 • Terrace, park, car park. Credit cards not accepted, no dogs allowed

10 JAS DES NEVIÈRES

M. Duermael

Route de Saint-Pierre
04300 Pierrerue
Tel. 04 92 75 24 99
Fax 04 92 75 03 75
duermael @ wanadoo.fr
http://jas-des-nevieres.com

Closed from 1 Nov to 31 Mar • 4 rooms, 2 of which are on the ground floor with shower/WC, the 2 upstairs have bath/WC • €65 (€60 low season), breakfast included • No table d'hôte • Terrace, car park. Credit cards not accepted • Outdoor swimming pool

We most liked: Only tell special friends about this enchanting monastery.

The fragrance of lavender and rosemary is all around you as you make your way up the winding lane to this superb monastery surrounded by oak trees. The spacious rooms, which overlook the cloisters and pool or the valley, are so quiet, you may well wonder if the monastery is still cloaked in its vow of silence. Deep sofas and a billiards table set the scene in the sitting room. It's the sort of place you want to tell everyone about and then worry that it might get overcrowded!

We most liked: "Baa, baa, black sheep have you any wool?"

The thick stone walls of this former sheepfold in the heart of the hamlet hide an undreamt-of haven of style and sophistication. We were unable to find fault with the refined good taste of the lovely bedrooms. Breakfast is served on a delightful inner patio, which echoes to the chirping of cicadas in the summertime. From the pool, you will be able to enjoy an uninterrupted view of mile upon mile of open fields.

Access : 6km to the north-west of Moustiers on the D 952

Access : 6km eastbound from Forcalquier on the D 12 then the D 212

 11 LA FERME DU COUVENT
M. Riehl

Les Molanes
04400 Pra-Loup
Tel. 04 92 84 05 05
Fax 04 92 84 05 05
info @ ferme-du-couvent.fr
www.ferme-du-couvent.com

Closed 1 week in Jun • 4 rooms • €70, breakfast included, half board available • Table d'hôte €18 to €25 • Garden • Tennis

 12 LE PRIEURÉ DE MOLANES
M. Paradis

Les Molanes
04400 Pra-Loup
Tel. 04 92 84 11 43
Fax 04 92 84 01 88
hotel.leprieure @ wanadoo.fr
www.prieure-praloup.com

Closed from 15 Apr to 5 Jun and 15 Sep to 15 Dec • 14 rooms on 2 floors, with bath/WC or shower/WC, all have television • €60 to 75 (€55 to €70 low season); breakfast €8; half board available • Menus €21 to €45 • Terrace, garden, car park. No dogs allowed in restaurant • Summer swimming pool

 A 100 % authentic Ubaye farmhouse.

In the heart of the resort, this 14C farm is a welcome surprise among the string of modern chalets. The farm's venerable age is still visible inside, in its low door-frames, floor made out of larch logs, narrow windows and cool rooms. Each of the simple bedrooms has its own terrace overlooking the valley, Barcelonette and the peaks. We particularly liked the fireside dinners.

 Did you notice the owner's name? What more shall we say?

May the devil take you if don't find happiness in this 17C priory! All the more so, as the chairlift of this alpine resort overlooking the lovely valley of Ubaye is on the doorstep of a superb skiing domain which unabashedly claims to be "a top resort for top people"! If the thrill of swooping down a powdery slope doesn't appeal, slap on the sun cream and relax on the south-facing terrace! A cheerful fire burns in the restaurant where you can sample a wide range of tasty dishes.

Access : In the resort

Access : 8.5km to the south-west of Barcelonnette, on the D 902, then the D 908 and right on the D 109

 13 LE VIEUX CASTEL
M. et Mme Léonardi

1 route des châteaux
04500 Roumoules
Tel. 04 92 77 75 42
Fax 04 92 77 75 42
vieuxcastel @ free.fr
http://vieuxcastel.free.fr

Open all year • 5 non-smoking rooms, all have bath/WC • €50, breakfast included, half board available • Table d'hôte €17 • Garden, sitting room. Credit cards not accepted, no dogs allowed

 14 LE PETIT PORT
M. et Mme Beaucamps

Les Fenières
04500 Sainte-Croix-de-Verdon
Tel. 04 92 77 77 23
Fax 04 92 77 77 23
saintecroixlac @ chez.com
www.chez.com/saintecroixlac

Open all year • 5 rooms, all have bathrooms • €50 to €70, breakfast included • No table d'hôte • Credit cards not accepted, no dogs allowed

 An afternoon's reading in the family library.

Planted over three hundred years ago, the mature chestnut trees still stand guard in front of this 17C house, formerly the property of the Clérissy family, inventors of Moustiers porcelain. The bedrooms have coffered ceilings and are decorated with hand-painted stencils; all are non-smoking. Arches, a fireplace and period furniture in the dining room set-off the ornate stone patterned floor.

The sandy beaches of Lake Ste-Croix, just a step away.

This tastefully renovated country villa stands in the heart of a little village which seems to cling to the mountainside. Lovely, warm hues adorn the bright bedrooms, equipped with spanking new bathrooms; two enjoy a view over the turquoise waters of Lake Ste-Croix. Don't even attempt to resist the delicious breakfasts served on the terrace in summer, you'll regret it!

Access : 4km to the north-east of Riez, Moustiers-Ste-Marie road (D 952), on the way into the village of Roumoules

Access : In the village

 15 **DOMAINE DES RAYES**
M. Masure

04200 Saint-Geniez
Tel. 04 92 61 22 76
Fax 04 92 61 06 44
les.rayes@wanadoo.fr
www.lesrayes.fr

Closed from Oct to Apr (except groups) • 5 rooms • €61 to €68 (€55 to €62 low season), breakfast included • Table d'hôte €17 • Car park. No dogs allowed • Outdoor swimming pool, children's play area

 Blessed with silence.

Exceptional is the only word to describe the location of this 17C sheepfold perched at an altitude of 1 300m and surrounded by open heath. Quiet, often immense bedrooms are decorated in a bold local palette. Wining and dining in the inviting dining room, reading in the superb vaulted sitting rooms or daydreaming on the terrace which commands a stunning view of the Durance Valley; all offer their own particular pleasure.

Access : 17km to the north-east of Sisteron, Saint-Geniez road on the D 3

 16 **MOULIN DU CHÂTEAU**
M. et Mme Staempfli-Faoro

Le Village
04500 Saint-Laurent-du-Verdon
Tel. 04 92 74 02 47
Fax 04 92 74 02 97
info@moulin-du-chateau.com
www.moulin-du-chateau.com

Closed early Nov to late Feb • 10 rooms, one with disabled access, with shower/WC, half have television • €76 to €102, breakfast €8, half board available • Restaurant closed Mon, Thu and lunchtime, menus (guests only) €30 • Terrace, garden. Dogs not admitted to the restaurant, but allowed in rooms (€7) • Library, billiards

 The friendly guesthouse atmosphere.

The former oil mill, built in the 17C and nestled in an extensive wooded garden, adjoins the castle of this town located in the heart of the Verdon regional nature reserve. The press and millstone continue to take pride of place in the middle of the spacious sitting room. Immaculate walls, wrought-iron beds, brightly-coloured fabrics and small cane armchairs preside over the deliberately unfussy bedrooms. The set menu is served in a rustic dining room or on the delicious terrace.

Access : Behind the château

479

 17 LA GIRANDOLE
M. Morel

Brunissard
05350 Arvieux
Tel. 04 92 46 84 12
Fax 04 92 46 86 59
lagirandole @ tiscali.fr
lagirandole.info

Closed from 15 Nov to 15 Dec • 6 non-smoking rooms with shower/WC and bath/WC and 2 gîtes • €66, breakfast included • No table d'hôte • Garden, car park. Credit cards not accepted, no dogs allowed • Outdoor swimming pool

 18 LES PEUPLIERS
M. Bellot

Chemin de Lesdier
05200 Baratier
Tel. 04 92 43 03 47
Fax 04 92 43 41 49
info @ hotel-les-peupliers.com
www.hotel-les-peupliers.com

Closed from 12 Apr to 5 May and from 29 Sep to 21 Oct and Tue lunchtime • 24 rooms, 6 of which are non-smoking, with bath/WC or shower/WC and television • €46 to €50 (€41 to €45 low season); breakfast €7; half board available • Menus €15 to €34 • Terrace, car park • Outdoor swimming pool, boules

 Well-situated on the "Sundial Route" – a themed tour of the villages of Haute-Provence.

Both the architecture and the sundial which adorns the façade of this old farmhouse are typical of the valley of Arvieux. The interior has been tastefully refurbished with old furniture and objects, colourful prints and fabrics, a piano and soft sofas in the sitting room. The rooms display a more uncluttered style with plain white walls and have balconies with a variety of views over the pleasant hilly landscape. Guests have the use of a kitchen.

 As welcoming in winter as in summer.

This alpine chalet enjoys a wonderful position surrounded by mountains and overlooking the lake of Serre Ponçon. The rooms are a cheerful mixture of sturdy, hand-painted furniture and bold regional fabrics; those on the second floor with a lake-view balcony were our favourite. Stone and wood feature prominently in the alpine dining room. Put your feet up on the shaded, south-facing terrace after a couple of hours energetic hiking, mountain biking or cross-country skiing, depending on the season!

Access : 3km northbound on the D 902

Access : Leave the N 94 towards Les Orres, then Baratier, in the village, take the second turning on the right

PROVENCE, ALPS AND THE FRENCH RIVIERA

 19 LES CHEMINS VERTS
Mme Dubois

05500 Buissard
Tel. 04 92 50 57 57
lescheminsverts @ free.fr
www.lescheminsverts.fr

Open all year • 4 rooms and one gîte • €44 to €50, breakfast included • Table d'hôte €13 • Terrace, car park. Credit cards not accepted, no dogs allowed

 20 LES BARTAVELLES
Mme Pernin

Le Clos des Pommiers
05200 Embrun
Tel. 04 92 43 20 69
Fax 04 92 43 11 92
info @ bartavelles.com
www.bartavelles.com

Closed from 3 to 14 Jan, Sun evening and Mon lunchtime from 1 Nov to 31 Mar • 43 rooms, 12 of which are in a separate wing, with bath/WC or shower/WC, all have television • €68 to €98 (€48 to €78 low season); breakfast €9; half board available • Menus €20 (weekdays) to €38 • Garden, car park, garage • Swimming pool, tennis

 Fill your lungs with fresh mountain air.

At an altitude of 1 200m, this pretty 18C farmhouse, run by amiable, helpful hosts, surveys the Drac valley and the rocky bastion of Dévoluy massif. The tasteful rooms are comfortable; the one called "Fleurette" has the best view. A brand new apartment is also available and the sitting room and panoramic terrace are worthy of note.

 The list of activities is endless.

Even though the impressive outline of this 1970s "cottage" may lack character, the rooms, decorated in true Queyras style and combining tranquillity with comfort, the bungalow apartments for families and the immense leafy garden overlooking the surrounding summits are enough to make you want to stay. In the summer you can choose between a quick snack on the terrace or dining indoors in the more traditional restaurant.

Access : 1km eastbound from Saint-Julien-en-Champsaur on the D 15

Access : 3km to the south-west on the D 94, on the Gap road

21 LE PARLEMENT
M. et Mme Drouillard

Charance
05000 Gap
Tel. 04 92 53 94 20
Fax 04 92 53 94 20
www.maisondhotes-leparlement.com

Open all year • 5 rooms • €60 to €80, breakfast included
• No table d'hôte • Car park. No dogs allowed
• Swimming pool, sauna, billiards, play area and climbing wall for children

22 LES BARNIÈRES
Famille Garcin

05600 Guillestre
Tel. 04 92 45 04 87
Fax 04 92 45 28 74
hotel-lesbarnieres@wanadoo.fr
www.hotel-lesbarnieres.com

Closed from 15 Oct to 26 Dec • 40 rooms with bath/WC and television • €75 to €80 (€75 to €78 low season); breakfast €10; half board available • Menus €18 (weekdays) to €32 • Garden, car park. No dogs allowed
• Swimming pool, tennis, table-tennis, boules, mini-golf

This establishment democratically offers something for everyone!

This appealing 18C house surrounded by greenery was formerly an outbuilding of the castle of Charance. Although only a few minutes from Gap, it is quiet and peaceful. The rooms are spacious, sophisticated and quite spotless; some command a view of the town. The basement has been fitted out with a wide range of activities including billiards, games room with a climbing wall for children and a sauna. The owner, an alpine and mountain-bike guide, will happily give you ideas for outings.

The sweeping view over the Durance Valley and the Alps.

In the upper reaches of Guillestre, this hotel is comprised of two chalets facing the mountains in the distance. The main wing is currently being tastefully renovated, but the summer wing has already been finished. Make the most of the garden and its leisure activities: swimming pool, tennis courts and pétanque and we can guarantee that you won't need to count the sheep at night.

Access : From Gap, 4km towards Orange and Valence (D 994), at the Rond Point des 3 Cascades, drive towards the Charance domain

Access : On the way out of the village, by the road

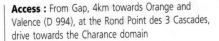

482

 23 LE CHALET D'EN HÔ
M. Baudoux

Hameau des Chazals - Le Roubion
05100 Névache
Tel. 04 92 20 12 29
Fax 04 92 20 59 70
chaletdenho @ aol.com
www.chaletdenho.com

Closed from 3 Apr to 10 Jun, 11 Sep to 21 Oct and 1 Nov
to 16 Dec • 14 non-smoking rooms with bath/WC or
shower/WC and television, most have a balcony • €79
to €114; breakfast €9; half board available • Menu €20
(dinner only) • Car park. No dogs allowed • Singing
courses, cross-country skiing, hiking, sauna

 24 AUBERGE LA NEYRETTE
M. et Mme Muzard

05250 Saint-Disdier
Tel. 04 92 58 81 17
Fax 04 92 58 89 95
info @ la-neyrette.com
www.la-neyrette.com

Closed from 13 to 30 Apr and from 15 Oct to 15 Dec
• 12 rooms with bath/WC or shower/WC, all have
television • €62 to €70; breakfast €8; half board available
• Menus €20 to €40 • Terrace, garden, car park • Pond
with trout fishing, play area

 **Breakfast on the terrace overlooking
the valley's multitude of wild flowers.**

The climb up to this larchwood chalet will reward you
with lovely bedrooms named after the mountains and
lakes you can see from the balconies. A tasteful marriage
of walls lined in pine and local draperies and the dining
room is adorned with tools which recall the local
tradition of woodworking. The nature-loving owners are
always happy to pass on tips and expert advice on
exploring the lovely Clarée Valley.

 **Fancy a nap under a tree
in the company of the local marmots?**

This inn lies in a secluded spot on Dévoluy's high plateau
at the foot of an arid crest of peaks. The recently
renovated rooms are decorated in keeping with their
wild flower names. The peaceful garden boasts a pond
where you can fish for your own trout, the house
speciality. In the summer, meals are served on the
terrace overlooking the solitary stone fortress. In the
winter, the ski slopes of Superdévoluy are just a short
drive away.

Access : Northbound from Briançon, leave the N 94
for the D 994G that follows the Clarée, turn right at
Roubion

Access : On leaving the village, on the Superdévoluy
road

 CHAMBRE D'HÔTE MADAME FARAUT
Mme Faraut

 14 rue de l'Agachon
06530 Cabris
Tel. 04 93 60 52 36
Fax 04 93 60 52 36

Closed from 1 Oct to 31 Mar • 5 rooms • €50 to €60, breakfast included • No table d'hôte • Credit cards not accepted

  LES JARDINS FRAGONARD
M. Mombeck

 12 rue Fragonard
06800 Cagnes-sur-Mer
Tel. 04 93 20 07 72
Fax 04 93 20 07 72
jardinsfragonard@hotmail.com

Open all year • 4 rooms with bath/WC • €72 to €85 (€55 to €80 low season), breakfast included • Table d'hôte by reservation • Sitting room, terraces, garden, car park. Credit cards not accepted, no dogs allowed • Outdoor swimming pool, billiards. Tennis and golf nearby

 Wandering around the lanes of this old village so popular with contemporary artists.

The yellow walls of this tiny village house are bound to catch your eye. The restful rooms are painted a spotless white; some of them enjoy a view of the Esterel massif and St-Cassien Lake, as does the sitting room. A light-hearted atmosphere also prevails in the beams and fireplace in the breakfast room and the countryside almost seems to creep in through the large bay window.

Conveniently located near the Renoir Museum.

Trees indigenous to the south fill the park of this secluded 1925 villa perched on the heights of Cagnes. An equally authentic Provençal look prevails in the brightly coloured rooms, often furnished in cane; all have brand new bathrooms. Depending on the season, breakfast is served on the terrace or inside, at a large communal table. The shaded garden and swimming pool are ideal for quiet, relaxing afternoons.

Access : In a lane in the village

Access : Near the Renoir Museum

27 VILLA L'ÉGLANTIER
M. et Mme Daran

14 rue Campestra
06400 Cannes
Tel. 04 93 68 22 43
Fax 04 93 38 28 53

Open all year • 4 rooms with bath/WC • €75 to €100,
breakfast included • No table d'hôte • Terrace, garden.
Credit cards not accepted

28 LA JABOTTE
M. April et M. Mora

13 avenue Marx-Maurey
06160 Cap-d'Antibes
Tel. 04 93 61 45 89
Fax 04 93 61 07 04
info@jabotte.com
www.jabotte.com

Closed Nov, 1 week at Christmas and Sun afternoon
• 10 non-smoking rooms with shower/WC • €75 to €80,
breakfast €7 • No restaurant • Terrace, garden, car park

A haven of peace and quiet within walking distance of the Croisette.

This large white villa hidden away on the heights of
Cannes is set in a lovely garden planted with palm,
orange and other exotic trees. Built in the 1920s, its
original Art Deco soul can still be felt. The guestrooms,
spacious, quiet and tastefully decorated, all have large
bathrooms. The White, Green and Blue rooms upstairs
have a balcony or a terrace, while the Red room, on
the ground-floor, opens onto the garden.

Superbly located just a stone's throw from a lovely sandy beach.

This establishment, well located in a quiet side street
at right angles to Salis Beach, is home to tastefully
decorated trim bedrooms. Their tiny terraces all overlook
a pleasant gravelled patio adorned with plants. The work
of one of the owners, a calligraphist in his spare time,
can be seen in some of the rooms and in the smart
sitting room where delicious breakfasts are served.
Warm, friendly welcome.

Access : On the heights of Cannes

Access : 100m from Salis Beach

COARAZE - 06390   LA BRIGUE - 06430

 29 L'AUBERGE DU SOLEIL
Mme Jacquet

 Dans le village
06390 Coaraze
Tel. 04 93 79 08 11
Fax 04 93 79 37 79
auberge.du.soleil@wanadoo.fr

Closed from 1 Jan to 15 Feb • 8 rooms with bath/WC
• €61; breakfast €8; half board available • Menus €20
to €25 • Garden • Outdoor swimming pool

 30 LE MIRVAL
M. et Mme Dellepiane

 3 rue Vincent-Ferrier
06430 La Brigue
Tel. 04 93 04 63 71
Fax 04 93 04 79 81
www.lemirval.com

Open from 1 Apr to 2 Nov • 18 rooms on 2 floors, most
have bath/WC, all have television • €42 to €62; breakfast
€8; half board available • Restaurant closed Fri lunchtime,
menus €19 to €25 • Terrace, garden, car park. No dogs
allowed • Mountain biking, white-water sports, walks
and 4-wheel drive excursions

 **Delicious little Provençal dishes
cooked by the lady of the house.**

This lovely mansion was built in 1863 and its
atmosphere of quiet serenity can only be reached on
foot. The immaculate rooms are a happy combination
of old and new; four enjoy a view of the valley and the
terraced fields. The immense dining room and conservatory also command an impressive vista. Madame uses
only fresh produce in her cooking, whose reputation
extends throughout the region. As for relaxation, look
no further than the billiard table, garden, orchard and
pool.

 **Anglers will not be able to resist
trying to hook a silver trout in the
torrents of the Levense.**

A late-19C alpine inn in a picturesque medieval village
close to the Italian border. Nearly all the modern,
practical rooms have been renovated. The restaurant-
veranda is nothing special in itself, but does offer a
superb view over the tiny stone bridge spanning the
village's renowned trout-stream. The owner organises
excursions in the Vallée des Merveilles (Marvels) either
in a four-wheel drive or on foot.

Access : Between the Turini Pass (D 2566) and
l'Escarène (D 21), at La Cabanette take the D 2566
towards Saint-Roch Pass, then the D 15

Access : 6.5km southbound from Tende on the
D 204, then at St-Dalmas-de-Tendre take a left on the
D 143

 31 LA BASTIDE DE SAINT-DONAT
M. Rosso

 Route du Pont-de-Pierre, parc Saint-Donat
06480 La Colle-sur-Loup
Tel. 04 93 32 93 41
Fax 04 93 32 80 61

Open all year • 5 rooms with shower or bath • €61 to €92, breakfast included • No table d'hôte • Terrace, garden. Credit cards not accepted, small dogs admitted

 32 AUBERGE DU BON PUITS
M. et Mme Corniglion

 06450 Le Suquet
Tel. 04 93 03 17 65
Fax 04 93 03 10 48

Closed from 1 Dec to 15 Apr and Tue except from 15 Jul to 30 Aug • 8 rooms, 2 of which are non-smoking, with bath/WC, air-conditioning and television • €60 to €73 (€58 to €61 low season); breakfast €9; half board available • Air-conditioned restaurant; menus €20 to €30 • Terrace, park, car park. Credit cards not accepted • Animal park, play area, white-water sports and fishing, scenic-path walks

 Dawdling on the terrace overlooking the river.

The stone walls of this sheepfold built in 1850 hide a wealth of ornate interior decoration. The ground floor has been beautifully restored in keeping with local traditions, including arcades, columns, fireplace and terracotta floor tiles. The pastel shades of the bedrooms are a perfect contrast to the old beams and furniture; some have a balcony. As you sit on the terrace, you will be able to listen to the river babbling gently below.

 The joyful shouts of the pony riders in the small animal park.

Children are welcomed with open arms in this old stone coaching inn complete with a play area and a lovely animal park on the banks of the Vésubie. Since 1890, the rooms have been constantly smartened up and embellished by the owners and their forebears. The kitchen is also a family affair and the delicious recipes have been handed down from mother to daughter for generations. Meals are served under the well-polished beams of the gleaming dining room.

Access : 2km southbound from Saint-Paul on the D 6

Access : On the D 2565, between Plan-du-Var and Bollène-Vésubie

PROVENCE, ALPS AND THE FRENCH RIVIERA

 33   **PIERROT-PIERRETTE**
M. Mitolo

 Place de l'Église - Monti
06500 Menton
Tel. 04 93 35 79 76
Fax 04 93 35 79 76
pierrotpierrette @ aol.com

Closed from 6 Dec 2004 to 15 Jan 2005 and Mon except
Easter • 7 rooms, 4 of which are in a separate wing, all
have shower/WC, no television • €67 to €76; breakfast
€8; half board available • Menus €27 to €39 • Garden
• Swimming pool

 34   **ARMENONVILLE**
Mme Moreilhon

 20 avenue des Fleurs
06000 Nice
Tel. 04 93 96 86 00
Fax 04 93 44 66 53
nice @ hotel-armenonville.com
www.hotel-armenonville.com

Open all year • 13 rooms with bath or shower, all have
television • €73 to €95 (€59 to €77 low season);
breakfast €9 • No restaurant • Garden, private car park.
No dogs allowed

 Your northern pallor will soon turn a lovely golden brown under Menton's bright sun.

This delightful little inn perched in the upper reaches
of a peaceful hamlet lies just outside Menton. Most of
the family-sized simply-furnished rooms have balconies.
The rustic dining room has its charm, but guests
generally come back for the luxurious garden, full of
exotic southern plants and sweet-scented roses, and the
swimming pool overlooking the valley of Carei.

 The old "Russian" district of Nice and its Orthodox cathedral.

This 1900 villa stands at the end of a cul-de-sac in the
old Russian quarter. A faded charm emanates from the
high-ceilinged rooms of varied sizes decorated with
"old-fashioned" furniture from the opulent Negresco
Hotel. Some overlook the flowers and palm trees in the
garden where breakfast is served on sunny days, i.e.
almost every day of the year. A pretty iron stove takes
pride of place in the sitting room.

Access : 5km northbound from Menton, on the
D 2566 towards Sospel

Access : From the Promenade des Anglais, take
Boulevard Gambetta, then turn left

 35 DURANTE
Mme Stramigioli

 16 avenue Durante
06000 Nice
Tel. 04 93 88 84 40
Fax 04 93 87 77 76
info@hotel-durante.com
www.hotel-durante.com

Open all year • 24 rooms, 19 of which have kitchenettes, all are air-conditioned with bath/WC or shower/WC and television • €69 to €125; breakfast €9 to €10 • No restaurant • Garden, car park

 36 VILLA LA TOUR
Mme Barbara Kimming

4 rue de la Tour
06000 Nice
Tel. 04 93 80 08 15
Fax 04 93 85 10 58
reservation@villa-la-tour.com
www.villa-la-tour.com

Open all year • 16 air-conditioned rooms with bath/WC or shower/WC and television • €59 to €125, breakfast €3.50 • No restaurant • No dogs allowed

 Breakfast on the terrace amid the tangy perfume of citrus fruit trees.

The pink façade and mascarons (carved caricatures) over the windows of this elegant abode, in a quiet cul-de-sac near the railway station are a reminder that Italy is just down the road. It is a pleasure to sleep with the window wide open, because all the rooms, recently refurbished in a Mediterranean flavour, overlook a terracotta tiled terrace-garden lined with rows of palm, orange and lemon trees.

 Enjoy the luxury of being a few steps from the heart of historic Nice.

This small hotel is delightfully located in a former 18C convent and is ideally located for all those who appreciate the picturesque appeal of historic Nice. Guests praise the personalised welcome and tastefully decorated rooms, thoughtfully soundproofed and insulated from the hot Riviera sun. They are all comfortably equipped, with the exception of the least expensive which is more basic but equally appealing. A tiny terrace commands a lovely rooftop view over Nice.

Access : From the railway station, take Av Durante and turn left in the cul-de-sac after Rue Alsace-Lorraine

Access : In the heart of the old town

PROVENCE, ALPS AND THE FRENCH RIVIERA

  37 LE BOSQUET
M. Cattet

74 chemin des Périssols
06580 Pégomas
Tel. 04 92 60 21 20
Fax 04 92 60 21 49
hotel.lebosquet@wanadoo.fr
www.pegomas.com

Open all year • 16 rooms with bath/WC or shower/WC and television • €45 to €60, breakfast €7 • No restaurant • Private car park, park. No dogs allowed • Swimming pool, tennis

   38 HOSTELLERIE DES REMPARTS
M. Tibaud

72 rue Grande
06570 Saint-Paul
Tel. 04 93 32 09 88
Fax 04 93 32 06 91
h.remparts@wanadoo.fr
www.stpaulweb.com

Closed from mid-Jan to mid-Feb, Sun evening and Mon • 9 rooms with bath/WC or shower/WC • €39; breakfast €7; half board available • Restaurant closed Mon to Fri evenings in winter; menu €12 to €30 • Car park

 The fruit orchards, regularly plundered for the delicious homemade jams served at breakfast.

Bougainvillaea, oleander, lavender, bamboo, lawns and tall trees make up the multicoloured backdrop that encircles this hotel a few kilometres outside Cannes. A clientele of regulars return annually, drawn by the establishment's peaceful atmosphere, friendly, relaxed welcome and swimming pool. A pleasantly subdued Provençal flavour echoes throughout the rooms, located in two buildings. A studio complete with kitchenette is also available for rent.

 Saint-Paul and this old hotel are everything you expect Provence to be.

Beautifully preserved stone walls, antique furniture, rustic earthenware tiles, bright colours and a faultless welcome paint the picture of this delightful hotel, hidden in a narrow street in historic St-Paul. Each of the personalised rooms is named after a flower and the largest offer a fine view of the countryside. It is hard to leave the shade of the lovely covered terrace.

Access : North-eastbound on the Mouans Sartoux road

Access : In the part of Rue Grande situated between Rue de l'Étoile and Rue des Pontis

 39 MAS DES CIGALES

M. Prieur-Gelis

1673 route des Quenières
06140 Tourrettes-sur-Loup
Tel. 04 93 59 25 73
Fax 04 93 59 25 73
lemasdescigales@free.fr
www.le-mas-des-cigales.com

Closed from 30 Oct to 1 Mar • 5 rooms • €92, breakfast included • No table d'hôte • Garden, car park. Credit cards not accepted, no dogs allowed • Outdoor swimming pool, tennis, bikes, wi-fi internet access

 40 BLANCHE NEIGE

M. et Mme Kretchmann

10 avenue de Valbery
06470 Valberg
Tel. 04 93 02 50 04
Fax 04 93 02 61 90

Closed in Nov, Mon evening and Tue in low season • 17 rooms with shower/WC, some have bath/WC, all have television • €75 to €85 (€65 to €75 low season); breakfast €8; half board available • Restaurant closed out of season; menu €25 • Terrace, garage, car park. No dogs allowed • Skiing, hiking

 The surrounding countryside, perfect for taking a stroll.

This pleasant villa perched on a hillside of pine trees commands a wonderful view of the Riviera coast. Hand-painted furniture adorns the personalised rooms named after local fauna and flora: Nasturtium, Peony, Butterfly, Violet and Olive. You can choose between a covered veranda overlooking the garden or (in summer) a poolside table for breakfast. If you lean slightly over the terrace, you will catch sight of a small waterfall and the property's tennis courts.

 Hey Ho, Hey Ho, it's out to play we go!

Once upon a time there was a chalet whose green and yellow shutters looked onto a forest of larch trees. Legend has it that these small rooms decorated with hand-quilted bedspreads and painted furniture were formerly the home of seven cheerful dwarves and their guest, Snow White – the hotel's namesake. Nowadays the region's white gold – 50km of slopes between 1 500 and 2 000m – has stolen the limelight from the princesses of yesteryear. Snug restaurant and spacious terrace overlooking the road.

Access : 2km from Tourrettes, Saint-Jean road

Access : At the entrance to the resort

PROVENCE, ALPS AND THE FRENCH RIVIERA

 41 MAS DE CLAIREFONTAINE
M. et Mme Lapostat

 3196 route de Draguignan
06530 Val-du-Tignet
Tel. 04 93 66 39 69
andre.lapostat @ wanadoo.fr
http://masdeclairefontaine.online.fr

Open all year • 3 rooms with bathrooms and television
• €79 to €100, breakfast included • No table d'hôte
• Terrace, park, car park. Credit cards not accepted, no
dogs allowed • Outdoor swimming pool. Nearby are
Provençal villages, fishing or sailing on the lake

 42 AUBERGE DES SEIGNEURS
Mme Rodi

 Place du Frêne
06140 Vence
Tel. 04 93 58 04 24
Fax 04 93 24 08 01

Open from Mar to Oct • 6 rooms with shower/WC • €70
to €85; breakfast €10; half board available • Menus €30
to €42

We most liked
**As you drive up to the mas, wind
down your window and listen
to the cicadas chirping!**

The picture of the stone mas and its terraced garden
dotted with umbrella pines and clumps of reeds will
make you reach for your camera. The Provençal-style
bedrooms and bathrooms are strewn with delightful
details such as delicately scented Fragonard soaps,
postcards and sweets, that make you feel you were
expected. The Iris room has its own private terrace. In
the summer months, guests are invited to eat outside
in the welcome shade of the oak tree.

We most liked
**Ladies are offered a flower
after the meal.**

This historic 17C inn next door to the Château de
Villeneuve is said to have enjoyed the patronage of
famous people such as François 1st, who died in 1547!
"But, but", you stammer as you quickly compare dates.
However the original decoration of this house has been
so skilfully preserved that you would be forgiven for
falling into the trap! Whatever the case, a taste of the
superb spit-roasted lamb from the open fire is bound
to reconcile you with the hotel's miraculous past.

Access : 10km to the south-east of Grasse,
Draguignan road

Access : In the grounds of the old town, near the
castle

 43 **MIRAMAR**
M. Varlet

167 avenue Bougearel
Plateau Saint-Michel
06140 Vence
Tel. 04 93 58 01 32
Fax 04 93 58 20 22
resa @ hotel-miramar-vence.com
www.hotel-miramar-vence.com

Closed from 15 Nov to 15 Dec • 18 rooms with bath/WC or shower/WC and television • €78 to €145 (€68 to €135 low season); breakfast €12 • No restaurant • Terrace, car park • Outdoor swimming pool, table-tennis, boules

 44 **QUATRE DAUPHINS**
M. Lafont

54 rue Roux-Alphéran
13100 Aix-en-Provence
Tel. 04 42 38 16 39
Fax 04 42 38 60 19

Open all year • 13 rooms with bath/WC or shower/WC, all have television • €65 to €78; breakfast €9 • No restaurant

 The magnificent view of the Baous mountain range and St Jeannet.

The interior of this pleasant pale-pink villa, built in 1927 on the doorstep of Vence, has just been renovated from top to bottom. Its pretty rooms, named after the region's flowers, are decorated with friezes and frescoes. A pleasant Mediterranean lounge-bar equipped with a large-screen TV is perfect for a drink before dinner. Outside, the breakfast terrace, garden and swimming pool all command the same lovely view of the Baous and the Riviera.

You won't regret opting for the romantic rooms under the eaves, however stifling in summer!

The tiny lanes lined with lovely old 17C and 18C mansions, the busy café terraces of the Cours Mirabeau, a multitude of tiny restaurants and colourful street markets – it could only be Aix en Provence! Turn a deaf ear to the noise, steel yourself to the heat and immerse yourself from head to toe in the charm of this hotel's tiled floors and painted furniture, only a step from the graceful little square of the Quatre Dauphins.

Access : On the plateau overlooking the road: from the centre, on Avenue du Général Leclerc (Cagnes road) then turn right

Access : In a quiet, small street in the Mazarin area

 45 SAINT-CHRISTOPHE
M. Bonnet

 2 avenue Victor-Hugo
13100 Aix-en-Provence
Tel. 04 42 26 01 24
Fax 04 42 38 59 17
saintchristophe @ francemarket.com
www.hotel-saintchristophe.com

Open all year • 58 air-conditioned rooms, 6 are split-level and one has disabled access. Rooms have bath/WC and television • €78 to €115 (€75 to €112 low season); breakfast €9 • Menu €21 (weekdays) to €26 • Garage. No dogs allowed in restaurant

 46 L'AMPHITHÉATRE
M. Coumet et M. Piras

 5 rue Diderot
13200 Arles
Tel. 04 90 96 10 30
Fax 04 90 93 98 69
contact @ hotelamphitheatre.fr
www.hotelamphitheatre.fr

Open all year • 28 rooms on 3 levels, most have shower/WC, all have television • €49 to €79 (€45 to €69 out of season); breakfast €7 • No restaurant

 Admire the paintings by a local artist on the walls of the comfortable lounge-bar.

The smart pink walls of this small building were home to a garage before the Bonnet family bought the premises in 1936 and turned them into a hotel-restaurant. Most of the rooms echo the establishment's Art Deco origins, but several are more Provençal in inspiration. The restaurant and conservatory-terrace have adopted the spirit of a Parisian brasserie, serving a somewhat eclectic range of dishes, including the house special of choucroute!

 Breakfasting on fresh fruit juice, crusty croissants and home-made fruit preserves.

A line of plane trees masks this small 17C house whose façade is adorned with a statue of the Virgin Mary. All the airy, tasteful and well cared-for rooms have just been treated to a facelift with painted and wrought-iron furniture and lovely draperies. The sitting and breakfast room feature the same happy blend of old walls, modern décor and bright southern colours. The hotel is ideally situated to explore Arles' countless treasures.

Access : In the town centre, near the tourist office and the Cours Mirabeau

Access : In the historical centre, near the Roman Theatre and Arena

494

 47 CALENDAL
Mme Jacquemin

5 rue Porte-de-Laure
13200 Arles
Tel. 04 90 96 11 89
Fax 04 90 96 05 84
contact@lecalendal.com
www.lecalendal.com

Closed from 2 to 24 Jan • 38 rooms, all have bath/WC or shower/WC and television • €45 to €99; breakfast €7 • Restaurant only open at lunchtime in season; buffet €14 • Garden. No dogs allowed

 48 LA MUETTE
M. Deplancke

15 rue des Suisses
13200 Arles
Tel. 04 90 96 15 39
Fax 04 90 49 73 16
hotel.muette@wanadoo.fr
http://perso.wanadoo.fr/hotel-muette

Closed during Feb school holidays • 18 rooms on 2 floors, with shower/WC, some have bath/WC, all have television • €51 to €54 (€48 to €51 low season); breakfast €6 • No restaurant • Garage

 Proof that France also drinks tea!

Teatime, something of an institution in this establishment, means tasty pastries and a wonderful selection of teas from one of France's most famous tea houses, served in a light, airy room with veranda, which also doubles as a breakfast room when the weather is not fine enough to enjoy the shade of the palms on the terrace. The rooms overlook either the garden, the Antique theatre, or, for a lucky few, the Arena; ask for one with a view when booking. All are decorated in bright, warm colours.

 The friendly, unaffected greeting.

This rather austere edifice, on a little square in the historic town, dates from the 12C and 15C; exposed stonework, regimental lines of beams and narrow bay windows bear witness to its age. A handsome spiral staircase leads up to the rooms, most of which are on the old-fashioned side, some do, however, sport Provençal prints and period furniture. Breakfast is served in a delightful rustic room, under the somewhat unnerving glare of a stuffed bull's head.

Access : Between the Antique theatre and arena

Access : On a small square in the heart of the historic centre

 49 LE CLOS DES ARÔMES
M. et Mme Bonnet

 10 rue Abbé Paul-Mouton
13260 Cassis
Tel. 04 42 01 71 84
Fax 04 42 01 31 76

Closed from Jan to Feb • 14 rooms, most have shower/WC, some have bath/WC, all have television • €63 to €73; breakfast €7; half board available • Restaurant closed Tue and Wed lunchtimes and Mon; menus €23 to €35 • Terrace, garden, garage. No dogs allowed

 50 LA GALINIÈRE
M. et Mme Gagnières

 Route de Saint-Maximin
13790 Châteauneuf-le-Rouge
Tel. 04 42 53 32 55
Fax 04 42 53 33 80
lagaliniere@aol.com
www.lagaliniere.com

Closed Sun evening from Oct to Apr • 18 rooms overlooking the courtyard or the garden, most have bath/WC, all have television • €55 to €80; breakfast €9 to €10, half board available • Menus €26 to €53 • Terrace, garden, two car parks, one of which is private • Swimming pool, stud farm, horse-riding

 Epitome of the best of life in Provence.

 45 acres of grounds and a riding centre with horses and ponies for the kids.

The doors of this pretty blue-shuttered house lead into a cheerful, flowered garden. Provençal prints and colours adorn the tasteful, well-soundproofed rooms, one of which is perfect for families. The meals, equally southern in flavour, are served in the bright dining room or, in the summer, under the shade of plane trees on the terrace.

Built in the 17C on the ruins of a Templar chicken farm, La Galinière was initially a coaching inn and Pope Pius VII slept here on two occasions, in 1809 and 1814. At the foothills of the Ste-Victoire mountain, immortalised by Cézanne, the estate's elegant wrought-iron gate, still flanked by the stones designed to protect it from the carriage wheels, leads into the inn, which now offers rooms decorated in a rustic style and a characterful restaurant in an old outhouse with a carriage door.

Access : From the town centre: on Place de la République, take Rue A Thiers then continue straight on past the church

Access : By the N 7, 2km from Châteauneuf-le-Rouge, towards St-Maximin-la-Sainte-Baume

 51 VAL MAJOUR
M. Güell

22 avenue d'Arles
13990 Fontvieille
Tel. 04 90 54 62 33
Fax 04 90 54 61 67
contact @ valmajour.com
www.valmajour.com

Open all year • 32 rooms with bath/WC or shower/WC and television • €58 to €150 (€42 to €92 low season); breakfast €10 • No restaurant • Park, garage, private car park • Outdoor swimming pool, tennis, table-tennis, boules

 52 PARC
M. et Mme Robin

Vallée de Saint-Pons
13420 Gémenos
Tel. 04 42 32 20 38
Fax 04 42 32 10 26
hotel.parc.gemenos @ wanadoo.fr
www.hotel-parc-gemenos.com

Open all year • 13 rooms with bath/WC and television • €57 to €87; breakfast €6.50; half board available • Menus €16 to €48, children's menu €11 • Garden, terrace, private car park

 The trees in the park are home to dozens of busy squirrels.

A stay in this regional house built on the doorstep of Alphonse Daudet's village is always a pleasant prospect. The spacious, rustic rooms are decorated with cheerful Provençal patterns; some have a terrace, while others have a balcony overlooking the park's many trees. On the leisure side, you can choose between a dip in the superb swimming pool or a friendly tennis match in the cool of the evening.

 Cool down in the refreshing shade of Saint Pons Park in the summer.

This enchanting Provençal home stands in a haven of greenery just as you leave town. The rooms are modern and appealing; some enjoy a view of the park. The large bay windows of the dining room–conservatory open onto a cheerful flowered garden. The shade of the plane trees is most welcome in the heat of the summer. Friendly and unaffected.

Access : On leaving the town, by the Arles road

Access : 1km on the Sainte-Baume road (D 2)

53 **DOMAINE DU BOIS VERT**
M. et Mme Richard

Quartier Montauban
13450 Grans
Tel. 04 90 55 82 98
Fax 04 90 55 82 98
leboisvert@hotmail.com
www.domaineduboisvert.com

Closed from 5 Jan to 15 Mar • 3 rooms • €65 to €72, breakfast included • No table d'hôte • Terrace, park, car park. Credit cards not accepted, no dogs allowed • Outdoor swimming pool, table-tennis

54 **LE CADRAN SOLAIRE**
Mme Guilmet

Rue du Cabaret-Neuf
13690 Graveson
Tel. 04 90 95 71 79
Fax 04 90 90 55 04
cadransolaire@wanadoo.fr
www.hotel-en-provence.com

Open all year, but by reservation only from Nov to Mar • 12 rooms with bath/WC or shower/WC • €53 to €78; breakfast €8 • No restaurant • Breakfast terrace, garden, private car park

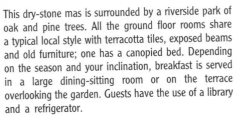

The award-winning friendly owners.

This dry-stone mas is surrounded by a riverside park of oak and pine trees. All the ground floor rooms share a typical local style with terracotta tiles, exposed beams and old furniture; one has a canopied bed. Depending on the season and your inclination, breakfast is served in a large dining-sitting room or on the terrace overlooking the garden. Guests have the use of a library and a refrigerator.

The lady of the house treats her guests like friends of the family.

A glance at the sundial on the façade of this three-hundred-year-old post house will explain the establishment's name. Not content merely to represent the timeless charm of Provence, the energetic lady of the house was determined to breathe a new lease of life into her property, and the result is impressive! Enchanting small rooms are decorated with taste and a profusion of delicate details, the bathrooms have been redone and the wrought-iron terrace surrounded by plants is a joy to behold.

Access : 7km southbound from Salon on the D 16 and then towards Lançon (D 19)

Access : In a residential area, on the way into the village

 55 **LE MAS DES RIÈGES**
M. Ducarre

Route de Cacharel
13460 Les Saintes-Maries-de-la-Mer
Tel. 04 90 97 85 07
Fax 04 90 97 72 26
hoteldesrieges@wanadoo.fr
www.hoteldesrieges.com

Closed from 5 Jan to 5 Feb and 15 Nov to 15 Dec • 20 rooms on the ground floor with bath/WC or shower/WC, all have television • €62 to €86 (€56 to €72 low season); breakfast €7 • No restaurant (snacks available around the pool on sunny days) • Garden, car park • Swimming pool

 56 **VILLA MARIE-JEANNE**
Mme de Montmirail

4 rue Chicot
13012 Marseille
Tel. 04 91 85 51 31
Fax 04 91 49 55 74

Open all year • 3 rooms, one of which has a terrace • €50 to €65, breakfast included • No table d'hôte • Garden, car park. Credit cards not accepted, no dogs allowed • Outdoor swimming pool

 Step out of your ground floor room and straight into the Camargue.

Just a few minutes from the tourist bustle of the town centre and already surrounded by marshes, you won't be able to miss this hacienda-style house set in a large garden full of flowers and trees. The lovely rustic-inspired rooms are adorned with Provençal fabrics and all have a private terrace. Treat yourself to a session in the beauty institute, complete with hammam, balneotherapy and a sun bed. Horse-riding possible.

 Not far from the famous "Stade-Vél", home of Olympique Marseille football club!

A rare pearl in the heart of a residential district that has gradually merged with the village of Saint Barnabé. The interior of this tasteful 19C house features a pleasant blend of traditional Provençal colours, old furniture, wrought-iron and contemporary works of art. The rooms are in the outbuildings and overlook the plane trees in the garden; one has a private terrace. Not to be missed!

Access : In the heart of the marshes, 1km from Saintes-Maries-de-la-Mer, on the Cacharel road, then a minor road

Access : From Marseille, take Boulevard de la Blancarde eastbound

57 LE BERGER DES ABEILLES
Mme Grenier

Route de Cabanes
13670 Saint-Andiol
Tel. 04 90 95 01 91
Fax 04 90 95 48 26
abeilles13 @ aol.com
berger-abeilles.com

Closed from 1 Nov to Easter • 8 rooms upstairs, with bath/WC or shower/WC, all have television • €75 to €98; breakfast €10; half board available • Restaurant closed Mon and every lunchtime except Sun; menus €30 to €52 • Terrace, garden, car park

58 L'AMANDIÈRE
M. Fougerolle-Jacquemet

Avenue Théodore Aubanel
13210 Saint-Rémy-de-Provence
Tel. 04 90 92 41 00
Fax 04 90 92 48 38
http://pers.wanadoo.fr/hotel.amandiere

Closed from early Nov to late Mar • 26 rooms, one of which has disabled access, with bath/WC or shower/WC and television • €53 to €64, breakfast €7 • No restaurant • Private car park, garden. No dogs allowed • Swimming pool

Ask the lady of the house why the house is named "The bee shepherd"...

The authenticity of this peacefully situated mas, off the busy N7, cannot be doubted. The charm is enhanced by a wonderful flowered terrace, shaded by a majestic plane tree. The rooms, some of which are furnished with old pieces, are comfortable and well looked after; three open directly into the garden. The rustic dining room is equally appealing, as is the lady of the house's pleasant welcome.

The owners clearly have their guests' welfare at heart.

Guests invariably fall in love with this discreet hotel tucked away in a sleepy, residential area. Trees and flowers adorn the garden which surrounds the recently built regional-style house. The rooms' fixtures and fittings are unostentatious and practical as is their sober, rustic style. Depending on the floor you will have either a balcony or a private terrace overlooking the garden. Homemade cakes often find their way onto the generously laden breakfast table. Lovely swimming pool.

Access : 2km to the north-west of Saint-Andiol, towards Avignon, leave the N 7 and take the D 74 E towards Cabanes

Access : Near the town centre, drive down Avenue Mirabeau then Avenue de Lattre de Tassigny

59 CASTELET DES ALPILLES
Mme Canac-Roux

6 place Mireille
13210 Saint-Rémy-de-Provence
Tel. 04 90 92 07 21
Fax 04 90 92 52 03
hotel.castel.alpilles@wanadoo.fr
www.castelet-alpilles.com

Open from late Mar to early Nov • 19 rooms in 2 buildings. Most rooms have bath/WC, all have television • €66 to €89 (€62 to €84 low season); breakfast €9 • No restaurant • Garden, private car park

60 ANGLETERRE
M. Ferrandino

98 cours Carnot
13300 Salon-de-Provence
Tel. 04 90 56 01 10
Fax 04 90 56 71 75
hoteldangleterre@wanadoo.fr
www.hotel-dangleterre.biz

Closed from 20 Dec to 6 Jan • 25 rooms on 3 levels, 15 of which are air-conditioned, with bath/WC or shower/WC, all have television • €45 to €51; breakfast €6 • No restaurant

 Just a five minute walk from St-Rémy, home to Nostradamus and Van Gogh.

This handsome early-20C house was built very near the antique site of Glanum. Some of the comfortable rooms possess a loggia and those on the second floor command a fine view of the Alpilles, a lovely chain of limestone hills. The immense sitting and dining rooms are decorated in true local style, but in the summer, guests generally prefer to breakfast in the lovely shaded garden.

 The "Château de l'Empéri": former residence of the archbishops of Arles.

This former convent dates back to the early years of the 20C and enjoys a matchless location in the heart of the old town and close to the museums. The simple, but comfortable rooms, with double-glazing and air-conditioning, lie behind well-restored walls. Breakfasting under a glazed dome has a distinctly "Empire" feel. Attentive, friendly service.

Access : On leaving the town drive towards the site of Villa Glanum

Access : In the town centre, near the pedestrian area

61 RUE DU CHÂTEAU
M. et Mme Laraison

24 rue du Château
13150 Tarascon
Tel. 04 90 91 09 99
Fax 04 90 91 10 33
ylaraison @ wanadoo.fr

Closed from 2 Nov to 25 Dec • 5 rooms • €76 to €85, breakfast included • No table d'hôte • Credit cards not accepted, no dogs allowed

Faultless, down to the tiniest detail.

A porch and heavy door guard the entrance to this 18C edifice in a quiet side street leading up to the castle of Good King René - a truly great Renaissance man. The beautifully restored rooms are of an extremely high standard; two are reached via a lovely medieval-style staircase. As soon as the sun is warm enough, breakfast is served on a lovely flowered patio with ochre-red walls.

Access : Near the castle

62 ALEGRIA
M. et Mme Ruys

59 chemin du stade
83630 Aups
Tel. 06 32 20 15 37
Fax 04 94 70 00 41
alegria-aups @ wanadoo.fr
www.alegria.tk

Closed in Jan • 5 non-smoking rooms with bathrooms, some with disabled access • €110, breakfast included • Table d'hôte €35 by reservation and for 6 people minimum • Play area, terrace, car park • Swimming pool

The young owners' determination to provide high-quality accommodation.

Treat yourself to this haven of well-being in a typical-style mas run by a young Flemish couple. The panoramic swimming pool is set in a peaceful garden of olive trees. The generously-sized bedrooms are subtly decorated: the most inviting in soft ochre colours, rich Sienna shades for the most romantic, olive green for the most modern, while the cheerful family room sports bright contrasting tones. Last but not least, the oriental suite leads onto a secluded Provençal terrace.

Access : 500m from the town centre

  63 LA CORDELINE

M. Dyens

14 rue des Cordeliers
83170 Brignoles
Tel. 04 94 59 18 66
Fax 04 94 59 00 29
lacordeline @ ifrance.com
www.lacordeline.com

Open all year • 5 rooms with bathrooms • €65 to €80, breakfast included • Table d'hôte €25 (by reservation Wed and Sat evening) • Terrace, garden. No dogs allowed

  64 L'AUMÔNERIE

M. et Mme Menard

620 avenue de Fontbrun
83320 Carqueiranne
Tel. 04 94 58 53 56
www.guidesdecharme.com

Open all year • 4 rooms • €75 to €110, breakfast included • No table d'hôte • Garden, car park. Credit cards not accepted, no dogs allowed • Direct access to the beach

 Listen to the birds singing and the fountain murmuring in the garden.

A haven of well-being right in the heart of town. This splendid 17C mansion offers immense rooms furnished with family heirlooms; all have new bathrooms and a small private sitting room. As soon as the sun begins to shine, breakfasts are served outside on the terrace under the trellis.

 Take a seat in the garden and dangle your feet in the Mediterranean!

The total lack of signposts, in fact signs of any kind, bears witness to this establishment's desire to preserve the quiet tranquillity that reigns within its walls. The rooms are tastefully appointed and breakfast will be served either in your room or, whenever the weather permits, under the shade of the terrace's tall pine trees. The garden which has a tiny staircase down to the sea, was what we liked best, however. All that now remains is to enjoy the luxury of your very own private beach.

Access : In the town centre

Access : In a park by the seaside, 5km from Hyères

  65 **DOMAINE DE NESTUBY**
M. et Mme Roubaud

Route de Montfort
83570 Cotignac
Tel. 04 94 04 60 02
Fax 04 94 04 79 22
nestuby@wanadoo.fr
www.sejour-en-provence.com

Closed from 15 Nov to 1 Mar • 5 rooms • €70 to €80, breakfast included, half board available • Table d'hôte €22 (closed weekends) • Car park. Credit cards not accepted

  66 **LES OLIVIERS**
M. et Mme Favero

Route de Flayosc
83300 Draguignan
Tel. 04 94 68 25 74
Fax 04 94 68 57 54
hotel-les-oliviers@club-internet.fr

Closed 5 to 25 Jan • 12 ground-floor rooms with shower/WC and television, 1 with disabled access • €54 to €58, breakfast €8 • No restaurant • Small sitting room, terrace, garden, car park • Outdoor swimming pool

 Nathalie and Jean-François love introducing guests to their estate's red, white and rosé wines.

You know you're in for a treat as soon as you catch sight of this lovely 19C property surrounded by vineyards. The pastel coloured rooms, furnished with items picked up in second-hand and antique shops, are named after the region's grape varieties. The large country dining table is in the old cow-shed, surrounded by mangers and a fireplace. In the summer, you will appreciate the shade of the plane trees and the cool spring water of the large pond.

 What better start to a summer's day than breakfast on the terrace overlooking the garden?

The nearby road will vanish as soon as you put down your suitcase in this recently-built hotel inspired by regional architectural traditions. Its cosy rooms are all excellently soundproofed and some sport the warm bright colours of Provence. A few overlook the swimming pool and a well-tended garden, planted, unsurprisingly enough given the establishment's name, with Mediterranean plants including olive trees!

Access : 5km southbound from Cotignac towards Brignoles

Access : 4km on the road to Flayosc then the D 557

67   **LES VERGERS DE MONTOUREY**
Famille Artaud

Vallée du Reyran
83600 Fréjus
Tel. 04 94 40 85 76
Fax 04 94 40 85 76
arttotos@wanadoo.fr

Open from Feb to 1 Nov • 6 non-smoking rooms with bath/WC and television • €55, breakfast included • Table d'hôte €20 drinks included (Mon, Wed and Fri) • Terrace, garden, park, car park. Credit cards not accepted • Table-tennis, children's bicycles, slide.

Getting into the spirit of life on the farm.

This delightful maison d'hôte in the Reyran Valley does full justice to its former farming function. The spacious, beautifully cared-for rooms are named after and decorated in the colours of fruit grown on the estate: strawberry, cherry, plum, peach, almond and fig. Home-grown produce takes pride of place on the great breakfast and dinner table, where owners and guests all sit down together, either in a country-style dining room or on the terrace. Excellent advice for tourists. Children welcome.

Access : In Montourey neighbourhood

68   **LA TOSCANE**
M. et Mme Leroy

RD 44- quartier de l'Avelan
83310 Grimaud
Tel. 04 94 43 24 11
latoscane@free.fr
www.la-toscane.com

Closed 1 week in Nov, opens in low season on request • 4 non-smoking rooms with bathroom • €75 for minimum stay of 2 nights in season (€80 for 1 night in low season); breakfast included • No table d'hôte • Terrace, garden, car park. Credit cards not accepted, no dogs allowed • Swimming pool

The care taken with the outdoor fixtures and interior decoration.

The roughcast ochre-orange walls, the patio (complete with well) of this lovely villa all bring Tuscany to mind. Relax in one of the exquisitely decorated rooms (stained wood furniture, quilted bedspreads, glazed lava tiles), each one named after a colour: off-white, yellow, orange and lavender. All have a pergola and terrace equipped with deckchair and wrought-iron furniture. Teak sun beds await guests around the pool, and there is a beautifully tended garden. (Well-behaved) children welcome!

Access : 4km north-east of Grimaud on the D 14 and the D 44 towards Plan-de-la-Tour

 69 LES CANCADES

M. et Mme Zerbib

 1195 chemin de la Fontaine-de-Cinq-Sous
83330 Le Beausset
Tel. 04 94 98 76 93
Fax 04 94 90 24 63
charlotte.zerbib@wanadoo.fr

Open all year • 4 rooms • €60 to €70, breakfast included
• No table d'hôte • Garden, car park. Credit cards not
accepted, no dogs allowed • Outdoor swimming pool

 70 LA HAUTE VERRERIE

M. Brun

Route de Saint-Tropez
83340 Le Cannet-des-Maures
Tel. 04 94 47 95 51
Fax 04 94 47 95 51
lahauteverrerie@aol.com

Open all year • 3 rooms • €50, breakfast included • No
table d'hôte • Garden, car park. Credit cards not
accepted • Outdoor swimming pool

 Breathe in the scent of pine, olive and cypress trees.

A steep, narrow lane takes you up to this Provençal villa surrounded by pine and olive trees in a quiet, wooded residential district. Designed by the owner, a retired architect, the tasteful rooms are of varying sizes; two have a terrace overlooking the sumptuous swimming pool. The summer kitchen is in a cabin in the pleasant garden.

 Right on the edge of the Forest of Maures.

A stream runs at the foot of this delightful mid-18C house, originally built as a glass-blowing workshop. The outbuildings are now home to individually decorated rooms. We loved the one under the eaves of the old attic, which has its own sun-deck, and the tiny stone cottage in the garden. A fireside adds character to the sitting room and the swimming pool in the small garden is also very welcome.

Access : 3km eastbound from Castellet, then opposite the Casino supermarket take chemin de la Fontaine de Cinq-Sous

Access : 6km eastbound from Luc on the D 558, towards Saint-Tropez

 71 LE HAMEAU DE CHARLES-AUGUSTE
Mme Gaudin

 Chemin de Baraouque
83340 Le Luc
Tel. 04 94 60 79 45
Fax 04 94 60 79 45
margaud @ wanadoo.fr

Open all year • 4 non-smoking rooms • €58 to €80, breakfast included • No table d'hôte • Terrace, garden, car park. Credit cards not accepted, no dogs allowed • Swimming pool

 72 DOMAINE DE LA FOUQUETTE
M. et Mme Aquadro

 83340 Les Mayons
Tel. 04 94 60 00 69
Fax 04 94 60 02 91
domaine.fouquette @ wanadoo.fr
www.domainedelafouquette.com

Closed from Nov to Feb • 3 non-smoking rooms, 1 with disabled access • €55, breakfast included, half board available • Table d'hôte €18 (evenings only except Sun) • Terrace, garden, car park

Listening to the owner's tales of the house.

Not a real hamlet as such, it is more a collection of buildings built over time around the original 18C farmhouse. All have been restored with a great deal of taste and warmth, and the comfortable, individually decorated rooms are most appealing, furnished with old family heirlooms and pieces picked up here and there. In fine weather, breakfast is served by the swimming pool in the shade of plane and chestnut trees. A perfectly charming spot and a faultless welcome.

Diving into this oasis of tranquillity and recharging our batteries.

A wine-growing estate surrounds this isolated but welcoming farm on the edge of the Maures mountain range. The quiet bedrooms are simply decorated in a Provençal style and the rustic restaurant sports a fireplace and a terrace commanding a superb view. A number of the aperitifs and some respectable little Côtes de Provence wines are produced on the estate and local delicacies have naturally found pride of place on the table d'hôte. Nearby are Tortoise Village and the Mayons Forest.

Access : 5min southbound of Luc, towards the public swimming pool, turn right before the pool towards the Source de la Pioule

Access : 10km south-east of Luc on the D 33 and the D 279 on the edge of the Maures mountains

73 LES PINS
Mme Perin

3630 route de Saint-Antonin
83510 Lorgues
Tel. 04 94 73 91 97
Fax 04 94 73 91 97
www.ehol.com

Open from 15 Mar to 15 Nov • 5 non-smoking rooms with bath/WC and shower/WC • €40 to €56, breakfast included • Table d'hôte €20 (evenings only except Sun and only 3 evenings/week in summer) • Terrace, car park. Credit cards not accepted, no dogs allowed • Swimming pool, play area

74 LE MAS DES OLIVIERS
M. Leroy

Chemin des Grands-Prés
83390 Puget-Ville
Tel. 04 94 48 30 89
Fax 04 94 48 30 89
sapori @ club-internet.fr

Open all year • 3 rooms • €65, breakfast included • Table d'hôte €23 • Terrace, garden, car park. Credit cards not accepted, no dogs allowed • Outdoor swimming pool, horse-riding, cycling

The family atmosphere and bursts of laughter from the children in the pool.

A grove of pines shades this sprawling villa built in the style of a mas next to a small vineyard. The terraces of the three suites in the annex overlook the swimming pool. The other two rooms, more basic but equally immaculately kept, are located in the main building and also decorated in the same Provençal style as the three suites. Countless leisure activities for children who are made particularly welcome by this establishment.

The unmistakable stamp of Provence.

Situated in the heart of the Vars countryside and in the midst of nearly 10 acres of vineyards and olive groves, this mas will delight travellers in search of peace and quiet. Good-sized, well-kept rooms sport the colours of southern France and the bathrooms are very pleasant. The distinctive flavour of Provence can also be tasted in the ochre colours and terracotta decoration of the sitting rooms. Bicycling and horse-riding can be organised on request.

Access : 4km north-west of Lorgues on the D 50 towards Entrecasteaux

Access : 2.5km on the N 97 Cuers road

RAMATUELLE - 83350

SALERNES - 83690

 75 LEÏ SOUCO
M. Giraud

Le Plan - Plaine de Camarat
83350 Ramatuelle
Tel. 04 94 79 80 22
Fax 04 94 79 88 27
www.leisouco.com

Closed from 15 Oct to 31 Mar • 6 rooms (2 air-conditioned) with bath/WC and television • €75 to €106 (€70 to €88 low season); breakfast included • No table d'hôte • Terrace, park, car park. Credit cards not accepted • Tennis

 76 LA BASTIDE ROSE
M. et Mme Henny

Chemin Haut Gaudran
83690 Salernes
Tel. 04 94 70 63 30
Fax 04 94 70 77 34
labastiderose @ wanadoo.fr
www.bastide-rose.com

Closed Oct to mid-Mar • 6 non-smoking rooms • €68, breakfast included • Table d'hôte €25 including beverages • Terrace, park, garden, car park. Credit cards not accepted, no dogs allowed

 A quiet night's sleep, far from the hubbub of the coast.

Olive, pine and other Mediterranean trees surround this Provençal house set in a wine-growing estate off the main road between Ramatuelle and St Tropez. Most of the rooms are on the ground-floor and enjoy private terraces overlooking the vineyards. The interior decoration is pleasantly sober and under-stated with immaculate walls, red tiles, bare beams, rustic furniture and bathrooms which sport Salernes tiles.

 The rustic charm of the spot.

A stony path leads up to this delightful farm, deep in a landscape of vineyards, orchards and sweet-smelling hillsides. Enjoy a quiet night or two in its rooms and suites fitted out with bathrooms decorated with Salernes tiles; some of the rooms are split-level and have their own private terrace. The Dutch farming couple extends a warm friendly welcome to all. Delicious home-made produce features prominently on the table d'hôte: chicken, goose, olives, wine, eggs, fish, apricots, plums.

Access : 3.5km east of Ramatuelle, on the D 93 towards Saint-Tropez

Access : 3km south-west of Salernes on the D31 towards Entrecasteaux, go through la Bresque towards La Colle or Riforan for 2.5km, then left

  77 VILLA LOU GARDIAN
M. et Mme Castellano

646 route de Bandol
83110 Sanary-sur-Mer
Tel. 04 94 88 05 73
Fax 04 94 88 24 13
www.lougardian.com

Closed from 15 Oct to 1 Apr • 4 rooms, 2 of which are in the garden • €78 (€68 low season), breakfast included • No table d'hôte • Garden, car park. Credit cards not accepted, no dogs allowed • Outdoor swimming pool, tennis

 78 LA BERGERIE DU MOULIN
M. et Mme Guillot

Chemin du Vieux Moulin
83460 Taradeau
Tel. 04 94 99 91 51
Fax 04 94 99 98 98
bergerie.moulin @ wanadoo.fr
www.bergeriedumoulin.com

Open all year • 6 non-smoking rooms, air-conditioned upstairs, with bath/WC or shower/WC, satellite television and mini-bar • €85 to €105, breakfast included • Table d'hôte €29 to €35, drinks included (reservation only) • Terrace, garden, private car park. Credit cards not accepted • Outdoor swimming pool, billiards

 Conveniently located near the sandy beach of La Gorguette.

Despite the nearby road, this recent villa surrounded by palm trees and a pleasant garden is quiet and peaceful. The bedrooms are colourful and well-soundproofed and all have lovely bathrooms; we preferred those near the large swimming pool. Meals are served on the patio. Tennis courts and table-tennis available in the grounds.

 The owners' excellent tourist and gastronomic tips.

This characterful house nestles in a peaceful village not far from Arcs-sur-Argens and Lorgues. Rustic outer stone walls overgrown with climbers, Provençal-style bedrooms, kitchen-cum-dining room in the former sheepfold and a lovely outdoor sitting room overlooking the pool and arbour, where meals are sometimes served in the summer. The chirping of the crickets and murmuring stream which used to turn the millwheel are likely to be the only sounds you will hear!

Access : On the Bandol road

Access : 6km from Arcs-sur-Argens on the D 10

PROVENCE, ALPS AND THE FRENCH RIVIERA

  79 CHÂTEAU DE VINS
M. Bonnet

Les Prés du Château
83170 Vins-sur-Caramy
Tel. 04 94 72 50 40
Fax 04 94 72 50 88
chateau.de.vins@wanadoo.fr
http://perso.wanadoo.fr/chateaudevins/

Closed from Nov to Mar • 5 rooms with bathrooms • €70, breakfast included • Garden, car park. Credit cards not accepted • Cultural events organised, music courses and summer concerts

  80 DE BLAUVAC
Mme Chapron

11 rue de la Bancasse
84000 Avignon
Tel. 04 90 86 34 11
Fax 04 90 86 27 41
blauvac@aol.com

Open all year • 16 rooms, most have bath/WC and a mezzanine, some have shower/WC, all have television • €63 to €73; breakfast €7 • No restaurant • No dogs allowed

 A listed historic castle with an emphasis on culture, music in particular.

Saved from ruin and lovingly restored by its owner, this 16C château, complete with towers on all four corners, now offers moderately sized, but beautifully appointed and utterly peaceful rooms, each of which is named after a musician. The former hunting room is now the dining room. Art exhibitions, concerts and music courses take place throughout the year in the other elegantly restored rooms.

 A stay in the heart of Avignon without the fuss of a busy town.

The Marquis de Blauvac built this 17C house in a quiet street near the Palais des Papes, from where Avignon's medieval "antipopes" defied Rome for almost 70 years. Its elegant wrought-iron balustrade and thick stone walls are typical of the period: the breakfast room is decorated in a Louis XV style. Most of the rooms, simply furnished but full of character, have a mezzanine with an extra bed.

Access : 9km from Brignoles on the D 24, Thoronet road

Access : In the town centre, in a side street leading to Place de l'Horloge (town hall)

 81 LA FERME
Mme Wawrzyniak

Chemin des Bois - Ile de la Barthelasse
84000 Avignon
Tel. 04 90 82 57 53
Fax 04 90 27 15 47
info @ hotel-laferme.com
www.hotel-laferme.com

Closed from 1 Nov to 20 Mar • 20 rooms, 3 of which are non-smoking, with bath/WC or shower/WC, air-conditioning and television • €77 to €88 (€65 to €70 low season); breakfast €10; half board available • Restaurant closed Mon and Wed; menus €23 to €38 • Terrace, private car park. No dogs allowed • Swimming pool

 If you come here, you will have to learn the nursery rhyme "Sur le pont d'Avignon..."

This handsome farm is located near to the Papal City on the Island of Barthelasse, one of the largest in Europe and a haven of greenery in Avignon. The tastefully decorated rooms ensure that the only sounds you will hear are those of the dawn chorus. The dining room features enormous beams, thick stone walls and a huge fireplace, while out on the terrace you can relax in the shade of the ancient plane tree.

Access : 5km northbound, on the Ile de la Barthelasse, by the D 228 then a minor road

 82 LE MÉDIÉVAL
M. Philippe Robert

15 rue Petite-Saunerie
84000 Avignon
Tel. 04 90 86 11 06
Fax 04 90 82 08 64
hotel.medieval @ wanadoo.fr
www.hotelmedieval.com

Closed from 23 Dec to 23 Jan • 34 rooms, all have bath/WC or shower/WC and television, most have a kitchenette • €53 to €84; breakfast €7 • No restaurant • No dogs allowed • Patio

 The kitchenettes in the rooms come in handy for a long stay during the festival.

This late-17C mansion built for a cardinal was formerly linked to the Papal Palace by an underground passage. A statue of the Virgin Mary stands in an alcove of its beautiful stone façade. A period staircase leads up to the rooms, a touch outdated but furnished in a rustic style. We recommend booking one of those overlooking the flowered patio, particularly during the summer. Multilingual staff.

Access : In a side street in the heart of the town, from the Porte St-Lazare, take Rue Carreterie and turn right

 83 LA MAISON
Mme Laurelut

Hameau de Piolon
84340 Beaumont-du-Ventoux
Tel. 04 90 65 15 50
Fax 04 90 65 23 29

Closed from Jan to Mar and Nov to Dec; every lunchtime in high season except Sun; Mon and Tue in low season • 3 rooms with separate entrances, on the courtyard, with bath/WC or shower/WC • €60 to €70 (€58 to €68 low season); breakfast €9 • Menus €29 • Terrace. No dogs allowed in rooms

 84 LA GARANCE
M. et Mme Babinet

Hameau de Sainte-Colombe
84410 Bédoin
Tel. 04 90 12 81 00
Fax 04 90 65 93 05

Closed from 15 Nov to 1 Apr (except by reservation) • 13 rooms located upstairs and on the ground floor, with bath/WC or shower/WC, all have television • €55 to €65 (€50 to €60 low season); breakfast €8 • No restaurant • Car park • Swimming pool, hiking

 You won't find a warmer welcome anywhere.

This old farm in the region of Malaucène has been transformed into an attractive Provençal house with blue shutters. Each of the three tastefully decorated rooms has its own independent access. The smart dining room is proudly decorated in bright southern colours, but it is the exquisite terrace that will remain in our memory. Dining by candlelight or lunching under the shade of a wonderful lime tree was sheer bliss.

 Take on the ascent of Mont Ventoux on foot... or by car!

It is a pleasure to drive into this pretty hamlet surrounded by vines and orchards and up to the front door of the farmhouse. Inside, the rooms' furnishings are modern and the tiles are old. You will be able to wake up and feast your eyes on Mont Ventoux, before tripping down to breakfast on the terrace or in the brightly-coloured dining room. Afterwards embark on the assault of this "giant of Provence" along signposted footpaths. Well worth writing home about.

Access : 4km to the north-east of Malaucène on the D 153

Access : Head for Bédoin on the D 19 from Malaucène or the D 974 from Carpentras, then drive towards Mont-Ventoux

 85 **LE COMTADIN**
M. Van Orshoven

65 boulevard Albin-Durand
84200 Carpentras
Tel. 04 90 67 75 00
Fax 04 90 67 75 01
le.comtadin@wanadoo.fr
www.le-comtadin.com

Closed from 23 Dec to 1 Feb, 12 Feb to 21 Feb
• 19 rooms, 2 of which are non-smoking, one has
disabled access. Rooms have bath/WC or shower/WC, all
have air-conditioning and television • €72 to €78;
breakfast €11 • Menus €20 to €35 • Patio, garage

 **86** **LES FLORETS**
M. et Mme Bernard

Route des Dentelles
84190 Gigondas
Tel. 04 90 65 85 01
Fax 04 90 65 83 80
www.hotel-lesflorets.com

Closed 1 Jan to 31 Mar, Mon evening, Tue from Nov to
Apr and Wed • 15 rooms with bath/WC and television
• €90 to €125; breakfast €12; half board available
• Menus from €24 to €38 • Terrace, garden, car park
• Near to the Dentelles de Montmirail

 Breakfasting on the patio.

This late-18C mansion stands on the ring road round
the busy capital of the Comtat region. Recently
refurbished, it proudly sports wrought-iron furniture,
high-quality materials and a contemporary decorative
style. Most of the rooms overlook the peaceful patio
which echoes to the murmur of the fountain in the
centre. The reception is home to orchids, the owners'
pride and joy.

 **The delightful, flower-decked shady
terrace.**

This inviting hostelry, lost in the countryside at the foot
of the Montmirail range, has been run by the same
family for three generations. The handsome edifice was
recently renovated and now sports a Provençal-coloured
façade, a pleasant sitting room-bar, a snug rustically
furnished dining room and very comfortable and
tastefully spruced-up bedrooms. The wines from the
family estate (Gigondas, Vacqueyras and Côtes du
Rhône) are the perfect accompaniment to the chef's
delicious regional cuisine.

Access : On the ring-road

Access : 3km eastbound of Gigondas on a minor
road

 AUBERGE DE CARCARILLE
M. Rambaud

 Route d'Apt par D2
84220 Gordes
Tel. 04 90 72 02 63
Fax 04 90 72 05 74
carcaril @ club-internet.fr
www.auberge-carcarille.com

Closed Dec, Jan and Fri (Fri evenings only from Apr to Sep) • 11 rooms with bath/WC or shower/WC and television • €60 to €75; breakfast €10, half board available • Menus €18 to €42 • Private car park, garden, terrace. No dogs allowed • Swimming pool

 LA BADELLE
Mme Cortasse

 84220 Gordes
Tel. 04 90 72 33 19
Fax 04 90 72 48 74
badelle @ club-internet.fr
www.la-badelle.com

Closed in Jan • 5 rooms • €74 to €92 (€68 to €84 low season), breakfast €5 • No table d'hôte • Garden, car park. Credit cards not accepted, no dogs allowed • Outdoor swimming pool

Taking life easy on the private terrace of your room.

The beauty of Gordes is no longer a secret, but this discreet country inn is worth keeping to yourself! Installed in a dry-stone construction on the edge of a garden, painted furniture and an elegant Provençal style set the scene for the impeccably kept rooms. Regional dishes take pride of place on the menu and are served in the light, colourful dining room. The terrace is equally appealing.

A beautiful combination of old and new.

A tiny country road leads to this ancient farmhouse. The rooms in the outbuildings have been entirely redone and all feature the same whitewashed walls, rustic earthenware tiles, old furniture and excellent bathrooms. Four open onto the swimming pool. In the summer guests are offered the use of a practical kitchen.

Access : Beneath the village towards Apt

Access : 7km southbound from Gordes on the D 104 towards Goult

 89 **AUBERGE DU CHEVAL BLANC**
M. et Mme Moullet

84240 La Bastide-des-Jourdans
Tel. 04 90 77 81 08
Fax 04 90 77 86 51
provence.luberon @ wanadoo.fr

Closed in Feb and on Thu • 4 rooms with bath/WC, air-conditioning and television • €70 to €90; breakfast €10; half board available • Restaurant air-conditioned; menus €27 to €37 • Terrace, private car park

 90 **LES FENOUILLETS**
M. Courrege

Quartier Revol
84240 La Tour-d'Aigues
Tel. 04 90 07 48 22
Fax 04 90 07 34 26
mail @ lesfenouillets.com
www.lesfenouillets.com

Closed from 31 Oct to 27 Mar • 15 rooms, one of which has disabled access, most have bath/WC, some have shower/WC, all have television • €65; breakfast €10; half board available • Menu (dinner only) €26 • Terrace, garden, private car park. No dogs allowed in restaurant

 The Luberon Regional Park is riddled with paths.

In just a few years, this former post house has been elegantly transformed into an up-to-date country inn. Exposed beams, thick stone walls and tiled floors set the scene for the spacious, welcoming rooms, some of which have a small cane-furnished sitting room. Warm, sunny colours adorn the elegant dining room which leads into the dappled shade of a quiet terrace.

 Relax in the shade of a mulberry tree on the terrace.

Wherever you turn, the eye is greeted with the distinctive charm of hand-printed cotton fabrics, reminiscent of the work of the Souleïado workshop, reputed for its designer Provençal prints and cotton. These fabrics adorn the rooms, restaurant and terrace, adding a lovely hint of gaiety to the modern and unusual architecture. The garden is as well-tended as the rest of the establishment, which welcomes growing numbers of regulars who appreciate the care and attention.

Access : On the main road of the village

Access : At Pertuis, leave the D 973 for the D 956: after 5km the hotel is on the bend before the Tour d'Aigues

 **91** LA MAISON DES SOURCES
Mme Collart

Chemin des Fraisses
84360 Lauris
Tel. 04 90 08 22 19
Fax 04 90 08 22 19
contact @ maison-des-sources.com
www.maison-des-sources.com

Open all year • 4 rooms with bathrooms • €82 to €84, breakfast included • Table d'hôte €25 (occasionally) • Sitting room, garden, car park. Credit cards not accepted • Hiking, horse-riding, mountain biking

92 LES GÉRANIUMS
M. Awada Huw

Place de la Croux
84330 Le Barroux
Tel. 04 90 62 41 08
Fax 04 90 62 56 48
les.geraniums @ wanadoo.fr

Closed Jan and Feb • 22 rooms located in 2 buildings, with bath/WC or shower/WC • €55 to €60; breakfast €10; half board available • Menus €18 (weekdays) to €46 • Terrace, garden, private car park. No dogs allowed • Llama farm in the village

 Breakfast in the welcome shade of acacia trees.

This old farmhouse, built against a cliff face riddled with caves, is hidden in the midst of vineyards, orchards and olive groves in the Luberon foothills. After some major restoration work it was saved from ruin and now offers brightly coloured rooms, the most curious of which features no less than four four-poster beds. The sitting and dining rooms have fine old vaulted ceilings and the somewhat unruly garden only adds to the appeal.

 Hiking through vineyards and olive groves in the foothills of the Montmirail.

This impressive stone house stands in the heart of a fortified village overlooking the Comtat plain. The spotless rooms are furnished in a rustic style; some have balconies facing the valley. The chef's delicious recipes, made with local produce, are definitely worth sampling, either on the spacious terrace which overflows with geraniums or in the dining room decorated with paintings left by an artist and regular visitor to the establishment.

Access : 4.5km to the south-west of Lourmarin on the D 27

Access : In the centre of the village

 93 HOSTELLERIE FRANÇOIS JOSEPH
M. Pochat

Chemin des Rabassières
84330 Le Barroux
Tel. 04 90 62 52 78
Fax 04 90 62 33 54
hotel.f.joseph@wanadoo.fr
www.hotel-francois-joseph.com

Open from 1 Apr to 2 Nov • 12 rooms, 6 are apartments, 5 are studios and one has disabled access. All have bath/WC or shower/WC and television • €70 to €103; breakfast €12 • Menus €22 (evening only) • Park, car park. No dogs allowed • Outdoor swimming pool

 94 MAS DE LA LAUSE
M. et Mme Lonjon

Chemin de Geysset
84330 Le Barroux
Tel. 04 90 62 33 33
Fax 04 90 62 36 36
maslause@provence-gites.com

Closed from Nov to Mar • 5 rooms with shower/WC • €57, breakfast included • Table d'hôte €16 • Garden, car park. Credit cards not accepted

 Snoozing under the umbrella pines.

In the heart of the countryside, this group of modern buildings has remained true to local architectural tradition. The modern rooms are brightened up by cheerful fabrics; half have loggias or ground floor terraces and families can book one of two cottages. A happy mixture of unruly bushes cohabit peacefully with perfect lawns in the garden and from the swimming pool, you can admire the view of Mont Ventoux.

 Apricot rooms, apricot trees, apricot jam and nectar of apricot.

Nestled among vineyards and apricot trees, this mas built in 1883 has been renovated in true Provençal fashion. The bright sunny rooms, recently repainted, echo their evocative names. Sunflower and Iris overlook the castle of Barroux and the Comtat plain, while Apricot faces the orchards. How about a quick game of pétanque before sampling the tasty regional cooking under the shade of an arbour?

Access : 2km from Barrous on the Monastères Ste-Madeleine road

Access : 800m towards Suzette

 95 LE MAS DE MAGALI
M. et Mme Bodewes

 Quartier Chante-Coucou
84110 Le Crestet
Tel. 04 90 36 39 91
Fax 04 90 28 73 40
masmagali@wanadoo.fr

Open from 28 Mar to 16 Oct • 11 rooms with bath/WC and television • €78 to €85; breakfast €9; half board available • Restaurant closed Wed; menus €28 to €34 (evenings only) • Terrace, garden, car park; No dogs allowed in restaurant • Outdoor swimming pool

 96 LE MAS DE GUILLES
M. et Mme Lherm

 Route de Vaugines
84160 Lourmarin
Tel. 04 90 68 30 55
Fax 04 90 68 37 41
hotel@guilles.com
www.guilles.com

Open from early Apr to mid-Nov • 28 rooms with bath/WC and television • €80 to €115; breakfast €12; half board available • Menu €42, evenings only • Terrace, garden, private car park. No dogs allowed in restaurant • Outdoor swimming pool, tennis

 The heady perfume of Provence's vegetation.

The utter peace and quiet, magnificent view of Mont Ventoux and the remote Vaucluse landscape, colourful blue and yellow dining room and spacious rooms, some with terraces: this modern mas captures all that is best in Provence. Magali, the lady of the house, oversees every aspect of your stay from pétanque and pastis to a quiet afternoon nap.

 The perfect peace and quiet.

A stony, but driveable path, leads to a delightful Provençal mas nestled in the midst of vineyards and orchards. The eye is drawn to the enchanting swimming pool surrounded by lawns where deck-chairs invite visitors to settle back and relax. Lovely old wardrobes, period furniture and warm yellow colours set the tone for the bedrooms. The chef's classical cuisine is served in an attractive, vaulted dining room or - weather permitting - on the sun-drenched terrace.

Access : Leave Vaison-la-Romaine on the D 938 (towards Malaucène) and after 3.5km, turn right (D 76)

Access : 2km from Lourmarin

 97 LE DOMAINE DES TILLEULS
M. Chastel

Route du Mont-Ventoux
84340 Malaucène
Tel. 04 90 65 22 31
Fax 04 90 65 16 77
info @ hotel-domainedestilleuls.com
www.hotel-domainedestilleuls.com

Open all year • 20 rooms, half of which overlook the park, all have bath/WC or shower/WC and television • €75 to €90; breakfast €9 • No restaurant • Park, private car park • Outdoor swimming pool, numerous footpaths nearby

 The lovely swimming pool surrounded by foliage.

The enormous rooms of this former Templar stronghold are now adorned with bold fabrics, pastel colours and earthenware tiles. The thick stone 18C walls make air-conditioning thankfully unnecessary even during heat waves. Ask for a room facing the lime, plane and chestnut trees in the enormous park. Walkers will be happy to learn that the young owners can indicate endless paths between Mont Ventoux, the "Giant of Provence" and the ragged crests of the Dentelles de Montmirail.

 98 LE MANOIR
M. ou Mme Caillet

Avenue Jean- Moulin
84550 Mornas
Tel. 04 90 37 00 79
Fax 04 90 37 10 34
lemanoir @ ifrance.com
www.hotel-le-manoir.com

Closed in Jan • 25 rooms located in 2 wings with bath/WC or shower/WC, some have air-conditioning and television • €48 to €53; breakfast €7; half board available • Restaurant closed Mon and Tue lunchtimes from Jun to Sep; Sun evening, Mon and Tue lunchtime from Oct to May; menus €17 (weekdays) to €30 • Terrace, car park, garage

 Wining and dining by candlelight on the patio.

This impressive 18C mansion stands at the foot of a steep cliff, dominated by the outline of Mornas fortress. The new owners have so far concentrated their restoration efforts on the restaurant, but they plan to redo the rooms shortly. That said, beautiful old wardrobes and marble fireplaces add a great deal of old-fashioned charm to the rooms. The verdant patio and flowered terrace echo to the light-hearted, sunny disposition of Provence.

Access : At Malaucène drive towards Mont-Ventoux, the hotel is on the left

Access : Beside the N 7 through the village

99 LES HAUTS DE VÉRONCLE
M. et Mme Del Corso

84220 Murs
Tel. 04 90 72 60 91
Fax 04 90 72 62 07
hauts.de.veroncle @ wanadoo.fr
http://hauts.de.veroncle.free.fr

Closed from 4 Nov to 29 Mar • 3 rooms • €42 to €53, breakfast included • Table d'hôte €20 • Sitting room, terrace, garden, car park. Credit cards not accepted

100 MAS DES AIGRAS
M. et Mme Davi

Chemin des Aigras
84100 Orange
Tel. 04 90 34 81 01
Fax 04 90 34 05 66
masdesaigras @ free.fr

Closed from 1 to 15 Jan, 26 Oct to 11 Nov, Tue, Wed and Sat lunchtime from Apr to Sep • 12 rooms, 8 of which are air-conditioned, all have bath/WC or shower/WC and television • €70 to €106; breakfast €11; half board €72 to €90 • Menus €18 (weekdays) to €50 • Terrace, garden, private car park. No dogs allowed • Outdoor swimming pool

Ever longed to be somewhere no-one could find you?

In the middle of nowhere – there is no other way to describe the peaceful tranquillity of this blue-shuttered mas with its dry stone walls, fragrant garrigue and chirping cicadas. A sophisticated cuisine is served by the fireside in winter or under the wisteria in the summer. If you feel like a walk, ask Mr or Mrs Del Corso to point you towards the path of the seven mills which runs alongside the gorges of the Véroncle.

The amazing botanical garden of a leading 19C entomologist, J-H Fabre.

The stone walls of this mas are hidden amid vineyards and fields on the outskirts of Orange. The cheerful young owners have thrown themselves into the task of rejuvenating their property, adding colourful cotton fabrics and hand-painted walls. Little by little, the rooms are regaining their rightful Provençal colours and are also being treated to air-conditioning. Organic produce figures prominently on the up-to-date menu, served in a dining room or on a teak and wrought-iron furnished terrace.

Access : 8km to the north-east of Sénanque on the D 177, the D 244 then the D 15

Access : 4km northbound from Orange on the N 7, then take a minor road (100m from the bypass)

 101 L'HERMITAGE
Mme Oury

 Route de Carpentras
84210 Pernes-les-Fontaines
Tel. 04 90 66 51 41
Fax 04 90 61 36 41
hotel.lhermitage @ libertysurf.fr
www.hotel-lhermitage.com

Closed in Dec, Jan and Feb • 20 rooms upstairs, most have bath/WC, all have television • €74 to €105 (€61 to €90 low season); breakfast €9 • No restaurant • Park, private car park. Supplement payable for dogs • Swimming pool

 102 LES AUZIÈRES
 M. Cuer

84110 Roaix
Tel. 04 90 46 15 54
Fax 04 90 46 12 75

Closed late Oct • 5 rooms with bathrooms, separate WC and television • €77, breakfast included • Table d'hôte €25 (from Mon to Fri only by reservation) • Sitting room, car park • Outdoor swimming pool, boules, table-tennis, billiards

 A refreshing drink from one of the 36 fountains of the "pearl of the Comtat".

Once the property of a relative of the famous Captain Dreyfus, whose court-martial divided public opinion in 1890s France and inspired Emile Zola's famous counterblast "J'accuse", this 19C house has retained a characteristically Provençal atmosphere. Majestic trees, statues and fountains abound in the immense park, together with a host of shaded corners, perfect for a quiet pastis. The colourful rooms are gradually being refurbished. The sitting rooms are decorated with period furniture.

 A sweeping view of the valley.

It would be hard to find a more secluded spot than this Provençal farm perched on a hillside in the midst of vineyards, olive groves and lavender fields. The spacious, cool bedrooms are spotless and utterly tranquil. Sample the traditional cooking at a huge wooden table in the dining room or on the terrace, facing Mont Ventoux and the jagged peaks of the Dentelles de Montmirail.

Access : Set back from the road, 2km northbound from Pernes-les-Fontaines, towards Carpentras on the D 938

Access : 6km westbound from Vaison on the D 975 towards Orange

103 LES SABLES D'OCRE
M. Hilario

Les Sablières
84220 Roussillon
Tel. 04 90 05 55 55
Fax 04 90 05 55 50
sablesdocre@free.fr
www.roussillon-hotel.com

Closed from 15 Nov to 15 Mar • 22 rooms with balcony, or terrace on the ground floor, 2 have disabled access, all have bath/WC or shower/WC, air-conditioning and television • €62 to €75 (€55 to €65 low season); breakfast €10 • No restaurant • Garden, car park • Outdoor swimming pool

104 L'ÉVÊCHÉ
M. et Mme Verdier

Rue de l'Évêché
84110 Vaison-la-Romaine
Tel. 04 90 36 13 46
Fax 04 90 36 32 43
eveche@aol.com

Closed from 15 Nov to 15 Dec • 3 rooms and 2 gîtes • €70 to €80, breakfast included • No table d'hôte • Sitting room, terrace. Credit cards not accepted, no dogs allowed

 Walk along the "ochre footpath" to the breathtaking Giants' Causeway.

The colourful walls of this modern hotel pay homage to the "red villages" of Roussillon and their picturesque houses. The mas built in 1998 on the outskirts of the village offers rooms which are handsomely equipped and have a balcony or garden-level terrace, even though they do rather lack character; some have brass beds. 400m away, the old Mathieu factory has been turned into a pigment conservatory – tours and courses.

 A warm country welcome after a hard day's sightseeing.

This former Episcopal palace, dating from the 16C, stands in the medieval part of town. Most of its countless rooms, on a variety of levels, overlook a tiny terrace. The breakfast room is the largest and it offers a wonderful view of the lower town. A lovely spiral staircase winds up to the well-furnished and tasteful rooms. Don't forget to take a look at the interesting collection of prints originally from a treatise on lockmaking.

Access : Around 10km from Apt, towards Avignon, leave the N 100 and turn right onto the D 149 for 4.5km

Access : In the old town

VIOLÈS - 84150

 **105** LA FARIGOULE
Mme Favrat

Le Plan-de-Dieu
84150 Violès
Tel. 04 90 70 91 78
Fax 04 90 70 91 78
www.la-farigoule.com

Closed from Nov to Mar • 5 rooms, including one studio, with shower/WC • €45 to €55, breakfast included • No table d'hôte • Sitting room, garden, car park. Credit cards not accepted • Play area, table-tennis

 106 MAS DE BOUVAU
M. et Mme Hertzog

Route de Cairanne
84150 Violès
Tel. 04 90 70 94 08
Fax 04 90 70 95 99

Closed from 2 to 31 Jan, 20 to 30 Dec, evenings from Nov to Feb, every lunchtime in Jul-Aug, Sat, Sun evenings and Tue lunchtime • 6 rooms with bath/WC or shower/WC and television • €59 to €69 for 2 (2 for 4 people); breakfast €9; half board available • Menus €25 to €35 (by reservation) • Terrace, garden, car park. No dogs allowed in rooms

 The erudite atmosphere of this characterful house.

This 18C wine-growers' house has lost none of its authenticity over the years. A fine staircase leads up to antique furnished rooms, each of which is named after a writer with Provence connections, including Frédéric Mistral, Alphonse Daudet and Marie Mauron; you won't be surprised to discover that your hosts used to own a book shop. Breakfasts are served in a lovely vaulted room. As for free time, there is a play area for children and the hotel rents out bicycles (including tandems).

 Daydreaming as you gaze on the jagged peaks of the Dentelles de Montmirail.

This old farmhouse is surrounded by the vineyards of the Plan de Dieu plateau which have been cultivated since the Middle Ages. The sober rooms are furnished with sturdy country pieces. Sample the traditional menu in one of the Provençal dining rooms or on the terraces – our favourite is in the old barn. The wine-list is a credit to the region.

Access : 10km westbound from Gigondas on the D 80 towards Orange, then the D 8 and the D 977 towards Violès

Access : Northbound from Violès, leave the D 977 and turn left towards Cairanne

RHÔNE-ALPES

A land of contrasts and a crossroads of culture, the Rhône-Alpes region offers visitors a thousand different faces. Its lofty peaks are heaven on earth to skiers, climbers and hikers attracted by the sublime beauty of its glittering glaciers, torrential streams and tranquil lakes, while its fashionable resorts, like Chamonix and Courchevel, set the tone in alpine chic. If you can tear yourself away from the roof of Europe, venture down past the herds of cattle grazing on the rich mountain grass and into the intense bustle of the Rhône valley, symbolised by its fast-flowing waters. From Antique Roman roads to high-speed inter-city trains, the main artery between north and south has forged the reputation of this region's economic drive. Rhône-Alpes lies on the route taken by hordes of holidaymakers every summer, and those in the know always make a point of stopping in the region to taste its culinary specialities. The area abounds in restaurants, from three-star trend-setters to Lyon's legendary neighbourhood *bouchons*, whose standards and traditions have made the region the kingdom of cuisine.

- Ain (01)
- Ardèche (07)
- Drôme (26)
- Isère (38)
- Loire (42)
- Rhône (69)
- Savoie (73)
- Haute-Savoie (74)

RHÔNE ALPES

1 AUBERGE DES BICHONNIÈRES
M. Sauvage

Route de Savigneux
01330 Ambérieux-en-Dombes
Tel. 04 74 00 82 07
Fax 04 74 00 89 61
bichonnier@aol.com
www.aubergedesbichonnieres.com

Closed 15 Dec to 15 Jan, Sun (except in Jul and Aug), Mon except summer evenings and Tue lunchtime • 9 rooms with bath/WC or shower/WC and television • €48; breakfast €8; half board available • Menus €15 to €31 • Terrace, garden, private car park

2 HÔTEL DE FRANCE
M. et Mme Maillard

19 place Bernard
01000 Bourg-en-Bresse
Tel. 04 74 23 30 24
Fax 04 74 23 69 90
info@grand-hoteldefrance.com
www.grand-hoteldefrance.com

Open all year • 44 rooms with bath/WC and shower/WC and television, 16 are non-smoking • €79; breakfast €9.50 • Restaurant facilities available next-door at "Chez Blanc" • Garage

 The charm of the "Route des étangs" (Pond Route).

Guests are pampered within the cob walls of this old farm, typical of the Dombes region. The rooms overlooking the courtyard, although a little on the small side, are refreshingly quiet. The cuisine draws on local traditions and ingredients and is served in a rustic dining room near an old stove or under a canopy on the terrace. Rows of crimson geraniums brighten up the peaceful garden.

 The happy marriage between contemporary fittings and the charm of yesteryear.

The glass canopy that adorns the elaborate façade of the hotel and the attractive mosaic in the lobby remind visitors that the building dates from the early 20C. The bedrooms were completely modernised recently and now sport wood furniture, old-fashioned wardrobes painted white, pastel-coloured walls, silky fabrics and beautifully appointed bathrooms. As for the breakfast buffet, it is sure to satisfy you both in terms of quality and quantity.

Access : On leaving the town, on the Ars-sur-Formans road

Access : In the town centre

3 FERME DES GRANDS HUTAINS
M. et Mme Veyron

Le Petit Brens
01300 Brens
Tel. 04 79 81 90 95
Fax 04 79 81 90 95

Closed in Nov and on Sun • 4 non-smoking rooms with bath/WC • €40 to €45 (€37 to €43 low season), breakfast included • Table d'hôte €13 • Terrace, car park. Credit cards not accepted, no dogs allowed

4 AUBERGE DE CAMPAGNE DU MOLLARD
M. Decré

01320 Châtillon-la-Palud
Tel. 04 74 35 66 09
Fax 04 37 61 11 72
f.decre@wanadoo.fr

Open all year by reservation • 4 rooms • €65, breakfast included • Menus €16 to €35 • Car park. Credit cards accepted in restaurant, no dogs allowed

 Enjoyable meals of beautifully cooked garden-fresh vegetables.

The farmhouse and pergola are delightful. The rooms under the eaves are snugly welcoming, furnished with family heirlooms and decorated in an old-fashioned style; all are non-smoking. The dining table, which shows the chef's preference for home-grown produce, is located in a welcoming room where a fire is lit in winter, or when the weather allows, around a stone table in the garden under the shade of an oak and birch trees.

 The religiously preserved rustic appeal.

A tiny country lane will take you up to this attractive farmhouse and courtyard-garden bedecked with flowers – a sight to behold in the spring. The four rooms in an outbuilding have wonderful carved wooden beds, but have a shared bathroom. Meals are served in a country-style dining room with a fireplace and a huge cauldron. The tasty family cooking focuses on local produce.

Access : 3km southbound from Belley on the D 31A

Access : 14km north-east of Pérouges on the D 984 and the D 904, towards Chalamont, then a lane on the left

5   **CLOS DE LA TOUR**
M. et Mme Rassion

01400 Châtillon-sur-Chalaronne
Tel. 04 74 55 05 12
Fax 04 74 55 09 19
hotellatour@free.fr

Closed one week before Christmas • 15 rooms, 1 has disabled access and 5 are air-conditioned • €115 to €145, breakfast included, half board available • La Tour Restaurant (same owner) 200m away; air-conditioned, menus €18 (weekday lunchtimes) to €58 • Garden, private car park • Swimming pool

6   **CHAMBRE D'HÔTE M. SALMON**
M. et Mme Salmon

150 place du Champ-de-Foire
01400 Châtillon-sur-Chalaronne
Tel. 04 74 55 06 86
Fax 04 74 55 42 56
alsalmon@club-internet.fr
www.chambresdhotes.fr/salmon/

Closed from 22 Dec to 8 Jan • 5 rooms • €50 to €53, breakfast included • No table d'hôte • Garden, car park. Credit cards not accepted, no dogs allowed

The spacious tree-lined garden through which the Chalaronne runs.

Just 200m from the Hotel de la Tour stands its lovely annex, the Clos de la Tour, made up of three beautifully restored old buildings, including a 16C mill. Shabby-chic walls, bare floorboards, exquisite fabrics, canopy beds, unusual light fittings and bathrooms which sport mosaics and the occasional "old-fashioned" bath tub set the picture for the delightful bedrooms. Guests invariably praise the peace and quiet of this charming address.

A breakfast worth getting up for!

Old wardrobes, a wooden staircase, huge beams and floral wallpaper: the stage is set and the curtain can rise on this welcoming home. Bunches of fresh flowers and well-polished wooden furniture greet you in the rooms. Make sure you get up early and have had time to work up an appetite, if you want to do justice to the substantial mounds of croissants, walnut bread, pancakes and no less than thirty home-made jams!

Access : In the town centre

Access : In the town centre

RHÔNE ALPES

7 L'AUBERGE CAMPAGNARDE
Mme Merloz

01230 Évosges
Tel. 04 74 38 55 55
Fax 04 74 38 55 62

 auberge-campagnarde@wanadoo.fr

Closed from 1 Jan to 1 Feb, Sep and 11 Nov to 1 Dec
• 15 rooms with bath/WC or shower/WC, all have television • €40 to €65; breakfast €7; half-board available • Menus €22 (weekdays) to €48 • Terrace, garden, car park • Outdoor swimming pool, mini golf, table tennis, play area, fishing

8 LA MAINAZ
M. Part

Route du col de la Faucille - N 5
01170 Gex
Tel. 04 50 41 31 10
Fax 04 50 41 31 77

mainaz@club-internet.com
www.la-mainaz.com

Closed Sun evening and Mon except during school holidays and from 1 Nov to 10 Dec • 22 rooms with bath/WC and shower/WC and television • €60 to €90; breakfast €12; half board available • Restaurant closed Sun evening, Mon and Tue lunchtime; menus €25 (weekdays) to €52 • Car park • Swimming pool

 Ideal for nature lovers with energetic children.

This old family farmstead in a remote village of Bugey has been turned into a lovely country inn with rustic or modern-style rooms and an inviting restaurant with stone walls and a fireplace. Children however generally prefer the shaded garden with play area, mini-golf and swimming pool.

 Contemplating the view of Lake Geneva and the Alps in the distance.

The same family has been presiding over the destiny of this high-perched chalet leading up to the Col de la Faucille for three generations. Some of the rooms command a superb view of the region, as do the restaurant terrace and swimming pool. Varnished pine panelling and 70s furniture gives an idea of the general decorative style, but some of the rooms were recently spruced up and a few also boast balconies. Fill up your lungs with sweet mountain air!

Access : Leave the N 504 (Ambérieu-Belley) between St Rambert-en-Bugey and Argis and follow the D 34

Access : 1km from the Col de la Faucille, on the N 5, towards Gex

RHÔNE ALPES

9 LA VILLA DU RHÔNE
Jean Cabardi

Chemin de la Lune
01700 Miribel
Tel. 04 78 55 54 16
Fax 04 78 55 54 16
contact@lavilladurhone.com
www.lavilladurhone.com

Open all year • 4 rooms • €70 to €80, breakfast included • Table d'hôte €25 • Garden, car park. Credit cards not accepted • Outdoor swimming pool

10 CHAMBRE D'HÔTE DE BOSSERON
Mme Rivoire

325 route de Genève
01160 Neuville-sur-Ain
Tel. 04 74 37 77 06
Fax 04 74 37 77 06
arivoire@free.fr

Open all year • 4 rooms with bathrooms • €58, breakfast included • No table d'hôte • Park, car park. Credit cards not accepted, no dogs allowed • Fitness room, billiards

 Peace and quiet on the threshold of Lyons.

This modern villa on the heights of Miribel commands a superb view of the Rhône and the valley. Two of the three rooms overlooking the swimming pool have their own private terrace with a view of the landscape. The redbrick walls of the sitting room on the veranda, complete with indoor garden and fireplace, are full of appeal. Breakfast on the terrace in the summer is a pure joy.

 Immaculately decorated.

You won't regret your decision to stay here when you see the impressive manor house and the five acres of parkland on the banks of the Ain. Good taste and a flair for interior decoration have resulted in comfortable, well-soundproofed rooms. A fitness room and billiards table in the outbuildings are for the sole use of guests. Your gracious hostess certainly knows how to make visitors feel welcome.

Access : 12km to the north-east of Lyon, A 46 towards Geneva, leave Miribel-Jonage Park, then D 71 towards the Mas Rillier and the Madone Campanile

Access : 8km to the north-east of Pont-d'Ain on the N 84

 11 SNC LES CHARMETTES
Mme Vincent

 La Vellaz, Saint-Martin-de-Bavel
01510 Virieu-le-Grand
Tel. 04 79 87 32 18
 Fax 04 79 87 34 51

Open all year • 3 rooms, one of which has disabled access
• €42, breakfast included • No table d'hôte • Car park.
Credit cards not accepted • Hiking and mountain biking

 12 LE JEU DU MAIL
M. et Mme Arlaud

 07400 Alba-la-Romaine
Tel. 04 75 52 41 59
Fax 04 75 52 41 59
lejeudumail@free.fr
http://lejeudumail.free.fr

Closed in Jan • 5 rooms • €52 to €68, breakfast included
• No table d'hôte • Garden, terrace, car park. Credit
cards not accepted, no dogs allowed • Outdoor swimming pool

Mother Nature at her best.

Why not treat yourself to a stay in this lovely farmhouse
and enjoy the superb surrounding countryside? The
snug, comfortable rooms are in the beautifully restored
stables and one is equipped for disabled guests. Visitors
have the use of a fitted kitchen and dining and sitting
rooms in a separate wing. The owner is extremely
knowledgeable about his region's tourist attractions.

A lengthy lunch under the trellis or in the shade of the plane tree.

The owners of this former 19C Templar stronghold were
among the precursors of the Ardèches chambre d'hôte
phenomenon in the 1970s. Since then, they have never
stopped taking great pleasure in entertaining guests. All
the rooms are very pleasant and each has been given
a name which relates to the property's history, including
Émilie, Jesuit's suite and Servants Quarters. In the
summer, breakfast and lunch, served under a shaded
trellis or plane tree, are sheer delight.

Access : 11km northbound from Belley on the N 504
as far as Chazey-Bons, then take the D 31C

Access : In the village

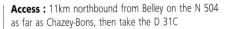

RHÔNE ALPES

 13 LA SANTOLINE
M. et Mme Espenel

07460 Beaulieu
Tel. 04 75 39 01 91
Fax 04 75 39 38 79
info@lasantoline.com
www.lasantoline.com

Open from 1 May to 30 Sep • 8 rooms (some have a balcony), one of which is a suite, all have bath/WC, some have air-conditioning • €65 to €130; breakfast €10; half board available • Terrace, garden, car park. No dogs allowed in restaurant • Outdoor swimming pool

14 AUBERGE LES MURETS
M. Rignanese

Lengarnayre
07230 Chandolas
Tel. 04 75 39 08 32
Fax 04 75 39 39 90
dominique.rignanese@wanadoo.fr
www.aubergelesmurets.com

Closed from 3 Jan to 10 Feb, 20 Nov to 10 Dec, Mon and Tue from 15 Nov to 30 Mar • 7 air-conditioned rooms with bath/WC or shower/WC and television • €55; breakfast €7, half board available • Air-conditioned restaurant; menus €16 to €26 • Car park, park, terrace. No dogs allowed • Swimming pool

 The lovely view of the Ardèche countryside and the Cévennes foothills.

 The restful swimming pool overlooking the Ardèche landscape.

Farm? Stronghold? Hunting lodge? Whatever the case, these 16C walls now house a hotel in a remote spot of garrigue that will appeal to urbanites in search of authenticity and tranquillity. The cheerful Provençal rooms would be quite at home in a glossy home-decoration magazine. Some have air-conditioning, but to our mind the thick dry-stone walls are more than sufficient to keep the scorching heat firmly outside. Vaulted restaurant, pretty terrace and a swimming pool surrounded by greenery.

Vineyards and 5 acres of grounds provide the setting for this lovely regional farm built in the 18C and recently turned into a family hotel. Attractive warm colours and bamboo furniture grace the majority of the rooms. Depending on the season, meals are served in vaulted dining room or on the terrace under the welcome shade of an old mulberry tree. The cuisine does full justice to the region's renowned culinary reputation and the buffet breakfast makes a perfect way to start the day.

Access : To the south-east, 1km on a small gravelled lane

Access : 6km northbound on the D 208, the D 104, then a minor road

MERCUER - 07200   **SAINT-DÉSIRAT - 07340**

 15 LE MAS DE MAZAN

M. Croze

 07200 Mercuer
Tel. 04 75 35 41 88
Fax 04 75 35 41 88
 masdemazan @ wanadoo.fr

Open all year • 5 rooms • €43, breakfast included • No table d'hôte • Car park. Credit cards not accepted, no dogs allowed

 16 LA DÉSIRADE

M. et Mme Mennier

 07340 Saint-Désirat
Tel. 04 75 34 21 88
contact @ desirade-fr.com
 www.desirade-fr.com

Closed Christmas and 1 Jan. Bookings only • 6 rooms • €45, breakfast included • Table d'hôte €17 • Terrace, garden, car park. Credit cards not accepted

 The owner takes guests round his pride and joy, a silk-worm farm.

This typical Cévennes farm has been lovingly restored by a farming couple, who enthusiastically greet all new guests. The spot is stunningly tranquil and the view of the valley, wooded hills and the village is matchless. The rooms are inviting and well restored but all, sadly, do not enjoy the wonderful view. The owner breeds silk worms and loves explaining the finer points of his "hobby".

 The lady of the house's culinary skills.

This fully renovated 19C mansion among Saint Joseph's trees and vineyards is a feast for the eyes. The simple, light and airy rooms overlook the magnolia tree in the courtyard, or the park and vineyard. Your cordon-bleu hostess loves surprising her guests with tasty regional recipes. A perfect base camp from which to explore the Ardèche.

Access : 5km to the north-west of Aubenas on the D 104 and the D 435

Access : 15km eastbound from Annonay on the D 82, towards Andance, then take a minor road

RHÔNE ALPES

 CHAMBRE D'HÔTE BOURLENC
M. et Mme Ventalon

Route de Saint-Andéol
07200 Saint-Julien-du-Serre
Tel. 04 75 37 69 95
Fax 04 75 37 69 95
bourlenc07@free.fr

Closed from Nov to Feb (open weekends by reservation)
• 5 rooms • €54, breakfast included • Table d'hôte €24
• Garden. Credit cards not accepted, no dogs allowed

  LA PASSIFLORE
Mme Luypaerts

07460 Saint-Paul-le-Jeune
Tel. 04 75 39 80 74
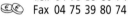 Fax 04 75 39 80 74

Open all year • 3 rooms • €42, breakfast included • No table d'hôte • Garden, car park. Credit cards not accepted, no dogs allowed

 A chance to taste forgotten varieties of fruit and vegetables.

It is impossible not to wind down during a stay at this house perched on a rock and surrounded by acacias. Colourful wardrobes, whitewashed walls and earthenware tiles add a delightful southern accent to the interior. The Pass of Lescrinet can be seen from the light, airy and generously proportioned rooms. Farm-grown fruit and vegetables take pride of place on the appetising dining table.

 The owners bend over backwards to make their guests feel at home.

This Flemish couple clearly care about their guests and want to make sure their stay in the Vans region is memorable. Despite the nearby road, the well-isolated house is a haven of peace. The agreeable rooms are extremely well-soundproofed and guests can choose from countless delightful sitting rooms. As to the breakfasts, served under an arbour near the mulberry tree and aviary, you'll certainly pass your plate for more...

Access : 3.5km from Saint-Julien-du-Serre on the D 218 towards Saint-Andéol-de-Vals

Access : 13km southbound from Vans on the D 901, then the D 104 towards Alès

  19 **HOSTELLERIE « MÈRE BIQUETTE »**
Mme Bossy

Les Allignols
07580 Saint-Pons
Tel. 04 75 36 72 61
Fax 04 75 36 76 25
merebiquette @ wanadoo.fr
www.logis-d-ardeche.com/merebiquette

Closed from 14 Nov to 12 Feb and Sun evening from Oct to Mar • 9 rooms in a separate wing, with bath/WC and television • €59 to €78; breakfast €7 to €8.50; half-board available • Restaurant closed Mon lunchtime, Wed lunch (except public holidays) menus €18 to €38 • Terrace, garden, car park • Outdoor swimming pool, tennis

  20 **VIVARAIS**
Mme Brioude

Avenue Claude-Expilly
07600 Vals-les-Bains
Tel. 04 75 94 65 85
Fax 04 75 37 65 47

Closed in Feb • 47 rooms on 5 levels, with bath/WC or shower/WC, all have television • €78 to €98; breakfast €9; half board available • Menus €30 to €58 • Terrace, private car park. No dogs allowed in rooms • Outdoor swimming pool

Tucking into the appetising breakfast buffet.

This old country farm is named after a goat's cheese formerly produced here: "la mère biquette" (a biquette is a kid goat) was sold by the current owners' parents in the local markets. It's a perfect hideaway to build up your strength in well-appointed rooms overlooking the chestnut trees or vineyards, a stone and wood rustic-styled restaurant, a shaded terrace overlooking the valley and a superb swimming pool.

Lounging on the balcony overlooking the fast-flowing Volane.

Near the casino, this old pink building is adorned with a frieze and terraces decked in flowers. The delightfully old-fashioned floral wallpaper and mahogany furniture in the bedrooms, the original bathrooms and elegantly dated atmosphere of the restaurant all add to the appeal. The mistress of the house's love of her region and its culinary traditions makes cooking with local produce, such as mushrooms, chestnuts and goat's cheese, a point of honour.

Access : Leave the N 102 between Villeneuve-de-Berg and Le Teil, take the D 293, through Saint-Pons and on for 4km

Access : Next to the casino

21 **LA TREILLE MUSCATE**
M. Delaitre

26270 Cliousclat
Tel. 04 75 63 13 10
Fax 04 75 63 10 79
latreillemuscate@wanadoo.fr
www.latreillemuscate.com

Closed from 5 Dec to 12 Feb and Wed • 12 rooms, 6 of which overlook the countryside, with bath/WC or shower/WC, most have television • €55 to €120; breakfast €9; half board available • Menu €15 to €26 • Terrace, small garden, private car park

  22 **LA MARE**
Famille Chaix

Route de Montmeyran
26800 Étoile-sur-Rhône
Tel. 04 75 59 33 79
Fax 04 75 59 05 20

Open all year • 4 rooms • €44, breakfast included • No table d'hôte • Garden, car park. Credit cards not accepted, no dogs allowed

 The fruit trees in blossom in the spring.

Midway between Valence and Montélimar just off the A 7 motorway, this village lying in the hills of the Drôme valley is home to an inn, made up of two old stone houses with lilac shutters. Terracotta tiled floors and second-hand furniture adorn the uncluttered, individually styled bedrooms. Sunny Provence can be felt in the dining room and the lovely terrace is hidden in a secret garden. However, if you are unable to resist the temptation of a motorway hotel, then have it your own way...

 The warm-hearted hospitality of this farming family.

On the threshold of the south of France, this lovely stone house run by a farming family is a unique chance to taste the legendary "savoir-vivre" of the region first-hand. The comfortable, appealing rooms are fitted with home-made furniture. Garden-produce features prominently in the delicious, generous helpings of home cooking. We also appreciated the friendly greeting and the modest prices.

Access : Leave the Valence-Montélimard road (N 7) between Loriol-sur-Drôme and Saulce-sur-Rhône for a minor road eastbound

Access : 15km to the south-east of Valence on the D 111 and the D 111B

 23 **BELLIER**
Mme Bellier

 26420 La Chapelle-en-Vercors
Tel. 04 75 48 20 03
Fax 04 75 48 25 31
www.hotel-bellier.fr

Closed Jan to 1 Apr (except by reservation), Tue evening and Wed except in summer • 13 rooms with bath/WC and television • €58 to €64.50 (€46 to €55 low season); breakfast €6; half board available • Menus €25 to €30 • Terrace, garden, car park • Outdoor swimming pool. In winter, cross-country skiing, snowshoe hiking

 24 **GÎTE DU VAL DES NYMPHES**
M. et Mme Andruejol

 Domaine de Magne
26700 La Garde-Adhémar
Tel. 04 75 04 44 54

Open all year • 5 rooms • €48 to €65, breakfast included • Table d'hôte €18 • Terrace, garden. Credit cards not accepted • Outdoor swimming pool

We most liked **Right in the heart of the Vercors, in nearly 450 000 acres of Regional Park.**

Air raids and fires took their toll on the village in 1944, which explains why the spruce chalet on a rocky outcrop over the road only dates from 1946. The majority of the spacious, welcoming rooms have a balcony. A mountain flavour adds warmth to the dining room and the fireplace in the sitting room is very welcome after a long day's skiing. In the summer, tables are laid round the swimming pool.

We most liked **Filling a basket with fruit from the estate.**

This mouth-watering fruit farm is built on a hillside in immense grounds which formerly included the Chapelle des Nymphes. The rooms are located in a small independent house overlooking the orchards. Meals are served in a vaulted dining room where old farm tools and family photos hang on the walls. Music lovers can try the family piano, while others may prefer to lounge in the garden. Before leaving, fill your basket with freshly picked peaches and apricots.

Access : In the village, on a rocky outcrop overlooking the road

Access : 1km on the Chapelle du Val des Nymphes road

539

 25 LA CAPITELLE
M. et Mme Terlin

Le Rempart
26270 Mirmande
Tel. 04 75 63 02 72
Fax 04 75 63 02 50
capitelle @ wanadoo.fr
www.lacapitelle.com

Closed from 1 Dec to 28 Feb, Tue and Wed lunchtime • 11 rooms, all have bath/WC or shower/WC and television • €79 to €160; breakfast €12; half board available • Menus €27 to €42 • Terrace

 26 SPHINX-HÔTEL
M. et Mme Harnichard

19 boulevard Desmarais
26200 Montélimar
Tel. 04 75 01 86 64
Fax 04 75 52 34 21
reception @ sphinx-hotel.fr
www.sphinx-hotel.fr

Closed from 23 Dec to 10 Jan • 24 rooms on 2 floors, all have bath/WC, air-conditioning and television • €50 to €63; breakfast €6 • No restaurant • Inner courtyard, private car park

 Breakfast on the ramparts.

This Renaissance house was a Templar stronghold before it became the home of Cubist artist, André Lhote, thereby attracting a whole host of other painters and rescuing from certain ruin the rest of this superb hilltop village. Furniture picked up in local antique shops adorns the rooms which gaze down on the tiny narrow streets or across the landscape of orchards; some have mullioned windows. Vaulted dining room and pleasant terrace.

 Mornings in the lovely inner courtyard.

This 17C mansion stands on Montélimar's tree-lined Allées Provençales, now a busy pedestrianised shopping area. Lofty ceilings, parquet floors, wainscoting and huge beams bear witness to the home's stately origins, while individual air-conditioning, greatly appreciated in the summer, is a small concession to modernity. All the rooms will soon have been refurbished.

Access : Leave the N 7 southbound from Saulce-sur-Rhône for the D 204

Access : In the town centre, alongside the Allées Provençales

 27 LA CARAVELLE
M. et Mme Allignol

 8 rue des Antignans
26110 Nyons
Tel. 04 75 26 07 44
Fax 04 75 26 07 40

Closed in Jan and in Nov • 11 non-smoking rooms with bath/WC or shower/WC and television • €70 to €95; breakfast €9 • No restaurant • Garden, private car park. No dogs allowed

 28 GINIÈS
M. et Mme Giniès

 38114 Allemont
Tel. 04 76 80 70 03
Fax 04 76 80 73 13
hotel-ginies@wanadoo.fr
www.hotel-ginies.com

Closed Fri evening and Mon • 15 rooms, one of which has disabled access, all have bath/WC or shower/WC and television • €53; breakfast €7; half board available • Menu €20 (weekdays) to €29 • Terrace, garden, car park. No dogs allowed in restaurant • Mini-golf

 A quiet read in the unusual garden.

The sign outside and a series of portholes from the battleship 'Jean-Bart' are the legacy of the former hotel owner who had a reputation as something of an old seadog. If you then add the unusual architecture of this 1900 villa and its curious garden full of Indian bean trees, you will be prepared for a stay in the earthly paradise of the olive kingdom but minus the traditional Provençal style. Quiet, well-cared for rooms.

 Ideally located near some of the best skiing domains in the Alps.

A sleepy village in the valley of the Eau d'Olle is home to this inn and its recent wing. The rooms are spacious, practical and well looked-after and some have balconies. You will have a choice of dining rooms, ranging from stones and beams in a rustic room to two more modern rooms with a view of the garden. A recently redone mini-golf course completes the picture.

Access : On the Promenade de la Digue

Access : In the village, 9km northbound from Bourg-d'Oisans on the N 91 then right on the D 526

RHÔNE ALPES

29 AU COQ EN VELOURS
M. et Mme Bellet

1800 route de Saint-Genix
38490 Aoste
Tel. 04 76 31 60 04
Fax 04 76 31 77 55
contact@au-coq-en-velours.com
www.au-coq-en-velours.com

Closed from 1 to 27 Jan, Sun evening and Mon • 7 rooms
with bath/WC or shower/WC, all have television • €60
to €65; breakfast €7 • Menus €26 to €54 • Terrace,
garden, car park

30 CHÂTEAU DES MARCEAUX
M. et Mme Rocca

38650 Avignonet
Tel. 04 76 34 18 94
Fax 04 76 34 18 94
eric.rocca@wanadoo.fr
http://monsite.wanadoo.fr/chateau
desmarceaux

Closed from Jan to mid-Apr and from Nov to late Dec
• 3 rooms • €67 to €74, breakfast included • No table
d'hôte • Park, car park. Credit cards not accepted, no
dogs allowed

 Ever tasted "rooster in velvet breeches"?

This smart village inn run by the same family since 1900
receives its guests in style. The bedrooms, named after
different species of the hotel's namesake (rooster), all
overlook the rear; those with a bathtub are the most
spacious. Fowl take pride of place in the dining room,
as a glance at the menu, paintings and ornaments will
quickly confirm: unsurprisingly perhaps, the house
speciality is "cockerel"! Pleasant terrace under the tall
trees in the garden and near a refreshing ornamental
pool.

Access : 2km to the north-east of Aoste on the
N 516, at the Gare de l'Est

 Superbly original rooms.

The diversity of architectural styles in this 18C château
is such that the ensuing variety of bedroom styles seems
perfectly natural. The first room, in the old dovecote,
is most spectacular with a superb staircase and walls
adorned with hundreds of roosting places. Original
parquet floors and high ceilings set the tone for the
second in the square tower, while the third in an
independent cottage is simply enormous. Look out for
the fresco in the dining room, painted by the
owner-artist himself.

Access : From the road, take the lane to the castle
gates

 31   **AUBERGE AU PAS DE L'ALPETTE**
M. Letellier

Bellecombe
38530 Chapareillan
Tel. 04 76 45 22 65
Fax 04 76 45 25 90
lepasdelalpette@libertysurf.fr
 www.alpette.com

Closed late Nov, Sun evenings and Wed except in season
• 13 rooms with shower/WC • €41 to €45; breakfast €7;
half board available • Menus €12 (weekdays) to €34
• Garden, car park • Outdoor swimming pool

 32   **AUBERGE DU VERNAY**
M. et Mme Raoul

Route d'Optevoz
38390 Charrette
Tel. 04 74 88 57 57
Fax 04 74 88 58 57
aub.vernay@libertysurf.fr
www.fhr.fr/charrette

Closed from 13 to 28 Jun, 5 to 13 Sep, Sun evening and
Mon • 7 rooms, one of which has disabled access, all
have shower/WC and television • €53 (€46 low season);
breakfast €7; half board available • Menus €15 to €25
• Terrace, car park

 A sumptuous view of Mont Blanc.

This isolated alpine inn in a remote corner of the
Chartreuse massif enjoys a stunning view of the
"rooftops of Europe". Wood prevails inside lending it a
warm, welcoming air. The rooms have sloping ceilings
and are neat and spotless. Local delicacies, such as
cheese specialities including wild goat's cheese in
mushrooms, feature prominently on the menu. Depending on the weather, diners can choose between a
wood-lined dining room or the terrace around the
swimming pool.

 Halcyon days in the countryside.

The spruce white stone walls of this 18C farmstead have
been given a new lease of life. All the delightful rooms
are decorated individually. In the restaurant, old
flagstones, a huge fireplace large enough to roast a
whole cow, sandblasted beams, cheerful paintings and
multicoloured modern chairs provide an amusing and
appealing mixture of tastes and styles. Outside, the old
bread oven can still be seen on the shaded terrace.

Access : Between Montmélian and Pontcharra (N 90)

Access : After the town hall drive towards Optevoz

RHÔNE ALPES

 33 CHÂTEAU DE PASSIÈRES
M. Perli

 38930 Chichilianne
Tel. 04 76 34 45 48
Fax 04 76 34 46 25

Closed from mid-Nov to late Feb and Sun evening and Mon out of season • 23 rooms, all have bath/WC or shower/WC, half have television • €49 to €66; breakfast €8; half board available • Menus €19 to €32 • Terrace, garden, car park • Outdoor swimming pool, tennis

 34 FERME DE RUTHIÈRES
M. Sauze

 Lieu-dit Ruthières
38930 Chichilianne
Tel. 04 76 34 45 98
Fax 04 76 34 45 98
fsauze@aol.com
 www.fermederuthieres.com

Closed from 20 to 27 Dec • 4 rooms upstairs • €44; breakfast included; half board available • Meals only by reservation (€14) • Garden, car park. Credit cards not accepted

 Watch a climbing party make the ascent of Mont Aiguille (3842m) from the comfort of your deck-chair!

The turrets of this small 14C manor house look out onto a hamlet in the shadow of Mount Aiguille. Most of the 23 bedrooms are contemporary in style, but three furnished with old pieces and lined in dark wood have more character. The owner, a professional footballer in his day, is a fan of 19C art as the numerous oils on the restaurant and sitting room walls illustrate.

 A strong focus on farm-grown produce.

This young farming couple extends a warm, unaffected welcome to guests to their farmhouse. The cow-shed has been turned into enormous guest bedrooms furnished in a country style; two enjoy a view of the Vercors. Regional art exhibitions are regularly held in the vaulted dining room complete with fireplace and columns: try the delicious home-grown produce.

Access : Leave the N 75 after 12km southbound from Monestier-de-Clermont, at "La Gare" take the D 7

Access : 4km to the north-west of Chichilianne on a minor road

 35 LE DOMAINE DE CLAIREFONTAINE
M. et Mme Girardon

Chemin des Fontanettes
38121 Chonas-L'Amballan
Tel. 04 74 58 81 52
Fax 04 74 58 80 93
domainedeclairefontaine @ yahoo.fr
www.domaine-de-clairefontaine.fr

Closed from 12 Dec to 15 Jan • 28 rooms, 2 of which have disabled access, with bath/WC and television • €45 to €115; breakfast €12; half board available • Air-conditioned restaurant closed Mon and Tue out of season; menus €35 (lunchtime weekdays) to €100 • Terrace, park with aviaries, private car park. No dogs allowed in restaurant • Tennis

 A ten-acre park surrounds this elegant manor house, two minutes from the A 7.

Formerly a convalescent home for the bishops of Lyons, these walls have been standing since 1766. Perhaps it is no surprise that the rooms look a little old-fashioned, but the sophisticated cuisine and the dining room more than compensate. A blend of contemporary 19C styles, the dining room leads onto a terrace overlooking mature parkland. For just a few euros extra, you may be interested to know, there is an exquisitely-decorated room which has been built in the old walnut-drying room.

Access : 9km southbound from Vienne on the N 7

 36 LA GABETIÈRE
M. Neyret

D 502
38780 Estrablin
Tel. 04 74 58 01 31
Fax 04 74 58 08 98

Open all year • 12 rooms with bath/WC or shower/WC and television • €52 to €64 (€50 to €62 low season); breakfast €8 • No restaurant • Park, private car park • Outdoor swimming pool

 An easy-going 16C manor.

On the outskirts of Vienne, trees and parkland surround this little 16C manor. A stone staircase in the tiny tower leads up to individually decorated boudoir bedrooms, recently equipped with double-glazing which cuts out the noise of the nearby road. Character also abounds in the exposed beams and late 17C fireplace in the breakfast room.

Access : 8km eastbound from Vienne on the D 41, then the D 502

 37   **LE CHÂLET HÔTEL PRAYER**
M. Prayer

 38650 Gresse-en-Vercors
Tel. 04 76 34 32 08
Fax 04 76 34 31 06
lechalet @ free.fr
http://lechalet.free.fr

Closed from 7 Mar to 8 May, 10 Oct to 24 Dec and Wed except school holidays • 20 rooms and 5 suites, all have bath/WC or shower/WC and television • €56 to €80; breakfast €9; half board available • Menus €18 to €49 • Terrace, garage, car park. No dogs allowed • Outdoor swimming pool, boules

 Botanical walks in the high mountain pastures.

Despite its name and warm atmosphere, this hotel bears more resemblance to a prosperous farm than a chalet. The bedrooms are being progressively renovated and all have a view of the village and the mountains. Take a seat in one of the comfortable dining rooms and tuck into large helpings of traditional cuisine. A glance at the visitors' book reveals a number of famous patrons, including actor Gérard Départieu and Albert II of Belgium.

Access : In the centre of the village

 38   **LE VAL FLEURI**
M. Bonnard

 730 avenue Léopold-Fabre
38250 Lans-en-Vercors
Tel. 04 76 95 41 09
Fax 04 76 94 34 69
 levalfleuri @ aol.com

Open from mid-May to 20 Sep and from 20 Dec to 20 Mar • 14 rooms, all have bath/WC and television • €32 to €57; breakfast €7; half board available • Menus €21 (weekdays) and €26 on Sun • Terrace, garden, garage, car park. No dogs allowed in restaurant

 An action-packed resort perfect for energetic children!

The old belfry of the church stands guard over the blue shutters of the Val Fleuri Hotel, built in the 1920s. Almost as if defying time to take its toll of the delightfully old-fashioned interior, the decoration of the dining room is exactly as it was when the establishment opened and some of the beautifully-kept bedrooms still boast their original Art Deco furniture or lamps. The fresh mountain air on the terrace, under the lime trees in the flowered garden, will whet your appetite.

Access : On the main road, behind the church

39 LES BALCONS DU LAC
M. Ferrard

145 chemin de Béluran
Lieu-dit Vers-Ars
38730 Le Pin
Tel. 04 76 06 68 82
Fax 04 76 06 68 82

Open all year • 5 rooms with bathrooms • €42, breakfast included • Table d'hôte €15 (evenings only) • Credit cards not accepted

40 LES SKIEURS
M. et Mme Jail

38700 Le Sappey-en-Chartreuse
Tel. 04 76 88 82 76
Fax 04 76 88 85 76
hotelskieurs@wanadoo.fr
www.lesskieurs.com

Closed in Apr, Nov, Dec Sun evening and Mon • 18 rooms with bath/WC or shower/WC and television • €65; breakfast €10; half board available • Menus €25 (weekdays) to €39 • Terrace, garden, car park. No dogs allowed • Outdoor swimming pool

Watch Lake Paladru change colour throughout the day.

Half the windows of this gradually restored old farmhouse face Lake Paladru, while the other half gaze out over fields and woods. The majority of the snug, simple bedrooms enjoy a view of the lake's deep waters; three have a kitchenette and all have spanking-new bathrooms. In the morning, you will breakfast in an enormous living room, in the centre of which stands a pyramidal fireplace. Warm and friendly.

Save room for the tempting cheeses and home-made desserts.

A curtain of fir trees conceals this pretty house lost in the remote high pastures of the Chartreuse. The wainscoted walls inside lend that unmistakable alpine touch, which fits the feeling of the snug little bedrooms. The welcoming restaurant has a huge stone fireplace for spit-roasting and chargrilling and the chef's generous regional cooking attracts gourmets from far and wide. A balcony-terrace overlooks the valley.

Access : 1km to the south-west of Paladru Lake on the D 17

Access : On leaving the village drive towards the Porte Pass

RHÔNE ALPES

 LE RELAIS DU ÇATEY
M. Ducretet

10 rue du Didier - Le Bourg
38080 L'Isle-d'Abeau
Tel. 04 74 18 26 50
Fax 04 74 18 26 59
relaiscatey@aol.com
www.le-relais-du-catey.com

Closed 6 to 23 Aug, 26 to 31 Dec • 7 rooms with bath/WC or shower/WC and television • €52 to €60; breakfast €6; half board available • Restaurant closed Mon lunchtime and Sun; menus €20 to €45 • Terrace, garden, car park

 LE PANORAMIQUE
M. Keesman

38142 Mizoen
Tel. 04 76 80 06 25
Fax 04 76 80 25 12
info@hotel-panoramique.com
www.hotel-panoramique.com

Closed from 11 Apr to 14 May and 19 Sep to 22 Dec • 9 rooms, 5 of which are non-smoking, all have bath/WC or shower/WC and television • €65 to €70; breakfast €10; half board available • Menus €20 to €24 • Terrace, garden, car park. No dogs allowed • Sauna

 Sample the chef's creative recipes on the terrace.

This elegant Louis XV house surrounded by trees and flowers lies in a residential district, only 10min from the international airport of Lyons. The cosy comfort of the bedrooms has recently been enhanced following high-quality renovation work. Wrought-iron and tasteful paintings adorn the contemporary restaurant, further set off by the original flagstones. Lime and Indian bean trees shade the pleasant terrace. Excellent, imaginative cuisine.

 If you're lucky, you may catch a glimpse of the chamois who live in the mountains.

In the summer, window boxes laden with geraniums adorn the balconies of this hillside chalet. Recently purchased by a young couple from the Netherlands who speak Dutch, French, English, German and Spanish, the atmosphere is decidedly polyglot. Among the establishment's numerous appeals are the warm mountain-style adopted in the bedrooms, a south-facing terrace, sauna and a superb panoramic view of the town, Oisans Valley and surrounding mountains.

Access : North-west of Bourgoin-Jallieu

Access : Between Le Freney-d'Oisans and the Barrage du Chambon tunnel, leave the N 91 and take the D 25

43 **DOMAINE DE LA COLOMBIÈRE**
Mme Carle

Château de Moissieu
38270 Moissieu-sur-Dolon
Tel. 04 74 79 50 23
Fax 04 74 79 50 25
colombieremoissieu@hotmail.com
www.lacolombiere.com

Closed from 20 Dec to 4 Jan • 21 air-conditioned rooms, 2 of which have disabled access, all have bath/WC or shower/WC and television • €69 to €112; breakfast €12, half board available • Air-conditioned restaurant closed Sun evening and Mon; menus €28 to €65 (special menu on national holidays) • Car park, park, terrace • Swimming pool

 Ideal for nature-lovers.

This handsome abode, built in 1820, stands in over 10 acres of well-tended grounds. Cleverly restored and turned into a hotel, the establishment offers spacious, brightly coloured rooms, each of which is named after a famous painter and a copy of each artist's paintings, painted by the lady of the house, hangs on the walls of the rooms. The restaurant, located in the estate's only contemporary construction, has a terrace overlooking the idyllic countryside.

44 **LES BASSES PORTES**
M. et Mme Giroud-Ducaroy

Torjonas
38118 Saint-Baudille-de-la-Tour
Tel. 04 74 95 18 23
mirvinc@wanadoo.fr

Closed from mid-Nov to late Jan • 3 rooms • €49, breakfast included • Table d'hôte €17 • Terrace, park, car park. Credit cards not accepted, no dogs allowed

 A happy marriage of past and present.

Extensive renovation work has restored this old farmhouse without removing any of its rustic charm. Whenever possible, the old stones, beams and parquet floors have been preserved. The somewhat surprising style of the bedrooms features a happy blend of old and new, in addition to brand-new bathrooms. A perfect base camp to explore the Île Crémieu.

Access : Near the village

Access : 2km northbound on the D 52B

 45 LE CHÂTEAU DE PÂQUIER
M. Rossi

38650 Saint-Martin-de-la-Cluze
Tel. 04 76 72 77 33
Fax 04 76 72 77 33
hrossi @ club-internet.fr

Open all year (by reservation in winter) • 5 rooms • €60 to €80, breakfast included • Table d'hôte €20 • Garden, car park. No dogs allowed.

 46 AU SANS-SOUCI
M. Maurice

38650 Saint-Paul-lès-Monestier
Tel. 04 76 34 03 60
Fax 04 76 34 17 38
au.sans.souci @ wanadoo.fr

Closed from 20 Dec to 31 Jan, Sun evening and Mon • 12 rooms, all have bath/WC or shower/WC and television • €52 to €58; breakfast €8; half board available • Menus €17 (weekdays) to €45 • Terrace, garden, private car park • Outdoor swimming pool, tennis

 Unaffected and welcoming.

The owners have clearly put their body and soul into the restoration of the Renaissance castle and pretty garden and the result happily does justice to their efforts. Countless decorative features have been preserved, such as the exposed beams, wooden ceiling, spiral staircase and mullioned windows. The spacious rooms are beautifully decorated and furnished; one affords you a rare opportunity of sleeping in an old chapel. Garden produce and meat chargrilled on the open fire.

 Alpine, cross-country and water-skiing: depending on the season, take your pick!

This former sawmill in a quiet hamlet was turned into a hotel-restaurant in 1934 by the grandfather of the current owners. Whether you prefer contemporary or alpine-style, book one of the renovated rooms, which are the largest. Tasty dishes made with fresh local produce are served in the rustic dining room, decorated with farming implements and old wooden skis from the early days. Mount Aiguille looms down over the shaded terrace, garden, tennis court and swimming pool.

Access : 12km northbound from Monestier-de-Clermont on the N 75 and a minor road

Access : On leaving Monestier-de-Clermont (towards Grenoble), leave the N 75 and turn left on the D 8

47 LE CHÂTEAU D'HERBELON
M. Castillan

Lac de Monteynard
38650 Treffort
Tel. 04 76 34 02 03
Fax 04 76 34 05 44
chateaudherbelon@wanadoo.fr
www.chateau-herbelon.fr

Closed from 20 Dec to 4 Mar, Mon and Tue except Jul-Aug • 9 rooms, all have bath/WC and television • €54 to €75; breakfast €7.50; half board available • Menus €19 to €34 • Terrace, garden, car park. No dogs allowed in rooms • Ideally located for wind-surfing

The 20km-long lake is renowned for its windsurfing.

This traditional country house covered in Virginia creeper and climbing roses stands on the banks of the Monteynard reservoir lake. A great deal of care and attention has clearly been lavished on the sizeable, usefully equipped rooms. An old stone fireplace adds character to the restaurant, while a lovely vaulted room in the basement is regularly rented out for weddings, communions and other family banquets. Children's play area in the walled garden.

Access : By the lake, 3km on the D 110E

48 LES MÉSANGES
M. Prince

Route de Bouloud
38410 Uriage-les-Bains
Tel. 04 76 89 70 69
Fax 04 76 89 56 97
prince@hotel-les-mesanges.com
www.hotel-les-mesanges.com

Closed from 20 Oct to 1 Feb • 33 rooms with bath/WC or shower/WC and television • €54 to €66; breakfast €8; half board available • Restaurant closed Mon, Tue and Sun evening from Feb to Apr; Mon lunchtime and Tue from 1 May to 20 Oct; menus €22 to €50 • Terrace, garden, car park. No dogs allowed • Swimming pool, table-tennis, boules, play area

Savouring the utter peace and quiet.

The villa overlooks the spa resort and castle. Ask for one of the renovated, practical rooms with balcony and enjoy the view over the Chamrousse or Vercors mountain ranges. A light, airy dining room in a modern style, pleasant terrace shaded by plane trees, peaceful garden with a play area and swimming pool complete the facilities of this family-run establishment.

Access : Avenue des Thermes, drive along the park, turn left onto the Chamrousse road, then at the spa hospital, turn right on Bouloud road

 49 CHÂTEAU DE CHAPEAU CORNU
M. Regnier

38890 Vignieu
Tel. 04 74 27 79 00
Fax 04 74 92 49 31
chapeau.cornu@wanadoo.fr
www.chateau-chapeau-cornu.fr

Closed from 19 Dec to 10 Jan and Sun evening except in Jul and Aug • 21 rooms (and 2 suites) with bath/WC or shower/WC and television • €67 to €150; breakfast €9 to €12; half board available • Menus €22 to €57 • Terrace, park, private car park. No dogs allowed in rooms • Outdoor swimming pool

 50 CHÂTEAU BLANCHARD
M. Bonnidal

36 route de Saint-Galmier
42140 Chazelles-sur-Lyon
Tel. 04 77 54 28 88
Fax 04 77 54 36 03
chateau-blanchard@wanadoo.fr

Closed from 7 to 26 Aug • 12 rooms, all have bath/WC and television • €57 to €80; breakfast €8; half board available • Restaurant closed Sun evening, Mon and Fri evening; menus €20 to €30 • Garden, car park

 If only a night in this fairy-tale castle could turn our fortunes from rags to riches!

The names of the former owners of this 13C fortified castle, Capella and Cornutti, explain the origins of the castle's amusing name which translates as Battered Hat. The rooms, which are gradually being treated to a new coat of paint, tasteful fabrics and wrought-iron furniture all have antique wardrobes; some also boast a four-poster bed. A stone-vaulted dining room, attractive inner courtyard terrace and a 10-acre park with ornamental pools and tree-lined paths complete the picture.

 The Hat Museum's collection shows off hats and caps of the rich and famous!

This rambling, elegant period house built in a shaded park once belonged to a family of milliners and after extensive renovation, it once again shines with the glow of its former youth. Inside, a marble staircase will take you up to comfortable bedrooms decorated individually in a contemporary flavour. The restaurant has opted for a traditional repertoire.

Access : From Bourgoin-Jallieu take the N 6 (towards Lyon), then right on the D 522 as far as Flosaille, then the D 19 and 5km after Saint-Clef, turn right

Access : On the way into the village, on the Saint-Galmier road

 51 LA BUSSINIÈRE
Mme Perrin

 Route de Lyon
42110 Feurs
Tel. 04 77 27 06 36
Fax 04 77 27 06 36
la-bussiniere@wanadoo.fr
 www.labussiniere.com

Open all year • 3 rooms • €40, breakfast included • Table d'hôte €15 (evenings only) • Garden, car park. Credit cards not accepted

 52 DOMAINE DE CHAMPFLEURY
Mme Gaume

 Le Bourg
42155 Lentigny
Tel. 04 77 63 31 43
Fax 04 77 63 31 43

Closed from 11 Nov to 1 Mar. Booking advisable in winter • 1 room, 1 two-room suite, 1 two-person gîte • €72, breakfast included • No table d'hôte • Park, car park. Credit cards not accepted, no dogs allowed

 The lady of the house's ceaseless quest for perfection.

The comfort of this renovated farmhouse leaves nothing to be desired: everything has been designed with the welfare of the guest in mind, from the digicode-access on the main gate and the excellent soundproofing to the high quality bedding. Huge beams and tasteful colours adorn the stylish bedrooms, which have immaculate bathrooms. Meals are taken around the large table in the dining room.

 Explore the secrets of the park.

This 19C country house stands proudly in a luxurious park planted with a wide range of trees. The guest rooms are light and airy; two can be turned into a family suite. Tennis courts and a large games room await guests and whenever the weather is fine enough, you can picnic in the park and lounge on the deckchairs.

Access : 3km eastbound from Feurs on the D 89, towards Lyon

Access : 8km to the south-west of Roanne on the D 53

SAINT-MAURICE-SUR-LOIRE - 42155

SAINT-PIERRE-LA-NOAILLE - 42190

53 L'ÉCHAUGUETTE
M. et Mme Alex

Ruelle Guy-de-la-Mûre
42155 Saint-Maurice-sur-Loire
Tel. 04 77 63 15 89
contact@echauguette-alex.com
www.echauguette-alex.com

Open all year • 4 rooms • €60 to €70 breakfast included
• Table d'hôte €24 • Credit cards not accepted, no dogs
allowed

54 DOMAINE DU CHÂTEAU DE MARCHANGY
Mme Grandeau

42190 Saint-Pierre-la-Noaille
Tel. 04 77 69 96 76
Fax 04 77 60 70 37
contact@marchangy.com
www.marchangy.com

Open all year • 3 rooms with bath/WC and television
• €80 to €95, breakfast included • Table d'hôte €30
• Park, car park. Credit cards not accepted • Swimming
pool

 Watch the pleasure boats on the lake.

It is difficult to resist the charm of these three houses
hidden in a medieval village opposite the peaceful
waters of Lake Villerest. All the tastefully decorated
rooms are different: one has a fireplace, the other enjoys
a view of the lake encircled by hills, while the last
overlooks the keep and church. Breakfasts are served
on the terrace or behind the kitchen's bay windows: a
feast for the palate, and the eyes.

 A life of luxury - for just a few euros!

An oak-lined drive leads up to this idyllic 18C château
in front of which is a large courtyard. The rooms, located
in the former outhouses of the estate, are quiet and
brimming with charm: restored parquet floors, family
furniture, rugs, canopy beds, curios and paintings. The
park, overlooking the countryside, is home to hundred-
year-old trees and a splendid swimming pool. A few
rows of vines produce a table wine that can only be
tasted on the property.

Access : 12km to the south-west of Roanne on the
D 53 and the D 203

Access : 5.5km north-west of Charlieu on the D 227
on a minor road

 55 CASTEL-GUÉRET
M. Coulaud

42220 Saint-Julien-Molin-Molette
Tel. 04 77 51 56 04
Fax 04 77 51 59 13
contact @ domaine-castelgueret.com
www.domaine-castelgueret.com

Open all year • 5 non-smoking rooms • €69 to €77, breakfast included, half board available • Table d'hôte €20 to €25, only by reservation • Park, car park. Credit cards not accepted, no dogs allowed • Outdoor swimming pool

 56 LA RIVOIRE
M. et Mme Thiollière

42220 Saint-Julien-Molin-Molette
Tel. 04 77 39 65 44
Fax 04 77 39 67 86
info @ larivoire.net
www.larivoire.net

Open all year • 5 rooms • €55, breakfast included, half board available • Table d'hôte €18 (evenings only) • Terrace, garden, car park. Credit cards not accepted, no dogs allowed

 Lording it for a weekend.

Nearly five acres of ancient trees surround this 19C château, painstakingly restored in keeping with the spirit of the period. Original parquet floors, marquetry work and antiques set the scene for the refined interior. All the Louis XV or Louis XVI-style rooms have their own private sitting room; the quality of the bedding and bathrooms deserves a special mention. When it comes to relaxing in the open air, the surrounding countryside offers numerous opportunities for long walks.

 Cottage-garden vegetables and local meats on the menu.

A circular stone tower and enormous kitchen garden contribute to the appeal of this lovely stately home, thought to date from the 15C. It enjoys a lovely position in the Nature Park of Pilat, overlooking the fir trees of the Ardèche hillsides, which is the view you will have from the cheerful rooms. Three sitting rooms, complete with piano, board games and a television, are reserved for the use of guests.

Access : 1km northbound from Saint-Julien-Molin-Molette on the D 8 towards Le Besset

Access : 5km eastbound from Bourg-Argental on the N 82

  57 SAINT-ROMAIN
M. et Mme Levet

Route de Graves
69480 Anse
Tel. 04 74 60 24 46
Fax 04 74 67 12 85
hotel-saint-romain @ wanadoo.fr
www.hotel-saint-romain.fr

Closed from 28 Nov to 9 Dec and Sun evening from early
Nov to late Apr • 24 rooms, most have bath/WC, all have
television • €47 to €55; breakfast €7; half board available
• Menus €19 (except Sunday lunchtime) to €46
• Terrace, garden, private car park

  58 LA MAISON DE NOÉMI
Mme Noëlle Pierre

 Le Pothu
69690 Brullioles
Tel. 04 74 26 58 08
noelle.pierre @ free.fr

Open all year • 3 rooms with bathrooms • €37, breakfast
included • No table d'hôte • Garden. Credit cards not
accepted

 Make sure you don't get lost in the labyrinthine passages of the village's 13C castle.

Don't pass up the chance of a visit to this lovely stone
farmhouse in the heart of the Beaujolais region, where
only the wind whispering through the foliage disturbs
the silence. The somewhat faded air of the rooms is
balanced by their spotless upkeep, while a welcoming
rustic dining room leads onto a summer terrace, always
packed in the high season. Your taste-buds may already
be watering at the prospect of sampling the inspired
meals rustled up by your owner-chef.

 Druids were said to dwell in the neighbouring wood.

At a height of 750m in the upper part of the village,
this 17C farmstead commands a superb view of the
Lyonnais mountains. The spotless and soberly decorated
rooms lie in a separate wing and all have bathrooms.
A communal living room is equipped with practical
cooking facilities. The mistress of the house, who used
to work for the Tourist Board, is a treasure-trove of
information about the region.

Access : Set back from the village, near
the gendarmerie (police station)

Access : 10km westbound from La Brevenne on the
N 89 and the D 81

59 CHEZ LA ROSE
M. et Mme Alizer

Place du Marché
69840 Juliénas
Tel. 04 74 04 41 20
Fax 04 74 04 49 29
info @ chez-la-rose.fr
www.chez-la-rose.fr

Closed from 8 to 28 Feb • 8 rooms with bath/WC or shower/WC and television, 5 of which in a separate wing • €50 to €100, breakfast €9, half board available • Restaurant closed lunchtime except Wed, Sat, Sun and public holidays and Mon evening from Oct to Apr; menus €25 to €60 • Terrace, private car park

60 LES PASQUIERS
M. et Mme Gandilhon

69220 Lancié
Tel. 04 74 69 86 33
Fax 04 74 69 86 57
ganpasq @ aol.com
www.bonadresse.com

Open all year • 4 rooms with disabled access • €80, breakfast included • Table d'hôte €25 • Sitting room, garden, car park. Credit cards not accepted • Outdoor swimming pool

 Sampling the delicious country fare washed down with a very drinkable bottle of Juliénas.

If France is so popular with tourists, it is partly because of this type of inn which offers such good value for money. Sylvette and Bertrand bend over backwards every day to ensure that their kitchen serves the best local fare and that their cellar is stocked with choice local vintages, all of which are served in their attractive rustic dining room or on the peaceful flower-decked terrace.

 A step back in time to Second Empire France.

High walls protect this lovely old house and garden from prying eyes. Many of the decorative features inside are original, such as the moulded ceilings, fireplace, carpets, library and grand piano in the sitting room. The rooms in the main house are furnished with 19C antiques, while those in the outbuilding have been reworked to a more modern design with coconut matting, bathrooms hidden by Japanese screens and children's drawings. The terrace is laid next to the swimming pool.

Access : In the heart of the village, opposite the roundabout

Access : 2km southbound from Romanèche-Thorins

 61 DOMAINE DES QUARANTE ÉCUS
M. et Mme Nesme

 Les Vergers
69430 Lantigné
Tel. 04 74 04 85 80
Fax 04 74 69 27 79
bnesme @ wanadoo.fr

Open all year • 5 rooms with bathrooms • €48 (€36 low season), breakfast included • No table d'hôte • Garden, car park. Credit cards not accepted, no dogs allowed • Outdoor swimming pool. Wine cellars, sales and tasting of the domain's wine

 62 CHAMBRE D'HÔTE M. ET MME BONNOT
M. et Mme Bonnot

 Le Bourg
69430 Les Ardillats
Tel. 04 74 04 80 20
Fax 04 74 04 80 20

Closed in Jan • 5 rooms • €42, breakfast included, half board available • Table d'hôte €16 • Garden, car park. Credit cards not accepted, no dogs allowed

 Sipping a glass of the estate's red or white Beaujolais.

The French common name of the ginkgo biloba tree – known as Maidenhair in English – in front of the house gave the estate its name. The bedrooms, furnished with old and new pieces and hung with reproductions of works by Van Gogh, overlook the vineyards or the garden and orchards of peach, cherry, apricot and plum trees. Breakfast is served in a rustic dining room, embellished by a dresser. The owners happily invite guests to look around the cellars and sample and purchase the estate's wine.

 Pamper your taste-buds in this lovely Beaujolais home.

This handsome farm on the doorstep of a sleepy country village is the sort of place you dream of. Its thick stone walls and natural wooden shutters immediately catch the eye, which is further treated to the vision of a lovely country interior. Bright colours and thick beams paint the juicy picture of the rooms, each of which is named after a fruit – raspberry, pineapple, plum, grapefruit and mandarin. Sample the delicious home cooking, washed down with a fruity glass of Beaujolais.

Access : 4km eastbound from Beaujeu on the D 78

Access : 5km to the north-west of Beaujeu on the D 37

 63 ARTISTES
Mme Lameloise

8 rue Gaspard-André
69002 Lyon
Tel. 04 78 42 04 88
Fax 04 78 42 93 76
hartiste @ club-internet.fr
www.hoteldesartistes.fr

Open all year • 45 rooms, all have bath/WC or shower/WC and television • €81 to €111; breakfast €9 • No restaurant • No dogs allowed

 64 CHAMBRE D'HÔTE GÉRARD LAGNEAU
M. et Mme Lagneau

Huire
69430 Quincié-en-Beaujolais
Tel. 04 74 69 20 70
Fax 04 74 04 89 44
jealagneau @ wanadoo.fr

Open all year • 4 non-smoking rooms upstairs, all have bathrooms • €52 to €57, breakfast included • Garden, car park

 Old Lyons' giant maze of "traboules"
– covered pedestrian passages.

This delightful hotel is located right in the heart of Lyons, on the peninsula opposite Fourvière Hill. The rooms are light and airy and make up in practicality what they lack in luxury; some overlook the Célestins Theatre, hence the hotel's name. The breakfast room is adorned with a fresco inspired by Cocteau. A nearby public car park is also most appreciated.

 A genuine wine-growing atmosphere.

A hamlet encircled by vineyards is the scene for the pleasant stone-built home of this wine-growing family who bend over backwards to make you feel at home with them. The rooms upstairs are simply decorated and spotlessly clean. You will breakfast under the beams of a rustic room. The icing on the cake is, however, the 16C cellar. Where better to sample the house vintages?

Access : Near Place Bellecour (and Bellecour car park), opposite the theatre

Access : In the middle of the vineyards

65 DOMAINE DE ROMARAND
M. et Mme Berthelot

69430 Quincié-en-Beaujolais
Tel. 04 74 04 34 49
Fax 04 74 04 35 92

Closed Christmas and New Year • 3 rooms • €53 to €56, breakfast included • Table d'hôte evenings only; menus €18 to €22 • Garden, car park • Outdoor swimming pool. Wine tasting and sales

66 HOSTELLERIE LE SAINT-LAURENT
M. Lavault

8 rue Croix-Blanche
69720 Saint-Laurent-de-Mure
Tel. 04 78 40 91 44
Fax 04 78 40 45 41
le.st.laurent @ wanadoo.fr

Closed from 26 Dec 2004 to 2 Jan 2005, 1 to 8 May, 16 May, 13 to 16 Jul, 1 to 21 Aug, 11 Nov and day before national holidays • 30 rooms with bath/WC or shower/WC, all have television • €57 to €110; breakfast €7; half board available • Menus €20 (weekdays) to €56 • Terrace, park, 2 car parks, one of which is private. No dogs allowed

 The overwhelming bouquet of fine wines.

This lovely stone house run by a wine-growing couple is set in a U-shaped courtyard overlooking a flowered rock garden and the vineyards: all the modern, comfortable rooms enjoy this same rural view. The rafters, fireplace, huge wooden table and maps of the Beaujolais region add character to the dining room. A profusion of home-made pastries and jams adds that little extra to breakfast time.

 Entirely devoted to guests' welfare.

This 18C mansion and its flowered park make an ideal stopover for weary travellers. It offers small, comfortable rooms – those in a separate wing are more modern. At mealtimes, you can choose between the warmth of maple wood or immense bay windows overlooking the greenery. In fine weather, the shade of the three-hundred-year-old lime tree is sheer bliss.

Access : 9km to the south-east of Beaujeu on the D 37 and the D 9, then drive towards Varennes

Access : 15km from Lyon, set back from the N 6

 67 **LA TERRASSE**
M. et Mme Arnette

 Le Bourg - Marnand
69240 Thizy
Tel. 04 74 64 19 22
Fax 04 74 64 25 95
francis.arnette @ wanadoo.fr
 www.laterrasse-marnand.com

Closed during Feb and Nov half-terms, Mon (except the hotel) and Sun evening • 10 rooms, one of which has disabled access, with bath/WC and television • €42; breakfast €6; half board €39 • Menus €12 (weekdays) to €43 • Terrace, car park • Children's games room

 68 **LA FERME DU POULET**
M. et Mme Rongeat

 180 rue Georges-Mangin
69400 Villefranche-sur-Saône
Tel. 04 74 62 19 07
Fax 04 74 09 01 89
la.ferme.du.poulet @ wanadoo.fr

Closed from 5 to 20 Aug, from 23 Dec to 2 Jan, Sun evening and Mon • 10 rooms, all have bath/WC and television • €80; breakfast €10 • Menus €34 • Terrace, car park. No dogs allowed in rooms

Just six kilometres from the water-sports of Lake Sapins.

This old textile factory, typical of the Beaujolais region, has been turned into a hotel. The agreeable rooms with terraces open directly onto the garden; each is named after a flower or aromatic plant and the decoration, even the fragrance, matches the theme. Two modern, soberly decorated dining rooms and a spacious terrace overlooking the mountains of the Lyonnais complete the picture: their modern menu features regionally inspired recipes.

A cheerful blend of rustic and contemporary flavours.

A sanctuary of greenery in the heart of an industrial estate, this beautifully-restored 17C fortified farm is protected from the bustle of urban life by a wall. All the spacious, functional rooms have excellent bedding. Multicoloured tableware livens up the magnificent old beams of the dining room. Pleasant inner courtyard terrace.

Access : 2km to the north-east on the D 94, on the way into Bourg-Marnand, opposite the town hall

Access : North-east of Villefranche, in the Industrial Zone (ZI) near the exhibition park

 69 AUBERGE SAINT-SIMOND
M. et Mme Mattana

 130 avenue Saint-Simond
73100 Aix-les-Bains
Tel. 04 79 88 35 02
Fax 04 79 88 38 45
auberge@saintsimond.com
www.saintsimond.com

Closed in Jan, Nov school holidays and Sun evening
• 28 rooms, 2 of which have disabled access, all have
bath/WC or shower/WC and television • €48 to €70;
breakfast €8 • Menus €20 (weekdays) to €32 • Car park,
terrace, garden. No dogs allowed in restaurant

 70 LA CROIX DU SUD
Mme Collot

 3 rue du Docteur-Duvernay
73100 Aix-les-Bains
Tel. 04 79 35 05 87
Fax 04 79 35 72 71
lacroix-sud@wanadoo.fr
 www.hotel-lacroixdusud.com

Closed from 1 Jan to 9 Apr and 5 Nov to 31 Dec
• 16 rooms, some have bath/WC or shower/WC and
television • €26 to €39; breakfast €6 • No restaurant
• Small courtyard-garden. Credit cards not accepted
• Television room with a small library

 **The garden lined with trees and flowers.**

For over a century, travellers have been resting their weary legs in this former post house then inn, just a few minutes from the Lac du Bourget. Eight rooms have been renovated and treated to soundproofing and new furniture, bedding and decoration. The others are comfortable if a little plain; some have a balcony; we recommend those overlooking the garden. Local dishes are served in the dining room-veranda which extends onto a terrace shaded by lovely old plane trees.

 The faded charm of the early 20C.

Could it be to conjure up memories of his trips to distant lands that the former owner built up this collection of hats from the world over? Equally popular with tourists and "patients" come to take the waters, this hotel is renowned for its faultless hospitality. The generously-dimensioned and rather faded bedrooms are most stylish.

Access : Near the town centre

Access : In the town centre, in a small, quiet street

 71 SOLEIL
M. Montaz

 15 rue de l'Église
73500 Aussois
Tel. 04 79 20 32 42
Fax 04 79 20 37 78
www.hotel-du-soleil.com

Closed from 21 Apr to 15 Jun and 30 Sep to 17 Dec • 22 rooms, one of which has disabled access, with bath/WC or shower/WC, all have television • €72 to €84 (€65 low season); breakfast included; half board available • Menus €20 to €22 (evenings) • Terrace, car park; No dogs allowed in rooms • Cinema room, sauna, hammam, jacuzzi, souvenir shop, billiards, skiing in season

 Discover the thrill of the 2 560m Via Ferrata rock-climbing course – the longest in France.

Next door to the church, whose bells are considerate enough to remain silent after nightfall, the walls of this austere chalet hide a warm interior. The rooms enjoy superb views of the village and the Vanoise range; ask for one of the renovated chalet-style rooms with light wood and pretty fabrics. There is no lack of outdoor activities from the roof terrace sun deck, open air jacuzzi, giant chess board and skittles, while indoors, you can sample the sauna, hammam and home cinema facilities.

Access : Near the church

  72 À LA PASTOURELLE
M. Blanc

 73480 Bonneval-sur-Arc
Tel. 04 79 05 81 56
Fax 04 79 05 85 44
www.pastourelle.com

Closed one week in May and on 1 Nov • 12 rooms with bath/WC • €52 to €58; breakfast €6; half board only in season • Restaurant closed out of season; menus €12 to €17 • Library-sitting room. No dogs allowed • Skiing and hiking nearby

On the doorstep of one of France's most beautiful skiing domains.

The roof of schist tiles and the name, which means cowgirl, both bear witness to the house's dedication to local traditions. Whether a one-night stopover on your journey through the French Alps or a base camp for breathtaking races down the slopes of La Vanoise, it will provide that little extra to make each day just perfect. The rooms are snug and cosy and the dining room is rich with the perfume of savoury cheese raclettes, fondues and sweet pancakes.

Access : In the upper part of the resort

RHÔNE ALPES

73 L'AUTANTIC

Mme Bourgeois

69 route d'Hauteville
73700 Bourg-Saint-Maurice
Tel. 04 79 07 01 70
Fax 04 79 07 51 55
hotel-autantic@wanadoo.fr
www.hotel-autantic.com

Open all year • 29 rooms, 2 of which have disabled access, with bath/WC (2 have shower/WC) and television • €40 to €130; breakfast €8 • No restaurant • Car park • Sauna

Tasting the thrills of white-water rafting on the Bourg.

The stone walls and narrow windows of this sturdy house, in the style of a traditional mountain chalet, were built recently in a quiet district of Bourg St Maurice, near the futuristic funicular railway up to the Arcs resort. The rooms, decorated with roughcast walls and pine furniture, overlook the peaceful valley and four have a balcony. Friendly staff and breakfast on the terrace are among the other perks of this modern chalet.

Access : On the way into the village, a little set back from the road

74 LE CAPRICE DES NEIGES

Famille Borrel

Route du Col des Saisies
73590 Crest-Voland
Tel. 04 79 31 62 95
Fax 04 79 31 79 30
info@caprice-des-neiges.com
www.caprice-des-neiges.com

Closed from 15 Apr to 19 Jun and 15 Sep to 20 Dec • 16 rooms with bath/WC, some have television • €83; breakfast €8; half board available • Menus €15 to €38 • Terrace, garden, car park. No dogs allowed in rooms • In summer: tennis, fly fishing, mini-golf; in winter: skiing and snowshoe hiking

Little teddy bears adorn some of the rooms of this friendly, family establishment.

The soft warm hues of wood greet the eye wherever you look in this exquisite chalet, just outside the village but at the foot of the slopes. Step into its welcoming doll's house interior and feast your eyes on the lovely fabrics, ornaments and Savoyard furniture. The rooms on the second floor have been renovated and it is planned to refurbish the others in the near future. All offer spectacular views of the Aravis and the mountain pastures. Regional delicacies.

Access : On the road from Col des Saisies, 1km from the resort and 50m from the ski lift

 75 CHALET LE PARADOU
M. Hanrard

 Pré Bérard
73210 La Côte-d'Aime
Tel. 04 79 55 67 79
Fax 04 79 55 67 79
hanrard @ aol.com

Closed from 3 May to 26 Jun and from 5 Sep to 19 Dec
• 5 rooms, 4 of which overlook a large terrace • €59,
breakfast included, half board available • Table d'hôte
€15 to €20 • Garden, terrace, car park. Credit cards not
accepted, no dogs allowed

 76 FLOR'ALPES
M. Bibollet

 73590 La Giettaz
 Tel. 04 79 32 90 88

Open from 15 Jun to 15 Sep and 20 Dec to 10 Apr
• 11 rooms, 7 with balcony, with bath/WC or
shower/WC • €34 to €39; breakfast €6, half board
available • Menus €16 to €24 • Garden

 An impeccably-run mountain chalet.

This superb wooden chalet perched at an altitude of
1 000m commands a stunning view of the Tarentaise
Valley and Mount Pourri. The spotlessly clean, comfortable rooms open onto a large terrace. The
wood-lined sitting room, complete with piano, matches
the alpine spirit that prevails throughout the establishment. Skiing packages are available in the winter, and
in the summer, you can laze about in the flowered
garden.

**The authentic Savoyard character of
this village.**

Tucked away between the village church and school, this
welcoming boarding house owes its success to the
faultless care and attention that the lady of the house
lavishes on all her guests. The rooms, simple but
pristine, all have a flower-decked balcony and a
wonderful view, which more than compensates for the
absence of television! Simple, home cooking with a
regional tang is served in a rustic dining room
overlooking the garden.

Access : 3km to the north-east of Aime on the D 86

Access : On a small square between the town hall
and the school

77 LES AIRELLES
M. Boyer

Rue des Darbelays - BP 25
73710 Pralognan-la-Vanoise
Tel. 04 79 08 70 32
Fax 04 79 08 73 51
hotellesairelles@free.fr
www.hotel-les-airelles.fr

Closed from 17 Apr to 4 Jun and from 24 Sep to 17 Dec
• 22 rooms with bath/WC or shower/WC and television
• €66 to €81; breakfast €8; half board available • Menus
€19 to €26 • Terrace, garage, car park. No dogs allowed
in restaurant • Outdoor swimming pool, sauna, spa bath,
billiards, table-tennis, shuttle to the ski lifts

78 BEAUSOLEIL
M. et Mme Vermeulen

73530 Saint-Sorlin-d'Arves
Tel. 04 79 59 71 42
Fax 04 79 59 75 25
info@hotel-beausoleil.com
www.hotel-beausoleil.com

Closed from 15 Apr to 30 Jun and 1 Sep to 15 Dec
• 23 rooms on 3 floors, 2 of which have balconies. All
have bath/WC or shower/WC and television • €48 to
€60; breakfast €8.50; half board €59 to €66 (€48 to €59
low season) • Menus €15 to €26 • Terrace, garden, car
park. No dogs allowed in the restaurant • Walks in the
Croix de Fer Pass and mountain sports

**Pralognan combines the charm of a
village with the facilities of a
top-class ski resort.**

This chalet, built on the outskirts of the resort, is
encircled by the ridges and crests of the Vanoise massif.
The mountain view from the rooms and balconies never
fails to bring gasps of admiration. In the kitchen, the
talented young chef's recipes provoke further cries of
approval. On the leisure side, the swimming pool is
heated, and the owner, an enthusiastic hiker, never tires
of indicating paths and trails to eager guests.

**Sunshine and powdery snow: what
more could you want?**

You know you're in for a treat right from the moment
you begin to climb the road by the Combe Genin or the
Croix de Fer Pass, driving past snowy peaks or pastures
of wild mountain flowers up to this remote mountain
chalet. Families are welcome in the practical, attractively
furnished rooms. After a long day out in the open air
you will be ready to feast on the delicacies rustled up
by your cheerful host.

Access : In the upper part of the resort, next to the
Granges forest

Access : Away from the centre of the resort,
towards the Col de la Croix-de-Fer

 79 LA FERME BONNE DE LA GROTTE
M. Amayenc

 73360 Saint-Christophe-la-Grotte
Tel. 04 79 36 59 05
Fax 04 79 36 59 31
info@ferme-bonne.com
www.gites-savoie.com

Open all year • 5 rooms, some have mezzanines • €66 to €89, breakfast included • Table d'hôte €18 to €27 • Terrace, park, car park. Credit cards not accepted (except Eurocard), no dogs allowed

 80 CHÉ CATRINE
Mme Finas

 88 rue Saint-Antoine
73500 Villarodin-Bourget
Tel. 04 79 20 49 32
Fax 04 79 20 48 67
info@che-catrine.com
che-catrine.com

Open all year • 3 rooms and 2 suites, all have bath/WC • €79 to €105 (€60 to €80 low season), breakfast included, half board available • Table d'hôte €28 • Garden. Credit cards not accepted

Irresistibly Savoyard in spirit and flavour.

In the space of a year, this three-century-old farm at the foot of the Échelles caves has become a must in the region. The renowned cuisine has remained true to its Savoyard roots and the gourmet chef takes great pleasure in watching his guests devour his tasty home cooking. The immense but still cosy rooms are all graced with painted furniture; some also boast a mezzanine.

Savour the good things of life in this superb mansion.

This country house, built in 1524, and restored in keeping with Savoyard traditions, is a gem of a find. You will immediately feel at home in the rooms and suites, decorated with solid pine furniture. Meals are served in the vaulted stables and the lounge-bar – hewn out of solid rock – is a delight for the eyes. The chef makes it a point of honour to use only garden vegetables and meat from the Maurienne Valley. Definitely worth writing home about, unless you'd rather keep it to yourself!

Access : 4km to the north-east of Échelles on the N 6, Chambéry road

Access : Motorway A 43, exit Modane, then after Modane 2km on the RN 6 towards the Haute Maurienne

RHÔNE ALPES

 81 **L'AIGUILLE DU MIDI**
M. et Mme Farini

479 chemin Napoléon - Les Bossons
74400 Chamonix-Mont-Blanc
Tel. 04 50 53 00 65
Fax 04 50 55 93 69
hotel-aiguille-du-midi@wanadoo.fr
www.hotel-aiguilledumidi.com

Closed from 12 Apr to 20 May and 20 Sep to 20 Dec
• 40 rooms with bath/WC and television • €69 to €80;
breakfast €12; half board available • Menus €21
(weekdays) to €44 • Terrace, garden, car park. No dogs
allowed in restaurant • Outdoor swimming pool, tennis,
fitness room, sauna, jacuzzi

 The view of the Bossons glacier from the shade of the park.

This impressive old country chalet has been a hotel since
1908. Behind the Tyrolean-style frescoes are wainscoted
rooms, most a little faded, but all overlooking the
wonderful Mont Blanc range. The circular dining room
and the terrace with wooden furniture and a giant
parasol give onto a lovely flowery park. Make sure you
look up and admire the beautiful carved ceiling in the
sitting room. Numerous leisure activities.

Access : 3km southbound from
Chamonix-Mont-Blanc

  82 **BEAUSOLEIL**
M. et Mme Bossonney

 Le Lavancher
74400 Chamonix-Mont-Blanc
Tel. 04 50 54 00 78
Fax 04 50 54 17 34
info@hotelbeausoleilchamonix.com
www.hotelbeausoleilchamonix.com

Closed 10 to 26 May and 20 Sep to 20 Dec • 17 rooms
on 2 levels, with bath/WC or shower/WC and television
• €84 to €94, breakfast €9, half board available
• Restaurant closed Thu lunchtime in summer and
lunchtimes from 20 Dec to 20 Jun; menus €13 to €28
• Terrace, garden, car park. No dogs allowed in
restaurant • Tennis, table-tennis

 The tranquillity of this secluded chalet.

Are you more of a winter- or a summer-mountain type?
The Bossonney family, who have run the hotel for three
generations, are guaranteed to make you feel at home
in their inviting chalet, whatever the season. The small,
wainscoted, refreshingly simple rooms are faultlessly
kept and a few boast balconies with a view of
snow-capped peaks or green pastures. Tasty home
cooking and cheese-based specialities are served in a
country-style dining room which opens onto the terrace
and garden.

Access : 6km on the N506, towards Argentière, then
minor road on the right

83   **LE KANDAHAR**
Mme Vuarand

Route du Linga
74390 Châtel
Tel. 04 50 73 30 60
Fax 04 50 73 25 17
lekandahar @ wanadoo.fr
www.lekandahar.com

Closed from 17 Apr to 3 May, 30 May to 4 Jul and 1 Nov to 24 Dec; Tue evening and Wed • 20 rooms, 13 of which with kitchenettes, all have bath/WC and television • €58 to €68 (€55 to €60 low season); breakfast €9; half board available • Menus €13 to €32 • Terrace, garden, car park • Fitness room, sauna

84   **LE CORDONANT**
M. et Mme Pugnat

Les Darbaillets
74700 Cordon
Tel. 04 50 58 34 56
Fax 04 50 47 95 57
lecordonant @ wanadoo.fr

Closed from mid-Apr to mid-May and from Oct to Dec • 16 rooms with balconies, bath/WC (2 have shower/WC) and television • €75.50 to €80; breakfast €7; half board available • Menus €22 (weekdays) to €28 • Terrace, car park. No dogs allowed in restaurant • Fitness room, sauna, jacuzzi

The family atmosphere of this alpine chalet.

This hotel on the border of Switzerland is renowned for the hospitable, welcoming aspect of its rooms. Within easy reach of the ski slopes thanks to frequent, free shuttles to the Linga, it is also surrounded by gentler hillsides for the less energetic, but the breathtaking viewpoints over the Chablais definitely require the efforts of serious walkers. In the kitchen, the chef sets-to with a will, to restore and revive body and soul with delicious local specialities.

The ear-splitting silence and stunning view from the valley windows.

The pink roughcast walls and creamy coloured wood-work of this smart chalet stand on the heights of the "Mont Blanc balcony". The rooms have been refurbished in a contemporary Savoyard style with wood-lined walls, painted furniture and pretty fabrics. From the dining room, you will be able to enjoy a breathtaking view of the "rooftops of Europe" as you sample the appetising, generous cooking, before settling down for a nap in the sun in the flowered garden.

Access : 1.5km to the south-west, on the Bechigne road, then left on the Linga road

Access : 4km to the south-west of Sallanches on the D 113

 85 LES GENTIANETTES
M. et Mme Tringaz

Route de Chevenne
74360 La Chapelle-d'Abondance
Tel. 04 50 73 56 46
Fax 04 50 73 56 39
bienvenue @ gentianettes.fr
www.gentianettes.fr

Closed from Easter to 1 Nov and 20 Sep to 18 Dec 2005
• 32 rooms with bath/WC or shower/WC and television,
2 have disabled access • €70 to €95, breakfast €9, half
board available • Menus €19.54 to €61 • Terrace, car
park. Dogs accepted at a supplement • Indoor swimming
pool, sauna, fitness room, hammam

 **Sampling the chef's mouth-watering
cooking after a day in the open air.**

A faultless welcome, well-proportioned cheerful bedrooms with wainscoting and balconies, a pleasantly
mountain-style dining room, impeccable regional cuisine
and generous breakfasts - what more could one ask from
this pretty chalet built in 1994? Those lucky enough to
come to La Chapelle-d'Abondance in the summertime
may catch sight of a gentian flower, the high-altitude
herbaceous plant which gave the hotel its name. In
winter, alpine sports are more the order of the day!

Access : North of Chapelle-d'Abondance

 86 LE BOIS JOLI
M. et Mme Birraux

74500 La Beunaz
Tel. 04 50 73 60 11
Fax 04 50 73 65 28
hboisjoli @ aol.com
www.hotel-bois-joli.com

Closed from 15 Oct to 20 Dec and Apr • 29 rooms, 8 of
which are in a separate wing, all have bath/WC or
shower/WC and television • €72 to €82 (€60 to €74 low
season); breakfast €9; half board available • Restaurant
closed Sun evening and Wed; menus €20 (weekdays) to
€48 • Terrace, garden, car park • Outdoor swimming
pool, tennis, sauna, table-tennis, billiards

 **The country appeal of this panoramic
chalet.**

The bedrooms, dining room and terrace all enjoy a view
of the Dent d'Oche, Mount Billiat and the summits of
the Chablais. In the summer, activities include a
swimming pool surrounded by foliage and a tennis court,
in the winter the ski slopes are nearby while year-round
activities include a children's play area and billiards
room with Lake Léman and its prestigious spa resorts
just a few kilometres away. Idyllic in any season.

Access : Below the road, 1.5km from Bernex on the
D 52

87 FLORALP
Mmes Pollet

74220 La Clusaz
Tel. 04 50 02 41 46
Fax 04 50 02 63 94
info @ hotel-floralp74.com
www.hotel-floralp74.com

Open from 28 Jun to 15 Sep and from 20 Dec to 14 Apr • 20 rooms, all have bath/WC or shower/WC and television. Front-facing rooms have balconies. • €50 to €85 (€45 to €70 low season); breakfast €8; half board available • Menus €15 (weekdays) to €26 • Car park. No dogs allowed in restaurant • Billiards room

A traditional mountain chalet.

The simple rooms at the front have an east-facing balcony and are much sought after by all the chalet's numerous regular guests. The region is riddled with beautiful, immaculate peaks, dales covered in rhododendron bushes and high rocky ranges. Tangy Tomme and Reblochon cheeses tempt the palate at lunchtime and dinners enable your hostesses to show off the full scope of their culinary skills. The sitting room with bar, billiard table and fireside is the perfect place for a nightcap.

Access : At the entrance to the resort, coming from Annecy on the D 909, take a right

88 LA CROIX DE SAVOIE
M. et Mme Tiret

768 route du Pernand
74300 Les Carroz-d'Araches
Tel. 04 50 90 00 26
Fax 04 50 90 00 63
info @ lacroixdesavoie.fr
www.lacroixdesavoie.fr

Closed Sun evening and Mon lunchtime • 19 rooms with shower/WC, most have a balcony • €73 to €77 (€45 to €48 low season); breakfast €8; half board available • Menus €17 to €38 • Terrace, garden, car park

Savour the tranquillity and the view of the Aravis and lose track of time.

This establishment, ideally located in the ski resort, is a haven of friendliness. The rooms, nearly all of which have a balcony, are an excellent combination of simple comfort and warm wood-panelling. Wood is also the predominant feature of the restaurant which serves regional dishes. Winter guests can head for the immense skiing domain and in the summer, walkers set off to explore the mineral kingdom of Platé. If you're lucky, you may catch a glimpse of a wild ibex following your climb.

Access : In the upper part of the resort, 1km from the centre, towards Flaine

89 GAI SOLEIL
Mme Mermoud

288 chemin des Loyers
74170 Les Contamines-Montjoie
Tel. 04 50 47 02 94
Fax 04 50 47 18 43
gaisoleil2 @ wanadoo.fr
www.gaisoleil.com

Closed from 20 Apr to 14 Jun and 15 Sep to 20 Dec
• 19 rooms with bath/WC or shower/WC, no television
• €51 to €70 (€48 to €68 low season); breakfast €10;
half board available • Menus €19 to €26 • Garden, car
park. No dogs allowed in restaurant • Fondue evenings
and films on mountain life

90 BEAU SÉJOUR
M. et Mme Blanc

Allée des Tennis
74290 Menthon-Saint-Bernard
Tel. 04 50 60 12 04
Fax 04 50 60 05 56

Open from 15 Apr to late Sep • 18 rooms, 14 of which
have shower/WC, 4 have bath/WC • €65 to €73;
breakfast €7 • No restaurant • Garden, private car park
• Table-tennis, reading room. Tennis, golf and water
sports nearby

 **Mount Joly and the snowy peaks of
the Miage greet you in the morning.**

The painting on one of the beams bearing the date
1823, was the work of the chalet's original owner. The
Gai Soleil's website joyfully relates this family farm's
intriguing history – an English version is in the pipeline,
we're told. Ask for one of the rooms refurbished in a
mountain style with wood walls and pine furniture. The
south-facing terrace is popular in winter and summer
alike. Attractive garden.

 Visit the fairytale castle of Menthon.

One hundred metres from Lake Annecy, this early-20C
villa stands in an enormous park. The bedrooms with
balcony, the most spacious, have recently been
renovated, doing away with the distinctive hallmarks of
the seventies. The bay windows of the breakfast room
overlook the flowered garden where meals are served
whenever the weather is warm enough. Friendly, family
service.

Access : In the upper part of the resort

Access : 100m from the lake

 91 FLEUR DES NEIGES
M. Archambault

 74110 Morzine
Tel. 04 50 79 01 23
Fax 04 50 75 95 75
fleurneige @ aol.com
www.fleurdesneiges.com

Closed from 10 Apr to 1 Jul and 5 Sep to 20 Dec • 33 rooms, all have bath/WC or shower/WC and television • €62 to €80 (€46 to €66 low season); breakfast €9; half board available • Menu €20 to €25 • Terrace, garden, car park. No dogs allowed • Indoor swimming pool, tennis, fitness room, sauna, table-tennis, boules

 92 AUBERGE DE L'ORANGERIE
M. Liboureau

 3 carrefour de la Charlotte
74700 Sallanches
Tel. 04 50 58 49 16
Fax 04 50 58 54 63
 auberge-orangerie @ wanadoo.fr

Closed from 5 to 27 Jan and 2 to 24 Jun • 7 rooms with bath/WC or shower/WC and television • €40 to €55, breakfast €8 • Restaurant closed Sun evening, Mon, and Tue, Wed and Thu lunchtimes; menus €24 to €58 • Private car park, garden, terrace

We most liked **Soothing your aching muscles in the pool after a day on the slopes.**

This chalet-style building is a little out of the centre of Chablais' tourist capital, Morzine. When booking, ask for one of the renovated rooms with wood-lined walls, pine furniture and matching fabrics; plans are afoot to redecorate the rather dour dining room in the near future. The hotel's facilities – fitness room, sauna, tennis court, swimming pool (indoor in winter) – reflect the resort's combination of sport and leisure activities.

We most liked **Gazing up at the mountains from one of the snug rooms.**

In the summertime, the façade of this chalet at the foot of the Côte de Passy is a riot of flowers. The well-renovated rooms guarantee that your nights will be quiet and peaceful: pine-panelling, excellent sound-proofing against the noise of the road, big beds piled high with duvets, inviting armchairs and fully tiled bathrooms. Some have a balcony. The owner-chef's cuisine, served in the rustic dining room, displays his creative flair for mixing traditional recipes and local dishes.

Access : Slightly out of the centre, on the Thonon-les-Bains road

Access : Outside the town at the foot of the Côte de Passy

 93 **GORGES DE LA DIOSAZ**
M. Vandenkoornhuyse

 "Sous le Roc"
74310 Servoz
Tel. 04 50 47 20 97
Fax 04 50 47 21 08
info@hoteldesgorges.com
www.hoteldesgorges.com

Closed from 8 to 22 May, Sun evening and Wed
• 7 rooms with bath/WC or shower/WC and television
• €65 (€52 low season); breakfast €7; half board
available • Menus €21 to €40 • Terrace. No dogs allowed

 94 **AU GAY SÉJOUR**
M. et Mme Gay

 Le Tertenoz
74210 Seythenex
Tel. 04 50 44 52 52
Fax 04 50 44 49 52
hotel-gay-sejour@wanadoo.fr
www.hotel-gay-sejour.com

Closed from 15 Nov to 15 Dec, Sun evening and Mon
(except holidays) • 11 rooms with bath/WC and television • €68 to €110; breakfast €12; half board available
• Menus €26 (weekdays) to €72 • Terrace, car park. No
dogs allowed in rooms • Snowshoe hiking. Annecy Lake
and ski slopes nearby

 **Francine and Sébastien greet guests
energetically and warmly.**

This traditional mountain chalet decked in flowers stands
on the edge of the gorges of the Diosaz. The restful
rooms have been refurbished in a sober, contemporary
alpine style and the windows of the inviting rustic dining
room overlook the Mont Blanc range. Wood prevails in
the sitting room and bar, where you can gratefully relax
with a glass of mulled wine after a hard day on the
slopes.

 **A summer vista of lush mountain
pastures or a winter picture of fields
of snow.**

This 17C farm, nestling in a peaceful medium-altitude
hamlet, has been turned into a pleasant family inn
where you can be sure of a lung-full of pure mountain
air. Though hardly stylish, the rooms are nonetheless
wonderfully peaceful and some enjoy a lovely view of
the valley. In the restaurant, the focus is on immaculate
service and well-judged traditional cooking.

Access : In the centre of the village, near the post
office

Access : 4km to the south-east of Faverges

  95 LE VIEUX LOGIS
M. Jacquier

Rue des Remparts
74140 Yvoire
Tel. 04 50 72 80 24
Fax 04 50 72 90 76
contact @ levieuxlogis.com
www.levieuxlogis.com

Closed from 1 Jan to 15 Feb • 11 rooms, all have
bath/WC and television • €60 to €70; breakfast €8
• Restaurant closed Sun evening and Mon; menus €23
(weekdays) to €42 • Terrace, private car park

**The Maze-Garden of the Five Senses
in the medieval village.**

This "old abode" of character, run by the same family
for four generations, is set right in the ramparts. The
rooms are practical and those on the first floor have a
balcony; thick 14C walls keep the interior cool, even
during the hot summer months. Under the vaulted
ceiling and well-worn beams of the dining room, you
will be invited to sample the house speciality of fillets
of perch. In the summer, meals are also served on the
lovely shaded terrace.

Access : On the way into the old town, set in the
ramparts

 So that you can treat yourself without having to break open your piggy bank, we have selected hotels and chambres d'hôte which offer a warm welcome, pleasant setting and character combined with affordable prices. The coin symbol next to an establishment indicates that it is a hotel or maison d'hôte with rooms at a maximum price of €40 per night for two (breakfast included in the maisons d'hôte, but extra in hotels).

Good food is of course an essential prerequisite for a successful holiday and we should know! We have therefore decided to point out all the hotels and maisons d'hôte whose cuisine is in some way outstanding. The hotels have all been awarded either one or more "Stars" for excellent cooking or a "Bib Gourmand" for good food at moderate prices by the Michelin Red Guide. In the maisons d'hôte, you will tuck into delicious home cooking, often prepared using home-grown produce.

ACTIVITY BREAKS

Feel like getting away from it all? Ready for a change of scenery? Want to get out into the countryside and work off some stress or extra pounds? The hotels and maisons d'hôte listed below all have a swimming pool at the very least and generally one or several other sports facilities or activities, either on site or very nearby. These include themed or signposted walks, fishing, tennis, golf, a fitness room/mini-gym, or riding, so check out each establishment to discover what is on offer.

583

ALPHABETICAL INDEX OF HOTELS AND MAISONS D'HÔTE

PHOTO CREDITS

Photographs of hotels and maisons d'hôte in the guide and on the cover:

Project Manager – Production: Alain LEPRINCE
Agence ACSI – A CHACUN SON IMAGE
2, rue Aristide Maillol, 75015 Paris – Tél. : (33) 01 43 27 90 10
Photo Credits : Romain Aix, Lawrence Banahan/ACSI©2004

The Regions – captions and credits

ALSACE : *Andlau, the Route du Vin* R. Mattes/MICHELIN

AQUITAINE : *Bassin d'Arcachon* A. Thuillier/MICHELIN

AUVERGNE : *Ambert town hall* J. Damase/MICHELIN

BURGUNDY : *Briare canal bridge* Ph. Gajic/MICHELIN

BRITTANY : *Port du Palais, Belle-Île* G. Guégan/MICHELIN

CENTRE AND UPPER LOIRE VALLEY : *Château d'Ussé* Ph. Gajic/MICHELIN

CHAMPAGNE-ARDENNE : *Place Ducale, Charleville-Mézières* Ph. Gajic/MICHELIN

CORSICA : *Bonifacio* G. Magnin/MICHELIN

FRANCHE-COMTÉ : *Château de Joux* G. Benoît à la Guillaumen/MICHELIN

ÎLE-DE-FRANCE AND PARIS : *Place de la Concorde* B. Kaufman/MICHELIN

LANGUEDOC-ROUSSILLON : *Le Cirque de Navacelles* B. Kaufman/MICHELIN

LIMOUSIN : *Sénoueix bridge* S. Sauvignier/MICHELIN

LORRAINE : *Bitche* R. Mattes/MICHELIN

MIDI-PYRÉNÉES : *Albi Cathedral* B. Kaufman/MICHELIN

NORD-PAS-DE-CALAIS : *International Kite Festival at Berck* Y. Tierny/MICHELIN

NORMANDY : *The Auge countryside* G. Targat/MICHELIN

PAYS-DE-LA-LOIRE : *Harvesting salt at Noirmoutier* M. Thiery/MICHELIN

PICARDY : *Marquenterre nature reserve* S. Sauvignier/MICHELIN

POITOU-CHARENTES : *Port d'Arçais, Marais poitevin* D. Mar/MICHELIN

PROVENCE-ALPS - FRENCH RIVIERA : *Calanque de Sormiou* G. Magnin/MICHELIN

RHÔNE-ALPES : *Notre-Dame de la Vie, Saint-Martin de Belleville* S. Sauvignier/MICHELIN

46, avenue de Breteuil – 75324 Paris Cedex 07
☎ 01 45 66 12 34
www.ViaMichelin.fr

Manufacture Française des Pneumatiques Michelin
Société en commandite par actions au capital de 304 000 000 EUR
Place des Carmes-Déchaux, 63 Clermont-Ferrand (France) - R.C.S. Clermont-Fd B 855 200 507
Michelin et Cie, Propriétaires-Editeurs - Dépôt légal Novembre 2004 – ISBN 2-06-710966-9

No part of this publication may be reproduced in any form without the prior permission of the publisher

Printed in France 10-2004/3.1

Typesetting: Maury Malesherbes (France)
Printing: ISTRA, Schiltigheim

Layout: Studio Maogani
4, rue du Fer à Moulin, 75005 Paris - Tel : 01 47 07 00 06

Published in 2005

YOUR OPINION MATTERS!

To help us constantly improve this guide, please fill in this questionnaire and return to:
Michelin Charming Places to Stay 2005
Michelin Travel Publications – Hannay House 39 Clarendon Road
WATFORD Herts WD17 1JA – U.K.

❯ 1- Have you ever bought other Michelin guides?

Yes .... ❏   No .... ❏

If yes, which one(s)?

Red Guide (hotels and restaurants) .... ❏

Green Guide (tourism) .... ❏

Other (please specify) .... ❏

❯ 2- Did you buy this guide:

For holidays .... ❏

For short breaks or weekends .... ❏

For business purposes .... ❏

As a gift .... ❏

❯ 3- Will you be travelling:

In a couple ... ❏   With family .... ❏

Alone .... ❏   With friends ... ❏

Other .... ❏

❯ 4- You are a:

Man .... ❏   Woman .... ❏

< 25 years old .... ❏   25 – 34 years old .. ❏

35 – 50 years old .. ❏   > 50 years old ..... ❏

Profession: ....

❯ 5-How would you rate the following aspects of the guide?

1 = Very good   *2* = Good   *3* = Acceptable   *4* = Poor   *5* = Very poor

	1	2	3	4	5
Selection of establishments	❏	❏	❏	❏	❏
Number of establishments	❏	❏	❏	❏	❏
Hotel/Maison d'hôte mix	❏	❏	❏	❏	❏
Prices of rooms	❏	❏	❏	❏	❏
Practical Information (prices, etc.)	❏	❏	❏	❏	❏
Description of the establishment	❏	❏	❏	❏	❏
Photos	❏	❏	❏	❏	❏
General presentation	❏	❏	❏	❏	❏
Distribution of establishments across France	❏	❏	❏	❏	❏
Themed indexes	❏	❏	❏	❏	❏
Cover	❏	❏	❏	❏	❏
Other (please specify)	❏	❏	❏	❏	❏

❯ 6-Please rate the guide out of 20:   / 20

❯ 7- Which aspects could we improve?

....
....
....
....
....
....
....
....
....
....
....
....
....
....
....
....
....
....